COPYRIGHT IN THE RENAISSANCE

STUDIES
IN MEDIEVAL AND
REFORMATION THOUGHT

FOUNDED BY HEIKO A. OBERMAN †

EDITED BY

ANDREW COLIN GOW, Edmonton, Alberta

IN COOPERATION WITH

THOMAS A. BRADY, Jr., Berkeley, California
JOHANNES FRIED, Frankfurt
BRAD GREGORY, University of Notre Dame, Indiana
BERNDT HAMM, Erlangen
SUSAN C. KARANT-NUNN, Tucson, Arizona
JÜRGEN MIETHKE, Heidelberg
M. E. H. NICOLETTE MOUT, Leiden

VOLUME C

CHRISTOPHER L.C.E. WITCOMBE

COPYRIGHT IN THE RENAISSANCE

COPYRIGHT
IN THE RENAISSANCE

PRINTS AND THE *PRIVILEGIO* IN
SIXTEENTH-CENTURY VENICE AND ROME

BY

CHRISTOPHER L.C.E. WITCOMBE

BRILL

LEIDEN · BOSTON

2004

This book is printed on acid-free paper.

Library of Congress Cataloging-in-Publication Data

Witcombe, Christopher L. C. E.
  Copyright in the Renaissance : prints and the privilegio in sixteenth-century Venice and Rome / by Christopher L.C.E. Witcombe.
    p. cm. — (Studies in medieval and Reformation thought, ISSN 0585-6914 ; v. 100)
  Includes bibliographical references and index.
  ISBN 90-04-13748-3 (hbk.)
    1. Copyright—Italy—History—16th century. 2. Copyright—Italy—Venice—History—16th century. 3. Copyright—Italy—Papal States—History—16th century. I. Title. II. Series.

KKH1160.W58 2004
346.4504'82'09031—dc22

2004043594

ISSN 0585-6914
ISBN 90 04 13748 3

PRINTED IN THE NETHERLANDS

For Rosemary, Giulia, Alexia

CONTENTS

LIST OF ILLUSTRATIONS

Fig. 1. Cornelis Cort, *Holy Trinity* (after Titian). 1567. Engraving. Photo: Rijksmuseum.

Fig. 2. Cornelis Cort, *Diana Discovering Callisto's Pregnancy* (after Titian). 1566. Engraving. Photo: The Metropolitan Museum of Art, Harris Brisbane Dick Fund, 1949 (49.97.541).

Fig. 3. Cornelis Cort, *Rape of Lucretia* (after Titian) 1571. Engraving. Photo: The Metropolitan Museum of Art, Harris Brisbane Dick Fund, 1949 (49.97.539).

Fig. 4. Ugo da Carpi, *Death of Ananias* (after Raphael). 1518. Chiaroscuro woodcut. Photo: Warburg.

Fig. 5. Ugo da Carpi, *Aeneas and Anchises* (after Raphael). 1518. Chiaroscuro woodcut. Photo: Warburg.

Fig. 6. Giacomo di Argentina, Caesar on a Chariot, one of 12 woodcuts of the *Triumph of Caesar*. c. 1504. Third State, with text. Photo: The Metropolitan Museum of Art, Harris Brisbane Dick Fund, 1927 (27.54.124).

Fig. 7. Ugo da Carpi, *Sacrifice of Abraham* (after Titian). c. 1515. Woodcut. Photo: Staatliche Museen, Berlin.

Fig. 8. Anonymous, Submersion of *Pharaoh's Army in the Red Sea* (after Titian). Woodcut. Late impression dated 1549. Photo: Courtesy of the Fogg Art Museum, Harvard University Art Museums. Gift of W. G. Russell Allen.

Fig. 9. Girolamo Pennacchi da Treviso, *Susannah and the Elders* (after Titian). c. 1515. Woodcut. Photo: Statens Museum for Kunst, Copenhagen.

Fig. 10. Lucantonio degli Uberti, *The Martyrdom of the Ten Thousand Christians on Mount Ararat*, c. 1515–1520. Woodcut. Photo: Princeton University Art Museum. Gift of Junius S. Morgan, Class of 1888 (?). Photo Credit: Clem Fiori © 1988. Photo: Trustees of Princeton University.

Fig. 11. Nicolas Beatrizet, *Circus Maximus* (after Ligorio). 1553. Engraving. Photo: The Metropolitan Museum of Art, Harris Brisbane Dick Fund, 1941 (41.72.(1) plate 68).

Fig. 12. Nicolas Beatrizet, *Circus Flaminius* (after Ligorio). 1553. Engraving. Photo: Warburg.

LIST OF ABBREVIATIONS

ABGU = Archivio della Biblioteca delle Gallerie degli Uffizi, Florence
ASASL = Archivio Storico, Accademia di San Luca, Rome
ASC = Archivio Storico Capitolino, Rome
ASF = Archivio di Stato, Florence
ASR = Achivio di Stato, Rome
ASV = Archivio di Stato, Venice
AVR = Archivio Vicariato, Rome
ASVat = Archivio Segreto, Vatican
acc. = accession
Arm. = Armadio (Archivio Segreto Vaticano)
BA, Vatican = Biblioteca Apostolica Vaticana
BM, London = British Museum, London
BN, Paris = Bibliothèque Nationale de France, Paris
BN, Florence = Biblioteca Nazionale, Florence
c. = circa
Calcografia, Rome = Calcografia, Istituto Nazionale per la Grafica, Rome
Casanatense, Rome = Biblioteca Casanatense, Rome
CCXN = Capi del Consiglio de' Dieci, Notatorio (Archivio di Stato, Venice)
CN = Collegio, Notatorio (Archivio di Stato, Venice)
CNC = Collegio Notai Capitolino (Archivio di Stato, Rome)
CX = Consiglio dei Dieci (Archivio di Stato, Venice)
ECBC = Esecutori contro la Bestemmia, Capitolari (Archivio di Stato, Venice)
Farnesina, Rome = Gabinetto Nazionale delle Stampe e Disegni, Farnesina, Rome
Fogg, Harvard = Fogg Art Museum, Harvard University, Cambridge, Mass.
fol. = folio
Houghton, Harvard = Houghton Library, Harvard University, Cambridge, Mass.
inv. = inventory
Marciana, Venice = Biblioteca Nazionale Marciana, Venice
Marucelliana, Florence = Biblioteca Marucelliana, Florence

MFA, Boston = Museum of Fine Arts, Boston

MM, New York = Metropolitan Museum of Art, New York

m.v. = *more veneto*. The year as given in Venetian archival records when the New Year began in March.

n. = note

NG, Washington – National Gallery of Art, Washington, D.C.

n.n. = new numbering (newer page numbers in archival registers)

no. = number

o.s. = old style. The year as given in records when the New Year began other than on January 1.

r. = recto

reg. = Registro

RSP = Riformatori dello Studio di Padova (Archivio di Stato, Venice)

SB = Secretarium Breviarum (Archivio Segreto, Vatican)

ST = Senato Terra (Archivio di Stato, Venice)

v. = verso

PREFACE

The emergence of copyright in the late fifteenth century and the expansion of its use over the course of the sixteenth century is an important but, until now, little understood phenomenon in the history of prints. This book presents a survey of copyright in sixteenth century Venice and Rome, with a special focus on copyright and printed images. It also addresses the related matters of licensing and censorship. Although no claim is made to inclusion of all the many copyrighted prints issued in the sixteenth century, enough examples have been gathered to permit a clear sense of how copyright functioned with respect to printed images.

The need to address the issue of copyright became unavoidable when I was conducting research for another project concerning print publishing in sixteenth-century Rome. As I encountered more and more prints carrying the enigmatic phrase "cum privilegio," it became clear that I could not proceed with an analysis of the commercial aspects of print publishing without understanding what a *privilegio* was and how it worked in the sixteenth century. In one sense, this book has been written mostly for my own edification; but the information it contains will be of considerable interest to others, both art historians and historians of books, printing, and publishing.

I am grateful to the many kind and generous people in numerous museums, libraries, archives in the United States and Europe who assisted me while I was conducting research for this study. You may not remember me, but I remember you. The opportunity to travel to these institutions, and the ability to purchase the photographs used as illustrations, were made possible with grants and a fellowship from Sweet Briar College. I especially want to thank Francesca Consagra for her tips regarding material in the Vatican Archives in the early stages of this project. I am also grateful to Claudia Chang and Mike Richards at Sweet Briar for their encouragement in the very early stages of writing. I owe a special debt of gratitude to Lisa Johnston and the Interlibrary Loan staff at Sweet Briar without whose help this study would not have reached any timely completion. Thanks are due above all to my wife, Rosemary, and my daughters, Giulia and Alexia, for their love, support and forbearance. This book is dedicated to them. I only wish my father, Frederick Ewart Witcombe (1922–2003), was alive to see this book in print.

C.L.C.E.W.
Ca' Badoer dei Barbacani, Venice

INTRODUCTION

In 1566, the Venetian painter Titian commissioned the Dutch engraver Cornelis Cort to produce prints of several of his designs. Titian was evidently concerned, however, that the prints would be copied by other engravers and so he decided to apply for copyright protection. A system of copyright had emerged nearly a century earlier, soon after the appearance of the printing press. It existed in the form of a *privilegio*, literally a "privilege," that was granted on an individual basis under the authority of the government. By 1566 it was well established in Venice.

In order to obtain a *privilegio*, Titian had to submit a supplication to the Venetian government. Before he could do this, however, it was necessary to obtain a license, and before a license could be issued, the content of the prints Titian wanted to publish had to be approved by an official censor. Titian initiated the process by submitting a copy of one of his printed designs, the *Holy Trinity* (Fig. 1), to the Riformatori dello Studio di Padova.[1] The Riformatori dello Studio di Padova had been established in 1545 by the Council of Ten as the official body to which publishers of books and prints were obliged to submit requests for approval of the material they wished to print.[2] It was the task of the Riformatori to decide whether or not the material submitted to them was acceptable on religious,

---

[1] Cort had engraved the print presumably after a *modello* of the *Holy Trinity* as the original painting, which Titian had executed for Charles V, had been shipped to Brussels in 1554. It was subsequently taken to the monastery of Yuste by Charles V on his retirement and is now in the Prado in Madrid (no. 432). The print is mentioned by Giorgio Vasari, *Le Vite*, 6: 451, and catalogued in Bierens de Haan, *L'oeuvre gravé de Cornelis Cort*, 9, and cat. no. 111. Domenico Lampsonius, writing from Liège, refers to Cort's print (together with five other prints by Cort) in a letter to Titian dated 13 March 1567 (the letter is reprinted in Gaye, *Carteggio inedito d'artisti*, 3: 242, no. 218). Three months later, on 15 June 1567, Titian himself wrote a letter to Margaret, Duchess of Parma and Regentess of Flanders, accompanied by a proof of the print. In the letter, Titian states "havendo io nelli giorni prossimamente passati fatto metter in stampe di rame il disegno della pittura della Trinità che feci già di comandamento dell'Imperatore . . ." Titian's letter was first published by Müntz in *Archives des Arts* 1 (1890), 69.

[2] The establishment of this function of the Riformatori dello Studio di Padova is recorded in ASV, CX, Comuni, Busta 36, fol. 124r.

Fig. 1. Cornelis Cort, *Holy Trinity* (after Titian). 1567. Engraving.
Photo: Rijksmuseum.

moral, and political grounds. Because of its religious subject matter, the Riformatori had Titian's print examined by the inquisitor Fra Valerio Faenzi. In a brief report to the Riformatori dated 4 January 1567 [1566 m.v.], Faenzi stated that he had seen the print and made the observation that "it is very decorous and properly represents the Holy Trinity." He also added that in his estimation it was "worthy of being seen for the honour of God," and concluded that it was "deserving of every privilege."[3]

With the approval of the Riformatori dello Studio di Padova now in hand, Titian's next step was to obtain a license. A system of licensing had been instituted by the Council of Ten in 1506.[4] Anyone who wanted to print or have printed in Venice any new work (both books and prints) had to obtain first a license from the Chiefs of the Council of Ten (*Capi del Consiglio dei Dieci*, a body of three men internal to and comprised of members of the Council of Ten). And so, on 8 January 1567 [1566 m.v.], four days after receiving the approval of the Riformatori dello Studio di Padova, Titian submitted a request for a license to Chiefs of the Council of Ten. It was granted two weeks later on 22 January.[5]

The document of his request for a license does not survive, but in it Titian evidently asked for approval to publish not only the *Holy Trinity* but also other prints as well. In the wording of the license that was subsequently issued, reference is made to Titian having designed and made various engraved copperplate prints, and notes that he intends also to make other designs from time to time and to make other prints ("havendo egli dissegnato, et fatto intagliar diverse stampe di rame, et intendendo anco di dissegnar di tempo in tempo, et farne stampar dell'altre"). With regard to the other prints, the license states that he is obliged to show ("mostrar") each one of the prints, as well as those that will be printed from time to time, to the Chiefs of the Council of Ten so they can be inspected

---

[3] The document recording Faenzi's report was first published by Paul Kristeller, "Tizians Beziehungen zum Kupferstich," *Mitteilungen der Gesellschaft für vervielfältigende Kunst* 34 (1911): 24. Kristeller, however, was unsure of the wording on the reverse of Faenzi's report and transcribes the text incompletely and incorrectly: "Alli cla.mi s.ri Reformatori dello con . . . di pa . . . miei signori colendissimi." He was thus unaware that the report was addressed to the Riformatori dello Studio di Padova.

[4] The document recording the proclamation is in ASV, CX, Proclami, Busta 1.

[5] The granting of the license is recorded in ASV, CCXN, reg. 21, fol. 68r. The document is transcribed in Kristeller, 25.

for any obscenity. Titian was also required to leave a copy of each print in the office of the Chiefs of the Council of Ten so that it can be seen each time if the print had been counterfeited. Moreover, each submitted print must be undersigned by the secretaries of the Council.

The number of such stipulations had increased in recent years as the Venetian government stepped up its efforts to control the content of printed material. In 1537, the Council of Ten had instituted the magistracy of the *Esecutori contra la bestemmia* ("Executors against Blasphemy") whose principal task was to prosecute blasphemers.[6] A special area of scrutiny was the products of the printing industry and whether books and prints contained anything against religion, morality, and "il buon costume" (good morals, or customary moral conduct). In 1543, the penalties for failing to obtain a license were made more stringent by the Executors with fines and punishments.[7] Four years later, in 1547, fines were increased and it was decreed that all unlawful and unlicensed books would be confiscated and publicly burnt.[8] The following year, the Council of Ten issued another proclamation against the printing and selling of books contrary to the Catholic faith.[9] A few months before Titian submitted his request for a license, the Executors added a new requirement that anyone who already had a license to print, before undertaking the printing project, must go to the office of the Executors and there, without charge, register the work in a special book.[10] Further requirements were introduced in the following decades (see Chapter 3).

On 22 January 1567 [1566 m.v.], the same day he was granted a license by the Chiefs of the Council of Ten, Titian submitted his

---

[6] The Esecutori contra la bestemmia is discussed in Renzo Derosas, "Moralità e giustizia a Venezia nel '500–'600. Gli Esecutori contro la bestemmia," in *Stato, società e giustizia nella Repubblica veneta (secc. XV–XVIII)*, ed. Gaetano Cozzi (Rome, 1980), 1: 431–528; and G. Cozzi, "Religione, moralità e giustizia a Venezia: vicende della magistratura degli esecutori contro la bestemmia (sec. XVI–XVII)," *Ateneo Veneto* 177 (n.s. 29) (1991): 7–95.

[7] The document is recorded in ASV, ECBC, Busta 54, vol. 1, fol. 36r.–v., 37r. Giuliano Pesenti, "Libri censurati a Venezia nei secoli XVI–XVII," *La Bibliofilia* 58 (1956): 16, reproduces part of the document but with several errors in transcription. It is also noted in Paul Grendler, *The Roman Inquisition and the Venetian Press, 1540–1605* (Princeton, 1977), 78.

[8] The document is recorded in ASV, CX, Comuni, Busta 43, fol. 24v.; and in ASV, ECBC, Busta 54, vol. 1, fol. 37r.

[9] The document is recorded in ASV, CX, Comuni, Busta 45, fol. 36r.

[10] The document is recorded in ASV, ECBC, Busta 54, vol. 1, fol. 37v.

supplication for a *privilegio* to the Senate of Venice. In his supplication, Titian refers to the print of the *Holy Trinity* (called "paradiso" in the supplication) that he had recently had printed and to "various other pieces" of his own invention ("un disegno del paradiso, et diversi altri pezzi di diversi altre inventioni") which he states he produced through his own "great labour and expense." He also explains that he produced these prints "for the communal convenience of those who study painting" ("à comun comodo de' studiosi della pittura"). He goes on to ask that no one else, without his permission, be permitted to re-engrave his designs or sell them in any form for fifteen continuous years in Venice or elsewhere.

A fortnight later, on 4 February 1567 [1566 m.v.], the Senate granted the *privilegio* to Titian with a vote of 167 in favour, 14 against, and 7 abstentions.[11] The *privilegio* claimed effectiveness within the Republic of Venice and carried a penalty of a fine of fifty ducats for each counterfeited plate and one ducat for each print printed from that plate, be it in the hands of the person who engraved the plate or in those of the person selling the print. Of the sum collected, the plaintiff, Titian, would receive one third, while the other two-thirds would be divided equally between the Arsenal and the Ospedale della Pietà.

With the *privilegio* now in hand, Titian published the *Holy Trinity*. It is inscribed with Titian's name, "Titianus," in the lower right and the date, "1566," in the lower left. Only the words "cum privilegio" indicate the print's approved and protected status. The duration of the *privilegio* is not given; only from the granting document is it learned that the period of coverage was fifteen years. Besides the *Holy Trinity*, Titian had the words *cum privilegio* inscribed on three other prints by Cort, all dated 1566: *Mary Magdalen, Prometheus Enchained on Mount Caucasus*, and *Diana Discovering Callisto's Pregnancy* (Fig. 2).[12]

---

[11] Titian's *privilegio* is recorded in ASV, ST, reg. 46, fol. 111r. (135r. n.n.). The document is transcribed in Kristeller, 24.

[12] The print of *Mary Magdalen* is listed in Bierens de Haan, no. 143. The painting of *St. Mary Magdalen in Penitence* had been shipped to Madrid in 1561. It was destroyed in a fire in London in 1873. The print, however, does not exactly resemble the painting and it is believed by some that it may reproduce another lost painting by Titian. The *Diana Discovering Callisto's Pregnancy* is listed in Bierens de Haan, no. 157. Of the two versions of Titian's painting of *Diana and Callisto*, that in the Kunsthistorisches Museum, Vienna, is more closely reproduced in Cort's print. The *Prometheus Enchained on Mount Caucasus* is listed in Bierens de Haan, no. 192. Titian's painting of *Prometheus* (more properly identified as *Tityus*) is now in the Prado Museum, Madrid.

Fig. 2. Cornelis Cort, *Diana Discovering Callisto's Pregnancy* (after Titian). 1566. Engraving. Photo: The Metropolitan Museum of Art, Harris Brisbane Dick Fund, 1949 (49.97.541).

The *privilegio* also appears on two other prints by Cort, both of which, however, are dated 1565: *St. Jerome Reading in the Desert*, and *Roger Saving Angelica*.[13] Presumably in both cases the plates had not yet been published. The *privilegio* also appears on Cort's *Martyrdom of St. Lawrence*, and *Rape of Lucretia* (Fig. 3), both dated 1571, and on an anonymous engraving of Titian's *Cyclops Forging the Arms of Brescia* dated 1572.[14] Presumably this is the same *privilegio* issued in 1566, which would indicate that the arrangement whereby Titian submitted for approval other prints as they were produced continued to remain in effect five or more years after the privilege was granted.[15]

The example of Titian's *privilegio* and the steps required in order to obtain it reveals the existence of a system by which the Venetian government and ecclesiastical authorities sought to control the production of books and prints. It governed in various ways the activities of publishers and printmakers and affected what they could and could not produce. It also influenced, though in ways that are difficult to document, matters of quality as well as choice and treatment of subject matter.

From the outset, the license functioned as a tool of control over material that was being printed, and in that respect also served as an effective censoring device. The *privilegio*, on the other hand, served primarily as a means of protecting the financial investment in a printing project. While a license was required, a *privilegio* was optional.

---

[13] The *St. Jerome Reading in the Desert* and *Roger Saving Angelica* are listed in Bierens de Haan, nos. 134 and 222, respectively. The print of *St. Jerome Reading in the Desert* does not correspond with any known painting by Titian. The *Roger Saving Angelica* is after a drawing by Titian now in Musée Bonnat, Bayonne.

[14] The *Rape of Lucretia* is listed in Bierens de Haan, no. 193. Bierens de Haan, however, confuses the history of the original painting in the Fitzwilliam Museum, Cambridge, reproduced in the print, and a version in the Musée des Beaux-Arts, Bordeaux. The *Martyrdom of St. Lawrence* is listed in Bierens de Haan, no. 139. The *Cyclops Forging the Arms of Brescia* is listed in Bierens de Haan, no. 156. The print, inscribed "EX ARCHE-/TYPO PALLATII/BRIXIENSIS/1572" in the lower left (and the words "Cum Priuilegio" to the right of the lion's head in the lower center), would appear to be after one of a series of paintings of *Allegories of Brescia* painted by Titian in the Great Hall of the Palazzo Comunale in Brescia and destroyed by fire in 1575.

[15] Carlo Ridolfi, *Le meraviglie dell'arte*, 1: 203, gives virtually the same list when recounting the prints engraved by Cort of Titian's work: "fece trasportare nelle stampe il Paradiso già dipinto per lo Imperadore; il martirio di San Lorenzo fatto per lo Rè Cattolico; la Maddalena pentita nell'eremo; il San Girolamo nel deserto; il bagno di Calisto con molte Ninfe; Prometeo lacerato dall'Aquila; Andromeda legata al sasso liberata da Perseo [i.e. Roger Saving Angelica]; & altre inventioni . . ."

Fig. 3. Cornelis Cort, *Rape of Lucretia* (after Titian) 1571. Engraving.
Photo: The Metropolitan Museum of Art, Harris Brisbane Dick Fund,
1949 (49.97.539).

Many prints were published in the sixteenth century without a *privi-legio*. Why did Titian apply for one? Towards the end of his supplication Titian gives the reasons why his designs should be protected from copyists:

> As some men ignorant of art, in order to avoid the work and out of greed for profit put themselves to this task [of copying prints, thereby] defrauding the honour of the inventor of the prints by depreciating them and profiting from the labours of others; besides cheating the public with a forged print of little value . . .

From these statements it is clear that Titian saw the *privilegio* as serving two interconnected purposes. First and foremost it protected his commercial rights, his investment of time and money in the project, by prohibiting copyists from profiting from his labours. Second, he clearly felt that it also protected in some measure his artistic rights by preventing the copyist from "defrauding" his "honour" as an artist. A copy made by those "ignorant of art" would be inferior in quality and would thereby devalue Titian's original invention. At stake, or so Titian claimed, was his "honour" as an artist, which may be understood to mean the perception of his standing as an artist in the eyes of the public. The public, of course, were the people who purchased prints. From the commercial point of view, if inferior copies were allowed to circulate, then not only would they diminish the profits Titian could make from his original print, but the inferior quality of the copy would also serve to lower the public's estimation of Titian as an artist and thereby depreciate the value of his work. In Titian's view, the copyist not only cheated him out of his commercial rights but also cheated the public with a "forged print of little value."

Besides Titian, a number of other individuals evidently regarded the *privilegio* as a useful device to protect their rights. What were these rights, exactly? Other questions also need to be addressed: When was copyright first used to protect printed images and under what circumstances was it granted? Who could apply for copyright, what was the application procedure, and did this vary from one granting authority to another? What sorts of prints were covered; was subject matter or quality an issue? For how long was a print protected by copyright? What legal steps were available to a holder of copyright when it was infringed? What penalties were incurred by transgressors? Was copyright an effective deterrent against counterfeiting? Why were some prints published with a *privilegio* and others not?

While copyright for books has received some attention from scholars, the issuance of the *privilegio* for printed images – woodcuts, engravings, etchings – during the same period (fifteenth and sixteenth centuries) has not been examined in depth.[16] Previous research on copyright in Italy during the Renaissance has focused primarily on its application to printed books, and, because of a relative wealth of archival material from the earliest period, on books printed in Venice. Archival research in the Venetian archives, undertaken mostly in the latter part of the nineteenth century, brought to light many pertinent documents that showed, among other things, that initially supplications for a *privilegio* had been submitted to the College (*Collegio*), but later, after 1517, they were submitted to the Senate (*Senato*). Records of the granting of privileges by the College were recorded in the registers of the *Notatorio del Collegio*, while those granted by the Senate were recorded in the registers of the *Senato Terra*.[17] Licenses granted for printing were recorded in the registers of the Chiefs of the Council of Ten (*Capi del Consiglio dei Dieci*).

Some two hundred and fifty-six documents, dating from 1469 to 1526, culled mostly from the records of the College, Senate, and Chiefs of the Council of Ten, were published in summary form by Rinaldo Fulin in 1882.[18] Several of these same documents, from the years 1469 to 1515, were published in complete transcriptions by Carlo Castellani in 1888.[19] These publications, together with much additional archival material, served as the basis for Horatio Brown's comprehensive study of the Venetian printing press published in 1891.[20] The Venetian archives were also explored by the Duc du

---

[16] David Landau and Peter Parshall, *The Renaissance Print: 1450–1550* (New Haven and London, 1994), examine the history of printmaking in both Italy and the Northern Europe and provide a valuable discussion of a handful of well-known examples of the Venetian *privilegio*. A few early examples of the *privilegio* granted for prints are briefly reviewed in Thomas Würtenberger, *Das Kunstlerfälschertum: Entstehung und Bekämpfung eines Verbrechens vom Anfang des 15. bis zum Ende des 18. Jahrhunderts* (Weimar, 1940), 186–188.

[17] Records of the supplications are to be found in the associated *filze*.

[18] Rinaldo Fulin, "Documenti per servire alla Storia della Tipografia Veneziana," *Archivio Veneto* 23 (1882): 84–212.

[19] Carlo Castellani, *La Stampa in Venezia dalla sua origine alla morte di Aldo Manuzio* (Venice, 1889).

[20] Horatio Brown, *The Venetian Printing Press 1469–1800* (London 1891). In preparation for this study, Brown compiled a manuscript list of privileges found in the Venetian archives dating from 1527 to 1597 which today is preserved under the title "Privilegi veneziani per la stampa (1527–1597)" in the Biblioteca Nazionale Marciana, Venice, cod. ital. VII, 2501 (12078).

Rivoli and Charles Ephrussi who, in an article on Venetian wood-cuts published in 1891, the same year Brown's study appeared, include references to a number of those documents concerning prints that Fulin had already published plus several others dating to after 1526 (Fulin's latest) and as late as 1547 (most of which were known also to Brown).[21] Rivoli and Ephrussi were not concerned directly with copyright *per se* but used several of the supplication and *privilegio* documents to argue that publishers produced their own wood-cuts to illustrate their books (see Chapter 4). Most of the published documents and several others in the Venetian archives besides were examined afresh in preparation for this present study. While further material, usually in the form of particular documents pertaining to individual publishers, continues to be published, no comprehensive study of the Venetian *privilegio* has yet been undertaken.

By the turn of the fifteenth-century, the Holy See in Rome was also granting copyright. In the sixteenth century, Venice and Rome were the principal granting authorities in Italy, if not Europe. They were also the first authorities to grant copyright for individual prints. In contrast to the Venetian *privilegio*, the papal *privilegio* has received only slight attention from scholars. In 1929–30, Pierina Fontana provided a sampling of documents pertaining to copyright that she had discovered in the Vatican Secret Archives.[22] The documents she included cover a period of twenty-four years, from 1515 to 1539.

---

[21] Le Duc de Rivoli and Charles Ephrussi, "Notes sur les Xylographes Vénetiens du XVᵉ et XVIᵉ siècles," *Gazette des Beaux-Arts* 32 (1891): 494–503.

[22] Pierina Fontana, "Inizi della proprietà letteraria nello Stato Pontifico (Saggio di documenti dell'Archivio Vaticano)," *Accademie e biblioteche d'Italia* 3 (1929–1930): 204–221. As an introduction to the early history of papal copyright, however, her research is flawed and inadequate. Research undertaken for this present study shows that Fontana failed to discover a number of important documents. In her claiming that the earliest known papal *privilegio*, discovered by her, is dated 26 February 1515, she evidently missed earlier examples, including two dating as early as 1509. Moreover, Fontana's reliability is brought into question when on one page she dates the *privilegio* "26 febbraio 1515" but three pages later gives the date of the same document as "9 settembre 1515." This error is compounded by the fact that nei-ther date corresponds to that given in the text of the *privilegio* printed in the book for which it was granted: 21 September 1515 (Fontana, 207, 210). The book, *De sermone Latino, et Modis Latine loqvendi* by Adriano Castellesi, titular cardinal of San Crisogono and bishop of Bath, was printed in Rome by Marcello Silber the fol-lowing month in October, 1515. According to Alberto Tinto, *Gli annali tipografici di Eucario e Marcello Silber (1501–1527)* (Florence, 1968), 124, n. 1, the book was in fact a second edition of the *De sermone Latino*, with the *De modis Latine loquendi* added. Tinto gives the correct date of the *privilegio* in the book, and also notes Fontana's errors.

More recently, Maria Grazia Blasio has also examined the papal
privilegio and the matter of licensing, covering the years 1487 to
1527.[23] Blasio's research is mostly bibliographic and contains little
or no original archival documentation. To my knowledge, no attempt
has been made to conduct a comprehensive search of the Vatican
Secret Archives for documents pertaining to copyright during the
period of the Renaissance.

As in Venice, the papal *privilegio* was applied for through a supplication, addressed to the pope himself. The *privilegio* was issued as
a *motu proprio* in the form of a papal *breve* ("brief") drawn up by the
Office of the Secretariate of Latin Briefs. A *motu proprio* (meaning literally "on one's own initiative") is a papal document personally signed
by the pope, while a *breve* is a type of papal letter by which apostolic secretaries transmitted papal commands. The Office of the
Secretariate of Latin Briefs had been established in the fifteenth century and functioned initially as part of the Apostolic Secretariate and
later as part of the Secretariate of State. Its primary task was the
preparation of the Latin text of letters (briefs) to be sent by the pope.
The Office of the Secretariate of Latin Briefs was presided over by
a prelate who belonged to the pontifical anticamera and was of
necessity a proficient Latinist. When issuing a brief, the Office of
the Secretariate of Latin Briefs also made a copy of the brief, "Ad
futuram rei memoriam" ("that the matter may be known in the
future" or "for future reference"), for its own records. The phrase
"Ad futuram rei memoriam" is one of the features that serve to distinguish the papal brief from the papal bull, which employs instead
the formula "Ad perpetuam rei memoriam ("that the matter may
be perpetually known") in the superscription. Bulls also employed
doubled-sided seals that were appended to the document on strings
sealed with lead. In contrast, briefs were sealed with wax imprinted
with the papal privy signet ring called the "Annelo Piscatoris"
("fisherman's ring," a gold ring holding the pope's private seal). In
the Archives of Secret Briefs, besides a copy of the original brief,
occasionally a copy of the *motu proprio* may be found together with,
towards the end of the sixteenth century, a copy of the original letter of supplication submitted by the supplicant.

---

[23] Maria Grazia Blasio, "Privilegi e licenze di stampa a Roma fra Quattro e
Cinquecento," *La Bibliofilia* 90 (1988): 147–159; and idem, *Cum gratia et privilegio: programmi editoriale e politica pontificia Roma 1487–1527* (Rome, 1988).

The Archive of Secret Briefs in the Vatican contains some seven thousand bound volumes of briefs dating from 1566 to 1846. Before 1566, the collection of briefs is less complete, as is made apparent by the existence of numerous published books carrying notice of papal *privilegio* but for which an archival record was not to be found. The search for briefs granting privileges is greatly facilitated by 'Indexes' compiled more or less at the time of issuance by the Office of the Secretariate of Latin Briefs which contain summary descriptions of the purpose or contents of each brief together with the name of the person or persons to whom it had been issued and the date of issuance. Both the Indexes and the volumes of briefs were incorporated into the Vatican Secret Archives in 1908.

Briefs were issued for many different purposes besides privileges for prints. The present Archive of Secret Briefs contains consistorial documents, marriage dispensations, indulgences, honours granted to corporations, ecclesiastics, and laymen, dispensations from canonical prescription, grants for privileged altars, and so on. The briefs are mostly filed under "Secretarium Breviarum," but may also be found (before 1580) in "Armadio."

Research conducted for this present study included a systematic and thorough search through the Indexes in the Vatican Archives from 1484 (the beginning of the papacy of Innocent VIII) to 1605 (the death of Clement VIII). A number of privileges for both books and prints were discovered among the many thousands of papal briefs issued during this period. The earliest papal *privilegio* found for single prints (i.e. issued independent of books) is dated 1575. Before 1575 the archive is less complete to the extent that despite the evidence on prints that the papal *privilegio* was being granted, corresponding documents have not been found. Although some problems regarding the papal *privilegio* before 1575 remain insoluble without the archival records, the largely complete documentation surviving for the last quarter of the sixteenth century provides the basis for an accurate assessment and analysis of the papal *privilegio* for this period.

*   *   *

Copyright was first introduced in Venice with the purpose of protecting the investment made in the commercial production of printed books. At some early point before the end of the century it was extended to, or was simply understood to include, prints made from woodcuts and copper plates. Although there are obvious differences between a woodcut or an engraving and a book, both were products of the printing press, and so from the outset it would appear that no significant legal distinction was made between the two. Apart from having a similar means of production, they were also closely linked in other ways: books were often illustrated with woodcuts and engravings, and books and prints could be published by the same individual. Books comprised mostly or entirely of prints also blurred distinctions. For legislators in fifteenth-century Venice, therefore, copyright laws were written to pertain equally to both books and prints. This equality extended to the procedure for application, which was done through the same authorities, and to the content of the granting document, which carried virtually the same restrictions, indemnities, mandates, penalties, and so on.

However, although technically equivalent in the eyes of the law, books were nonetheless considered to be of far greater importance than prints. Much more time, money, and effort was expended in their production, and it was with the protection of this larger investment that copyright was mostly concerned. By dint of the production process, prints were an incorporate part of the copyright system, but they occupied a secondary place in it. The primary concern was with books; prints *per se* do not appear to have had any significant influence on the content of copyright legislation. Copyright granted for prints, then, was inextricably bound up with that granted for books. It is therefore both necessary and appropriate in order to better comprehend the form of copyright protection available for prints to pay close attention to the larger context of copyright for books.

The notion of what constitutes a 'print' is treated broadly. In this study, a print includes 'fine art' prints of works of art (both original and reproductive), prints of antiquities, architectural prints, portraits, geographical maps, views of cities and fortresses, and prints with so-called "popular" subject matter. Also included are woodcuts and engravings produced as book illustrations and page decorations. Because it was possible to acquire copyright protection for each of these different types of prints, they have all been included in this study.

The chapters in Part 1 survey the early history of copyright and attempt to answer the questions posed earlier. The chapters in Part 2 are mostly compilations of the various recipients of copyright grouped initially by area and period, and then by subject type. No claim is made to completeness and the reader should not assume that the list of recipients includes everyone who received a *privilegio* during the years covered. A chronologically ordered handlist of prints granted and/or published with a *privilegio* is provided in Appendix A.

Although the focus of this study is prints and copyright granted in Venice and Rome, it should not be overlooked that the Venetian government and the Holy See were not the only authorities granting the *privilegio* in Italy in the sixteenth century. Nor indeed was the *privilegio* exclusively an Italian phenomenon but was available also in other countries. A study of copyright in Europe, or even in Italy besides Venice and Rome, in the sixteenth century is beyond the scope of this present book. Until such a study is undertaken, however, a few brief notes are offered in Appendix B on some of the first examples of copyright granted elsewhere in Italy and in various parts of Europe. Most of these authorities were granting copyright for books throughout the sixteenth century. A few, however, mostly in the latter half of the century, were also issuing the *privilegio* for prints.

PART ONE

SURVEY

CHAPTER ONE

PRINTMAKING IN SIXTEENTH-CENTURY ITALY

From its inception in the fifteenth century printmaking was pre-
dominantly a commercial activity. The production of prints in Italy
grew from a small trickle at the beginning of the sixteenth century
into a great flood by the end. Before embarking on an examination
of prints and copyright, it is important to get a sense of these developments in the making and distribution of prints in the sixteenth
century in order to understand the circumstances that gave rise to
the need for copyright.

Giorgio Vasari supplies the most comprehensive contemporary survey of printmaking in Italy up to 1568 in his *vita* of Marcantonio
Raimondi, which appeared in the expanded second edition of his
Lives of the Painters, Sculptors, and Architects.[1] Vasari also provides a
revealing example of the growing awareness of the revolution that
was occurring in the expanding production of prints and the growth
in the print market. Significantly, Vasari all but ignored prints in
the first edition of the *Lives* published eighteen years earlier in 1550.
He had included sections that discuss the production of *nielli* and
chiaroscuro prints made from woodblocks, and devoted a *vita* to Valerio
Vicentino, an engraver of stones and cameos, but had little to say
about prints made from copper plates, except to point out that copperplate engraving was derived from the technique developed for
engraving *nielli*. Nothing is said about the many Italian and German
prints that could be seen in Italy at the time he was writing. Of the
many Italian and German engravers, Vasari mentions only Albrecht
Dürer, Marcantonio Raimondi, Marco da Ravenna, Iacopo Caraglio,
Enea Vico, and the obscure Girolamo Fagiuoli.[2]

---

[1] Vasari, 1568, 5: 395–442. Vasari and prints are discussed in Evelina Borea,
"Vasari e le stampe," *Prospettiva* 57–60 (1989–90): 18–38.

[2] Dürer, Marcantonio, Marco da Ravenna, and Ugo da Carpi are mentioned
by Vasari in the *vita* of Raphael in the 1550 edition of *Le Vite*, 2: 658–59. Ugo da
Carpi's chiaroscuro woodblock prints are discussed at greater length in the section
"De le Stampe di legno . . ." (1550, 1: 109–110). Enea Vico and Girolamo Fagiuoli
[Vasari gives the name as Ieronimo de Fagiuoli] are both mentioned at the end

By 1568 the revolution occurring in the production of printed images could no longer be ignored.[3] At the outset Vasari acknowledges his omission of a discussion of the technique of copperplate engraving in the 1550 edition, states that he now wishes to correct that oversight, and includes an entire chapter devoted to Marcantonio Raimondi "and other engravers of prints" ("e altri intagliatori di stampe"). However, although the chapter, in keeping with the structure of the book, is ostensibly a biography of Marcantonio Raimondi, Marcantonio's *vita* serves largely as a framework and context for what amounts to a survey of the history of printmaking from its origins down to Vasari's own day. It is clear that Vasari felt compelled to attempt this in part because of the significant changes in the production of engraved prints that had occurred soon after the middle of the century. Between 1550 and 1568 prints had achieved a new prominence in Rome due largely to the entrepreneurial activities of the print publisher Antonio Lafrery (1512–1577) who, as Vasari himself observed, had organized the production of engravings into a large-scale business that issued prints singly, in sets, or collected into books, in a variety of sizes and subjects.[4] Moreover, a number of the prints that Lafrery had in stock had been produced earlier in the century, catering, it would appear, to a new interest in prints as something collectible. The appeal of the print as a collector's item would have been impressed upon Vasari by the Netherlandish painter and writer Dominicus Lampsonius who enthusiastically discussed prints in these terms in at least one letter to Vasari in 1565.[5] Indeed, Vasari explains at the end of the chapter on Marcantonio that he had undertaken the writing of it "in order to please not only connoisseurs of our arts, but especially those who take delight in works

---

of the *vita* of Valerio Vicentino (1550, 2: 864), and Iacopo Caraglio in the *vita* of Perino del Vaga (1550, 2: 928). To this list should perhaps be added the Bolognese sculptress Properzia de Rossi whom Vasari says also engraved copperplate prints ("intagliar stampe di Rame") (1550, 2: 776).

[3] Vasari's attitude towards prints is discussed by David Landau, "Vasari, Prints and Prejudice," *Oxford Art Journal* 6 (1983): 3–10.

[4] The extent of Lafrery's print publishing activities can be gathered from Franz Ehrle, *Roma prima di Sisto V* (Rome, 1908); François Roland, "Un Franc-Comtois Editeur et Marchand d'Estampes a Rome au XVIᵉ Siècle: Antoine Lafrery (1512–1577)," *Mémoires de la Société d'émulation du Doubs* (Besançon) (1911): 320–378; and Christian Huelson, "Das Speculum Romanae Magnificentiae des Antonio Lafreri," in *Collectanea Variae Doctrinae Leoni S. Olschki* (Munich, 1921), 121–170.

[5] Lampsonius's letter, dated 25 April 1565, is reproduced in Frey, *Der literarische Nachlass Giorgio Vasaris*, 2: no. 492, 158–162.

of this kind."[6] This statement contributes to the impression that the chapter was written primarily as a sort of handbook for those interested in prints, and in particular for collectors. Collectors, who arguably comprised a small but select segment of the market for prints, purchased prints primarily for aesthetic reasons. They sought out the works of recognized engravers by name (Vasari having identified for them the collectible engravers), and were generally concerned more with the quality of the engraving and printing than with the subject matter. Collectors (and curators of prints in museums today) were primarily interested in prints of high quality produced by the original engraver whose name they would know.

The very existence of Vasari's chapter on prints, together with the increase in the production of prints, the concomitant growth in the print market, plus the appearance of print dealers and publishers and the emergence of print collectors, all serve as evidence of widespread and well-formed consumer taste for prints by the middle of the sixteenth century. Canons of taste were already established in various areas of the decorative arts, and this had immediate economic effects. The purchasing of prints by collectors and others had the effect of channeling wealth into a luxury consumption, which resulted in its transformation into human capital in the form of an increase in the number of skilled engravers and printers practicing their trade, the expansion in the range of their skills (including the development of new skills and techniques such as chiaroscuro printing and etching), and the stimulus this brought about in the exercise of those skills. The increase in the number of active engravers over the course of the sixteenth century is evidence not only of increasing demand for prints but also that printmaking was an attractive trade with tangible rewards. The popularisation of prints and the increase in their consumption almost certainly had a significant economic impact on the cities of Venice and Rome, a fact which the government of Venice clearly recognized and cultivated from the outset in part through the introduction of copyright laws. Richard Goldthwaite has stressed the centrality of the decorative arts to the transformation of the social structure of the economy in the sixteenth century.[7] The success of the printmaking and print publishing industry

---

[6] Vasari, 1568, 5: 442: "per sodisfare non solo agli studiosi delle nostre arti, ma a tutti coloro ancora che di così fatte opere si dilettano."

[7] Richard A. Goldthwaite, *The Building of Renaissance Florence: An Economic and Social*

contributed to this transformation and to the formation of consumer tastes for luxury material goods.[8] It is within this context that Vasari composed his *vita* of Marcantonio.

Vasari had apparently already intended to include a *vita* of Marcantonio in the new edition of the *Lives*, when, in 1564, judging by the contents of a note written to himself on the back of a letter he had received in April of that year, he decided to expand it to include other Italian printmakers and also German and French engravers.[9] In the chapter, Vasari attempts to treat both the Italian and the northern engravers on a more or less chronological basis. This chronology is divided into roughly three segments. The first spans the period from 1460 to around 1510, the latter date apparently coinciding in Vasari's mind more or less with the beginning of Marcantonio's career in Rome. This section opens with the fifteenth-century Italian *niellist* Maso Finiguerra whom Vasari credits with the invention of the technique for producing prints. This technique was then employed by another Florentine, the goldsmith Baccio Baldini who, because he utilized the designs of Sandro Botticelli in his prints, may be identified as the first reproductive engraver. It was these developments that encouraged Andrea Mantegna to begin making prints after his own works. It is at this point in the development of engraving, Vasari explains, that "the invention then passed to Flanders" and he turns to the prints of Martin Schongauer and Albrecht Dürer.[10] At the end of this first chronological segment, as a sort of culmination of the developments he had been discussing, Vasari introduces Marcantonio and the pre-Rome part of his career. He mentions the early years spent apprenticed to Francesco Francia in Bologna, but concentrates more on his trip to Venice and his discovery, and plagia-

---

History (Baltimore, 1980); and idem, *Wealth and the Demand for Art in Italy, 1300–1600* (Baltimore, 1993).

[8] Chandra Mukerji, *From Graven Images: Patterns of Modern Materialism* (New York, 1983), who studied pictorial prints as a way of analysing the historical development of consumerism during the period of the Renaissance, has argued that consumerism helped to create capitalism, not the other way round.

[9] Frey, 2: 78. The note reads: "Nomi di maestri delle stampe di rame Todeschi, Taliani et Franzesi. Bisogna rifare la vita di Marca[n]tonio Bolognese per metterci tutti questi maestri" ("Names of German, Italian and French masters of copperplate engraving. Must redo the life of Marcantonio to include all these masters").

[10] Vasari, 1568, 5: 396. This claim, which asserts that engraving was invented by the Italian Maso Finiguerra, has been generally discarded in the face of prints dating to before 1460 both in the North and in Italy.

rism, of Albrecht Dürer's woodcuts (for Vasari's story of Marcantonio's plagiarism of Dürer's prints, see Chapter 4).

The second chronological segment, which spans the period from *circa* 1510 to around 1530, opens with the notice of Marcantonio going to Rome, but then turns immediately to discuss the activities of Lucas van Leyden and his interaction with Dürer. Lucas's prints are highly praised by Vasari, but when he returns to Marcantonio, he remarks that Marcantonio's prints were held in much higher estimation than the Fleming's. The reason for this, Vasari explains, was because of Marcantonio's good design.[11] This, in Vasari's judgement, is what distinguished Marcantonio from his contemporaries Dürer and Lucas, who were admired chiefly for their technical mastery. It was the technique of Dürer and, to a lesser extent, that of Lucas that Marcantonio had learned earlier in his career. But, after his arrival in Rome, he added to this *buon disegno* and thus, in Vasari's eyes, surpassed his northern rivals.

The period of Marcantonio's activity in Rome is subdivided into two parts consisting of that before Raphael's death, in 1520, and that after. These sections are separated by a discussion of the activities of two pupils of Marcantonio, Marco da Ravenna (Marco Dente) and Agostino Veneziano. The final chronological segment deals with the period beginning with the death of Marcantonio (or with his departure from Rome soon after the Sack of 1527), down to the time Vasari was writing. It opens with a section devoted to chiaroscuro woodcuts, which appear to have been the only type of prints Vasari liked, but then turns to a discussion of engraving "after Marcantonio" which includes not only Italian engravers such as Jacopo Caraglio, Giovanni Battista Scultori, Enea Vico, Giulio Bonasone, Battista Franco, Giorgio Ghisi, and Giovanni Battista de' Cavalieri, but also numerous "oltramontani," including the italianized Nicolas Beatrizet (Nicolo Beatricetto), René Boyvin, Lambert Suavius, Hans Liefrinck, George Pencz, and Jacob Binck.[12] Vasari also mentions some

---

[11] Vasari, 1568, 5: 411: "ch'erano molto più stimate le cose sue pel buon disegno che le fiaminghe." A few pages earlier Vasari had pointed out that when Marcantonio arrived in Rome, he "gave his whole attention to design" (5: 406: "si diede tutto al disegno"). The significance of the notion of design (*disegno*) in Vasari's thinking is discussed in Moshe Barasch, *Theories of Art from Plato to Winckelmann* (New York, 1985), 217–219.

[12] Vasari devoted an entire section to Ugo da Carpi and the technique of chiaroscuro prints in the 1550 edition (see above). He again discusses the prints of Ugo

important publishers of prints: Baviera, Tommaso Barlacchi, and Antonio Lafrery, who operated shops in Rome, and Hieronymus Cock (who was also an engraver-etcher) in Antwerp.

Vasari's survey, however, is by no means comprehensive and numerous engravers have been omitted. No mention is made, for example, of the Venetians Jacopo de' Barbari, Giulio and Domenico Campagnola, and Giulio Musi. He also neglects to include several Italian engravers at work around the time he was writing, such as Mario Cartari, Sebastiano del Re, Michele Lucchese, Andrea Marelli, Mario Labacco, and Adamo Scultori. He also ignores a number of non-Italian engravers working in Italy: the Frenchmen Georges Reverdy, who was in Italy around 1530, Jacques Prévost, who was already in Rome by 1535, Philippe Soye, who worked in Rome in the 1560s, and Etienne Dupérac, who began working in Rome in 1559. Nor is mention made of the Belgian Jacob Bos, who was in Rome already by 1549, or the Dutch engraver Cornelis Cort, who arrived in Rome from Venice in 1566, or the Dalmatian engraver Martin Rota, who worked in both Venice and Rome before moving to Vienna in 1568.

However, even with these omissions, Vasari's chapter on the life of Marcantonio Raimondi provides a sense of the rapid growth in the production of prints in the first half of the sixteenth century. From the handful of engravers identified at the outset, the numbers more than double with each successive generation. At the beginning of the century in Italy Marcantonio stands virtually alone. In the second and third decades he is joined in Rome by Agostino Veneziano, Marco da Ravenna, Jacopo Caraglio, and the chiaroscuro woodcut specialist Ugo da Carpi. In the fourth and fifth decades the numbers increase again to include Giovanni Battista Scultori, Enea Vico, Giulio Bonasone, Giorgio Ghisi, Battista del Moro, Luca Penni, Antonio da Trento, Battista Franco, Nicolas Beatrizet, and Giovanni Battista de' Cavalieri. Vasari's list is by no means complete, but a survey otherwise conducted of engravers active in Italy during the first half of the century would show a similar increase in numbers.

---

da Carpi in the 1568 edition, together with a selection of those by Baldassare Peruzzi, Parmigianino, Antonio da Trento, and Domenico Beccafumi. In his *vita* of Beccafumi, Vasari states that he possessed one of Beccafumi's chiaroscuro woodcut prints. This is the only instance where Vasari mentions owning a print himself (see Landau, "Vasari, Prints and Prejudice," 4).

Not all these printmakers, of course, were equally productive, but the significant increase in the number of producers of prints over the course of a few decades would indicate the development of a market for prints capable of supporting ever-increasing numbers of practitioners. Vasari's survey stops in 1568, but the pace in the production of prints continues unabated into the seventeenth century. This level of growth, which could be sustained only if there was sufficient demand, provides some notion of the size of the market available for prints.

A further and perhaps more telling indication of the size of the market is the number of copies of prints made during the same period. The sheer number of copies suggests that the market for prints was perhaps more complex than is presumed. Moreover, besides what they may reveal about the composition of the print market (i.e. who was purchasing prints), copies of prints raise important questions about popularity and taste.

The market for prints was discovered, or one could almost say created, by the painter Raphael, who subsequently exploited it with great efficiency through his chief engraver Marcantonio. It is generally presumed that Marcantonio's prints were purchased by *cognoscenti* and collectors. The notion that such individuals comprised the chief market for prints is supported by Vasari's statement, noted above, that his chapter on Marcantonio was written largely in order to satisfy "all those who delight in works of that kind."

Copies of prints, on the other hand, which were often produced by anonymous engravers and were usually inferior in quality to the original, would not have interested Vasari's collectors. A great many copies were produced, however. Their existence suggests that there was a second market, different from that composed of *cognoscenti* and collectors for whom Vasari was writing, and more extensive and diverse, that was capable of sustaining a number of copyists whose products varied considerably in quality. Conceivably, prints were produced to satisfy all levels of society, with the majority finding their way, in the latter half of the century, into the hands of the general public.

The existence of copies is also indicative of the popularity of the original. It can be argued that the more copies of a print produced, the more popular must have been the original. Whatever the impression left by Vasari, printmaking was primarily a commercial activity. Beauty of design and quality in the engraving were certainly factors taken into consideration, but it should not be overlooked that prints were used by artists, engravers, and publishers alike chiefly as a means of making money. The commercial value of a print is based on its popularity in the market place. Its popularity in the market place, in turn, was based, it would appear, not exclusively on its technical and aesthetic qualities, or on the name of its engraver, but, with these factors contributing to the effect, on the appeal of its subject matter. This is made abundantly clear in Antonio Lafrery's inventory of prints available at his shop in Rome in 1573. Significantly, whereas Vasari, writing for collectors, discusses prints largely in terms of the engravers and their artistic accomplishments, Lafrery lists his prints according to subject matter, and then size.[13]

The majority of prints produced in the sixteenth century were reproductive in that they were based on, or 'interpreted' in imaginative ways, designs produced by someone other than the engraver himself. In his inventory of 1573, Lafrery regularly omits the names of the engravers, but he occasionally includes the name of the artist whose design was reproduced in the print. Initially, we are confronted with the intriguing question of what a print was thought to be in the sixteenth century. When someone purchased a print, did they think they were acquiring, say, an engraving by Marcantonio after Raphael, or a Cornelis Cort after Titian, or an actual design by Raphael or Titian? Was a print seen as an engraved drawing of a design, or as a 'reproduction' of a drawn or painted design?[14] This raises questions about attitudes towards originality and invention, about notions of artistic property, and about the rights of both artists and engravers. Copyright, by its very nature, may be understood to reflect prevailing ideas about copying and what constituted 'originality' and thus provides a way of understanding what these concepts meant in the production and reproduction of images.

---

[13] This point is also made by Michael Bury, "The Taste for Prints in Italy to c. 1600," *Print Quarterly* 2 (1985): 13. Evelina Borea, "Stampa figurativa e pubblico dalle origini all'affermazione nel Cinquecento," 319–413, discusses the early appearance of categories of subject matter. Lafrery's inventory is reproduced in Ehrle, *Roma Prima di Sisto V* (Rome, 1908), 54–59.

[14] Michael Bury, "The Taste for Prints in Italy to c. 1600," has argued that prints were regarded in the same way as drawings. Reproductive printmaking and the issue of how the prints were perceived are discussed in Evelina Borea, "Le stampe che imitano i disegni," *Bollettino d'arte* 7 (1992): 87–122; Michael Bury, "On Some Engravings by Giorgio Ghisi Commonly Called 'Reproductive'," *Print Quarterly* 10 (1993): 4–19; and Landau and Parshall, *The Renaissance Print*, 293–294.

All these issues—copying, imitation, originality—are to a certain degree fundamental to the concept of copyright. In other words, the concept of an original needs to be in place before you can establish that a copy or an imitation has been made of it. At first glance, the study of copyright would seem to offer an exciting way for the art historian to discover what an 'original' was thought to be in the Renaissance, and thereby what a work of art was conceived as being. Upon further scrutiny, however, it can be seen that this line of reasoning will not produce the desired result. First of all, of course, while a work of art may be an original, an original is not always a work of art, in the modern sense. In copyright, the original is simply that which has been copyrighted. In a copyright supplication, a print may be claimed to be the first of its kind, and therefore the original, but the designation carries no particular claim to it being a work of art. It would be erroneous to think that copyright was applied only to 'works of art' as we understand them today.

These observations also broach the perplexing issue of why some prints were issued with copyright protection and others not. For example, while the *privilegio* appears on several prints engraved by Diana Mantuana between 1575 and 1577 (see Chapter 8), such as *Christ and Mary Magdalen at the Table of Simon the Pharisee* after Giulio Campi, dated 1576, it does not appear on either the *Madonna with Blessing Christ Child* after Durante Alberti nor the *Madonna Kneeling Embracing the Christ Child* after Francesco Salviati, both dated the same year. Of three prints by Diana Mantuana dated 1577, the *privilegio* appears on a *Holy Family in Egypt* after Correggio, but not on either the *Martyrdom of St. Agatha* or the *Penitent Magdalen*. In the case of the painter and printmaker Federico Barocci, to choose just one other example out of many, the *privilegio* appears on his *Pardon of Saint Francis* but not on any of his other prints. Why is this? Why are some prints singled out for copyright protection and others ignored?

One reason might be that the selection was based on aesthetic considerations and quality. Put more simply, only the best prints were copyrighted. But who made the initial selection? Judging from the supplications, where in many instances individual prints are named, the decision over which prints to publish with copyright was made by the supplicant. Certainly quality was an important issue for Titian, who saw the *privilegio* as a means of protecting the plates engraved for him by Cort against copyists who would produce prints of inferior quality (see the Introduction). However, it may be guessed

that the process of selecting prints for copyright protection was based
not solely on matters of aesthetics and quality but was also influenced
by other forces, notably the print market and the Church. It is clear,
both from the point of view of aesthetic appreciation and from the
nature and purpose of copyright as it is examined in this study, that
the *privilegio* itself was not issued on the basis of quality. Perhaps a
case could be made from the few copyrighted prints surviving from
the early part of the century that quality was taken into consideration, but this could not be sustained in the latter part of the century. Although the quality of many copyrighted prints is high, others
are noticeably substandard in terms of design and execution. This
is not to say, however, that for the people who purchased prints the
notice of copyright may not have indicated some measure of quality, much in the same way as a 'by royal appointment' label on
British goods, or a guarantee notice, are perceived by the average
consumer today.

However, although the presence of a copyright notice on a print
seems not to have been necessarily a signal of quality, might it not
nonetheless be regarded as a measure of taste? Arguably, publishers
sought copyright for prints they believed were going to be popular
in the market place and thus more prone to being plagiarized. If
popularity reflects taste, then the *privilegio* provides a unique insight
for the art historian into popular taste at the time. However, the
market was not the only or even the dominant determining force of
control in the sixteenth century. There was no 'invisible hand' freely
at work, but instead the very visible hand of the Church that over
the course of the century, and especially after the Council of Trent
and throughout the period of the Counter-Reformation, came to
exercise increasing control over the printing industry through licensing and censorship (see Chapter 3). To a large degree it can be
stated that as much as copyrighted prints may reflect contemporary
popular taste, they also functioned at the same time as one of the
means by which the Church, and also secular power structures, could
manipulate that taste, in much the same way taste is both reflected
in and manipulated by the media today.

The significant increase in Italy in the number of prints with religious subject matter after the Council of Trent supportive of Catholic
Counter-Reformation views may reflect an increased piousness in the
general populace but it also manifestly served the aims of the Church.
The principal means of control, however, was through licensing,

which was required of all publishers, rather than the *privilegio*, which was an optional 'extra' once a license had been obtained. Copyrighted prints, then, may be regarded as useful indicators of popular taste but with the understanding that within the dominant socio-religious context this 'taste' was focused primarily on subject matter, with aesthetic appreciation and quality playing a less significant part.

It may be the case, therefore, that the choice of which prints would carry a notice of copyright, and which not, was based on perceived market potential that resided more in the choice of subject matter than in purely aesthetic considerations. Of course, it may be argued that aesthetic appeal and marketability were more closely linked in the sixteenth century than they might seem today, but the situation should not be oversimplified. It is worth recalling the distinctions in the print market between collectors, whose acquisitions were based largely on aesthetic considerations and for whom Vasari wrote his *vita* of Marcantonio, and everyone else (the 'public', for want of a better word) who purchased prints at shops, like the one operated by Antonio Lafrery in Rome, largely according to subject matter and, it may be guessed, under the influence of prevailing popular taste. By and large, copyrighted prints fall into the latter category, although a collector's cultured taste and popular taste may at times coincide.

* * *

Finally, it is useful to explain, to the extent that it can be understood today, the various circumstances by which prints were brought into existence in the sixteenth century. All prints may be divided initially into two categories: those that were commissioned and those that were produced at the initiative of the engraver. This can be an important distinction for art historians. In most cases it has absolutely no bearing on the quality of the print, but it can affect one's appreciation of the creative forces involved by making one aware of possible restraints, or lack thereof, that may have affected the final result. It can be argued that when at work on a non-commissioned print, the engraver was free to exercise his or her creative talents without restriction. At the same time, though, in a non-commissioned print the engraver need hold only to his own standards. As far as I am aware, none of the 'original' prints produced in the sixteenth century (i.e. prints in which the engraver is producing or reproducing his own design) was commissioned. An exception might be engravers employed at court, such as Jacques Callot in the Medici ducal court in Florence at the end of the sixteenth century. The extent to which his prints were entirely 'original' or were directly 'commissioned' by his employer is not clear.

Non-commissioned prints, especially those produced by a painter, such as Federico Barocci, are often among the most admired today. This does not mean that prints produced on commission lack creativity and are less admirable. A commissioned print links the engraver to at least one other person. In many instances this other person was a print publisher whose particular requirements in a print imposed certain restrictions on the engraver. In other instances, the other person who commissioned prints was an artist who, in seeking to translate his own ideas and designs into prints, worked closely with the engraver. Several of Marcantonio Raimondi's prints after Raphael, for example, appear to be the result of a collaborative effort directed by the artist.

A plate that has been commissioned usually remained the property of whoever had commissioned it. This might be a book publisher who had commissioned a frontispiece or illustrations for a book, or the writer of a book who commissioned engravings for the same purpose but at his own expense. Or it might be an artist who had commissioned engravings of his own work. It is in the latter category that art historians most frequently encounter commissioned prints in the sixteenth century, although those produced for books are probably more numerous.

It seems likely that anyone who commissioned a plate would want to have copyright protection. It is not surprising therefore to find among the prints granted a *privilegio* in the second half of the sixteenth century a large number of commissioned plates. In these cases the *cum privilegio* inscription is frequently combined with the publisher's name-and-date inscription. A corollary of this observation is that with the development of the print publishing industry, especially in Rome, and the increasing number of plates commissioned by print publishers, there is a commensurate increase in the latter half of the century in the number of privileges granted.

The *privilegio* was designed to inhibit copyists. In the sixteenth century copying prints was widespread and was one of the ways an engraver might earn a living. To a certain extent, copying was also understood to be the means by which a beginner might learn technique. In his well-known account of Marcantonio's plagiarism of

Dürer's prints in Venice (see Chapter 4), Vasari conveys the impression that it was through this exercise that Marcantonio learned his engraving technique. A similar situation would seem to apply to Agostino Veneziano who, at the outset of his career in Venice, copied prints by both Giulio Campagnola and Dürer. In 1514, for example, he made a copy of Campagnola's *Astrologer* (Campagnola's print is dated 1509). He also copied Campagnola's *The Young Shepherd* and two versions of *The Old Shepherd*. Agostino signed his full name, "AGVSTINO DI MVSI," in the upper right of the latter version of *The Old Shepherd*. In 1514, Agostino copied Dürer's *Last Supper*. He also copied Dürer's *Virgin with the Monkey*, and composed another print with the animals that appear in Dürer's engraving *Adam and Eve* and the two standing dogs in his *Vision of St. Eustace*.[15] An example from later in the century would be Cherubino Alberti whose copies of prints by Cornelis Cort appear among his earliest engravings.

But, it should not be overlooked that although artistic admiration and desire to emulate may have been among the reasons why an engraver might choose to copy a print, it was the commercial value of the original that made it attractive, and it was this that the copyist (or his employer) hoped to usurp in part for himself. Moreover, copying was a two-way street. Whatever was successful in the market place was liable to be copied, whether the print was by the 'master' or the 'pupil'. In the case of Marcantonio and his 'pupils', for example, it has long been assumed that Agostino Veneziano and Marco da Ravenna were invariably the copyists of the master's prints. The belief has been that Marcantonio produced the original and when occasion demanded (a worn-out plate, for example), Agostino or Marco were employed to reproduce it. This simple explanation has been challenged by John Spike who argued that in some cases it was Marcantonio who copied the prints of Agostino and Marco. According to Spike, Marcantonio copied Agostino's *Warrior with a Standard*, his *Man Carrying the Base of a Column*, and his *Three Marys Lamenting the Dead Christ* (two versions by Agostino). He also made a copy of Marco da Ravenna's *Venus Wounded by a Thorn*.[16] The truth

---

[15] The prints are listed in Bartsch, 14: nos. 408, 409, 411, 414, and 458, and Passavant, 6: 65, no. 182. Agostino's copies of both Campagnola and Dürer are discussed in Dieter Kuhrmann, "Frühwerke Agostino Venezianos."

[16] John Spike, Marcantonio's Relationship to His School, Qualifying Paper Presented to the Department of Fine Arts, Harvard University, 1974. The prints

of the matter is that Agostino, Marco, and Marcantonio copied each other's prints. A print by one that proved popular in the market place was copied in the hope of cashing-in on its commercial success.

To this end, one finds the initially curious situation in which an engraver might also copy his own work. This phenomenon is easily explained, however. It was noted earlier that in the case of a print that had been commissioned the engraved plate was the property of whoever commissioned it. Money from sales of the print went to the owner of the plate. If the engraver was both covetous and unethical, he could engrave a copy of his own print for his own financial advantage. The most controversial example of this is Marcantonio's copy of his own print of the *Massacre of the Innocents*. In this instance, the original plate (the version 'without the fir tree') had been commissioned by Raphael. Later, possibly after Raphael's death in 1520, Marcantonio copied the print, keeping the plate and all profits earned through sales to himself. Interestingly, this explanation is also found in an anecdote, dismissed as apocryphal by modern scholars, recorded by Carlo Cesare Malvasia in the seventeenth century, in which it is reported that Marcantonio was murdered in Bologna (following his departure from Rome after the Sack in 1527) by a Roman nobleman who had commissioned the *Massacre of the Innocents* and was angered because Marcantonio, contrary to the contractual agreement, had made a copy of it for his own profit.[17] The story purports to explain two issues that are treated as connected: one is the demise of Marcantonio, and the other the two versions of the *Massacre* print. Without additional documentation, it is impossible to say whether the story of Marcantonio's murder is true or not. For the same reasons, and contingent upon the truth of the first issue, it is equally impossible to determine whether or not the motivation for the murder was that given in the story. However, although the story of the murder may be untrue, the situation that is described as having provoked the murder is perfectly plausible.

The extent to which copying was tolerated is difficult to judge.

---

are listed in Bartsch, 14: nos. 481, 482; nos. 476, 477; nos. 37, 38, 39; no. 321. The issue of repetitions and copies is also discussed in Landau and Parshall, 131–142.

[17] Carlo Cesare Malvasia, *Felsina Pittrice*, 8. The anecdote is repeated by Filippo Baldinucci, *Cominciamento, e progresso dell'arte dell'intagliare in rame*, 22; and again by Baldinucci in *Notizie dei professori del disegno*, 52.

Because it was so widespread it would no doubt have been hypocritical to complain. Marcantonio, for example, who had blatantly copied Dürer's prints, could hardly make a fuss about Agostino Veneziano copying his pieces. The market for prints, however, was growing and with it grew competitiveness not just among engravers, but also between rival publishers who, in addition to the artist and the engraver, began to emerge as the important third arm in the commercial production of prints.

Publishers were often also printers whose activities may be divided into three categories: a) those who merely printed plates, either independently or at the behest of someone else; b) those who also owned and printed plates; and c) those who did one or both of the above, but also commissioned plates. If a printer owned plates (many of which, acquired through purchase, would have already been printed at least once before by another printer or a publisher), it was frequently the case that he also commissioned plates. If he then printed a commissioned plate himself, or had someone else print it, he became thereby also a publisher. Many of the plates owned by printer-publishers, such as Antonio Lafrery, had not been commissioned by them, and a number had already been commercially printed at least once before being acquired at a later date either from the engraver, from printers, or from other publishers. Beginning with the printer-publisher Antonio Salamanca, in the late 1530s, it became customary for publishers (and printers who owned plates) to add their name (or 'address') to the plates they owned.

From the many sixteenth-century prints issued without a publisher's address on the first state, it would appear that engravers generally worked independent of commissions, producing prints at their own expense. From an engraver's point of view, although working on commission provided, per commission, a more or less guaranteed source of income with few expenses, it could be less profitable in the long run. It was to the advantage of the engraver to undertake the expense of purchasing and engraving his own plate, paying for its printing, and selling the prints through dealers than to receive a one-time payment for engraving a plate that on completion became the property of the individual who had commissioned it. In the former case, if the print was commercially successful, the engraver earned money; in the latter case, it was the plate's new owner who profited.

When a print was not commissioned, the plate remained in the possession of the engraver who, if he or she wished, could sell it at any time. It was no doubt also the case that an engraver would engrave a plate in the hope of selling it immediately upon completion. Artists, book and print publishers, and whoever owned plates could also sell them. The purchasers were usually print publishers, some of whom, like Antonio Lafrery in Rome, built up large inventories.

Besides commissioned and non-commissioned work by 'freelance' engravers, a large number of plates in the sixteenth century were produced by anonymous engravers employed by printer-publishers. At an early stage in many an engraver's career, time may have been spent doing hack work in a printer-publisher's shop. Tommaso Barlacchi and Antonio Lafrery, according to Vasari, hired young engravers to work for them, and it may be assumed that Antonio Salamanca did the same.[18] It was no doubt the ambition of these young engravers eventually to become freelance, as some certainly did.

A freelance engraver in the early sixteenth century might earn a living in four different ways, and evidence indicates that an engraver frequently pursued all four. One was to produce prints independently for the open market. This was a financially risky proposition, but a handsome profit could be made if the print was successful. Another option was to engrave a plate and attempt to sell it immediately to a publisher or other interested party. A third possibility was to be occasionally employed by a book publisher to produce illustrations for books. This sort of work was usually executed anonymously but offered a more-or-less guaranteed income over a short period while the publishing project was underway. A fourth option was to accept commissioned work from whomever needed engraving done. Before the emergence in the 1520s of the printer-publisher who specialized in prints, employment in this last category came mostly from artists who would engage the engraver to produce one or more plates of his work. Presumably in most cases the cost of the copper plate was covered by the artist who also paid for the printing and distribution. The engraver was most likely paid a predetermined amount based perhaps on such factors as the difficulty of the design, number of figures, size of the plate, and so on. Although artists continued

---

[18] Vasari, 1568, 5: 431.

through the sixteenth century to engage engravers to produce prints of their work, this role of reproducing the inventions of artists increasingly came under the control of publishers. Whereas at the beginning of the century artists such as Raphael, Giulio Romano, and Baccio Bandinelli had influenced what would be printed, by the second half of the century it was the publishers who determined in large measure what would be engraved. And their judgement in this matter came increasingly under the influence of market forces.

During the 1530s and 1540s, as the print publishing industry began to organize around a rapidly expanding print market, the counterfeiting of prints for commercial reasons became rampant. One of the results, that continues to stigmatize later sixteenth-century Italian prints, was an increase in the number of poorly executed prints, a situation that Vasari blamed on the avarice of the printers, "eager more for gain than for honour."[19] It was this counterfeiting, and the avarice of printers, that the *privilegio* was intended to check.

To a certain degree, guilds were supposed to prevent pirating, especially among their own members, but this did not include, apparently, the reproduction in prints of paintings and drawings. A patron or owner of a particular work of art, especially one in a position of power, might perhaps inhibit the activities of counterfeiters, but again this does not seem to have extended to prints. In some cases it might be decreed that a painting cannot be copied, such as was the case with Raphael's painting of the *Visitation* executed for the Church of S. Silvestro in Aquila. On 2 April 1520, soon after the painting was completed, the town council of Aquila decreed that it was forbidden under any pretense whatever to make copies of the work. According to Crowe and Cavacaselle, this decree apparently remained in force until 1610 when it was repealed in favour of Giovanni Andrea Urbani of Urbino.[20]

At the same time, however, a painter could be commissioned to imitate directly the painting of another. For example, when Raphael

---

[19] Vasari, 1568, 5: 430. Arthur Hind, *A History of Engraving and Etching* (Boston and New York, 1923), 118, laments that "The middle years of the sixteenth century was nowhere a time of great achievement in engraving, and, unhappily for the student, the deficiency in quality was far from being accompanied by a paucity of production. There has never, perhaps, been a period more prolific in prints of all sorts."

[20] Crowe and Cavalcaselle, *Raphael: His Life and Work*, 2: 480.

was commissioned in 1505 to paint a Coronation of the Virgin for the nuns at the convent of Monteluce in Perugia, the contract obliged him to reproduce, as accurately as possible, the panel of the same subject painted by Domenico Ghirlandaio in 1486 for the church of S. Girolamo in Narni.[21]

---

[21] See Umberto Gnoli, "Raffaello e la 'Incoronazione' di Monteluce," *Bollettino d'arte* 11 (1917): 134, and doc. 1 for the contract, dated 12 December 1505, which reads in part: "Magister Rafaiel Iohannis sanctis de urbino . . . facere construere et dipingere una tavola sive cona [ancona] sopra l'altare grande de la chiesa de fuore de dicta chiesa de quilla perfectione proportione qualita et conditione della tavola sive cona existente in nargne nel la chiesa de san Girolamo del luoco menore et omne de colore et figure numero et più et ornamenti commo in dicta tavola se contiene et de migliore perfectione si è possibele . . ." It can be noted that in 1507 the same subject was also commissioned of Giovanni Spagna by the Observant Friars of Monte Santo of Todi who also expressly required Spagna to reproduce Ghirlandaio's panel in Narni ("cum coloribus et aliis rebus ad speciem et similitudinem tabulae factae in Ecc. Sancti Ieronymi de Narnea . . ."). Spagna was called upon by the Observant friars of S. Martino di Trevi to paint yet another copy. The painting was copied again in 1541 by Spagna's pupil and son-in-law, Jacopo Siculo, for the Observant church of the Annunziata outside Norcia.

CHAPTER TWO

COPYRIGHT IN VENICE AND ROME

Monopolies, Patents, and Copyright

Venice, already a centre of book production in the fifteenth century, was the first city to introduce copyright legislation in a form of the *privilegio*. Copyright, however, was only one of three different types of printing *privilegio* that can be identified in Venice in the latter part of the fifteenth century. The first type to be issued took the form of a temporary monopoly, of which there is only one example. On 18 September 1469 the College granted the German printer Joannes de Spira (Johannes of Speyer or Johann von Speier) the exclusive privilege to print books in Venice for a period of five years.[1] At the time of the granting, Spira had already published the letters of Cicero and Pliny's *Natural History*, noted in the document granting the *privilegio*, and was preparing to print other important books. The intent behind the *privilegio* evidently was to secure Spira's services, which were seen as beneficial to the city. The disadvantage of the monopoly, however, was that it effectively discouraged other printers from setting up shop in Venice. The Venetian authorities evidently recognized this and when Spira died shortly after receiving the monopoly, the *privilegio* was not transferred to Vindelius (Wendelin or Vindelin) de Spira, his brother and co-worker, nor was it ever again granted in Venice.

Another type of *privilegio* was the patent that conferred exclusive rights over an invention or process for a specified length of time. The patent was quite specific, which prevented it from being too restrictive. Patents were granted only occasionally, usually for developments or improvements in the art of printing. One of earliest examples granted in Venice was for printing Greek. Aldo Manuzio (Aldus Manutius) had requested a patent on 25 February 1496 [1495 m.v.]

---

[1] The document is recorded in ASV, CN, reg. 11, fol. 55r. [Fulin, "Documenti," no. 1].

for a period of twenty years for his new Greek typeface.[2] A patented feature of Aldo Manuzio's Greek type was a new way of arranging the accents and breathing marks separately over the letters by means of kerning or overhanging. Five years later on 23 March, 1501, Manuzio submitted another supplication for a ten-year patent for his new chancery cursive typeface.[3] On 17 December 1502, Manuzio was also granted a papal patent by Pope Alexander VI for both his Greek and cursive type. Initially it was granted for ten years and was valid throughout Italy. When it was renewed by Julius II in January 1513, the period of duration was extended to fifteen years and its area of application was claimed to be all of Christendom. Following the death of Julius, it was re-confirmed by Leo X in November 1513.[4] Besides Manuzio, a ten-year patent was also granted on 21 September 1498 to Nicola Vlastò (Nikolaos Vlastos) from Candia, Crete, for a new type of Greek letters which had their accents attached.[5]

Innovations in the printing of music were also granted patents. On 25 May 1498, a patent for printing music notation was granted for twenty years to the music publisher Ottaviano dei Petrucci da Fossombrone who had invented a way of printing organ music.[6] Petrucci's first book printed under the new patent, the *Harmonicae Musices Odhecaton A*, was published by Amadeo Scoto and Niccolò di Raphael in 1500. The following year Petrucci published *Canti B. numero Cinquanta*. In granting the *privilegio* to Petrucci, the College explained that it wanted to stimulate inventiveness and new inventions that it regarded as being for the public good. On 26 June 1514, Petrucci

---

[2] The document is recorded in ASV, CN, reg. 14, fol. 133v. (137v. n.n.) [Fulin, "Documenti," no. 41]. It has been transcribed in Giovan Battista Gasparini, "La Natura Giuridica dei Privilegi per la Stampa in Venezia," 116, no. 4.

[3] The document is recorded in ASV, CN, reg. 15, fol. 33v. (35v. n.n.) [Fulin, "Documenti," no. 111]. It has been transcribed in Gasparini, 117, no. 5.

[4] All three privileges were reproduced in Niccolò Perotti's commentary on Martial, *Cornucopia, sive commentaria linguae latinae*, issued in November 1513. They are reprinted in Antoine-Auguste Renouard, *Annales de l'Imprimerie des Alde, ou histoire des trois Manuce et de leurs éditions*, 3rd ed. (Paris, 1834), 505–8.

[5] The *privilegio* is recorded in ASV, CN, reg. 14, fol. 177v. (181v. n.n.) [Fulin, "Documenti," no. 85]. Vlastos subsequently had four books printed for him by his countryman and associate the printer Zacharias Kalliergês between 1499 and 1500.

[6] The *privilegio* is recorded in ASV, CN, reg. 14, fol. 170r. (174r. n.n.) [Fulin, "Documenti," no. 41]. Petrucci's supplication is transcribed in Anton Schmid, *Ottaviano dei Petrucci da Fossombrone*, 10–11. Petrucci's publications are listed in Augusto Vernarecci, *Ottaviano de' Petrucci da Fossombrone*, 66–67, 69.

submitted a request to extend it another five years.[7] The previous year, on 22 October 1513, Petrucci also applied for and was granted a fifteen-year papal patent for the printing of organ music.[8] Petrucci's Venetian and papal patents evidently remained effective to the extent that the printer-publisher Francesco Marcolini, in his supplication to the Senate for a *privilegio* on 1 July 1536, complained that for thirty years Petrucci had been printing music using his patent and that for the last twenty-five years no one else could do so.[9]

Patents were also granted for new printing techniques. For example, on 14 February 1568 [1567 m.v.], Andrea Brugone was granted a twenty-year *privilegio* for his invention of a method for printing in red and black "at one time without removing the paper from the drum."[10] Another example is the patent issued to the printmaker Ugo da Carpi on 24 July 1516 for his newly invented technique of chiaroscuro printing.[11] In his supplication, da Carpi explains that he has invented a new way of printing "chiaro et scuro" which he says has never been done before. He describes it as a beautiful thing and useful to many who like drawing. Moreover, he adds that he has engraved, and had engraved, things never done before, or even thought of, by others. He then asks for a *privilegio* that nobody counterfeit any of his designs and engravings and if anybody presumes to do so, and wants to print them here [i.e. in Venice] or elsewhere, that they not be permitted to sell them in any place subject to the Dominion of Venice. The only chiaroscuro prints produced by Ugo da Carpi carrying a notice of the Venetian patent are the *Death of Ananias* and *Aeneas and Anchises* after designs by Raphael (Figs. 4, 5).

---

[7] The *privilegio* is recorded in ASV, CN, reg. 17, fol. 92r. (94r. n.n.) [Fulin, "Documenti," no. 193]. The complete text is given in Schmid, 19–20, and Vernarecci, 120–121.

[8] The *privilegio* is transcribed in Schmid, 16–18, and Vernarecci, 115–119, and noted in Claudio Sartori, *Bibliografia delle opere musciali stampate da Ottaviano Petrucci*, 17–18. The document was signed by Cardinal Pietro Bembo.

[9] Marcolini's *privilegio* is recorded in ASV, ST, reg. 29, fol. 38v. (54v. n.n.). The text of Marcolini's supplication reads "per esser circa xxx anni che fu uno Ottaviano da Fossombrono che stampava la musica nel modo che se imprimono le let[te]re, et è circa xxv. anni che tal opera non si fa, alla quale impresa si è messo non pur l'Italia ma l'alemagna et la franza, e non l'hanno potuto ritrovare." It is also noted in Brown, 107.

[10] The document is recorded in ASV, ST, reg. 46, fol. 188r. (212r. n.n.). It is also noted in Brown, 98.

[11] The document is recorded in ASV, CN, reg. 18, fol. 32v. (33v. n.n.) [Fulin, "Documenti," no. 209].

Fig. 4. Ugo da Carpi, *Death of Ananias* (after Raphael). 1518. Chiaroscuro woodcut. Photo: Warburg.

Fig. 5. Ugo da Carpi, *Aeneas and Anchises* (after Raphael). 1518.
Chiaroscuro woodcut. Photo: Warburg.

The prints were published in Rome in 1518 after Ugo, who had moved to the city, had also acquired a papal patent protecting his chiaroscuro technique. Both prints are inscribed:

> RAPHAEL. VRBINAS. QVISQVIS. HAS. TABELLAS. INVITO. AVTORE. IMPRIMET EX. DIVI. LEONIS X. AC. ILL. PRINCI[N]PIS. ET. SENATVS. VENETIARVM. DECRETIS. EXCOMVNICATIONIS. SENTE[N]TIA[M]. ET. ALIAS. PENAS. INCVRRET. ROME. APVD. VGVM. DE. CARPI. I[N]PRESSA[M]. M. D. XVIII.[12]

Other chiaroscuro prints by Ugo, however, do not carry notice of copyright. His two-tone (grey-green and black) chiaroscuro woodcut of *St. Jerome in Penitence* after a design by Titian (inscribed "TICIANVS" and "VGO"), for example, which was evidently produced before he left Venice, is not protected by the Venetian patent.

The third type of *privilegio* was that granted for copyright which gave a special concession or right to reproduce specified works in printed form for a specified length of time. Opinions vary on how many types of copyright *privilegio* were available. In the area of book publishing, Horatio Brown has identified two different types: one granted to the author of a manuscript or to a translator, and the other to an editor or a printer.[13] Leonardas Vytautas Gerulaitis, on the other hand, recognizes three types, one granted to editors, another to translators, and a third to authors, while Giovan Battista Gasparini identifies instead one type which guaranteed literary property to authors for their work (which he regards as analogous to copyright proper), another guaranteeing printing rights to editors for work not their own, and a third type protecting authors, editors, and printers from foreign competition.[14]

Although each of these features and types of applicant (authors, editors, translators, printers, etc.) are in evidence in the documents they do not necessarily serve to distinguish one type of *privilegio* from another. This becomes apparent when one attempts to group the documents according to any one of these criteria. From the surviv-

---

[12] The inscription has been translated in Landau and Parshall, *The Renaissance Print*, 150, as follows: "Raphael from Urbino. Whoever will print these images without permission of the author will incur the excommunication of Pope Leo X and other penalties of the Venetian Senate. Printed at Rome at Ugo da Carpi's 1518."

[13] Brown, 53, 54.

[14] Gerulaitis, *Printing and Publishing in Fifteenth-Century Venice*, 34; Gasparini, 106.

ing documents it is clear that there was one basic type of *privilegio* in which the language used for the details was simply adjusted to suit the demands of each individual applicant. This study focuses on the privileges granted to publishers of prints and books. But the same concession or 'privilege' was granted to others in a variety of circumstances. For example, on 28 May 1565, a *privilegio* was granted to Giovanni Battista Firussino that prevented others from making or making use of certain metal instruments he had invented each one of which was capable of grinding more than one *staro* of good farina grain per day. The *privilegio* was granted for ten years and carried the usual penalties of confiscation and fine.[15] This same type of *privilegio*, with virtually the same restrictions, indemnities, mandates, and penalties, will be recognized in the examples discussed below pertaining to prints and books.

The procedure for obtaining a *privilegio* in Venice was initiated with a supplication that, before 1517, was usually submitted to the College. A supplicant could be anyone with a proprietory claim to the commercial rights of the published work but was usually the person who was financially responsible for the printing project, be it of a manuscript or a new edition of a previously printed book, or of a woodcut block, or an engraved plate. The person who assumed the financial responsibility for a printing project may be called a publisher. In this study, the term 'publisher' is used broadly to describe the individual (or group of individuals in partnership) who paid for a printing project. As the *privilegio* was conceived first and foremost as a means to protect a publisher's financial investment in a printing project, every supplicant for copyright may be identified as a publisher of one kind or another. In other words, it was only publishers, in the broad sense of the term, who appled for copyright.

Publishers of prints may be divided into two categories. The first includes those individuals who either engraved their own designs, or had them engraved by someone else, or individuals who engraved someone else's designs in preparation for publication. For example, the painter Federico Barocci obtained copyright for a print he had engraved himself after his own design. Titian, on the other hand, hired the engraver Cornelis Cort to engrave his designs, while the

---

[15] Firussino's *privilegio* is recorded in ASV, ST, reg. 45, fol. 128v. (148v. n.n.). Money collected from the fine was to be divided among the *accusatore*, the Magistrate, and Ospedale degli Incurabili.

papal *privilegio* granted Diana Mantuana was for prints she engraved after designs by other artists (see Introduction and Chapter 8). In each case, the individual, instead of selling the plates to someone else and thereby relinquishing the commercial rights to them, decided to publish the prints him- or herself. Because the individual retained ownership of the plates, he or she could apply for copyright protection.

The second category comprises everyone who published prints engraved and designed by other people. It may be sub-divided into printer-publishers and merchant-publishers. Printer-publishers were individuals who operated their own presses. They might print material of their own choice at their own expense from plates they had acquired through purchase, or print material for others under contract or commission. Generally it is usual to find them printing material on their own presses, and it may be presumed that the owner of a press also operated it him- or herself (in some cases, however, the actual press machinery may be owned by someone other than a printer). Merchant-publishers, on the other hand, did not operate a press. They would acquire plates through purchase (or possibly occasionally as gifts or through inheritance), or would contract with the owners to publish a book or print, and undertake the printing at their own expense. As a category, merchant-publishers can include booksellers, dealers, traders (and, later, print sellers and dealers), as well as those individuals who, although otherwise unconnected in any obvious way with the publishing world, nonetheless wished to have a book or print printed and to hold the commercial rights to it. In the sixteenth century, there emerged several publishers in both Venice and Rome who specialized in the publication of prints (see Chapters 6 and 7).

The Privilegio *in Venice before 1517*

For the early period in Venice, before 1517, each supplication for a *privilegio* was treated more or less on an individual basis. Each *privilegio* was literally a special 'privilege' granted to the supplicant. In the index compiled for each register of the records for the Venetian Senate, individuals to whom privileges were granted for printing are listed in the section headed "Speciales Personæ." The supplicant usually asked that the *privilegio* be valid for a specific time period, that certain sanctions and fines of a specified amount be levied against the counterfeiter, and specifying, too, how the fine collected should be divided up and who should receive what portion of it. Despite this apparently open system, a certain conformity did apply to the extent that a 'typical' *privilegio* can be identified, however. A standard Venetian *privilegio* was usually valid for ten years during which time an apprehended transgressor would have all counterfeited copies of the book or print confiscated and a fine of twenty-five ducats levied for each copy printed. Usually, it was specified that the money collected from the fines be divided into thirds of which one third went most often to the "accusatore" (the person who identified the counterfeiter), another third to the supplicant, and the final third to the magistrate to whom the case was brought. However, there were numerous exceptions to this typical *privilegio* and developments in form and content are noticeable over the course of the period under examination.

Although by far the majority of privileges were valid for 10 years, some were for shorter periods (6, 5, 3, or 2 years, or for only six months), others for longer (12, 15, 20, and 25 years). As far as can be determined, there was no obvious correlation between the duration of the *privilegio* and the item for which it was granted. Possibly there was some formula that took into account the cost of production, the price of the book, and projected sales over so many years by which it could be calculated how long was needed to recover all expenses. However, it was clearly generally conceded, given the preponderance of instances, that ten years was sufficient in most cases. Those privileges granted for less than ten years appear simply to comply with the request stated in the supplication. There is no evidence, at least among the examples examined in this study, that the College ever increased the requested duration. However, there are several instances where the requested length of time was reduced. In a handful of cases, the period was reduced for no obvious reason from the by-no-means unusual request for 10 years to 5 years and 6 years.

There was no obvious system for applying sanctions against counterfeiters. It was generally the case, though, that the supplicant asked that all counterfeited books be confiscated and specified monetary penalties and fines be imposed. Counterfeited books could be confiscated not only from the publisher but also from the bookseller who sold or is selling them. The amount to be levied in penalties, the type of fine, and its division and disbursement seems to have been determined by the supplicant. The least common type of fine is that which imposes a single sum, usually for each infraction; they range from 200 to 500 ducats. No distinction appears to have been made between types of publishers.

The more common method was to impose a fine on each counterfeited book (or print) printed or sold. As mentioned above, the sum was usually 25 ducats, but 10 ducats was also common, sometimes 20, and occasionally 50 or even 100 ducats. In one instance, a fine of 50 ducats was charged for every five books counterfeited. Smaller fines were also common: mostly 1 ducat, but also 2, 3, 4, and 5 ducats. The amount of the fine seems to have been determined by the supplicant. Again, there is no obvious correlation between the amount of the fine and the actual cost of the book or print. Occasionally, both types of fine were imposed. A variation is the fine but also a penalty imposed on copies of books or prints printed outside the Republic of Venice but sold within the territory.

It was usually specified in the *privilegio* that the money collected from the fines be divided up and distributed to various specified people and institutions. Commonly, the sum collected was divided in thirds, though it could also be divided in half, or into fourths, or one of the thirds further divided in half. As was mentioned above, one portion would usually go to the person who identified the counterfeiter. Occasionally, it was requested that the identity of the accuser not be divulged. Another portion often went to the supplicant, and a third to the magistrate or office to which the case was brought. A large number of supplications specify that a portion be given to the Avogadori di comun (the public prosecutors) who would present the case to the magistrate. Some designate a portion for the Signori della Notte who dealt with matters of public order. With less obvious reasons, a similarly large number of supplications specified a portion go to the hospital of the Pietà, while a lesser number named the Venetian Arsenal. Portions were also designated for the hospital of S. Antonio, the Signoria, and the Monte Nuovo, as well as the Doge, S. Marco, the hospital of Gesù Cristo, the Cinque alla Pace, and the Treasury. In some cases, however, the supplicant left it up to the authorities to divide the money as they saw fit.

In the event that a copyist was apprehended, the supplicant could bring the case before any magistrate of his or her choosing. Occasionally a supplicant might request an unusual penalty. For example, the translator Matteo Berto requested that the counterfeiter be jailed for two months.[16]

The *privilegio* attempted to give notice of what constituted a copy. To forge or make a counterfeit copy is to produce an exact imitation of the original with the intent to defraud. But what was a counterfeit copy? Copies may vary from the original in any number of ways such as employing a different type, or a smaller type. Or did the copy merely have to bear a general resemblance to the original to be judged a copy? In various ways, the *privilegio* sought to describe what was not permissible. Size was evidently a factor. In the *privilegio* granted to the printer Bernardino Benalio in 1516 (see Chapter 5), for example, it is stated that the prints for which he was granted copyright could not be reproduced in the same size, or made larger, or smaller. Nor could the design be added to, changed, or diminished.

To a certain degree the College could also impose conditions on the publisher upon the fulfillment of which depended the validity of the *privilegio*. Brown identified three kinds: (1) those affecting the quality of the work, (2) those concerned with the rate of production, and (3) those which affected the copyrights of other publishers.[17] To this list can be added a fourth kind that concerns the condition of sale.

Concerning the quality of the work, besides correctness in the text and printing, it was required that the item be printed on good quality paper. Evidently poor quality paper was often used and continued to be used to the extent that on 4 June 1537 the Senate, in order to combat the "damnable and disgraceful practice" and to remedy a situation where "nearly all the books currently being printed in Venice do not hold the ink of whoever wants to write in them," passed a law that required printers to produce books with paper that did not blot. Those printers who failed to use good quality paper would be fined one hundred ducats, forfeit their *privilegio*, and have their books confiscated and burned in the Piazza di San Marco.[18]

---

[16] Matteo Berto had submitted a supplication to the College for a two-year *privilegio* for his translation into Italian of "tutti li misterij de la santa messa." His *privilegio* is recorded in ASV, CN, reg. 15, fol. 17v. (19v. n.n.) [Fulin, "Documenti," no. 101].

[17] Brown, 57.

[18] The document is noted in Giuseppe Fumagalli, *Lexicon typographicum Italiae: dictionnaire géographique d'Italie* (Florence, 1905), 496–7.

The second condition, which was only occasionally included in a *privilegio*, obliged the holder to have works printed within a year from the date of supplication, or specified that they be printed at a certain rate *per diem*. It was possible, however, for acceptable reasons, if a printer failed to print a work within the specified time period, to request an extension.

The third condition most frequently encountered was designed to protect publishers holding previously granted privileges, and to protect the College from the consequences of granting a *privilegio* to a publisher for a work that another publisher has already begun to print. The proviso is repeated constantly in different forms. As Brown points out, the position of the College on this point was so clearly understood that a declaration in support of it was sometimes inserted in the supplication.[19]

The fourth condition concerned the pricing of the books listed in the supplication. Privileges frequently included a clause admonishing the holder to sell his books at a fair price. As in the previous case, this proviso was stressed so much by the College that a statement to this effect was often included in the supplication. However, despite the demands of the College and promises of the publishers, the pricing of books was much abused and evidently excessive amounts were charged. After 1517, the Senate attempted to curb this abuse by requiring all publishers to submit a copy of the publication to the Provveditori di Comun who had the book priced for the market by experts.

Occasionally, a publisher submitted a supplication to the Senate asking for the right to sell a book at a stated price. Prints were also subject to pricing restrictions, as the supplication of the German merchant Anton Kolb attests. On 30 October 1500, Kolb submitted to the College a request for permission to sell each print of the large six-block woodcut view of Venice at three *fiorini*. In the same supplication, he also asked for the right to sell the print anywhere in the dominions of the Republic of Venice without having to pay duty on it. In his supplication, Kolb explains that because of the incredible labour involved in producing the print, the difficulties of composition in such a large subject, and the sheer size of the paper, to

---

[19] Brown, 57.

sell the print for less than three *fiorini* would not permit him to recover his costs. The request was granted for a four-year period.[20]

In several instances, following the death of the publisher, we find his heirs seeking a *privilegio* for work left unprinted. However, although the heirs might continue the printing activities of a deceased family member, or ask to take over the *privilegio*, the *privilegio* at the outset was usually not established as inheritable. In some instances, however, it was specified in the supplication that the portion of the fine due for the supplicant could be collected by the supplicant's successors.

There are several examples of supplicants seeking to renew a *privilegio*. For example, in 1509 [1508 m.v.], Leonardo Crasso submitted a request to renew for another ten years his ten-year *privilegio* for the *Hypnerotomachia Poliphili* which had been printed by Aldo Manuzio in 1499.[21] The reason Crasso gives for needing to renew his *privilegio* is that due to the disturbances of war sales have been slow. The same reason is given by Ottaviano dei Petrucci da Fossombrone who, in 1514, wished to extend for a further five years his twenty-year patent on printing music.[22] However, renewals were not always granted. After the death of Aldo Manuzio on 6 February 1515, and after the privileges granted to Manuzio (including the twenty-year *privilegio* he received in 1496 for his Greek type), and to Andrea Torresani d'Asola "and associates" for printing in Greek had expired, the College gave notice on 25 February 1517 [1516 m.v.] that the printing, and importing, of works in Greek would be henceforth open to all.[23]

* * *

---

[20] The document is recorded in ASV, CN, reg. 15, fol. 26r. (28r. n.n.) [Fulin, "Documenti," no. 105]. The College's action is recorded on 31 October 1500 in the diary of Marino Sanuto, *I Diarii*, 3: col. 1006. Although it is often referred to as such, Kolb's *privilegio* is not for copyright.

[21] Crasso's *privilegio* is recorded in ASV, CN, reg. 16, fol. 38r. (40r. n.n.) [Fulin, "Documenti," no. 173].

[22] Petrucci's *privilegio* is recorded in ASV, CN, reg. 17, fol. 92r. (94r. n.n.) [Fulin, "Documenti," no. 193].

[23] The document is recorded in ASV, CN, reg. 18, fol. 50v. (51v. n.n.) [Fulin, "Documenti," no. 213]: "Il. Ser^mo. Principe fa saper, et, e, p[er] deliberation del Exmo. Collegio, ch[e] cum ciosia chel sia finito ogni privilegio, et gratia p[er] il passato concessa al g. Aldo Manutio, Andrea da asola, et Compagni Impressori de libri greci, Al p[rese]nte, et damo Inanti el si concede libera faculta à cadauno si di stampar, et far stampar, come di condur in questa Cita libri greci, et Quelli usar, vender, et tener come meglio li parera senza alcuna molestia, over impedimenta."

It is clear that the *privilegio* was perceived from the outset as the means of granting the commercial rights for a printed item for a specific period of time. It is also clear that such rights were not granted simply for the asking. It was evidently understood by the supplicant that it was necessary to state that money, time, and effort had been invested in the project. The whole point of the *privilegio* was to establish a period of protection during which the holder of the copyright was given a fair chance through sales of his product to recover his initial expenses. The government of Venice, in other words, was prepared to protect investment in a printing project by legislating against unfair competition.

The financial investment was crucial to consideration: if a supplicant had no expenses, in theory at least, he was ineligible for copyright protection. It was therefore usual for the supplicant to point out how much money, time, and labour had gone into a project, and to stress how this investment might be jeopardized by counterfeiters. For example, in a supplication submitted on 22 February 1494 [1493 m.v.], the book-publisher Lazaro de' Soardi tells the College how he has composed at his own expense ("cum sue spese") new editions of two books the printing of which will cost him a great deal of effort and expense ("grandissima fatica e spesa").[24] In a supplication submitted on 7 June 1494, the editor-publisher Bernardino di Landriano explains that he has edited two books with great labour and expense, and on 15 July 1498 Democrito Terracina refers in his supplication to the very great and almost intolerable expense ("cum grandissima et quasi intollerabel spexa") he had incurred in the printing of works in several languages.[25] In 1500, the Brescian printer-publisher Bernardino Misinta explains that the manuscript of Pamphilo Sassi's *Sonetti e capitoli* cost him a great deal to purchase and will cost him a great deal to print.[26] Similarly, for prints, the *privilegio* granted to Benedetto Bordon on 30 March 1504 for a series of twelve woodcuts of the *Triumph of Caesar* (see Chapter 5), Bordon states that the project was undertaken with "a very large expendi-

---

[24] The document is recorded in ASV, CN, reg. 14, fol. 95r. (99r. n.n.) [Fulin, "Documenti," no. 22].

[25] Landriano's *privilegio* is recorded in ASV, CN, reg. 14, fol. 101v. (105v. n.n.) [Fulin, "Documenti," no. 27]. Terracina's *privilegio*, for works "in lingua arabica, morescha, soriana, armenicha, indiana, et barbarescha," is listed in Fulin, no. 82.

[26] Misinta's *privilegio* is recorded in ASV, CN, reg. 15, fol. 20v. (22v. n.n.) [Fulin, "Documenti," no. 102].

ture of time and money and at no small inconvenience to himself"
("uno grandissimo spacio de tempo cum dispendio, et incommodo
de la poca faculta sua"). He explains that he had the woodblocks
engraved, "for which he spent a large sum of money" ("et deinde
ha fatto intagliar quelli in ditto legname; Ne le qual opera ha exbur-
sato bona quantita de danari"). In 1516, Bernardino Benalio explains
that prints for which he was seeking a *privilegio* were produced at
"notable expense" (see Chapter 5).

It was the anticipated return from this investment that was threatened by the activities of counterfeiters. Counterfeiters not only usurped
the fruits of a publisher's investment but also benefited because less
money, time, and effort were put into the production of a copy. In
1498, Nicola Vlastò complained of counterfeiters who "seek to usurp
the labours of others with little expense and less work" ("circano
usurpar le fatiche daltri cum pocha spesa, et mancho faticha").[27] For
many publishers, one of the chief benefits of the *privilegio* was the
protection it afforded against the envy and unscrupulous rivalry of
their own colleagues in the fiercely competitive publishing business.
The bookseller Bernardino Rasma complains in 1496 that the situation had become worse in recent years and tells the College that:

> a pernicious and hurtful corruption has crept into the midst of the
> merchant printers of this glorious city, whereby not only in times past
> but now-a-days many of them are undone. For when one of them
> shall have set himself to produce a book of rare beauty—which entails
> the absorption of all his capital in it—should his brother merchants
> come to hear of it, they use every cunning device to steal the proofs
> of the new work from the hands of the pressmen, and set to, with
> many men and many presses, to print the book before the original
> designer of the book can finish his edition, which, when it is ready
> for issue, finds the market spoiled by the pirated edition.[28]

Lazaro de' Soardi explains that he, "having gone to the expense of
correcting and perfecting the work, would lose all the fruits of his
labours" to others who, not being honest, would copy his work "out
of envy and in order to undo [him]."[29] Similarly, Giovanni di Lorenzo

---

[27] The document is recorded in ASV, CN, reg. 14, fol. 166v. (181v. n.n.) [Fulin, "Documenti," no. 85].

[28] Brown's translation, 55–56. Rasma's *privilegio* is recorded in ASV, CN, reg. 14, fol. 133r. (137r. n.n.) [Fulin, "Documenti," no. 44].

[29] Soardi's *privilegio* is recorded in ASV, CN, reg. 14, fol. 99v. (103v. n.n.) [Fulin, "Documenti," no. 25]: "Non saria honesto, che altri per Invidia, et per disfare dicto

da Bergamo explains that, having gone to such "very great expense and labour," he does not want, after having printed the work, "someone else, finding the work already corrected and completed, re-printing it and selling it at a cheap price that will bring ruin to the supplicant, as often happens."[30] Gabriele Braccio da Brisighella and his associates wanted a *privilegio* because "many, out of envy and hate, will seek by any means to harm and oppress them."[31] Filippo Pincio regularly complained about the competition in publishing. In 1498, he said he needed a *privilegio* "so as not to be ruined by the usual teacherously rabid competition common in this miserable art" ("per non esser ruinato da la perfida rabia de la concorrentia consueta fra questa miserabel arte"). In 1512, he refers again to "the treacherous and rabid competition which is destroying this calamitous art" ("la perfida et rabiosa concorrentia, la quale et destruze questa calamitosa arte") which can be dispelled only through the benign help of the Venetian government ("La qual concorrentia solum mediante el benigno ajuto di Vostra Serenità potrà fugere"). And yet again, in 1515, he says he needs a *privilegio* because he would otherwise be ruined "by the treacherous and rabid competition that rules and destroys this calamitous art" ("dalla perfida e rabiosa concorrentia, la qual regan et destrugie questa calamitosa arte").[32] Democrito Terracina in 1498 comments on the competition, and in 1500 Aldo Manuzio complains of how after printing a work (in this case, the letters of St. Catherine) "with the highest diligence and very beautiful type" ("cum summa diligentia, et bellissima lettera"), others "finding it all done without any of their own labour make a competing copy" ("trovando la cosa fatta senza alcun loro fadiga li facia concorrentia").[33] In 1507, Paganino de' Paganini speaks

---

supplicante, habiando facta la spexa In far corezer, et redure dicte opera a bona perfection li fuse tolto el fructo de le suo fatiche, e spexe grande."

[30] Giovanni di Lorenzo's *privilegio* is recorded in ASV, CN, reg. 14, fol. 116v. (120v. n.n.) [Fulin, "Documenti," no. 32]: "grandissima spexa et fatiche, non voria che dapoy che'l havera Impressa, qualche uno altro, trovata za la opera correcta e compida, la restampisse et desse per vilissimo pretio a danno e ruina de lui supplicante come molto volte achade."

[31] Braccio da Brisighella's *privilegio* is recorded in ASV, CN, reg. 14, fol. 157r. (171r. n.n.) [Fulin, "Documenti," no. 76]: "molti per Invidia, et odio cercaranno per ogni via, et modo nocere, et opprimer dicta Compagnia"

[32] Pincio's privileges are in ASV, CN, reg. 14, fol. 158r. (173r. n.n.); reg. 16, fol. 100r. (106r. n.n.); and reg. 18, fol. 16r. (17r. n.n.), respectively [Fulin, "Documenti," nos. 77, 184, and 199, respectively].

[33] Manuzio's *privilegio* is recorded in ASV, CN, reg. 15, fol. 23v. (25v. n.n.) [Fulin, "Documenti," no. 104]. For Terracina's comments, see Fulin, no. 82.

of his dread of being ruined by the perfidious rivalry which he says prevails in this poor and miserable art ("la perfida concorrentia, laquale regna in questa povera, et miserabel arte") which has brought total ruin to his house ("che seria total ruina del casa sua").[34]

In addition to copying, Aldo Manuzio describes in his supplication submitted on 17 October 1502 some of the other tricks counterfeiters employ to circumvent local copyright laws such as printing a book in Brescia with a colophon for Florence, or in Lyons with a colophon for Venice.[35] In Venice Aldo Manuzio's books were counterfeited by the printers Gregorio de' Gregorii and Alessandro Paganino, among others.

Besides giving reasons why copyright should be granted, it was also somewhat incumbent upon the supplicant to offer an explanation why the work should be published in the first place. Frequently it is stated that the work had not been printed before in Italy. Lazaro de' Soardi, for example, says that the sermons of St. Vincent Ferrer, for which he sought a *privilegio*, had been "never before printed in Italy" ("maij piu stampati In Italia").[36] This could be understood simply as information directed to the College assuring them that the work was new and not covered by any previous *privilegio*, but the phrase also has about it an impressive air of importance, implying that its publication now is an exciting and momentous event; much as a ringmaster in a circus might introduce a new act as "never before seen in the United States." This singular event would also be described as enhancing the illustriousness of the Republic of Venice. On 16 January 1503 [1502 m.v.], Francesco Sechino explained that his publication of the never-before-printed Camaldolese missal would be "a thing that would bring honour to this city" ("cossa di honore a questa città").[37] In 1498, Gabriele Braccio of Brisighella informed the College that "by the culpable negligence and ignorance of printers, the texts of editions become every day more corrupt," adding that this is a "dishonour and a public injury to this glorious city." However, he, Braccio, and his associates, "ever solicitous for the

---

[34] Paganini's *privilegio* is recorded in ASV, CN, reg. 16, fol. 7r. (8r. n.n.) [Fulin, "Documenti," no. 162].

[35] The contents of Manuzio's 1502 supplication are noted in Fulin, no. 126.

[36] Soardi's *privilegio* is recorded in ASV, CN, reg. 14, fol. 99v. (103v. n.n.) [Fulin, "Documenti," no. 25]. The sermons, *Sermones sancti Uince[n]tij fratris*, were published in three parts in Venice by Soardi in 1496 (Sander, 3: no. 7610).

[37] Sechino's *privilegio* is recorded in ASV, CN, reg. 15, fol. 83v. (85v. n.n.) [Fulin, "Documenti," no. 129].

honor and welfare of this thrice glorious Republic, are resolved by means of a new and beautiful invention, to print both in Greek and Latin with every care and diligence." He goes on to explain that "In this useful and laudable undertaking they have spent much money, even more than they could afford, but they have done so in the hope of being favourably regarded by your most benignant and clement serenity."[38]

In the case of books, if a work had already been published, it was claimed that the earlier printing was full of mistakes that needed correcting, or that it had been printed on poor quality paper, or that the type was inferior. Lazaro de' Soardi, in the supplication mentioned above, says that previous editions of the works of Cicero were "up to now printed very incorrectly on poor paper and bad type" ("stampate Infino al presente Incorrectissime de cativa carta, et pessima littera"). Similarly, Gaspare di Colonia in 1502 states that current editions of the letters and works of Francesco Filelfo "are very corrupt" ("sono corruptissime") and, moreover, have been printed "on very bad paper and type" ("in pessima charta et lettera").[39]

Occasionally it is claimed that the work to be printed will be of some use. The merchant-publisher Geronimo Durante, for example, asserted that he wanted to publish the two books on Aristotle cited in his supplication for the general benefit.[40] The printer-publisher Giorgio Arrivabene from Mantua believed that his edition of the *Repertorium Bertachini* would be of use to lawyers.[41] Democrito Terracina extravagantly claimed that his books on languages to be "of utility to the Christian republic, and the exaltation of the faith, and the augmentation of the natural sciences, as well as medicine, in the conservation of the health of the soul and bodies of many and all faithful Christians."[42] The printer-publisher Giambartolomeo dalla

---

[38] Brown's translation, 56. The *privilegio* is recorded in ASV, CN, reg. 14, fol. 157r. (171r. n.n.) [Fulin, "Documenti," no. 76].

[39] Soardi's *privilegio* is recorded in ASV, CN, reg. 14, fol. 99v. (103v. n.n.) [Fulin, "Documenti," no. 25]. Gaspare di Colonia's *privilegio* is recorded in ASV, CN, reg. 14, fol. 80r. (82r. n.n.) [Fulin, "Documenti," no. 125].

[40] Durante's *privilegio* is recorded in ASV, CN, reg. 14, fol. 67r. (71r. n.n.) [Fulin, "Documenti," no. 7].

[41] Arrivabene's *privilegio* is recorded in ASV, CN, reg. 14, fol. 90v. (94v. n.n.) [Fulin, "Documenti," no. 16]. The first part of Joannes Bertachinus's *Repertorii* was published by Giorgio Arrivabeni in Venice in 1500; the second and third parts in 1501 (Adams, *Catalogue of Books Printed on the Continent of Europe in Cambridge Libraries*, 1: 117, no. 795).

[42] Terracina's *privilegio* is summarised in Fulin, no. 82.

Fontana believed all the books he had been publishing in Venice over the years were "of convenience to all students with no small usefulness for all the facts they contain" ("a comodità de tuti li studenti cum utilita non picola de tuti li datij, et intrade di quella"). Jacopo Pencio opined that his publications were "most useful to students" ("molto utile a li studenti"), while P. Benedetto, "having toiled in the study of the liberal arts" ("habiendosse longamente affaticato neli studij dele arte liberali"), believed that his works were "very necessary to young scholars" ("à li adolescenti scolastici molto necessarij").[43] In the case of prints, Benedetto Bordon, in 1508, describes his *mappamondo* as being "of marvellous utility" ("de mirabile utilità") to everyone interested in such things (see Chapter 5).

Sometimes very practical reasons are given. In 1504, Oldrato da Lampugnano, into whose hands had recently come a copy of Marcantonio Sabellico's *Chroniche*, and recognizing the work as the "food and sustenance of very learned men" ("cibo, et pasto de homeni doctissimi"), wanted to publish it because there were currently not enough copies available ("el numero de li quali è pochissimo").[44] In another instance, a book binder named Benedetto wanted to publish some books because other editions had become irreparable.[45]

A supplication might also include information clearly intended to influence the College's decision. On one level this might simply involve drawing attention to the fact that the supplicant has lived and worked a long time in Venice, or has published many books in the past. For example, Lazaro de' Soardi, who was originally from Savigliano (near Turin), described himself as "already a longtime resident of Venice" ("gia longo tempo habitante in Venexia"), as did

---

[43] Fontana's *privilegio* is recorded in ASV, CN, reg. 15, fol. 110v. (112v. n.n.) [Fulin, "Documenti," no. 139]. Pencio's *privilegio* is recorded in ASV, CN, reg. 15, fol. 153r. (155r. n.n.) [Fulin, "Documenti," no. 151]. Benedetto's *privilegio* is recorded in ASV, CN, reg. 15, fol. 101r. (103r. n.n.) [Fulin, "Documenti," no. 134].

[44] Lampugnano's *privilegio* is recorded in ASV, CN, reg. 15, fol. 134v. (136v. n.n.) [Fulin, "Documenti," no. 144]. Lampugnano had the *Chroniche* published in 1508. The title-page reads: "Chroniche che tractano de la Ori/gine de Veneti, e del Principio de/la Cita, e de Tutte le Guere [sic] da/Mare e Terra facte in Italia:/ Dalmacia. Grecia. e contra/tuti li infideli . . . volgariza/te per Matheo Vi/sconti . . ." with at the end: "Ad Instancia e/Impensa de Oldrato Lampugnano Stampate co[n] Gratia e Priuilegii . . ." See Max Sander, *Le livre à figures italiens depuis 1467 jusqu'à 1530* (New York, 1941), 3: no. 6650.

[45] Benedetto's *privilegio* is recorded in ASV, CN, reg. 16, fol. 38v. (40v. n.n.) [Fulin, "Documenti," no. 174].

Matteo de Codeca (Capodecasa) from Parma, while Bernardino da Vercelli pointed out he had been a resident of the city for many years ("habitante in Venetia za molti anni"). Bernardino da Landriano from Milan in 1496 says he had been living in Venice for five years, and Jacomo Ungaro, "intagliatore di lettere" and printer of figured song books, claimed to have lived in Venice for forty years. Giambartolomeo dalla Fontana informed the College that over many years he had printed numerous books in Venice. Andrea Torresani from Asola in Lombardy, besides stating that (in 1499) he had been in Venice for twenty-five years and that he had printed all sorts of books, also declared that he had paid his taxes ("pagando le tasse et angarie poste et occorse ala tera").[46]

At a more important level, the supplicant would refer to the interest or support of an important person. For example, Bernardino da Landriano was assisted in his supplication by the ambassador to the Duke of Milan, Taddeo Vimercati, while Girolamo Biondo had enlisted the support of the ambassador of Rimini, Antonio di Cauchorio. The supplication of the printer-publisher Silvestro de' Torti was recommended by the ambassador of Ferrara, Aldobrandino de' Guidoni. The printer-publisher Paganino de' Paganini says he was "beseeched and exorted by many distinguished doctors" ("pregado et exortado per molti dignissimi. Doctori") to print in portable form "li texti de rason canonica et civile," which, he adds, would be a "major convenience and utility for poor students" ("major commodità et utilità de li poveri studenti").[47]

---

[46] Soardi's *privilegio* is recorded in ASV, CN, reg. 14, fol. 95r. (99r. n.n.) [Fulin, "Documenti," no. 22]. Codeca's *privilegio* is recorded in ASV, CN, reg. 14, fol. 111r. (115r. n.n.) [Fulin, "Documenti," no. 34]. Bernardino da Vercelli's *privilegio* is recorded in ASV, CN, reg. 15, fol. 31r. (33r. n.n.) [Fulin, "Documenti," no. 110]. Landriano's *privilegio* is recorded in ASV, CN, reg. 14, fol. 144v. (148v. n.n.) [Fulin, "Documenti," no. 51]. For Ungaro's *privilegio*, see Fulin, no. 189. Fontana's *privilegio* is recorded in ASV, CN, reg. 15, fol. 110v. (112v. n.n.) [Fulin, "Documenti," no. 139]. Torresani's *privilegio* is recorded in ASV, CN, reg. 15, fol. 13v. (15v. n.n.) [Fulin, "Documenti," no. 96].

[47] Landriano's *privilegio* is recorded in ASV, CN, reg. 14, fol. 101v. (105v. n.n.) [Fulin, "Documenti," no. 27]. Biondo's *privilegio* is recorded in ASV, CN, reg. 14, fol. 103r. (107r. n.n.) [Fulin, "Documenti," no. 28], and noted in Brown, 1891, 57. Silvestro de Torti's *privilegio* is recorded in ASV, CN, reg. 14, fol. 109r. (108r. n.n.) [Fulin, "Documenti," no. 30]. Paganini's *privilegio* is recorded in ASV, CN, reg. 14, fol. 110r. (114r. n.n.) [Fulin, "Documenti," no. 33].

The Venetian Privilegio *after 1517*

By the second decade of the sixteenth century the existing system of application for privileges through the College had got out of hand. Not only were no records kept, other than the entry in the Notatorio del Collegio, of who had been granted a *privilegio*, for what it had been granted, its duration, and how many privileges had been granted to any individual, but there seems to have been no convenient way of checking whether a book had been granted a *privilegio* before, or if it had, if the *privilegio* had expired or was still in effect. The main problem, though, was the sheer number of privileges that had been granted over the years. A publisher might hold privileges for a number of books. In several cases a *privilegio* was granted for a list of books that a publisher merely hoped he could eventually get into print, but in several instances failed to do so. Thus, a number of authors, or titles, were effectively locked away. This situation was exacerbated by the College's willingness to grant a publisher a *privilegio* not only for works in press but also for works yet to be printed. Thus books could be held in a kind of limbo by a publisher, a situation that was occasionally remedied by a clause in the *privilegio* which obliged the holder to have works printed within a year from the date of the supplication, but which was, on the other hand, effectively perpetuated by the College stating in several instances that a *privilegio* would not start until the book had been printed, which conceivably might not be for several years after it had been granted. This particular abuse was not properly addressed until 3 January 1534 [1533 m.v.], when the Senate decreed that if a work was not published within one year of the granting of the *privilegio*, then the *privilegio* would be withdrawn.[48]

The proliferation of privileges threatened to paralyse the book trade in Venice. The system had already proved so prejudicial that several printers had been forced to abandon Venice and move elsewhere in Italy. Between 1505 and 1517, Simone Bevilaqua, Nicolò Brenta, Antonio de Zanchi, Zacharias Kalliergês, Ottaviano dei Petrucci, and Bernardino Guerraldo had all left Venice. In response to the situation, on 1 August 1517 the Senate introduced a law that revoked all earlier privileges and declared that thereafter the *privilegio*

---

[48] The document is recorded in ASV, ST, reg. 27, fol. 190.

could be granted only by the Senate.[49] The new law decreed that henceforth privileges were to be granted only to new works and to works that had not been printed before. Moreover, each supplication was to be voted on by the full Senate, with a two-thirds majority required for approval. Some publishers who had only recently been granted a *privilegio* through the College quickly sought to have it reconfirmed by the Senate.

Although it is reasonable to accept the argument that it was the throttling effect of too many privileges that precipitated this drastic legislation, the new law may have been introduced also in partial response to the papal bull issued in 1515 by Leo X which sought to impose a form of universal censorship (this bull is discussed in Chapter 3). In light of this papal concern over the content of published books (and this on the eve of the Lutheran heresy), the lack of administrative rigour and oversight in the granting of privileges before 1517 may have induced the Venetian government to adopt a role of increased responsibility over what it was officially willing to endorse in the form of a *privilegio*. The year before, in 1516, the Council of Ten had already established a rudimentary form of literary censorship for all works in Humanity (see Chapter 3).

The form of the *privilegio* after 1517 remained the same as it had been before, both in terms of duration and penalties imposed. However, noticeably fewer supplications were submitted, and it would appear that privileges were harder to obtain.

A condition that is stressed much more than it had been in the past is that the grantee of a *privilegio* be required to print the work in the Republic of Venice. Indeed, on occasion it is a stated condition that the work not only be printed but also sold in Venice and its territories. However, it soon became the case that the Senate was willing to grant a *privilegio* provided the work was printed in Venice. Initially, this requirement made perfect business sense. Later, however, it came to be seen as too restrictive. What it hampered was the book sellers in Venice whose trade, in an increasingly international market, included not only books published in Venice but also those printed elsewhere. A publisher in Rome, or Lyons, or Antwerp, however, might hesitate to have his wares sold in Venice because, unable to acquire a Venetian *privilegio* due to the foreign printing,

---

[49] The document is recorded in ASV, ST, reg. 20, fols. 58v.–59r. (73v.–74r. n.n.).

his books were open game for counterfeiters. The Venetian government soon recognized this problem and consequently made its *privilegio* available to anyone qualified to apply for it whether or not they published in Venice.

A contributing factor no doubt to these deliberations in Venice was the decision made by the Holy See in Rome to begin making available papal privileges for works printed outside the Papal States. The papal *privilegio*, which offered concessions supported by threats of both financial and spiritual punishment, claimed effectiveness throughout the Christian world, including Venice, a situation which continued to rankle in Venice throughout the sixteenth century. Compared with the Venetian *privilegio*, the papal *privilegio* granted more extensive protection and carried stiffer penalties (see below). However, although the papal *privilegio* may be seen as effectively overshadowing the Venetian *privilegio*, it did not replace it in Venice. Instead, publishers began to apply for both.

For publishers in Venice, in most cases a Venetian *privilegio* would be acquired first. Lodovico Ariosto, for example, had been granted a Venetian *privilegio* on 25 October 1515, and then, five months later, on 27 March 1516, was granted a papal *privilegio* by Pope Leo X for his book *Orlando Furioso*.[50] In other cases, it was the other way around; having been granted a papal *privilegio*, a publisher then sought a Venetian *privilegio*. For example, in his supplication dated 23 April 1515 to the College in Venice for a *privilegio* for several books he had translated from Hebrew, the Augustinian monk and converted Jew, Fra Felice da Prato, pointed out that he had already been granted a papal *approbatio* and a *privilegio*. He describes how he had supplicated "at the feet of his Holiness the Pope" and been granted a papal *privilegio*. The ten-year papal *privilegio*, granted by Leo X, appears on the title-page of *Psalterium ex Hebraeo diligentissime ad verbum fere traslatu[m]: fratre Felici ordinis Heremitarum sancti Augustini i[n]terp[re]te,*

---

[50] Ariosto's Venetian *privilegio* is recorded in ASV, CN, reg. 18, fol. 23r. (24r. n.n.) [Fulin, "Documenti," no. 203]. The Venetian *privilegio* granted him by the College, however, was revoked on 1 August 1517. On 7 January 1526, Ariosto submitted a new supplication to the Venetian Senate explaining that because of the revocation of his original *privilegio* his book had been printed by others with many errors ("e stata stampata da molti incorrettissima"). He asked for all the concessions that had been granted him on 25 October 1515, which were duly granted anew by the Senate. The new document is recorded in ASV, ST, reg. 24, fol. 227v.–228r. (245v.–246r. n.n.).

published in Venice on 5 September 1515.[51] Fra Felice evidently felt that his rights would be better protected in Venice with a Venetian *privilegio*. His request does make it appear as if he felt the papal *privilegio* was not sufficient. Another example of a book printed in Venice but having more than one *privilegio* is the fortune-telling book *Triompho di Fortuna*, published in Venice in 1526, for which its author Sigismondo Fanti from Ferrara obtained first a papal *privilegio* from Clement VII, and then, on 19 November 1526, a ten-year Venetian *privilegio*.[52]

After 1517 there is also evidence that privileges could be 'purchased', with the supplicant offering a sum of money to the Senate. An interesting case is that of the Jewish merchant-publisher Daniel Bomberg. On 7 December 1515, Bomberg was granted a ten-year *privilegio* for "certain books in Hebrew" ("certi libri hebrei") and a patent for Hebrew cuneate type. When all privileges were revoked in 1517, Bomberg successfully had his reconfirmed by the Senate in 1518.[53] When the *privilegio* expired in 1525, Bomberg applied for renewal for five years but the Senate, fearing complications with the ecclesiastical authorities because of the Hebrew subject matter, failed to pass the motion.[54] A second attempt, submitted by Bomberg four days later on 12 October of 1525 also failed. According to Marino Sanuto, "The motion was put to the vote and lost, and this for the second time; and it was well done, and I had my hand in it; for he printed books in Hebrew that were against the faith."[55] With his second submission Bomberg had offered one hundred ducats for the

---

[51] Fra Felice's *privilegio* is recorded in ASV, CN, reg. 18, fol. 2v. (3v. n.n.) [Fulin, "Documenti," no. 197]. The book was printed by Peter Liechtenstein at the expense of Daniel Bomberg.

[52] Fanti's Venetian *privilegio* is recorded in ASV, ST, reg. 24, fol. 134v. (152v. n.n.). In his supplication, Fanti pointed out that he had already been granted a papal *privilegio* by Clement VII. This information is repeated in the text of the Venetian *privilegio* ("... si come ancho egli e stata concessa p[er] sua Immensa humanita dalla San[it]ta del N[ostro] S[igno]re Clement papa VII come per breve appare"). The book is catalogued in Ruth Mortimer, *Italian 16th Century Books*, no. 180. The colophon reads: "Impresso in la inclita Citta di Venegia per Agostino Portese. Nel anno dil virgineo parto MDXXVI. Nel mese di Genaro, ad instatia di Iacomo Giunta Mercatate Florentina. Con il Privilegio di PAPA CLEMENTE VII e del Senato Veneto a requisitione di L'AVTORE, come appare nelli suoi Registri."

[53] Bomberg's 1515 *privilegio* is recorded in ASV, CN, reg. 18, fol. 24r. (25r. n.n.) [Fulin, "Documenti," no. 204]. The 1518 document confirming it is recorded in ASV, ST, reg. 20, fol. 116r. (131r. n.n.) [Fulin, "Documenti," no. 217].

[54] The Senate's decision was recorded by Marino Sanuto, *I Diarii*, 40: cols. 56–57.

[55] Sanuto, 40: col. 45. The translation is by Brown, 105.

privilegio. When this failed, with his third submission, made the following day, 17 October, he increased the amount to one hundred and fifty ducats. The motion failed again. On 8 March 1526, Bomberg tried once more, offering this time three hundred ducats, but again failed. Finally, on March 27, he was able to overcome the religious scruples of the Senate with an offer of five hundred ducats and was granted a ten-year *privilegio*.[56]

The Privilegio *in Rome*

The earliest papal privileges would appear to be those granted during the reign of Alexander VI (1492–1503). On 23 July 1498, for example, the *Commentaria super omnia diversorum auctorum de antiquitatibus loquentium* by Johannes Annius Viterbiensis (Annio da Viterbo, i.e. Giovanni Nanni da Viterbo) was printed by Eucario Silber with a ten-year *privilegio* that was valid within the Papal States and carried a penalty of confiscation of all printed copies.[57] It was during the reign of Alexander VI's successor, Julius II (1503–1513), however, that the *privilegio* became firmly established. The majority of privileges granted by Julius II (and by Alexander VI) were for the publication of various official acts and texts of a public nature issued by, or under the auspices of, one or another of the Vatican bureaus. For example, on June 1504, soon after Julius's election, Eucario Silber printed "cum Priuilegio" the *Regole* of the Cancelleria Apostolica, and, four months later, at the end of October, a *Formularium terminorum* for the Rota Romana.[58] Notice of copyright also appears on numerous papal bulls, such as *Bulla reformationis Tribunalium Urbis*, printed on 28 March 1512 by the merchant-publisher Jacopo Mazzocchi, on *Bulla reformationis officialium Romane Curie*, printed two

---

[56] Sanuto, 40: col. 76; and 41: cols. 55 and 118. The 150 ducats of Bomberg's third submission, is recorded in the records of the Council of Ten on 16 October 1525 (ASV, CX, Criminal, Busta 5, reg. 48, fol. 76).

[57] The *privilegio* is noted in Blasio, "Privilegi e licenze di stampa," 147, and idem, *Cum gratia et privilegio*, 80. The book is listed in *Scrittura, biblioteche e stampa a Roma nel Quattrocento*, 218, no. 1583. It is worth noting that the following year, in 1499, Alexander VI appointed Annio da Viterbo Master of the Sacred Palace (see Chapter 3).

[58] The books are catalogued in Alberto Tinto, *Gli Annali Tipografici di Eucario e Marcello Silber (1501–1527)*, no. 16 and no. 18. The privileges are noted in Blasio, "Privilegi e licenze di stampa," 150; and idem, *Cum gratia et privilegio*, 40.

days later on 30 March by Marcello Silber, and on *Bulla prorogationis generalis Concilii* printed by Mazzocchi the following April.[59]

However, the *privilegio* was also being granted for other works. In 1506, a *privilegio* was issued to Mazzocchi who financed the printing of Cristoforo Persona's translation of Procopius's *De bello Gottorum* (printed by Giovanni di Besicken: "Impressum per Ioannem Besickem Alemanum Impensa Iacobi Mazzochii Romanæ Academiæ Bibliopole"), and in 1509, a twenty-five-year *privilegio* was granted to Mazzocchi for financing the printing of Raffaele Maffei's translations of Procopius's *De bello persico, liber primus*.[60] The notice of copyright, printed on the verso of the last page, reads:

IULIUS II PONT MAX EDICTO VETUIT NE/QUIS HUNC LIBRUM IMPRIMAT NEVE IM/PRIMI PERMITTAT. SIQUIS CONTRA HINC/AD XXV. AN. FECERIT ANATHEMA SIT./ NOXAMQUE IACOBO MAZOCHIO/BIBLIOPOLAE PENDAT.

The earliest papal *privilegio* for which a record survives in the Vatican archives is that granted by Julius II on 26 January 1509 to Giovanni Jacobo Luchinus, a book printer living in Venice.[61] Six months later, on 9 July 1509, Julius II issued a ten-year *privilegio* to Tommaso Pighinucci da Pietrasanta, a writer of apostolic briefs, for an edition of *Medicina Plinii*, which was printed in Rome by Stephano Guillereti (Étienne Guillery).[62] Pighinucci had edited and financed the printing of the text, which was a previously unpublished compendium on medicine erroneously attributed to Pliny the Elder.

In 1510, a ten-year *privilegio* was granted to Ludovico di Varthema and his heirs for his *Itinerario* which was printed by Stephano Guillereti in collaboration with Hercole Nani at the expense of Ludovico degli Arrighi Vicentino (for Arrighi, see also Chapter 12).[63] The *privilegio*

---

[59] Fernanda Ascarelli, *Annali Tipografici di Giacomo Mazzocchi*, nos. 47, 48; idem, *Le Cinquecentine Romane*, 146; Tinto, *Eucario e Marcello Silber*, no. 121. See also Blasio, "Privilegi e licenze di stampa," 151, n. 11. For two more bulls published at this time (13 December 1511, and 2 May 1512), see Adams, 2: 156, nos. 719–720. For other bulls of Julius II, see Ascarelli, *Le Cinquecentine Romane*, 145–147.

[60] *De bello persico* was published bound together with *De bello Gottorum* by Eucario Silber in Rome on 7 March 1509.

[61] The *privilegio* granted Luchinus is recorded in ASVat, Arm. 39, vol. 27, fol. 127r.–v. (130r.–v. n.n.).

[62] The *privilegio* granted to Pighinucci is recorded in ASVat, Arm. 39, vol. 27, fol. 430v., 431r.–v.(436v., 437r.–v. n.n.). The date of printing in the book is given as 1 July 1509, nine days before the *privilegio* was granted.

[63] The book is listed in Francesco Barberi, "Stefano Guillery e le sue edizione

carried a fine of one hundred gold ducats to be divided between the Camera Apostolica and the rightful beneficiaries. Seven years later, in 1517, the book was re-published and a new *privilegio* was issued, for another ten years and valid within the territory of the Papal States. However, it was granted not to Varthema but to Guillereti with the explanation that the earlier edition was now exhausted and that Ludovico di Varthema was dead without heirs.[64] On 4 February 1510, Mazzocchi printed Francesco Albertini's *Opusculum De mirabilibus novae et veteris Urbis Romae* with the words "CUM PRIVILEGIO" on the title-page.[65]

Besides those already mentioned, Mazzocchi, Silber, and Guillereti also printed various works of ancient literature. Raffaele Maffei's translation into Latin of Homer's *Odyssey*, for example, was printed with a *privilegio* by Mazzocchi on 12 September 1510.[66] After the election of Leo X, the number of papal privileges granted for learned and literary works increased significantly, with a special interest shown in writings both in Greek and translations from the Greek. Among the first privileges granted by Leo X was one for Giovanni Lorenzi's

---

romane," in *Studi offerti a Roberto Ridolfi*, 98, and discussed in Emanuele Casamassima, "Ludovico degli Arrighi detto Vicentino copista dell'*Itinerario* del Varthema," *La Bibliofilia* 64 (1962): 117–162. The full title reads: *Itinerario di Ludovico de Varthema Bolognese nello Egypto, nella Surria, nella Arabia deserta et felice, nella Persia, nella India et nella Ethiopia . . . Stampato in Roma per maestro Stephano Guillireti de Loreno et maestro Hercule de Nani Bolognese ad instantia de maestro Lodovico de Henricis de Corneto Vicentino. Nel Anno M. D. X. a di VI de Decembrio.*

[64] The contents of the papal *privilegio* are noted in Blasio, *Cum gratia et privilegio*, 86. In the colophon of the 1517 edition is written: "Cum gratia & privilegio del S. Signore N. S. Leone pp. X in suo anno quinto." Varthema's *Itinerario* appears to have been published simultaneously in Venice by Giorgio Rusconi on 6 March 1517.

[65] The book is listed in Ascarelli, *Annali tipografici di Giacomo Mazzocchi*, no. 24. Mazzocchi printed it again in 1515. In 1529 the book was reprinted with woodcut illustrations and with the title *Mirabilia Rome. Opusculum de mirabilibus nove et veteris urbis Rome editum a Francisco Albertino Florentino cum privilegio* in Lyon by Jean Marion for Romain Morin. Curiously, Albertini's *Septem mirabilia orbis et urbis Romae et florentinae civitatis* issued by Mazzocchi three days later, on 7 February 1510, was published without a *privilegio*.

[66] The book is listed in Ascarelli, *Annali Tipografici di Giacomo Mazzocchi*, no. 28; and Adams, 1: 551, no. 795. It may be mentioned with respect to the printing of Greek texts in Rome, that in a letter written in May the following year (1511), Angelo Colocci discusses the printing in Rome of books in Greek, and the foundation of an Academy, perhaps along the lines of that of Aldo Manuzio in Venice. See Vittorio Fanelli, "Il ginnasio greco di Leone X a Roma," in Vittorio Fanelli, *Ricerche su Angelo Colocci e sulla Roma cinquecentesca*, 93. There is evidence that Colocci tried to attract Aldo Manuzio to Rome.

translation from Greek into Latin of Plutarch's *Libellus aureus quomodo
ab adulatore discernatur amicis*, printed "Cum gratia et privilegio" in
1514 by Mazzocchi.[67] Other Greek works followed. On 15 January
1516, for example, Zacharias Kalliergês published in Rome with a
ten-year papal *privilegio* a Greek edition of the *Idylls* of Theocritus.[68]
Leo X actively promoted Greek studies in Rome and granted numerous privileges, especially for works printed by the press belonging to
the Greek Academy, the Stamperia Greca del Ginnasio Mediceo,
which opened in the house of Angelo Colocci and remained active
until 1519. The first book to issue from that press was the *scholia* on
Homer's *Iliad*, printed in 1517, for which Leo X granted a *privilegio*.[69]
Others followed.

Besides Greek works, the *privilegio* was also granted for other publications. In 1515, notice of copyright appears in several books printed
by Stephano Guillereti, including the *Svma de arithmetica, geometria prac-
tica utilissima* by the Spanish mathematician Juan de Ortega, and
Filippo Beroaldo's *editio princeps* of the first six books of Tacitus's
Annales. The latter was published 1 March 1515 by Guillereti under
the title *Libri quinque nouiter inuenti atque cum reliquis eius operibus editi*.
According to the well-known story, the codex containing the six
books by Tacitus (the so-called "Mediceo primo" [Lauretianus 68, I])
had been stolen from the monastery of Corvey in Westphalia. In
1508 it was in the hands of Francesco Soderini from whom it was
acquired by Cardinal Giovanni de' Medici (the future Leo X). In
1515, after becoming pope, Leo X granted Beroaldo the exclusive
rights to the printing of the book.[70] One of the printed books Leo

---

[67] The book is listed in Ascarelli, *Annali Tipografici di Giacomo Mazzocchi*, nos. 73,
83; and the *privilegio* noted in Blasio, *Cum gratia et privilegio*, 81.
[68] The book is catalogued in Mortimer, *Italian 16th Century Books*, no. 497; and
the *privilegio* noted in Blasio, *Cum gratia et privilegio*, 90.
[69] The book is listed in Emile Legrand, *Bibliographie hellenique*, 1: 159, no. 56
(the text of the *privilegio* is reproduced on pp. 161–162); and Anthony Hobson, "The
Printer of the Greek Editions *In Gymnasio Mediceo ad Caballinum Montem*," 334. The
scholia was based on Vatican manuscripts which Janus Lascaris had borrowed on 9
June 1516 and 4 May 1517. A copy of the book, *Scholia in Homeri Iliadis*, is in the
Collegio Greco, Rome.
[70] Beroaldo had been Cardinal Giovanni de' Medici's secretary. In 1514, after
becoming pope, Leo X nominated Beroaldo *praepositus* of the Accademia Romana.
In 1516, Leo X further nominated Beroaldo to the post of "curatore dei privilegii
di Santa Romana Chiesa" in Castel Sant'Angelo, and made him prefect of the
Vatican Library. These nominations are recorded in two papal briefs dated 5
September and 16 September 1516 (ASVat, Arm. 39, vol. 36, fols. 36, 105v.).

sent to the Abbey of Corvey, together with a plenary indulgence, as a replacement for the 'borrowed' manuscript. Much to the annoyance of Leo X, the Milanese scholar and publisher Alessandro Minuziano ignored the papal *privilegio* and reprinted Beroaldo's edition of Tacitus word-for-word. Minuziano was duly summoned to Rome to answer directly to the Pope. His detailed apology, however, appeased Leo X's anger and, with a papal letter of absolution, Minuziano was permitted to publish the work, provided he came to terms with Filippo Beroaldo.[71]

Like the Venetian *privilegio*, the form of a papal *privilegio* was fairly standard. It was usually divided into four parts the first of which identified the supplicant and the item or items being covered and often stating the reason why protection was being sought. This was followed in the second part by a section granting indemnity ("Indemnitate") to the supplicant, and frequently also to his or her heirs and successors, usually for a period of ten years, occasionally fifteen, during which time it was prohibited to copy the said work or works without the license, sometimes in writing, of the supplicant, or the supplicant's heir and successor.

The third part, usually beginning with the word "Inhibentes," concerned general and particular restrictions, the geographical area of enforcement, and penalties. Restrictions were usually applicable to "one and all" ("omnibus et singulis") of whatever status, rank, order, or condition, but often citing in particular one or more among book sellers, printers, engravers, and dealers depending on the situation. In contrast to the Venetian *privilegio*, the geographical range of effectiveness claimed in a papal *privilegio* extended beyond Rome and the Papal States ("in Urbe quam in totu statu Ecclesiastico") to all of Italy and beyond ("tam in Italia, quam extra Italiam"); in fact it was held to be enforceable in all the territories and regions subject to the Holy Roman Church ("Sanctae Romanae Ecclesiae mediate vel immediate subiectus").[72] The penalty for transgressors was usually

---

[71] The incident is noted in Pierina Fontana, "Inizi della proprietà letteraria nello Stato Pontifico (Saggio di documenti dell'Archivio Vaticano)," *Accademie e biblioteche d'Italia* 3 (1929–1930), 208–09; Francesco Barberi, "Libri e Stampatori nella Roma dei Papi," *Studi Romani* 13 (1965), 438; and in Norton, *Italian Printers*, xxvii–xxviii. Landau and Parshall, 302, explain that the reason for Leo X's anger was that he had purchased the original manuscript for the enormous sum of 500 ducats.

[72] The extent of the papal claim of effectiveness, especially the phrase *tam in Italia, quam extra Italiam*, was, in fact, objected to by Venice in the case of the publisher Domenico Basa in 1594. The case is discussed in Brown, 140–42.

500 gold ducats *de Camera*, though sums of 200 and 300 are also recorded. The sum was usually divided between the plaintiff and the Camera Apostolica, but there are also a number of instances where the sum would be divided equally into thirds with one third each going to the plaintiff and the Camera Apostolica and that remaining being paid to the person who denounced the counterfeiter. Not infrequently fees were automatically deducted to cover the cost of the authority hearing the case. In this respect, the penalty was not unlike that administered in Venice, and also included confiscation of all copies of counterfeit books, or plates and prints, together with, occasionally, equipment. The papacy, however, unlike the secular government of Venice, was also able to impose another penalty, that of 'automatic' excommunication ("excommunicationis latae sententiae"). Although considered a singular and overly harsh punishment today, it was not such an unusual threat in the sixteenth century. It had been used in earlier times against debtors to the Camera Apostolica, and although the use of an interdict against debtors was limited under Pope Pius V in 1570, excommunication *latae sententiae* in special cases remained *in forma Camerae* as late as the eighteenth century. The papal *privilegio* was regarded as a type of contractual obligation for which, if it was violated, the transgressor was subject to 'automatic' excommunication.

The fourth section of a papal *privilegio* concerned the mandate ("Mandato") issued with respect to the *privilegio* to those directly beholden to and responsible for enforcing papal authority, both spiritual (Archbishops, Bishops, and their vicars and officials), and secular (Legates, Vicelegates, Nuncios, Governors, Judges, Magistrates, etc.), requiring all to render the supplicant every assistance, should he or she need it, in the prosecution of his or her case against transgressors.

Indication of the *privilegio* on the print varied in form. The most familiar is the simple inscription *cum privilegio*, making it easy to confuse it with a *privilegio* granted in Venice. Occasionally before 1575, but fairly consistently after this date, the inscription also included the name of the pope granting the *privilegio*, and its duration.

Prints and the Papal Privilegio

The first printed book illustrated with woodcuts, Johannes de Turre-cremata's *Meditationes*, was printed in Rome in 1467 (see also Chapter 4).

In 1478, twenty-seven engraved maps by Conrad Sweynheym (the partner of Arnoldo Pannartz) were featured in a Latin edition of Ptolemy's *Cosmographia* published in Rome by Arnoldus Buckinck. After copyright became available, numerous books illustrated with prints were published with a papal *privilegio*. On 30 November 1517, for example, Mazzocchi was granted a six-year *privilegio* for his edition of Andrea Fulvio's *Illustrium imagines*.[73] The book is illustrated with 204 woodcut portraits in medallions of Roman, Byzantine, and German emperors and other illustrious ancient personages. The woodcuts have been ascribed tentatively to Ugo da Carpi.[74] The *privilegio* also included Mazzocchi's own edition of *Epigrammata antiqvae vrbis* which contains twenty-one illustrations, including a full-page woodcut of the Pantheon.[75]

With the exception of Ugo da Carpi's patent, however, no examples of independent prints carrying a papal *privilegio* have come to light before 1546. Moreover, there is no corresponding archival documentation available before 1575. Without archival support, it is difficult to say how many privileges were granted for prints during the first three-quarters of the century. Without archival documentation, it is also difficult to identify the person to whom the *privilegio* was granted. In most of the examples before 1575, one can only guess the identity of the grantee. And as the case of Anthonie van Santfoort and the prints of Cornelis Cort makes clear, guessing on the basis of names that appear on the print can be completely off the mark (see Chapter 9). The Santfoort case, plus examples in the other chapters, should also alert us to the problem of the date of the *privilegio*, which may not be the same as that which appears on the print. Dates, indeed, are another issue with copyrighted prints before 1575. In several cases, the print is undated so there is no way of telling when the period of copyright protection began, or, perhaps more importantly, when it ceased to be effective. And to

---

[73] Fulvio's book is listed in Ascarelli, *Annali Tipografici di Giacomo Mazzocchi*, no. 116; and catalogued in Mortimer, *Italian 16th Century Books*, no. 203. Although the *privilegio* is dated 30 November 1517, the publication date is given as 15 November 1517, fifteen days before the *privilegio* was granted.

[74] Luigi Servolini, "Ugo da Carpi Illustratore del Libro," *Gutenberg-Jahrbuch* (1950): 202.

[75] The book, which was not published until April 1521, is listed in Ascarelli, *Annali Tipografici di Giacomo Mazzocchi*, no. 144; and catalogued in Mortimer, *Italian 16th Century Books*, no. 297.

confuse matters further, the duration of the copyright is rarely indicated. This situation changes soon after the election Gregory XIII
(1572–1585) who evidently brought to the administration of papal
privileges a new rigour that required all prints to carry proper notice
of copyright giving both the date when the print was issued and the
duration of the *privilegio*.

CHAPTER THREE

PROPRIETORSHIP, LICENSING, CENSORSHIP

Before turning to an examination of privileges granted for prints, it is necessary to address the issues of licensing and censorship. First, though, a few comments are in order concerning the question of whether during this period copyright incorporated notions of intellectual or creative property. Did the *privilegio* protect an author's or an artist's ideas from being used by someone else? Generally speaking, the answer to this question is, no; there was no concept yet in sixteenth-century Italy of ideas constituting property. The main purpose of copyright during the Renaissance was to protect the financial investment made in a printing project. Only much later, beginning in the eighteenth century, was it extended to include authors and artists by recognizing their rights over the reproduction of their own creations and allowing them the opportunity to protect those rights through copyright. However, the Renaissance *privilegio* did incorporate a notion of proprietorship.

Books and Proprietorship

That the book-privilege incorporated a notion of literary proprietorship was first argued by Horatio Brown in the case of the author-publisher Marcantonio Sabellico to whom the Venetian College had granted the first recorded book-privilege on 1 September 1486.[1] Although more recently Rudolf Hirsch has questioned Brown's argument, the case Brown makes for an incipient form of literary proprietorship is compelling.[2]

A clause in the *privilegio* granted to Sabellico states that the author may consign his manuscript to the printer of his choice ("alicui

---

[1] Brown, 53. Sabellico's *privilegio* is recorded in ASV, CN, reg. 13, fol. 115v. [Fulin, "Documenti," no. 3].

[2] Rudolf Hirsch, *Printing, Selling and Reading 1450–1550* (Wiesbaden, 1967), 81, believes that Brown "was mistaken when he considered this privilege a recognition of literary property."

diligenti impressori qui opus illud imprimat suis sumptibus et edat et nemini præter eum liceat opus illud imprimi facere"). In granting Sabellico the right to select a printer, Brown argues that the College thereby recognized simultaneously Sabellico's proprietory rights to his own manuscript. The *privilegio* made it illegal to print Sabellico's manuscript without his permission, and that anyone caught doing so would be prosecuted and fined 500 ducats. The printer selected by Sabellico was Andrea de' Torresani da Asola who published the work in 1487. Other author-publishers were accorded this same right. On 3 January 1492 [1491 m.v.], Pietro Francesco da Ravenna was granted a *privilegio* in which it was stated that no one could print his book "excepto dumtaxat illo impressore, quem prefatus doctor preelegerit."[3] On 10 March 1513 the author-publisher Nicolò Liburnio was granted a *privilegio* for ten years during which time nobody could print his book *Le Selvette* except Jacopo Pencio, and which in fact Pencio printed the following May.[4] Similarly, in a supplication submitted in August 1515, the author-publisher Giovanni Aurelio Augurello [Johannes Aurelius Augurellus] expresses his right to have his book *Chrysopaea* printed by whomever he pleases and names Simone de Luere.[5]

The concept of literary proprietorship, however, was by no means securely established and was evidently often infringed upon by printer-publishers. In response to continuing abuse, a new law was enacted which included a provision designed to protect authors from having their work printed and sold without their permission. On 7 February 1545 [1544 m.v.] the Council of Ten declared that henceforth anyone seeking to print a work must present documentary proof of the author's consent to the Riformatori dello Studio di Padova in order to obtain a license.[6] (For the Riformatori dello Studio di Padova and licensing, see below.) The new law was aimed directly at printer-

---

[3] Pietro Francesco's *privilegio* is recorded in ASV, CN, reg. 14, fol. 49r. (53r. n.n.) [Fulin, "Documenti," no. 4]. It is discussed by Rinaldo Fulin, "Primi privilegi di stampa in Venezia," *Archivio Veneto* 1 (1871), 161. The short, fourteen-page book on how to improve one's memory, titled *Libellus de artificiosa memoria FOENIX dictus*, was printed on 10 January 1492 [1491 m.v.] by Bernardino de' Cuori da Cremona.

[4] Liburnio's *privilegio* is recorded in ASV, CN, reg. 17, fol. 40v. (42v. n.n.) [Fulin, "Documenti," no. 187].

[5] Augurello's *privilegio* is recorded in ASV, CN, reg. 18, fol. 18v. (19v. n.n.) [Fulin, "Documenti," no. 201]. The book, *Chrysopoeiae libri III et Geronticon liber primus*, was indeed published by Luere ("impressit Simon Luerensis") in 1515.

[6] The document is recorded in ASV, CX, Comuni, Busta 36, fol. 124r.

publishers for whom the matter of proprietorship was less clearly defined. Printer-publishers usually printed new editions of previously printed works or manuscript works written, translated, or edited by someone else. In contrast to the author, translator, or editor, the printer-publisher may not actually own the manuscript to be published. And the question of ownership appears central to the notion of proprietorship. It may be presumed that author-publishers and translator-publishers owned their own manuscripts. Similarly, a number of editor-publishers might own the manuscripts they wished to have printed, such as Giovanni Domenico Negro, a doctor of medicine, who explains in his supplication for a *privilegio* that he had personally acquired the two codices he wishes to have printed. He was granted a *privilegio* for both books on 24 January 1492 [1491 m.v.].[7]

But what about printer-publishers? In most cases it is usually impossible today to establish whether or not a manuscript was owned by the printer-publisher at the time of the printing. One of the earliest examples of a *privilegio* granted to a printer-publisher is that issued on 17 August 1492 to Bernardino Benalio who wished to publish Bernardo Giustiniani's *De origine urbis Venetiarum*.[8] Giustiniani, a member of the old, aristocratic Venetian family, had died three years earlier in 1489. Did Benalio acquire the manuscript after Giustiniani's death, or did he perhaps come to some arrangement with Giustiniani's heirs to print the manuscript, which nonetheless remained in their hands? Benalio could have published the work under a contract with Giustiniani's heirs in an arrangement that permitted him to claim commercial rights to the printed book to protect his expenses (which, besides printing costs, may also have included the payment of a fee to the Giustiniani). Under these circumstances, although Benalio may not have owned the Giustiniani manuscript, he was eligible to seek a *privilegio*. Such a contractual arrangement was not unusual, and indeed could be more complicated than that suggested in Benalio's

---

[7] Negro's *privilegio* is recorded in ASV, CN, reg. 14, fol. 50r. (54r. n.n.) [Fulin, "Documenti," no. 5]. The two codices are "Haliabas" (or *Aliabatte*, i.e. the *Liber medicinae, sive, Regalis dispositio* of the tenth-century Persian physician ‘Ali ibn al-‘Abbas al-Majusi, translated by Stephanus Antiochenus), and "Xantis de Pisauro, de venenis," i.e. *De Venenis* written in Venice by Santes de Ardoynis (Sante Arduino da Pesaro) between 1424 and 1426. Both were published, at Negro's expense ("impensa . . . Johannis Dominici de Nigro") in 1492 by Bernardino Ricci da Novara.

[8] The *privilegio* granted Benalio is recorded in ASV, CN, reg. 14, fol. 66r. (70r. n.n.) [Fulin, "Documenti," no. 6].

case. For example, the majority of the letters and orations of St. Catherine of Siena were not owned by Aldo Manuzio when he published them in 1500. In a contract drawn up on 17 April 1499, it would appear that the original manuscript volumes (and one printed volume) were in the possession of an unnamed monastery. Manuzio entered into negotiations for their printing with Margarita Ugelheimer, the widow of Peter Ugelheimer, from whom she had received the manuscript volumes. In the contract drawn up with Manuzio, she acknowledges her satisfaction with the arrangements Manuzio has made with Antonio Condelmera, a representative of the unnamed monastery, for the payments which are to be made to the monastery for the privilege of printing each volume. The contract also specified that Manuzio had to return the manuscripts and the printed book after he had finished using them as copy-text. The contract makes it clear that the financial burden for the project was on Manuzio. The following year, on 23 July, he submitted a supplication to the College for a *privilegio* which was duly granted and Manuzio published the *Epistole* the following 15 September.[9]

That someone could have copyright for something owned by somebody else might seem confusing at first. This situation, however, highlights the nature of copyright in sixteenth-century Italy and also brings to light a fundamental difference between a *privilegio* for a book and a *privilegio* for a print. Copyright for books may be understood to serve an interlocked double function. First of all it served to protect the printed book from being copied without permission over a specified period of time. At the same time, in the case of authors, translators, and editors, in the very act of being granted, the *privilegio* established the proprietory rights of these individuals to the 'original manuscript' in their possession. The term 'original manuscript' is introduced here to identify the work the supplicant wished to print or have printed; it could be a recently penned piece, an old codice, or a revised, emended, or annotated edition of a previously published book. Unlike today, proprietory rights were not believed

---

[9] Manuzio's *privilegio* is recorded in ASV, CN, reg. 15, fol. 23v. (25v. n.n.) [Fulin, "Documenti," no. 104]. The publishing project is discussed by M. H. Laurent, "Alde Manuzio l'Ancien, Éditeur de S. Catherine de Sienne (1500)," *Traditio* 6 (1948): 357–363; and Henri D. Saffrey, "Les Images Populaires de Saints Dominicains à Venise au XVe siècles et l'Édition par Alde Manuce des 'Epistole' de Sainte Catherine de Sienne," *Italia medioevale e umanistica* 25 (1982): 241–312.

to exist *ipso facto* in the 'original manuscript' but were created in the process of obtaining copyright. In other words, copyright could be obtained only if the 'original manuscript' was to be printed. It is important to understand that copyright applied only to the book in its printed form. Proprietory rights to the 'original manuscript' were established only if the 'original manuscript' was printed. Sabellico's *privilegio* could be invoked only if the published version of his manuscript (produced by Sabellico's designated printer) was reproduced by another printer without his permission. The *privilegio* protected his 'original manuscript' *per se* only in so far as it recognized it to be his property to which copyright pertained after it had been printed. Once granted the *privilegio* continued to provide copyright protection for the book for the time specified.

A book is produced in what is essentially a three-step process. First there is the 'original manuscript'. The 'original manuscript' is then recreated in moveable type from which the book is then printed.

In effect, for different lengths of time the book exists in three different forms. After completion, the book, of course, continues to exist, and probably so does the 'original manuscript'. The type into which the 'original manuscript' has been transformed, and from which the book was printed, however, is removed from the bed of the press, broken up, and returned to its cases. The object of copyright, that which has been copyrighted, may be said literally to exist only on paper. This obvious point is made in order to contrast it with the situation found in copyrighted prints.

Prints and Proprietorship

A print (woodcut or engraving) is also produced in a three-step process. First, there is the design, which would be drawn directly onto the woodblock or copper plate. In many cases, this drawing reproduced an already existing design or image. In other cases, however, the drawing which exists on the woodblock or plate is the only record of the design. The design is then reproduced by being cut into a woodblock, or engraved into a copper plate, which is then printed to produce the print.

In contrast to the production of the book, when the process is completed, a different configuration of elements remains. The design, if it was a reproduction of another design, such as a drawing or a painting, continues to exist. If, however, it existed only in the drawing on the woodblock or plate, it is now lost in its original form. But more importantly, not only does the finished product, the print, exist, but so does the woodblock or plate from which it was produced. Unlike books for which the 'original manuscript' in whatever form was integrally part of the copyright grant, for prints it is the woodblock or plate, and not the original design, which serves as the basis for the claim to copyright.

For all practical purposes, the process of application for a *privilegio* and the restrictions, penalties and so forth contained in the document issued were essentially the same for prints as they were for books. What is fundamentally different is the basis for the claim for copyright. In place of the 'original manuscript' we have instead the notion of the 'original plate'. In a legal sense the 'original plate' was not unlike the 'original manuscript'. As in the case with the 'original manuscript', the owner of the block or plate, or someone with the necessary permission from the owner, can submit a supplication for a *privilegio*. However, this similar legal status should not be allowed to conceal a fundamental difference that has a direct bearing on the perceived rights of artists and printmakers. Whereas with copyright for books the notion of proprietory rights applied to the 'original manuscript', and with it the first stirrings of a concept of literary or intellectual rights, with prints, proprietory rights, such as they were, applied only to the 'original plate'. In other words, with the focus on the 'original plate', there was no basis for a claim to proprietory rights for the drawing or painting that the block or plate reproduced. There was no equivalent in prints of literary proprietorship, of what might be called artistic proprietorship or artistic rights. The *privilegio* for prints protected neither the original drawn or painted design nor the idea or image reproduced but merely the rights of the owner of the block or plate. Neither the inventor of the idea or image, nor the engraver or woodcutter who reproduced it, had any claim to 'artistic' rights.

Licensing and Censorship in Venice

At the outset, it would appear that the only requirement for a printing project was a legal claim to the 'original manuscript' or 'original plate' one wished to print. By the beginning of the sixteenth century, however, other 'requirements' began to adhere to the process that were to become the basis for a system of licensing and censorship. What first occurred in isolated incidences, but which was soon deemed to be applicable in all cases, was the approval by a competent authority of the content of the works that the government was otherwise protecting through the granting of privileges. Initially, a publisher might bring to the College's attention the fact that the work for which he sought a *privilegio* had been approved or affirmed by an authority in order to fortify his supplication. In 1494, Bernardino Benalio, for example, evidently submitted, along with his petition for a *privilegio* for the works of Lorenzo Giustiniani and Alessandro Tartagni da Imola which he wished to print, the written approval of the rector of the law school and a number of lecturers at the University of Padua.[10] The *privilegio* duly recorded that the College "visis attestationibus rectoris iuristarum, et complurium doctorum legentium in Florentissimo Gymnasio Patavino affirmatium opera." In a petition submitted in 1506, a Dominican, Fra' Silvestro da Prierio, pointed out that the works he wished to publish had been approved by a brother Dominican appointed by the general of his order to examine Fra' Silvestro's work.[11]

However, while this sort of approval no doubt influenced the decision of the College, in the area of books with religious subject matter, it was the official approval of the Patriarch and of the Inquisitor that was to become crucial. It is in this official ecclesiastical approval that can also be recognized the first stirrings of censorship. The early history of licensing and censorship in Venice is one that is both a process of accommodation to ecclesiastical concerns and the development of a system of quality and content control that served not

---

[10] ASV, CN, reg. 14, fol. 94v. (98v. n.n.) [Fulin, "Documenti," no. 20]. Benalio's *privilegio* is noted in Martin Lowry, *The World of Aldus Manutius, Business and Scholarship in Renaissance Venice* (Oxford, 1979), 23. The approval had been granted for the book *Doctrina della Vita Monastica*, which Benalio published on 20 October 1494. A copy is in the Marciana, Venice, Miscell. 1018[2].

[11] Fra' Silvestro da Prierio's *privilegio* is recorded in ASV, CN, reg. 15, fol. 158r.–v. (160r.–v. n.n.) [Fulin, "Documenti," no. 111].

only to protect the Church's doctrines and Christian sensibility, but
at the same time also to maintain the viability of the publishing
industry.

The first formally authorized right to censor books was issued by
Sixtus IV in a brief, *Accepimus literas*, dated 17 March 1479. It was
addressed to the rectors of the University of Cologne and granted
them the authority to use ecclesiastical censures against heretical and
erroneous books. The rectors soon thereafter developed the *imprimatur* which certified that a book did not contain matter the Church
found objectionable. Notice of approval, indicated by the term *approbatio*, began to appear in the 1480s in the colophon of books printed
in Cologne, usually in the phrase "admissum et approbatum ab alma
Coloniensi universitate" or something similar.[12]

In Italy, the earliest instance of a work receiving an ecclesiastical
approbatio is *Nosce te*, a devotional book by Joannes Carthusiensis
[Giovanni di Dio Certosino], published by Nicolaus Jenson in Venice
in 1480.[13] As yet, however, there was no obvious connection between
the *approbatio* and the *privilegio*. The *approbatio* was not regarded as a
prerequisite for a *privilegio*, nor was it necessarily granted with the
view to obtaining a *privilegio*. Neither Joannes Carthusiensis nor
Nicolaus Jenson, for example, sought a *privilegio*.[14]

In 1487, Pope Innocent VIII issued a bull, *Inter multiplices*, which
was the first significant attempt to impose a general censorship
throughout Christendom: "tam in Romana Curia, quam in reliquis
Italiae, Germaniae, Franciae, Hispaniarum, Angliae et Scotiae alia-
rumque nationum quarunlibet Christianarum civitatibus, terris, cas-
tris, villis et locis."[15] The concern was with the diffusion of material

---

[12] This early instance of censorship is noted in Rudolf Hirsch, "Pre-Reformation
Censorship of Printed Books," *Library Chronicle* 21 (1955): 100–105; idem, *Printing,
Selling and Reading 1450–1550* (Wiesbaden, 1967), 87; and Paul Grendler, *The Roman
Inquisition and the Venetian Press, 1540–1605* (Princeton, 1977), 71.

[13] The *approbatio* is noted in Brown, 61, and Putnam, *The Censorship of the Church
of Rome*, 1: 78. The 'approval' was granted by: "Philippus rota juris utriusque doctor; Joannes gusmaci, archipresbyter monte Silicis, ac plebanus Sanctae Mariae nove
de Venetiis; Petrus frigerius artium et theologie doctor, archiepiscopus Corphiensis;
Mapheus girardo, Patriarcha Venetiarum, Dalmatieque primas; Gabriel Crunus,
ordinis minorum theologorum, Inquisitor." Besides *Nosce te*, the book also contains
Certosino's *Corona senum; De immensa charitate dei; De humilitate interiora et patientia vera*;
and *Libellus qui flos vitae interpretatur*.

[14] Brown, 61, reports not finding any record of a *privilegio* for *Nosce te* in the
archives of the College or the Senate.

[15] The full text of the bull is given in Joseph Hilgers, *Der Index der verboten Bücher*,

printed in books that was contrary to the Catholic religion or deemed scandalous. The bull ordered that printers and authors, under pain of excommunication *latae sententiae* and heavy fines, not publish any works that have not first been submitted for examination by the ecclesiastical authorities and duly approved by them or by their delegates. It also ordered the Master of the Sacred Palace in Rome and diocesan ordinaries throughout Christendom to watch diligently to prevent books that were heretical, impious, or scandalous from being published. Books that were deemed heretical or otherwise dangerous were to be burned. In 1501, Alexander VI promulgated an almost identical bull under the same Incipit, *Inter multiplices*, that extended censorship specifically to the cities of Magdeburg, Cologne, Mainz, and Trier. Addressing the Archbishop of Magdeburg and the rulers of the three other ecclesiastical principalities, Alexander VI explained that:

> The art of printing can be of great service in so far as it furthers the circulation of useful and tested books; but it can bring about serious evils if it is permitted to widen the influence of pernicious works. It will, therefore, be necessary to maintain full control over the printers so that they may be prevented from bringing into print writings which are antagonistic to the Catholic faith, or which are likely to cause trouble to believers.[16]

In Venice, the papal legate to the Venetian Republic, Niccolò Franco, Bishop of Treviso, published a decree in 1491 that forbade anyone to print, or cause to have printed, or permit to have printed, any books dealing with ecclesiastical and doctrinal matters, except ordinary devotional works.[17] All such works were ordered to be submitted for approval to the bishop or vicar-general. A specific instance of censorship during this period is the decree issued on 21 February 1497 by the Patriarch of Venice, Tommaso Donà, intended to censor nude figures in Luc'Antonio Giunta's edition of Ovid's *Metamorphoses*.

480–82. It is noted in Pasquale Lopez, *Sul libro a stampa e le origini della censura ecclesiastica* (Naples, 1972), 63–64; and Putnam, 1: 78. The bull itself was printed in Rome by Eucario Silber.

[16] The translated passage is from Putnam, 1: 80–81. The bull is also noted in Rudolph Hirsch, "Bulla Super Impressione Librorum, 1515," *Gutenberg-Jahrbuch* (1973): 249.

[17] The decree, noted in Putnam, 1: 79–80, also ordered that two titles be burned: Antonio Rosselli's *Monarchia sive de potestate imperatoris et papae et de materia conciliorum* (Venice, 1487), and Pico della Mirandola's nine hundred theses (Rome, 1486). Pico's theses had been banned by Innocent VIII in 1487.

The decree begins: "Reverendissimus dominus Patriarcha mandavit Luce Antonio del Zonta qui imprimere facit (nec non Ioanni Rubeo de Verzellis impressori) opus vulgare Ovidii Methamorphosii cum figuris inhonestis . . ."[18] Under threat of automatic excommunication ("sub pena excomunicationis late sententie"), Giunta agreed to modify the figures. It is a measure of the direct effect of the decree that in the 1497 Giunta edition the figures were in fact retouched with the offending areas blotted out in ink. In successive editions in 1501 and 1508 the illustrations were more modest.[19] On 10 February 1510, another decree was issued by the Patriarch Antonio Contarini. This one was more general in scope, calling for the prohibition of books printed with immoral illustrations. Single prints produced independent of books must also have been subject to similar demands for censorship.

The response of the Venetian government to the issue was to establish its own system of licensing and censorship. It became necessary for publishers to obtain permission to print from the Council of Ten, which was granted following approval by an appropriate authority. In 1505, the printer-publisher Jacopo di Pencio da Lecco, for example, was granted permission ("concessa facultà") by the Council of Ten to print *Tre Questione* by Bernardino Zane, the Archbishop of Spalato (Split), which had been previously approved by the Patriarch ("et approbate dal Reverendissimo Patriarcha").[20] The following year, a system of licensing was instituted. On 11 October 1506, the Council of Ten proclaimed that henceforth no one in the city of Venice could print, or have printed, any new work without first obtaining a license from the Chiefs of the Council of Ten (*Capi del Consiglio dei Dieci*).[21] In cases where authors touched on politics and affairs of state, the Chiefs of the Council of Ten evidently felt competent to make its own decision over whether or not

---

[18] The decree is noted in Antonio Niero, "Decreti pretridentini di due patriarchi di Venezia su stampa di libri," *Rivista di storia della chiesa in Italia* 14 (1960): 450; and Grendler, 72.

[19] Giunti's 1497 edition, entitled *Metamorphoseos Libri: volgarizzamento antico toscano*, had been printed by Giovanni Rossi (the "Ioanni Rubeo de Verzellis impressori" named in the decree). Niero, 450, n. 5, suggests that Savonarolan propaganda at this time against the nude figure probably contributed to the reaction to Giunta's illustrations.

[20] Pencio's *privilegio* is recorded in ASV, CN, reg. 15, fol. 153r. (155r. n.n.) [Fulin, "Documenti," no. 151].

[21] The document recording the proclamation is in ASV, CX, Proclami, Busta 1.

to grant a license to print. For example, it relied on its own authority when it issued a license to Luc' Antonio Giunta on 16 July 1507 to print one of three orations delivered by Joannes Rebler, ambassador from Emperor Maximilian, before the Doge and the Signoria.[22] On other occasions, however, the Chiefs might ask someone of authority to examine a work to make sure it did not contain any religious or moral errors. For example, in the text of the license issued to Gregorio de' Gregorii on 31 August 1508 for *Universalis de anima traditionis opus* . . . by Cristoforo Marcello, the Chiefs noted that it had had the work examined by Vincenzo Quirini who had found nothing in it contrary to Catholic truth.[23] In the *privilegio* granted to Bartholamio di Cori on 13 October 1510, it is recorded that the book he wished to print, *La Obsidione de Padua*, had been granted a license by the Chiefs, and that it had been examined in particular by Marco Antonio Lauredano, one of the Chiefs.[24]

The situation soon emerged, however, that notices of ecclesiastical approval came to play a central role in the decisions of the Chiefs of the Council of Ten in the authorization to print particular books and prints. By the beginning of the second decade of the century, it was becoming necessary for publishers to obtain a license, and ecclesiastical approval if necessary, prior to submitting a supplication for a *privilegio*. Meanwhile, too, the Chiefs of the Council of Ten came to acknowledge as definitive the judgement of the eclesiastical authorities in the area of religious books and to accept tacitly their approval as a prerequisite to the granting of a license. What this meant in practice is that the Chiefs of the Council of Ten could

---

[22] The document recording the issuance of the license to Giunta is in ASV, CCXN, reg. 3, fol. 28r. (33r. n.n.) [Fulin, "Documenti," no. 163]. The four-page book, *Oratio ad Principem & senatum Venetum Illustris. habita*, was sold in Venice for the price of one *soldo*, according to the diarist Marino Sanuto, *I Diarii*, 7: col. 132.

[23] The document is recorded in ASV, CCXN, reg. 3, fol. 85r. (90r. n.n.) [Fulin, "Documenti," no. 166]. The passage reads: "quod Doctor Vicenzo Querini cui per capita opus ipsum datum fuit revidendum et bene examinandum, affirmavit nihil in ipso opere esse quod repugnet vel alioquin contrarium sit catholicae veritati." Brown, 62, regards this as "the first instance of a religious censorship exercised by a secular government." Quirini, a former Venetian ambassador to Spain and the Empire, was also a monk in the austere Camaldolese order.

[24] The document recording the *privilegio* is in ASV, CN, reg. 16, fol. 68r. (74r. n.n.) [Fulin, "Documenti," no. 180]. The pertinent passage reads: "et havendo havuto licentia da li magnifici Capi proximi passadi di lo Excellentissimo Conseglio di X di stampar la prefata opereta, per esser stà udita dal magnifico messere Marco Antonio Lauredano, uno de dicti magnifici Capi."

exercise only partial control over the licensing of religious books. The Council could still refuse to license a book which had already been granted ecclesiatical approval, but it could hardly grant a license to a book denied it.

If in the area of religious censorship the Chiefs of the Council of Ten was willing to accept the role of ecclesiastical authorities, who functioned independently of the Council, censorship of other types of books remained in the hands of the Council of Ten. On 30 January 1516 [1515 m.v.], the Council took the first steps towards codifying censorship and issued a general order in which an officially appointed censor, Andrea Navagero, was given the task of supervising all books printed in the humanities:

> In all parts of the world, and in the famous cities not only of Italy but also of barbarous countries, that the honour of the nation may be preserved, it is not allowed to publish works until they shall have been examined by the most learned persons available. But in this our city, so famous and so worthy, no thought has yet been bestowed upon this matter. Hence it comes to pass that the most incorrect editions which appear before the world are those issued in Venice, to the dishonour of the city. Be it, therefore, charged upon our Noble Andrea Navagero to examine all works in humanity which, for the future, may be printed; and without his signature in the volumes they shall not be printed, under pain of being confiscated and burned, and a fine of three hundred ducats for him who disobeys this order.[25]

Licensing, however, remained an issue. Despite the earlier proclamation, on 3 July 1519, the Council of Ten found it necessary to state again the prohibition against all works being printed without a license from the Chiefs of the Council of Ten.[26] Eight years later, on 29 January 1527 [1526 m.v.], the Council of Ten issued another proclamation stating that no books could be printed in prose or in verse without first having obtained a license from the Chiefs of the Council of Ten.[27] The proclamation apparently had been precipitated in reaction to the scandal that had developed as a result of a

---

[25] The translation is in Brown, 65. The original document is ASV, CCXN, Misti, filza 39, fol. 39v. Seven months later, on 31 July 1516, the edict, signed by the three Chiefs of the Council of Ten, was repeated in language directed especially at publishers. This second edict is recorded in ASV, CCXN, reg. 4, fol. 123r. (126r. n.n.) [Fulin, "Documenti," no. 210].

[26] The document is recorded in ASV, CX, Proclami, Busta 2, fol. 33.

[27] The document is recorded in ASV, CX, Comuni, Busta 4, fol. 108; and in ASV, ECBC, Busta 54, vol. 1, fol. 36r.

complaint made by the Franciscans of S. Francesco della Vigna in Venice against a book, *Libro della origine delli volgari proverbii*, for which the author, Luigi Cinzio (Aloyse, or Alvise, Cinzio del Fabritii), had been granted a *privilegio* by the Senate on 5 October 1526.[28]

In 1545, official approval was also being granted by the Riformatori dello Studio di Padova, a body associated with the university in that city which, since 1405, had been part of the dominion of Venice.[29] On 7 February 1545 [1544 m.v.], the Council of Ten declared that henceforth the Riformatori dello Studio di Padova would serve as the official body to which publishers were obliged to submit requests for approval of the material they wished to print.[30] The Riformatori decided whether or not the submitted material was acceptable on religious, moral, and political grounds. On 24 January 1545 [1544 m.v.], for example, a license for the publication of Ludovico Dolce's comedy, *Il Capitano*, was granted by the Chiefs of the Council of Ten after the work was approved by the Riformatori.[31] In another example, on 1 August 1553, the Chiefs of the Council of Ten stated that the Riformatori dello Studio di Padova had found nothing contrary to the laws ("non vi è una cosa alcuna contraria alle leggi") in an oration by Paulo Novello and duly granted it a licence.[32]

An indication of increasing concern over the content of printed material is the decision made on 20 December 1537 by the Council of Ten to institute the magistracy of the *Esecutori contra la bestemmia*

---

[28] Cinzio's *privilegio* is recorded in ASV, ST, reg. 24, fol. 117v. (135v. n.n.) [Fulin, "Documenti," no. 253]. The complaint is reported in documents recorded by the Chiefs of the Council of Ten in ASV, CCXN, reg. 7, fols. 111v. and 161r., and recorded in the diary of Marino Sanuto (43: 448). It is discussed in Brown, 67–71, 74–75; and noted in Gerulaitis, *Printing and Publishing in Fifteenth-Century Venice*, 53–54.

[29] The studio at the university had been re-opened in 21 February 1517 [1516 m.v.], and given definitive form as a magistracy by the Venetian Senate on 22 September 1528 with the election of Andrea Mocenigo and Nicolo Tiepolo as "Doctori, proveditori, et reformatori del studio de Padoa." The following month, on 17 October, however, the earlier election was revoked and instead three "riformatori" were elected. The documents are recorded in ASV, ST, reg. 25, fol. 71v. (89v. n.n.), and ASV, ST, reg. 25, fol. 75v. (93v. n.n.), respectively. The election of the Riformatori dello Studio di Padova is discussed in Giuseppe Cappelletti, *Storia di Padova* (Padua, 1875), 2: 107–112.

[30] The document is recorded in ASV, CX, Comuni, Busta 36, fol. 124r.

[31] The license is recorded in ASV, CCXN, reg. 13, fol. 189v. Dolce's book was printed two years later, in 1547, by Gabriele Giolito de' Ferrari.

[32] The dcocument is recorded in ASV, CCXN, reg. 14, fol. 37v. A number of original notices of approval, dating mostly only to the decade of the 1550s however, survive in the archive of the Riformatori dello Studio di Padova in the Archivio di Stato in Venice (Filze 284, "Licenze per stampe").

("Executors against Blasphemy") to prosecute blasphemers against God, the Virgin Mary, and the "celestial court." The Council of Ten had been preoccupied with the repression of blasphemy since the early sixteenth century. During the first thirty or so years of the century they intervened in blasphemy cases at least eight times and sanctioned new penalties against blasphemers.[33] A special area of scrutiny was the products of the printing industry and whether books contained anything against religion, morality, and "il buon costume."

There were, indeed, many books and other printed material that were found to be "against the honour of God and the Christian faith" and so, on 12 February 1543 [1542 m.v.], the earlier requirement of a license introduced by the Council of Ten was made more stringent by the Executors with an increased fine of 50 ducats for printers and 25 ducats for sellers who failed to comply. In addition, it was stated that anyone caught selling books or other material that is both unlicensed and of unlawful content will be whipped from the Rialto to San Marco and then imprisoned for six months. And furthermore, anyone who has printed or is printing such material will be imprisoned for one year and fined one hundred ducats, and will not be released from prison even after one year until the fine has been paid; and upon release, they will be banished from the Venetian state.[34]

Despite the harsh penalties, however, the requirement of obtaining a license was evidently largely disregarded. Four years later, on 17 May 1547, it was re-iterated, with the added feature that all unlawful and unlicensed books will be confiscated and publicly burned, while the fine was increased to two hundred and fifty ducats. The following year, on 18 July, the Council of Ten issued another proclamation against the printing and selling of books contrary to the Catholic faith.[35] If, however, only passages in books were found offensive or

---

[33] The Esecutori contra la bestemmia are discussed in Renzo Derosas, "Moralità e giustizia a Venezia nel '500–'600. Gli Esecutori contro la bestemmia," in *Stato, società e giustizia nella Repubblica veneta (secc. XV–XVIII)*, vol. 1, ed. Gaetano Cozzi (Rome, 1980), 431–528; and Gaetano Cozzi, "Religione, moralità e giustizia a Venezia: vicende della magistratura degli esecutori contro la bestemmia (sec. XVI–XVII)," *Ateneo Veneto* 177 (n.s. 29) (1991): 7–95.

[34] The document is recorded in ASV, ECBC, Busta 54, vol. 1, fol. 36r.–v., 37r. Pesenti, 16, reproduces part of the document but with several errors in transcription. The document is also noted in Grendler, 78.

[35] The 17 May 1547 document is recorded in ASV, CX, Comuni, Busta 43, fol. 24v.; and in ASV, ECBC, Busta 54, vol. 1, fol. 37r. The 18 July 1548 document is recorded in ASV, CX, Comuni, Busta 45, fol. 36r.

unlawful they could be excised and the revised book re-submitted for approval and licensing. On 13 March 1554, for example, the Chiefs of the Council of Ten referred to Luca Gaurico's treatise on astrology printed "altre fiate" by Bartolomeo Cesano in 1552 but which had run afoul of the Executors.[36] All the offending clauses and particulars were subsequently removed ("dapoi levare da quello tutte le clausule et particole"); the revised book had then received the approval of the Riformatori del Studio di Padova, and now the Chiefs granted it a license ("conciedono licentia che possa essere stampato in questa Cita levate da quello le cose che li predetti S^{ri}. contra le biastema hanno giudicato dever esser ut supra levate").

In other instances, though, the offender was imprisoned. On 26 January 1579, the Executors gave notice against Stefano Bindoni who had been jailed for having copied with intention to print some pieces from the "indecent and prohibited" works of Pietro Aretino. Several offending pieces are mentioned, including in particular the 'discussion' of Nana and Antonia (from Aretino's *Ragionamenti* in which prostitutes in Rome reveal to each other the moral failings of important men, published in 1534–36), as well as Aretino's *I Dialoghi* (in which the carnality and corruption of Rome is further examined in dialogue form). Bindoni was now awaiting the eighth tribunal of the Inquisition.[37]

Although most of the attention was focused on books, there is evidence that printed images were also included under the surveillance of the Executors against Blasphemy. On 9 September 1568, for example, the engraver Domenico Zenoi, who two years earlier had been granted a *privilegio* for some maps (see Chapter 10), was fined ten ducats for having engraved several very indecent prints ("alcune figure dishonestissime") which had been printed together with indecent sonnets ("sonetti dishonesti"). The prints had been found in the shop of Giovanni Francesco Camocio, who was also ordered to pay five ducats for having had and sold the engravings.[38] From the description,

---

[36] The document is recorded in ASV, CCXN, reg. 15, fol. 108r. The book, *Tractatus astrologicus in quo agitur de prætertis multorum hominum, accidentibus per proprias eorum genituras ad unguem examinatis. Quorum exemplis consimilibus vnusquisq[ue] de medio genethliacus vaticinari poterit de futuris, quippe qui per uarios casus artem experientia fecit, exemplo monstrante viam,* had been printed in Venice in 1552 (the colophon reads "Venetiis apud Batholomæum Cæsanum. Anno M D LII").

[37] The document is recorded in ASV, ECBC, Busta 56, fol. 159v.

[38] The document is recorded in ASV, ECBC, Busta 56 [formerly Busta 3], Notatorio, fol. 41v.

it seems very likely that the indecent engravings were copies made
by Zenoi of the series of prints known as *I Modi* engraved by
Marcantonio Raimondi after designs by Giulio Romano and printed
with indecent sonnets composed by Pietro Aretino.[39]

As a means of combatting continued abuse, on 17 November
1566, the Executors added a new requirement that anyone who
already had a license to print, before undertaking the printing project, must go to the office of the Executors and there, without charge,
register the work in a special book.[40] Three years later, on 28 June
1569, yet another requirement was introduced. Evidently the Executors
had found that in some cases, in the process of preparing a book
for publication, the text of books finally published had been altered,
usually by the compositors, from that which the Executors had previously approved and which the Chiefs of the Council of Ten had
licensed at the outset of the project, and that in some instances these
changes overstepped the bounds of what was acceptable. To deal
with this problem, the Executors now required that anyone wanting
to print a new work, in order to obtain a license, was obliged first
to submit two copies of the book, one to be reviewed for conformity to censorship requirements, and the other to be consigned to
the office of the Riformatori dello Studio di Padova where it would
be used later to compare with the final printed book to check for
alterations. Any alterations made by the compositor must be approved
by the Riformatori. A fine of one hundred ducats was imposed for
non-compliance.[41]

The respective competence of the Executors against Blasphemy,
on the one hand, and that of the Inquisition, on the other, with
regard to judging heretical blasphemy became an issue in the latter
half of the century. In Venice, the Executors against Blasphemy
served as a secular tribunal which in practice was subordinate to the
Inquisitors. At the end of the century, a law passed by the Senate

---

[39] Marcantonio's prints are commented on by Vasari, 1568, 5: 418. The engravings are discussed in *I Modi nell'opera di Giulio Romano, Marcantonio Raimondi, Pietro
Aretino e Jean-Frédéric-Maximilien de Waldeck*, ed. Lynne Lawner (Milan, 1984); and
Bette Talvacchia, *Taking Positions: On the Erotic in Renaissance Culture* (Princeton, 1999).
[40] The document is recorded in ASV, ECBC, Busta 54, vol. 1, fol. 37v.
[41] The document is recorded in ASV, ECBC, Busta 54, vol. 1, fol. 38r.–v. It is
worth noting that it is also stipulated that the books given into the hands of the
Riformatori, and judged suitable by them, would be placed in a public library ("li
libri che resteranno presso di loro Reformatori, et saranno da essi giudicati degni
della Libraria publica, siano posti nella libraria sodetta").

in 1596 sought to give the Executors more complete autonomy and power. Three years earlier, two new laws were issued by the Council of Ten concerning printing. According to the first, issued on 12 May 1593, besides the need for a license furnished by the Council of Ten, it was established that if the contents of the book had passed the examination of the Riformatori dello Studio di Padova and contained nothing unlawful from both the religious and the political point of view, on publication each book must also contain the names of the Inquisitors, the secretary, and of the "lettor pubblico" who had examined it. The second law, passed two months later on 14 July, instituted further bureaucratic controls, with the compliance of the Inquisition.[42]

Although the focus of legislation in licensing and copyright was books, it is clear from documented cases that independent prints were also subject to the same requirements and procedures. The obligation to comply with the increasingly restrictive licensing regulations must have had a stifling effect on print production. However, it is also evident, both from the government's need to make more stringent established requirements and to add new regulations, and by the fact that print publishing flourished during this same period, that these efforts to regulate and control the products of the print industry were ineffective and largely ignored by publishers. Nevertheless, publishers, whether or not they complied with the licensing regulations some of the time or not at all, worked within an industry closely scrutinized and regulated by secular and ecclesiastical authorities, and this must have had an impact on their activities.

Licensing and Censorship in Rome

Despite the bulls promulgated by Innocent VIII in 1487 and Alexander VI in 1501, noted earlier, by the second decade of the sixteenth century there was growing criticism of secular learning and the publication of books containing errors in doctrine and material contrary to Christian teaching. In response, the tenth session of the Fifth Lateran Council addressed the issue and on 4 May 1515 Leo X promulgated the papal bull, *De Super impressione librorum* (also known as *Inter*

---

[42] These laws are noted in Cozzi, 43–44.

sollicitudines) on the matter of censorship of printed material. Ludwig
von Pastor has summarized the contents of the bull as follows:

> In highly enthusiastic terms the Pope celebrates the benefits to mankind
> and the Church conferred through the favour of heaven by this dis-
> covery [of printing] which had come down as a gift from God to
> earth. By means of printing everyone for little money can buy many
> books, the study of gifted minds is made easy. Catholic scholars too
> (and the Catholic Church prays that they may be many) can be edu-
> cated thereby and thus win over unbelievers to the truth. But in
> different countries many masters of this new craft misuse it by the cir-
> culation of works containing errors of faith and attacks on persons in
> high station, which are not only unedifying to their readers, but inju-
> rious to their religious and moral life, as experience has shown and
> in the time to come will show more clearly still. But the Head of the
> Church must take heed that that which was invented for God's glory,
> for the exaltation of the faith, and for the diffusion of art and learn-
> ing, does not become a curse instead of a blessing, and endanger the
> salvation of the faithful, that the good seed and the cockle, the med-
> icine and the poison, are not mingled together. Therefore the Pope
> forbids, with the approval of the Council, under pain of excommuni-
> cation and of heavy fines, the printing of any book without the appro-
> bation of the Bishop and the Inquisitor, and in Rome of the Cardinal
> Vicar and the Master of the Palace. Every book printed contrary to
> these regulations shall be burned.[43]

Besides burning the books, the publisher and/or printer were also
to be fined one hundred ducats, which went towards the building
of St. Peter's ("ac centum ducatorum fabricae basilicae"). The decree
was all-embracing and universal in application ("tam in Urbe nostra, quam aliis quibusvis civitatibus et diocesibus"). The regulations
were to be enforced by the bishops and their delegates, or the inquisitor ("episcopo ad id deputandum, ac inquisitorem haereticae pravitatis"). Although similar in many respects to the earlier and virtually
identical bulls issued by Innocent VIII in 1487 and by Alexander
VI in 1501, Leo X's bull omits some of the earlier provisions, such
as the prohibition of binding and holding, but is more specific in its
prohibition of libelous writings (the previous bulls referred only in
general terms to "scandalous" texts). That it was felt necessary to
re-issue the basic concerns and prohibitions of the earlier bulls suggests that the requirement that all printed books be approved by the

---

[43] Pastor, *The History of the Popes*, 8: 397–8.

appropriate designated authority was not being fulfilled by the printers and publishers, a situation that may have also troubled Clement
VII, who had Leo X's bull printed again in 1523.

The control of printing and the selling and diffusion of printed
texts was also an important facet of the Inquisition, established by
Paul III in 1542 with the bull *Licet ab initio*. The following year, on
12 June 1543, an official edict was issued by the Roman inquisitors
addressed to book sellers, printers, and customs officers.[44] In Rome,
it had been decreed since 1487 that all books were to be submitted
for approval to the Cardinal Vicar and the Master of the Sacred
Apostolic Palace ("Magister Sacri Palatii Apostolici"). The Master of
the Sacred Palace was the pope's official theologian or "master" in
theology. One of the official functions of the Master of the Sacred
Palace was the selection of who was to preach in the papal chapel.
This particular right had been conferred on the Master of the Sacred
Palace in the papal bull *Dudum ex pluribus* issued by Pope Eugene IV
on 3 October 1437 and addressed to the then Master of the Sacred
Palace, Giovanni Torquemada. It was renewed by Calixtus III in
the bull *Licet ubilibet* in 1456, and confirmed in the constitution on
the reform of the Curia by Pius II (1458–64). The duty involved the
supervision of the content of sermons, and included the provision
that copies of each sermon were to be submitted to the Master of
the Sacred Palace before they were delivered in order to ascertain
the identity between the approved redaction and the sermon as ver-
bally presented. It was the duty of the Master of the Sacred Palace,
whose alternate title was *haereticae pravitatis inquisitor*, to examine the
sermons to ensure they were of sound doctrine and conformed to
the rules of the faith.

Over the course of the sixteenth century (and in the following
centuries), the authority and influence of the Master of Sacred Palace
grew greater and greater. As was noted above, in the bull of 1487
Innocent VIII conferred on the Master of the Sacred Palace the
right to examine manuscripts destined to be printed in Rome. The
Master of the Sacred Palace thereby had special jurisdiction over
the printing and sale of books and prints in Rome; every book or
print produced in the city required the permission and license, the

---

[44] See J. M. De Bujanda, *Index de Rome 1557, 1559, 1564. Les premiers index romains
et l'index di Concile de Trente (Index des Livres Interdits, VIII)* (Sherbrooke, Québec, 1990),
27. The text of the edict is given in Hilgers, 483–88.

imprimatur or *publicetur*, of the Master of the Sacred Palace. Evidence that this requirement was being fulfilled by some publishers can be found in books they published. For example, in 1492, during the reign of Pope Alexander VI, the statement "Licenziate per lo maestro del sacro palatio de Alexandro sexto l'anno primo" appears at the end of the text of Giuliano Dati, *Stazioni e indulgenze di Roma*, printed by Andreas Fritag. In 1494, the Master of the Sacred Palace granted Fritag another license, this time to print *Judicium anni*, a book by the Polish astrologer Ladislau de Cracovia (alias Tenczynski). The colophon reads: "Impressum Rome ex licentia magistri sacri Palatij Apostolici per me Andream Fritag de Argentina, Die IIII Januarij MCCCCLXXXXIIII."[45]

Another duty of the Master of the Sacred Palace was to establish the sale price of books. In the *privilegio* granted on 9 July 1509 to Tommaso Pighinucci da Pietrasanta, it is requested that the price of the book be determined by the Master of the Sacred Palace who, at that time, was Giovanni Raffanelli.[46] The circumstances, however, may have been unusual because Pighinuccio was an employee of the apostolic administration and a member of Julius's household (he is described in the document granting the *privilegio* as "apostolorum scriptori, et familiari nostro"). The duties of the Master of the Sacred Palace are also made clear in a letter from Rome dated 24 March 1524 in which Cardinal Corner reported that a *bando* had been issued against printers printing anything without the approval of the Master of Sacred Palace ("Qui è stato pubblicato un bando, che niuno stampatore ardisca stampare cosa alcuna nuova né latina, né volgare, che non sia approbata dal Maestro del Sacro Palazzo").[47] A *bando*, like an edict, was a public notice, an official proclamation of command. In this instance, the *bando* served as the means by which the stipulation set out in the papal bull (that all printed books be approved

---

[45] Noted in Blasio, *Cum Gratia et Privilegio*, 80 and 156 respectively. The books are listed in *Scrittura, biblioteche e stampa a Roma nel Quattrocento: aspetti e problemi*, 174, no. 1260, and 196, no. 1424 respectively. Ladislau de Cracovia's book is discussed in Bronislaw Bilinski, "Judicium Ladislai de Cracovia (Teneczynski) stampato a Roma nel 1494," in *Italia Venezia e Polonia tra Medio Evo e età moderna*, ed. Vittore Branca and Sante Graciotti (Florence, 1980).

[46] The *privilegio* is recorded in ASVat, Arm. 39, vol. 27, fol. 430v., 431r.–v. (436v., 437r.–v. n.n.).

[47] The letter is cited in Blasio, *Cum gratia et privilegio*, 73. The letter goes on to explain that the reason for the *bando* was a recently printed *Elegia* by an anonymous author regarding the capture of Francis I, king of France.

by the appropriate authority) was made public knowledge. Besides
the *bando* issued in 1524, other *bandi* addressing the same matter continued to be issued, though only a few examples from the last years
of the sixteenth century can now be found in Vatican Secret Archives.[48]

On 27 March 1570, Pius V instituted the Congregation of the
Index (Congregazione dell'Indice) of prohibited books, with the Master
of the Sacred Palace as its permanent secretary. The Congregazione
dell'Indice produced the *Index Librorum Prohibitorum* ("Index of Forbidden
Books"), a list of books condemned by the Church as harmful to
the faith and to morals and which the faithful were prohibited to
read or even possess. Lists of forbidden books had been published
before 1562, however. The first had been drawn up in 1544 by the
Faculty of Theology at the University of Paris. Others followed in
France, as well as in Spain and Portugal. In Venice, on 16 January
1549 [1548 m.v.], the Council of Ten had issued a decree for the
printing of a catalogue of heretical and suspect books.[49] The catalogue was published in Venice by the apostolic nuncio Giovanni
Della Casa (and printed by Vincenzo Valgrisi). In Rome, the first
Index had been published under Paul IV in 1559 by the Sacred
Congregation of the Roman Inquisition.

Notice of License

With the election of Pope Gregory XIII in 1572, papal copyright
took a new turn. The Council of Trent, which concluded in 1563,
had recommended that a number of reforms be undertaken by the
Church. In the process there emerged stricter licensing and greater
control over the issuance of copyright. From the evidence of inscriptions on books and prints in the second half of the century, it became
a requirement that receipt of the license be indicated on both books
and prints. Whereas previously the phrase most often encountered
is "Con Gratia e Privilegio," during the reign of Pius V (1566–1572)
books began to appear inscribed with words indicating that they had

---

[48] Evelyn Lincoln, Printing and Visual Culture in Italy, 1470–1575, Ph.D. diss.,
University of California, Berkeley, 1994, 218, n. 69, reports that the archive of the
Master of the Sacred Palace in the Vatican Secret Archives contains little material
before the eighteenth century.

[49] The document is recorded in ASV, CX, Comuni, reg. 47, fol. 195r.

been published *cum licentia* ("with license") as well as *cum privilegio*. For example, Vasari's 1568 edition of the *Vite* was published by the Giunti "Con Licenza e Privilegio di N. S. Pio V et del Duca di Fiorenza e Siena." Examples of this form continued into the 1580s.

Under Gregory XIII, it soon became common to see the phrase take the form of "Con Licentia de' Superiori" or "Con Licenza de' Superiori" or "Cum Licentia Superiorum." It might also take the form "Permissu Superiorum" (or "Superiorum permissu") or "Superiorum Licentia," or occasionally "Auctoritate Superiorum." The *approbatio* and the *licenza* amounted to the same thing and were issued by the same papal office, that of the Master of the Sacred Palace. Either or both terms might be used in documents and inscriptions. A note on the supplication of Philippe Thomassin, dated 7 December 1599, regarding Aliprando Capriolo's *Centum Armorum Duces*, for example, states that the book had been printed with the license and approbation of the Master of the Sacred Palace ("liber fuit Impressus cum licentia et approbatione Magistri Sacri Palatij") (see Chapter 8).

Beginning during the reign of Gregory XIII, notice of license also begins to appear on prints, often in conjunction with the *privilegio*. An early example is Philippe Thomassin's print of *St. Paul First Hermit* after Bernardino Passari, which carries the notice of a ten-year *privilegio* granted by Gregory XIII, plus official approval ("Motu proprio D. PAPA GREG. XIII per annos X superiorum permissu") (for the print, see Chapter 8). Direct reference to the approval of the Master of the Sacred Palace also begins to appear in the text of the document granting the *privilegio*. Besides the example of Thomassin's *privilegio* cited above, in the *privilegio* granted to Francesco Villamena on 8 October 1596, it is stated that his prints "fuerint a sacri Palatij nostri Apostolici Magistro approbatas modo et forma praemissis per totum statum Ecclesiasticum" (see Chapter 8). A similar phrase is found in the text of the *privilegio* granted to Jacopo Lauro on 17 March 1598 (see Chapter 8). In his supplication for a *privilegio* granted on 23 June 1599, Giovanni Antonio di Paolo stated that he intends to print many engravings of every sort, "with the approval of the sacro Palazzo." In the text of the *privilegio* itself reference is made to the publishing of the prints "postquam a Magistro sacri Palatii recognite et approbate" (see Chapter 8).

CHAPTER FOUR

PRINTED IMAGES AND COPYRIGHT IN VENICE BEFORE 1517

Prints Illustrating Books

The illuminated manuscript determined early in the history of printing a taste for illustrations in books. Even before the introduction of
moveable type block books carried woodcut illustrations. Pictorial
woodcut illustrations soon began to appear in printed books together
with other decorative designs such as initials, bars, and borders. As
was noted in Chapter 2, the first printed book illustrated with woodcuts, thirty-one of them, was Johannes de Turrecremata's *Meditationes*
printed in Rome in 1467 by Ulrich Hahn.[1] The first engraved illustrations appeared ten years later, in 1477, when three were included
in Antonio Bettini da Siena's *Monte Santo di Dio* printed in Florence
that year by Niccolo di Lorenzo.[2] The following year, 1478, twenty-
seven engraved maps by Conrad Sweynheym (the partner of Arnoldo
Pannartz) were featured in a Latin edition Ptolemy's *Cosmographia*
published in Rome by Arnoldus Buckinck.[3] Soon thereafter, wood-
engraved and copperplate engraved illustrations began appearing in
books printed in Florence.

---

[1] According to the colophon, the woodcuts reproduce a series of now lost frescoes painted in the cloisters of S. Maria sopra Minerva in Rome. However, Franz
Unterkircher, "Der erste illustrierte italienische Druck und eine Wiener Handschrift
des gleichen Werkes (Hain 15722, Cod. Vindob. 3805)," in *Hellinga: Festschrift,
Feestbundel, Mélanges: Forty-three Studies in Bibliography Presented to Prof. Dr. Wytze Hellinga*
(Amsterdam, 1980), 498–516, has argued that the illustrations must have been based
on an illuminated manuscript.
[2] The engraved illustrations in Monte Santo di Dio are discussed in Hind, *Early
Italian Engravings*, 1: 97–98; and Alfred William Pollard, *Early Illustrated Books* (New
York, 1927), 86.
[3] The engraved illustrations for Ptolemy's *Cosmographia* are noted in Demetrio
Marzi, "I tipografi tedeschi in Italia durante il secolo XV," in *Festschrift zum fünfhundertjährigen Geburtstage von Johann Gutenberg*, ed. Otto Hartwig (Leipzig, 1900), 505–578
(repr., Lichtenstein: Nendeln, 1968, 514–515); Tony Campbell, *The Earliest Printed
Maps, 1472–1500* (Berkeley and Los Angeles, 1987), 122–30; Arthur Robert Hinks,
"The Lettering of the Roman Ptolemy of 1478," *Geographical Journal* 101 (1943):
188–190; and Pollard, 82, n. 1.

Despite the taste for illustrations in books, printers in Venice did not begin to produce them intensively until the last decade of the fifteenth century. For many of these books, the illustrations were a significant feature. In those cases where the publisher sought a *privilegio*, the fact that the book was illustrated was mentioned in the supplication and *privilegio*. Among the books for which Tommaso di Venezia was granted a *privilegio* in February 1495 [1494 m.v.], for example, was an edition of Livy's *Historiae romanae decades* containing over three hundred illustrations ("cum figuras, ultra trecentas").[4] Later that year, Francesco Cattaneo sought a *privilegio* for an illustrated edition of Vitruvius ("cum el greco et figure sue").[5] On 10 February 1496 [1495 m.v.], Stefano Römer explains that he had gone to much time, trouble and expense "to recover, correct and make the illustrations" for an edition of *Epitoma in Almagestum Ptolomaei* by Joannis de Monte Regio (Johann Müller Regiomontanus), which was printed in Venice by Johannes Hamman [or Hertzog] on 31 August 1496.[6]

In 1497, and again in 1498, the Venetian printer-publisher Lazaro de' Soardi refers to printing a number of books "with figures" ("cum figure").[7] Also in 1498, Antonio di Zanoti lists several books, "all historiated with borders and figures and with engraved miniatures" ("tute istoriade, cum frixi et figure et in miniadore facto de intajo").[8] In 1506, Paolo da Canale wanted to print with a *privilegio* a new edition of Ptolemy's books on geography "with plates" ("cum le sue tavole").[9] In 1510, the printer Bartolomeo de' Zanni submitted a request to publish several books, all with illustrations, including an *Opera Omnia* of Virgil, which was published by Zanni, "Cum Gratia

---

[4] Tommaso di Venezia's *privilegio* is recorded in ASV, CN, reg. 14, fol. 115v. (119v. n.n.) [Fulin, "Documenti," no. 38]. The book is probably the edition of Marcus Antonius Sabellicus printed in Venice in 1495 by Filippo Pincio.

[5] Francesco Cattaneo's *privilegio* is recorded in ASV, CN, reg. 14, fol. 130r. (134r. n.n.) [Fulin, "Documenti," no. 39]. The book is possibly that published by Cristoforo Pensa [Christophorus de Pensis] in 1496, listed in Sander, 3: no. 7693. For later editions of Vitruvius, see below and Chapter 11.

[6] Stefano Römer's *privilegio* is recorded in ASV, CN, reg. 14, fol. 134r. (138r. n.n.) [Fulin, "Documenti," no. 40]. The book is listed in Sander, 3: no. 6399. The frontispiece is discussed in Hind, *History of Woodcut*, 2: 498.

[7] Soardi's two privileges are recorded in ASV, CN, reg. 14, fol. 147v. (151v. n.n.) and fol. 161r. (176r. n.n.) [Fulin, "Documenti," nos. 61 and 78] respectively.

[8] Zanoti's *privilegio* is recorded in ASV, CN, reg. 14, fol. 155v. (169v. n.n.) [Fulin, "Documenti," no. 74].

[9] Canale's *privilegio* is recorded in ASV, CN, reg. 15, fols. 160v.–161r. (162v.–163r. n.n.) [Fulin, "Documenti," no. 156].

& Priuilegio," in Venice on 20 June 1510.[10] The following year, 1511, Giovanni Tacuino from Cerreto submitted a supplication for a *privilegio* to print Giovanni Giocondo's edition of Vitruvius's *De architectura* with illustrations, and an illustrated Sallust.[11]

Throughout this period book illustrations were mostly woodcuts. In the majority of cases neither the designer of the woodcut nor the name of the cutter is known. Occasionally a name appears, such as "VGO" (identified as Ugo da Carpi), but more frequently (though still a small percentage of the total number of woodcut illustrations) a woodcut is signed with a monogram which in some instances can be identified, such as "IA" or "ZA" for Zoan Andrea.[12]

Among the identified cutters at work in Venice illustrating books during this period are Ugo da Carpi, Lucantonio degli Uberti, Giovanni da Brescia, Domenico Campagnola, Benedetto Montagna, Jacopo Ripanda, Florio Vavassore, and Giacomo di Argentina. The Duc de Rivoli and Charles Ephrussi have attempted to identify other cutters. They have argued that from the wording in a supplication it is in certain cases clear that the cutting was being done by the person submitting the supplication. The publisher who also produced his own woodcuts always said *far* ("made") in the supplication, whereas if the cutting was done by someone else the words *fatto far* ("had made") or *far intagliar* ("had engraved") were used.[13] Thus Stefano Römer, who said "far le sue figure," was responsible for woodcuts in Johann Müller Regiomontanus's edition of *Epitoma in Almagestum Ptolomaei* printed in 1496 (noted above). Similarly, the phrase "Et per haver etiam facto le figure . . ." ("and for having made the figures . . .") means that Giorgio di Rusconi produced his own woodcuts for the

---

[10] Zanni's *privilegio* is recorded in ASV, CN, reg. 16, fol. 38v. (40v. n.n.) [Fulin, "Documenti," no. 172]. The woodcuts illustrating the Virgil are discussed in Mortimer, *Italian 16th Century Books*, no. 524. Works by Lucan, Suetonius, Plautus, Juvenal, Priscian, and Plutarch were also included in the *privilegio*.

[11] Tacuino's *privilegio* is recorded in ASV, CN, reg. 16, fol. 80v. (86v. n.n.) [Fulin, "Documenti," no. 182]. The edition of Vitruvius was printed by Tacuino on 22 May 1511. The title-page reads: "M. VITRVVIVS/PER/IOCVNDVM SO/LITO CASTIGA/TIOR FACTVS/CVM FIGVRIS ET TABVLA/VT IAM LEGI ET/INTELLIGI POS/SIT." The book is catalogued in Mortimer, *Italian 16th Century Books*, no. 543. For Vitruvius, see also Chapter 11.

[12] The problem of the identity of "ZA" has been recently discussed in Suzanne Boorsch, "Mantegna and His Printmakers," in *Andrea Mantegna* (Milan, 1992), 56–66.

[13] Rivoli and Ephrussi, "Notes sur les Xylographes Vénetiens du XVᵉ et XVIᵉ siècles," *Gazette des Beaux-Arts* 32 (1891): 498.

Supplementum Chronicarum, for which he received a *privilegio* in 1506.[14]

The same problem of identification also applies to engraved illustrations in books which, it should be added, were rare before 1514. The earliest signed engraved illustrations printed in Venice are four full-page maps and plans of Nola printed in Ambrogio Leone's *De Nola* in 1514. The first plate is signed "HIE. MOCE," the abbreviated name of Girolamo Mocetto, who is also named in Leone's preface to the book.[15] Among the engravers known by name working in northern Italy at this time (though not all of them necessarily also as book illustrators), including several of the woodcutters mentioned above, are Lucantonio degli Uberti, Giulio Campagnola, Domenico Campagnola, Benedetto Montagna, Jacopo de' Barbari, Girolamo Mocetto, Zoan Andrea, Giovanni Antonio da Brescia, Giovanni Maria da Brescia, Nicoletto da Modena, Marcantonio Raimondi, and Giovanni Pietro da Birago.

Copyright and Prints Independent of Books

Besides prints used as illustrations in books, throughout the period woodcuts and engravings were also being produced independent of books. It is these latter prints that are the main focus of interest in this present study, and in particular those for which it was deemed necessary to seek a *privilegio*. Between 1498, when the first print-privilege was issued, and 1517, a period of nearly twenty years, the *privilegio* was granted for at least fourteen, possibly seventeen, named prints, and for an unknown number of other prints otherwise unnamed in the supplications. Of this number, only five have survived, and of these only one is preserved in the first impression; three more appear to be later states and the fifth survives only in copies. Of the rest, including four maps, there is no trace. Before saying anything else, it is sobering for art historians to realize how few prints have survived.

The five surviving prints—the *Triumph of Caesar* published by Benedetto Bordon in 1504, the *Submersion of Pharaoh's Army,* the *Susanna,*

---

[14] Rusconi's *privilegio* is recorded in ASV, CN, reg. 15, fol. 159v. (160v. n.n.) [Fulin, "Documenti," no. 153].

[15] Mocetto and the illustrations are discussed in Hind, *Early Italian Engravings,* 469–70, nos. 15–18.

and the *Sacrifice of Abraham* originally published by Bernardino Benalio in 1515, and the copies of the *Triumph of Christ* first published by Benalio in 1516 (each discussed in Chapter 5)—all have one thing in common: size; all are multi-block productions. Among the prints that have not survived, there is reason to suspect from the titles given them in the supplications that they too were also large prints made from two or more blocks. For example, it seems likely that Giovanni da Brescia's "History of Emperor Trajan" was illustrated in several scenes. The "Triumph of the Virgin" named by Benalio was probably conceived in a horizontal multi-block design similar to that of the *Triumph of Christ*, while the "Last Judgement," also named by Benalio, may have employed a more vertical format but still on a large scale. The manner in which the subjects are listed in Gregorio de' Gregorii's 1516 supplication suggests that they were all part of the same, and therefore large, design. Similarly, Fra Ippolito's supplication appears to describe a single print of "the *storia* of Sodoma and Gomorra *with* that of pharaoh persecuting the people of Israel." And finally, from the evidence of the several surviving but uncopyrighted examples of large maps from this period, including Jacopo de' Barbari's twelve-block *View of Venice* published by Anton Kolb, it is reasonable to suggest that the four maps—one of Venice, two of Italy, one a *mappamondo*—were also large prints. It may be surmised, therefore, either that the *privilegio* during this period was issued exclusively to large prints, or that only the publishers of large prints applied for copyright.

Their size may also explain why so few have survived. How were such prints viewed? Later in the sixteenth century there is evidence that smaller prints were pasted into special albums or placed in drawers. Most of the prints under discussion here, however, would have to be folded to fit into an album or lie in a drawer.[16] An alternative method of display was to glue the print onto canvas or wood and, perhaps also with the addition of a frame, to hang it on the wall. They could also have been pasted directly onto the wall. In Bernardino Benalio's testament, drawn up in November 1517, mention is made of him dealing with coloured woodcuts.[17] The possibility

[16] The viewing and storing of prints is discussed in Michael Bury, "The Taste for Prints in Italy to c. 1600," *Print Quarterly* 2 (1985): 12–26.

[17] Benalio's testaments of 14 September 1516 and 17 November 1517 are recorded in ASVen, Not.ᶜ Test. B. 974, n. 7. They are discussed by Bartolomeo Cecchetti, "La pittura delle stampe di Bernardino Benalio," *Archivio Veneto* 33 (1887): 538–39.

that the *Sacrifice of Abraham*, the *Susanna*, and the *Submersion of Pharaoh's Army in the Red Sea*, which he printed in 1515, may have been coloured is striking. When also imagined as hanging on a wall, these large woodcuts begin to rival paintings and perhaps served as a relatively inexpensive substitute for paintings in the decoration of rooms. Their appeal would have been not as prints *per se*, but as pictures. The manner in which they were displayed must have greatly decreased their chances of survival.

Large multi-block prints were difficult to make and costly to print. Anton Kolb in his supplication explained that besides the problems encountered in the composition of a large subject, the technique of printing from large blocks, which required large sheets of paper, was extremely difficult. No doubt it was the great labour and expense involved in producing large prints that made possession of a *privilegio* desirable. The evidence, or lack of it in the form of documents or prints carrying a *privilegio* inscription, suggests that publishers at this time did not bother to seek copyright for small, single-block prints.

It might be asked under these circumstances why a *privilegio* was considered necessary; after all, the sheer size and difficulties of production would surely have inhibited would-be plagiarists. The perceived threat, however, may have been copies produced on a smaller scale which could be printed more easily and sold for much less. That this was in fact occurring is suggested by the inclusion in the *privilegio* document of a clause stating that the copyrighted item could not be printed or sold in whole or in part, with additions or diminutions or with any alterations. The production of smaller scale or reduced copies is also suggested through the example of Benalio's *Triumph of Christ*. The now lost original was most likely a ten-block print, but Gregorio de' Gregorii's copy was composed in five blocks, and Lucantonio degli Uberti's in nine (see Chapter 5).

Approximately a quarter of the prints issued with a *privilegio* between 1498 and 1517 were maps, all now untraced. This is not surprising; maps were extremely popular in the sixteenth century and privileges for maps far outnumber those in every other category of prints (see Chapter 10). These early Venetian privileges signal the beginning of a widespread demand for maps of all kinds. The taste for maps later in the century is clearly indicated in the inventory of prints available for sale at Antonio Lafrery's print shop in Rome in 1573 which places maps first and lists over one hundred examples.

Besides maps, the subject matter of two of the early copyrighted prints was drawn from ancient Roman history: Bordon's *Triumph of Caesar*, and Giovanni da Brescia's *History of Emperor Trajan*. The remaining prints illustrated Biblical subjects, drawing upon both the Old Testament and the New Testament.

Effectiveness: The Case of Marcantonio Raimondi and Albrecht Dürer

At this point, it is appropriate to ask whether the *privilegio* as a legal instrument of protection was an effective deterrent against counterfeiting. The answer to this question is somewhat elusive and difficult to assess. No documents have yet come to light that record a suit brought against a print counterfeiter. However, there is one instance, recorded by Vasari, of a printmaker lodging a complaint about a counterfeiter. The story of Albrecht Dürer bringing suit against Marcantonio Raimondi for plagiarising his prints is well known. It appears to present a clear case of copyright infringement and is worth examining in detail. In the process, it may be necessary to adjust the current interpretation of events and the date of the affair.

According to Vasari, while Marcantonio was in Venice there arrived in the city some "fiaminghi" with many prints ("carte intagliate"), both woodcuts and engravings, by Albrecht Dürer.[18] Marcantonio saw these prints for sale in Piazza di San Marco and, "amazed by their style and Dürer's technique" ("stupefatto della maniera del lavoro e del modo di fare d'Alberto"), spent most of his money on buying them. Vasari specifically states that among the prints he purchased was the *Passion of Christ* in thirty-six woodcut *quarto* sheets (identified today as *The Small Passion*) which, he adds, began with the sin of Adam and the expulsion from Paradise and ended with the scene of the Pentecost.[19] Marcantonio then counterfeited in copperplate all thirty-six prints. He also added Dürer's monogram, "AD," and the prints were sold and purchased as Dürer's work. News of this was sent to Dürer in Nürnberg together with one of the plagiarised sheets.

---

[18] Vasari, 1568, 5: 405. Vasari was under the mistaken impression that Dürer was from Flanders. He begins his account of Dürer by describing him as working in Antwerp ("cominciò Alberto Duro in Anversa") and elsewhere locates him in "Fiandra." The "fiaminghi" print merchants are probably Germans.

[19] *The Small Passion* is actually comprised of thirty-seven prints. Vasari omits mention of the 37th print, the *Last Judgement*.

Greatly angered, Dürer traveled to Venice, appealed to the Signoria, and brought an action against Marcantonio. The case was heard, but the only satisfaction Dürer won was an injunction against Marcantonio that he include neither Dürer's name nor his monogram on the plates he copied.

There are two problems with Vasari's account. The first is that Marcantonio's copies of *The Small Passion* carry not Dürer's monogram but Marcantonio's blank tablet. Modern scholars, in fact, believe that Vasari erred in his identification of the prints Marcantonio counterfeited and that the series he copied that provoked Dürer's ire was the *Life of the Virgin*.[20] The second problem is that, according to Vasari, upon learning of Marcantonio's counterfeiting activities, Dürer traveled to Venice to bring his suit. It is known that Dürer visited Venice twice in his career and that his second visit occurred in 1506. Moreover, on two of the seventeen counterfeited prints can be seen the date 1506.[21] Although Dürer's twenty-print set comprising the *Life of the Virgin* was not formally published until 1511 (see below), it has been assumed, largely on the basis of Marcantonio's copies, that Dürer must have completed by 1506 at least the seventeen prints Marcantonio had counterfeited by that year.

However, it has recently been shown that the date 1506 which appears on two of Marcantonio's copies, and which has been used to date the counterfeiting, was added to the engraved plates much later in the eighteenth century.[22] Without this date as an anchor, it is possible that Vasari erred not only in his identification of the coun-

---

[20] The prints are listed in Bartsch, 14: nos. 621–637. Marcantonio's counterfeiting of Dürer's *Life of the Virgin* is discussed in Henri Delaborde, *Marc-Antoine Raimondi* (Paris, 1888), 14–20.

[21] Bartsch, 14: no. 627 (no. "7" *Annunciation*) and no. 630 (no. "10" *Adoration of the Magi*). Examples of these prints can be examined in the collection of the MM, New York, inv. no. 41.1.228. It is also argued, by Innis Shoemaker, *The Engravings of Marcantonio Raimondi*, exhib. cat., The Spencer Museum of Art, Lawrence, Kansas, 1981, xiv; and Bernice Davidson, Marcantonio Raimondi: the Engravings of his Roman Period, Ph.D. dissertation, Harvard University, Cambridge, Mass., 1954, 9, for example, that the presence of the mark of the Venetian publishers Nicolò and Domenico Sandri, brothers from Jesu ("fratelli dal Jesu"), on the last print copied by Marcantonio (Bartsch, 14: no. 637) also indicates an early date. However, according to Norton, *Italian Printers*, 150, the Sandri brothers were active as booksellers and publishers throughout the period from 1501 to 1520.

[22] See Konrad Oberhuber, "Raffaello e l'incisione," in *Raffaello in Vaticano* (Milan, 1984), 342, n. 21. All seventeen of Marcantonio's counterfeited plates are preserved today in the Calcografia, Rome, inv. no. 1684.

terfeited prints that caused Dürer to bring suit against Marcantonio but also in stating that Dürer came to Venice to do so. It is worth recalling that Dürer was in residence in Venice from 1505 to 1507 and in his surviving letters from the period makes no mention of the incident recounted by Vasari. Moreover, according to the now discredited 1506 date, Marcantonio would have been counterfeiting Dürer's prints while Dürer himself was in the city and so Dürer presumably would have come to know about them directly (there would have been no need to write to him) and would not have needed to undertake a special journey from Nürnberg. Could Marcantonio's copies have been made later than is assumed?

Bearing this possibility in mind, the question pertinent to this study can now be asked: On what basis was Dürer able to bring suit against Marcantonio? In other words, did Dürer possess some form of copyright protection for his prints? The circumstances described by Vasari strongly suggest that Dürer's complaint had some sort of legal support which the Venetian government recognized and acted upon. No documents have come to light that show that Dürer had a Venetian *privilegio*, but he did have an imperial *privilegio*, which may have prompted the Venetian government to take steps on Dürer's behalf.

It should be remembered that the *Life of the Virgin* and *The Large Passion* (both printed in folio) as well as *The Small Passion* (printed in quarto) were all published in 1511 in the form of books with text printed on the reverse side of each image. At this same time, Dürer also republished the fifteen plates of the *Apocalypse* that he had first published in 1498 with the title: *Die heimliche Offenbarung Johannes*, with a text in German.[23] The *Life of the Virgin* was accompanied by Latin verses by Chelidonius (the latinized name of Benedict Schwalbe) and published with the title *EPITOME IN DIVAE PARTHENICES MARI/AE HISTORIAM AB ALBERTO DVRERO/NORICO PER FIGVRAS DIGES/TAM CVM VERSIBVS ANNE/XIS CHELIDONII.* The title-page has the title above Dürer's woodcut of the *Madonna and Child in the Crescent* with ten lines of verse below. The following

---

[23] On the verso of the last page are printed the words: "Gedrücket zu Nurnbergk durch Albrecht durer, maler, nach Christi geburt M. CCCC und darnach im xcviij. iar." The 1511 edition has the text in Latin, filling two columns of each page opposite the woodcut. The prints are listed in Bartsch, 6: nos. 60–75. An example of the 1511 edition can be examined in the BA, Vatican, Cicognara IX.2022.int. 3.

pages open with a woodcut on the right and accompanying verse on the left.[24] The *Small Passion* included verses by Chelidonius and other authors and was published with the title *Passio Christi ab Alberto Durer Norimbergensi effigiata, cum varii generis carminibus Fratrum S. Benedicti, Chelidonii, Mesophili.*[25] The *Large Passion* was accompanied by verses by other authors collected together by Chelidonius, and was published with the title *Passio domini nostri Jesu. ex. hieronymo Paduano. Dominico Mancino. Sedulio. et Baptista Mantuano. Per fratrem Chelidonium collecta. cum figuris Alberti Dureri Norici pictoris.*[26] The colophon of each reads: "Impressum Nurnberge per Albertum Durer pictorem. Anno christiano Millesi/mo quingentesimo vndecimo." Importantly, the colophon also includes notice of an imperial *privilegio* that Dürer had evidently been granted by Emperor Maximilian I some time before 1511. The original document of the *privilegio* is lost (and the date of its granting) but a copy of the text made in the eighteenth century survives in the Staatsarchiv in Nürnberg.[27] Though lacking precise dates (a date for the granting of the imperial *privilegio*, and the date Marcantonio produced his counterfeit prints), Vasari's story would indicate that there was an overlap of one with the other and that Dürer was in possession of an imperial *privilegio* when Marcantonio produced his copies. It therefore seems likely that the granting of

---

[24] Bartsch, 7: nos. 76–95. The pages can be examined in the BA Vatican, Cicognara IX.2022.int. 1. One of the prints, the *Meeting of Anna and Joachim at the Golden Gate*, is dated 1509 (Bartsch, 6: no. 79, however, reads this date as 1504); two others, the *Death of the Virgin* (Bartsch, 6: no. 93) and the *Assumption and Coronation of the Virgin* (Bartsch, 6: no. 94) are dated 1510.

[25] The prints are listed in Bartsch, 7: nos. 16–52.

[26] The prints are listed in Bartsch 6: nos. 1–15. The pages can be examined in the BA, Vatican, Cicognara IX.2022.int. 2. According to Vasari, 1568, 5: 410: "l'anno 1510 parte della Passione di Cristo, cioè ne condusse, con animo di fare il rimanente, quattro pezzi: la Cena, l'esser preso di notte nell'Orto, quando va al Limbo a trarne i Santi Padri, e la sua gloriosa Resurrezione." As Vasari correctly observes, these four prints—*Last Supper, Arrest of Christ, Christ in Limbo*, and *Resurrection*— are dated 1510.

[27] Staatsarchiv, Nürnberg, S.I, L.79, Nr. 15, Fasz. 2. The text is given in Hans Rupprich, *Dürers Schriftlicher Nachlass*, vol. 1 (Berlin, 1956), 79, no. 26: Heus tu insidiator ac alieni laboris: & ingenij surreptor ne manus temerarias/his nostris operibus inicias caue Scias enim a gloriosissimo Romano/rum imperatore Maximiliano nobis co[n]cessum esse ne quis/suppositicijs formis has imagines imprimere seu/impressas per imperij limites vendere aude/at q. si per co[n]temptum seu auaricie cri/men sec[us] feceris post bonoru[m] co[n]/fiscatio[n]em tibi maximum per/iculu[m] subeundum/esse certissime/scias.

the *privilegio*, and the subsequent counterfeiting, probably occurred no earlier than 1510.[28]

* * *

Vasari's story provides only the slightest indication of the effectiveness of copyright in the area of printed images. In the case of books, however, there are examples of legal steps taken against copyright infringement. For example, the book *Continens Rasis* (by the Moslem physician Abu Bakr Muhammad ibn Zakariya Razi, c. 865–925), for which the editor-publisher Amedeo Scotti (the son and heir of Ottaviano Scotti) had obtained a *privilegio* on 20 November 1500, was evidently being copied by the printer-publisher Bernardino Benalio. On the 3 October 1503, Scotti was able to prosecute and the Signori di Notte al Civil ordered Benalio to cease printing the book.[29] In 1503 the merchant-publisher Gironimo [or Girolamo] Durante made an "intimazione e protesta" against Andrea Torresani d'Asola who had printed some books for which Durante had been granted a twelve-year *privilegio* on 19 August 1492. Andrea Torresani was found guilty and fined five hundred ducats, the amount stipulated in the *privilegio*.[30]

It may be surmised from indirect evidence that the *privilegio* was regarded as a useful form of protection against counterfeiters and must therefore have been effective to some degree. In Venice it is clear that the possession of a *privilegio* was understood to afford the holder some pecuniary advantage as is indicated by the occasional

---

[28] Richard Rogers Bowker, *Copyright: Its History and Its Law* (Boston and New York, 1912), 11–12, notes that in 1512, when copies or imitations or engravings (it is unclear exactly what was being referred to) by Dürer, with a forged signature, appeared in Nürnberg, the magistrates ordered them confiscated. In 1528, the authorities in Nürnberg granted Dürer's widow exclusive "rights" to Dürer's works, including Dürer's four books on human proportion, *Hierinn sind begriffen vier Bücher von menschlicher Proportion*, which had been published posthumously in Nürnberg that year. Four years later, in 1532, the city magistrates placed restraints on the re-engraving of Dürer's prints.

[29] Scotti's *privilegio* is recorded in ASV, CN, reg. 15, fol. 28r. (30r. n.n.) [Fulin, "Documenti," no. 106]. The case against Benalio is recorded in ASV, Signori di Notte al Civil, Busta 120, reg. 1, fol. 204r. The document is noted in Carlo Volpati, "Gli Scotti di Monza tipografi-editori in Venezia," *Archivio storico Lombardo* 59 (1932): 370. Nonetheless, an edition of *Continens Rasis* was printed by Benalio six years later in 1509.

[30] Durante's "intimazione e protesta" is recorded in ASV, CN, reg. 14, fol. 67r. (71r. n.n.) [Fulin, "Documenti," no. 7]. Torresani's fine is recorded in ASV, Signori di Notte al Civil, Busta 120, reg. 1, fol. 81v.

supplication that claims financial distress due to an accident or the
need to support a large family. In 1496, for example, the printer-
publisher Filippo Pincio drew attention to his miserable situation
after a fire that year destroyed his house with all his books and supplies.[31] Or Benedetto Fontana, who described himself as an orphan
with three unmarried sisters.[32] Evidently the printer-publisher Melchior
Sessa also believed in the advantages of possessing a *privilegio* and
requested one after a series of tragedies beginning with the death of
his father, the printer Giovanni Battista Sessa, which left Melchior
an orphan, followed by a fire with damages estimated at two thousand ducats.[33] Similarly, later in 1529, after a fire in the monastery
of San Stefano that destroyed all his printed books stored in "un
magazen" there, Bernardino Benalio submitted a new supplication
to the Senate for a ten-year *privilegio*, which was granted on 22 April.[34]

It was also clearly worth going to some pains in order to procure
a *privilegio* including, if necessary, paying large sums of money. As
was noted in Chapter 2, in 1526 Daniel Bomberg, in order to per-
suade the Senate to grant him a *privilegio*, was prepared to 'give' or
'lend' to the Senate (Marino Sanuto uses the words "donar" and
"prestar") the sum of five hundred ducats. For Bomberg, possession
of a *privilegio* evidently warranted such an expenditure, which serves
to indicate how highly the *privilegio* was valued. Bomberg's case raises
the larger question of fees for privileges. Were supplicants required
to pay a fee? There is no archival evidence recording fees paid for
privileges in either Venice or Rome, but it is difficult to believe that
the system operated entirely *gratis*.

---

[31] Pincio's *privilegio* is recorded in ASV, CN, reg. 14, fol. 153v. (157v. n.n.) [Fulin,
"Documenti," no. 68].

[32] Benedetto Fontana's *privilegio* is recorded in ASV, CN, reg. 14, fol. 138r. (142r.
n.n.) [Fulin, "Documenti," no. 47].

[33] Sessa's *privilegio* is recorded in ASV, CN, reg. 16, fol. 53v. (59v. n.n.) [Fulin,
"Documenti," no. 179].

[34] Benalio's misfortune is discussed in Vittorio Rossi, "Un incendio a Venezia e
il tipografo Bernardino Benalio," *Libro e la stampa* 4 (1910): 51–55. Benalio's *privilegio* is recorded in ASV, ST, reg. 26, fol. 15r.

PART TWO

RECIPIENTS

CHAPTER FIVE

PRINTS GRANTED COPYRIGHT
IN VENICE BEFORE 1517

Girolamo Biondo

The earliest example in surviving documents of a *privilegio* granted for a print is that issued on 5 April 1498 to the merchant-printer Girolamo Biondo (or Biondi) for a map. Biondo, who was originally from Florence, worked in Venice primarily as a printer of books. His first *privilegio* had been granted on 23 June 1494 for two books: *De celesti vita* by Giovanni Manardi [Johannes Manardus Ferrariensis], and the *Epistolae* of Marsilio Ficino.[1] Soon thereafter, Biondo evidently entered into partnership with Giovanni Battista da Borgofranco Pavese whose name appears together with Biondo's on another *privilegio* granted on 16 February 1495 [1494 m.v.] for two more books described in the supplication as an "Evangelia ac epistolas annuales" and "epistolas S. Catherine de Senis."[2] The following year, the names of Biondo and Giovanni Battista da Borgofranco Pavese again appear together on a *privilegio* granted in April 1496 for three books: some works translated from Greek into Latin by Marsilio Ficino, a Martianus Capella, and a translation from Latin into Italian of *De oculo morali*, an ethical treatise on the eye by Peter of Limoges [Petrus Lacepiera].[3]

Two years later, on 5 April 1498, Biondo, alone this time, was

---

[1] The *privilegio* is recorded in ASV, CN, reg. 14, fol. 103r. (107r. n.n.) [Fulin, "Documenti," no. 28]. Biondo's supplication had been supported by the ambassador of Rimini, Pandolfo Malatesta. Manardi's book was printed in Venice by Matteo Capodecasa for Girolamo Biondo in 1494. Ficino's *Epistolae* was printed by Capodecasa for Biondo the following year. On the verso of the title-page appear the words "PRIVILEGIVM HIERONYMI BLONDI."

[2] The *privilegio* is recorded in ASV, CN, reg. 14, fol. 115v. (119v. n.n.) [Fulin, "Documenti," no. 38]. Copies of neither book can be traced, although the letters of St. Catherine were published five year later by Aldo Manuzio (for which, see Chapter 3).

[3] The *privilegio* is recorded in ASV, CN, reg. 14, fol. 138v. (142v. n.n.) [Fulin, "Documenti," no. 48]. *De oculi morali* was published as *Libro de locchio morale et spirituale vulgare* in Venice in 1496.

granted another *privilegio* for two more books, but also for a newly drawn and engraved view of Venice.[4] In his supplication, Biondo explains that this view, showing "the city of Venice, just as it lies and is situated," he had caused to be designed and cut with great pains and diligence. No mention is made of the map's designer, nor is the cutter identified. This would appear to be the first instance of a *privilegio* granted for an independent print, in this case a map. It is clear from the supplication that Biondo is referring not to a drawing of the map, but to the already completed print. No examples of the print have survived.

Benedetto Bordon

Unlike Girolamo Biondo, who was a printer, Benedetto Bordon [or Bordone] from Padua was a miniaturist by training and active principally as an illuminator of liturgical texts. In the last decades of the century, as printing blossomed in Venice into a major commercial activity, and illustrated books especially surged in popularity, Bordon, while continuing to work as a miniaturist, enterprisingly turned his particular skills in small-scale design to the production of designs for prints which would then be cut by someone else and either sold independently or used for illustrations in books. His role as the designer of prints is made explicit in the undated two-block woodcut of *The Virgin and Child with Saints Sebastian and Roch* where, in a tablet in the upper left, appears the words "BENEDICTVS PINXIT" (i.e. "painted," or designed, by Benedetto), while in the upper right of the same print is another tablet inscribed with the words "IACOBVS FECIT" (i.e. "made," or cut, by Jacobus). The Jacobus in this case has been identified as the German woodcutter Giacomo di Argentina [Jacobus Argentoratensis].[5] It seems likely that the project was ini-

---

[4] The *privilegio* is recorded in ASV, CN, reg. 14, fol. 170v. (174v. n.n.) [Fulin, "Documenti," no. 79]. The full text of the *privilegio* has been transcribed in Juergen Schulz, "Jacopo de' Barbari's view of Venice. Map Making, City Views and Moralized Geography before the year 1500," *Art Bulletin* 60 (1978): 429, n. 10. The books listed in the *privilegio* are Servius's commentary on Terentius and the works of Turrecremata.

[5] The identification of "JACOBVS" as Giacomo di Argentina is discussed in Jean Michel Massing, "Jacobus Argentoratensis: Étude préliminaire," *Arte Veneta* 31 (1977): 43; and Hind, *History of Woodcut*, 2: 434. Hind, however, identifies "BENEDICTVS" as the painter Benedetto Montagna. The print under discussion here may possibly be identified with that listed in the inventory of Alessandro Rosselli's print shop in

tiated by Bordon, who probably first drew the design on the block and then engaged Giacomo di Argentina to cut it.

Bordon first emerges as a publisher on 3 May 1494 when he submitted a supplication to the College for a *privilegio* for some works by Lucian which, he says, had never before been printed and which cost him a lot of time and money to collect and edit.[6] He requested a *privilegio* for ten years. The book, which is a compendium of Lucians' witty and satirical stories, can be identified as the *Opera Varia*, published in Venice by Simone Bevilaqua on 25 August 1494, approximately four months after Bordon received the *privilegio*.[7] The book has a printed text with black-ground woodcut ornamental borders around painted illustrations. The borders were presumably designed by Bordon, and the paintings executed by him directly.[8] Another edition, published in Venice by Giovanni Battista Sessa in 1500 carries the note "Seq. Supplicatio Benedicti Miniatoris ad Principem Venetiarum pro edendis operibus Luciani et subsequens concessio."[9] No doubt the *privilegio* was intended to protect Bordon's illustrations as much as Lucian's text.

Ten years later, on 30 March 1504, Bordon submitted another supplication for a *privilegio*, in this case for "designs [or drawings] of the triumph of Caesar."[10] This would appear to be the first *privilegio* issued for a figurative print, and the first granted to a painter. In his supplication, Bordon explains that he drew the designs on the

---

Florence as "1ª Vergine Maria e San Rocho e San Bastiano, in dua pezi di legno." See Iodoco Del Badia, "La bottega di Alessandro di Francesco Rosselli merciaio stampatore (1525)," in *Miscellanea Fiorentina di Erudizione e di Storia* (Florence, 1894), 26.

[6] The *privilegio* is recorded in ASV, CN, reg. 14, fol. 99v. (103v. n.n.) [Fulin, "Documenti," no. 26].

[7] The book is catalogued in G. Mariani Canova, *La Miniatura Veneta del Rinascimento 1450–1500* (Venice, 1969), cat. no. 143; and Sander, 2: no. 4037. The book includes Lucian's *de ueris narrationibus, de asino auro, philosopho[rum] uite, Scipio, tyranus, schaphidium, palinurus, Charon, Diogenes, Terpsion, hercules, nirtus* [sic] *Dea, in amorem,* and *Timon.* Editions of Lucian had been published as early as 1475 in Naples. Hirsch, *Printing, Selling and Reading,* 85, notes an edition printed in Venice in 1493, the year before Bordon was granted his *privilegio.*

[8] The woodcut border of the frontispiece is discussed in Myriam Billanovich, "Benedetto Bordon e Giulio Cesare Scaligero," *Italia medioevale e umanistica* 11 (1968): 203–204. A copy of Lucian in the Nationalbibliothek, Vienna, inv. no. 4G.27, was printed on parchment and hand-illuminated by Bordon for a member of the Mocenigo family in Venice.

[9] The book is listed in Hain, *Repertorium Bibliographicum,* 3: no. 10263 (given incorrectly by Fulin, "Documenti," as no. 10262).

[10] The *privilegio* is recorded in ASV, CN, reg. 15, fol. 116r. (118r. n.n.) [Fulin, "Documenti," no. 141].

blocks himself, a task, he says, that took him a great deal of time. He also explains that he has had the woodblocks cut which, he adds, cost him a great deal of money. He asks that no one in the city of Venice, or in any other place or location within the Dominion be permitted to print a similar woodcut triumph like his own, and that anyone who prints a copy outside the Dominion of Venice not be permitted to sell it or have it sold either in the city of Venice or anywhere else within the Dominion. The penalty for those who produce counterfeit prints, and those who sell them within the Dominion, is the irremisible loss of all woodcuts and a fine of ten ducats for each counterfeited print printed or sold. A third of the fine was to go to the "accusador," another third to the magistrate who will hear the case, and the final third to Bordon himself. The cutter is not identified in the document, but, as Jean Michel Massing has convincingly argued, it appears very likely that it was Giacomo di Argentina who produced a series of twelve woodcuts of the *Triumph of Caesar* (Fig. 6).[11]

But, are the prints that survive today the original ones for which the *privilegio* was granted? Three editions of the series are known. The existence of what may have been a first 'state' is known only through Heinecken who, in 1786, referred to a now-lost impression on the first block of which was inscribed the words: "Manibus propriis hoc preclarum opus in lucem prodire fecit Jacobus Argentoratensis germanus architypus solertissimus. Anno virginei partus M.D.III. Idibus februarii su hemisphaero Veneto finem imposuit." According to Massing, the problem with the inscription with respect to Bordon's *privilegio* is that it identifies Giacomo di Argentina as the publisher and not Bordon.[12] More precisely, in fact, the inscription names Giacomo di Argentina as the *maker* of the prints, a situation that does not preclude identifying Bordon as the publisher. Moreover, according to the date recorded in the inscription, 13 February 1504 [1503 m.v.], the woodcuts were completed about six weeks *before* Bordon requested the *privilegio*. Although Giacomo di Argentina may have completed the cutting of the blocks by 13 February 1504 and begun printing them, they were most likely not published, that is

---

[11] Jean Michel Massing, "Jacobus Argentoratensis," 42–52; and idem, "*The Triumph of Caesar* by Benedetto Bordon and Jacobus Argentoratensis Its Iconography and Influence," *Print Quarterly* 7 (1990): 4–21.

[12] Massing, "*The Triumph of Caesar* by Benedetto Bordon," 4.

Fig. 6. Giacomo di Argentina, Caesar on a Chariot, one of 12 woodcuts of the *Triumph of Caesar*. c. 1504. Third State, with text. Photo: The Metropolitan Museum of Art, Harris Brisbane Dick Fund, 1927 (27.54.124).

put out for sale, by Bordon until he had been granted the *privilegio* on March 30. At that point Bordon presumably would have had Giacomo di Argentina add the notice of copyright to the blocks.

Unfortunately, Heinecken does not record the existence of a *privilegio* inscription. Nor does such an inscription appear on the second and third 'states'. Morover, although the third impression may be a later state of the second, it is difficult to say whether they are later 'states' of the impression described by Heinecken. As in the case with books, notice of copyright on prints was generally indicated with a short inscription, usually simply the words *cum privilegio*, which was cut into the block or engraved on the metal plate. As a matter of practical consideration, it may be noted that it must have been necessary to reserve a space on a woodblock for an anticipated *privilegio* inscription. It is clear from Bordon's supplication that the blocks for the *Triumph of Caesar* were already cut before the request for the *privilegio* was submitted. Unless some aforethought had been given to the cutting and a space on the block left uncut, it would be difficult once the block was finished to add a *privilegio* inscription. In the few surviving inscribed examples from the early sixteenth century (see below) it would appear that space was left intentionally in the form of a tablet or some similar device.

On the evidence of these same surviving examples, there is reason to believe that the addition of a *privilegio* inscription was the accepted means of indicating copyright protection. In other words, every print that was granted a *privilegio* was inscribed with a notice to this effect. Possible exceptions are books of prints and prints issued in sets where the inscription might be seen only on the cover sheet or frontispiece, if there was one. With respect to Giacomo di Argentina's *Triumph of Caesar*, as none of the surviving impressions carry a *privilegio* inscription, we cannot be sure that they are precisely those for which Bordon was granted a *privilegio* in 1504; they are either later states, from which the inscription has been removed, or they are copies.

Four years later, on 19 September 1508, Bordon was granted another *privilegio*, this time for two woodcut maps, one of the "whole province of Italy" and the other a *mappamondo*.[13] Bordon explains that he had spent a lot of time, money, and effort on the project.

---

[13] The document is recorded in ASV, CN, reg. 16, fols. 29v.–30r. (31v.–31r. n.n.) [Fulin, "Documenti," no. 168].

Of particular interest is his description of the *mappamondo* as being "round in the shape of a ball" ("in forma rotonda de balla"). This reference to a ball-like shape is also found in the inventory of Alessandro Rosselli's print shop in Florence compiled in 1527 where is listed a ball-shaped coloured *mappamondo* ("appamondo in palla cholorito").[14] Possibly it was intended for mounting on a globe, like the example listed in Antonio Lafrery's inventory in 1573, which is described as a "Mappamondo in doi tondi per metter sopra una palla" ("mappamondo in two roundels for putting on a ball [or globe]").[15] Besides being fitted over a globe, it is also possible that, like the example listed in Rosselli's inventory, Bordon's *mappamondo* was intended to be coloured.

Bordon says that he designed both maps with very great subtlety showing the lines of longitude and latitude, and with the appropriate names inscribed for each place, river, mountain, and "every other thing necessary for the complete understanding of everyone" ("et ogni altra cossa necessaria ad compita intelligentia de ognuno"). He adds that the project was difficult and that he spent a lot of money on the woodcutting because it is his way to bring such things to perfection. The *privilegio* was valid for ten years with a penalty that included the confiscation of all the prints printed, and their woodblocks, and a fine of ten ducats for each one printed. As before, a third of the fine was to go the "accusador," a third to the magistrate, and a third to Bordon. Bordon's map of Italy was evidently printed as it is described in 1560 by Bernardini Scardeone, who saw an example of it with a dedication to the Venetian nobleman Francesco Corner.[16] Impressions of neither print, though, have survived.

---

[14] The entry in Alessandro Rosselli's inventory is recorded in Iodoco Del Badia, 25. It should be noted in the case of Bordon's *mappamondo*, that Rivoli and Ephrussi, "Notes sur les Xylographes Vénetiens du XVe et XVIe siècles," *Gazette des Beaux-Arts* 32 (1891): 498, transcribe the passage in the document incorrectly as: "et etiam lo Apamondo in forma rotonda de bella [sic] cosa et nova . . ."

[15] This observation has also been made by Roberto Almagià, "Alcune stampe geografiche italiane dei secoli XVI e XVII oggi perdute," *Maso Finiguerra* 5 (1940): 98, and repeated by Lilian Armstrong, "Benedetto Bordon, *Miniator*, and Cartography in Early Sixteenth-Century Venice," *Imago Mundi* 48 (1996): 76. It should be noted that Almagià gives the date of Bordon's request incorrectly as 1509. The listing in Lafrery's inventory is given in Ehrle, *Roma prima di Sisto V*, 54.

[16] Bernardini Scardeone's report is noted in Almagià, "Alcune stampe geografiche italiane," 99.

Giovanni da Brescia

On 20 April 1514, Giovanni da Brescia, who describes himself as a painter ("Zuan da Brexa depentor"), submitted a supplication to the College for a ten-year *privilegio* for a print produced by himself in woodcut after his own design of the history of Emperor Trajan.[17] No prints of this subject that might be identified with the one named in the document have yet come to light. In his supplication, Giovanni complains that some of his trial proofs were pirated. He says that he had printed some of his work experimentally to see how it would turn out, but the proofs were immediately stolen by others, who began to produce counterfeit copies. Although he refers to having made one drawing or design ("uno desegno") from which he made a woodcut, he goes on to point out that so far he has only printed part of his work, but intends to print all of it. From these comments it may be inferred that his design was cut on more than one block (and that his trial proofs were made from single blocks).

It is not difficult to imagine, especially given the subject matter, that the design was laid out in a horizontal format and printed from several blocks, much like Bordon's *Triumph of Caesar*. Possibly the prints reproduced scenes from the Column of Trajan in Rome. According to Raffaello Maffei, "il Volaterrano," in his *Commentariorum Urbanorum Libri XXXVIII*, published in Rome in 1506, drawings of all the reliefs from top to bottom ("circum machinis scandendo") had been made by Jacopo Ripanda of Bologna.[18] Without the print in hand, however, it is impossible to know whether or not Benalio was reproducing these particular drawings.

---

[17] The *privilegio* is recorded in ASV, CN, reg. 17, fols. 87v.–88r. (fols. 89v.–90r. n.n.) [Fulin, "Documenti," no. 192]. It was first fully transcribed in Gaye, *Carteggio inedito d'artisti*, 2: 136, doc. 81.

[18] Giuseppe Fiocco, "Jacopo Ripanda," *L'Arte* 23 (1920): 28. Fifty-five pen drawings illustrating the entire column and preserved in the library of the Istituto dell'Archeologia e Storia dell'Arte, Palazzo Venezia, in Rome, have been attributed to Ripanda by Roberto Paribeni, "La Colonna Trajana in un codice del Rinascimento," *Rivista del R. Istituto d'archeologia e storia dell'arte* 1 (1929): 9–28. More recently, the same drawings have been attributed to Giulio Romano by Jacob Hess, "A proposito di un libro di Girolamo Muziano," *Maso Finiguerra* 2 (1937): 73. These and other drawings of the Column of Trajan are discussed in Chapter 9 below in connection with a series of prints of the reliefs produced under the direction of the painter Girolamo Muziano.

Bernardino Benalio

The publishing activities of Bernardino Benalio, a printer from Bergamo, appear to have begun as early as 1483 when he published the first edition of Jacopo Filippo Foresti's *Supplementum Chronicarum.* Foresti's book, it may be noted, contains numerous outline woodcuts of imaginary cities. Three years later, in 1486, another edition of the *Supplementum Chronicarum* was published containing an additional seventy panoramic vignettes of Venice and other cities, notably Florence and Rome, plus three figurative woodcuts of the *Creation of Eve*, the *Fall and Expulsion from Paradise*, and the *Story of Cain and Abel.* Benalio's first *privilegio* was granted on 17 August 1492 for the publication of Bernardo Giustiniani's *De origine urbis Venetiarum.*[19] Two years later, in 1494, he received another, and a third in 1499, which was issued jointly to him and Francesco di Baldassari from Perugia. A fourth *privilegio* was granted to Benalio alone in 1500. A gap of fourteen years then appears in the records before he again receives a *privilegio*, in 1514. All of the privileges granted Benalio up to this point had been for books.[20] It is therefore surprising to find that in a supplication for a ten-year *privilegio* granted on 9 February 1515 [1514 m.v.], besides three books, are included an unspecified number of prints, which Benalio claims "have never before been printed in Venice."[21]

> Item el ditto fa designare & intagiare molte Belle hystorie deuote çioe la submersione di pharaone la hystoria de Susanna: la hystoria del sacrifitio de abraham, et altre hystorie noue ch[e] non sono mai piu sta stampate nel Dominio de S[ua] Sub[limi]^{ta}.

Three of the prints are: a *Submersion of Pharaoh's Army in the Red Sea*, a *Susanna*, and a *Sacrifice of Abraham*. The *Sacrifice of Abraham* can be convincingly identified as the four-block woodcut by Ugo da Carpi (Fig. 7). It is known in at least five editions of which the first is

---

[19] The *privilegio* is recorded in ASV, CN, reg. 14, fol. 66r. (70r. n.n.) [Fulin, "Documenti," no. 6]. It is also noted in Rinaldo Fulin, "Primi privilegi di stampa in Venezia," *Archivio Veneto* 1 (1871): 162.

[20] These privileges are recorded in ASV, CN, reg. 14, fol. 94v. (98v. n.n.) [Fulin, "Documenti," no. 20] and ASV, CN, reg. 15, fol. 6v. (8v. n.n.) [Fulin, "Documenti," no. 95]; ASV, CN, reg. 15, fol. 16r. (18r. n.n.) [Fulin, "Documenti," no. 99]; and ASV, CN, reg. 17, fol. 87v. (85v. n.n.) [Fulin, "Documenti," no. 191].

[21] The document is recorded in ASV, CN, reg. 17, fol. 103r. (105r. n.n.) [Fulin, "Documenti," no. 196].

Fig. 7a. Ugo da Carpi, *Sacrifice of Abraham* (after Titian). c. 1515. Woodcut.
Photo: Staatliche Museen, Berlin.

Fig. 7b. Ugo da Carpi, *Sacrifice of Abraham* (after Titian),
detail of *privilegio* inscription.

undoubtedly that surviving in a unique impression in the Staatliche Museen in Berlin (inv. no. 868–100) and carries the inscription:

> In Uenetia per Ugo da carpi/Stampata per Bernardino/benalio: Cu[m] priuilegio c[on]cesso per lo Illustrissimo Senato./Sul ca[m]po de san Stephano.

The inscription explains succinctly that the woodcut is by Ugo da Carpi and was printed by Bernardino Benalio with a *privilegio* granted by the Venetian Senate. The Campo di San Stefano is presumably the location where the print could be purchased. This is the earliest surviving example of a print carrying a *privilegio* inscription. In later states the inscription was erased and replaced by other inscriptions that identify Titian as the designer. A third state, for example, carries the inscription "SAGRIFICIO DEL PATRIARCA/ABRAMO/DEL CELEBRE TIZIANO," while the fourth state is inscribed simply "TIZIANO." The copyright protection afforded Benalio by the *privilegio* would have lasted only two years, however. In 1517 all privileges granted up to then were revoked (see Chapter 2).

Of the other two prints, the *Submersion of Pharaoh's Army in the Red Sea* would appear to survive only in a later impression published by Domenico dalle Greche in 1549 (Fig. 8). David Rosand and Michelangelo Muraro have suggested that the woodcut's twelve blocks may have been acquired by Dalle Greche from Benalio's heirs.[22] A fragment (the right half of the middle block on the right side) possibly of the original print is in the Museo Correr in Venice.[23] Unlike the 1549 impression, the woodblock from which the Correr fragment was printed was free of wormholes and other indications of age. Besides wormholes, the age of the blocks used to print the 1549 impression is also apparent in the cracks, a break in one corner, and the outlines of an inserted plug. The age of the blocks, together with the fact that the later impression matches cut for cut the Correr fragment, increases the likelihood that the 1549 impression is a later state of the original rather than a copy. The inscription on the bottom, second block from the left below the floundering Egyptian horsemen reads:

---

[22] Rosand and Muraro, *Titian and the Venetian Woodcut*, 70. The date of Benalio's death was unknown to Rosand and Muraro. It can now be reported that Benalio died in 1546 (see note 33 below), making it quite conceivable that Dalle Greche could have acquired the wood blocks from Benalio's widow soon thereafter.

[23] Museo Correr, Venice, Stampe A15, fol. 39, no. 39.

Fig. 8. Anonymous, *Submersion of Pharaoh's Army in the Red Sea* (after Titian). Woodcut. Late impression dated 1549. Photo: Courtesy of the Fogg Art Museum, Harvard University Art Museums. Gift of W. G. Russell Allen.

La crudel persecutione del ostinato Re, contro il populo tanto da Dio/amato, Con la sommersione di esso Pharaone goloso dil inocente/ sangue. Disegnata per mano dil grande, et immortal Titiano./In venetia p[er] domeneco dalle greche depentore Venitiano./M.DXLIX

As in the case of the *Sacrifice of Abraham*, the original *privilegio* inscription was removed and replaced with the one there now. As Rosand and Muraro surmise, it seems likely that the identification of Titian as the designer was not part of the original inscription.

The *Susannah and the Elders* may be identified as the four-block woodcut of which the only known single complete impression is that in Copenhagen (Fig. 9), and the two sheets of the bottom half in the British Museum in London. The print is signed with a monogram that has been identified as that of Girolamo Pennacchi da Treviso (1497?–1544).[24] The plaque in the lower right in both the Copenhagen and British Museum impressions, where a *privilegio* inscription was most likely located, has clearly been erased, which suggests the possibility that these impressions are a later state of the original rather than copies (counterfeit copies would not reproduce the erased area as seen in the Copenhagen and British Museum sheets).

As for the "altre hystorie noue" unnamed in Benalio's supplication, there are no clues to their identity. However, it can be suggested that perhaps one of the prints was the eight-block woodcut of the *Martyrdom of the Ten Thousand Christians on Mount Ararat* signed with the monogram (L*) of Lucantonio degli Uberti of which only late impressions survive (Fig. 10).[25] The original print, which has been dated to around 1515–1520, was almost certainly larger. This is suggested by the fact that the cartouche in the lower right corner appears arbitrarily trimmed; two more blocks (an upper and a lower) could have extended the block to the right. The cartouche, now blank in surviving editions, could well have contained Benalio's address and the *privilegio* inscription.

In his supplication, Benalio asks that no one other than himself be permitted to print, or engrave, the said works and "historie" for the next ten years, and that anyone who makes counterfeit copies

---

[24] The monogram is identified by Franca Zava Boccazzi, "Tracce per Gerolamo da Treviso il Giovane in alcune xilografie di Francesco de Nanto," *Arte Veneta* 12 (1958): 71.

[25] The print is catalogued in Rosand and Muraro, cat. no. 14, who identify the monogram as Lucantonio degli Uberti's. The print has also been attributed to Domenico Campagnola.

Fig. 9. Girolamo Pennacchi da Treviso, *Susannah and the Elders* (after Titian). c. 1515. Woodcut. Photo: Statens Museum for Kunst, Copenhagen.

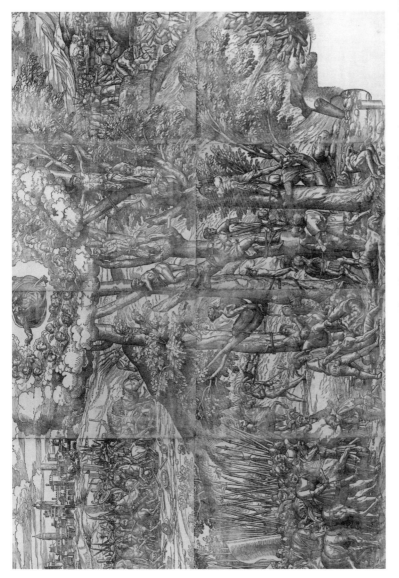

Fig. 10. Lucantonio degli Uberti, *The Martyrdom of the Ten Thousand Christians on Mount Ararat*, c. 1515–1520. Woodcut. Princeton University Art Museum. Gift of Junius S. Morgan, Class of 1888 (?). Photo Credit: Clem Fiori © 1988. Photo: Trustees of Princeton University.

outside the dominion of Venice not be permitted to sell them in the city or in any part of the dominion under penalty of a fine of two ducats for each item. A third of the fine was to go the Arsenal, another third to the "accusador," and a third to the Signori di Notte.

Sixteen months later, on 6 May 1516, Bernardino Benalio submitted another supplication for a *privilegio* to publish three more prints, listing this time a *Last Judgement*, printed on two sheets, "with the angelic choir and blessed orders and an infinite number of damned and demons," a *Triumph of the Virgin Mary*, and "the imaginary procession of Our Lord [printed] on eight royal sheets with very beautiful ornaments" ("la processional visione imaginaria del Salvator nostro in octo fogli reali cum bellissime ornamenti"). He added that these works are "certainly deserving of commendation and favour for their new spiritual and very devotional invention."[26]

Neither the *Last Judgement* nor the *Triumph of the Virgin* can be traced.[27] The last print mentioned on the list, though, may be identified as the ten-block woodcut *The Triumph of Christ* by an anonymous cutter after a design by Titian that exists in several editions. The connection between Benalio's *privilegio* and the woodcut was first put forward by Fabio Mauroner in connection with an edition signed by Lucantonio degli Uberti.[28] Rosand and Muraro, however, rejected this as unlikely on the basis that the inscription suggests that Lucantonio was the publisher, not Benalio.[29] This may well be the case for this edition, but Rosand and Muraro's argument should not serve as the basis for negating any connection between Benalio's *privilegio* and the *Triumph of Christ* woodcuts.

The initial problem in linking the two is Vasari's statement that the *Triumph of Christ* was issued in a woodcut by Titian in 1508.[30] Carlo Ridolfi, however, writing in 1648, dates the work later, to

---

[26] The *privilegio* is recorded in ASV, CN, reg. 18, fol. 32r. (33r. n.n.) [Fulin, "Documenti," no. 208].

[27] The description of the *Last Judgement*, however, does call to mind one of Alessandro Rosselli's engravings of the subject based on Fra Angelico's painting on panel now in the Museo di San Marco, Florence. Rosselli's single-sheet print, however, has been dated to c. 1480–90 by Jay A. Levenson in *Early Italian Engravings from the National Gallery of Art* (Washington, D.C., 1973), cat. no. 12, which is too early to be considered in connection with this *privilegio*.

[28] Fabio Mauroner, *Le incisioni di Tiziano*, 2nd ed. (Padua, 1943), no. 1, 3 (pp. 34–35).

[29] Rosand and Muraro, 39.

[30] Vasari, 1568, 7: 431: "L'anno appresso 1508 mandò fuori Tiziano in istampa di legno il Trionfo della Fede . . ."

when Titian was in Padua (i.e. around 1510–11). Ridolfi associates
the print with a frieze painted by Titian in a house he was renting
in Padua.[31] No earlier sources can be found, however, that corrob-
orate Ridolfi's statement. Even if Ridolfi is correct, though, it should
not be assumed that the print was made immediately after the painting was completed; five years could easily have passed before the
design was cut into woodblocks. It is also perfectly feasible, however,
within the context of Titian's stylistic development, to date the design,
whatever its original source, to the months (or possibly even a year
or more, given the size of the project) prior to May 1516. Benalio,
of course, had just recently published other designs by Titian, the
privilegio for which, granted in February 1515 (see above), he brought
to the attention of the College in his new supplication. It must
be assumed that the edition for which Benalio was granted a *privilegio* was the first (it is unlikely that he would have sought a *privilegio* for a work already published). This first edition, however, is
evidently lost as there are no surviving impressions that carry a *privilegio* inscription.

   In his supplication, so that his work would not be copied by "invid-
ious ignoramuses" ("invidi ignoranti"), Benalio had asked for an "invi-
olabile privilege" that "for ten years nobody other than him under
whatever conditions, can, with or without permission, in Venice, or
anywhere on land or sea in the Venetian State, make or have made
prints of these subjects, either the same size, or made larger, or
smaller, and that neither could the design be added to, changed, or
diminished" ("per anni diese niuno altro che mi de qualunque conditione & Stato sia, possa cum gratia, ò senza gratia in questa Emi-
nentissima Cita de Venetia, ò qualunque altro loco de Terra, ò da
mar de questo perpetuo duraturo Stato, ò far fare stampe de questa
materia in equal, mazor, ò minor forme, addendo, mutando, ò min-
uendo"). Moreover, other than Benalio, "nobody could print, or have
printed, nor could they print to sell or have sold, in Venice or elsewhere, nor in any way trade" the prints listed in the *privilegio* ("ne
quelle facte imprimer, ò far imprimer, ne quelle ancora in dicte
Terre, ò terre aliene impresse vender, ò far vender, ne per modo
alcuno mercandar"). Benalio asks that each and every time a print

---

[31] Carlo Ridolfi, *Le meraviglie dell'arte* (Venice, 1648), 156: "Trasferitosi poscia à
Padova, dicono, ch' ei ritraesse il Trionfo di Christo nel giro d'vna stanza della
casa da lui presa, che si vede in istampa in legno disegnato di propria mano . . ."

is counterfeited, a fine of three hundred gold ducats be paid, and
that the blocks ("stampe") and the printed sheets be confiscated from
the counterfeiter. The money collected from the fines should be
divided between the Avogadori de Commun, the Signori di Notte,
and himself and his heirs, or someone in his stead. For some unex-
plained reason, the College halved the ten years requested by Benalio
to five.

In August 1517, just over a year after the *Triumph of Christ* was
printed, the *privilegio* protecting it was revoked by the Venetian Senate
(see Chapter 2). Without this protection the print was evidently immediately copied. Perhaps first off the mark was Gregorio de' Gregorii
who issued a five-block copy in 1517, which was followed by the
nine-block copy by Lucantonio degli Uberti mentioned above.[32]
Possibly the revocation of his privileges and the subsequent copying
of his prints soured Benalio on print publishing. His foray into the
field was ill-timed and probably turned out to be not as lucrative as
he had hoped. After 1517, he evidently abandoned prints and returned
to publishing only books, an activity which kept him busy until his
death in 1546.[33]

Giacomo di Argentina

It will be recalled that Giacomo di Argentina had produced a series
of twelve woodcuts of the *Triumph of Caesar* for Benedetto Bordon in
1504. Now, eleven years later, on 25 July 1515, he submitted his

---

[32] Rosand and Muraro, 38, 2, 3, date the Lucantonio copy to soon after 1517.
Paul Kristeller, *Il Trionfo della Fede: Holzschnittfolge nach Tizians Zeichnung* (Berlin, 1906),
believes the 1517 de' Gregorii version to be the earliest, followed by that of
Lucantonio degli Uberti. More recently Michael Bury, "The 'Triumph of Christ'
after Titian," *Burlington Magazine* 131 (1989): 188–197, has also argued that the 1517
de' Gregorii version is the earliest. It may be noted that according to a document
in ASV, CX, Busta 2, on 7 January 1513, Lucantonio degli Uberti had been condemned for blasphemy ("bestemmia") by the Council of Ten. His punishment was
jail for one year and then banishment from Venice for three years ("Luca Antonio
de Uberti fiorentino stampatore condannato dal Consiglio dei X ad un anno di
carcere . . . e poi per anni tre bandito da Venezia . . . per bestemmia"). Evidently
he returned to Venice at the end of this period, in 1517.

[33] Benalio must have died shortly before 8 August 1546, which is the date on a
document (ASV, Procurator Nobili, Busta 15, fol. 143r.) recording the inventory
drawn up for his widow ("Elisabetta vedova de Bernardino de Benalio stampatore").

own supplication for a *privilegio* to publish a map or view of Venice.[34] As part of his expression of his need for a *privilegio*, he pointed out that he was poor and had nine small children. In his supplication, he stated that in order to print his map and so that no one else will copy it, he was appealing "as a poor supplicant" at the feet of the Council members that for the next ten years no one be permitted to print his work or have it printed, so that he can support his poor children and his family. The penalty was set at twenty-five *lire* "piccoli" for each counterfeit map printed. No trace of the print survives, however.

Gregorio de' Gregorii

The printer Gregorio de' Gregorii, who published works both alone and in association with his brother Giovanni, had been granted his first *privilegio* for books in 1494.[35] More privileges followed, but only intermittently. His next was not granted until 1507. In 1508 he received a license from the Council of Ten to print a theological work, and in 1512 he was granted another *privilegio* for a new way to print missals and breviaries.[36] Four years later, on 22 April 1516, he again submitted a supplication to the College but this time included not only a request for a book, the *Offices of the Blessed Virgin Mary*, but for also "alcune Cose dj desegno," and listed first a "triumph, and the nativity, death, resurrection and ascension of our most merciful Saviour," which, he added, "will be a very beautiful invention."[37] He went on to list the "destruction of the holy City of Jerusalem" and "many other various and beautiful inventions" which he said had not been printed before.

---

[34] The *privilegio* is recorded in ASV, CN, reg. 18, fol. 16r. (17r. n.n.) [Fulin, "Documenti," no. 198].

[35] The *privilegio* is recorded in ASV, CN, reg. 14, fol. 101v. (105v. n.n.) [Fulin, "Documenti," no. 29].

[36] The *privilegio* granted in 1507 is recorded in ASV, CN, reg. 16, fol. 16v. (18v. n.n.) [Fulin, "Documenti," no. 164]. The license granted in 1508 is recorded ASV, CCXN, reg. 3, fol. 90r. [Fulin, "Documenti," no. 166]. The *privilegio* granted in 1512 is recorded in ASV, CN, reg. 17, fol. 11v. (13v. n.n.) [Fulin, "Documenti," no. 185].

[37] The *privilegio* is recorded in ASV, CN, reg. 18, fol. 31v. (32v. n.n.) [Fulin, "Documenti," no. 207].

The phrase "which *will be* a very beautiful invention" ("la quale *sera* bellissima inventione") in the supplication indicates that the publication of these prints was a project Gregorio de' Gregorii was planning for the future, and indeed later in the *privilegio* reference is made to "the designs [drawings] that he *will* make." The reference in the first phrase ("la quale sera . . .") is to something singular which suggests that the "triumph, and the nativity, death, resurrection and ascension of the most merciful Saviour" all appear in one print. This was how it was understood by Mauroner who tentatively identified the print as the *Triumph of Christ* published by Gregorio de' Gregorii in 1517.[38] However, the inexact correspondence between the description and the print, acknowledged also by Mauroner, makes the identification unconvincing, and it now seems more likely that the *privilegio* for the *Triumph of Christ* was that granted to Bernardino Benalio (see above).

No print or prints resembling that described by Gregorio de' Gregorii can be traced. The implication that the scenes described— "triumph, and the nativity, death, resurrection and ascension of our most merciful Saviour"—all appeared in one print suggests a long frieze-like design. However, it is also possible that Gregorio de' Gregorii is describing not a single print with several scenes but a series of separate images which he intended to publish together as a set, to which he refers in the singular. Rivoli and Ephrussi believe that the prints were in fact illustrations for the book, the *Offices of the Blessed Virgin Mary*, named at the beginning of the supplication.[39] This is certainly possible. Although Gregorio de' Gregorii had already published the *Offices of the Blessed Virgin Mary* in earlier editions, he describes this new edition as having a revised format. This revision appears to be linked to a new method and form for producing prints: "Et etiam ha trovata modo et forma de stampare alcune Cose dj desegno." Rivoli and Ephrussi go on to argue that in the phrase "modo et forma de stampare alcune cose di desegno" the word "stampare" should be understood not in the sense of to print (i.e. merely to publish) but as meaning to pull prints. In other words, Gregorio de' Gregorii was actually involved in the making and production of the prints. The case Rivoli and Ephrussi want to make

---

[38] Mauroner, no. 1, 2.
[39] Rivoli and Ephrussi, 495.

is that the prints listed in the supplication were cut by Gregorio de' Gregorii himself, a claim they believe is supported in a passage in the supplication that refers to "the designs that *he will make*." Confirmation of this supposition is provided by the woodcuts signed with the initials "G.G.," which Rivoli and Ephrussi identify as Gregorio de' Gregorii, illustrating a *Missale aquilejensis Ecclesie* published by Gregorio de' Gregorii in Venice on 15 September 1519. It can be added that the same initials also appear on a border piece between Evangelists Mark and John in a breviary printed in Venice on 31 October 1518 by Gregorio de' Gregorii for Kristóf Frangepán.[40] However, whether or not Gregorio de' Gregorii himself made the print or prints, it remains unclear if they were printed as independent sheets or served as illustrations in the *Offices of the Blessed Virgin Mary*.

Gregorio de' Gregorii was evidently interested in publishing prints at this time as his name appears as publisher on the copy of the *Triumph of Christ* in 1517, noted above, and on a woodcut signed by Lucantonio degli Uberti of the *Madonna and Child with Saints John the Baptist and Gregory the Great*, both of which are inscribed "Gregorius de gregoriis/excusit. M.D.XVII."[41] Neither of these prints, however, can be associated with those listed in the *privilegio*. The print described as the "destruction of the holy City of Jerusalem" has not been identified; nor have any of the "many other various and beautiful inventions" mentioned in the supplication.

In his supplication, Gregorio de' Gregorii asked that for ten years, beginning when he had completed them, nobody be permitted to print or, having printed, sell copies in the city of Venice or in Venetian territory. The penalty for counterfeiters was confiscation of the copies and a fine of ten ducats for each one found printed. The fine was to be divided into three parts between the magistrate to whom the denunciation was made, the hospital of the Pietà, and the person who made the denunciation.

Fra Ippolito

On 15 May 1516, a Fra Ippolito di Pregnachi from Brescia of the Humiliati, exiled from his place of birth, submitted a supplication

---

[40] The breviary is catalogued in Mortimer, *Italian 16th Century Books*, no. 88.

[41] The prints are catalogued in Rosand and Muraro, cat. no. 2, 2, and cat. no. 11.

to the College for a *privilegio* for two prints (or possibly one print combining the two scenes) of "the story of Sodom and Gomorrah with that of the pharaoh persecuting the people of Israel," which, he explains, "he has already engraved."[42] For this, Fra Ippolito asks that nobody be permitted to engrave the said histories for the next ten years on pain of a fine of one hundred ducats. Neither of these prints has been traced.

---

[42] The document is recorded in ASV, CN, reg. 18, fol. 38v. (39v. n.n.).

CHAPTER SIX

PUBLISHERS OF PRINTS AND BOOKS
IN VENICE AFTER 1517

The most prolific publishers of printed images (including maps) in the sixteenth century were printers. Many of the books they printed were profusely illustrated with woodcuts and engravings to which special reference was sometimes made in the privileges granted for them. Several printers in the period after 1517 also issued independent prints. Among the more notable publishers in this activity are Gabriele Giolito, Michele Tramezzino, Giovanni Francesco Camocio, members of the Bertelli family, Nicolo Nelli, and Giacomo Franco.

Gabriele Giolito de' Ferrari

Gabriele Giolito de' Ferrari, who had been printing books with privileges since 1539, published numerous books with illustrations.[1] Especially noteworthy is the supplication he submitted to the Venetian Senate on 16 December 1541 for a *privilegio* to cover specifically the ornamentations and designs in a new edition of Ariosto's *Orlando Furioso*.[2] The profusely illustrated book, published the following year, 1542, was dedicated by Giolito to the Duc d'Orléans, the husband of Catherine de' Medici, and later King Henry II of France. The book evidently made an impression on Giorgio Vasari who refers to it in the *Vita* of Marcantonio Raimondi.[3] The engraver of the illustrations, however, remains unknown.[4]

---

[1] The printing activities of Gabriele Giolito are discussed in Bongi, *Annali di Gabriel Giolito de'Ferrari da Trino di Monferrato, stampatore in Venezia*; and Giuseppe Dondi, "Una famiglia di editori a mezzo il secolo XVI: i Giolito," *Atti dell'Accademia delle Scienze di Torino* 102 (1968): 589–701.

[2] The document is recorded in ASV, ST, reg. 31, fol. 177r. (198r. n.n.). The *privilegio* also included a new edition of Petrarch. Ariosto's earlier privileges for *Orlando Furioso*, the last of which had expired in 1536 (and Ariosto himself had died in 1535), are noted in Chapter 2.

[3] Vasari, 1568, 5: 435: "Non furono anco se non lodevoli le figure che Gabriel Giolito stampatore de' libri, mise negli Orlandi Furiosi, perciocchè furono condotte con bella maniera d'intagli."

[4] Ariosto's book is noted in Bongi, 1: 43. The prints in the 1542 edition are

A decade later, on 26 February 1553 [1552 m.v.], Giolito was granted a fifteen-year *privilegio* by the Senate for Ludovico Dolce's translation into Italian in "ottava Rima" of Ovid's *Metamorphoses*, which Giolito intended to print "with illustrations."[5] The same *privilegio* also included annotated and illustrated editions of Dante and Petrarch, and Francesco Baldelli's translation of Caesar's commentaries, also printed with illustrations (for which, see Chapter 11). On 12 September 1555, Giolito published Enea Vico's engravings in *Discorsi di Enea Vico Parmigiano sopra le Medaglie de gli Antichi* (see Chapter 8). Besides illustrated books, Giolito also published prints, including several maps (see Chapter 10).

Michele and Francesco Tramezzino

The brothers Michele and Francesco Tramezzino operated presses in both Venice and Rome. They were both in Rome in 1527 when their names appear in a census in which they are both identified as book dealers.[6] At the time of the sack of Rome in 1527, they moved to Venice, but on 5 July 1528 Francesco returned to Rome and set up a shop on via del Pellegrino. Michele stayed in Venice, where, in the latter part of the 1530s, he began operating his own press. In a supplication to the Senate submitted in 1536, Michele Tramezzino describes himself as a "seller of books" ("venditor dei libri").[7] On 10 October 1538, he was granted a *privilegio* for Pandolfo Collenuccio's *Compendio delle historie del regno di Napoli*, which he printed in Venice in May 1539 ("Stampate in Vineggia per Michele Tramezino"), and on 24 August 1543, he received another *privilegio* for a translation of

---

briefly discussed in Ugo Bellocchi and Bruno Fava, *L'Interpretazione Grafica dell'Orlando Furioso* (Reggio Emilia, 1961), 16–17, and plates 8 (canto 26, stanza 129) and 9 (canto 33, stanza 126); and Philip Hofer, "Illustrated Editions of 'Orlando Furioso'," in *Fragonard Drawings for Ariosto* (New York, 1945), 27–40.

[5] The document is recorded in ASV, ST, reg. 38, fol. 193r. (214r. n.n.). Giolito published the book in 1557 with the Italian title *Le transformationi*. The same year Giolito also published Dolce's *Dialogo della pittura intitolato l'Aretino*, the license for which had been granted on 15 July, 1557 (ASV, CCXN, reg. 16, fol. 225v.).

[6] D. Gnoli, "Descriptio urbis o censimento della popolazione di Roma avanti il Sacco borbonico," in *Archivio della R. Societa romana di storia patria* 17 (1894): 466: "Michael Tramesino libraro" and "Francisco Tramesino libraro." The publishing activities of the Tramezzino brothers are discussed in Tinto, *Annali tipografici dei Tramezzino* (Rome, 1966).

[7] The document is recorded in ASV, ST, reg. 29, fol. 2r. (23r. n.n.).

Andrea Fulvio's *De antiquitatibus urbis.*[8] While a number of books were printed in Venice, others the brothers (mostly Michele) paid to have printed in Rome (in the colophon, the location "Roma" is followed by "impensis" or "sumptibus" Michele Tramezzino). In most cases, books published by the Tramezzino brothers carry privileges from both the Senate in Venice and the pope in Rome. Several books carry in addition privileges from Charles V and the King of France, and some also privileges from the Duke of Florence and the Duchess of Mantua.[9]

By the early 1550s, Michele Tramezzino was also publishing prints. On 2 June 1551, he was granted a *privilegio* for, among other things, a printed design entitled "The Way, the Truth, and the Life" ("Via, Verità, et Vita"), and another of the Resurrection ("Christo resuscitante").[10] He also developed an interest in publishing works on both antique and modern Rome. On 30 July 1548, he was granted a ten-year *privilegio* for Lucio Fauno's *Delle antichita della città di Roma.*[11] When the book was published in 1553, it included in it also Fauno's *Compendio di Roma antica*, which Tramezzino had published separately the previous year. Tramezzino had been granted a separate *privilegio* for the *Compendio di Roma antica*, and also for an engraved map of Rome, on 12 December 1551.[12] Besides the Venetian *privilegio*,

---

[8] The *privilegio* granted for Collenuccio's book is recorded in ASV, ST, reg. 30, fol. 45r. The book is listed in Tinto, *Annali tipografici dei Tramezzino*, 3, no. 2. The Biblioteca Marciana in Venice has the 1541 edition (141.D.223) and later editions. It may be noted that on 3 September 1550, Tramezzino was granted another *privilegio* for printing "l'historia del Regno de Napoli di .D. filippo argentone Comineo, Insieme co[n] q[ue]lla di Colenuccio" (ASV, ST, reg. 37, fol. 45v. [66v. n.n.]). The *privilegio* for Andrea Fulvio's *De antiquitatibus urbis* is recorded in ASV, ST, reg. 32, fol. 193r. For works by Fulvio published in Rome, see Chapter 2.

[9] Books carrying French royal and imperial privileges are listed in Tinto, *Annali tipografici dei Tramezzino*, 5–7, nos. 7, 9, 10, 11. All were published in 1540 and inscribed: "Cautum est aedicto Summi Pontificis, & Caroli. V. Imp. ac Regis Franciae, necnon Illus. Sen. Veneti. [. . .] intra Decennium Imprimere, aut venalia alibi impressa habere audeat." Two books, both by Paolo Giovio and carrying also ducal privileges, are listed in Tinto, 25, no. 59; 30, no. 77. The inscription reads: "Cum privilegio summi Pontificis, Caroli V. Imperat. Regis Franciae. Illustrissimi Senatus Veneti, nec non Excellentissimorum Florentiae, & Mantuae Ducum." For privileges issued elsewhere in Italy and Europe, see Appendix B.

[10] The document is recorded in ASV, ST, reg. 40, fol. 131v. (152v. n.n.). These prints are not listed in Tinto, *Annali tipografici dei Tramezzino*, and have not been identified.

[11] The document is recorded in ASV, ST, reg. 35, fol. 172r. The book is listed in Tinto, *Annali tipografici dei Tramezzino*, no. 120.

[12] The document is recorded in ASV, ST, reg. 38, fol. 51 (72 n.n.). The book is listed in Tinto, *Annali tipografici dei Tramezzino*, no. 121.

both Fauno's books also carry a papal *privilegio* granted by Julius III.

The following year, 1553, Tramezzino published in Venice a little book on ancient circuses, theatres, and amphitheatres by the Italian architect, painter and antiquarian Pirro Ligorio. Printed in the book is the text of a ten-year papal *privilegio* granted by Julius III on 23 October 1550, and the text of a twenty-year Venetian *privilegio* issued by the Senate on 19 December 1552.[13] The Venetian *privilegio* included not only Ligorio's book, but also eight prints designed by Ligorio, including two maps:

> We concede to our loyal Michele Tramezzino that others may not print, or have printed, or sell without our permission in this city or in other places or cities of our dominions for the next twenty years, the maps or true designs of ancient Rome, of modern Rome, the Circus Maximus, the Circus Flaminius, Italy, or the Praetorian fortress designed by M. Pirro Ligorio, painter of Naples, and similarly the map of Hungary and Transylvania composed by Peter Apian and the map of Germany and its frontiers on each side, prepared for the most reverend Cardinal d'Augusta, nor may there be engraved, either in copper or in wood, either larger or smaller extracts or passages from the above maps or the book by Pirro Ligorio on the Antiquities of Rome, namely, the circles, theaters, and amphitheatres . . .[14]

The prints listed in the *privilegio* are among the first printed by Tramezzino and initiate a period of intense print publishing activity by him that spans the next ten years. Seven of the eight prints named in the *privilegio* can be identified. On each print notice is also given of the papal *privilegio*. The first print mentioned, "Roma antica," can be identified as the map of *Rome* engraved by Giulio de Musi Veneziano (very possibly the son or nephew of the engraver Agostino

[13] The Venetian *privilegio* is also recorded in ASV, ST, reg. 38, fol. 174r.–v. (195r.–v. n.n.). With the approval of the Riformatori dello Studio di Padova, the Chiefs of the Council of Ten had granted Tramezzino a license five days earlier, on 14 December. The title-page of the booklet reads: "LIBRO/DI M. PYRRHO/LIGORI NAPOLITANO,/DELLE ANTICHITÀ DI ROMA, NEL QVALE SI TRATTA DE'/Circi, Theatri, & Anfitheatri./CON LE PARADOSSE DEL MEDESIMO/auttore, quai confutano la commune opinione/sopra varii luoghi della città di Roma./Co'l privilegio del Sommo Pontefice Giulio III. & del=/l'Illustrissimo Senato Veneto per anni XX." The colophon (p. 51r.) reads: "IN VENETIA per Michele Tramezino/MDLIII." A copy is in the BA, Vatican, Barberini O. VI. 98. Another copy is in the Marciana, Venice, 66.1.194. The "Libro" is printed on pages numbered 1–23, with the "Paradosse" following on pages 25–51.
[14] The translation is given in Roberto Almagià, "Pirro Ligorio Cartografo," *Rendiconti della Classe di Scienze morali, storiche e filologiche* serie 3, vol. 11, fasc. 3–4 (1956): 51.

de Musi Veneziano).[15] The second print, "Roma moderna," can be identified as the map of Modern Rome, dated 1552.[16] The "Circo Massimo" is the *Circus Maximus* engraved by Nicolas Beatrizet (Fig. 11).[17] Although it is named in the Venetian *privilegio*, only the papal *privilegio* is indicated in the inscription on the print. The "Circo Flaminio," which was also engraved by Beatrizet, carries similar inscriptions (Fig. 12).[18] It has been argued, not unreasonably, that the print of the *Circus Flaminius* (and, presumably, also that of the *Circus Maximus*) was originally intended for use as an illustration in Ligorio's book.[19] Ligorio's book, however, is thin and small, measuring only 160 × 110 mm., whereas the print of the *Circus Flaminius* measures 370 × 555 mm. It seems unlikely, therefore, that the print (or prints) was to be folded in. The book was otherwise published without illustrations.

The print described in the *privilegio* as "dell'Italia" may be a map of Italy, but it has not been identified. The "Castro Pretorio" is a print by an anonymous engraver inscribed: "CASTRVM PRÆTORIVM/CVM PRIVILEGIO/SVMMI PONT./ET SENAT. VENET./MICH. TRAMEZINI/FORMIS MDLIII."[20] Of the two

---

[15] The print is listed in Robert W. Karrow, *Mapmakers of the Sixteenth Century and Their Maps* (Chicago, 1993), 351, no. 51/2; Tinto, *Annali tipografici dei Tramezzino*, 47, no. 127; Christian Huelsen, *Saggio di bibliografia ragionata delle piante icnografiche e prospettiche di Roma dal 1551 al 1748*, rev. ed. (Florence, 1933), 43, no. 15; Ronald V. Tooley, "Maps in Italian Atlases of the Sixteenth Century," *Imago Mundi* 3 (1939): 41, no. 485; and Fabia Borroni Salvadori, *Carte, piante e stampe storiche delle raccolte lafreriane della Biblioteca nazionale di Firenze* (Rome, 1980), 70, no 213.

[16] The print is inscribed "VRBIS ROMA SITVS IIS QVAE/ADHUC CONSPICIVNTVR/VETER. MONVMENT. RELIQVIIS/PYRRHO LIGORIO NEAP. INVENT./ROMAE MDLII." It is listed in Karrow, 349, no. 51/1; Tinto, *Annali tipografici dei Tramezzino*, 44, no. 119; Huelsen, *Piante icnografiche e prospettiche di Roma*, 41, no. 2; Tooley, 41, no. 484; and Marcel Destombes, "Les cartes de Lafréri et assimilées (1532–1586) du Départment des Estampes de la Bibliothèque nationale," *Nouvelles de l'Estampe* 5 (1970): 250, no. 99. Inscribed in the lower left of the map is the monogram ("GLA") of the English cartographer George Lily ("Georgius Lilius Anglus"), then resident in Rome. An example is in the BA, Vatican, St. Geogr. I.144.

[17] The print is listed in Bartsch, 15: 271, no. 105.

[18] Bartsch, 15: 271, no. 104. Overlooked by Tinto, *Annali tipografici dei Tramezzino*. Ligorio's reconstruction of the *Circus Flaminius* is examined in Donat De Chapeaurouge, "Eine Circus-Rekonstruktion des Pirro Ligorio," *Antike und Abenland* 8 (1973): 89–96.

[19] The suggestion was put forward in Erna Mandowsky, "Pirro Ligorio's Illustrations to Aesop's *Fables*," *Journal of the Warburg and Courtauld Institutes* 24 (1961): 330.

[20] The print is listed in Tinto, *Annali tipografici dei Tramezzino*, 45, no. 122; and Christian Huelsen, "Das Speculum Romanae Magnificentiae des Antonio Lafreri,"

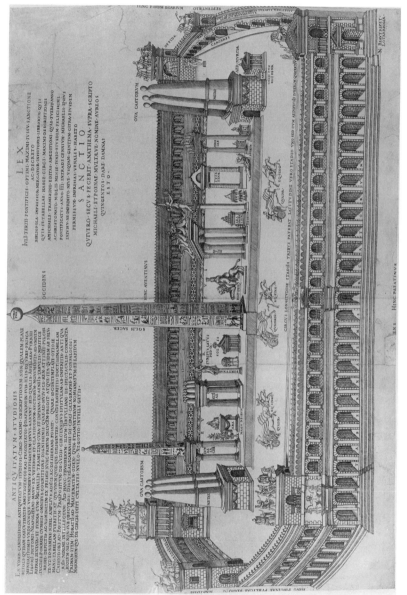

Fig. 11. Nicolas Beatrizet, *Circus Maximus* (after Ligorio). 1553. Engraving. Photo: The Metropolitan Museum of Art, Harris Brisbane Dick Fund, 1941 (41.72.(1) plate 68).

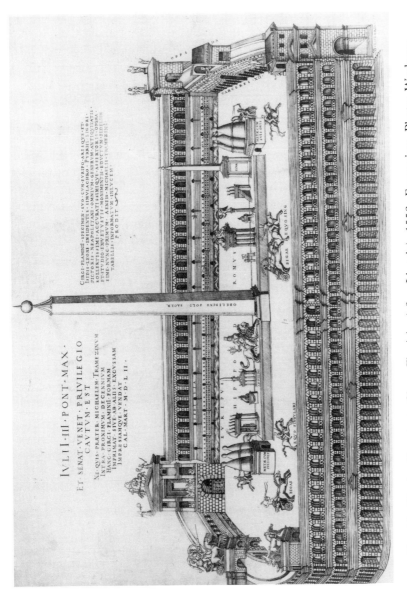

Fig. 12. Nicolas Beatrizet, *Circus Flaminius* (after Ligorio). 1553. Engraving. Photo: Warburg.

maps, the first, "la carta dell'Ongaria, et Transilvania composta per M. Pietro Appiano," has been identified by Roberto Almagià as the map of Hungary engraved by Sebastiano del Re (Sebastiano a Regibus). Apiano's map, "Tabula Hungarie ad quatuor latera," which Sebastiano del Re had copied, had been printed in 1528 by Johann Cuspinianus in Ingolstadt with an imperial *privilegio* granted to the cartographer Georg Tanstetter.[21] Sebastiano del Re's map is inscribed: "NOVA DES/CRIPTIO TOTIVS/HUNGARIAE/Pyrrho Ligorio Neap. auc-tore/ROMÆ. M. D. LVIII./Michaelis Tramezini for-/mis, cu[m] priuilegio Summi/Pont. & Veneti Sena/tus ad decen[n]ium." The date, given as "M. D. LVIII," is most likely an error and should be M. D. LIII. The "carta de Germania co' suoi confini da ogni parte, drizzata al Reverendissimo Cardinal d'Augusta" is the map of *Germany* dated 1553 engraved by Nicolas Beatrizet.[22] The title inscription includes, as stated in the *privilegio*, a dedication to Cardinal of Augusta (i.e. Otto Truchsess von Waldburg, Cardinal and Bishop of Augsburg).

It may be observed in the prints of Roman antiquities that Tra-mezzino has given special prominence to the *privilegio* inscription. On Beatrizet's print of the *Circus Maximus* the notice of *privilegio* is spelled out in large capital letters and includes the warning that the print

in *Collectanea Variae Doctrinae Leoni S. Olschki* (Munich, 1921), 50, no. 35. Lawrence McGinniss, *Catalogue of the Earl of Crawford's "Speculum Romanae Magnificentiae" now in the Avery Architectural Library* (New York, 1976), no. 138, cites an anonymous reverse copy published by Bolognino Zaltieri.

[21] The map is listed in Almagià, "Pirro Ligorio Cartografo," 52, 56. Apiano's 1528 map is listed in F. Van Ortroy, "Bibliographie de l'oeuvre de Pierre Apian," *Le Bibliographe moderne* 5 (1901): 89–156, 99, no. 4; and in Karrow, 54, no. 7/6. The map was also the basis for another of the same published in 1552, and another published in 1556 by the Viennese historiographer Wolfgang Lazius. It was also published anonymously by Giovanni Andrea Vavassore.

[22] The map is listed in Tinto, *Annali tipografici dei Tramezzino*, 46, no. 124; Tooley, 30, no. 252; Borroni Salvadori, *Carte, piante e stampe*, xx, and 27, no. 72; Almagià, "Pirro Ligorio Cartografo," 52; and Karrow, 226, no. 30/70.1. It is not listed in Bartsch. The print is signed in the lower left corner with the monogram "NB" which at times has been identified as Natale Bonifacio. Roberto Almagià, "Intorno all'opera cartografica di Natale Bonifaco," *Archivio storico per la Dalmazia* 14 (January, 1933): 481, describes it as the earliest known print by Bonifacio. Besides the fact that Bonifacio was only fifteen years old in 1553, there are also other reasons for identifying the monogram as that of Nicolas Beatrizet. Silvia Bianchi, "Apporti per Natale Bonifacio," *Rassegna di studi e di notizie* 10 (1982): 191, n. 32, also doubts that Bonifacio was the engraver (but mistakenly repeats Almagià's error in describing the print as published in Venice by Niccolò Tramezzino, rather than Michele Tramezzino). The print also carries the monogram of the English cartographer George Lily ("GLA" = Georgius Lilius Anglus), then resident in Rome, who made the map.

is protected by papal decree for ten years and that anyone copying or selling the print without permission will be excommunicated and fined five hundred gold ducats. Interestingly, although Tramezzino was in possession of a twenty-year Venetian *privilegio*, only the ten-year papal *privilegio* is referred to in the inscription; an indication that Tramezzino thought more highly of the papal *privilegio* than the Venetian *privilegio*. The prominence given to the papal *privilegio*, however, may also have been because the prints were no doubt also being sold (and possibly even printed) in Rome, where interest in prints of antiquities was much higher than in Venice. There was also considerable competition in Rome for prints in this category at this time, notably from the print publisher Antonio Lafrery (see Chapter 7), who was not above having copies made of unprotected prints issued by his rivals.

In the meantime, the Tramezzino brothers continued to publish books. On 24 September 1552, a *privilegio* was granted to Michele for works by Pietro Lauro, and five days later, on 29 September, another was granted to both Michele and Francesco for more books.[23] Then, two years later, on 28 July 1554, Michele alone published with a Venetian *privilegio* (and a papal *privilegio*) a two-part, circular *mappamondo* engraved by Giulio de Musi.[24]

Besides this *mappamondo*, Michele Tramezzino also published other prints, including several of Ligorio's restored antiquities and maps. On 3 November 1554, he was granted a twenty-year *privilegio* to print Pirro Ligorio's restored perspective view of the *Antique Port of Ostia*, engraved by Giulio de Musi.[25] Three years later, he was granted a *privilegio* for Ligorio's restored views of the *Theatre of Marcellus*, engraved by Jacob Bos and dated 1558, as well as for six maps:

---

[23] The *privilegio* for works by Pietro Lauro are recorded in ASV, ST, reg. 38, fol. 147r. (168r. n.n.), and ASV, RSP, Filze 284, nos. 4, 5. The *privilegio* granted to both Michele and Francesco Tramezzino is recorded in ASV, ST, reg. 38, fol. 147r.–v. (168r.–v. n.n.).

[24] The *privilegio* is recorded in ASV, ST, reg. 39, fol. 146r. (167r. n.n.). The map is listed in Tinto, *Annali tipografici dei Tramezzino*, 49, no. 133; Tooley, 17, no. 18; and Borroni Salvadori, *Carte, piante e stampe*, 82, nos. 248–49.

[25] The document is recorded in ASV, ST, reg. 39, fol. 187r. (208r. n.n.). The print is listed in Karrow, 351, no. 51/4; Tinto, *Annali tipografici dei Tramezzino*, 49, no. 134; Bartsch, 15: 508, no. 1. Huelsen, "Speculum Romanae Magnificentiae," 147, no. 25, lists a second edition dated 1558. An undated anonymous print showing a reconstruction of the harbour based on Ligorio's perspective view was published by Bolognino Zaltieri.

Norway (1558), *Gelders* (1558), *Flanders* (1555), *Brabant* (1568), *Holland* (1558), and *Naples* (1558).[26] At this time, Tramezzino also printed with a *privilegio* Bos's engraving of the *Baths of Diocletian and Maximian,* dated 1558, and Bos's map of *Frisia* (1558).[27]

The maps listed in the 1557 *privilegio,* and others published later, were issued either by Michele Tramezzino alone or in conjunction with his brother Francesco. Each one carries both a papal and a Venetian *privilegio.* Other maps designed by Pirro Ligorio include *France* (1558), *Belgium* (1558), and *Friuli* (1563).[28] Maps not designed

---

[26] The *privilegio* is recorded in ASV, ST, reg. 41, fols. 27v.–28r. (42v.–43r. n.n.): "i paesi di Narvegia, Gheldria, Fiandra, Brabantia, et holanda; Il Theatro di Marcello, et il Regno de Napolj." The print of the *Theatre of Marcellus,* labelled *THEATRVM-MARCELLI,* is inscribed in the upper right "PYRRO, LIGORIO.NEAP. INVE./ROMAE. M.D.L.VIII" and "Michaelis Tramezini formis/Cum privile Summi pont." An example is in the Farnesina, Rome, 44H30, inv. no. 70324. Of the six maps, the first, "Narvegia" (Norway) has not been identified, although it may be the map identified as *Northern Europe,* dated 1558, listed in Tinto, *Annali tipografici dei Tramezzino,* 61, no. 169; Tooley, 19, no. 40; and Borroni Salvadori, 34, no. 92. The map is a reduced copy of the large nine-sheet map by Cornelis Anthoniszoon. The map of *Gelders* is listed in Tinto, 53, no. 144; Tooley, 29, no. 231; and Borroni Salvadori, 29, no. 78. The map reproduces a nine-sheet map of Gelders compiled by Jacob van Deventer in 1542–43, though not printed (in Antwerp) until 1556. The map of *Flanders* is listed in Karrow, 380, no. 56/6.1; Tinto, 50, no. 136; Tooley, 27, no. 198; and Borroni Salvadori, 30, no. 80. The print is a copy on a reduced scale of Mercator's four-sheet map of Flanders published in 1540. The map of *Brabant* is listed in Tinto, 52, no. 142; Tooley, 24, no. 142; and Borroni Salvadori, 28, no. 75. It is a copy of map by Jacob van Deventer compiled in 1536 though not printed until 1546. The map of *Holland* is listed in Tinto, 53, no. 145; Tooley, 33, no. 298; and Borroni Salvadori, 29, no. 79. The map of *Naples* is listed in Karrow, 352, no. 51/5; Tinto, 55, no. 151; Almagià, "Pirro Ligorio Cartografo," 52, who gives the date as 1557; Carlo Castellani, *Catalogo ragionato delle più rare o più importanti opere geografiche a stampa che si conservano nella Biblioteca del Collegio romano* (Rome, 1876), 249, no. 123a; Tooley, 38, no. 403; and Borroni Salvadori, 23, no. 59.

[27] The *Baths of Diocletian and Maximian* is listed in Tinto, *Annali tipografici dei Tramezzino,* 61, no. 170; and in Huelsen, "Speculum Romanae Magnificentiae," 150, no. 37. The map of *Frisia* is listed in Tinto, 52, no. 143 (who gives the date as 1556); Tooley, 28, no. 218; and Borroni Salvadori, *Carte, piante e stampe,* 31, no. 82. The map is based on one compiled by Jacob van Deventer in 1545.

[28] The map of *France* is listed in Karrow, 352, nos. 51/6 and 177, 27/3.8; Tinto, *Annali tipografici dei Tramezzino,* 58, no. 161; Almagià, *Monumenta cartografica Vaticana,* 2: 21; Almagià, "Pirro Ligorio Cartografo," 54; Castellani, *Catalogo ragionato,* 241, no. 12a; Nils Adolf Eril Nordenskiöld, *Facsimile-Atlas to the Early History of Cartography* (Stockholm, 1889; repr., Liechtenstein, 1970), 119, no. 19; Tooley, 27, no. 208; and Borroni Salvadori, *Carte, piante e stampe,* 13, no. 33. Although the print is inscribed "Pyrrho Ligorio Neap auctore," the map is a copy reduced in size from the four-sheet woodcut copy by Giovanni Andrea Vavassore, dated 1538, of the original map by Oronce Fine first produced in 1525. The map of *Belgium* is listed in Karrow,

by Ligorio were also published, such as a map of *Portugal* by the mathematician and cartographer Fernando Alvares Seco, produced for the Spanish scholar Achilles Statius (or Stazio, i.e. Aquiles Estaço, 1524–1581) and dedicated by him to Cardinal Guido Ascanio Sforza, which was engraved by Sebastiano del Re and published in 1561.[29]

On 3 February 1561 [1560 m.v.], Michele and Francesco Tramezzino together were granted a *privilegio* for four maps by Pirro Ligorio of Ancient Rome, Greece, Spain, and Hungary.[30] Ligorio's map of *Ancient Rome* was engraved by Jacob Bos and published jointly by Michele and Francesco Tramezzino in 1561.[31] The map of *Greece* was engraved by Sebastiano del Re and dated 1561. The map of *Spain*, however, is dated 1559. Both were published also with a papal *privilegio*.[32] The same *privilegio* included engraved designs of the *Visitation of Our Lady* and a map of the city of *Antwerp*, but these prints have not been identified.

Meanwhile, on 25 June 1557, Michele Tramezzino was granted a *privilegio* by the Venetian Senate for a "cronica de Romani Pontificj" by Onofrio Panvinio, and on 29 August 1561 received another *privilegio*

352, no. 51/7; Tinto, 56, no. 156; Almagià, "Pirro Ligorio Cartografo," 55; Castellani, 248, no. 113a; Tooley, 23, no. 132; Borroni Salvadori, 15, no. 37. It is a reverse copy of an anonymous Italian copy of a lost French original by Gilles Boileau de Bouillon (Aegidius Boleanuus Bolionius). The map of *Friuli* is listed in Karrow, 356, no. 51/12; Tinto, 73, no. 200; Almagià, "Pirro Ligorio Cartografo," 59; Castellani, 249, no. 119a; Tooley, 29, no. 231; and Borroni Salvadori, 18, no. 46.

[29] The map is listed in Karrow, 472, no. 67/1; Tinto, *Annali tipografici dei Tramezzino*, 67, no. 190; Castellani, *Catalogo ragionato*, 248, no. 111a; Nordenskiöld, 122, no. 127; Tooley, 40, no. 456; Borroni Salvadori, *Carte, piante e stampe*, 12, no. 29.

[30] The document is recorded in ASV, ST, reg. 42, fol. 42v. [62v. nn]. The Tramezzino's supplication is transcribed in Howard Burns. "Pirro Ligorio's Reconstruction of Ancient Rome: The *Anteiqvae Vrbis Imago* of 1561," in *Pirro Ligorio: Artist and Antiquarian*, ed. Robert W. Gaston (Florence, 1988), 47, n. 21.

[31] The map, titled ANTEIQVAE VRBIS IMAGO ACCVRATISSIME EX VET-ERIBVS MONVMENTEIS FORMATA, is listed in Karrow, 354, no. 51/11; and Huelsen, *Piante Icnografiche e Prospettiche di Roma*, 52, VIIIa. An example is in BA, Vatican, St. Geogr. S. 97. Ligorio's reconstruction of Ancient Rome is discussed in Burns, 19–92. A reduced copy in two sheets was made by an anonymous engraver and published in Cologne in 1588.

[32] The map of *Greece* is listed in Karrow, 354, no. 51/10. The map of *Spain* is listed in Tinto, *Annali tipografici dei Tramezzino*, 62, no. 173. According to Marcel Destombes, "La grande carte d'Europe de Zuan Domenico Zorzi (1545) et l'activité cartographique de Matteo Pagano à Venise de 1538 à 1565," in *Studia z Dziejów Geografii i Kartografii*, ed. Jósef Babicz (Warsaw, 1973), 128, the map of Spain is a copy of that for which Fra Vincenzo Paletino de Curzole had been granted a Venetian *privilegio* in 1550 (see Chapter 10).

for Panvinio's edition of Platina's *Lives of the Popes*.[33] On 6 September 1567, he was granted a twenty-year *privilegio* by the Senate to print "the treatise of the edifices built by Pope Pius IV" by Pirro Ligorio. The book, however, does not appear to have been printed.[34] Besides maps and prints of antiquities and architecture, Michele Tramezzino also published in 1553 a print of the *Sacrifice of Iphigenia*, engraved by Nicolas Beatrizet, on which appears notice of papal copyright: "ROMÆ/MICHAELIS TRAMEZINI FORMIS/CVM PRIVILE-GIO SVMMI PONT/M D LIII."[35]

Giovanni Francesco Camocio

Unlike Michele Tramezzino, Giovanni Francesco Camocio was primarily a bookseller. On 18 July 1552, he and his partners, who described themselves as "book dealers residing in this illustrious city of Venice," had been granted a *privilegio* for fifteen years for two books, both translations from Greek into Latin.[36] Although Camocio

---

[33] Tramezzino's 1557 *privilegio* is recorded in ASV, ST, reg. 41, fol. 28r. (43r. n.n.). His 1561 *privilegio* is in ASV, ST, reg. 43, fol. 99v. (119v. n.n.). It may be noted that in 1557 Jacobus de Strada had published in Venice at his expense Panvinio's *Epitome pontificum romanorum* (from St. Peter to Pius IV) with both an imperial and Venetian *privilegio* (noted in Dennis Rhodes, *Silent Printers*, 194). Eleven years later, in 1568, Antonio Lafrery published ("Antonii Lafrerii formeis") in Rome Panvinio's *XXVII Pontificum Maximorum elogia et imagines accuratissime ad vivum aeneis typeis delineatae*. The series of engraved portraits of popes begins with Urban VI (portrait on right page, text on left). The last portrait, of Pius V, is signed by the engraver Philippe Soye in the bottom left corner ("Philippus Soius fecit"). A copy is in the Houghton, Harvard, Typ 525.68.672F (catalogued in Mortimer, *Italian 16th Century Books*, no. 356). Panvinio's activities are discussed in Clare Robertson, *'Il Gran Cardinale' Alessandro Farnese, Patron of the Arts* (New Haven and London, 1992), 220–223. For a map of *Antique Rome* by Panvinio, see Chapter 10.

[34] The document is recorded in ASV, ST, reg. 46, fol. 156v. (180v. n.n.). The book is not listed in Tinto, *Annali tipografici dei Tramezzino*.

[35] The print is listed in Bartsch, 15: 261, no. 43. The plate is preserved in the Calcografia, Rome, inv. no. 1143. It has been suggested by Evelina Borea, "Stampe da Modelli Fiorentini nel Cinquecento," in *Firenze e La Toscana dei Medici nell'Europa del Cinquecento: Il Primato del disegno* (Florence, 1980), 272, no. 729; and by Stefania Massari and Simonetta Prosperi Valenti Rodinò, *Tra mito e allegoria: immagini a stampa nel '500 e '600* (Rome, 1989), 250, no. 96, that the print is after a drawing by Francesco Salviati.

[36] Camocio's *privilegio* is recorded in ASV, ST, reg. 38, fol. 133r. (154r. n.n.). The first of the two books, *Meletii Philosophi. Natura structuraque hominis opus*, etc., was printed in 1552 (the colophon reads: "Venetiis ex officina Gryphii, sumptibus vero Francisci Camotii et sociorum. Anno MDLII"). The second book, *Commentarii in Aristotelis libros metheorologicos Io. Bapt. Camotio interprete*, however, was not printed until

continued to publish books over the next fifteen years, he also operated a copperplate printing press at his bookshop located at S. Leo
where he printed many engravings, including numerous maps. The
earliest, dated 1560, include a *Planisfero* by Giacomo Gastaldi, a nau-
tical map of the *New World* by Niccolò de' Nicolai (both engraved
by Paolo Forlani), and a map of *Lombardy*.[37] In order to protect these
activities, in 1567 he submitted a supplication to the Senate for a
privilegio. He states in his supplication that he wishes:

> to put forth for the public advantage various drawings both of devo-
> tion, countries and combined or separate provinces, both in large and
> small format, by the hand of various men of merit, which I have now
> had engraved in copper and since it has occurred to me during the
> past time to cause many fine works to be put forth at great expense,
> which have immediately been counterfeited by others thereby causing
> great losses to me, I, Giovanni Francesco Camocio, on my knees,
> entreat Your Highness that all kinds of pictures, both devotional and
> portraits, geographies, both combined and individual, and all kinds of
> drawings [i.e. designs] which I shall cause to be engraved in copper
> and which have not been made by anyone else, nor of those made in
> the form and size I shall make during a period of 15 next years, no
> one else than me, or else depending on my will, may make, nor cause
> to be made, nor, if made by others, sell nor cause to be sold all the
> types mentioned in this supplication either in this glorious city or in
> the territories and areas of Your Illustrious Dominion under penalty
> of losing the engravings . . .[38]

The *privilegio* was granted on 2 October 1567 ("a Gio. franc.o Camocio
per diversi dissegni di figure, come paesi, provincie . . .).[39] The following year Camocio submitted another supplication for *privilegio*,
also for "diversi dissegni di figure," which the Senate granted him
on 12 October 1568.[40] Among the prints issued by Camocio with
this last *privilegio* were a *Resurrection* engraved by Martino Rota in

---

1556 and, according to the inscription on the frontispiece, which reads simply "apud
Fr. Camotium," was published by Camocio alone. The translation, from Greek into
Latin, was by the famous Hellenist Giovanni Battista Camocio, who is not to be
confused with Giovanni Francesco Camocio, although both came from Asola.
[37] The two Forlani maps are listed in David Woodward, *The Maps and Prints of
Paolo Forlani: A Descriptive Bibliography* (Chicago, 1990), 1, no. 01.01; and 2, no. 03.01.
The map of *Lombardy* is listed in Borroni Salvadori, *Carte, piante e stampe*, 17, no. 43.
[38] The translation of Camocio's supplication is given in Rodolfo Gallo, "Gioan
Francesco Camocio and his Large Map of Europe," *Imago Mundi* 7 (1950): 93–94.
[39] The document is recorded in ASV, ST, reg. 46, fol. 168v. (192v. n.n.).
[40] The document is recorded in ASV, ST, reg. 47, fol. 50v. (71v. n.n.), and filza.

1569, and perhaps also Rota's undated *Virgin at the Foot of the Cross* after Michelangelo.[41] Camocio also appears to have published with a *privilegio* an anonymous copy of Cornelis Cort's 1567 engraving of the *Visitation*, possibly after Marco Pino.[42] In 1570, he published with a *privilegio* an anonymous engraving (sometimes attributed to Giovanni Battista Scultori) of *Attilius Regulus in the Barrel* after a design by Giulio Romano.[43]

Camocio published several maps with the *privilegio*. Two of them are of Europe, both dated 1568: *Europa brevis, ac novissima descriptio*, and *Europa in forma piccola*, engraved by Domenico Zenoi. A map of *Morea* with a *privilegio* is dated 1569, as is a map of *Istria*. A *privilegio* also appears on a map of *Cyprus* published by Camocio in 1570.[44]

Giovanni Andrea Vavassore

The Venetian publisher Giovanni Andrea Vavassore (or Valvassore; also called Guadagnino) began his career as a printmaker, but around 1530 also took up printing.[45] Before November 1530 he produced

---

[41] Rota's *Resurrection* is not listed in Bartsch, but is listed in Passavant, 6: 185, no. 115; and in Zani, 2, 9: 69. An example is in the BN, Paris, Eb 12, fol. p. 11. The print is inscribed "Apud Ioanne[s] Franciscu[m] Camociu/Cum Privilegio." Camocio's address also appears, without a *privilegio*, on Rota's *Baptism of Christ* (Bartsch, 16: 3), *St. Jerome* (Passavant, 6: 185, no. 118); and Michelangelo's *Pietà*. Rota's *Virgin at the Foot of the Cross* is listed in Bartsch, 16: 25; and Zani, 2, 8: 198. A document in the Venetian archives records Martino Rota's presence in Venice as early as 10 April 1543 (ASV, Cancelleria Inferiore, Archivio del Doge, Lettere, reg. 10, fol. 9r.).

[42] Cort's print is listed in Bierens de Haan, 51, no. 27a.

[43] The print is listed in Bartsch, 15: no. 36. It is inscribed "VENETIIS/Apud Joannum Franciscum Camocium/M.D.LXX" with below "Cum privilegio."

[44] The maps of Europe and of *Morea* are listed in Gallo, "Gioan Francesco Camocio," 96. The map of *Morea* is inscribed "co[n] privilegi. Appresso Gioan Francesco Camocium. In Vinegia 1569." The maps of *Istria* and *Cyrpus* are listed Karrow, 123, no. 21/27.2; 8, no. 1/58. The date of the map of *Istria* is given incorrectly as 1562 by Gallo, "Gioan Francesco Camocio," 95.

[45] Vavassore's name as printmaker first appears on a set of prints of the *Labours of Hercules* ("Opera di Giovanni Andrea Valvassori detto Guadagnino"), and on the frontispiece of two books: "Sovan [sic] Andrea de Vavasori" on the title-page of *La Conuersione De Sancta Maria Madalena e La Vita De Lazaro e Marta. In ottaua Rima Hystoriata. Co[m]posta p[er] Maestro Marcho Rasiglia Da Foligno* printed in Venice in 1513, and "Jovan Andrea de Vavassori F." on the frontispiece of *Thesauro spirituale volgare in rima et hystoriato*, printed in Venice in 1518. Both books were printed by Nicolò Zoppino (i.e. Nicolo d'Aristotile detto Zoppino) and Vincenzo di Paolo da Venezia. He also produced numerous prints of maps, though none with a *privilegio*. Vavassore's maps are described in Leo Bagrow, *Giovanni Andreas di Vavassore. A*

and published a block book, *Opera nova contemplativa per ogni fidel christiano*, the one hundred and twenty illustrations in which have been attributed to Giovanni Andrea Vavassore's brother, Florio.[46] Passavant believes that the initials "F.F.," which appear on three sheets of a set of seven woodcuts of the planets published by Giovanni Andrea, are Florio's.[47] The brothers also published works jointly.

On 9 May 1553, Giovanni Andrea submitted a supplication to the Senate in which he stated that he had, with very great labour and expense, gathered together "figures designed by the excellent masters" ("figure designate da Maestri eccelenti") which he had engraved for inclusion in new editions of Petrarch, Boccaccio, and Ariosto's *Orlando Furioso*.[48] On 15 March 1560, he was granted another *privilegio* for the book *Della guerra di Campagna di Roma, et del Regno di Napoli, nel Pontificado di Paolo III* . . . by Alessandro Andrea Napolitano, which he published the same year.[49] In 1557 he published a quarto edition of Lorenzo Spirito's fortune-telling book, *Libro de la ventura*.[50] Vavassore also printed and published pattern books (see Chapter 12). On 23 March 1566, he received a *privilegio* for several more books.[51]

Venetian Cartographer of the 16th Century. A Descriptive List of His Maps (Jenkintown, 1939).

[46] The block book is catalogued in Mortimer, *Italian 16th Century Books*, no. 518; and Hind, *History of Woodcut*, 2: 239–40. The illustrations are noted in Prince d'Essling [Victor Massena], *Études sur l'art de la gravure sur bois à Venise. Les livres à figure vénitiens de la fin du XVᵉ siècle et du commencement du XVIᵉ* (Florence, 1907–1914), pt. 3, 114.

[47] Passavant, 5: 89. It may be noted that the initials "F.F." also appear on a map of Wittenburg, dated c. 1568 (Borroni Salvadori, *Carte, piante e stampe*, 65, no. 197) and on an undated map of Siena (ibid., 73, no. 223).

[48] The *privilegio* is recorded in ASV, ST, reg. 39, fol. 17v. (38v. n.n.) and filza. The *privilegio* refers to "nove figure, & nove additioni sopra Il Furioso dell' Ariosto, Il Petrarcha, et il Boccaccio." According to Hofer, "Illustrated Editions of 'Orlando Furioso'," 31, Vavassore's edition of Ariosto's *Orlando Furioso* was published in 1548. The *privilegio*, therefore, must refer to a later revised edition (with "nove figure et nove additioni") not mentioned by Hofer. Only the 1553 edition is discussed by Enid T. Falaschi, "Valvassore's 1553 illustrations of *Orlando furioso*: the development of multi-narrative technique in Venice and its links with cartography," *La Bibliofilia* 77 (1975): 227–251.

[49] The *privilegio* is recorded in ASV, ST, reg. 42, fol. 123r.–v. (142r.–v. n.n.).

[50] Vavassore's 1557 edition of Lorenzo Spirito's fortune-telling book, *Libro de la ventura*, is not included in Tammaro de Marinis, "Le illustrazioni per il *Libro de le sorte* di Lorenzo Spirito," in Tammaro de Marinis, *Appunti e ricerche bibliografiche* (Milan, 1940), 69–83.

[51] The *privilegio* is recorded in ASV, ST, reg. 46, fol. 15r. (39r. n.n.).

Giovanni Ostaus

On 30 June 1556, a *privilegio* was granted to the German publisher Giovanni Ostaus for a book *Contemplatio totius vitae et passionis Domini Nostri Iesv Christi*, which was published the following year, and for a design of the *Crucifixion* "con alcune scritture intorno" by the painter Giuseppe Porta Salviati. The book consisted of forty-nine half-page woodcuts of the life of Christ each with an accompanying Latin distich, a selection from the Bible, and a prayer. Salviati's print of the *Crucifixion* had been approved by the Riformatori dello Studio di Padova and a printing license granted for it by the Chiefs of the Council of Ten on 19 May 1556.[52] The same *privilegio* also covered a book of embroidery patterns, with an illustration by Salviati, that Ostaus published the same year (see Chapter 12).

The Bertelli

The Bertelli family published mostly books, some of them with a *privilegio*. Luca Bertelli, for example, who is described as a "libraro" in Padua, was granted a *privilegio* on 23 March 1566 for an edition of Hippocrates's *De capitis vulneribus* by the anatomist Gabriele Fallopio.[53] The Bertelli also published numerous prints, some of which were granted a *privilegio*. On 5 June 1582, for example, a *privilegio* was granted to Luca Bertelli for a copperplate engraving of the *Martyrdom of Santa Giustina* by Paolo Veronese. The print, engraved on two sheets by Agostino Carracci, reproduces Veronese's altarpiece, the *Martyrdom of Santa Giustina*, painted in 1565 for the private chapel of the abbot of the Benedictine monastery and church of Santa Giustina in Padua. Bertelli was evidently granted also a Royal *privilegio* and a papal *privilegio*.[54]

---

[52] The *privilegio* granted Ostaus is recorded in ASV, ST, reg. 40, fol. 120v. (140v. n.n.). The license for the *Crucifixion* is recorded in ASV, CCXN, reg. 16, fol. 126r. The print is catalogued in Rosand and Muraro, cat. no. 85.

[53] The document is recorded in ASV, ST, reg. 46, fol. 15r. (39r. n.n.). Bertelli published the book the same year as *In Hippocratis librum de vulneribus capitis Gabrielis Falloppii medici clarissimi expositio*.

[54] The document is recorded in ASV, ST, reg. 54, fol. 28r. (69r. n.n.). The painting is now in the Museo Civico, Padua. The print is catalogued in Bohlin, *Prints and Related Drawings by the Carracci Family* (Washington, D.C., 1979), cat. no. 105. It is inscribed "Cum Privilegijs/Summi Pontificis Caes Maestatis Regis Catholici et Senatus Veneti." An inscription in the margin concludes "Venetijs Kal. Iun. MDLXXXII Clmae D.V. Addictissimi Lucus Bertellus, et socius Aug.s Car. fe."

Another member of the family, Donato Bertelli, who was also a "libraro," printed Gastaldi's map of Asia in 1559 (see Chapter 10). In 1564, Ferando Bertelli issued with a *privilegio* a large sheet illustrating various proverbs engraved by Nicolo Nelli.[55]

Nicolo Nelli

Nicolo Nelli worked as both an engraver and a publisher. In 1563, he published two prints engraved by Gaspare Osello (Gasparo ab Avibus) copied from prints by Giorgio Ghisi, a *Diana and Endymion* and *Apollo and the Muses*, both after designs by Luca Penni.[56] In 1564, he issued two more prints engraved by Osello, a *Venus and the Rose*, also after Penni, and a *Last Supper* after Lambert Lombard.[57] Ghisi's print of Lombard's *Last Supper* had been published with an eight-year imperial *privilegio* (evidently ignored by Osello or Nelli) by Hieronymus Cock in Antwerp in 1551 (see also Appendix B). All four prints were later acquired by Lafrery and re-published by him in Rome. In 1565, Nelli published Osello's copy of Giorgio Ghisi's print of Raphael's fresco of the *Disputà* which had been published in 1552 also with an eight-year imperial *privilegio* by Cock.[58] The same year, he printed Osello's engraving of the *Holy Family with St. Anne* after Giorgio Vasari.[59] In 1567, Nelli published an anonymous copy of Marco Dente's print of the *Madonna Reading with the Christ Child* after Raphael.[60]

---

[55] An example of the print is in the BN, Paris, Ba 1 (XVI), vol. 5.

[56] The *Diana and Endymion* is listed in Bartsch, 15: 402, no. 43-copy; and in Boorsch and Lewis, *The Engravings of Giorgio Ghisi* (New York, 1985), 91, no. 21. The print is a reverse copy of Ghisi's print of 1556. An example with Nelli's address is in the BN, Paris, Eb 11a, fol. The *Apollo and the Muses* is listed in Bartsch, 15: 406, no. 458-copy; and in Boorsch and Lewis, 99, no. 23, Copy 2.

[57] The *Venus and the Rose* is listed in Bartsch, 15: 400, no. 40-Copy; and in Boorsch and Lewis, 95, no. 22. The print is a copy of Ghisi's print of 1556. The *Last Supper* is listed in Bartsch, 15: 387, no. 6; and in Boorsch and Lewis, 64, no. 12, Copy.

[58] Ghisi's original print is listed in Bartsch, 15: 394, no. 23. Osello's copy is listed in Boorsch and Lewis, 68, no. 13, Copy.

[59] The print is listed in Borea, "Stampe da Modelli Fiorentini nel Cinquecento," 282, no. 777.

[60] Marco Dente's original print is listed in Bartsch, 14: 54, no. 48. The anonymous copy published by Nelli is listed in Stefania Massari, et al., *Raphael invenit* (Rome, 1985), 196, 3.

Giacomo Franco

Giacomo Franco (1550–1620) was an engraver but worked primarily as a publisher. He was the natural son of the painter and engraver Giovanni Battista Franco (also known as Battista Franco and by the nickname "il Semolei," c. 1510–1561). His earliest *privilegio* would appear to be that granted on 17 June 1586 for a print of the *Miraculous Virgin of Treviso* (the Madonna Grande di Treviso) with her miracles in both copperplate and woodcut.[61] In the following decade, he also published a book on costumes worn by Venetian women, a sewing manual, and a writing book (see Chapter 12). In the early seventeenth century, Franco was evidently granted a *privilegio* for prints of drawings, including drawing studies of parts of the human body, entitled *Regole per imparar a disegnar i corpi humani* by the painter Jacopo Palma the Younger (also known as Palma Giovane, c. 1548– 1628). The book had first been published in Venice in 1608 in collaboration with Odoardo Fialetti (1573–1638) with the title *Il vero modo et ordine per dissegnar tutte le parti et membra del corpo humano.* Two years later, in 1611, Franco published *Regole per imparar à disegnar i corpi hvmani diuise in doi libri.* Each of the etched plates of studies is inscribed "Iacobus Franco formis con Priuilegio."[62]

Franco's name as publisher and holder of the *privilegio* also appears on a book of drawing studies by his father Giovanni Battista Franco. The book, *De excellentia et nobilitate delineationis libro duo*, which is a compilation of various prints by his father of antique cameos and animals, was published in "Venetijs aput Jacobus Franco ad signum solis con Privilegio."[63] The dedication is dated 20 September 1611.

---

[61] The *privilegio* is recorded in ASV, ST, reg. 57, fol. 54r.–v. (76r.–v. n.n.).

[62] The illustrations are listed in Bartsch, 16: nos. 2–27. An edition printed in Venice by Marco Sadeler in 1636 is catalogued in Carlo Pasero, "Giacomo Franco, editore, incisore e calcografo dei secoli XVI e XVII," *La Bibliofilia* 37 (1935): 352, no. 29.

[63] Prints from the book are listed in Bartsch, 16: nos. 81 ("Giacomo franco forma"), 82, 83, 84, 85, and 86. Giacomo Franco had earlier published a number of his father's engravings (see Bartsch, vol. 17).

CHAPTER SEVEN

PUBLISHERS OF PRINTS AND BOOKS IN ROME

Antonio Lafrery

Born in Orgelet in the parish of Besançon, France, in 1512, Antonio Lafrery (Antoine Lafrére) first emerges as a publisher in Rome in 1544. At the outset, he issued prints in three general subject categories: mythological, religious, and the antique. Within a few years, he expanded this range to include maps and plans, contemporary architecture, and portraits. Possibly as early as 1547, Lafrery had conceived the idea of collecting the prints he owned of antique architecture and sculpture, together with some contemporary (i.e. sixteenth-century) examples, and publishing them bound together in a single volume with the title-page *Speculum romanae magnificentiae*. Over the next six years, 1547–1553, Lafrery evidently focused almost exclusively on producing prints for the *Speculum*. During these same years he further increased his collection of plates by having copies made in his shop of prints that his principal rival in Rome, Antonio Salamanca, was publishing. In 1553, Salamanca went into partnership with Lafrery.[1]

Of the many prints issued by Lafrery over the course of his career, only a few carry a *privilegio*. The earliest would appear to be an anonymous engraving dated 1555 of an antique marble statue identified by Lafrery in his 1573 inventory as *Adonis* (Fig. 13).[2] The statue, then in the Palace of the Bishop of Aquino, according to the inscription on the print ("Antiquum ex pario marmore, in aedibus Hadriani episcopi Aquinatus"), is now in the Vatican. The print is inscribed

---

[1] Lafrery's career and printing activities are discussed in François Roland, "Un Franc-Comtois Editeur et Marchand d'Estampes a Rome au XVIᵉ Siècle: Antoine Lafrery (1512–1577)," *Mémoires de la Société d'émulation du Doubs* (Besançon) (1911): 320–378; Franz Ehrle, *Roma prima di Sisto V. La pianta di Roma Du Pérac-Lafréry del 1577* (Rome, 1908); and Christian Huelsen, "Das Speculum Romanae Magnificentiae des Antonio Lafreri," in *Collectanea Variae doctrinae Leoni S. Olschki* (Munich, 1921), 121–170.

[2] Ehrle, *Roma prima di Sisto V*, 56, line 242: "Adone statua di marmo nel palazzo del Vescovo d'Aquino."

Fig. 13. Anonymous, *Adonis*. 1555. Engraving.
Photo: Avery Architectural and Fine Arts Library, Columbia University
in the City of New York.

"Con gratia et privilegio Ant. Lafrerius Sequanus R.M. DLV."[3] Ten years later, in 1565, the *privilegio* appears on another print issued by Lafrery of the *Temple of Antoninus and Faustina* by an anonymous engraver (Fig. 14).[4] Identified as "Hoc templum in foro Romano," and including a plan below, the print is inscribed: "Ant. Lafreri aeneis formis cum gratia et/privilegio Romae an. M.D. LXV."

Besides antiquities, Lafrery also published prints with religious subjects. The *privilegio* appears inscribed on Philippe Soye's engraving of the *Madonna del Silenzio* after Michelangelo dated 1566 (Fig. 15).[5] He also issued prints of 'historical subjects'. The *privilegio* appears, for example, on Cornelis Cort's engraving of the *Battle of Hannibal and Scipio* after Giulio Romano dated 1567.[6] The inscription "Cum Gratia et Privilegio 1567" appears in the lower right. The print was published by Lafrery for Tommaso Cavalieri, but it is unclear to whom the *privilegio* was granted.[7]

Lafrery also published books illustrated with prints. On 16 October 1557, he had been granted a Venetian *privilegio* for Juan de Valverde's *Historia de la composicion del cuerpo humano*. The book had been approved by the Riformatori dello Studio di Padova on 4 October, and been granted a license by the Chiefs of the Council of Ten on 9 October 1557. It included anatomical engravings by Nicolas Beatrizet.[8] In his

---

[3] The print is listed in Huelsen, "Speculum Romanae Magnificentiae," 155, no. 63. An example without the *privilegio* inscription is in the Casanatense, Rome, vol. 20.B.I.73/426.

[4] Huelsen, "Speculum Romanae Magnificentiae," 144, no. 9. The print is listed in Lafrery's inventory as "Tempio di Antinino et Faustina" (Ehrle, *Roma prima di Sisto V*, 55, line 174).

[5] The print is inscribed "Philippus Sericus fecit" and "Ant. Lafrerij formis Romae MDLXVI cum privilegio." It is listed in Lafrery's inventory as "Madonna di Mich. Ang" (Ehrle, *Roma prima di Sisto V*, 57, line 438).

[6] The print is listed in Bierens de Haan, 180, no. 197. It is listed in Lafrery's inventory as "Battaglia d'elefanti di Annibale et Scipione di Raf" (Ehrle, *Roma prima di Sisto V*, 56, line 296).

[7] The main inscription (bottom centre) reads: "EX ARCHETYPO RAPHAELIS VRBINATIS/QVOD EST APVD THOMAM CAVALERIVM PATRICIVM ROMANVS/EXCVDERABAT ROMAE ANTONIVS LAFRERIVS SEQVANI."

[8] The approval is recorded in ASV, RSP, Filze 284, no. 122. The license is recorded in ASV, CCXN, reg. 16, fol. 251v. The *privilegio* is in ASV, ST, reg. 41, fol. 52v. (67v. n.n.). The document granting the *privilegio* reads: "ad Antonio Lafrerij per l'istoria dell'anotomia de'l corpo humano composte in lingua latina Italiana, et spagnola dal Dottor Gio. di Valverde spagnolo." Italian editions of the book were published in 1558, 1559, and 1560. Bartsch refers to another Italian translation published in Venice by Giunti in 1586, and another Latin edition published by Giunti in 1589. According to Passavant, 6: 119, no. 115, all later editions, published in 1560, 1566, and 1589 in Venice and Antwerp, were printed with copies of Beatrizet's engravings. The engravings are listed in Bartsch, 15: 262, nos. 45–86.

Fig. 14. Anonymous, *Temple of Antoninus and Faustina*. 1565. Engraving.
Photo: Avery Architectural and Fine Arts Library, Columbia University
in the City of New York.

Fig. 15. Philippe Soye, *Madonna del Silenzio* (after Michelangelo). 1566.
Engraving. Photo: Courtesy of the Fogg Art Museum, Harvard
University Art Museums. Gift of Belinda L. Randall from the
collection of John Witt Randall.

supplication to the Venetian Senate, Lafrery specifically mentions the copperplate engravings ("con le figure intagliate in rame"). The project was most likely initiated by Lafrery's partner at the time, Antonio Salamanca, who had previously published books in Spanish.

In 1569 Lafrery issued an edition of engravings, attributed to Agostino Veneziano, of antique busts (beginning with Heraclitus and ending with that of Janus) published in Rome under the title *Inlustrium virorum ut exstant in urbe expressi vultus*.[9] The frontispiece of the second edition is inscribed "Cum Privilegio Sum: Pont:" with below "Formis Antonij Lafrerj." The first edition was dedicated to Cardinal Granvelle (Antoine Perrenot) by Achilles Statius (Aquiles Estaço), who had compiled the prints and supplied a preface.

Two years later, in 1571, Lafrery published with a papal *privilegio* Cort's print on two sheets of the *Annunciation with Four Prophets* after Federico Zuccaro's now lost fresco in the demolished Jesuit church S. Maria Annunziata, Rome (Fig. 16).[10] A *Portrait of Giovanni Parisotto di Valetta*, Grand Master of the Knights of Malta at the time of the Siege of Malta in 1565, engraved by Martino Rota, was published by Antonio Lafrery with a *privilegio* in 1575.[11]

Pietro Paolo Palumbo

Pietro Paolo Palumbo from Novara worked primarily as a print publisher. By 1586, his shop had been inherited by his heir Gaspare

---

[9] The book is listed in Lafrery's inventory as "Libro de Termini et Filosofi, cauati da marmi antichi, con la prefatione di messer Achille Tatio" (Ehrle, *Roma prima di Sisto V*, 59, line 592). An earlier edition contained forty busts, which was increased to fifty-two in the 1569 edition. Copies of this second edition can be examined in the BA, Vatican, Cicognara, VI, 2120, int. 2; and the Houghton, Harvard, Typ 525.68.672F (see Mortimer, *Italian 16th Century Books*, no. 173). The attribution of the engravings to Agostino Veneziano is doubtful.

[10] The print is listed in Bierens de Haan, 50, no. 26. An example is in the BN, Paris, Bb 16a, fol. 32 (and Ec 34, fol.). The print, which is mentioned by Carel van Mander, *Het Leven der doorluchtighe Nederlandtsche en Hoogduytsche schilders* (Haarlem, 1604), fol. 186, and Baglione, 271 (2nd ed., 388), is dedicated to Antoine Perrenot (Cardinal Granvelle), Viceroy of Naples. It is probably that listed as "Annunciata di Federico" in Lafrery's inventory (Ehrle, *Roma prima di Sisto V*, 57, line 387). The church of S. Maria Annunziata was demolished in 1626 to make room for the church of S. Ignazio.

[11] An example of the portrait is in the BN, Paris, Eb. 12, fol. p. 37. It is inscribed "ILLVSTRISS. F. IO. DE VALLETA SAC. RELIGIONIS HIEROSOL/M. M. MELITA. A. TVRCIS OBSESSA./M.D. LXV" and "Ant. Lafrerj formis Romæ cum Privilegio."

Fig. 16. Cornelis Cort, *Annunciation with Four Prophets* (after Federico Zuccaro). 1571. Engraving. Photo: Bibliothèque nationale de France.

Alberti who published a number of Palumbo's plates in a second
state. It would appear that Palumbo first began to publish prints in
1563 when he issued with a *privilegio* an anonymous engraving *Man
of Sorrows* (his earliest dated print). It is inscribed "Palumbi Navarien
curabat Romae 1563 cum privilegio."[12] The following year he published, also with a *privilegio*, an anonymous *Adoration of the Shepherds*
("Palumbi Novarien' curabant/Romae 1564 cum Privilegio").[13] He
continued to publish prints through the 1570s, sometimes in conjunction with Ascanio Palumbo.

Among the prints issued by Palumbo in the 1570s are two that
he reprinted in a second state with the original *privilegio*. Cornelis
Cort's print of the *Stoning of St. Stephen* after Marcello Venusti was
published by Palumbo in 1576 ("Romae apud P. Paulum Palumbum
Novarien A.D. MDLXXVI") with the words "forma prima" added to
the *privilegio* inscription. The following year, the print was issued again
("Romae apud P. Paulum Palumbum Novarien A.D. MDLXXVII"),
inscribed with the words "Cum Privilegio forma secunda" (Fig. 17).[14]
The following year, the same thing occurs again with Cort's engrav-
ing of Livio Agresti's *Last Supper* which Palumbo printed "Cum
Privilegio Forma Prima" in 1578, and in "forma secunda" in 1580.[15]
This use of the terms "forma prima" and "forma secunda" with a
privilegio would appear to be unique. In the meantime, Palumbo also
published Cort's 1577 print of *St. George Killing the Dragon* after Giulio
Clovio with a *privilegio* in 1578, and probably around the same time
Cort's print of Federico Zuccaro's *Birth of the Virgin*.[16]

---

[12] The print is listed in Zani, 2, 7: 254.

[13] Zani, 2, 5: 37. The print has been attributed to Beatrizet.

[14] The print is listed in Bierens de Haan, 110, no. 102; and in Zani, 2, 9: 204.
It was dedicated to Alessandro Sforza di Santa Fiora, Cardinale di Santa Maria in
Via. The print was re-issued again in a third state by Gaspare Alberti. Baglione,
21, mentions the print in his *vita* of Venusti.

[15] The print is listed in Bierens de Haan, 89, no. 76, who, however, believes the
"forma secunda" version to be not a later state but a copy of Cort's print by
Michelangelo Marelli. An example of the "Forma Prima" version is in the MFA,
Boston, Parker Coll. No. 1.555. The print, after Agresti's fresco in the Oratorio
del Gonfalone in Rome, was dedicated to Giulio Antonio Santori, Cardinal of
S. Severino. The plate is listed in the inventory of Cort's possessions compiled after
his death. Zani, 2, 7: 96, refers to a second state of the "forma prima" dated 1587,
and a third state with Gaspare Alberti's address. Heinecken, *Dictionnaire des Artistes*,
1: 58, lists an example published by Gaspare Ruspa in 1582 ("Casp. Rutz excud.
1582").

[16] The print of *St. George Killing the Dragon* is listed in Bierens de Haan, 138, no.
130; and in Arnolfo Bacotich, "Giorgio Giulio Clovio, 1498–1578 (Dalmatia?),"

Fig. 17. Cornelis Cort, *Stoning of St. Stephen* (after Marcello Venusti).
1577. Engraving. Photo: The Metropolitan Museum of Art, Harris
Brisbane Dick Fund, 1953 (53.601.345).

Bartolomeo Faletti

Bartolomeo Faletti was active as a print publisher in Rome in the 1560s. A document dated 1562, in which he is described as "Bartolomeo Faletti, book seller near Sant'Agostino," associates him with Antonio Salamanca and another book publisher named Vincenzo Luchini.[17] Faletti published mostly maps. In 1560, for example, he published an anonymous map of *Cyprus*, and in 1561, Giovanni Antonio Dosio's map of *Rome* engraved by Sebastiano del Re.[18] He also published Giovanni Battista de' Cavalieri's *Portrait of Pius IV*, which was printed with a *privilegio* in 1560.[19] Seven years later, in 1567, Faletti printed with a *privilegio* Stefano Dupérac's four engravings of Michelangelo's architecture on the Campidoglio (see Chapter 11).

Lorenzo Vaccari

Like Palumbo, Lorenzo Vaccari worked exclusively as a print publisher. He first emerges in the mid-1570s in Rome where he established a printing house that was continued into the seventeenth century by his sons Andrea and Michelangelo Vaccari. In the Jubilee Year of 1575 Vaccari published with a *privilegio* a series of prints of antique Rome engraved by Stefano Dupérac: "I VESTIGI/DELL'ANTICHITA DI ROMA/RACCOLTI ET RITRATTI IN PERSPETTIVA/CON OGNI DILIGENTIA/DA STEFANO DV PERAC PARISINO." Below is written: "IN ROMA appresso Lorenzo della Vaccheria alla/insegna della palma Con priuilegio del. Som. Pont./L'ANNO MDLXXV."[20] Two years later, in 1577, Vaccari printed with a *privilegio* Cornelis Cort's engraving of *St. Jerome in the*

Archivio Storico per la Dalmazia 20 (January 1936): 438, no. 1. The print of Federico Zuccaro's *Birth of the Virgin* is listed in Bierens de Haan, 45, no. 20. The print, like that of Livio Agresti's *Last Supper*, was dedicated to Giulio Antonio Santori, Cardinal of S. Severino. The second state carries the address of Gaspare Alberti.

[17] The document is recorded in ASR, Collegio Notai Capitolini, Busta 1520, Saccocius (1562), fol. 308r. Vincenzo Luchini also published prints (see Chapter 11).

[18] The map of *Cyprus* is listed in Borroni Salvadori, *Carte, piante e stampe*, 42, no. 122. The map of *Rome* is listed in Huelsen, "Speculum Romanae Magnificentiae," 142, no. 3; and in Borroni Salvadori, 104, no. 310.

[19] The *Portrait of Pius IV* is inscribed "PIVS. IIII. PONT./OPT. MAX./Typis Bart. Faleti. ROMÆ M.D. LX./cum privilegio." In the lower right is "Ioannes baptista de Caualeriis incid." An example is in the BN, Paris, Eb. 10, fol.

[20] The edition is noted in Thomas Ashby, "Le Diverse Edizioni dei 'Vestigi dell'Antichità di Roma' di Stefano Du Pérac," *La Bibliofilia* 16 (1915): 401–421.

Desert with Two Angels after Jacopo Palma il Giovane, and Cort's *Coronation of the Virgin with Saints Lawrence, Damasus* [this saint is also sometimes identified as St. Sixtus], *Peter, and Paul* after Federico Zuccaro's altarpiece on the main altar in the church of S. Lorenzo in Damaso in Rome.[21]

Claudio Duchetti

Claudio Duchetti (Claude Duchet), like his uncle Antonio Lafrery, was from Besançon in France. The earliest appearance of his address ("Claudii ducheti formis") is on a print of the Council of Trent titled "Congregatio patrum generalis sacri et oeucumenici tridentini concilii" printed in Venice and dated 1565 ("VEN. ANNO MDLXII-III").[22] Although the inscription would appear to indicate that Duchetti issued the print in Venice (and this in fact is most likely the case), it is also clear that Duchetti merely altered the date, and added his own address, to a print that had originally been published in Venice in 1563. However, at this time, and for the next ten years, Duchetti was indeed in Venice. His presence in the city a few years later, in 1570, is indicated by the appearance of his address (and the date) on a re-issued print of Paolo Forlani's map of the world, titled "Vniversale descrittione di tvtta la terra conoscivta fin qui," and on Martino Rota's print of *Mary Magdalen* after Titian.[23] At this time, his address also appears on several maps of islands: *Majorca* (1570), *Minorca* (1570), *Cyprus* (1570), *Crete* (1570), *Rhodes* (1570), and *Corfu* (1572), as well as on maps of *Constantinople* (1570), *Morea* (1570), *Germany* (1570), and *Europe* (1571), plus two undated maps: *Siena*, and *Jerusalem*, but datable to this period.[24] His address also appears on

---

[21] The prints are listed in Bierens de Haan, 139, no. 131; 147, no. 141.

[22] The print is noted in Borroni Salvadori, *Carte, piante e stampe*, xli; and listed in Huelsen, "Speculum Romanae Magnificentiae," 166, no. 131.

[23] The map of the world is listed in Borroni Salvadori, *Carte, piante e stampe*, 90, no. 269. Forlani's map, which had been issued by Fernando Bertelli in 1565 (listed in Karrow, 241, no. 30/93.1; and Rodney Shirley, *The Mapping of the World: Early Printed World Maps 1472–1700* (London, 1993), 133, no. 115), was in turn a new rendering of Gastaldi's map of 1546 in a larger format (Karrow, 218, no. 30/3; Shirley, 96, no. 85). Another version, dated 1571, has printed tablets containing texts on the wanderings of the apostles St. Peter and St. Paul. Rota's print of *Mary Magdalen* is listed in Bartsch, 16: 24.

[24] The maps are listed in Tooley, 36, no. 357; 37, no. 393; 26, no. 186 (not no. 181, as in Borroni Salvadori); 26, no. 178; 41, no. 465; 25, no. 156; 38, no. 400;

later states of maps of *Antwerp*, *Calais*, and *Tripoli*, and, with the date 1571, on a later state of Sebastiano del Re's engraving of Pirro Ligorio's map of *France*, first published in 1558 by Michele Tramezzino (see Chapter 6).[25]

Archival evidence indicates that Duchetti left Venice in 1576 and moved to Rome where he went to work in the print shop of his uncle Antonio Lafrery.[26] Before long, however, his suspicious nature and his accusations of stealing led to unrest among the other members of the workshop and Lafrery asked him to leave. By 1577, he was evidently working in Sicily, where he was joined by one of Lafrery's former assistants Giacomo Gherardi (Jacques Guérard). While in Sicily, news reached Duchetti that Lafrery had died in Rome and that he was the heir to Lafrery's estate, together with his cousin, Stefano [Étienne] Duchetti. Shortly after receiving the news, Duchetti, together with Gherardi, returned to Rome, arriving at the shop on Via del Parione on 9 October 1577. On 28 November began the difficult and protracted process of dividing up Lafrery's estate (Lafrery had died intestate) between Claudio and Stefano, which was not completed until 1581.

Meanwhile, during the years the estate was being settled, Claudio Ducchetti continued to issue prints from the shop in Rome. As he had earlier in Venice, he continued to publish maps. During these same years, the engraver Ambrogio Brambilla engraved several prints for Duchetti. The earliest of these are two prints dated 1579 of the *Vatican Palace and Gardens* (which is a copy of Mario Cartari's view of the same dated 1574), and *Castel S. Angelo with la Girandola*.[27] Over

---

30, no. 257 (the print is inscribed: "Opera di Iacopo di gataldi Cosmografo" and "Per Claudio ducheto 1570"); 19, no. 39 (the print, inscribed "Claudio Ducheto exc. L'anno M.D. LXXI," was dedicated by Forlani to Franco Morandi); 43, no. 522; 35, no. 339, respectively. Most of the maps are also listed in Borroni Salvadori, *Carte, piante e stampe*, 41, no. 116; 40, no. 115; 39, no. 110; 39, no. 109; 80, no. 242; 38, no. 105; 26, no. 71; 8, no. 17; 21, no. 54; and 81, no. 246.
[25] The maps are listed in Borroni Salvadori, *Carte, piante e stampe*, 66, no. 200; 88, no. 265 (the print was first issued by Lafrery); 105, no. 315 (the print is a later state of that published by Lafrery in 1560); 13, no. 33.
[26] This and the following information is drawn from a document in ASR, Archivio de Tribunale del Governatore di Roma, vol. 255, Costituti dal 26 Ottobre 1577 al 18 Gennaro 1578, D. Ascanius Caracciolus pro Charitale Notus, fol. 11v.ff. The document has been partially transcribed and its contents discussed in Gian Ludovico Masetti Zannini, "Rivalità e Lavoro di Incisori nelle Botteghe Lafréry-Duchet e de la Vacherie," in *Les Fondations nationales dans la Rome pontificale* (Rome, 1981), 547–566.
[27] The print of the *Vatican Palace and Gardens* is listed in Huelsen, "Speculum Romanae Magnificentiae," 166, no. 129; and in McGinniss, no. 264. It is inscribed

the next three years Duchetti published numerous other prints by Brambilla (see below). Between 1580 and 1582, he also published prints by Pietro Perret, Diana Mantuana, and Natale Bonifacio.

It was at the height of this activity that Duchetti applied for a papal *privilegio*. Although a copy of the granting document has not come to light, the entry in Index 752 for the month of May 1582 records that a ten-year *privilegio* was granted to Duchetti for two books of prints, one of popes and one of emperors.[28] The latter book would appear to be that printed by Duchetti in 1582 containing 135 small portraits of emperors, from Julius Caesar to Rudolf II, engraved by Ambrogio Brambilla, with the title *OMNIVM IMPERATORVM A C. IVLIO CAESARE VSQVE AD ANNVM PRAESENTEM ICCONES* [sic], although it does not carry a notice of *privilegio*.[29] The book of popes presumably is that entitled *OMNIVM PONTIFICIVM A S. PETRO VSQVE AD PRAESENTEM* with engraved portraits by Ambrogio Brambilla. The earliest edition known to Christian Huelsen, however, is dated 1585 and contains 237 small portraits of popes from St. Peter up to Sixtus V (elected in 1585).[30] Very possibly Duchetti issued an earlier edition, soon after 1582, with 236 portraits up to Gregory XIII.

Bartolomeo Grassi

On 1 October 1584, the publisher Bartolomeo Grassi was granted a *privilegio* the text of which includes references to two books illustrated

---

"Vero dissegno deli Stupendi Edefitii Giardini Boschi Fontane Et Cose Maravigliose di Belvedere in Roma" and "Romae Claudii duchetti formis 1579." The *Castel S. Angelo with la Girandola* is listed in Huelsen, 166, no. 127; and in McGinniss, no. 273. It is inscribed "Claudii Duchetti formis" and "Io. Ambr. Bram. inven. fec./1579." An example is in the BN, Paris, Ba 1 (XVI).

[28] The *privilegio* is indexed in ASVat, Index 752, fol. 129r.

[29] The book is listed in Huelsen, "Speculum Romanae Magnificentiae," 166, no. 134. The book is very probably that listed under "Libri diversi" in the inventory of Duchetti's heir, Giacomo Gherardi, in 1594 as "De retratti d'Imperatori..." (Ehrle, *Roma prima di Sisto V*, 48, line 56).

[30] Huelsen, "Speculum Romanae Magnificentiae," 166, no. 135. Subsequent editions were brought out by Duchetti's heirs as new popes assumed the throne. Portraits of Urban VII and Gregory XIV were added in an edition published by the heirs of Claudio Duchetti ("Apud hered. Cl. Ducheti"), and in 1592 another edition added Innocent IX and Clement VIII. This last edition is probably that listed under "Libri diversi" in the inventory of Duchetti's heir, Giacomo Gherardi, in 1594: "De Pontefici sino a Clemente ottavo" (Ehrle, *Roma prima di Sisto V*, 48, line 52).

with engravings by Mario Cartari.[31] One of the items listed is for a
book of the antiquities of Pozzuoli ("Antiquitates Puteolor[um]"). The
book was printed by Grassi in 1584 with twenty engraved plates by
Cartari, plus a map of Pozzuoli titled *Explicatio . . . Puteolis spectantur*.[32]
The text, in both Latin and Italian which accompanies the plates,
was provided by Alfonso Ciaccono (Alonso Chacón).

The other book named in the *privilegio* was the seven works of
mercy ("septem opera misericordiae corporalis, et sp[irit]ualis"), which
was published with the title *Icones operum misericordiae*. The two parts
of the book, the *pars prior* and the *pars posterior*, were printed together
with a text by Julius Ruscius (or Roscius) [Hortini] (i.e. Giulio Roscio
Ortini). The frontispiece of the first part, showing the Seven Acts of
Mercy in rectangular panels down the sides and along the bottom,
was engraved by Cristofano Cartari ("C. Cart. fe."). The frontispiece
of the second part was engraved by Mario Cartari, who was also
responsible for engraving the remaining sixteen plates. The designs
for the plates in the first part were copied from a series of prints,
the first titled "Septem opera misericordia corporalia . . .," engraved
by Philippe Galle in 1577.[33] Grassi had the book printed by Bartolomeo
Bonfadino in 1585.[34]

On 19 November 1585, Grassi was granted another *privilegio* by
Sixtus V, this time for several books, among them an edition of the
works of Lucius Annaeus Seneca, corrected and emended by the
French humanist and scholar Marc Antoine Muret ("opera Lucij
Annei Senece correcta et emendata cum annotationibus Marci Antonij
Muretti"), and an Italian translation of Juan Gonzalez de Mendoça's
history of China, *Dell'historia della China*.[35] Of special interest, how-

---

[31] The *privilegio* is recorded in ASVat, SB, 60, fol. 376r.–v., 379r.–v.; *Motu proprio*, fols. 377v.–378r.

[32] The map of Pozzuoli is listed in Destombes, 249, no. 91. It may be noted that in a letter dated 24 December 1589, Philippus van Winghe in Rome wrote to Abraham Ortelius informing him that Cartari's map was among those he had recently acquired (noted by Borroni Salvadori, "Cartaro, Mario," in *Dizionario biografico degli Italiani*, 20: 798).

[33] Evidence of this is found in a copy of the *Icones* in the Houghton, Harvard, Typ 525.86.752F.

[34] The colophon is dated 1585: "Ex Typographia Bartholomaei Bonfadini, In via Peregrini. M.D. LXXXV." A copy is in the BA, Vatican, R.G. Teologia II. 370. The *Icones* was dedicated by Grassi to Claudio Aquaviva, the general of the Jesuits.

[35] The *privilegio* is recorded in ASVat, SB, 116, fol. 414v. Seneca's book is listed in Fernanda Ascarelli, *Le cinquecentine romane*, 257; and in Adams, 2: 202, no. 889. It was printed by Francesco Zannetti in 1585. *Dell'historia della China*, which Grassi

ever, in this same *privilegio* document is a book described as "librum de allusionibus stemmatibus seu impressis et emblematibus super armis seu insignibus a Dilecto filio Principio fabricio Canonico Aprutinensis utriusque Iuris Doctore compilatum." This can be identified as Principio Fabricio's *Delle allusioni, imprese, et emblemi del Sig. Principio Fabricii da Teramo sopra la vita, opere, et attioni di Gregorio XIII Pontefice Massimo libri VI* printed by Grassi with 256 engraved illustrations (including the frontispiece) by Natale Bonifacio.[36] The book was slow to appear (it was not published by Bartolomeo Grassi and Giacomo Ruffinelli until 1588), which Fabricio himself blamed on the slowness of the engravers in preparing the plates and the problems involved in printing a book with engraved illustrations. Fabricio complained that the process was time-consuming because it required two separate printings on different presses, once for the letters on one press and again for the plates on another ("in due volte, cioè le lettere, & i Rami seperatamente, & in diuersi tempi, & tal'hora in diuersi luoghi . . .").[37]

A few words may be interjected here about the engraver Natale Bonifacio. The work undertaken for Fabricio was not the first of Bonifacio's engraving projects but it stands at the beginning of an intensely busy period of seven years terminating only with the engraver's death on 23 February 1592. The term "engraving" must be used loosely because Bonifacio appears to have made extensive use of etching and engraving together. In the contract drawn up with Andrea Bacci (see below), for example, reference is made to

---

had printed by Giovanni Martinelli in 1586, is a translation of *Historia de las cosas mas notables, ritos y costumbres del gran reyno de la China sabidas assi por los libros de los mismos Chinas, como por relacion de religiosos, y otras personas que han estado en el dicho reyno,* printed together with an Italian translation by Francesco Avanzo: *Viaggio fatto da Siviglia alla China dal P.F. Martino Egnatio . . .* (i.e. Martín Ignacio de Loyola). It had been first published, "Con Privilegio y Licencia de sa Sanctidad," in Valencia, Spain, in 1585.

[36] The frontispiece is inscribed below: "In Roma Appresso/Bartolomeo Grassi,/Con Licentia de Superiori,/Et Priuilegio. l'anno. 1588./Intagliati da Natal Bonifatio da Sib." The complete text of the *privilegio* is printed near the beginning of the book. Fabricii [or Fabrizi] dedicated the work to his lord and patron ("mio Signore, & padrone") Giacomo Boncompagni on 13 June 1588. A copy of the book is in the Houghton, Harvard, Typ 525.88.381. Another copy of the book is in the Casanatense, Rome, N. t.22 ccc. The colophon of the 1588 edition reads: "ROMÆ, Apud Iacobum Ruffinellum/M.D. LXXXVIII." Grassi was in partnership with Ruffinelli from 1584 to 1591.

[37] Noted in Mortimer, *Italian 16th Century Books*, no. 177.

Bonifacio's working in both engraving and etching ("a bulini ed acqua forte"). Originally from Sibenik in Dalmatia, and following a period of perhaps four years spent in Venice, Bonifacio had arrived in Rome probably in 1574 when his name appears on 19 March of that year among those proposed for membership in the Virtuosi al Pantheon.[38] Three years later, on 2 May 1577, he signed his name as witness to a document concerning the house Giovanni Battista de' Cavalieri was renting next to his print shop on the Vicolo Savelli towards the Via del Pellegrino.[39] Initially he seems to have worked for Antonio Lafrery whose address appears on Bonifacio's engraving of the *Saviour with the Globe*, dated 1577, and subsequently for Lorenzo Vaccari for whom he engraved *The Holy Shroud*, dated 1579, and possibly also some copies of prints by Cornelis Cort. By 1580 his plates were being printed by Claudio Duchetti. Duchetti's name as publisher appears, for example, on two prints dated 1580 by Bonifacio concerning the teachings of St. Augustine. In the same year Duchetti also printed Bonifacio's map of *Palermo*, and his engraving of the *Farnese Bull*, which Bonifacio himself dedicated to Cardinal Alessandro Farnese. A view of *Maastricht* shown under siege by Alessandro Farnese, printed by Vaccari, was engraved by Bonifacio in 1585. Two years later, in 1587, he produced a map of *Abruzzo* carrying the address

[38] Bonifacio was in Venice by 1570, which is the date on a map of Cyprus ("Venetiis M.D. LXX. Natal Bonifacio S.F.") and where he produced at least one "popular print," dated 1574, titled *Sentenze di Dio contra li Maldicenti raccolte dalle Sacre Lettere*, printed "Appresso l'Eccell. M. Borgarutio Barg.re." Bonifacio apparently also produced twelve small maps for a book *Disegni di alcune più illustri città et fortezze del mondo* published in Venice by Donato Bertelli in 1574. Bertelli printed the same book with a Latin title, *Civitatum aliquot insegniorum et locorum magis munitorum delineatio.* Presumably Bonifacio's engravings were added to the first edition of the book published by Ferdinando Bertelli in 1568 (which should not be confused with Giulio Ballino's *Disegni delle più illustri città et fortezze del mondo* published in Venice with a *privilegio* in 1569 by Bolognino Zaltieri). It is by no means clear, however, that Bonifacio engraved maps for the 1574 edition. The record of Bonifacio's membership in the Virtuosi al Pantheon is given in Orbaan, "Virtuosi al Pantheon," 28–29: "messer Natale Bonifatii, intagliatore in rame."

[39] The document is reproduced in Gian Ludovico Masetti Zannini, *Stampatori e librai a Roma nella seconda metà del Cinquecento: documenti inediti* (Rome, 1980), 106, 210, 130, n. 94. Bonifacio identifies himself in the document as "intagliatore." It may be noted that three years later, on 10 April 1580, Bonifacio's wife, "Madonna Madalena," was also proposed for membership in the Virtuosi al Pantheon (Orbaan, "Virtuosi al Pantheon," 29). The location of Cavalieri's house and shop is given in the records as "nel vicolo del palazzo dell'illustrissimo signor cardinale Savelli," which I am presuming is the narrow street off Via delle Botteghe Oscure (Via del Parione in the sixteenth century) today named Vicolo Savelli.

of Nicolaus van Aelst. His principal occupation, however, was supplying engraved illustrations for books. One of his first projects was to produce engravings for Andrea Bacci's projected book "D'Ordine Universi." A contract was drawn up on 7 November 1580 between Bacci, who is described as "medico romano," and "Natale del defunto Gerolamo Bonifacio da Sibenico in Dalmatia maestri e disegnatori in rame," according to which Bonifacio would engrave "una tavola di rame con figure et tavole scritte et altri disegni."[40] He was enjoined not to make other copies, but to produce his designs faithfully in both engraving and etching. He was also obliged to work in Bacci's house in "via de' Pontifice" and to finish the work in forty or fifty days.[41] If the work turned out well, the payment would be twenty-five *scudi*, besides the "tip" ("oltre la mancia"). The work referred to may be the book *Ordo universi et humanarum scientiarum prima monumenta* recorded in biographies of Bacci as printed in Rome in 1581.[42]

In 1586 and 1587, Bonifacio was at work on a series of prints recording the moving of the Vatican obelisk that Grassi printed with a papal *privilegio*, and, in 1589 and 1590, he provided prints for Domenico Fontana's book *Della trasportatione dell'obelisco Vaticano* and a plan of the basilica of St. Peter's for Tiberio Alfarani's book, *De Basilicae Vaticanae Antiquissima et Nova Structura* (see Chapter 11).

During these same years Bonifacio was also involved in other engraving projects. In 1587 he produced the title-page, a portrait of the author (with appended verses composed by Julius Roscius), and fifty-one engraved maps, plans, views, and details of pilgrimage churches for Jean Zuallart's *Il devotissimo viaggio di Gerusalemme* printed in Rome by Francesco Zanetti and Giacomo Ruffinelli. On the frontispiece it is stated that "Aggiontovi i dissegni di varii luoghi di Terra

---

[40] The contract is printed in Bertolotti, *Artisti veneti in Roma* (Venice, 1884), 35.

[41] It may be noted that Andrea Bacci's wife, Martia, is listed as a member of the Virtuosi al Pantheon ("Madonna Martia di messer Andrea Bacchi, medico"). Her and her husband's address in Rome is given as "alla strada de Pontefice al vicolo del cavaliere della Porta." The record is transcribed in Orbaan, "Virtuosi al Pantheon," 31.

[42] The book was reprinted by Theodor Galle in Antwerp in 1596. Lamberto Donati, "Natale Bonifacio," *Archivio storico per la Dalmazia* 3 (April, 1927), 33, believes that the print listed as "Doi fogli del Globo celeste e terrestre, intagliate da Natale Bonifacio" in the 1614 catalogue of Andrea and Michelangelo Vaccari (Ehrle, *Roma prima di Sisto V*, 62, line 289) must have been one of the plates for the book. Roberto Almagià, "Intorno all'opera cartografica di Natale Bonifaco," *Archivio storico per la Dalmazia* 14 (January, 1933), 492, illustrates the "globo terrestre" portion of the print which is inscribed "Roma Lorenzo della Vaccheria forma."

Santa & altri paesi. Intagliati da Natale Bonifacio Dalmatᵃ."[43] At this time he also prepared for Grassi the illustrations for Principio Fabricio's *Delle allusione, imprese, et emblemi sopra la vita, opere, et attioni di Gregorio. XIII. pontefice massimo libri iv*, mentioned above, and in 1589, he engraved the frontispiece and fifteen plates illustrating Giovanni Guerra's *Varii emblemi hieroglifici usati nelli abigliamenti delle pitture fatte in diversi luochi nelle fabriche del S.mo S.r Nostro Papa Sixto V P.O.M.*[44]

In 1590, Bonifacio engraved a map of *Abruzzi*, and probably early in the same year also a map of *Ancient Palestine*. Although undated, the map of Palestine carries the arms of Sixtus V, who died on 24 August 1590. It is also referred to in a letter dated 1 September 1590 written by Phillipus van Winghe in Rome to his friend the geographer Abraham Ortelius informing him that he had met Bonifacio in Rome and that the engraver had recently finished a map of Palestine which he had compiled himself with the aid of persons who had traveled there.[45] The letter explains that with the death of Sixtus Bonifacio now intended to dedicate the print to the new pope. Urban VII, however, died within a few months of assuming the chair of St. Peter, and his two successors, Gregory XIV and Innocent IX, also reigned for brief periods. The presence of empty cartouches to the left and right of the central one still containing the arms of Sixtus V suggests the Bonifacio abandoned his plan to dedicate the print.

Around this same time Bonifacio also produced a map of *East Africa*, which was published in 1591 by Grassi, together with eight plates showing women and men in African dress, animals, and exotic plants (attributed to Bonifacio), in Filippo Pigafetta's book describing observations made in the Congo by the Portugese Duarte (Odoardo)

---

[43] The Belgian Jean Zuallart (known in Italy as Giovanni Zuallardo) was a Knight of the Holy Sepulchre and had made the journey to Jerusalem in 1586. Zuallart dedicated the book to Odoardo Farnese on 20 May 1587. In the "proemio" Zuallart explains that he had made the original drawings for the engraved illustrations. One of Julius Roscius's prefatory verses is addressed to Bonifacio ("AD NATALEM BONIFACIVM æris incidendi artificem egregium"). A copy of the book is in the Houghton, Harvard, NC5.Z8111.587d (see Mortimer, *Italian 16th Century Books*, no. 559). The book was reprinted in Rome in 1595 by Domenico Basa.

[44] The book is listed in *Mostra del Libro Illustrato Romano del Cinquecento* (Rome, 1950), 36, no. 110.

[45] The letter is published in Jan Hendrik Hessels, *Abrahami Ortelii (geographi antverpiensis) et virorum eruditorum ad eundem et ad Jacobum Colium Ortelianum (Abrahami Ortelii sororis filium) epistulae. Cum aliquot aliis epistolis et tractatibus quibusdam ab utroque collectis, (1524–1628) Ex autographis mandante Ecclesia Londino-Batava edidit* (Cambridge, 1887; repr., Osnabrück, 1969), no. 170 (pp. 408–412).

Lopez from 1578 to 1587: *Relatione del Reame di Congo e delle circonvicine contrade Tratta dalli Scritti di Odoardo Lopez Portoghese Per Filippo Pigafetta Con disegni vari di geografia, di piante, d'habiti, d'animali, & altro.*[46] In 1591 Grassi also published Pigafetta's *Relatione dell'assedio di Parigi col disegno di quella città et de' luoghi circonvici,* an account of the siege of Paris by Henri IV in 1590, with plates, including a map of *Paris,* by Bonifacio.[47]

Tolomeo Veltronio

On 29 October 1588, Tolomeo Veltronio, a Knight of the Order of St. John in Malta, was granted a ten-year *privilegio* for the publication of the recently revised Statutes of the Order of St. John in Malta.[48] The book is of interest because it contains plates engraved by Philippe Thomassin and Gysbert van Veen. Besides the granting document, the Vatican Archives kept also a copy of Veltronio's letter of supplication.[49] In his supplication, Veltronio explains that, with the blessed approval of the pope and under the orders of his superiors, with great diligence and expense he has printed the statutes. The request continues by expressing concern that the book might be reprinted by others to the detriment of the Order and asks the pope to issue a *motu proprio* prohibiting others from printing the book in either Latin or Italian without the express permission and privilege

---

[46] A long inscription in the upper part of the map, which begins "Sisto PP. V. Prencipe magnanimo, et per bene della Rep:ca nato, spense/i ladroni dello Stato Ecc.co . . ." and concludes "impresa da non essere qui ramemorate," with Filippo Pigafetta's signature at the end and with Bonifacio's name as engraver below ("Natalis Bonifacius Incidebat"), praises the accomplishments of Sistus V in Rome (the obelisks, the columns of Trajan and Marcus Aurelius, the Scala Santa, etc.). The print was dedicated by Pigafetta on 25 April 1590 to Antonio Migliore, as is recorded in an inscription in the lower right which begins "Al molto Ill.re et Rmo Mons.re Antonio Migliori Vescovo di S. Marco, et/Commendatore di S. Spirito./Infino ad hora niuno ha cosi ben rappresentato in disegno l'Africa, & il Capo di buona Spe=/ranza . . ." and ends "come il nostro Sig.r Odoardo con la grande sua carte . . . Di Roma à 25 d'Aprile M.D. XC." The map is reproduced in Théophile Simar, *Le Congo au XVIe siècle d'après la relation Lopez-Pigafetta* (Brussels, 1919) (opposite page 40).

[47] The book was published by Grassi in partnership with Giacomo Ruffinelli. The frontispiece has "Appresso Bartolomeo Grassi" while the colophon has "Appresso Iacomo Ruffinello." Another edition was printed in Bologna in the same year.

[48] Veltronio's *privilegio* is recorded in ASVat, SB, 138, fol. 139r.–v., and SB, 137, fols. 139r.–v., 140r.–v. (1740 copy).

[49] Veltronio's supplication is recorded in ASVat, SB, 138, fol. 104r.

of the Cardinal Grand Master. After it was submitted, the request was evidently scrutinized by Cardinal Antonio Carafa whose name appears in the lower part of the document.

Interestingly, in his supplication Veltronio asks that the *privilegio* carry the same penalties ("le medesime pene") as those in a *motu proprio* granted by Pope Sixtus V to "Girolamo Cathena nella vita di Pio V" and lists excommunication, a fine of five hundred gold ducats, and the confiscation of all books. The book Veltronio was referring to is Catena's *Vita del gloriosissimo papa Pio Quinto*, which had been published in Rome the previous year with a *privilegio* granted in July of 1586.[50] The significance of Catena's book for Veltronio may have been because it also treated, much to the interest of the Knights of St. John in Malta, the Battle of Lepanto in 1571, listing, as is indicated on the title-page, "the names of galleys and of the Christian and Turkish captains that took part in the naval battle."

The circumstances surrounding the publication of the Statutes of the Order of St. John in Malta, and the *privilegio* granted it, were unusual and may be recounted briefly.[51] The unusual event in the history of the Order of St. John in Malta was the elevation to cardinal by Pope Sixtus V of the Grand Master, Hugues Loubenx de Verdalle (or Ugo de Verdala, as he was known in Italy).[52] The ceremony took place in Rome on 18 December 1587. Traveling from Malta, Verdalle had made a grand entry into the city on 8 December. He was received with every sign of special consideration by Sixtus whose hospitality included the provision of lodgings in the Vatican

---

[50] The *privilegio* is recorded in ASVat, SB, 120, fol. 262. The book, *Vita del gloriosissimo papa Pio Quinto . . . con una raccolta di lettere di Pio V a diversi principi & le risposte, con altri particolari. E i nomi del le galee & di capitani così christiani come turchi che si trovarono alla battaglia navale . . .*, was printed in Rome by Vincenzo Accolti in 1586. The following year it was printed again by Alessandro Gardane and Francesco Coattino. A copy is in the BA, Vatican, R. G. Vite V. 647. It is listed in Ascarelli, *Le Cinquecentine Romane*, 55. A later edition was published in Rome in 1647 by Filippo de Rossi (BA, Vatican, Papi IV, XVI, Pio V, 3, cons). Catena's biography of Pius V is discussed in Pastor, 17: 420–423.

[51] The following discussion also appears in Witcombe, "Privilegio Papale per la pubblicazione degli statuti dell'Ordine di San Giovanni di Malta (Roma, 1588)/The *Privilegio* for the Publication of the Statutes of the Order of St. John in Malta (Rome, 1588)." *Rivista Internazionale del Sovrano Ordine di Malta* 23 (1991): 28–38.

[52] According to Giovanni Biasiotti and Gustavo Giovannoni, "La Vita a Roma dei Cavalieri di San Giovanni di Gerusalemme," in *Atti del IIº Congresso nazionale di studi romani*, vol. 2 (Rome, 1931), 360, Verdalle was only the second Grand Master ever to be created cardinal.

apartment of Innocent VIII. Ten days later Verdalle was created Cardinal of S. Maria in Portico in Rome.[53]

Born in Toulouse, France, Verdalle had been elected Grand Master of the Knights of St. John of Jerusalem (the Knights Hospitalers) in Malta in 1582. Early in his magistracy he set about revising and re-codifying the Statutes of the Order. Verdalle confirmed the completed revision on 23 July 1584. The revised statutes were then taken to Rome where they were presented for approval to Pope Gregory XIII by the Order's Orator (ambassador) at the Holy See, Fra Giovanni Rondinelli. They were subsequently inspected by Cardinal Antonio Carafa, and approved on 20 March 1586 by Sixtus V (who had succeeded Gregory XIII on 24 April 1585).[54]

Presumably it was the intention to publish the statutes as soon as they were approved, but for reasons that are unclear the project was delayed. Perhaps with knowledge of the pending nomination of Verdalle as cardinal it was decided to wait until after the ceremony had taken place. They were finally published with the title *Statuta Hospitalis Hierusalem* in Rome at the Vatican's own press, the Tipografia del Popolo Romano, in 1588.[55] It seems likely that the project, again because of Verdalle's nomination as cardinal, was expanded beyond what may originally have been a much simpler plan to include a number of engraved plates. The decision to include engraved illustrations was evidently made after 18 December 1587 for Verdalle appears in more than one plate as a cardinal, including one, immediately following the title page, in which he is depicted kneeling before Pope Sixtus V who is shown in the act of placing a cardinal's hat on Verdalle's head.[56]

---

[53] Verdalle's entry into Rome was described by the papal Master of Ceremonies, Paolo Alaleona (Arch. dei Cerimonieri, App. No. 37, 1587, pp. 497–499; cited by Biasiotti and Giovannoni). According to Pastor, 21: 238, note 3, an *avviso* of 9 December 1589 describes Verdalle's entry and reception by Sixtus on 8 December 1587. Information about Cardinal Verdalle is provided in Lorenzo Cardella, *Memorie storiche de cardinali della Santa romana chiesa* (Rome, 1793), 5: 288–289.

[54] This information is found in *The Order of St. John in Malta* (Valletta, 1970), no. 346.

[55] A copy is in Houghton, Harvard, Typ 525.88.552F. The book is catalogued in Mortimer, *Italian 16th Century Books*, no. 273. The publication date is given incorrectly as 1586 in *The Order of St. John in Malta*, no. 346. Other editions of the *Statuta* are listed in Ferdinand Heller von Hellwald, *Bibliographie méthodique de l'Ordre souv. de St. Jean de Jérusalem* (Rome, 1885), 213–216.

[56] Illustrated in Mortimer, *Italian 16th Century Books*, 396.

Verdalle is portrayed prominently throughout the book. Following the text of the address by Giovanni Battista Canobbio to Sixtus V, dated 20 March 1586 (the date Sixtus approved the revised statutes, and not, as is sometimes thought, the date the statutes were published), are thirteen plates of miniature portraits in oval medallions of fifty-one Grand Masters of the Order. The first twelve plates, engraved by the French engraver Philippe Thomassin, have four portraits each. The thirteenth, engraved by Gysbert (or Gijsbert, or Gisberto in Italy) van Veen, has three portraits, the last being of Verdalle shown as a cardinal.[57] Immediately following is another plate with a full-page medallion portrait of Verdalle, with his coat of arms included within the architectural design of the border. A further twenty-one copperplates, all within woodcut borders, illustrating various important occasions and significant features of life in the Order, include several with Verdalle shown officiating at ceremonies.[58]

Although unsigned, all twenty-one plates, and the title-page with the figures of Faith, Charity, and Hope, are believed to have been engraved by Philippe Thomassin, who also executed the medallion portraits. The fact that Thomassin was French (he had been born in Troyes and had come to Rome in 1584; see Chapter 8), like Verdalle, may have been a factor in the choice of him to engrave the illustrations. Thomassin's engravings are thought to be based on drawings by Giuseppe Cesari (the Cavaliere d'Arpino), possibly with

---

[57] The portraits are preceded by a plate engraved with the title: "Effigies magistror[um] Hospitalis" on a banderole and showing God the Father, angels and cherubs. In the catalogue *The Order of St. John in Malta*, no. 346, the number of medallion portraits is given incorrectly as forty-seven. Thomassin's plates are catalogued in Edmond Bruwaert, *Recherches sur la vie et l'oeuvre du graveur troyen Philippe Thomassin* (Troyes, 1876), 117, nos. 246–284.

[58] According to the catalogue *The Order of St. John in Malta*, no. 346, scenes depicted in the plates include Reception of a Knight into the Order; the great ward in the Sacred Infirmary at Valletta; the reception of Sisters of the Order; the Church of St. John; a map of the island of Malta with the Turkish fleet at sea; the Common treasury; sessions of the Chapter General; sessions of the Council; the Grand Master; the Grand Master and Bailiffs; Priors; the election of the Grand Master; a Commandery; the sealing of contracts; the leasing of land by the Order; justice; a map of Valletta. There are four different border designs, the first of which is based on the title-page of Antonio Blado's edition of the *Statuta Hospitalariorum S. Ioannis Hierusalem* published in Rome in 1556 (noted in Mortimer, *Italian 16th Century Books*, no. 395; and in Emerenziana Vaccaro Sofia, *Catalogo delle edizioni romane di Antonio Blado Asolano ed eredi (1515–1593)* (Rome, 1961), 4: 389, no. 1656).

the assistance of a collaborator (Paris Nogari and Cesare Nebbia have been suggested).[59]

Appended with its own title-page to the *Statuta* is an "Index materiervm" composed by Tolomeo Veltronio himself. Veltronio is believed to have composed also the elegiac Latin verses in honor of Sixtus V and Verdalle that appear in a cartouche beneath the scene of Verdalle being made cardinal by Sixtus V.[60] Within a border depicting scenes from the life of St. John, the title-page shows in the lower part the arms of Verdalle surmounted by a cardinal's hat below which is printed the words "ROMÆ. CVM PRIVILEGIO. 1588."

Marc' Antonio Rossi

Marc' Antonio Rossi is perhaps best known for his writing manual, *Giardino de scrittori*, published in 1598 (see Chapter 12). That same year, however, on 27 March 1598, Rossi was also granted a papal *privilegio* for a print which he describes in his supplication as a "Carta di Gloria" (and described in the *privilegio* as a "Cartam Gloriae in Excelsis"), engraved on two separate plates by the Flemish engraver Martin Van Buyten.[61] On one of the plates was engraved the words "lavabbo inter innocentes etc," and on the other "In principio etc" (i.e. the opening lines of the Gospel of St. John: "In principio erat verbum . . ."). Possibly these two prints may be identified as those listed in the index of prints for sale at the "stamperia" of Andrea and Michelangelo Vaccari in 1614 as "L'*In principe* di S. Giouanni intagliato in lettera," and "Il lavabo inter innocentes, intagliato in lettera."[62] These entries suggest that both prints were composed primarily of text. Interestingly, Rossi explains that these prints were for

---

[59] Herwarth Röttgen, *Il Cavalier d'Arpino* (Rome, 1973), 172–173, no. 1. Röttgen, 146, no. 68, and tav. 68, discusses in particular a drawing attributed to Cesari in the collection of Janos Scholz, New York, for the figure of S. Giorgio which appears in the border of the full-page plate with the portrait of Verdalle on page 20 (Röttgen, fig. 1b). Cesari is believed to have also supplied drawings for the plates on pages 12, 18, 30, 64, 76, 90, 104, 134, 144, 162, 168, 174, and 180. A drawing for the kneeling Knights in the plate on page 90 is in the Graphische Sammlung, Munich (inv. no. 2610).

[60] *The Order of St. John in Malta*, no. 346.

[61] The supplication and the *privilegio* are recorded in ASVat, SB, 269, fol. 34r.–v., 35v.

[62] These entries in the 1614 inventory of Andrea and Michelangelo Vaccari are given in Ehrle, *Roma prima di Sisto V*, 65, lines 272, 273.

placing on either side of an altar ("da ponersi dall'una, et l'altra parte dell'altare").

Four years later, on 19 August 1602, Rossi was granted another *privilegio* in this case for a corrected edition of the *Directorium chori* by Giovanni Guidetti which had first been published twenty years earlier in 1582. In his supplication Rossi explains that he has had all the notes re-engraved ("fatto intagliare tutte le note di nuove").[63]

Giovanni Antonio di Paoli

Giovanni Antonio di Paoli was a print dealer and sometime publisher active in Rome in the last decade of the sixteenth century and the first decades of the seventeenth. The earliest notice of his name would appear to be 15 October 1596 when it is listed among the creditors of Altiero Gatti, a "libraro" from Siena, who had died on 8 September.[64] His latest dated work is Luca Ciamberlano's print of *St. Charles Borromeo Visiting St. Philip Neri*, which Di Paoli dedicated to Federico Borromeo in 1612. This print, and another, that of *Sine Cerere et Baccho Frigo Venus*, engraved by Raffaello Guidi after a design by Bartholomeus Spranger, were published by Di Paoli in their first state.[65] Most of the prints carrying Di Paoli's address, however, were issued in later states. Some of these prints had once belonged to Antonio Lafrery and later to Paolo Graziani (Lafrery's chief printer and later the principal inheritor of Lafrery's plates after the death of Claudio Duchetti) who issued several of them in conjunction with the printer Petri de Nobilibus in the early 1580s. This is also the case for Giovanni Battista de' Cavalieri's large two-sheet engraving *Miracle of the Loaves and Fishes* after Raphael, and Giorgio Ghisi's engraving *Death of Procris* after Giulio Romano.[66] Other prints issued

---

[63] Rossi's supplication and the *privilegio* are recorded in ASVat, SB, 324, fols. 253r.–v., 254r., 256r. A copy of the 1582 edition of Guidetti's book is in the BA, Vatican, Racc.I.V.1039: *Directorium chori ad usum sacrosanctae Basilicae Vaticanae & aliarum cathedralium & collegiatarum Ecclesiarum collectum opera Ioannis Guidetti . . .* Romae, 1582.

[64] The 1596 document is noted and transcribed in Masetti Zannini, *Stampatori e librai*, 112, 181, and 309 (Appendix 40, 6).

[65] An example of *St. Charles Borromeo Visiting St. Philip Neri* is in the Casanatense, Rome, vol. 20.B.I.89/68. An example of the *Sine Cerere et Baccho Frigo Venus* is in the Farnesina, Rome, vol. 35.H.1. inv. no. 36627. The latter print is mentioned by Baglione, 392.

[66] An example of the *Miracle of the Loaves and Fishes* is in the Farnesina, Rome, vol. 40.H.6, inv. no. 49895. An example of the earlier Graziano/Nobilibus state is

by Di Paoli, however, such as Lorenzo Penni's *Death of Adonis*, were printed only in their second state.[67]

In his supplication for a *privilegio*, dated 4 June 1599, Di Paoli identifies himself as a printer located near the church of S. Maria della Pace.[68] He explained that it was his intention to publish a number of copperplate prints "of every kind," including "devotional" prints, "curious" prints, and "exemplars such as of the Lord, of male and female saints, of pious and generous princes." Perhaps to encourage a favorable outcome to his supplication, Di Paoli was not beyond a little flattery and adds to his list of exemplars "and in particular one of Your Holiness" (i.e. Clement VIII). The *privilegio*, which Di Paoli asked be good "for a few years," was granted on 23 June 1599 for the usual ten-year period.[69] The only print that has so far come to light bearing this *privilegio* is one engraved by Francesco Villamena titled "SANCTA MARIA A SVCVRSO," dated 1599, which Di Paoli dedicated to Ferdinando Farnese, Bishop of Parma ("Ioannes Antonius de Paulis D. D. 1599").[70] At some later date, presumably after 1610, Di Paoli was evidently granted another *privilegio*. A *Portrait of Emperor Matthias*, dated 13 June 1612, carries Di Paoli's address ("Ioan Antonij de Paulis Formis") and a papal *privilegio* ("Cum Privilegio S. Pon.").[71]

---

inv. no. 49896. The *Death of Procris* is listed in Bartsch, 15: no. 61. Di Paoli's address ("Ioan Antonij de Paulis for. Roma") appears on the sixth state. The plate is in the Calcografia, Rome, inv. no. 634.

[67] The *Death of Adonis* is listed in Stefania Massari, et al., *Tra Mito e Allegoria* (Rome, 1989), 320, cat. no. 118.

[68] Di Paoli's supplication is recorded in ASVat, SB, 284, fol. 197v.

[69] The *privilegio* is recorded in ASVat, SB, 284, fols. 191r.–v., 198r.

[70] An example is in the BN, Paris, Eb. 15, fol. 20.

[71] The print is listed in Bartsch, 17: no. 126 (as Cherubino Alberti). The print, which employs an oval frame engraved by Cherubino Alberti for a *Portrait of King Henry IV of France*, and shows a bust of the emperor, is inscribed: "MATTHIAS. I.—DEI GRA. ROMANOR/IMPERATOR BOHE-MIAE ET HVNGARIAE RE/Archidux Austriae et c. electus—Anno 1612 die 13 Junij."

CHAPTER EIGHT

ENGRAVERS AND COPYRIGHT
IN VENICE AND ROME

Perhaps not surprisingly, the largest group besides printers to take advantage of copyright in the sixteenth century is comprised of engravers who used it to protect their own work. Most of them were located in Rome, where they applied for the papal *privilegio*. Because several of the engravers seeking copyright are not well known, even to scholars in the field, supplementary information has been included about their careers and printmaking activities.

Venice

Apart from those submitted before 1517 (see Chapter 5), supplications from individual engravers do not begin to appear until the 1540s. Only a handful of engravers in Venice take advantage of copyright. Enea Vico began to apply for privileges in 1546, mostly to cover prints in books. Domenico Zenoi was granted a *privilegio* for maps. Nicolo Nelli, who worked primarily as a publisher (see Chapter 6), was also granted privileges for his engravings. In the latter part of the century, the engraver Giacomo Franco was granted privileges for several items.

Enea Vico

On 19 November 1546, the engraver Enea Vico submitted a supplication for a *privilegio* to the Venetian Senate in which he explains that in order to make a living, he has made some very beautiful and rare designs never before seen in prints ("alcune bellissimi et rarissimi disegni non più veduti ne stampati"). He now wants to engrave and publish them for the benefit and use of painters and sculptors and other virtuous persons ("i quali volendo lui intagliare et mandare in luce a benefitio et utile di tutti li pittori et altre virtuose persone"). He was duly granted a ten-year *privilegio* with the usual penalties of a fine of two hundred ducats and confiscation of prints, and the division of the fine into thirds, with one third for the "accusador," one third for the supplicant, and one third for the magistrate.[1] Interestingly, in his supplication Vico specifically asks that his name be protected from use on designs he did not make. His request is re-stated in the *privilegio*: "that no one *in perpetuo* can put the supplicant's [i.e. Vico's] name on designs not made by him" ("che alcuno in perpetuo non possa poner il nome di esso supplicante sotto li dissegni non fatti da lui proprio supplicante"). In other words, Vico was seeking copyright not against forgers of his own designs, but against forgers who put his name on prints he did not design. The *privilegio* made it unlawful for anyone to place Vico's name on prints that had not been made by him. The type of *privilegio* granted Vico appears to have been intended not to prevent copying as such, but rather to prohibit prints being sold as his, and the passing off as his designs and prints that he had not invented or produced himself.

Vico does not name in his supplication any of the prints he planned to engrave and publish. Soon after 1546, though, several of his engravings carry a *privilegio* inscription on the plate. The earliest to do so is *King Henry II of France*, dated 1547.[2] This same *privilegio* may also have covered two other prints. The first, dated 1548, is of *Proserpine Changing Aesculapius into an Owl* after Parmigianino (Fig. 18). The print is inscribed: "FRANC. PARM. INV./AEN. VIC. PARM. F./M.D. XLVIII. CON/PRIVILEG. VEN." Although Bartsch describes the print with the *privilegio* notice as a copy ("copie fort trompeuse"), the very presence of the *privilegio* inscription almost certainly signifies that this is the original impression by Vico.[3] The second of Vico's prints, produced two years later in 1550, is a large portrait print of *Giovanni de' Medici* (i.e. Giovanni dalle Bande Nere)

---

[1] The *privilegio* is recorded in ASV, ST, reg. 34, fol. 167v. [190v. n.n.] and filza. Vico's supplication has been partially transcribed by Rivoli and Ephrussi, "Notes sur les Xylographes Vénetiens du XVe et XVIe siècles," *Gazette des Beaux-Arts* 32 (1891): 500.

[2] The print is listed in Bartsch, 15: 337, no. 250. It was published probably very soon after March 1547 when Henry succeeded his father Francis I as king. The print was no doubt intended by Vico to cater to popular curiosity and the sudden interest shown in the man whose queen was the Italian Catherine de' Medici.

[3] The print is listed in Bartsch, 15: 303, no. 45, second copy.

Fig. 18. Enea Vico, *Proserpine Changing Aesculapius into an Owl* (after Parmigianino). 1548. Engraving. Photo: Warburg.

set in an oval within an elaborate frame surrounded by allegorical figures.[4]

The appearance of Vico's copyrighted engravings signals the beginning of a period of renewed interest in prints, and a concomitant increase in the number of privileges granted. This is true not only in Venice, but also in Rome and in other parts of Europe. Among the reasons for the rise in the number of prints carrying a *privilegio* inscription at this time may be the interest increasingly shown in collecting prints. Significantly, Enea Vico's prints were admired and actively collected by his contemporaries. For example, the writer Anton Francesco Doni praised Vico's work in a letter to him datable to 1545. In the same letter, Doni names other 'collectible' engravers— Schongauer, Dürer, Lucas van Leyden, Marcantonio, Caraglio, Marco da Ravenna, whom he refers to as "le più valenti intagliatori che abbin tagliato rami insino a oggi"—whose prints Doni already had examples of in his own collection. In a letter written in Venice to the painter Francesco Salviati, dated August 1545, Pietro Aretino similarly praised Vico, in the same breath as he praised Marcantonio Raimondi.[5] With such interest in his work, Vico no doubt wanted to ensure that only his authentic prints were available.

Vico also produced a number of engravings for books for which privileges were granted. On 6 July 1548, Antonio Zantani submitted a supplication to the Senate for a twenty-year *privilegio* to print "images of the ancient Emperors," which he published as *Le Imagini con tutti i riversi trovati et le vite de gli Imperatori tratte dalle medaglie et dalle historie de gli antichi*. Zantani identifies himself as the author of the two prefatory epistles. The book is comprised of plates engraved by Vico of copper, silver, and gold medals dating from the reign of Julius Caesar to that of Domitian.[6] In addition to the Venetian *privilegio*, Zantani also acquired an imperial *privilegio*, a royal *privilegio*, and

---

[4] The print is listed in Bartsch, 15: 338, no. 254.

[5] Doni's letter is transcribed in Bottari, *Raccolta di lettere*, 3: 350, no. 167. The letter also appears in Anton Francesco Doni, *Il Disegno* (Venice, 1549), fol. 52r.–52v. Aretino's letter is in Bottari, 3: 142, no. 49. Aretino wrote directly to Vico once in 1546 and twice in 1548 (Bottari, 3: 152, no. 57; 169, no. 72; and 170, no. 73).

[6] Zantani's *privilegio* is recorded in ASV, ST, reg. 35, fol. 165v. The prints are listed in Bartsch, 15: 344, nos. 322–406. Vico's name appears below on the frontispiece: "ENEA VICO PARM. F./L'ANNO MDXLVIII." The prints of medals are grouped according to whether they are in copper ("IN RAME"), silver ("IN ARGE[N]TO") or in gold ("IN ORE"). The book was published again in 1601 by Giacomo Franco with a new *privilegio* and with the title "Reliqua Librorum

a papal *privilegio*, each for ten years. Seven years later, Vico provided the engraved illustrations for the *Discorsi di Enea Vico Parmigiano sopra le Medaglie de gli Antichi*, published in 1555, for which a fifteen-year *privilegio* had been granted not to Vico, as the book's title might suggest, but to the publisher Gabriele Giolito on 12 September 1555.[7]

Two years earlier, in 1553, it would appear that Vico himself had obtained four privileges—papal, imperial, Venetian, and one from the Duke of Florence—for his large engraving *The Lineage of the Twelve Caesars*.[8] Then, in 1557, following the approval of the Riformatori dello Studio di Padova on 4 June, and the granting of a license by the Chiefs of the Council of Ten the following 21 June, Vico was granted a *privilegio* on 29 August 1557 for the Italian edition of his *Le Imagini delle Donne Auguste*, which he published in partnership with Vincenzo Valgrisio in Venice in 1557.[9] Two years later, on 17 June 1559, Vico was granted a ten-year *privilegio* to print the "tabula hieroglyphica," the so-called Isiac Table or "tabula Bembina" engraved with hieroglyphic ornaments with an image of the Egyptian goddess Isis enthroned in the centre.[10] The book was published with the title

---

Aeneae Vici Parmensis ad Imperatorum Historiam ex antiquis nummis pertinentum a Iacobo Franco calcographo veneto in lucem edita." See Pasero, "Giacomo Franco, editore, incisore e calcografo dei secoli XVI e XVII," *La Bibliofilia* 37 (1935): 349, no. 23).

[7] The book had been approved by the Riformatori dello Studio di Padova and granted a license by the Chiefs of the Council of Ten on 26 March 1555 (the license is recorded in ASV, CCXN, reg. 16, fol. 5v.). The *privilegio* is recorded in ASV, ST, reg. 40, fol. 55r. (75r. n.n.).

[8] The print is listed in Bartsch, 15: 340, no. 256.

[9] The approval is recorded in ASV, RSP, Filze 284, no. 101, the license in ASV, CCXN, reg. 16, fol. 220r. (221r. n.n.), and the *privilegio* in ASV, ST, reg. 41, fol. 43v. (58v. n.n.). The prints are listed in Bartsch, 15: 342, no. 329. Anton Francesco Doni makes reference to "le medaglie" in a letter to Vico (Bottari, 3: no. 167). The book was later listed in Lafrery's inventory: "Libro delle medaglie delle Donne Auguste di Enea Vico" (Ehrle, *Roma prima di Sisto V*, 59, line 599). Several privileges were granted for the Latin edition of the book, *Augustarum Imagines*, published a year later in 1558 by Valgrisio. The frontispiece is listed in Bartsch, 14: 343, no. 321. Both editions are catalogued in Mortimer, *Italian 16th Century Books*, nos. 532 and 533. Vico included in the same *privilegio* a request also for "books on the various costumes of different nations of the world," for which see Chapter 12.

[10] Approval had been granted on 3 June by the Riformatori dello Studio di Padova (ASV, RSP, Filze 284, no. 205). The *privilegio* is recorded in ASV, ST, reg. 42, fol. 28r. (47r. n.n.). The rectangular table, probably from an ancient Roman temple or shrine of Isis, was discovered in Rome 1525 and acquired by Cardinal Bembo. The table, which is now in the Museo Egizio, Turin, is discussed in Ernesto Scamuzzi, *La 'mensa Isiaca' del Regio Museo di Antichità a Torino* (Rome, 1949), and

Vetvstissimae Tabvlae Aeneae Hieroglyphicis hoc est sacris Aegyptiorvm literis caelatae typus quem ex Torquati Bembi Mvsaeo a. M.D.LIX. Aeneas Vicus Parmensis edidit. It was copied and printed in Venice in 1600 by Giacomo Franco.[11] Besides the title-page, the book contains eleven double-page plates engraved by Vico.

Domenico Zenoi

For a *privilegio* granted the engraver Domenico Zenoi on 5 December 1566 for some maps, see Chapter 10.

Nicolo Nelli

Nicolo Nelli's work as a publisher of prints has already been noted in Chapter 6. Nelli's work as an engraver includes, besides the large sheet of proverbs he engraved for Ferando Bertelli (noted in Chapter 6), a map of *Malta* that was issued with a *privilegio* in 1565 (see Chapter 10). Two years later, in 1567, Nelli was granted a fifteen-year *privilegio* for an engraving of a family tree with a series of small portrait roundels of the principal Ottoman Turks.[12]

In 1568, Nelli engraved the frontispiece (inscribed "Nicolo Nelli Venetiano F. 1568") to Giulio Ballino's *Disegni delle più illustri città et fortezze del mondo*, which was published in Venice with a *privilegio* by Bolognino Zaltieri in 1569 (see Chapter 10). On 12 October 1569, Nelli himself was granted a twenty-year *privilegio* by the Senate for "li dissegni suoi novi."[13] Perhaps among the prints covered by this

---

Enrica Leospo, *La mensa Isiaca di Torino* (Leiden, 1978). Its hieroglyphs are discussed by Erik Iversen, *The Myth of Egypt and its Hieroglyphs in European Tradition* (Princeton, 1993), 55–56, 85.

[11] Franco's copy of the book is listed in Pasero, 348, n. 22; and in Adams, 2: 323, no. 639.

[12] The document is recorded in ASV, ST, reg. 46, fol. 112v. (136v. n.n.). The sheet is inscribed "SOMMARIO ET ALBORO DELLI PRINCIPI OTHOMANI/Con li loro veri Ritratti al naturale di Nicolo Nelli Venetiano. Con Priuilegio del Senato Veneto per anni XV" and "Nicolo Nelli Venet. F/1567. co[n] priuilegio del/Senato Veneto per/anno. 15." An example is in the BN, Paris, Ba 1 (XVI), vol. 5. The text accompanying the engraving was written by Francesco Sansovino (the son of the architect and sculptor Jacopo Sansovino). A few years earlier, in 1564, Sansovino had written (together with other contributors) a *Historia Universale dell'Origine et Imperio de Turchi* which included a section devoted to "le vite particolari de i principi Ottomani fino al tempo presente." Sansovino's book is noted in Rhodes, *Silent Printers*, 243.

[13] Nelli's *privilegio* is recorded in ASV, ST, reg. 47, fol. 137r. (158r. n.n.).

privilegio is an *Allegory of the Battle of Lepanto*, dated 1572, and a *Madonna and Child with Sts. Anne and Catherine* published two years later, in 1574.[14]

Rome

Rome had been a thriving centre of print production since the second decade of the sixteenth century. However, it is not until the 1540s that engravers working in Rome begin to avail themselves of copyright protection for their prints. The earliest example of a notice of *privilegio* appearing on a print published in Rome is Giulio Bonasone's large print of Michelangelo's *Last Judgement* (Fig. 19).[15] The print, which has been dated to 1546, is inscribed "Cum privilegio Summi Pontifici." It was dedicated by Bonasone to Cardinal Alessandro Farnese.[16] Possibly the *privilegio* was obtained with the assistance of the cardinal. The next example appears over a decade later, in 1557, on a *St. Jerome* engraved by Sebastiano del Re (Sebastiano a Regibus) after Marcello Venusti's painting based on a design by Michelangelo. The print is inscribed "M[ichael]. Ang[elo]. in[ventor]./Marcel[llo Venusti] Pin[xit] and Seb[astiano]. a Reg[ibus]. clo[diensis]. incid[ebat]/ Romae MDLVII/con privilegio."[17]

During the last thirty years of the century, however, several important engravers sought copyright for their prints. For some of them, though, such as Giovanni Battista de' Cavalieri, Mario Cartari, Cherubino Alberti, and Michaeli Grecchi Lucchese, on whose prints a notice of *privilegio* appears frequently, no record of the granting document has been found in the archives. Without the archival

---

[14] The *Allegory of the Battle of Lepanto* is inscribed "1572 In Venetia appreso Nicolo Nelli/con licentia de superiori et privilegio/per anni xx." The engraving has been attributed to Martino Rota. An example is in the BN, Paris, Eb 12 fol. p. 28. The print of the *Madonna and Child with Sts. Anne and Catherine* is inscribed "1574/In Venetia appresso/Nicolo Nelli Al segno/de Arca di Noe/con priuilegio." An example is in the BN, Paris, Ba 1 (XVI), vol. 5.

[15] The print is listed in Bartsch, 15: 132, no. 80.

[16] Clare Robertson, *'Il Gran Cardinale' Alessandro Farnese, Patron of the Arts* (New Haven and London, 1992), 158, believes Alessandro Farnese commissioned the engraving from Bonasone.

[17] The print is listed in Mario Rotili, ed., *Fortuna di Michelangelo nell'Incisione* (Benevento and Rome, 1964–1965), 72, no. 49. The plate was later acquired by Antonio Lafrery.

Fig. 19. Giulio Bonasone, *Last Judgement* (after Michelangelo). c. 1546.
Engraving. Photo: Warburg.

record, it is not always clear to whom the *privilegio* was granted. For the other engravers included in this chapter—Diana Mantuana, Leonardo Caccianemici, Aliprando Capriolo, Francesco Villamena, Jacopo Lauro, the Sadelers, Philippe Thomassin, Domenico Falcini, Mattheo Greuter, and Leonardo Parasole—surviving records in the Vatican Secret Archives provide valuable information about them and their activities.

Giovanni Battista de' Cavalieri

A native of the Val Lagherina (the valley of the Adige to the south of Trento) in northern Italy, Giovanni Battista de' Cavalieri worked in Rome both as an engraver and a publisher. Among his earliest dated prints are two dated 1561, one a large print of the *Massacre of the Innocents*, and the other a small print inscribed *Pacientia*.[18] Many other prints followed, mostly reproductive, some of which were published by Antonio Salamanca (including the *Massacre of the Innocents* just mentioned, and others presumably in the year before Salamanca's death in 1562) and others by Lafrery.

In 1561, if not before, Cavalieri began publishing prints of antique statuary collected together in the form of a book the first edition of which was entitled *Antiquarum Statuarum Urbis Romae, Liber Primus*. He subsequently published an enlarged edition, *Antiquarum Statuarum Urbis Romae, Primus et Secundus Liber* (undated), and later still a *Tertius and Quartus Liber*. The first edition was comprised of fifty-eight plates and a title-page with "ANTIQVARVM STATVARVM VRBIS ROMAE LIBER PRIMVS" inscribed in the upper cartouche and the lower cartouche left blank. In what has been described as the second edition, the lower cartouche carries a dedication to Otto Truchsess, Bishop of Augsburg and titular Cardinal presbyter of S. Maria in Trastevere, with below the words "Cum priuilegio" followed by Cavalieri's name as the engraver ("Ioanne Baptista de Cauallerijs lagherino incisore"). Otherwise lacking a date, the project may nonetheless be dated to between 14 April 1561, when Truchsess was made cardinal presbyter of S. Maria in Trastevere, and 18 May

---

[18] The *Massacre of the Innocents* is listed in Zani, 2, 5: 338. The plate is the Calcografia, Rome, inv. no. 27. An example of the *Pacientia* is in the Farnesina, Rome, 40.H.6, inv. no. 49914. The print is signed on a tablet in the lower right: *Ioannes baptis/ta de Cavaller/is lagerinus inci.*

1562, when he vacated this position on his elevation to the see of Albano. A 'third' edition, issued after Truchsess's elevation, with the dedication altered to read "August S.R.E. Cardinali Episcopo Albanensi Dicatus," was printed in Rome by Francesco Palumbo ("Apud Franciscum Palumbum Novariensem"). A second collection of one hundred entirely new plates entitled "ANTIQVARVM/STAT-VARVM/VRBIS/ROMAE/TERTIVS ET QVARTIVS/LIBER" and carrying a dedication (dated 1 June 1593) to Giacomo Paluzzi Albertoni, was published with a *privilegio* in 1594.[19]

In 1565, the *privilegio* appears on a *Martyrdom of St. Catherine* engraved by Cavalieri after Livio Agresti.[20] Four years later, in 1569, the *privilegio* is seen again on another print by Cavalieri after Livio Agresti, the large *Finding of the True Cross*.[21] Besides his own prints, Cavalieri occasionally also published the prints of others. Cornelis Cort's engraving dated 1572 of the *Creation of Eve* after Federico Zuccaro, for example, was published by Cavalieri with a three-year *privilegio*.[22]

Two prints by Cavalieri, each carrying notice of copyright, were issued on the occasion of the Jubilee in 1575. One is a large, two-sheet print showing, in the corners, the four Roman basilicas, S. Maria Maggiore, S. Giovanni in Laterano, S. Paolo fuori le Mura, and St Peter's, with a seated personification of "SANCTA ROMA" in a central oval with images of the Christian charities to either side.[23] On the other print by Cavalieri, which shows the façade of Old St. Peter's with the piazza in front and new St. Peter's rising behind, the inscription records that the *privilegio* granted was for three years. In the lower margin is a long dedicatory inscription by Cavalieri to Cardinal Lodovico Madruzzo.[24]

---

[19] The *Antiquae Statuae Urbis Romae* is discussed in Thomas Ashby, "Antiquae Statuae Urbis Romae," *Papers of the British School at Rome* 9 (1920): 107–158.

[20] The print is inscribed "Ioannes baptista de cavalleris/incidebat Cum privilegio." An example is in the Farnesina, Rome, vol. 40 H. 6, inv. no. 49907. The example in the BN, Paris, Eb. 10. fol., has the lower margin trimmed off.

[21] The print is inscribed: "Incidebat Ioa Bap^ta. de Cavallerijs/Cum privilegio Anno D[omi]ni 1569." An example is in the Farnesina, Rome, vol. 40 H 6, inv. no. 49910.

[22] The print is listed in Bierens de Haan, 35, no. 1. The print is inscribed "Cum privilegio ad triennium" and "Jo. Baptista de Cavallerijs aeneis formis Romae."

[23] An example is in the BM, London, inv. no. 1874–6-13–610. The print is inscribed "Joan Bapt. de Cavalleriis incidebat cu[m] gra[tia] et privilegio Romae An/ Iubilei 1575," and dedicated by Cavalieri to the Polish Cardinal Stanislaus Hosius.

[24] An example is in the Farnesina, Rome, Scat. 30, F.C. 49911. The dedicatory inscription ends with "Joannes Baptista de Cavallerijs hic repraesentat, coelestia

In 1580, Cavalieri's book of engravings of portraits of the popes, *Pontificum romanorum effigies*, was published in Rome with a *privilegio* by Domenico Basa.[25] Many of the portraits Cavalieri copied from Onofrio Panvinio's *XXVII Pontificum Maximorum elogia et imagines accuratissime ad vivum aeneis typeis delineatae* that had been published by Antonio Lafrery in 1568. Four years later, in June 1584, Cavalieri was granted a ten-year papal *privilegio* for a series of portraits of Emperors: *ROMA-NORVM IMPERATORVM EFFIGIES*.[26] The book contains 156 engraved portraits of the emperors, beginning with Julius Caesar, numbered "1" to "156" on the right-hand pages, with accompanying text on the left. Rudolf II (even though he had been emperor since 1576) was evidently included as a last minute addition (as number 157) and has no accompanying portrait. The accompanying text was supplied by Tomasz Treter (1550–1601), a canon at S. Maria in Trastevere in Rome and secretary to King Stephan of Poland.[27]

A *privilegio* dated 27 June 1584 also appears in two books with engravings by Cavalieri of martyrs and it seems safe to assume that it is the same *privilegio* listed in the Index of the Vatican Archives. The first book, *Ecclesiae anglicanae trophaea*, was printed in Rome in 1584 by the book publisher Bartolomeo Grassi ("Romæ Ex Officina Bartholomæi Grassi").[28] Cavalieri engraved the title-page and the thirty-five plates, numbered 2–36, which reproduce Niccolò Circignani's recently completed (1583–84) paintings of English martyrs in the English College, S. Tommaso di Canterbury (formerly S. Trinità

---

invisibiliaq[ue] mysteria contemplare. Romae V. Calend. Febr. Anno Jobilei [sic] M.D. LXXV."

[25] "Ex typographia Dominici Basae." The book was printed by Francesco Zannetti ("Rome, Apud Franciscus Zanettum, 1580") and dedicated to Cardinal Andrea of Austria. A copy is in the BA, Vatican, Barberini, T.VI.114. An edition dated 1585 is listed in *Mostra del Libro Illustrato Romano del Cinquecento* (Rome, 1950), 36, no. 109. Another edition is dated 1591, and another was published in Rome in 1595 by Bartolomeo Bonfadini (a copy is in the BA, Vatican, Cicognara III.2010).

[26] The *privilegio* is indexed in ASVat, Index 752, fol. 277r.: "Pro Joanne baptista de Cavalerijs Tridentin[ensis] De Imprimendo ad X^um. [i.e. decennium] effigies Imperati." The actual granting document has not been discovered.

[27] The title page reads "ROMANORVM/IMPERATORVM/EFFIGIES/Elogijs, ex diversis Scripto/ribus, per THOMAM Treteru[m]./S. MARIAE. Transtyberim Ca/nonicum collectis/Illustratae/Opera et Studio Io. Baptae./de Cavallerijs aeneis ta/bulis Incisae./ROMAE ANNO DOMINI/MDLXXXIII." The dedication, by Cavalieri to King Stephan, is dated 4 September 1583. A copy is in BA, Vatican, Cicognara III. 2009.

[28] An example is in the BA, Vatican, Cicognara.VI.2008. int. 2.

degli Inglesi) in Rome.[29] On the frontispiece is written: "Per Io. Bap. de Cavalleriis/aeneis typis repraesentatae/Cum Privilegio Gregorij XIII P[ontifex] M[aximus]."[30] Around the same time Cavalieri also printed a set of five plates showing scenes of martyrdom, each with annotated explanatory text below. The first plate in the series (which serves as the title-page), titled across the top "CRVDELITAS IN CATHOLICIS MACTANDIS," is inscribed below: "Ioa Baptista de Cauallerijs incidebat Romæ. Anno Domini. 1584."[31]

The second book, *Ecclesiae militantis triumphi*, was printed with a *privilegio* by Grassi the following year, in 1585.[32] Besides the title-page, the book contains thirty-one plates engraved by Cavalieri after Circignani's frescoes, completed in 1582, of scenes of martyrdom in the church of S. Stefano Rotondo (the Hungarian College) in Rome.[33]

---

[29] Circignani's frescoes are noted in Baglione, 41. The frescoes, and Jesuit iconography, are discussed in Thomas Buser, "Jerome Nadal and Early Jesuit Art in Rome," *Art Bulletin* 58 (1976): 428; and Leif Holm Monssen, "Rex gloriose martyrum: A Contribution to Jesuit Iconography," *Art Bulletin* 63 (1981): 130–37.

[30] In the main oval on the frontispiece is printed: "ECCLESIAE/ANGLICANAE/TROPHAEA/Siue/Sanctor[um] Martyrum qui pro CHRISTO/Catholicaeq[ue] fidei Veritate asserenda,/antiquo recentioriq[ue] Persecutionum/tempore, mortem in Anglia subierunt,/PASSIONES/Romae in Collegio Anglico per/Nicolaum Circinianum depictae . . ." In a cartouche below appears the name of Thomasz Tretero, "Canonico S. Mariae Transtyberim in Vrbe, et Ser. Regis Poloniae secretario." A copy is in the BA, Vatican, Cicognara VI.2008.int. 2. An example of the frontispiece alone is in the Farnesina, Rome, vol. 26.L.71, inv. 3700. An edition of the book may have been printed before the *privilegio* was granted (see also *Ecclesiae militantis triumphi* below). The British Museum also has an edition dated 1584 with the Rome imprint of Francesco Zannetti on the text leaf on which is written: "Descriptiones qvaedam illivs inhvmanae et mvltiplicis persecvtionis, quam in Anglia propter fidem sustinent catholicè christiani." Another example of the same is in the Casanatense, Rome (listed in *Mostra del Libro Illustrato Romano del Cinquecento*, 38, no. 122).

[31] A copy is in the BA, Vatican, Cicognara VI.2008.int. 3. The four plates following are numbered in the lower right corner with the title of each across the top: "1" "APPREHENSIONES CATHOLICORVM"; "2" "NOCTVRNÆ PER DOMOS INQVISITIONES"; "3" "TORMENTA IN CARCERIBUS INFLICTA"; "4" "IVDICIA ET CONDEMNATIONES."

[32] A copy is in the BA, Vatican, Cicognara VI.2008.int. 1. According to Mortimer, *Italian 16th Century Books*, no. 118, the British Museum has an edition without the name of a printer dated 1583, before the *privilegio* was granted.

[33] Bruno Passamani, "Cavalieri, Giovanni Battista," in *Dizionario biografico degli Italiani*, 22: 674, notes the existence of subsequent editions with various titles. The editions dated 1583, 1584, 1585 are dedicated to Stanislao Roscio, secretary of King Stephan of Poland. In 1586 Grassi also published fifteen plates engraved by Cavalieri showing the life of S. Apollinare of Ravenna after paintings by Circignani in the German and Hungarian College: "Beati Apollinaris martyris . . . res gestae prout Romae in eiusdem aede sacra apud Collegium Germanicu[m] et Ungaricu[m]

The *privilegio* also appears on the frontispiece of Cavalieri's booklet of prints of "monsters" printed in 1585.[34] See also Chapter 11 for Cavalieri's prints of the Santa Casa di Loreto.

Mario Cartari

Mario Cartari, and his brother Cristofano Cartari, had arrived in Rome in the early 1560s.[35] Mario Cartari's earliest dated print would appear to be a copy he made in reverse of Heinrich Aldegrever's

---

a Nicolao Circiniano depictae visu[n]tur a Ioanne Baptista de Cavalleriis typis aeneis expressae." A copy is in the BA, Vatican, Cicognara VI.2008.int. 4. Prints of Circignani's paintings in S. Stefano Rotondo were again published in 1589, with the addition of text by Julius Roscius [Hortini] (i.e. Giulio Roscio Ortini), in an edition, with a *privilegio*, entitled "TRIVMPHI MAR/TYRVM/IN TEMPLO D. STEPH/ANI CAELLI MONTIS/EXPRESSVS," and described as "the work and industry" of Cavalieri ("Opera et industria Jo. Baptistae de Cavalleriis"). The book, which Ortini dedicated to Prospero de la Baume (the dedication is dated 5 March 1589), was printed in Rome "Apud Alexandrum Gardanum & Franciscum Coattinu[m]." A copy is in the BA, Vatican, R.G. Arte-arch. V.5. The book reproduces in reverse all thirty-one plates from *Ecclesiae militantis triumphi* with text on the left page and the plate on the right. At the end a new page of text and a new plate have been added for S. Gabino (the plate shows S. Protus, S. Gabino, and S. Ianuarius). The reason for this addition is immediately made clear in the following several pages of text, translated, from Sardinian (Sardu) into Latin ("ex lingua Sardoa in latinam"), and entitled: "NARRATIO/DEDICATIONIS. TEMPLI/D. GABINI. MARTYRIS/TVRRIBVS. SARDINIAE." Evidently the "Narratio" had been first printed two years earlier, in 1587 ("Impressa Romæ anno M D XLVII"). Circignani's paintings are noted in Baglione, 41, and discussed in Leif Holm Monssen, "The Martyrdom Cycle in San Stefano Rotondo," *Acta ad archaeologiam et artium historiam pertinentia. Serie altera in 8o* 2 (1982): 175–317 (Part One); 3 (1983): 11–106 (Part Two).

[34] On the frontispiece is printed: "Opera nel quale vi e molti Mostri/de tute le parti del mondo antichi e moderni/con le dechiarationi a ciascheduno fina/al prese[n]te Anno 1585. Sta[m]pate in Roma/Cum privilegio/Ioanne Baptista de Cavalierijs lagherino incisore." An example is in the BM, London, inv. no. 46–5–9–249. The booklet contains seventeen sheets besides the frontispiece. Thomas Ashby, "Impiego degli stessi rami per opere diverse in alcune edizione romane," *La Bibliofilia* 27 (1925–26): 162, notes that for the frontispiece Cavalieri re-used the one he had employed for his *Antiquarum Statuarum Urbis Romae Liber Primus*.

[35] Cristofano Cartari has long been assumed to be the son of Mario Cartari (see, most recently, Borroni Salvadori, "Cartaro, Mario," *Dizionario biografico degli Italiani*. 20: 797, 799). A document in the State Archives in Rome, however, makes it clear that Cristofano and Mario were brothers (ASR, Archivio de Tribunale del Governatore di Roma, vol. 255, Costituti dal 26 Ottobre 1577 al 18 Gennaro 1578, D. Ascanius Caracciolus pro Charitale Notus, fol. 25v., in which Cristofano Cartari is quoted as saying that he lives in a house in Via del Parione in Rome with Mario Cartari "mio fratello").

Adoration of the Shepherds, dated 1560.[36] Besides prints of religious sub-
ject matter, he also produced maps, of which two of the earliest are
of *Cyprus* and *Crete*, both dated 1562 and published in Venice by
Ferando Bertelli.[37] The following year, 1563, Bertelli published Cartari's
map of *Palestine*.[38] Over the next three years he produced a print of
St. Catherine of Alexandria after Francesco Salviati, a *Penitent Mary
Magdalen* after Bartolomeo Neroni, called Riccio, dated 1564, and a
Madonna and Child after Giulio Clovio dated 1565.[39] He also engraved
portraits, for example that of *Pope Pius V Flanked by Saints Peter and
Paul*, which was published by Bartolomeo Faletti in 1567.[40]

Over the course of his career Cartari produced a number of maps,
of which several were printed with a papal *privilegio*. The earliest
would appear to be that of *Modern Rome* dated 1576.[41] The following year, 1577, he engraved a map of *Italy*, which was printed with
a ten-year *privilegio*.[42] Two years later, in 1579, a notice of a ten-year
privilegio appears on his map of *Antique Rome*.[43] In 1580, a ten-year

---

[36] The print is noted by Borroni Salvadori, "Cartaro, Mario," in *Dizionario biografico
degli Italiani*, 20: 796; and idem, *Carte, Piante e Stampe*, xxix, where the date is given
as 1563.

[37] The maps of *Cyprus* and *Crete* are listed in Borroni Salvadori, *Carte, Piante e
Stampe Storiche*, 42, nos. 120, 121 respectively; Destombes, "Les cartes de Lafréri,"
246, nos. 55 and 48, respectively; and Tooley, 26, nos. 182 and 175, respectively.

[38] The map of *Palestine* is listed in Borroni Salvadori, "Cartaro, Mario," *Dizionario
biografico degli Italiani*. 20: 797; Passavant, 6: 160, no. 53; Tooley, 39, no. 435; and
Reinhold Röhricht, *Bibliotheca Geographica Palaestinae* (Berlin, 1890), 605, no. 78. It
carries Cartari's monogram and is inscribed: "PALESTINÆ SIVE TERRE SANCTE
DESCRIPTION. MDLXIII Ferandvs Bertellvs Excvdebat Venetiis." The map is a
re-print of map of Palestine published in Rome in 1557 by Giovanni Francesco
della Gatta.

[39] The *St. Catherine of Alexandria* is listed in Bartsch, 15: no. 13. Another version
of the same subject is dated 1567 (Bartsch, 15: no. 12). Both the *Penitent Mary
Magdalen* and the *Madonna and Child* are unknown to Bartsch. All three prints are
noted in V. Federici, "Di Mario Cartaro Incisore Viterbese del secolo XVI," *Archivio
della R. Società Romana di Storia Patria* 21 (1898): 544, 545.

[40] The print is listed in Bartsch, 15: 529, no. 21.

[41] The map of *Modern Rome* is listed in Huelsen, *Piante Icnografiche e Prospettiche di
Roma*, 65, no. 72. The print is dedicated to Henry III of France. In the upper right
corner is inscribed: "ROMA RENASCES" with below "cum privilegio per anni
X." In the upper left is an inscription which concludes with the words: "Marius
Kartarius Viterbiensis . . . Anno MDLXXVI." The title in the upper margin reads:
"NOVISSIMA VRBIS ROMAE ACCVRATISSIMA DESCRIPTIO."

[42] The map of *Italy*, inscribed "Italia. Marius Cartarus Fecit. Romae Anno.
M.D.LXXVII. Cum Privilegio an. X," is listed Karrow, 237, 30/90.5.

[43] The map is listed in Huelsen, *Piante Icnografiche e Prospettiche di Roma*, 68, no.
76. In the upper margin is inscribed: "CELEBERRIMAE VRBIS ANTIQVAE/
FIDELISSIMA TOPOGRAPHIA POST OMNES ALIAS AEDITIONES

papal *privilegio* together with a *privilegio* granted by the Duke of Tuscany (i.e. Francesco I de' Medici) appear on Cartari's map of *Perugia* designed by Egnazio Dante and dedicated to Giacomo Buoncompagni.[44] A ten-year *privilegio* also appears on Cartari's "corografia" of the *Baths of Diocletian*, which Vincenzo Scamozzi dedicated to Giovanni Corraro, the Venetian envoy in Rome.[45]

Cartari also produced various illustrations for books. Mention can be made of plates signed with his monogram (and dated 1576) in Fulvio Orsini's *Familiae romanae quae reperiuntur in antiquis numismatibus* printed with a *privilegio* in Rome in 1577 by Giuseppe degli Angeli for the heirs of Francesco Tramezzino.[46]

It may be noted that Mario Cartari also pursued a career as a print publisher. A number of the prints he published (though none of them with a *privilegio*) were engraved by his brother Cristofano Cartari.[47] For example, an *Adoration of the Shepherds* after Bartolomeo Neroni (called Riccio) is inscribed "Cristofano Cartario Inc." and "Marius Cartarius EXC. Romae."[48] Mario Cartari also published anonymous copies of Giorgio Ghisi's *Farnese Hercules* and of Cort's *A Faun Carrying Young Bacchus*, both after antique statues.[49] In 1577

ACCVRATISSIME DELINEATA." In the upper left, as part of the dedicatory inscription, appears the name "Marius Cartarius Viterbiensis . . . AN. M.D.LXXIX," with below "Cum privilegio per anni X."

[44] The print is inscribed: "Descrittione del territorio di Perugia Augusta et dei luoghi circonvicini del P.M. Egnatio Danti da Perugia matematico dello Studio di Bologna." It is dedicated to "Iacopo Buoncompagni marchese di Vignola, duca d'Arci et di Sora, governatore di S. Chiesa." Fra Egnazio Dante (1536–1586) had come to Rome in 1580 after resigning his position of professor of mathematics at the University of Bologna to take up his appointment as papal cosmographer to Gregory XIII. Giacomo Buoncompagni, General of the Church, Marchese of Vignola, and Duke of Sora, was Gregory XIII's natural son.

[45] An example of the print is in the BA, Vatican, Arch. S. Rom. St. Pat. XXI (1898).

[46] The *privilegio* seems to have been granted to the heirs of Tramezzino: "Romae cum privilegio curantibus heredib. Francisci Tramezini." The colophon reads: "Romae impensis haeredum Francisci Tramezini. Apud Iosephum de Angelis. M.D.LXXVII." The book was dedicated to Cardinal Alessandro Farnese.

[47] It may be noted in passing that on 12 February 1581, "Messer Cristofano Cartaro, da Viterbo, intagliator di disegni in rame" was proposed for membership in the Virtuosi al Pantheon. Orbaan, "Virtuosi al Pantheon," 29.

[48] The print is listed in Zani, 2, 5: 105.

[49] Ghisi's original print of *Farnese Hercules* is listed in Bartsch, 15: 530, no. 24. Cartari's copy is listed in Bartsch, 15: 401, no. 41, Copy. It is also listed in McGinniss, no. 440; and Boorsch and Lewis, *The Engravings of Giorgio Ghisi* (New York, 1985), 189, no. 58. The inscription reads "Marius Cartarus exc. Rome." The *A Faun Carrying Young Bacchus* is listed in Bartsch, 15: 530, no. 25. The inscription on the

he published one of his own prints, a *Madonna and Child with St. Roch and St. Sebastian* after Filippo Bellini da Urbino.[50] In 1578 he published in a book, *Prospettive diverse*, a series of twenty-six prints of views, ruins, and bridges of Rome ("Mario Cartaro exc.").[51] The project, however, must have been conceived much earlier as the frontispiece includes a dedication to Cardinal Sforza who died in 1564.

Cherubino Alberti

Cherubino Alberti is usually linked in the minds of art historians with his brother, Giovanni, and remembered chiefly for a series of important fresco decorations undertaken jointly in Rome during the reign of Pope Clement VIII (1592–1605). He began his career, though, not as a fresco painter but as an engraver of copper plates. His earliest dated prints were produced soon after his arrival in Rome, at the age of fifteen, in 1568. Over the next fifteen years or so he devoted himself almost exclusively to engraving and during this period produced more than half of the approximately two hundred prints that can now be associated with him. There are indications, however, that his career as a printmaker was not wholly successful, and that in the 1580s he began to turn increasingly to painting. He continued to produce prints intermittently, however, down to within a few years of his death in 1615. His activity as a printmaker spans a period of more than forty years. For most of the first part of his career, up to the mid-1580s, he was active mostly as a reproductive engraver and over the course of his career engraved prints after such artists as Michelangelo, Raphael, Polidoro da Caravaggio, Andrea del Sarto, and the brothers Federico and Taddeo Zuccaro.

copy reads "Marius Cartarus. exc. Romæ." Cort's original print is catalogued in Bierens de Haan, 154, no. 149.

[50] The print is listed in Federici, 543; and Borroni Salvadori, "Cartaro, Mario," 797 (who notes that Passavant, 6: 159, no. 43, erroneously gives the inventor of the print as Filippo Bottini). The print is inscribed "Philippus Bellinus Urbinates invent" and "Marius Cartarius excudebat Romæ 1577." The print also carries the monogram of Mario Cartari, "MK." Filippo Bellini's work is discussed in Catherine Monbeig Goguel, "'Filippo Bellini da Urbino della Scuola del Baroccio'," *Master Drawings* 13 (1975): 347–370.

[51] The prints are noted in Passavant, 6: 157; and Borroni Salvadori, "Cartaro, Mario," 797.

In 1573, within a few years of his arrival in Rome, Alberti evidently applied for papal copyright, a notice of which, granted by the recently elected Pope Gregory XIII, appears on Alberti's engraving of *God the Father supporting the Dead Christ* after Taddeo Zuccaro's fresco in the Pucci Chapel in S. Trinità dei Monti.[52] The same inscription appears again the following year on Alberti's print after another fresco by Taddeo, the *Flagellation*, in the Mattei Chapel in S. Maria della Consolazione in Rome (Fig. 20), and also on the *Agony in the Garden* after Rosso Fiorentino (Fig. 21).[53] The *privilegio* appears again on four prints by Alberti dated 1575: an *Adoration of the Shepherds*, and a *Conversion of St. Paul*, both after Taddeo Zuccaro, a *Penitent St. Jerome* after Michelangelo, and *Tabernacle* after Rosso Fiorentino.[54] In 1582, a *privilegio* granted by Gregory XIII appears on a *Madonna and Child with St. Elizabeth and St. John* after Raphael.[55] Other examples of copyrighted prints by Alberti, however, are without

[52] The print is listed in Bartsch, 17: 57, no. 22. An example is in the Marucelliana, Florence, vol. 13, no. 37.

[53] The *Flagellation* is listed in Bartsch, 17: 56, no. 18. An example is in the Marucelliana, Florence, vol. 13, no. 23. The plate is in the Calcografia, Rome, inv. no. 1793–2. The print is referred to by Baglione, 131. The example of the *Agony in the Garden* illustrated here (in the New York Public Library, New York, inv. MERH) shows the state with the *privilegio* of Gregory XIII (unknown to Bartsch). Bartsch, 17: 56, no. 17, records a later state in which the *privilegio* of Gregory XIII erased and replaced a *privilegio* of Urban VIII in 1628, for which, see below.

[54] The *Adoration of the Shepherds* is listed in Bartsch, 17: 53, no. 10. Examples are in the BM, London, inv. no. 8–485–8–1874; the Marucelliana, Florence, vol. 13, no. 22; and the Uffizi, Florence, inv. no. 1570. The print, which in the second state carries the address of Nicolaus van Alest, appears later listed in the inventory of 1614 of Andrea and Michelangelo Vaccari. Zani, 2, 5: 119, records a state, unknown to Bartsch, with a dedication dated 1575 to Cardinal Paulo de Aretio ("Ded. Paulo De Aretio Car . . . Dicavit Romae MDLXXV") in the lower margin (the lower margin is missing in later states). The *Conversion of St. Paul* is listed in Bartsch, 17: 70, no. 57. Examples are in the BM, London, inv. no. 12–3444–10–1874; and the Marucelliana, Florence, vol. 13, no. 24. The notice of copyright reads only "cum privilegio," but I am assuming it was issued under Gregory XIII. A later state, with the address of Carlo Losi, 1774, is in the MM, New York, inv. no. 51.501.3247. The altarpiece of the *Conversion of St. Paul* is in the Frangipane Chapel in S. Marcello al Corso. The state of the *Penitent St. Jerome* in the BM, London (inv. no. 1979 U.835) is unknown to Bartsch, 17: 69, no. 54, who records a state inscribed "Cum privilegio Summi Pontificis." Another example of the same state is in the Marucelliana, Florence, vol. 13, no. 20. The *Tabernacle* is listed in Bartsch, 17: 73, no. 66. Examples are in the BM, London, inv. no. W3–133; and the Uffizi, Florence, inv. no. 1579.

[55] The print is listed in Bartsch, 17: 63, no. 40. Examples are in the BM, London, inv. no. 1977–12–10–1; and the Marucelliana, Florence, vol. 13, no. 19. The first state, unknown to Bartsch, has a lower margin in which is inscribed a dedication, dated 1582, to Alfonso Visconti.

Fig. 20. Cherubino Alberti, *Flagellation* (after Taddeo Zuccaro). 1574.
Engraving. Photo: Pineider.

Fig. 21. Cherubino Alberti, *Agony in the Garden* (after Rosso Forentino).
1574. Engraving. Photo: New York Public Library.

a date. Three undated prints, each carrying a *privilegio* granted by Gregory XIII, are of Michelangelo's Florence *Pietà*, Vasari's *Madonna of the Rosary*, and a *Resurrection* after 'Raphael' (the print is actually after a drawing by Perino del Vaga) (Fig. 22).[56]

The observant reader will have noticed that, although Alberti died in 1615, a number of his prints also carry notice of a *privilegio* granted by Urban VIII in 1628. Four examples printed with a *privilegio* granted by Gregory XIII, the *Flagellation* after Taddeo Zuccaro (see Fig. 20), the *Tabernacle* after Rosso Fiorentino, the *Madonna and Child with St. Elizabeth and St. John* after Raphael, and the undated *Resurrection* after 'Raphael' [Perino del Vaga] (see Fig. 22), have appended to Gregory XIII's *privilegio* also a *privilegio* granted by Urban VIII dated 1628. In another example, Gregory XIII's *privilegio* on the *Agony in the Garden* after Rosso Fiorentino was later erased and replaced with that of Urban VIII. Besides these examples, there are another eighty or so prints by Alberti inscribed with the phrase "cum privilegio Summi Pontificis," which, it is argued here, indicates the same 1628 *privilegio* granted by Urban VIII. How Alberti's prints came to be carrying the *privilegio* of Urban VIII, granted thirteen years after the engraver's death and for prints produced half a century earlier, can be closely documented.

Of the approximately two hundred prints Alberti produced over the course of his career, only about twenty-three (and exclusively his reproductive engravings) bear the imprint of a publisher. In each case, the plates for these were almost certainly owned by the publisher. Of the remaining plates there is good reason to believe that at least one hundred and forty of them remained in Alberti's hands until his death, at which point they were inherited by his daughters.

Alberti died in Rome on October 18, 1615. In a document described as a "Particola di Testamento di Cherubino Alberti," Alberti named as his sole heir his son, Carlo, but explains that if he, Carlo, should

---

[56] The *Pietà* is listed in Bartsch, 17: 58, no. 23. An example is in the BM, London, inv. no. 1874–6–13–600. The *Madonna of the Rosary* is listed in Bartsch, 17: 62, no. 37. Vasari's altarpiece, executed by Jacopo Zucchi (1569), is in the Capponi-Compagnia del Rosario Chapel in Santa Maria Novella, Florence (unknown to Bartsch as the source for the print). The *Resurrection* is listed in Bartsch, 17: 58, no. 24. Examples are in the BM, London, inv. no. 8–491–8–1874; and the Marucelliana, Florence, vol. 13, no. 59 (not no. 52, which mistakenly also cites Bartsch, 17: no. 24 as a reference). Perino del Vaga's drawing is discussed in Arthur Ewart Popham and Johannes Wilde, *The Italian Drawings of the XV and XVI Centuries in the Collection of His Majesty the King at Windsor Castle* (London, 1949), 340, cat. no. 972.

Fig. 22. Cherubino Alberti, *Resurrection* (after Perino del Vaga). Engraving. Photo: Warburg.

die a minor, or, after coming of age, die without legitimate and natural sons, born from a legitimate marriage, his complete inheritance, without any diminution, would pass to Alberti's surviving daughters in equal portions.[57] However, if at that time any of his daughters had entered a convent, they would be excluded, and the inheritance would go to the daughters who are married, or were getting married, while those who were not married by this time should become nuns and would not be recipients of the inheritance. The document concluded by stating that the daughters would also be bound and obliged to erect a chapel in the church of S. Francesco in Borgo Sansepolcro, the home town of Cherubino and the Alberti family.

As later documents make clear, Cherubino's son Carlo did in fact die without producing a legitimate male heir, and the inheritance was passed to Cherubino's four daughters, Benedetta, Dionora, Francesca, and Caterina. In the meantime, Francesca had married Lattantio Pichi, Dionora had married Giuseppe Maria Guelfi, and Caterina had married Giuliano Alberti (who was also her cousin, the grandson of her great-uncle Girolamo Alberti). Benedetta, however, had become a nun in S. Lorenzo in Sansepolcro, and was therefore excluded. Cherubino's engraved copperplates were therefore inherited by the three married daughters, and their husbands.

The date of Carlo Alberti's death is unknown. In any case, given that Dionora, the eldest, was only eleven years old in 1615, it is unlikely that the inheritance passed immediately to the daughters. There is reason to believe, in fact, that the matter was not settled until the mid-1620s, at which time Cherubino's heirs evidently decided to publish a number of the plates now in their hands. Details of the plan to publish the plates survives in the form of a letter, dated 8 June 1627, sent by Lattantio Pichi, the husband of Francesca, to Cassiano del Pozzo in Rome.[58] Pichi had evidently written earlier and was now replying to Pozzo's response. Pichi's initial letter to

---

[57] The document is recorded in ASF, Conventi Soppresse (S. Francesco), Busta 246, N. 1, loose sheet. The essential contents of Alberti's will are summarized in a document published by Michelangelo Gualandi, "Memorie intorno la celebre famiglia degli Alberti di S. Sepolcro," in *Memorie Originale Italiane Risguardanti le Belle Arti*, vol. 2, serie 6 (Bologna, 1845), 66. This latter document, though listed as in the Archivio della Biblioteca delle Gallerie degli Uffizi, Florence by Giustiniani Degli Azzi, "Archivio Alberti," *Gli Archivi della Storia d'Italia*, serie 2, vol. 4 (Rocca S. Casciano, 1915), 234, can no longer be found.

[58] The letter is published in Bottari, 1: 341, no. 131. It is also noted in Bartsch, 17: 46.

Pozzo, who was the friend and advisor to Urban VIII's nephew Cardinal Francesco Barberini, must have concerned the expression of his wish to dedicate some of the prints to the Cardinal. In the letter of June 8, Pichi stated that he wanted to print the plates and to procure for them a *privilegio* from the pope and, if necessary, from the Duke of Tuscany, while offering the work to the protection of Cardinal [Francesco] Barberini. Reference is also made to "the honour of the good memory of Cherubino Alberti, his father-in-law" and to profiting from the inheritance.

Sometime between 8 June and 6 October 1627, writing on behalf of the heirs of Cherubino Alberti, Pichi submitted a supplication asking for a *privilegio* for fifteen or twenty years for Alberti's engraved copperplates of various works of Polidoro da Caravaggio and others as well as works of Alberti's own invention.[59] On 6 October, under the name of Cardinal Francesco Barberini, the request was approved, for fifteen years, and on 3 January 1628 the *privilegio* was officially issued.[60] Pichi did not waste any time in having the notice of copyright added to the plates. In several cases, he also added dedications, as well as other names and dates, and in a few cases erased previous inscriptions.

Perhaps the first plate Pichi turned his hand to, erasing in the process Gregory XIII's *privilegio* and adding Urban VIII's and changing the date from 1574 to 1628, was *The Agony in the Garden* after Rosso (the earlier state is seen in Fig. 21).[61] In the lower margin Pichi also added a dedication by the heirs of Cherubino Alberti to Cardinal Francesco Barberini. Thereafter, though, with the other prints he simply added Urban's *privilegio* to the plate, leaving Gregory's intact. Also carrying dedications to Cardinal Francesco Barberini are *The Cumaean Sibyl* from the Sistine Chapel ceiling, *Perseus Changing Atlas into a Mountain with the Head of Medusa* after Polidoro da Caravaggio, the *Winged Genius Holding a Tablet*, the two-plate *Triumph of Two Roman Emperors* after Polidoro, and the title-page of the nine-print set of *Antique Vases* after Polidoro.[62] Each of these prints also carries the

---

[59] The supplication is recorded in ASVat, SB, 733, fol. 52r.

[60] The *privilegio* is recorded in ASVat, SB, 733, fols. 80r.–v, 81r.–v.

[61] Whether Pichi undertook the actual engraving himself is unknown, but the evidence presented so far strongly suggests that he at least oversaw the project.

[62] The *Cumaean Sibyl* is listed in Bartsch, 17: 76, no. 73. Examples are in the BM, London, inv. no. 18–64–5–1927; the Marucelliana, Florence, vol. 13, no. 180; and the Farnesina, Rome, inv. no. 26733. The inscription reads "Opus in Capella

same notice of *privilegio*, "cum Privilegio Summi Pontificis," which occurs in the same form on a large number of undedicated prints by Alberti (of which four are also dated 1628), from which it may be suspected that in each case it signals the *privilegio* granted by Urban VIII and thus was added to the plates in 1628.

Besides Cardinal Francesco Barberini, Pichi also dedicated a print of *Renown Sounding a Trumpet* (Alberti's own invention?) to Casciano del Pozzo.[63] For reasons that are less clear, Pichi also dedicated five prints to Cardinal Lorenzo Magalotti, who was the brother-in-law of Urban VIII's younger brother Antonio Barberini. Three of the five are after Polidoro: an *Expulsion of Adam and Eve*, an *Adam and Eve after the Expulsion*, and a *Sacrifice of Isaac*.[64] Also dedicated to Magalotti are a *Prometheus* after Cristofano Gherardi (not Michelangelo, as Bartsch believes), and the scenes of *Venus Ascending towards Mt. Olympus, and Venus and Jupiter* after Raphael's fresco in the vault of the Loggia di Psiche in the Villa Farnesina.[65]

Vaticani a M. Ang. B. Rota/depictu et à Cherubino Alberti incisum cuius/haeredes Illmo Principi FRANCISCO/CARD. BARBERINO/Romæ 1628." The *Perseus Changing Atlas into a Mountain with the Head of Medusa* is listed in Bartsch, 17: 85, no. 108. Examples are in the MM, New York, inv. no. 41.97.442a; the BM, London, inv. no. 8–531–8–1874; and the Marucelliana, Florence, vol. 13, no. 112. The plate is in the Calcografia, Rome, inv. no. 1793–29. The design shows a detail of Polidoro's façade decoration of the Casino del Bufalo in Rome. The *Winged Genius Holding a Tablet* is listed in Bartsch, 17: 102, no. 145. Three Barberini bees have been added to the globe. The *Triumph of Two Roman Emperors* is listed in Bartsch, 17: 109, no. 160. Examples are in the BM, London, inv. no. 13–285–12–1873; and the Marucelliana, Florence, vol. 13, nos. 110, 111. The plates are in the Calcografia, Rome, inv. nos. 1793–16, 1793–17. The design is from the façade of a house decorated by Polidoro in Piazza Madama. The set of *Antique Vases* is listed in Bartsch, 17: 110, no. 161. Examples are in the BM, London, inv. no. 8–561–8–1874; and the Marucelliana, Florence, vol. 13, no. 150. All ten prints (Bartsch, 17: nos. 161–170) were probably included in the dedication. According to the original inscription, the title-page, and presumably also the other nine prints in the set, were engraved by Alberti in 1582. The designs are based on the vases painted by Polidoro in a frieze between the first and second floors of the façade of the Palazzo Milesi in Rome. The plates are in the Calcografia, Rome, inv. no. 1793–30.

[63] The print is listed in Bartsch, 17: 106, no. 152. An example is in the MM, New York, inv. no. 51.501.646. The plate is in the Museo Civico, Sansepolcro. A copy in reverse, omitting the date and the *privilegio* inscription, is in the BM, London, inv. no. 8–554–8–1874.

[64] The *Expulsion of Adam and Eve* is listed in Bartsch, 17: 49, no. 2. The *Adam and Eve after the Expulsion* is listed in Bartsch, 17: 50, no. 3. The *Sacrifice of Isaac* is listed in Bartsch, 17: 50, no. 4. An example is in the MM, New York, inv. no. 59.570.336.

[65] The *Prometheus* is listed in Bartsch, 17: 80, no. 92. Examples are in the BM, London, inv. no. 8–519–8–1874; and the Marucelliana, Florence, vol. 13, no. 108. The print is after a fresco by Cristofano Gherardi executed in the so-called Prometheus

A number of prints not dedicated by Pichi but otherwise inscribed with Urban VIII's *privilegio* are worthy to be considered as candidates for re-issuance. The print showing the *Three Graces; Venus with Juno and Ceres*, for example, from Raphael's *The Story of Psyche* in the Loggia di Psyche, originally dedicated in 1582 by Alberti to Cardinal Alessandro Farnese was reprinted with the added inscription "Cum privilegio Vrbani VIII P.M."[66] Also, the *Winged Genius Seated on a Cloud, Sounding a Trumpet*, inscribed "1628 Cum Privilegio Summi Pontificis," and the six prints of Michelangelo's sibyls and prophets from the Sistine Chapel ceiling, including that showing the *Lybian Sibyl and the Prophet Daniel*, originally dedicated by Alberti to Duke Francesco de' Medici in 1577 and subsequently inscribed "Cum privilegio Summi Pontificis 1628."[67] Two of the prints in this series, *The Prophet Ezekiel* and *The Prophet Isaiah* (Fig. 23), however, broach an awkward problem.[68] Both prints are clearly unfinished and one wonders if they had in fact ever been published during Alberti's own lifetime. Moreover, for both these prints, and several others inscribed with Urban VIII's *privilegio*, such as *The Adoration of the Magi*, dated 1574, after Rosso Fiorentino, and the undated *Angel Supporting the Body of Christ*, no earlier states are known, raising the possibility that the copyrighted state is in fact the first state.[69] With other prints to which the notice of *privilegio* has been added, such as the ineptly

---

Room in the Castello Bufalini at S. Giustino, a few miles to the south of Sansepolcro. The print is signed and dated 1582 by Alberti. The *Venus Ascending towards Mt. Olympus, and Venus and Jupiter* is listed in Bartsch, 17: 85, no. 107. An example is in the BM, London, inv. no. 8–530–8–1874.

[66] The print is listed in Bartsch, 17: 84, no. 106. Examples are in the BM, London, inv. no. 8–529–8–1874; and the Marucelliana, Florence, vol. 13, no. 140. The landscapes in the lunettes appear to be Alberti's own invention.

[67] The *Winged Genius Seated on a Cloud, Sounding a Trumpet* is listed in Bartsch, 17: 101, no. 141. Examples are in the BM, London, inv. no. 8–547–8–1874; and the NG, Washington, acc. no. B-26,230. An earlier state without any lettering is in the BM, London, inv. no. 13–1827–12–1873. The *Lybian Sibyl and the Prophet Daniel* is listed in Bartsch, 17: 76, no. 72. An example is in the MM, New York, inv. no. 17.50.19–153. An example of an earlier state, unknown to Bartsch, is in the Marucelliana, Florence, vol. 13, no. 60.

[68] *The Prophet Ezekiel* is listed in Bartsch, 17: 77, no. 77. Examples are in the BM, London, inv. no. 18–68–5–1927; and the Marucelliana, Florence, vol. 13, no. 178. The plate is in the Museo Civico, Sansepolcro. *The Prophet Isaiah* is listed in Bartsch, 17: 77, no. 76. Examples are in the BM, London, inv. no. 18–67–5–1927, and V.2–66; and the Marucelliana, Florence, vol. 13, no. 176. The plate is in the Calcografia, Rome, inv. no. 1793–12.

[69] *The Adoration of the Magi* is listed in Bartsch, 17: 54, no. 12. Examples are in the MM, New York, inv. no. 62.602.302; the Marucelliana, Florence, vol. 13, no. 35;

Fig. 23. Cherubino Alberti, *The Prophet Isaiah* (after Michelangelo).
Engraving. Photo: Warburg.

engraved and unfinished *Young Tobias Brought Before the Virgin and Child*, one again wonders whether Alberti had ever intended to publish them at all during his own lifetime, and whether the activities of his son-in-law in 1628 were perhaps causing him to turn in his grave![70]

Although the case of Lattantio Pichi and Alberti's plates is an unusual one, it can be noted that Anthonie van Santfoort had been granted a *privilegio* for prints by Cornelis Cort that he had inherited from the engraver after his death and which, it seems likely, Cort had not published (see Chapter 9). In another instance, mentioned in the Introduction, the *privilegio* was added by Titian to two plates by Cort that had been engraved the previous year but, it is suggested, had not yet been published. These cases should alert the student of sixteenth-century prints to the possibility that the date of a *privilegio* may not necessarily indicate also the date a plate was engraved, and that a number of surviving prints may never have been published by their original owner.

Michaeli Grecchi Lucchese

Michaeli Grecchi Lucchese's career as an engraver appears to have been underway by 1547, which is the date on a set of prints of architectural fantasies. Later, the date 1553 appears on two of Lucchese's prints, one of the *Madonna di Loreto* after Raphael, and the other depicting *Romulus Ploughing the Confines of Rome* after a frieze panel painted by Polidoro da Caravaggio on the façade of the Palazzo Boniauguri in Rome. Lucchese also painted. On September 2, 1558, he is described as consul in the Accademia di San Luca in Rome.[71]

---

and the Uffizi, Florence, inv. no. 1571. The print is after a lost cartoon by Rosso. The *Angel Supporting the Body of Christ* is listed in Bartsch, 17: 57, no. 21. Examples are in the BM, London, inv. no. 8–489–8–1874; and the Marucelliana, Florence, vol. 13, no. 38.

[70] The *Young Tobias Brought Before the Virgin and Child* in listed in Bartsch, 17: 61, no. 32, where it is described as one of Alberti's first engravings. An early proof of the print (unknown to Bartsch), in which Alberti sketched in some ideas with pen and ink in the unfinished landscape background, is in the Marucelliana, Florence, vol. 13, no. 6. The plate is in the Calcografia, Rome, inv. no. 1793.15.

[71] Lucchese's career is discussed in Bernice Davidson, "Introducing Michaeli Grechi Lucchese," *Art Bulletin* 46 (1964): 550–552. The *Madonna di Loreto* is listed in Passavant, 6: 167, no. 4. Examples of the print of *Romulus Ploughing the Confines of Rome* are in the Farnesina, Rome, vol. 34 H. 27, inv. no. 31586; and in the BN, Paris, Ba I, XVI, vol. 5.

A number of his prints carry notice of copyright (usually written simply as *cum privilegio*) but with no date. Among his copyrighted prints are a *Moses Striking Water from the Rock*, a copy of Marcantonio's *Massacre of the Innocents* (without the fir tree), after Raphael, a copy of Marcantonio's *Martyrdom of St. Lawrence* after Baccio Bandinelli, and a copy of Agostino Veneziano's *The Climbers* after Michelangelo. The *privilegio* also appears on a print of Giulio Romano's altarpiece, *Holy Family with Saints* in Santa Maria del Anima in Rome, and on *The Mystery of Diana of Ephesus* after Polidoro da Caravaggio's painting on the façade of the Palazzo Gaddi on Via della Maschera d'Oro in Rome.[72] From what is known about his career, it may be surmised that his copyrighted prints most likely all date to after 1560.

* * *

For the following engravers, documents survive in the Vatican Secret Archives. However, there are a number of extant prints by these same engravers inscribed with a notice of copyright for which the appropriate archival document has not been found.

Diana Mantuana

One of the earliest surviving documents for a papal *privilegio* granted for prints is that issued to the engraver Diana Mantuana. Born in Mantua, probably in 1547, Diana was the daughter of the engraver

---

[72] The *Moses Striking Water from the Rock.* is inscribed "M.L. cum privilegio." Examples of states with Lucchese's monogram and notice of *privilegio* are in the Farnesina, Rome, vol. 34 H. 27, inv. no. 31540; the BN, Paris, Ba I, XVI, vol. 5. Passavant, 6: 167, no. 2, notes only the title and is perhaps referring to a state without the inscriptions, an example of which is also in the BN, Paris, Ba I, XVI, vol. 5. Examples of the copy of Marcantonio's *Massacre of the Innocents* are in the Farnesina, Rome, vol. 24 H. 27, inv. no. 131272, and 31582. The print is listed in Bartsch, 14: no. 20, Copy B. The copy of Marcantonio's *Martyrdom of St. Lawrence* is listed in Bartsch, 14: no. 104 Copy C. Examples are in the Farnesina, Rome, vol. 34 H. 27, inv. no. 31585; and the BN, Paris, Ba I, XVI, vol. 5. An example of the copy of Agostino Veneziano's *The Climbers* is in the Farnesina, Rome, vol. 34 H. 27, inv. no. 31590. The print is listed in Bartsch, 14: no. 487. An example of the *Holy Family with Saints* is in the BM, London, inv. no. 1856–12–13–59. The print is inscribed "IVLII. ROMANI. INVENTUM/MICHAELIS LVCENSIS OPERA" plus also Lucchese's initials "M.L.," but which also carries the monogram of Mario Cartari. Another example is in the BN, Paris, Ba 1, XVI, vol. 5, which also has the address of Antonio Lafrery. The plate is preserved in the Calcografia, Rome, inv. no. 623. An example of *The Mystery of Diana of Ephesus* is in the BN, Paris, Ba 1, XVI, vol. 5.

Giovanni Battista Scultori (also known as Giovanni Battista Mantuano) and the sister of the engraver Adamo Scultori. Her relationship to Giovanni Battista Scultori is made clear on her print *Descent from the Cross*, the designer of which she identifies as Giovanni Battista Scultori and herself, the engraver, as his daughter ("IO BAPTISTA SCVLP-TOR/MANTVANVS INVENTOR/DIANA FILIA INCIDEBAT").[73] Her first engravings may date as early as 1560 when she was perhaps only thirteen or fourteen years old. In 1565 the architect Francesco Capriani from Volterra came to Guastalla where he was employed on architectural projects by Cesare Gonzaga and probably in these same years also worked in Mantua. At this time, Francesco must have met Diana and the couple may have married soon thereafter.[74] By 1570 Francesco was in Rome where, in the service of Cardinal d'Este, he worked on projects in Tivoli and in the Palazzo del Quirinale.[75] It is likely that Diana was with him. In 1573, Francesco took out a freehold lease (*enfiteusi*) from the Convent of S. Agostino for a house in the Campo Marzio.[76] On 2 September 1578, the couple had a son, Giovanni Battista, who was baptized in the church of S. Agostino in Rome, with the painter Durante Alberti standing as his god-father. On 10 April 1580, "Madonna Diana Mantovana, moglie di messer Francesco Volterra" was proposed as a member of the Virtuosi al Pantheon.[77]

---

[73] The print is listed in Bartsch, 15: 435, no. 7. Vasari, 1568, 6: 490, also refers to Diana as the daughter of Giovanni Battista Mantovano. It may also be noted that in a letter dated 30 April 1583 written by Monsignor Aurelio Zibramonte in Rome to the court of Mantua, reference is made to "la famosa Diana figlia già di M. Gio. Battista Scultori." Zibramonte's letter is transcribed in Bertolotti, *Artisti in Relazione coi Gonzaga Duchi di Mantova nei secoli XVI e XVIII* (Modena, 1885), 17.

[74] According to Carlo D'Arco, *Istoria della vita e delle opere di Giulio Pippi detto Romano* (Mantua, 1838), 80, they were married in 1567. Valeria Pagani, "Adamo Scultori and Diana Mantovana," *Print Quarterly* 9 (1992): 75, however, states that this is pure conjecture. Evelyn Lincoln, "Making a Good Impression: Diana Mantuana's Printmaking Career," *Renaissance Quarterly* 50 (1997): 1101, gives their marriage date as 1575.

[75] Documents recording payments made to Francesco for his work at Tivoli for the years 1570, 1572, 1573, and 1577 have been published by David R. Coffin, *The Villa d'Este at Tivoli* (Princeton, 1960).

[76] The document is in ASR, Atti Romauli, 30 Notai Capitolini, off. 30, vol. 28 fol. 242v.–245r. The house had been granted to him by the friars at S. Agostino with the provision that he restore and maintain it. The façade of the house was painted by Raffaellino da Reggio (Baglione, 26) who was a very good friend of Francesco Capriani (Baglione, 49). Several examples of Raffaellino da Reggio's work were engraved by Diana Mantuana (see below).

[77] Her husband Francesco had been a member of the Virtuosi al Pantheon since 1577. It may be noted that together with Diana, Madalena, the wife of the engraver

On 5 June 1575, Diana Mantuana was granted a ten-year *privilegio* by Pope Gregory XIII for five prints she had engraved.[78] The granting document had been issued by Gregory XIII's Secretary for Briefs, Cesare Glorieri.[79] The document refers to Diana Mantuana as the wife of the architect Francesco Cipriani [sic], and a resident in Rome. Four of the five engravings listed can be readily identified among Diana's known oeuvre, an identification which can be confirmed in each case by the presence on each of the prints of a *privilegio* inscription. The first three are described as after designs by Giulio Romano. The first, "Historiam evangelij de adultera," may be identified as the large, single-plate *Christ and the Adultress* (Fig. 24).[80] In the lower left corner is inscribed the name Giulio Romano as the inventor, and Diana as the engraver: "IULIUS R./INVENTOR/DIANA F." In the bottom centre appears the *privilegio* inscription: "CON PRIVILEGIO DI PAPA GREGOR XIII/PER ANNI X." The second print, "Convivium Deorum," can be identified as the three-plate *Preparations for the Wedding Feast of Cupid and Psyche* after Giulio Romano's fresco in the Palazzo del Te.[81] On a plaque above the door on the left of the first print in the series is the inscription "IVLIVS/ROM/ INVENTOR/DIANA F." At the bottom left of the third print is the *privilegio* inscription: "D. GREGORII PP XIII/PRIVILEGIO AD DECEM/ROMAE MDLXXV." The third print listed in the granting document is described as a "Cursus, seu carceres equorum Triumphi Caesaris," which provides a more interesting and informative title to another three-plate print usually identified somewhat blandly as a *Procession of Roman Horsemen*.[82] In the lower left corner

---

Natale Bonifacio ("Madonna Madalena, moglie del Natale Bonifatio") was also proposed for membership. It is possible that she was also an engraver, though nothing of her work is known. Natale Bonifacio had been proposed as a member two years earlier on 9 February 1578. For Natale Bonifacio, see Chapter 7.

[78] The document is recorded in ASVat, Arm. 42, vol. 28, fol. 213r.–v.

[79] Glorieri occupied the position until 1584 when he was dismissed by Gregory XIII.

[80] The print is listed in Bartsch, 16: 434, no. 4; and catalogued in Stefania Massari, *Incisori Mantovani* (Rome, 1981), no. 150. The illustration in Fig. 24 here is of the second state to which has been added the address of Antonio Carenzano. Carenzano had purchased the plate for this print after Diana's death and reprinted it in 1613. The plate is preserved in the Calcografia, Rome, inv. no. 624.

[81] The print is listed in Bartsch, 16: 449, no. 40; and catalogued in Massari, *Incisori Mantovani*, no. 149; and Paolo Bellini, *L'Opera incisa di Adamo e Diana Scultori* (Vicenza, 1991), 201, no. 23.

[82] The print is listed in Bartsch, 16: 452, no. 45; and catalogued in Massari, *Incisori Mantovani*, cat. no. 146. Massari titles the prints "Trionfo di Sigismondo." One of the plates is in the Calcografia, Rome, inv. no. 643.

Fig. 24. Diana Mantuana, *Christ and the Adultress* (after Giulio Romano). 1575. Engraving. Photo: Warburg.

of the first print in the series is the inscription "IVLIVS/RO. IN./ DIANA/F." The notice of *privilegio* appears in the lower right of the third print: "SVM. PONT. PRIVILEGIO/ROMAE. M.D.LXXV." These three prints are the largest and most ambitious of Diana's engraving projects and were highly admired. In a letter to Francesco Capriani, Diana's prints are described as "mirabilissime" and the *Preparations for the Wedding Feast of Cupid and Psyche* in particular is praised as a "cosa stupenda."[83]

The fourth print is described as a *Nativity* designed by the miniaturist Giulio Clovio, but which has not been traced. The fifth and last print is a *St. Jerome*, described as being the "model and invention" of Daniele da Volterra. The print is inscribed "DANIEL VOLATER. INVENT. DIANA ROMAE INCIDEBAT" in the lower right, and "PRIVILEGIO. D. GREG. PP. XIII" in the lower left. A painting of *St. Jerome* that is clearly related to the engraving and possibly by Daniele da Volterra that was originally located in the church of S. Marta behind the Vatican, was identified recently by Paolo Bellini.[84]

It is reasonable to assume that the drawings for the first three engravings, which are of designs executed by Giulio Romano in Mantua, and perhaps also the prints themselves, were produced while Diana was in Mantua. The last two prints, however, after Giulio Clovio and Daniele da Volterra, both artists who were working in Rome during these years, were probably done after Diana's arrival in that city. The *St. Jerome*, it may be noticed, is inscribed as engraved by Diana in Rome ("DIANA ROMAE INCIDEBAT").

Besides being published with a papal *privilegio*, the three prints after Giulio Romano were all dedicated to members of the Gonzaga family. The *Preparations for the Wedding Feast of Cupid and Psyche* was dedicated to Claudio Gonzaga (of Borgoforte), at that time a prelate in Rome. From the dedicatory inscription in the lower left corner it is clear that Claudio Gonzaga assisted Diana in procuring the *privilegio*.[85]

---

[83] The letter is reproduced in Bottari, 4: 87.

[84] The discovery was first published by Paolo Bellini, "Alcuni dati sull'attività romana di Diana Scultori," *Paragone* 38 (1987): 56. The print had not been previously catalogued. It is discussed in greater detail in Bellini, *Adamo e Diana Scultori*, 208, no. 25. Evelyn Lincoln, "Diana Mantuana's Printmaking Career," 1119–1123, argues that both the engraving and the painting were based on a lost drawing by Daniele da Volterra. The painting is now in the Vatican Museum.

[85] The inscription reads: "All'Ill.mo S.r Claudio Gonzaga/Diana Mantuana/e cosa conveniente che questa mia fatica havendo ricevuto/l'essere sotto il dominio

The *Christ and the Adultress* was dedicated to Eleonora of Austria, the wife of Duke Francesco Gonzaga and Duchess of Mantua. The *Horsemen* was dedicated to Scipione Gonzaga. The dedicatory inscriptions on the first two are dated 1 September 1575, three months after Diana was granted the *privilegio*. If through the dedication of the *Wedding Feast* Diana wished to acknowledge the support of Claudio Gonzaga, her decision to dedicate the *Horsemen* to Scipione Gonzaga was perhaps in the hope of winning a future patron. In the 1560s Scipione Gonzaga was beginning to amass a collection of prints that by the time of his death in 1593 filled several large volumes.[86]

Besides the five prints listed in the papal document, the *privilegio* also appears on four other engravings by Diana. Evidently the *privilegio*, as we have seen elsewhere, was understood to extend to other works not mentioned in the initial document. Two of the prints are dated 1575: a *Sacrifice of Abraham* after Giulio Clovio, and a *Madonna and Child with the Young John the Baptist* after Raffaellino da Reggio.[87] A *Christ and Mary Magdalen at the Table of Simon the Pharisee* after Giulio Campi is dated 1576, and the fourth, a *Holy Family in Egypt* after Correggio, is dated 1577.[88]

Leonardo Caccianemici

On 1 March 1577, the obscure engraver Leonardo Caccianemici from Bologna was granted a ten-year *privilegio* by Gregory XIII for

---

dell'Eccell.ma casa vostra riceva ancora il ben essere sotto il nome di V. S. Ill.ma poiché hora ella/viene in luce favorita da lei con amplissimo Privilegio del/la S.ta di Nostro Sig.r Ricevila dunque con benigno animo/et con essa la servitu di casa mia in Roma il di' primo/dì di Setembre MDLXXV."

[86] Scipione Gonzaga's print collection is discussed in Alessandro Luzio, *La Galleria dei Gonzaga venduta all'Inghilterra nel 1627–28* (Milan, 1913), especially Appendix E, "La collezione di stampe del Card. Scipione Gonzaga. Lettere di Giorgio Alario," pages 273–74.

[87] The *Sacrifice of Abraham* is listed in Passavant, 6: 142, no. 47; and catalogued in Massari, *Incisori Mantovani*, 101, no. 154; and Bellini, *Adamo e Diana Scultori*, 193, no. 19. The *Madonna and Child with the Young John the Baptist* is listed Bartsch, 15: 440, no. 18; and catalogued in Massari, *Incisori Mantovani*, 100, no. 153; and Bellini, *Adamo e Diana Scultori*, 199, no. 22.

[88] The *Christ and Mary Magdalen at the Table of Simon the Pharisee* is listed in Bartsch, 15: 433, no. 3; and Passavant, 6: 142, no. 3; and catalogued in Massari, *Incisori Mantovani*, 101, no. 155; and Bellini, *Adamo e Diana Scultori*, 211, no. 28. The *Holy Family in Egypt* is listed in Bartsch, 15: 440, no. 19; and catalogued in Bellini, *Adamo e Diana Scultori*, 222, no. 36. An example of the print is in the MM, New York, inv. no. 29.49.19.

"figuras sanctorumque imagines et similia" among which are listed what appears to be a Deposition, a St. Cartherine "desponsatio," a "Jesus exeuntis de templo dilapidationis actus," Aesop, and a map: "Orbe Civitatum geographica."[89] Nothing is known about any of these prints, and very little about Leonardo Caccianemici. It seems likely he was the son or nephew of Vincenzo Caccianemici, a painter and printmaker also from Bologna who, according to Vasari, died in 1542. Vasari mentions only his work as a painter and refers to a now lost *Beheading of St. John the Baptist* in S. Petronio in Bologna.[90] A handful of prints have been associated with Vincenzo, including some etchings, a technique he may have learned from Parmigianino. Both Leonardo and Vincenzo may also be related to Francesco Caccianemici who worked as an assistant to Primaticcio at Fontainebleau.

Aliprando Capriolo

Like Giovanni Battista de' Cavalieri, Aliprando Capriolo was from the Trentino in northern Italy. He was in Rome by 1574 when his name appears in a list of *confrati* of the Virtuosi al Pantheon where he is described as an "engraver of copperplate prints."[91] Like many engravers of his generation working in Rome in the 1570s he was influenced by the engraving style of Cornelis Cort and may in fact have been one of his pupils. Like Cristofano Cartari's, the similarity of Capriolo's technique and style of treatment to Cort's has made difficult the attribution of unsigned prints.[92]

His earliest dated print, a *Last Supper* after Taddeo Zuccaro, was engraved in the Jubilee Year of 1575 and carries a dedication by Caprioli to Giovanni Federico Madruzzo.[93] A two-plate *Assumption of*

[89] The document is recorded in ASVat, Arm. 42, vol. 29, fols. 239r.–240r. The document was first published by Lamberto Donati, "Chi fu Leonardo Caccianemici?" *Maso Finiguerra* 1 (1936): 248–49.

[90] Vasari, 1568, 5: 238.

[91] Caprioli's membership of the Virtuosi al Pantheon is given in Orbaan, "Virtuosi al Pantheon," 32: "Messer Alibrando Caprioli, intagliatore di stampe in rame; 1574."

[92] Caprioli's life is discussed in Guido Suster, "Dell'incisore trentino Aliprando Caprioli," *Archivio Trentino* 18 (1903): 144–206. Bierens de Haan, 237, lists prints by Cristofano Cartari that are often mistaken for those of Cort.

[93] The print of the *Last Supper* is listed in Suster, 150, no. 1. Examples are in the Uffizi, Florence, inv. nos. 9757 and 1476. Giovanni Federico Madruzzo, the Conte di Challant, was the nephew of Cardinal Cristoforo Madruzzo. The second state carries the address of Philippe Thomassin and Giovanni Turpino [Jean Turpin] (for whom, see below).

the Virgin, after Taddeo Zuccaro's fresco in SS. Trinità dei Monti in Rome, dated 1577, was dedicated to Cardinal Theano. Both this print and that of *St. James Fighting the Moors in Spain* after Paris Nogari dated 1579, appear in Andrea and Michelangelo Vaccari's list of prints for sale in their shop in 1614.[94]

Besides single sheets, Capriolo also engraved sets of prints. A set of fifty prints (plus the frontispiece) he engraved after drawings by Bernardino Passari illustrating the life and miracles of St. Benedict was published "Cum licentia superiorum" in 1579 for the Spanish Benedictine Congregation at S. Benedetto di Valladolid under Cristobal de Agüero.[95]

On 2 April 1596, Capriolo was granted a papal *privilegio* for some unspecified prints, for his book *Centum Armorum Duces,* and for his set of twelve prints illustrating the *Articoli del Credo degli Apostoli.*[96] The *Centum Armorum Duces* is composed of one hundred engraved portraits of distinguished commanders each printed with a brief account written by Capriolo of their exploits on the battlefield.[97] The accounts were written by Capriolo using information drawn from a variety of historical sources listed on page four of the book. Among the sources cited, it may be noted, is a "Helia Capriolo," who wrote a history

---

[94] The print of the *Assumption of the Virgin* is listed in Suster, 153, no. 2. Examples are in the Marucelliana, Florence, vol. 11, no. 145; and the Uffizi, Florence, inv. no. 1475. The print of *St. James Fighting the Moors in Spain* is listed in Suster, 154, no. 3. The print had formerly been given to Cornelis Cort by Heinecken, 4: 348. An example is in the BN, Paris, Ec 34b, p. 34. The listing of these prints for sale in the Vaccari print shop is given in Ehrle, *Roma Prima di Sisto V,* 62, line 209: "Doi fogli dell'Assunto della Madonna di Taddeo Zuccaro, intagliata da Alibranzo Capriolo"; and 61, line 133: "San Giacomo contro i Mori in Spagna intagliata da Alibrazo Capriola."

[95] "VITA ET MIRACULA SANCTISSmi PATRIS/BENEDICTI Ex libro ii Dialogorum Beati/GREGORII Papae et Monachi/collecta. Et ad instantiam Devotorum/Monachorum Congregationis eius/dem S.ti. BENEDICTI Hispania/rum aeneis typis accuratissime/delineata./ROMAE—ANNO—M.D.LXX.VIIII." An example is in the Uffizi, Florence, inv. no. 95160. The book was dedicated to Cardinal Giacomo Savelli, the congregation's protector. The book was republished in Rome in 1584, 1594, 1596, and 1597 (edition of Paolo Arnolfini; an example is in the Casanatense, Rome, K.II.21.1.CCC), and in Florence in 1586. The book was reprinted in 1980 by the Abbazia di Praglia on the occasion of the fifteen-hundreth anniversary of the birth of St. Benedict.

[96] The *privilegio* is recorded in ASVat, SB, 238, fol. 28r.–v.

[97] "RITRATTI/DI/CENTO CAPITANI/ILLVSTRI/Intagliati/da Aliprando Capriolo/Con li lor fatti in guerra/da lui brevemente scritte/IN ROMA/1596/Con licenza de Superiori." The colophon reads: "IN ROMA/Per Domenico Gigliotti. M.D. XCVI/CON LICENZA DE' SVPERIORI."

of Brescia and who may in fact have been a scholarly relative of the engraver.[98] Starting with "Federico Primo Barbarossa," Capriolo includes among a selection of recent emperors, kings, and princes, various members of prominent Italian families: the Este, Sforza, Visconti, Orsini, and Gonzaga. Of this group, however, the Gonzaga are given special prominence with no fewer than eight members of the family included. Moreover, Capriolo dedicated the book to Vincenzo Gonzaga, the third Duke of Mantua.

Surviving letters written by Capriolo in Rome to Annibale Cheppio, Vincenzo Gonzaga's secretary in 1595 and 1596, provide an insight into the project.[99] Having already obtained the Duke of Mantua's support, Capriolo wrote on 27 May 1595 tactfully asking for advice on the series of Gonzaga commanders. He points out first that for "Francesco primo" and "Federigo terzo marchese" monsignor Giulio Capilupi had given him two portraits painted by Lorenzo Costa in the guardarobba of Cardinal Scipione Gonzaga, but wanted to know if he should also include Federigo da Bozzolo, "who never achieved the rank of general and was always unlucky in war."[100] In another letter dated 1 July 1595 concerning the accompanying text for each portrait Capriolo explains that it is enough for him to be sent only succinct notices of their deeds in war as this is all each will contain and no more.

The dedication inscription is dated 1 January 1596, and three months later, on 15 March, Capriolo sent some copies of the book to the Duke of Mantua, followed by some more copies on 30 March. The purpose of Capriolo's letters, dedication, and inclusion of Gonzaga family members among the illustrious warriors of recent history, it should not be forgotten, was to entice the Duke into acknowledging with a handsome reward the honour thereby bestowed on him and

---

[98] The book cited by Caprioli may be identified as *Delle historie bresciane di M. Helia Cavriolo libri dodeci . . . Fatti volgari dal molto rev. D. Patritio Spini . . . et aggiontovi doppo il Cavriolo, quanto è seguito sino all'anno 1585 . . .* which was published in Brescia, "appresso P. M. Marchetti" (i.e. Pietro Maria Marchetti) in 1585. A copy is in the BA, Vatican, Barberini Q XIII 21). Elia (or Helia) Capriolo (or Cavrioli) died in 1510.

[99] The letters were published by Bertolotti in "Lettere inedite di Aliprando Caprioli," *Archivio storico per Trieste, l'Istria e il Trentino* 3 (1884): 117–119. They were also published by Bertolotti in *Artisti Veneti in Roma* (Venice, 1884), 37–39.

[100] Besides Lorenzo Costa, Capriolo also used Dürer and Titian as sources for his portraits.

his family through Capriolo's exertions. In a letter dated 12 May 1596, Capriolo thanks the Duke for a gratuity of fifty gold *scudi*.

Besides the *Cento Capitani Illustri*, the *privilegio* also covered a series of twelve prints illustrating the articles of the Apostles Creed, the *Articoli del Credo degli Apostoli*. These plates, however, were not published until 1599 after they had been acquired by Philippe Thomassin following Capriolo's death (see below).

Francesco Villamena

According to Baglione, the engraver Francesco Villamena from Assisi arrived in Rome during the papacy of Sixtus V.[101] One his earliest dated prints is a copy of Cornelis Cort's (or perhaps Cristofano Cartari's) engraving of Correggio's *Madonna and Child with St. Jerome and Mary Magdalen*, dated 1586.[102] In 1588 his engraving of the *Vision of St. Catherine of Siena* after Ventura Salimbeni was issued with a *privilegio*, as was his print, dated 1589, of *King Alfonso Expelling the Moors from Spain* engraved after a design by Antonio Tempesta, which was printed in Rome by T. Moneta with a *privilegio* granted by Sixtus V.[103] In 1594, Villamena engraved the frontispiece and a series of fifty-one images in *S. Francisci historia cum iconibus in aere excusis*, published by Andrea de Puttis.[104]

Two years later, on 8 October 1596, Villamena was granted a ten-year *privilegio* by Clement VIII for a number of unnamed engravings of religious subjects.[105] This *privilegio* would appear to be that indicated on several prints issued in 1597. Two are after designs by Ferraù Fenzoni: *Moses and the Brazen Serpent* inscribed "Romae Cum Privilegio Summi/Pontificis Anno MDXCVII" in the lower left and "Superiorum Permissu" in the lower right, and *St. Francis with a Vision of the Madonna and Child*, with "Romae Cum Privilegio Summi Pontificis

---

[101] Baglione, 392.

[102] The print is listed in Bierens de Haan, 71, no. 50 (Copy b.). An example of a later state is in the BN, Paris, Eb. 15, fol. 21, with the address added of the Florentine printer Benedictus de Claro ("Benedictus de Claro Florentinus Formis Romae").

[103] An example of each print is in the BN, Paris, Eb 15, fol. 23 and fol. 68, respectively.

[104] The series is catalogued in Dorothee Kühn-Hattenhauer, Das Grafische Oeuvre des Francesco Villamena, Ph.D. diss., Freien Universität, Berlin, 1979, 24.

[105] The *privilegio* is recorded in ASVat, SB, 356, fols. 91r.–v, 92r. A copy of the *Motu proprio* is interleaved unpaginated between fols. 91 and 92.

et Superiorum permissu Anno" in the lower left, and the date "Sesquimillesimo Nonagesimo Septimo" [i.e. 1597] in the lower right.[106] The *privilegio* and the date 1597 also appear on Villamena's engraving of the *Stigmatization of St. Francis* after Federico Barocci, which Villamena dedicated to Paolo Sanvitale, Bishop of Spoleto, as well as on his *Rest on the Return from Egypt* after Girolamo Muziano.[107] It also appears on a print of the *Presentation in the Temple* after Paolo Veronese dedicated by Villamena to Marcello Vestrio Barbiano.[108] Villamena's chances of being granted a *privilegio* for this last print must have been greatly enhanced by the dedication; Marcello Vestrio Barbiano was the Papal Secretary of Latin Briefs (see below).[109] In the last two years of the century, the *privilegio* also appears on two prints engraved by Villamena after designs by Mario Arconio: an *Annunciation* dated 1598 and dedicated to Asdrubale Mattei, and a large sheet with a portrait of Clement VIII dated 1599.[110]

In the Jubilee year of 1600, several prints by Villamena appeared carrying a *privilegio*. One issued "Cum Priuilegio Summi Pontificis atq[ue] Superiorum Permisu. Anno Iubilei. 1600" depicts a triumphant

---

[106] The print of *Moses and the Brazen Serpent* is listed in Zani, 2, 3: 213. The print is also mentioned in Baglione, 393. An example is in the BN, Paris, Eb. 15, fol. 3. The print was dedicated by Villamena to Clementi Bartholo: "Per illustri D.D. Clementi Bartholo, Patricio Vrbinati, virtutum, a bonarum artium protectori praesantiss. Franciscus Villamena Viro optimo . . . dicavit." The plate was acquired and printed in a second state by Giovanni Marco Paluzzi ("Gio. Marco Paluzzi Formis romae"). An example is in the Casanatense, Rome, vol. 20.B.I.89/81. The print of *St. Francis with a Vision of the Madonna and Child* is listed in Kühn-Hattenhauer, 165. An example is in the BN, Paris, Eb. 15, fol. 57. The print was dedicated by Villamena to Fabio Orsini: "Ill.mo et R.mo Fabio—Ursino virtutem/omnium, et bonarum—artium Patrono/Franciscus—Villamena D.D." (in the lower margin with Orsini's coat of arms in the centre).

[107] The print of Barocci's *Stigmatization of St. Francis* is listed in Kühn-Hattenhauer, 172. Examples are in the Casanatense, Rome, vol. 20.B.I.69/119; and the BN, Paris, Eb 15, fol. 59. Kühn-Hattenhauer, 25, also notes a copy of Villamena's print engraved by Luca Ciamberlano ("Luca Ciamberlano fe"). The print of the *Rest on the Return from Egypt* is listed in Kühn-Hattenhauer, 195. Examples are in the Marucelliana, Florence, vol. 70, no. 11; and the BN, Paris, Eb 15, fol. 23.

[108] The print is listed in Kühn-Hattenhauer, 207. An example is in the BN, Paris, Eb. 15, fol. 13. The print is inscribed: "Quod opus de Christo Iesu in templo oblato Paulus Veronensis pictor eximius penicillo expressit Franciscus Villamena Assisias aere incisum." The dedication reads: "Admodum Ill. et R.mo Marcello Vestrio Barbiano Secretario Apostolico Virtutum Patrono D.D.D."

[109] Marcello Vestrio Barbiano's name first appears on papal briefs issued towards the end of the papacy of Sixtus V (1585–1590). He held the position of secretary of Latin briefs throughout the papacy of Clement VIII (1592–1605).

[110] An example of each print is in the BN, Paris, Eb 15, fol. 6 and fol. 45, respectively.

statue of Alexander the Great, dedicated to Ranuccio Farnese by Gaspare Celio, who did the drawing ("Gaspar Coelius delineator") and Villamena, who did the engraving ("Franciscus Villamena Scalptor [sic]").[111] Others include a labelled plan of the city of *Valletta* (Malta), a *Penitent St. Jerome* after Barocci, a *Crucifixion* drawn by Giovanni Baglione ("Ioannes Baglionus figuravit"), a large engraving of the relic of the tip of St. Longinus's lance, and a print filled with information about the seven churches of Rome ("SEPTEM VRBIS ECCLESIARVM DESCRIPTIO").[112]

After 1600 we find the *privilegio* appearing on several of Villamena's prints, including an engraving of Villamena's own design of *Barruffa defending himself against attacking Spaniards*, dated 1601 and dedicated by Villamena to Ciriaco Mattei, a *Madonna and Child with Sts. Anne, Elizabeth, and John the Baptist* after Raphael dated 1602, and *King David with his Harp* after Ippolito Andreasi, published by Philippe Thomassin in 1603.[113] The *privilegio* continues to appear on later prints by Villamena.

Jacopo Lauro

Little is known of Jacopo Lauro's early career. According to Giovanni Gori Gandellini, he was born in Rome in 1580, but a date twenty years earlier would be more feasible.[114] Antonino Bertolotti cites a document dated 6 July 1583 in which a barber reported having treated "Giacomo Lauro intagliatore di rame romano" after he had been injured in the jaw by a painter named Agostino.[115] Two years later, in 1585, his name appears as engraver on a print of *Perseus*

---

[111] Examples are in the Casanatense, Rome, vol. 20.B.I.90/41; and the BN, Paris, Eb 15, fol. 46. The engraving was printed in Rome "apud Ill.m Card.m Farnesium Filium./Simeonis Moschini Sculptoris egr." The address of Giovanni Marco Paluzzi ("Gio. Marco Palauzzi Formis Romæ") appears above.

[112] An example of each of the prints is in the BN, Paris, Eb 15, fol. 117, fol. 50, fol. 30, fol. 26, and fol. 44, respectively. The print of the *Crucifixion* is inscribed as "Il Vero ritratto della Gloriosa Madon[n]a delle Gratie de Canepina de Padri Carmelitani."

[113] An example of *Barruffa defending himself against attacking Spaniards* is in the Casanatense, Rome, vol. 20.B.I.89/74; and the BN, Paris, Eb 15. fol. 79. Examples of both the *Madonna and Child with Sts. Anne, Elizabeth, and John the Baptist* and the *King David with his Harp* can be found in the BN, Paris, Eb 15, fol. 17, and fol. 5, respectively.

[114] Gori Gandellini, *Notizie degli Intagliatori* (Siena, 1813), 11: 305.

[115] Bertolotti, *Giunti agli Artisti Belgi ed Olandesi in Roma* (Rome, 1885), 221.

published by Claudio Duchetti, and in 1590 on a late state of a print by Marco Dente da Ravenna after Raphael.[116]

The ten-year papal *privilegio* granted Lauro on 17 March 1598 was for an unspecified number of unnamed prints of religious subject matter.[117] One of the prints almost certainly covered by this *privilegio* is a *Septem Urbis ecclesiae cum earum reliquiis, stationibus et indulgentiis* engraved by Lauro after a design by Antonio Tempesta and dated 1599.[118] The print shows the traditional *Sette Basiliche* but also includes the *Tre Fontane* and the *Nunziatella*, thereby increasing the number shown to nine. Lauro's name also appears as the engraver on the first of the twelve small panels illustrating the *Apostles' Creed* published by Donato Rascicotti.[119]

In 1612 he published with a *privilegio* his *ANTIQVAE VRBIS SPLENDORIS*, dedicated to Ranuccio Farnese.[120] A *privilegio* also appears on a print dated 1614 of the *Garden of Ciriaco Mattei on Monte Celio*, designed by the architect Matteo Pampani, which Lauro dedicated to Mattei.[121]

---

[116] The print of *Perseus* is listed in Huelsen, "Das Speculum Romanae Magnificentiae," 165, no. 123. The later state of the Marco Dente print is listed in Leandro Ozzola, "Gli Editori di Stampa a Roma nei Secoli XVI e XVII," *Repertorium für Kunstwissenschaft* 33 (1910): 405.

[117] The *privilegio* is recorded in ASVat, SB, 268, fols. 451r.–v., 452r.

[118] An example is in the BA, Vatican, Riserva S.7. int. 136. Johann Jacob Merlos, *Kölnische Künstler in alter und Neuer Zeit* (Dusseldorf, 1895), col. 18, no. 57, lists a *Martyrdom of St. Sebastian* dated 1600 by Lauro, which he describes as a copy after a design by Hans von Aachen (corrected to "Al. Paduano" in Thieme-Becker, 22: 460) engraved by Johannes Muller and published by Hans Muller (no. 61). Merlos, however, does not say whether or not the print carried a *privilegio*.

[119] Titled "DVODECIM/ARTICVLI/SIMBOLI/APOSTOLICI/ICONIBVS/ EXPRESSI." The twelve small panels surround on three sides a large central panel showing the *Last Supper* engraved by Francesco Villamena after a design by Antonio Tempesta. The print carries a dedication by Rascicotti to Jacopo Danio, secretary to Grand Duke Ferdinand de' Medici. An example is in the BN, Paris, Eb. 15, fol. 27.

[120] An example is in the Farnesina, Rome, FC 32747, vol. 2921 (dated 1615). The full title-page reads: SERENISSIMI. PRINCEPS. RANVTII. FARNESII/PARMAE. ET. PLACENTIAE/INVICTISSIMI. DVCIS/AVSPICIO/ANTIQVAE VRBIS SPLENDORIS/CO[M]PLEMENTV[M]/... IN AERE GRAPHICE/DE SCRIBVNTVR ET ELEGANTER COMMENTARIIS EXPLICANTVR./IACOBO LAVRO ROMANO—AVTORE ET SCVLPTORE. Notice of the papal *privilegio*, and other privileges, appears below "Romae Cu[m] Privilegio—Sum[m]i Pontificis et Principum aliorum" with the date "ANNO DNI. MDCXV." Later editions are dated 1637 and 1641.

[121] An example is in the Farnesina, Rome, FC 66768. It may be noted that the obelisk shown in the garden was later moved and now stands at the top of the Spanish Steps in front of SS. Trinità dei Monti in Rome

Jan, Raphael, and Aegidius Sadeler

On 15 May 1598 the Flemish printers and engravers Jan, Raphael, and Aegidius Sadeler were granted a *privilegio* by Clement VIII for "diversas hystorias et figuras e novo et vetero testamento extractos etiam et alias prophanas hystorias."[122] There are a confusing number of Sadelers, but the ones to whom this *privilegio* was granted are certainly the two elder brothers, Jan I and Raphael I, and their nephew Aegidius (Gillis or Gilles, Egidius, or Egidio in Italy) II (the son of Gillis I). The first of the three, Jan (Joannes, Johannes, Hans, or Giovanni in Italy) Sadeler, was born in Brussels in 1550. In 1572 he was enrolled in the guild in Antwerp as a "coeper print snider." Raphael had been born in 1560 or 1561 in Antwerp, where his name appears in the guild for the first time in 1582. Aegidius had been born in Antwerp in 1570.

In 1580 Jan and his younger brother Raphael were in Cologne where Jan printed an engraving by Raphael, then nineteen years old, of an *Annunciation with Four Prophets* by Federico Zuccaro.[123] On 20 May 1580, Jan was granted a ten-year imperial *privilegio*, which appears, for example, on a set of twelve prints of the *Youth of Christ* engraved by Jan after designs by Martin de Vos.[124] Jan was still in Cologne in 1582, but by 1583 he was back in Antwerp.[125] Three years later, in 1586, Jan, together with Raphael and probably also

---

[122] The document is recorded in ASVat, SB, 270, fol. 119r.–v, 120r.; a copy of the *Motu proprio*, unpaginated, is interleaved between fols. 119 and 120.

[123] The print is a copy after Cort's engraving of the same (listed in Bierens de Haan, no. 26). It is inscribed "Joannes Sadeler excud. Coloniae Agrip. A.D. 1580.— Raphael Sadeler sculpsit aetatis suae 19." An example of the print in the MM, New York, inv. no. 53.601.16.

[124] The 1580 imperial *privilegio* is noted in Rodolfo Gallo, "Gli Incisori Sadeler a Venezia," *Rivista della Città di Venezia* 9 (1930): 38. The prints are listed in Hollstein, *Dutch and Flemish Engravings, Etchings and Woodcuts, ca. 1450–1700* (Amsterdam, 1980), 21: 105–107, nos. 160–171. Each print is inscribed with some form of the phrase "Cum gratia et privil S. C. M."

[125] It was at this time, between 1583 and 1586, that Jan produced the three sets of prints praised by Baglione, 388: (1) *Imago Bonitatis Illius* (eight prints, including title-page) showing the creation of the world, dedicated to Wilhelm, Duke of Bavaria (the prints are listed in Hollstein, 21: 85–86, nos. 9–16); (2) *Boni et Mali Scientia* (twelve prints, including title-page), dated 1583, which shows the history of the first men, dedicated to Francesco Maria della Rovere, Duke of Urbino (Hollstein, 21: 87–88, nos. 17–28); (3) *Bonorum et Malorum Consensio* (fifteen prints, including title-page), dated 1586, showing the history of the family of Seth, dedicated to Ferdinand, Archduke of Austria (Hollstein, 21: 89–90, nos. 29–43). Copies of all three sets are in the BA, Vatican, Cicognara, IV, 2141.

Aegidius, moved to Frankfurt, and then, in 1588, to Munich to take up the post of engraver to Duke Wilhelm V of Bavaria. It would appear that in Munich (if not before their arrival there), Jan and Raphael began issuing prints (usually in sets) in partnership. A series of eight allegorical prints (plus a title-page) of the *Virtues of Christ* engraved by Jan after designs by Martin de Vos, dated 1588, carries on the title-page a dedication to Julius Echter, Bishop of Würzburg, by both Jan and Raphael.[126]

Further evidence of this partnership is the granting, a few years later, in 1593, of a ten-year imperial *privilegio* jointly to both Jan and Raphael.[127] One of the items published by the brothers with this *privilegio* was a set of thirty-one prints (including the title-page) of hermits titled *Sylva Sacrae. Monumenta sanctoris philosophiae quam severa anachoretorum disciplina vitae et religio docuit.* Following designs supplied by Martin de Vos, the title-page and fifteen of the prints were engraved by Jan, and the remaining fifteen by Raphael.[128] On the title-page, besides the notice of the *privilegio*, is a dedication to Duke Wilhelm by Jan and Raphael dated 1594. Probably around this same time (or perhaps a little earlier inasmuch as it does not appear to have been issued with a *privilegio*) the brothers also published another set of thirty prints (including the title-page) of hermits, again after designs by Martin de Vos, titled *Solitudo sive vitae patrum eremicolarum.*[129] The brothers' names appear together on the title-page, while each print is inscribed simply "Sadeler excudit" (in various abbreviated forms). While still in Munich the brothers also began the practice of sharing the engraving of sets of prints. For example, for the set of four prints of personifications of *European Countries*, issued with an imperial *privilegio*, Jan engraved the plates for *Germania* and *Italia*, and Raphael those for *Francia* and *Hispania*.[130]

---

[126] The prints are listed in Hollstein, 21: 156–157, nos. 455–463.

[127] The *privilegio* is noted in Alfred Von Wurzbach, *Niederländisches Künstler-Lexikon* (Vienna and Leipzig, 1910), 2: 538.

[128] The prints are listed in Hollstein, 21: 150–151, nos. 407–422 (Jan); 240–242, nos. 118–132 (Raphael). Hollstein is incorrect in describing the set as composed of "Title and twenty-nine prints." There is a title-page, a page titled "PARAGRAMMA" (inscribed "In Sacras Sylvas Ioannis et Raphaelis Sadelerorum" and with thirty-six lines of text), and twenty-nine prints of hermits.

[129] The prints are listed in Hollstein, 21: 147–149, nos. 377–406.

[130] The prints are listed in Hollstein, 21: 164, nos. 497–498 (Jan); 249, nos. 176–177 (Raphael).

In 1595, in the wake of the bankruptcy of the Wilhelm's court in Munich, Jan and Raphael, accompanied by Aegidius (who between 1591 and 1593, while Jan and Raphael stayed in Munich, had traveled to Italy and returned to Munich), together with Jan's son, Justus, moved to Italy and set up shop in Venice. Aegidius stayed in Venice until 1598 (the papal *privilegio* makes it clear that all three, including Aegidius, were living in Venice at the time the *privilegio* was granted) when he was summoned to Prague, where he became imperial engraver to the court of Emperor Rudolf II, and where he died in 1629.[131] In 1600, two years after Aegidius's departure, Jan died. Raphael remained in Venice for a few years after his brother's death, but probably in 1604 he returned to Munich where he died in 1632.[132] Justus (or Jodocus), whose name is not listed in the 1596 *privilegio*, stayed on in Venice after the death of his father and the departures of his uncle and cousin, and ran the family's print publishing business until his death, in Leiden, while on a trip in the company of the Venetian ambassador to Holland, in October 1620.[133]

Jan and Raphael had continued to issue prints jointly after their move to Venice. As they had done previously, they divided up between them the engraving of sets of prints. For example, in 1597 they published a set of six prints (including the title-page) of allegorical figures, *Schema seu speculum principum*, where Jan engraved the title-page and the first two plates, *Arma* and *Litterae*, and Raphael the remaining three, *Nuptiae, Pietas*, and *Venatio*. The engravings, all after designs by Giovanni Stradano, were printed at the Sadeler's shop in Venice ("Venetijs ex ofici [sic] Sadelery"). Another example is a pair of prints, *Death Visiting the Poor*, engraved by Jan ("Ioann: Sadeler Scalpsit Venetijs"), and *Death Visiting the Rich* (Death Visiting a Rich Lady at a Banquet) by Raphael ("Raphael Sadeler scalpsit Venetijs"),

---

[131] Aegidius had been appointed imperial engraver in the autumn of 1597, but, it would now appear, on the evidence of the papal *privilegio*, that he did not depart Venice for Prague until the following year, after the *privilegio* had been granted.

[132] A testament drawn up in Venice by Jan is dated 17 August 1600 (Gallo, 53, doc. 2). A testament drawn up in Venice by Raphael is dated 16 April 1602 (Gallo, 46, and 54, doc. 3). The date of Raphael's death is variously given as 1628 or 1632.

[133] Justus's career in Venice is discussed in Philippe Sénéchal, "Justus Sadeler: Print Publisher and Art Dealer in Early Seicento Venice," *Print Quarterly* 7 (1990): 22–35.

both after designs by Giovanni Stradano ("Ioann: Stradan' Academic' Florentinus figuravit").[134]

It would appear that the imperial *privilegio* granted Jan and Raphael in 1593 could still be applied when needed. An undated set of four prints, two engraved by Jan and two by Raphael, of the *Four Seasons*, after designs by Jacopo Bassano, which were most likely printed in Venice soon after they settled there, carry the imperial *privilegio*. Another example is the series of three prints known as "The Kitchens of Sadeler" of which two, *Christ in the House of Mary and Martha*, dated 1598, and *The Rich Man and the Poor Lazarus* were engraved by Jan, while the third, *Christ at Emmaus*, was by Raphael.[135] All three, all after designs by Jacopo Bassano, carry an imperial *privilegio*.

Numerous prints issued by the Sadelers after 1598 continue to carry notice of the imperial *privilegio* but it is now frequently combined with the papal *privilegio*. Notice of the *privilegio* can be found on prints engraved by Jan and Raphael, as well as on those by Aegidius. After 1600, it also appears on prints by Justus.

Perhaps the first item issued by the Sadelers with the new papal *privilegio* was a set of fifty-one prints (including the title-page) treating once again the subject of hermits entitled *Trophaeum Vitae Solitariae*. Based on designs by Martin de Vos, twenty-five of the plates were engraved by Jan and twenty-five by Raphael. The title-page, engraved by Raphael ("Raphael Sadeler Scalpsit Venetijs 1598"), carries a dedication by "Ioann. et Raphael Sadeleri fratres" to Cardinal Enrico Gaetano (Caietan). Two years later, in 1600, the brothers produced another book of twenty-eight prints of hermits called *Oraculum Anachoreticum*. This time, Jan engraved the title-page ("Ioã Sadeler scalpsit Venetijs") and thirteen plates, and Raphael another thirteen, all after designs by Martin de Vos.[136] Altogether Jan and Raphael

---

[134] The prints in the *Schema seu speculum principum* are listed in Hollstein, 21: 171, nos. 533–535 (Jan); 254, nos. 203–205 (Raphael), as are the pair of Death prints: Hollstein, 21: 174, no. 553 (Jan); 256, no. 214 (Raphael).

[135] The prints of the *Four Seasons* are listed in Hollstein, 21: 166, nos. 507–508 (Jan); 249, nos. 178–179 (Raphael). Only Raphael's two prints of Spring and Autumn carry notice of the *privilegio*. "The Kitchens of Sadeler" are listed in Hollstein, 21: 112–113, nos. 199–200 (Jan); 223, no. 43 (Raphael). Hollstein notes a date of 1593 in the margin of the *Christ at Emmaus*, but this is too early and may be a mis-reading of 1598.

[136] The prints in the *Trophaeum Vitae Solitariae* are listed in Hollstein, 21: 152–152, nos. 423–436 (Jan); 242–243, nos. 133–144 (Raphael). Hollstein, 21: 244, states

together produced five books devoted to hermits (four of male hermits, one of female), all after designs by Martin de Vos: *Sylvae Sacrae; Solitudo Sive Vitae Patrum Eremicolarum; Trophaeum Vitae Solitariae; Oraculum Anachoreticum;* and *Solitudo Sive Vitae Foeminarum Anachoritarum.* Four of the books were known to Giovanni Baglione, who commented on them with admiration.[137] The plate following the title-page of the *Oraculum Anachoreticum* was devoted to a fifteen-line dedication by the brothers ("Ioh. et Raph. Sadelerii FS") to Clement VIII.

It is very likely that the *Oraculum Anachoreticum* was among those prints that Jan took to Rome in the summer of 1600 to show Pope Clement VIII. The purpose of the trip, in fact, may have been to submit new prints that Jan wished to publish with the papal *privilegio* for the required *imprimatur* of the Master of the Sacred Palace. No doubt another print included was the *Portrait of Clement VIII* engraved by Jan.[138]

On 22 May 1600, before making the arduous journey to Rome, Jan left instructions in a document drawn up by a notary that in the event of his death the plates jointly owned by him and Raphael, which are named in a list, should not be sold by his heirs but kept intact: "Che non possino detti rami in alcun modo mai partirsi, o dividersi, ma debbano stare e servarsi ad uno, e unitamente, e a commun utile, e beneficio."[139] Interestingly, the list includes many of the prints which Jan and Raphael had issued with a *privilegio*. Some of the prints listed the brothers had published earlier in Munich, such as the *Virtues of Christ* and two books of prints of hermits, the *Sylva Sacrae* and the *Solitudo sive vitae patrum eremicolarum.* More numerous are prints issued in Venice. These include the *Trophaeum vitae solitariae*, the *Oraculum anachoreticum*, the *Schema seu speculum principum*, the *Four Seasons*, the pair of *Death visiting the Poor* and *Death visiting the Rich*, and the three "Kitchens of Sadeler." Also included are the *Seven Liberal Arts* (eight prints, including title-page), the book of prints of flowers in vases, a series of eighteen prints (including the title-page) of female saints (*Speculum Pudicitiae*), *St. Narcissus, Patriarch of*

---

that "All the prints have the privilege." The prints in the *Oraculum Anachoreticum* are listed in Hollstein, 21: 153–155, nos. 437–450 (Jan); 244–245, nos. 145–157 (Raphael).

[137] Baglione, 389.

[138] The portrait is listed in Hollstein xxi, 181, no. 589. It is inscribed "cu[m] gratia et priuil. Sum[m]i Po[n]tif. et Caes. Maest."

[139] The document is transcribed in Gallo, 49–52: doc. 1.

Jerusalem in a landscape, three copies of prints by Cornelis Cort, and three entries as yet unidentified.[140]

The list, however, represents only those plates jointly owned by the brothers. Both Jan and Raphael evidently owned other plates independently of each other, a few of which were published with the papal *privilegio*. Jan's engraving of an *Adoration of the Shepherds* after Jacopo Bassano, for example, which is not on the list, was published with the papal and imperial *privilegio* in 1599. Other prints issued by Raphael before 1600, including those with a papal *privilegio*, also do not appear on the list. An *Adoration of the Magi*, engraved by Raphael after Jacopo Bassano was issued with the *privilegio* in 1598. Similarly, Raphael's engravings of the *Virgin and Child with S. Catherine of Siena*, after Polidoro da Lanciano, and *St. Francis*, after Felice Brusasorci, were both printed with the papal and imperial privileges in 1599.[141]

After the death of Jan Sadeler on 26 August 1600, Raphael evidently took over the shop in Venice and his name as publisher also appears on his own prints. Those carrying the papal and imperial *privilegio* include a *Holy Family* after Johannes Rottenhammer, a *S. Agnes* after Denys (Dionisio) Calvaert and dedicated to Clement VIII, and *The Little Milkmaid* after Jacopo Bassano, all three dated 1601. The latest dated appearance of the papal and imperial privileges on a print by Raphael is a half-length portrait of *Charles Borromeo* dated 1604 ("R. Sadeler fecit aᵒ 1604"), the same year Raphael left Venice and moved to Munich.[142]

The papal *privilegio* also appears on some prints by Aegidius who must have left Venice for Prague very soon after the *privilegio* had

---

[140] The three undentified entries are: "La Mad.a con li fratti di Egidio—no. 1," "Un libr.to apostolico, ramette sedici—no. 16," and "Un friso con l'inscrittion del lib. Geremitico—no. 1." The second item mentioned might be that referred to by Baglione, 389: "Gio. & Egidio insieme hanno dato fuori la carta di Christo, che chiama Andrea all'Apostolato, intaglio di Giovanni Sadeler." Baglione, however, refers to one print ("la carta"), whereas the list describes a booklet ("libretto") with sixteen small plates ("ramette sedici").

[141] The prints of the *Adoration of the Shepherds*, the *Adoration of the Magi*, and the *Virgin and Child with S. Catherine of Siena* are listed in Hollstein, 21: 109, no. 182; 216, no. 14; and 227, no. 60. The last print is inscribed "Polidorus de Lanzan pinxit. Raphael Sadeler Scalpsit. Venetiis," and "Cum priuilegio Sum. Pontificis et S.C.M." The *St. Francis* is also listed in Hollstein, 21: 235, no. 97. It is inscribed "R. Sadeler Fecit," "Foelix Brusasorzius Veron.is pinxit," and "Cum priuil. Sum Pontific. et S. Cae. M."

[142] The prints are listed Hollstein, 21: 231, no. 79; 233, no. 88; 257, no. 215; and 259, no. 225.

been granted. It appears on several prints he produced in his new position as court engraver to Rudolf II. One example is a portrait of *Emperor Rudolf II*, engraved by Aegidius after a design by Adriaen de Vries ("Adrianus de Vries Hagiensis Invent"), which is inscribed "Cum Priuil. Sui Pontif. et Sac. Cae. M^tis." The same inscription also appears on Aegidius's engraving of *The Three Maries at the Tomb*, dated 1600, after Bartholomeus Spranger's painting of the same, dated 1598, in the Imperial Chapel in Prague.[143]

A papal (and an imperial) *privilegio* also appears on a few engravings by Jan's son, Justus. One example, printed by the Sadeler shop in Venice, is a *Virgin and Child*, dedicated by Justus to the Duchess of Parma, and inscribed "I. Sad. Fecit. Cum priuil. Sum. Pont. et Sac. Caes. Maies." Another, of a *Holy Family in Egypt*, is inscribed "Iu. Sadeler excud. Venetijs cum priuil. Sum Pontif. et S. Caes. Mai."[144]

Philippe Thomassin

Some of Philippe Thomassin's earlier activities were noted earlier in this chapter. The *privilegio* appears on several prints engraved by Thomassin and on several published by him either alone or in partnership with Jean Turpin. Among the first prints executed by Thomassin soon after his arrival in Rome in 1584 are some carrying a *privilegio* inscription. One, dated 1585, is of *St. Paul First Hermit* after Bernardino Passari, which was printed with a ten-year *privilegio* granted by Gregory XIII.[145] However, as the print carries a dedication by Passari (to Pietro Fulvio), it seems likely that the *privilegio* had been granted to Passari rather than to Thomassin. That Passari had been granted a *privilegio* in 1585 is further indicated by a four-sheet print of the *Marriage of Isaac and Rebecca*, engraved almost certainly by Aliprando Capriolo, on which appears the *Motu proprio* of

---

[143] The portrait of *Emperor Rudolf II* is listed in Hollstein, 21: 69, no. 321. The print is mentioned by Baglione, 389. The *The Three Maries at the Tomb* is listed in Hollstein, 21: 21, no. 60 (with no reference to the *privilegio*).

[144] The *Virgin and Child* is listed in Hollstein, 21: 198, no. 9. Of the prints by Justus singled out by Baglione for mention is an *Adoration of the Magi* after Federico Zuccaro's painting in San Francesco della Vigna in Venice (Baglione, 388), but it does not carry a *privilegio* (Hollstein, 21: 198, no. 1). The *Holy Family in Egypt* is listed in Hollstein, 21: 202, no. 38.

[145] The print is listed in Edmond Bruwaert, *Recherches sur la vie et l'oeuvre du graveur troyen Philippe Thomassin* (Troyes, 1876), 101, no. 144. An example is in the BN, Paris, Ed. 10. rés. fol. 48, but without a *privilegio* inscription.

Gregory XIII (inscribed in the same form as it appears on the *St. Paul First Hermit*), which Passari dedicated to Cardinal Enrico Gaetano and which he also printed in 1585. This print, which was re-issued by Philippe Thomassin with a new *privilegio* in 1599, is discussed below.

Probably in the latter part of the reign of Sixtus V, Thomassin formed a publishing partnership with another Frenchman, Jean Turpin (or Giovanni Turpino as he was called in Italy; or Latinised to Johannes Turpinus Gallus) and together, it would appear, were granted a papal *privilegio* by Sixtus V in 1588. Notice of the *privilegio* appears on several prints. Two, dated 1588, are a *S. Anthony of Padua* after Antonio Tempesta, printed by Moneta, and *St. Mary of Egypt* after Ventura Salimbeni, which Thomassin both engraved and published.[146] The Sistine *privilegio* also appears on several prints dated 1589. A *Holy Family* engraved by Thomassin after Martin Fréminet, and a *St. Margaret* engraved by Thomassin after Raphael's painting, then at Fontainebleau, were both published with a ten-year *privilegio* by Thomassin and Turpin. A third print engraved by Thomassin, and issued with a *privilegio*, of *Four Martyrs* after Bernardino Passari, was printed the same year by Marcello Clodio, who also dedicated it to Giovanni Antonio Fachinetto, titular cardinal of the SS. Quattro Coronati. A print of *S. Maria Maggiore* dated 1589 also carries the *privilegio*.[147]

The same ten-year Sistine *privilegio* appears on Thomassin's engraving of Ventura Salimbeni's *Rest on the Return from Egypt*, and on a pair of prints, one of *Jesus Christ*, the other of the *Virgin Mary*, after Giulio Clovio published by Thomassin and Turpin. It also appears on an *Entombment* after Federico Barocci.[148] During the very brief

---

[146] The prints are listed in Bruwaert, 104, no. 206; and 108, no. 217.

[147] The *Holy Family* is listed in Bruwaert, 89, no. 93. The notice of *privilegio* reads: "Cu[m] priuil. S.mi D. N. PP. Sixti. V. p[er] a[nn]os. X." The print was dedicated by Thomassin to the French cardinal François de Joyeuse. An example is in the BN, Paris, Ed. 10. rés. fol. 18. The *St. Margaret* is listed in Bruwaert, 108, no. 218. The painting is now in the Louvre (inv. no. 1607). The print was dedicated by Thomassin to the scholar Giovanni Battista Raimondi. The *Four Martyrs* and the print of *S. Maria Maggiore* are listed in Bruwaert, 100, no. 141; 94, no. 127, respectively.

[148] The *Rest on the Return from Egypt* is listed in Bruwaert, 74, no. 22. Zani, 2, 6: 90, who attributes the engraving to Francesco Villamena, records a later state issued after Thomassin's partnership with Turpin was dissolved. The plate evidently remained in the hands of Turpin who erased Thomassin's name as engraver and his name as publisher leaving only "Io Turpinus socij excud." Thomassin's erased name can be seen faintly in the example in the BN, Paris, Ed. 10. rés. fol. 8. The prints of

reign of Gregory XIV, Thomassin and Turpin were evidently granted another ten-year *privilegio* which appears on numerous prints over the next decade. Among the first are Thomassin's engravings of the *Annunciation* and the *Flagellation*, both after paintings by the French painter Martin Fréminet, and the *Adoration of the Shepherds* after a painting apparently executed by Francesco Potenzano for Philip II of Spain (the inscription reads "Magnus Potenzanus inuen. et pinxit pro Rege Cattolico Philippo 2° Hyspaniarum. . . .").[149] It also appears on a *Virgin of the Rosary*, designed by Antonio Tempesta, an *Assumption* after Barocci, and a print of *S. Maria del Popolo*, dated 1592, showing the Virgin and Child with twelve medallions illustrating the history of the church of S. Maria del Popolo. Very probably it is this *privilegio* that also appears on an undated print of *St. Sebastian* after Fréminet ("Martinus Freminettus in.") issued by Thomassin and Turpin ("Cu[m] priuil. ad anos X./Phls et Io Turpinus socii excud. Romae").[150]

With this same ten-year *privilegio* Thomassin and Turpin published Thomassin's engraving of *The Wedding Feast at Cana* after the Flemish painter and draughtsman Denys Calvaert, dated 1592, and a *Baptism* after Martin Fréminet, also dated 1592.[151] Four years later, in 1596,

---

Jesus Christ, the *Virgin Mary*, and the *Entombment* are listed in Bruwaert, 87, nos. 85, 86; 84, no. 63, respectively.

[149] The *Annunciation* is listed in Bruwaert, 31. The print, dated 1591, includes some verse by Giulio Roscio Ortini and a dedication by Thomassin to Giulio Antonio Santori, Cardinal of S. Severino. An example is in the BN, Paris, Ed. 10. rés. fol. 12. The *Flagellation* is listed in Bruwaert, 80, no. 55. An example is in the BN, Paris, Ed. 10. rés. fol. 30. The print is dedicated by Turpin to Michaeli Bonello, Cardinal Alessandrino. The *Adoration of the Shepherds* is listed in Bruwaert, 71, no. 15. The print is dedicated to "Card. de Mendoza" (i.e. Ioan Gonzalez de Mendoça) by Turpino ("Ioannes Gallus S. D.D."). An example is in the BN, Paris, Ed. 10. rés. fol. 4.

[150] The *Virgin of the Rosary* is listed in Bruwaert, 93, no. 123. It is dedicated by Turpin to Michaeli Bonello, Cardinal Alessandrino. The *Assumption*, the print of *S. Maria del Popolo*, and the *St. Sebastian* are listed in Bruwaert, 92, no. 120; 94, no. 126; and 99, no. 139. An example of the *St. Sebastian* is in the BN, Paris, Ed. 10. rés. fol. 42, but with Thomassin's name and the word "socii" erased.

[151] *The Wedding Feast at Cana* is listed in Bruwaert, 77, no. 28. The print is inscribed "DIONISIVS CALVART BELGA INVEN." and "PHLS. TH. FE 1592." It was dedicated by Thomassin to "Don Leonardo Abeli Episcop. Sideniensi." An example is in the BN, Paris, Ed. 10. rés. fol. 28, but trimmed and with the Thomassin/ Turpin address erased. The *Baptism* is listed in Bruwaert, 75, no. 25. The print is inscribed "M. Freminet in Phls fe." and "Cu[m] priuil. ad an. x." An example is in the BN, Paris, Ed. 10. rés. fol. 24, but with lower margin with the dedicatory inscription trimmed off.

they published a *Christ After the Flagellation* after Paolo Brameri.[152] In 1597 appeared a *Holy Family with St. Anne at Home* after Francesco Vanni, a *Madonna with Sleeping Christ Child*, a *Conversion of St. Paul* after the Flemish painter Sébastien Vrancx ("Sebastianus Vrancxus inuen."), and a print of *St. Augustine* with the twenty-eight "sacri ordines" (*Sacri ordines XXVIII S. Augustini*).[153]

The following year, 1598, Thomasssin and Turpin were granted a new *privilegio* by Clement VIII, which is seen on two prints of *Rosaries*. The first, titled REGINA ROSARII, is inscribed "Phls et Io Turpin.s excud Romae cu priuil. Summi Pontificis ad decennium superior. pmissu." The second, titled ROSARIVM NOMINIS IESV, is inscribed "Bref de Clément VIII—Phls Thomassinus fe. Cu priuil. S. P. ad decennium 1598 supior pmissu."[154] At this time, they also published a *Martyrdom of St. Apollonia* after Riccardo Ripanelli, and probably (the last number of the date is unclear: "Phls. et Io. Turpinus exc. 159_") a *God the Father Supporting the Dead Christ with Angels holding the Instruments of the Passion*.[155] In 1599 appeared Thomassin's engraving of an *Adoration of the Magi* after Camillo Spalucci, and a *St. Sebastian* after the Flemish artist Pieter de Jode ("Petrus de Iode inuen.").[156]

In 1599, as the ten-year *privilegio* granted by Gregory XIV was about to expire, Thomassin applied for another, which was granted on 7 December 1599. In his supplication he asks for a *privilegio* for the plates he had acquired from the estate of the recently deceased Aliprando Capriolo (Thomassin's supplication now makes it clear that Capriolo, whose death-date was previously unknown, must have

---

[152] The *Christ after the Flagellation* is inscribed "Paulus Brameri Palerm. inven." and "Phls et Io. Turpinus excud. Romae 1596/Cu[m] priuil. ad anos x." An example is in the BN, Paris, Ed. 10, rés. fol. 29, but with Thomassin's name erased. Zani, 2, 7: 217, is almost certainly mistaken in identifying the engraver of the print as Philippe Soye.

[153] The first three prints are listed in Bruwaert, 75, no. 23; 89, no. 90; and 97, no. 135. Examples are in the BN, Paris, Ed. 10 rés. fol. 9; rés. fol. 13; and rés. fol. 40. The *St. Augustine* is listed in Bruwaert, 116, no. 245.

[154] The two prints of *Rosaries* are listed in Bruwaert, 93, nos. 124–125.

[155] The *Martyrdom of St. Apollonia* is listed in Bruwaert, 108, no. 216. An example is in the BN, Paris, Ed. 10. rés. fol. 46. An example of the *God the Father Supporting the Dead Christ with Angels holding the Instruments of the Passion* is in the Farnesina, Rome, 46.H.10, inv. no. 71866.

[156] The *Adoration of the Magi* is listed in Bruwaert, 72, no. 18. It is inscribed "Phls scalpsit 1599" and "Phls et Io Turpinus exc: Romae cu priuil Sumi Pontificis ad annos dece." An example is in the BN, Paris, Ed. 10. rés. fol. 6. An example of the *St. Sebastian* is in the BN, Paris, Ed. 10. rés. fol. 43.

died in 1599).[157] He points out first that Capriolo had been granted a ten-year *privilegio* for his "many sacred images, and a book entitled *Centum Armorum Duces Illustres*" (i.e. the *Ritratti di Cento Capitani Illustri*). He goes on to explain that on the death of Capriolo, he, Thomassin, purchased from Capriolo's heirs all the above-mentioned plates and prints and more, and he mentions in particular a *Marriage of Isaac and Rebecca* engraved in four and half sheets ("et di più l'Historia del Matrimonio di Isac et Rebecha sculpita in quattro fogli e mezzo"). Thomassin then asks for a *privilegio* so that these prints would not be usurped by others after he has gone to so much expense and the work it will take to print them all.

In the summary of the supplication made on the reverse of the same sheet, it is noted that Capriolo's heirs had sold everything to Thomassin.[158] Subsequently, several of Capriolo's prints were re-issued with the address of Thomassin and Turpino.[159] Significantly, only those prints that had been previously granted copyright were included in the new *privilegio*. The prints listed in the document granting the *privilegio* to Thomassin include the *Centum Armorum Duces Illustres*, the "symbolum fidei figuratum a Martino de Vos," and the "Historium Matrimonij Isaci et Rebecchae." The last print, a *Marriage of Isaac and Rebecca*, is identified as having been invented by Baldassare Peruzzi ("Baldassari Perutio Pictore Senen[sis] edita[m], et Inventa[m]").

The *Ritratti di Cento Capitani Illustri* was issued with the *privilegio* the following year, the title concluding with the inscription "Et dati in luce da Filippo Thomassino et Giovan Turpino con privilegio DI PAPA CLEMENTE VIII per anni dieci 1600 in Roma."[160] The

---

[157] The *privilegio* is recorded in ASVat, SB, 290, fol. 269r.–v, 272r. Thomassin's supplication is interleaved on fol. 271v.

[158] One of Capriolo's heirs may have been Pietro Capriolo (a son, or a nephew?) who, it would appear, took up print publishing in the very year of Aliprando's death. His address ("Petru Capriolus formis Romae 1599") appears on an anonymous copy of a print, sometimes attributed to Marco Dente da Ravenna, of Marcantonio Raimondi's engraving of the *Virgin of the Cradle* after Raphael (Bartsch, 14: no. 63)

[159] Several are listed in Suster, 150, no. 1; 156, no. 5; 159, no. 6; 160, no. 7; 165, no. 2; and 166, no. 4. Some examples can be found in the Farnesina, Rome, vol. 34.H.27. inv. nos. 31518, 31519. The partly erased address of Thomassin and "Io. Turpinu[m]" also appears on the print attributed to Capriolo of *Christ Raising the Son of the Widow of Naim* after Federico Zuccaro (an example is in the Farnesina, Rome, 46.H.10. inv. no. 71844; state unknown to Suster).

[160] The *Ritratti di Cento Capitani Illustri* is listed in Bruwaert, 127, no. 361; and Suster, 188. The dedication, to King Henry IV of France, is dated 12 March 1600.

"symbolum fidei," designed by Martin de Vos, is the set of twelve prints illustrating the *Articoli del Credo degli Apostoli* (the Apostles Creed) which Capriolo had not yet published before his death (see above). The *Credo* reproduces in large part prints designed by Martin de Vos which were engraved and printed with a royal *privilegio* ("cum privilegio regis") in 1579 by Jan Sadeler.[161]

Capriolo's print of *The Marriage of Isaac and Rebecca* after Peruzzi is most likely that described by Pietro Zani as engraved by Gisberto van Veen and published in Rome in 1585 by Bernardino Passari.[162] The print is on four sheets, the first of which carries a dedication by Bernardino Passari to Cardinal Enrico Gaetano below which is a ten-year *privilegio* granted by Gregory XIII ("Motu proprio Pont. Max. Gregorij XIII. per annos X. superiorum permissu"). Baldassare Peruzzi's name appears in verses inscribed below the *privilegio*. The third sheet is inscribed "Apud Bernardinum Passarum Romae Ann. D. 1585," while the fourth sheet carries a medallion portrait of Peruzzi around which is inscribed "BALTHASAR PERUCCIVS SENENSIS PICTOR ET EXCELLENS ARCHITECTVS INVEN." Under the circumstances, it seems likely that the *privilegio* had been granted Passari. Zani describes a second state in which the dedication has been changed and with, on the second sheet, the words "Cu[m] priuil Summi Pontificis" added. On the fourth sheet the *Motu proprio* of Gregory XIII has been erased. Zani makes no mention of the presence of the address of Thomassin and Turpin.[163]

By 1603 Thomassin appears to have been granted another *privilegio* that appears, for example, on Villamena's engraving of an *Annunciation* after a drawing by Ippolito Andreasi for his altarpiece, completed in 1602, in the church of S. Maria in Castello in Viadana ("Cu.

---

[161] Capriolí's prints of the *Credo* are listed in Suster, 193−201. Copies of all twelve prints are in the Farnesina, Rome, vol. 34.H.27. inv. nos. 31564−31580. The set was printed again by Callisto Ferrantes (example in the Farnesina, Rome, vol. 50.K.16. inv. nos. 91697−91708). They were also issued by Matteo Florimi with Vos acknowledged as the designer but without an engraver's name (example in the BA, Vatican. Cicognara IV 2141 int.6). Sadeler's prints of the *Credo* are listed in Hollstein, 21: 157−160, nos. 465−476.

[162] Zani, 2, 3: 37. Zani gives no reason for attributing the engraving to Van Veen.

[163] Zani, 2, 3: 39, does note that the print was copied "in piccolo" by Teodoro de Bry (i.e. Johann Theodor de Bry, 1561−1623), who also published it ("Ioan Theodori de Bry fe. et Excud."). An example of De Bry's print is in the Fogg, Harvard, Randall 2008.

privil. Sumi Pont. Philippus Thomassinus exc. Romae 1603").[164] By 1602, as his address makes clear, Thomassin was no longer in partnership with Turpin. Turpin, it seems, acquired a portion of the stock of plates which he re-issued, carefully erasing Thomassin's name in their joint address (though frequently leaving in place the word "socij" to produce the incongruous phrase "Io Turpinus socij excud.") and often maliciously erasing Thomassin's name as the engraver of the print. Thomassin continued to publish prints, often his own, with a *privilegio*, which appears on prints dated 1610, 1613, 1614, 1615, 1617, the plates of several of which are today in the Calcografia, Istituto Nazionale per la Grafica, Rome.

Domenico Falcini

In his supplication, dated 12 December 1603, the copperplate engraver Domenico Falcini explains that he has engraved a series of prints of all the Emperors from Julius Caesar to the present as represented on medals, and each printed with a brief *vita*. He goes on to explain that the work was reduced to a few sheets which could either be made into a book or put all together in a frame ("fatica grande ridotta in pochi fogli, che se ne puo fare libro, et anco metterli tutti insieme in un quadro"). The *privilegio* was granted five days after his supplication, on 17 December.[165] The prints have not been identified.

Falcini's activities are largely unknown. He apparently made woodcuts, including some three-block chiaroscuro prints. A large engraving of *St. John the Evangelist* in London (probably one of a series as the number "6" appears in the margin in the lower right), is signed "Dom^co falcini fecit."[166] In his supplication he describes himself as from "Ponte a Sieve in dominio Fiorentino," which corrects the long-held belief that he was originally from Siena. His Florentine origins are also signaled in the inscription, "Dom^cus. falcinus. fecit. flors.," found on the print of *St. Francis of Assisi* engraved by Falcini after a design by the painter Jacopo Ligozzi.[167] The print, which also car-

---

[164] The print is listed in Konrad Oberhuber, *Die Kunst der Graphik III: Renaissance in Italien 16. Jahrhundert* (Vienna, 1966), 209, no. 356.

[165] For the supplication and the *privilegio* are recorded in ASVat, SB, 340, fols. 347v., and 348v.

[166] The engraving of *St. John the Evangelist* is in the BM, London, C.56, inv. no. 1951–4–7–118.

[167] Examples of the print are in the MM, New York, inv. no. 49–62–11; and the Uffizi, Florence, inv. no. 4933.

ries a *privilegio* and a dedication dated 1 June 1612, served as the
frontispiece to a series of etched and engraved prints of the monastic community at Monte della Vernia (now known simply as La
Vernia) and some scenes from the life of St. Francis illustrating a
large guidebook with text published in Florence in 1612 by Fra Lino
Moroni entitled *Descrizione del Sacro Monte della Vernia*.[168] Moroni, a
provincial of the Observant Franciscans, had been invited to produce the book by Arcangelo da Messina, the archbishop of Monreale
and a general of the Observant Franciscan order, in 1608. Moroni
personally visited La Vernia, taking with him on the trip the artist
Jacopo Ligozzi from whom he commissioned drawings for the project. Moroni dedicated the book to Arcangelo da Messina. Seven of
the prints were etched by Raffaello Schiaminossi, and another fifteen
produced by an anonymous engraver.[169]

Falcini also published prints. A set of four engravings showing the
Labours of the Months (three months per print), engraved by Cesare
Bassano was published by Falcini and dedicated by him to Matteo
Grazini. The dedication, dated 14 August 1607, was composed in
Siena. Another example, inscribed "Domin. falcini formis flor.," is
a small engraving of *St Isidore the Farmer*, dated 1622, issued on the
occasion of the saint's canonization by Gregory XV on 4 March
that year.[170]

Mattheo Greuter

In his *vita* of Mattheo Greuter, Baglione states that the German
engraver had died in Rome in 1638 at the age of 72. His date of
birth would therefore have been 1566. According to Baglione, Greuter
had been born in Strassburg, had lived for a while in Lyons and
then in Avignon before coming to Rome. This same information
also appears in Greuter's supplication for a *privilegio*, granted on 11
December 1604, but with some important additional details that

---

[168] The book is noted in Ernst Philip Goldschmidt, *Catalogue of Illustrated Books
1491–1759* (London, n.d.), no. 69; and in Simonetta Prosperi Valenti Rodino, "La
Diffusione nell'iconografia Francescana attraverso l'incisione," in *L'Immagine di San
Francesco nella Controriforma* (Rome, 1982), no. 118.

[169] Schiaminossi's prints are listed in Bartsch, 17: nos. 130–136. Although the
dedicatory letter mentions 25 plates, only 22 were included (lettered A-Y), besides
Falcini's frontispiece.

[170] An example of the set of four prints of the *Labours of the Months* is in the
Uffizi, Florence, inv. nos. 1983–1986. An example of *St. Isidore the Farmer* is in the
Uffizi, Florence, inv. no. 12870.

Baglione does not provide. Greuter, a German in counter-reformation Rome, evidently felt it necessary to include a brief history of his life in his supplication in order to convince the papal authorities that he was free from the Lutheran heresy. The supplication reads in part:

> It is about ten years ago that Mattheo Greuter from Strassburg left the Lutheran heresy and embraced the truth of the Catholic faith, and so that he could live more securely in the said Catholic religion, abandoned his country and, with three of his children, that is, two boys and a girl, came to Catholic parts where, mostly in Avignon, he lived some years with much spiritual consolation, living by his art, which is that of engraver in copperplate, through which he acquired, besides his living, much fame and reputation. Now he is to be found in this City of Rome, and it is already 18 months that he has been supporting himself in it with his work, and he is sought out by many people wanting some things engraved that he has already drawn of his own design, because his engraving is very fine ("il suo intaglio è finissimo"), and unusual in this City.

Greuter continued by expressing concern over his work being counterfeited and humbly asked for a *privilegio*. On the verso of the following sheet, much of this information is repeated in summary form, but added to it is the fact that after Greuter moved to the "Catholic parts" he also lived in Lyons. The addition of information not found in the supplication (but known later to Baglione) would suggest that the papal authorities had conducted further investigation into Greuter's background. However, he was evidently found worthy and on 27 November 1604 received the approval ("approbata") of the Master of the Sacred Palace. The *privilegio* was granted a fortnight later.[171] Perhaps because of Greuter's history, the document was signed not only by Marcello Vestrio Barbiano, Clement VIII's secretary of Latin briefs, but also by Cardinal Aldobrandini.[172]

---

[171] Greuter's supplication and *privilegio* are recorded in ASVat, SB, 352, fols. 353r.–v., 354r., 356r. The translation of the supplication is mine.

[172] As noted earlier, Marcello Vestrio Barbiano, whose name first appears on briefs issued towards the end of the papacy of Sixtus V (1585–1590), held the position of secretary of Latin briefs throughout the papacy of Clement VIII (1592–1605). It will be recalled that Francesco Villamena had dedicated to Barbiano his engraving of Paolo Veronese's *Presentation in the Temple* (see above). According to a document in the Vatican Archives, Cardinal Pietro Aldobrandini (Clement VIII's nephew and Papal Secretary of State) was appointed "Praefectura Segretaria. Brevium secretarum" in June 1598 (a document recording the appointment is in ASVat, SB, 271, fol. 260). Aldobrandini's name also appears on the *privilegio* granted Domenico Falcini in 1603.

The papal *privilegio* granted Greuter on 11 December 1604 for ten years was for unnamed prints. Probably the first to be issued with the *privilegio* is a portrait of the short-lived Medici pope, Leo XI, dated 1605. The print shows Leo XI in the centre with portraits of four other Medici popes in each corner. It is signed "Matthaeus Gr. sc." and inscribed "cu[m] Privileg°. S. P. ad decennio/Romae 1605." Another example is a view of *S. Giovanni Laterano*, with features of interest inside the basilica shown in panels arranged around on three sides. It was most likely engraved by Paolo Maupino (Paul Maupain) after the design by Giovanni Maggio ("Io: Maggi' delin:"), which Greuter also published with the *privilegio*: "M. Greuter excudit cu[m] Priuilegio."[173]

Leonardo Parasole

Leonardo Parasole, a woodcutter and engraver, was the son of Agostino Parasole from Sant' Angelo di Visso near Spoleto and Norcia (he is occasionally referred to "Leonardo Norsino"). Information about Leonardo Parasole comes primarily from Baglione who includes in his *vita* of Leonardo also notices of the activities of his wife Isabella [sic] Parasole [i.e. Isabetta, or Elizabetta, Catanea Parasole], and their son Bernardino Parasole (for Isabetta Parasole, see Chapter 12).[174]

Baglione reports that during the reign of Sixtus V Leonardo produced numerous beautiful and lifelike woodcuts of plants for Castore Durante's *Herbario nuovo*.[175] According to Nissen, Leonardo made the woodcuts following designs produced by his wife Isabetta.[176] The

---

[173] An example of Greuter's portrait of Leo XI is in the Farnesina, Rome, vol. 58.N.4., inv. no. 120910. The print of *S. Giovanni Laterano* is undated. It is dedicated by Maupino to Christina of Lorraine, the Duchess of Tuscany.

[174] Baglione, 394–395.

[175] The title-page of the book reads: *HERBARIO/NVOVO/DI CASTORE DVRANTE/MEDICO, ET CITTADINO ROMANO/Con FIGVRE che rappresentano le viue Piante, che nascono in/tutta Europa, & nell' Indie Orientale, & Occidentale*. Durante dedicated the book to Cardinal Girolamo Rusticucci (dated 27 March 1585). The colophon reads: "IN ROMA/Nella Stamperia di Bartholomeo Bonfadino, & Tito Diani./MD LXXXV." A copy is in the BA, Vatican, Racc.I.II.104.

[176] Claus Nissen, *Die Botanische Buchillustration. Ihre Geschichte und Bibliographie* (Stuttgart, 1951), 2: no. 569. The only source for Parasole's association with the *Herbario* is Baglione. Parasole's name appears nowhere in the book, and none of the many plates (including the portraits of Giacomo Antonio Cortuse and Castor Durante, at age 56) is signed. Gian Ludovico Masetti Zannini, *Stampatori e Librai a Roma nella*

book was published in Rome by Giacomo Bericchia and Giacomo Tornieri in 1585.[177]

Baglione also reports that Leonardo produced some "intagli" for an Arabic *Evangelia* with designs by Antonio Tempesta. The book, which Baglione explains was printed "nella Stampa Medicea, sotto la cura di Gio. Battista Raimondi, grandissimo Letterato," is certainly the folio edition of the Gospels in Arabic, *Euangelium Sanctum Domini nostri Iesu Christi conscriptum a Quatuor Evangelistis Sanctis idest, Matthaeo, Marco, Luca, et Iohanne*, edited by Giovanni Battista Raimondi and printed at the Typographia Medicea in Rome in 1591.[178] Of the one hundred and forty-nine woodcuts printed from sixty-seven blocks contained in the book, fourteen carry both the monograms of Parasole ("P" or "L.P.") as cutter and of Antonio Tempesta as designer, plus another four that are signed by Leonardo Parasole alone.[179]

Parasole also developed for the Typographia Medicea a new method for printing books of plain chant for which he, and Fulgentio Valesino, were granted a *privilegio* on 16 September 1593.[180]

In 1594, Parasole contributed a single engraving to the second edition, printed in Latin, of Antonio Gallonio's *De SS. Martyrum cruciatibus liber, quo potissimum instrumenta et modi, quibus iidem Christi martyres olim torquebantur, accuratissime tabellis expressa describuntur*. The first edition, in Italian (*Trattato degli Strumenti di Martirio e delle varie maniere di martoriare usate da' gentile contro christiani*), which contained twenty-two prints of scenes of martyrdom engraved by Antonio Tempesta, had been published in Rome by Ascanio and Girolamo Donangeli

---

Seconda Metà del Cinquecento (Rome, 1980), 215, reports from a document that on the death of Leonardo's father, Agostino, all the family possessions were divided between his sons, Leonardo, Apollonio, Rosato, and Filippo, except the "stampe intagliate e disegnate," including the "herbario de Castor Durante medico," which were to remain "in comune."

[177] "IN ROMA/Per Iacomo Bericchia, & Iacomo Tonierij, MDLXXXV." The book was reprinted by Sessa in Venice in 1602 (a copy of this edition is in BA, Vatican, R.G. Med.II.161), and again in 1636.

[178] The reference is made by Baglione, 315, in his *vita* of Tempesta.

[179] The book is catalogued in Mortimer, *Italian 16th Century Books*, no. 64, and mentioned in Guglielmo Enrico Saltini, "Della Stamperia orientale Medicea e di Giovan Battista Raimondi," *Giornale Storico degli Archivi Toscani* 4 (1860): 272. The title-page is dated 1590. Examples of the prints are in the BM, London, inv. no. 163.a.23; and the Casanatense, Rome, vol. 20.B.I.73/200–240.

[180] The *privilegio*, granted "Pro Fulgentio Valesino ac Leonardo Parosolium," is recorded in ASVat, SB, vol. 207, fol. 50. The invention is discussed by Saltini, 281–283, and doc. 20.

in 1591. The second edition, to which was added three more plates, including the one by Parasole (for a total of twenty-five) was printed by Luigi Zannetti for the Congregazione dell'Oratorio at S. Maria in Vallicella.[181]

The following year, 1595, a *Pontificale Romanum Clementis VIII Pont. Max. iussu restitutum atque editum*, was printed by Giacomo Luna at the expense of Leonardo Parasole and his associates.[182] Both the title-page and the colophon carry the date 1595. Clement VIII's universal *privilegio*, "Ad perpetuam rei memoriam," dated 10 February 1596, is reprinted in the first pages. Confusingly, this is followed by a thirty-year limited *privilegio* ("Ad futuram rei memoriam") dated 13 February 1596, after the book's publication, in which Leonardo and his associates are named. Even more confusing is that two years later, on 30 July 1598, archival records show that a fifteen-year *privilegio* was granted to Parasole and his associates for the same book.[183]

The *Pontificale Romanum* has numerous illustrations. The title-page carries a border, with figures to the sides and the Aldobrandini papal arms above, by Francesco Villamena. Villamena's name in full or his initials only appear on other illustrations. A number of the prints (and perhaps all of them) appear to have been designed by Antonio Tempesta. His name as inventor appears on several, notably on those engraved by Camillo Grafico. Besides Villamena and Grafico, at least one illustration is signed "L. Lauro f." who might be a relative of Jacopo Lauro (see above). It would appear that not all the illustrations were ready when the book went to press as there are several blank spaces.

In this same vein, on 17 July 1600 Parasole was granted another *privilegio*, this time for an edition of Clement VIII's revised "cere-moniale episcoporum" which was published later that same year, in October, as *Caeremoniale episcopum iussi Clementis VIII. Pont. Max. novissime reformatum*.[184] According to Baglione, in the same Jubilee Year

---

[181] In an edition published in Paris in 1660, the designer of the prints is identified as Giovanni Guerra by Catherine Monbeig Goguel, "Giovanni Guerra da Modena, disegnatore e illustratore della fine del Rinascimento," *Arte Illustrata* 7 (1974): 16, and n. 16; and in Elena Parma Armani, et al., *Libri di immagini, disegni e incisioni di Giovanni Guerra (Modena 1544–Roma 1618)* (Modena, 1978), 90, no. 82.

[182] A copy of the book is in BA, Vatican, Chigi.I.519.

[183] The *privilegio* is recorded in ASVat, SB, 273, fol. 44r.–v., 45r.–v.

[184] The *privilegio* is recorded in ASVat, SB, 297, fol. 467r.–v., 468r. The *privilegio* was granted for a ten-year period and carried a fine of one thousand gold ducats "de Camera." Although there is little doubt that the *Caeremoniale episcopum iussi*

of 1600, Leonardo engraved three "historiette" for an *Offices of the Blessed Virgin Mary*. Based on designs by Antonio Tempesta, the three engravings showed the *Annunciation*, the *Visitation*, and *Christ Washing the Feet of the Apostles*.[185]

This brings us to 2 January 1605 when Leonardo submitted a supplication for a *privilegio* for set of woodcut prints of all the emperors "up to the present." Interestingly, in making his case for a *privilegio*, Leonardo points out that his woodcut prints cost less than those printed from copperplate. He asks for a *privilegio* for ten years during which time nobody but him, or with his written license, or his heirs or successors, may engrave in wood the images of the emperors, etc. The *privilegio* was granted on 10 February 1605, but as yet no trace of the prints has been found.[186]

To these years, or perhaps a little later, may be dated an undated series of fifty-six woodcuts illustrating a *Vita di S. Antonio Abbatis* of which several carry the monogram of Antonio Tempesta as designer and two the monogram of Leonardo as cutter. The book was printed by Mattheo Greuter.[187]

The activities of Leonardo's wife, Isabetta Parasole, are discussed in Chapter 12. As for Leonardo's son, Bernardino Parasole, a painter and pupil of Giuseppe Cesari (the Cavaliere d'Arpino), his name is brought forward as a suspect in a case of theft in 1611. On 5 October 1611, the "antiquario" Pietro Steffanoni from Vicenza, then living on the Corso in Rome near Monte di Brianza, declared that he had been robbed of various pieces of friezes by Polidoro da Caravaggio of which one, the *Story of Niobe*, had been painted on the Palazzo Milesi, and another, the *Rape of the Sabines*, had been painted on a house in Piazza Madama. Steffanoni states that he had also lost var-

---

Clementis VIII. Pont. Max. novissime reformatum is the book for which Parasole was granted the *privilegio*, it carries no mention of Parasole. His name appears nowhere and the many illustrations are unsigned. The book was published in Rome "Ex Typographia linguarum externarum." A copy is in BA, Vatican, Casimiri.IV.257.

[185] Baglione, 394. An example of the last mentioned print, *Christ Washing the Feet of the Apostles*, is in the BM, London, C.51, 1868.6.12.598–602. The British Museum also has a woodcut of *Christ Healing the Blind Man*, signed with Tempesta's monogram and Parasole's monogram, and an *Agony in the Garden*, signed with Parasole's monogram alone (BM, London, C.51, 1868.6.12.592–597).

[186] The supplication and *privilegio* are in ASVat, SB, 353, fols. 752r.–v., 753r., 755r.

[187] All fifty-six woodcuts are in the Farnesina, Rome, vol. 58.K.61., FC. 119842–119897. The two carrying Leonardo Parasole's monogram are inv. nos. 119883 and 119884.

ious drawings and four hundred medals. The prime suspect was "Bernardino figlio di Leonardo Parasoli." Leonardo is identified in the document as an "intagliatore alla fontana de Trevi," while Bernardino is described as being a painter, as is his companion in crime, Domenico. The frieze of the *Rape of the Sabines* was later seen in Piazza Navona in the shop of Antonio Caranzano, a seller of drawings.[188] Caranzano said he had acquired part of it from Bernardino Parasole and the other half from a certain painter, the brother of Terenzio, Cardinal Alessandro Montalto's painter.[189]

---

[188] The case, which was brought before the Tribunale del Governatore in Rome, is printed in Bertolotti, *Artisti Lombardi a Roma* (Milan, 1881), 1: 128–129. It is interesting to note in passing with respect to this case that Antonio Caranzano [or Carenzzano] who acquired the stolen friezes by Polidoro, in 1613 published eight prints engraved by Raffaello Guidi of Polidoro da Caravaggio's Gods in niches painted on Monte Quirinale. The first print of the series, that of "IVPPITER," is inscribed: "POLIDORVS de Caravaggio Pinxit Romae in Monte Quirinale Raphael Guidus sculpsit Romae 1613." The series was dedicated by Carenzano to "Hippolito Marchioni de Ruvere . . ." All eight prints are in the Farnesina, Rome, vol. 35.H.1, inv. nos. 36619–36626, and all eight plates are in the Calcografia, Rome, inv. no. 227. For Antonio Caranzano, see also n. 80.

[189] The painter Terenzio from Urbino is noted in Baglione, 157–158. Bertolotti, *Artisti Bolognese, Ferrarese ed alcuni altri* (Bologna, 1885), 156, cites a letter written to the Duke of Mantua on 20 July 1613 which is signed "Terentio Terentij pittore di Montalto." Terenzio's brother was Giulio Cesare Terenzio.

CHAPTER NINE

PAINTERS AND COPYRIGHT IN VENICE AND ROME

The copyright granted to painters was for prints that either they themselves had produced or prints they had commissioned from engravers. In the latter case, the print or prints may be of the painter's own inventions, or they may be of images designed under their direction.

Venice

Only a handful of painters in Venice took advantage of the protection afforded them by copyright. First and foremost among them was Titian whose *privilegio*, granted in 1567, is discussed in the Introduction. Besides Titian, the Venetian Senate also granted copyright to the painters Giuseppe Porta Salviati, Francesco Terzi, Ludovico Pozzoserrato (Lodewyk Toeput), and Cesare Vecellio.

Giuseppe Porta Salviati

For most of his career Giuseppe Porta worked as a painter and an occasional engraver. He had arrived in Venice from Florence in 1539 in the company of his master the painter Francesco Salviati. When Francesco Salviati returned to Florence in 1541, Giuseppe stayed in Venice (and later added the name Salviati to his own). One of the first projects he undertook soon after his arrival in the city was to produce the frontispiece and one hundred small wood-engraved illustrations of philosophers and allegorical figures for a for-tune-telling book, *Le Sorti di Francesco Marcolini intitolate Giardino dei Pensieri*, published by Francesco Marcolini in 1540. Several years later, he also supplied prints to the German publisher Giovanni Ostaus (see Chapters 6 and 12).

He was evidently also interested in architecture and engineering. Following the receipt of a license on 21 May 1552 from the Capi del Consiglio dei Dieci, he was granted a ten-year *privilegio* on 11

July for his own book on the Ionic capital, *Regola di far perfettamente col compasso la voluta et del capitello ionico et ogn'altra sorte. Per Iosephe Salviati pittore ritrovata.* The book, dedicated by Salviati to Daniele Barbaro, was printed in Venice by Francesco Marcolini.[1]

On 18 March 1575, he was granted another *privilegio*, but this time for a device for raising water. In Venice, water and the moving of water were a constant concern. Numerous privileges for such devices are recorded in the records of the Venetian Senate, including one granted to Galileo Galilei for "l'edificio di alzar acque."[2] Salviati's invention is described in the *privilegio* as capable of raising water from rivers to whatever desired height in order to irrigate land and to make fountains. It could also be used to drain water from marshy land. At this point in his career, Salviati is describing himself as both a painter and mathematician ("Pittore, et Matematico").[3]

Francesco Terzi

In the early 1550s, following a period when he worked in and around his native city of Bergamo, the painter Francesco Terzi travelled to Vienna where he joined the Hapsburg court of Ferdinand I, king of Bohemia and Hungary (and subsequently Holy Roman Emperor, 1558–1564). Terzio remained in Vienna for the next twenty-five years where he produced, among other things, numerous portraits of members of the court and other illustrious figures. He also worked on the production of a corpus of prints, engraved by Gaspare Osello (Gaspar Patavinus ab Avibus), recording the history of the Hapsburg dynasty. It was for this latter project that, on 2 December 1568, Terzio was granted a fifteen-year Venetian *privilegio*. The book, *Francisci*

---

[1] In the license, the Riformatori del Studio di Padova state that "il disegno della voluta del capitello Ionico et la regole di farla di Joseffe Salviati pittore non e cosa che sia contra le lezze nostre dano licentia che possa essere stampato." The *privilegio* is recorded in ASV, ST, reg. 38, fol. 125v. (146v. n.n.): "sia concesso à Joseph Salviati Pitor per Il disegno della voluta del capitello Ionico, et la regula di farla." The book, which is referred to by Vasari, 1568, 7: 47, is catalogued in Mortimer, *Italian 16th Century Books*, no. 456; and in Scipione Casali, *Annali della tipografia veneziana di Francesco Marcolini da Forlì* (Forlì, 1861), 219–224, no. 90.

[2] Galileo's *privilegio* is recorded in ASV, ST, reg. 64, fol. 107r.

[3] The *privilegio* is recorded in ASV, ST, reg. 50, fol. 127r.–v. (149r.–v. n.n.). The document is discussed in Bruce Boucher, "Giuseppe Salviati, Pittore e Matematico," *Arte Veneta* 30 (1976): 219–224.

Tertii Bergomensis, Serenissima Ferdinandi Archiducis Austriæ, Ducis Burgundiæ, cometis Trioli, etc. pictoris aulici, ad invictiss. Caesarem Maximiliarium II. Romanorum imp. Semper augustum . . . MDLXIX, was published the following year.[4]

Ludovico Pozzoserrato (Lodewyk Toeput)

On 4 July 1585, the Flemish painter Lodewyk Toeput, using the Italianized name Ludovico Pozzoserrato, was granted a *privilegio* for his copperplate print of the Piazza San Marco in Venice.[5] Born in Antwerp, Toeput had been working in Italy since 1573. By 1582, he appears to have settled in Treviso, near Venice.

Cesare Vecellio

On 9 January 1590, the painter and engraver Cesare Vecellio, a nephew of Titian, was granted a twenty-year Venetian *privilegio* for a costume book (see Chapter 12), and an engraving *La città di Venetia con tre piazze et la corte Ducale*.[6]

Andrea Vicentino

On 14 May 1594, a *privilegio* was granted to the painter Andrea (Michieli) Vicentino for his copperplate print of the *Marriage Feast at Cana*.[7] Vicentino had been working in Venice since the mid-1570s, joining the painters' guild in 1583. In the 1590s, he won a series of important state commissions for history paintings in the Doge's Palace, and also painted altarpieces for churches in Venice and on the mainland.

---

[4] Terzio's *privilegio* is recorded in ASV, ST, reg. 47, fol. 67v. (88v. n.n.). A copy of the book is in the BA, Vatican, Cicognara XI. 2114.

[5] The document is recorded in ASV, ST, reg. 56: "Lodovico Pozzo Sarata Fiamengo pittore . . . il dissegno nuovamente fatto da lui in rame della Piazza nostra di S. Marco."

[6] The *privilegio* is recorded in ASV, ST, reg. 59, fol. 165r. (195r n.n.). A print of the same type (but without a *privilegio*) of *The College of Venice*, published "IN VENETIA APPRESSO LVDOVICO ZILETTI. 1575" and signed with Vecellio's monogram "C.V." in the lower right corner, is catalogued in Rosand and Muraro, cat. no. 90.

[7] The document is recorded in ASV, ST, reg. 64, fol. 45v. (66v. n.n.): "sia concesso al fedel Andrea Vicentino Pittore per el dessegno delle Nozze in Canna Galilei stampato in rame."

Rome

As was the case in Venice, only a few of the many painters working in Rome in the sixteenth century sought copyright for their printing projects.

Girolamo Muziano

On 4 November 1569, the painter Girolamo Muziano was granted a ten-year papal *privilegio* for a book of prints illustrating the entire narrative sequence of the reliefs of the Column of Trajan.[8] The document granting the *privilegio* is especially important for the book itself, which was finally published in 1576, carries no notice of copyright.

At the time Muziano submitted his supplication for the *privilegio*, the prints that were to serve as illustrations for the book were far from completion. As in the case of Giovanni da Brescia who, in 1514, had been granted copyright in Venice for a *History of Emperor Trajan* (see Chapter 5), the *privilegio* was granted Muziano on the basis of a few prints in hand, with the expectation that more would be forthcoming.

According to Baglione, the drawings from which Muziano had the prints made were by Giulio Romano.[9] It has been argued that a series of fifty-five pen drawings formerly attributed to Ripanda illustrating the entire column preserved in the library of the Istituto di Archeologia e Storia dell'Arte in the Palazzo Venezia in Rome, furnished the designs for the prints, and may be attributed to Giulio Romano.[10] Another series of one hundred and twenty-four drawings

---

[8] The document is recorded in ASVat, Arm. 30, vol. 247, fol. 7 (18 n.n.).

[9] Baglione, 51: "Fu cominciata da Giulio Romano la nobilissima fatica di disegnare le attioni Romane, che nella Colonna Traiana sono rimaste scolpite; ma questo gran lavoro fu da Girolamo Mutiano honoratamente seguitato, e con sua molta gloria felicemente terminato sì, che in rame con diligenza fu rapportato il tutto; & Alfonso Ciaccone eccellentemente v'interpose le sue dotte esplicationi; onde lo studioso delle antichità Romane molto al Mutiano deve."

[10] The drawings were attributed to Giulio Romano by Jacob Hess, "A proposito di un libro di Girolamo Muziano," *Maso Finiguerra* 2 (1937): 73. They have also been attributed to Ripanda by Roberto Paribeni, "La Colonna Trajana in un codice del Rinascimento," *Rivista del R. Istituto d'archeologia e storia dell'arte* 1 (1929): 9–28. It may be noted that Raffaello Maffei, "il Volaterano," in his *Commentariorum urbanorum libri XXXVIII* (Rome, 1506), records that Ripanda had made drawings of all the reliefs from top to bottom: "Floret item nunc Romae Iacobus Bononiensis qui

of scenes from Trajan's Column in the Pinacoteca Estense in Modena have also been attributed to Giulio Romano.[11]

Soon after the project got underway, Muziano ran into unexpected trouble. According to a document published by Ugo da Como, to realize the project Muziano had entered into a partnership ("societatem") with Antonio de Gentile, "faventino aurifice in urbe," and Lorenzo de Rozoli (or Rosolis), "miniatore romano," whose task it was to produce etchings from Giulio Romano's drawings.[12] However, with about fifty of the plates etched, Lorenzo de Rozoli died. Unfortunately for Muziano, all the plates and drawings that Lorenzo had in his possession at the time of his death were inherited by the Hospital of S. Giacomo degli Incurabili in Rome. Moreover, the officials of the institution had then promptly sold them to a "Maestro Marino sartore de Tolentino." Fortunately, though, on 20 April 1573 Muziano was able to secure the return of all the plates and drawings. Muziano next arranged for a certain Leonardo to etch the remaining plates. These were evidently completed by 1576 when the book was published in Rome, without a notice of *privilegio*, by Francesco Zannetti and Bartolomeo Tosi in 1576.[13] It contained one hundred

---

Traianae columnae picturas omnes ordine delineavit, magna omnium admiratione, magnoque periculo circum machinis scandendo."

[11] The Pinacoteca Estense drawings are discussed in Mihail Macrea, "Un Disegno Inedito del Rinascimento Relativo alla Colonna Traiana," *Ephemeris dacoromana (annuario della Scuola romena di Roma)* 7 (1937): 77–116; and Maria Grazia Pasqualitti, "La Colonna Trajana e i disegni rinascimentale della Biblioteca dell'Istituto d'Archeologia e Storia dell'Arte," *Accademie e biblioteche d'Italia* 46 (1978): 159. In either case, these are possibly the drawings from which Giulio Romano drew his designs for the stucco frieze showing the Triumph of Emperor Sigismondo in a room in the Palazzo del Te in Mantua. Vasari, 1550, 2: 887–88. ("Vita di Giulio Romano"): "Si passa poi in una camera [in the Palazzo del Te], dove sono fregi di figure di basso rilievo di stucchi, con tutto l'ordine de' soldati, che sono nella colonna di Traiano." Vasari reports more or less the same in the 1568 edition (Vasari, 1568, 5: 540).

[12] The document is transcribed in Ugo da Como, *Girolamo Muziano, 1528–1592: note e documenti* (Bergamo, 1938), 178–79.

[13] The title page reads: "HISTORIA/CEV VERISSIMA/A CALVMNIIS MVLTO-/RVM VINDICATA/Quae refert Traiani animam precibus Divi Gregorij Pontificis/Romani a tartareis cruciatibus ereptam. AVCTORE F.ALFONSO CIACONO HISPANO/Doctore Theologo instituti praedictorum, & Romani/Pontificis Poenitentario." A secondary title-page reads: "HISTORIA/VTRIVSQVE BELLI DACICI/A TRAIANO CAESARE GESTI,/EX SIMVLACHRIS QVAE IN COLVMNA/EIVSDEM ROMAE VISIVNTVR COLLECTA." A copy is in the BA, Vatican, R. I., II, 919, int. 2, 1. The text, on pages numbered 1–34, describes each scene depicted in the prints, with numbered passages (1–320) corresponding

and thirty plates accompanied by an explanatory text by the Spanish scholar Alfonso Ciaccono (Alonso Chacón, 1540–1599). A second edition was published in Rome in 1616 by Jacopo Mascardi. According to Baglione, the prints in the second edition were retouched by Francesco Villamena.[14]

In the meantime, Muziano had sued for payments (totaling 300 *scudi*) with respect to the first contract with Lorenzo de Rozoli and over the next four years received from Mario Gabriele, "advocato concistoriale et del popolo romano," 12.50 *scudi* per month, beginning 3 May 1573. A notary document was drawn up on 29 May 1577 after the final payment was made, which Muziano formally acknowledged in a separate document.[15] The following year the entire matter appears to have been sorted out. In a document, dated 16 July 1578, Muziano also acknowledged having in hand, as per an agreement drawn up on 6 May 1573 with Mario Gabriele with respect to the "desegno della colonna," the following items: one hundred and thirty etched and engraved copper plates ("pezi de rame designare cento trenta"); the drawing for the "first column" on a rolled piece of paper; the column printed on a rolled sheet of paper; the *motu proprio* of the *privilegio* for the column; plus books with the one hundred and thirty plates printed with the history of the column in Latin.[16]

At some point before the completion of the Column of Trajan volume, it would appear that Giovanni Battista de' Cavalieri became briefly involved in the project. Inserted after the text are two fold-out prints, one showing the exterior elevation of the column, and the other a vertical section through the interior. On the latter appears

---

to numbers on each print. Following three pages of Index are 130 page-sized prints. Muziano's role in the project is mentioned briefly in the "LECTORI CANDIDO SALVTEM" following the dedication to Philip II: "Postrem Hieronymus Mutianus pictor Romae insignissimus, in quo quid potius commendes, & admireris, nescias: aut artis summam peritiam, aut religionis observantiam, mores candidissimos, multasque alias animi & corporis dotes, quibus ornatus existit; in publicam commoditatem & utilitatem pariter, in aes cuncta columnæ simulachra exprimi & incidi fecit, multis sumptibus in eare factis, multisque laboribus & fatigationibus susceptis."

[14] Baglione, 393. A third edition was issued by Pietro Sante Bartoli in 1672, and a fourth by Carlo Losi in 1773.

[15] These documents, evidently overlooked by Da Como, are to be found in ASR, CNC, no. 1770, 314r., 315r.–v., 316r.–v., 336r.–v., and 337v.

[16] The document is recorded in ASR, CNC, no. 1770, fol. 487r.–v.

an inscription indicating that it had been printed in Rome by Cavalieri, and for which he had also been granted a *privilegio* for ten years: "Romae imprementur apud Jo: Baptistam de Cavallerijs decem annorum priuilegio impetrato." It is also possible, however, that both these sheets were originally a separate project, for which Cavalieri had been granted a separate *privilegio*, that was subsequently incorporated into Muziano's book.[17]

By the looks of things, the printing of the plates was undertaken by Bonifazio Bregio, a painter and printer from Como, whose name appears on the first and last prints (those numbered "1" and "130").[18] Little is known of Bregio's activities. In the notary document of 16 July 1578 mentioned above, Bregio is identified as "bonifatio de bregii pictor" and referred to as living "in la strada del pellegrino" in Rome. This is the same address given in connection with a document referring to "Bonifacio pittor da Como Bregio" dated 1566. A "Bonifazio Bregio da Como pittore" is also mentioned in a document dated 30 April 1573.[19] He evidently died in 1582 when a document dated 15 March 1582 refers to the "heirs and sons of Bonifazio Bregio" ("gli eredi e figli di Bonifatio Bregi"). In the years before his death, he apparently operated a workshop with his younger brother Simone Bregio, and ten days after the previous notice, on 25 March, an inventory of the workshop materials was drawn up so that his part could be divided up among his heirs.[20]

---

[17] Hess, "A proposito di un libro di Girolamo Muziano," 73, identifies the sheet of the exterior elevation of the column as probably coming from Lafrery's *Speculum romanae magnificentiae*, and refers to Huelsen, "Das Speculum Romanae Magnificentiae des Antonio Lafreri," 148, no. 30. The print shows the column surmounted by a statue of Emperor Trajan. They may also have come from an undated set of eighty-seven plates of the reliefs printed by Cavalieri which Bruno Passamani, "Cavalieri, Giovanni Battista," in *Dizionario biografico degli Italiani*, 22: 675, believes were produced before Muziano's project was completed. It may be noted that Cavalieri appears to have received at least one *privilegio*, and perhaps others, already in the 1560s and early 1570s (see pages 162–163).

[18] The inscription "Bonifatio Breggi al Melone d'oro in Roma" appears above on the first page ("1") and again on the last page ("130"). On 20 January 1579, in a supplication addressed to Muziano with respect to the 16 July 1578 document drawn up by a notary for Bregio, mention is made of the one hundred and thirty etched plates of Trajan's Column ("et altre tavole cento trenta della colon[n]a traiana intagliare in acq[ua] forte") (ASR, CNC, no. 1770, fol. 491v.). The issue is pursued further in notary documents dating 15 March 1579 (ASR, CNC, no. 1770, fol. 492r.), and 27 August 1579 (ASR, CNC, no. 1770, fol. 492v.).

[19] Bertolotti, *Artisti lombardi a Roma* (Milan, 1881), 1: 123, 128.

[20] The inventory is transcribed in Gian Ludovico Masetti Zannini, *Pittori della seconda metà del Cinquecento in Roma* (Rome, 1974), 18. The document refers to "tutte

Between 1573–1575, before the Column of Trajan book was published, Bregio was evidently involved in printing a series of seven engravings by Cornelis Cort after drawings by Girolamo Muziano of saints in the wilderness.[21] Each plate is inscribed with Bregio's printer's address: "Bonifazio Bregio at the [sign of the] Golden Melon in Rome" ("Bonefatio breggi al melone doro in Roma"). One of the prints in the series, *St. Jerome Penitent in the Wilderness*, dated 1573, is inscribed "Moto proprio de papa gregorio XIII pontifice maximo" (Fig. 25).[22] On each of the other six plates the *privilegio* is written "PRIVILEGIO.D.GREG.PP.XIII": *St. Eustace in the Wilderness Encounters the Miraculous Stag*, 1575; *St. Francis of Assisi Penitent in the Wilderness*, 1575; *St. John the Baptist in the Wilderness*, 1574 or 1575; *St. Jerome Translating the Bible in the Wilderness*, 1573; *Mary Magdalen Penitent in the Wilderness*, 1573; and *St. Onuphrius Penitent in the Wilderness*, 1574.[23] Muziano also had in his possession in 1578 an eighth plate by Cort, dated 1567, of *St. Francis Receiving the Stigmata*.[24]

---

le robe mercantili della boteca delli heredi di qm messer Bonifacio de Bregi et di messer Simon di Bregi suo fratello per indivisio . . ."

[21] The series is referred to by Baglione, 388: "Tra le altre, ch'egli intagliò, furono quelle, che vengono da Girolamo Mutiano, con que' rari paesi, ch'è cosa degna a vederli, con franchezza e con nobil'intaglio per alto fatti, cioè il San Gio. Battista, il s. Girolamo, il s. Francesco, la s. Maria Maddalena, il s. Eustachio e il s. Honofrio co'loro romitorij, e paesi egregiamente incisi."

[22] The print is listed in Bierens de Haan, 127, no. 116; and Luisa Consonni, "Gerolamo Muziano e i suoi incisori," *Rassegna di sudi e di notizie* 11 (1983): 204, no. 32.

[23] The prints are listed in Bierens de Haan, 124, no. 113; 125, no. 114; 126, no. 115; 127, no. 117; 128, no. 118; and 129, no. 119. A notary document of 16 July 1578 refers to Muziano having in his possession eight engraved copper plates, six for printing in "foglio reale" engraved by the deceased Cornelis Cort and designed by Muziano, and two other engravings by another hand. The six prints are then each identified by the name of the saint: "le decte sei de cornelio son queste una de S. hieronimo unaltra de S. Io. bap.ta laltra de S.to heustachio, laltra de S.to Honofrio laltra de S. Gioacchino [sic] e la sesta della magdalena e una pure de uno foglio reale intagliato da un altro de S. Hier.° che scrive et l'actava piccola intagliata da un altro de la Matalana (ASR, CNC, no. 1770, fol. 485r.–v.). The document is transcribed in Da Como, *Girolamo Muziano*, 183–184. The eight plates are referred to again in a supplication addressed to Muziano with respect to the 16 July 1578 document drawn up by a notary for Bonifatio Bregio dated 20 January 1579 (ASR, CNC, no. 1770, fol. 491v.).

[24] Cort's *St. Francis Receiving the Stigmata* is listed in Bierens de Haan, 136, no. 128. Baglione, 388, refers to "un'altro bellissimo paese, ov'è S. Fra[n]cesco che riceve le stimmate."

Fig. 25. Cornelis Cort, *St. Jerome Penitent in the Wilderness* (after Girolamo Muziano). 1573. Engraving. Photo: The Metropolitan Museum of Art, Harris Brisbane Dick Fund, 1953 (53.600.2534).

Anthonie van Santfoort

When the engraver Cornelis Cort died in Rome in 1578, his possessions, including at least four engraved plates, were inherited by
his countryman Anthonie van Santfoort (or Santvoort; and known
in Italy as Antonio de Santfort).[25] Santfoort, who was also nicknamed
"Groene Anthonie" (or "Antonio Verde" in Italy), worked in Rome
as a painter.[26] In 1577, his name is recorded among the members
of the Accademia di S. Luca in Rome ("Maestro Antonio de Santforte,
pittore fiamingo"), where he is also identified as "Antonio de Gisan-
forte." In the same records, the following year, 1578, he is referred
to as the "heir of Cornelis Cort" ("Maestro Antonio... fiamingo
erede di Cornelio Cort").[27] Upon inheriting Cort's plates, Santfoort
evidently decided to publish those that had not yet been printed.
He also sought copyright for them. Following the submission of a
supplication, he was granted a ten-year papal *privilegio* on 13 February
1579.[28] Each of the prints mentioned in the granting document can
be readily identified.

The first print mentioned, a Virgin Mary after a design by Federico
Barocci, can be identified as the *Holy Family with a Cat* after Barocci's
painting now in the National Gallery, London (Fig. 26).[29] The print
is signed and dated by Cort in the lower right ("Cornelis Cort fec.
1577"), with Barocci's name below in the margin ("Federicus Barotius
Urbinensis Inventor"). Just above the margin, and in a hand different
from the other inscriptions, and no doubt added by Santfoort, is the
notice of copyright: "Di. Greg. PP. xiij ex Priuil.p.an.x."

---

[25] An inventory published by Bertolotti, *Giunte agli artisti belgi ed olandesi in Roma
nei secoli XVI e XVII* (Rome, 1885), 227, of prints left by Cort (but not plates engraved
by him) was drawn up 17 March 1578. The inventory also carries the note, dated
22 April 1578, referring to "dominus Anthonius de Santfort mechinensis heres
Cornelii Cort."

[26] Carel van Mander, *Het Leven der doorluchtighe Nederlandtsche en Hoogduytsche schilders*
(Haarlem, 1604), fol. 263v., refers to "Anthoni Santvoort, die men hiet den Groenen
Anthonis." Confusingly, Godefrid Hoogewerff, *Nederlandsche Schilders in Italië in de
XVIe Eeuw* (Utrecht, 1912), 139, also describes Santfoort as nicknamed "de Blauwe
Anthonis."

[27] The records are in ASASL, Libro degli Introiti dall'Anno 1534 fino all'anno
1653, fols. 74v., 75r., and 79v. The documents are noted in Godefrid Hoogewerff,
Bescheiden in Italië omtrent Nederlandsche Kunstenaars en Geleerden (The Hague, 1913),
24–25.

[28] The document is recorded in ASVat, Arm 42, vol. 37, fol. 243r.–244r.
(247r.–248r. n.n.).

[29] The print is listed in Bierens de Haan, 64, no. 44. An example is in the MM,
New York, inv. no. 17.50.16–169. The print is mentioned by Baglione, 271.

Fig. 26. Cornelis Cort, *Holy Family with a Cat* (after Federico Barocci). 1577. Engraving. Photo: The Metropolitan Museum of Art, Purchase, Joseph Pulitzer Bequest, 1917 (17.50.16−169).

The next print listed is a "beati Hieronymi a Bernardino Passaro alios Antino designate," which may be identified as Cort's *Body of St. Jerome Supported by Angels* after Bernardino Passari ("Barnardinus Passarus Jnventor") (Fig. 27).[30] The notice of *privilegio* appears in the lower left above the margin. Interestingly, although Passari is identified as the inventor, the copyright document states that the design was drawn by a certain Antino. Very possibly, this Antino is to be identified as Iacopo d'Antino who is mentioned in a letter dated 31 March 1579 written by Giovanni Antonio Dosio in Rome to Niccolò Gaddi.[31] In the letter, Dosio informs Gaddi that d'Antino had found a chest of many beautiful prints by Albrecht Dürer, Marcantonio, and others ("Iacopo d'Antino dice aver trovato un conserto di molte belle carte, e sono d Alberto, Marcantonio e altri"), a notice which links d'Antino to the world of prints in Rome. Circumstances suggest that the drawing for the print, in the collection of J. H. Beckmann in Brême, is by Antino, and not, according to the accepted attribution (based on Cort's print), Bernardino Passari.[32]

The "Annutiate Deipare Virginis" may be identified as the *Annunciation*, believed to be after a design by Titian, while the last print named, a "beati laurentij prothomartiris," is certainly the *St. Lawrence* after a design by the Flemish artist Hans Speckaert (Fig. 28).[33] It is clear from some unfinished areas in the print of *St. Lawrence* (the area between the hanging cloth and the pier on the right; the object held in the saint's left hand; the right side of the face; the saint's right foot; and elsewhere) that Cort had not completed the engraving at the time of his death.

Federico Barocci

On 11 January 1581, the painter Federico Barocci was granted a *privilegio* for his print known as *Il Perdono di S. Francesco d'Assisi* (Fig. 29).[34] The print, an etching, reproduces Barocci's own painting that he had completed in 1576 and was then to be seen on the high altar

---

[30] The print is listed in Bierens de Haan, 143, no. 137.

[31] The letter is reproduced in Bottari and Ticozzi, 3: 312, no. 147.

[32] The drawing is illustrated in Bierens de Haan, 142, fig. 39 (the caption for it, however, is given to the print in fig. 38, and vice versa).

[33] The *Annunciation* and the *St. Lawrence* are listed in Bierens de Haan, 48, no. 24; and 144, no. 138, respectively.

[34] The document is recorded in ASVat, SB, 70, fol. 7v.–8r.

Fig. 27. Cornelis Cort, *Body of St. Jerome Supported by Angels* (after Bernardino Passari). 1577. Engraving. Photo: The Metropolitan Museum of Art, The Elisha Whittelsey Collection, The Elisha Whittelsey Fund, 1959 (59.570.181).

Fig. 28. Cornelis Cort, *St. Lawrence* (after Hans Speckaert). 1577. Engraving.
Photo: The Metropolitan Museum of Art, The Elisha Whittelsey Collection,
The Elisha Whittelsey Fund, 1949 (49.95.1738).

Fig. 29. Federico Barocci, *Il Perdono di S. Francesco d'Assisi* (after Federico Barocci). 1581. Etching and Engraving. Photo: courtesy of the Fogg Art Museum, Harvard University Art Museums, Arnold Knapp Fund, by exchange.

of the church of S. Francesco in Urbino.[35] The subject is St. Francis requesting directly from Christ, who appears overhead in the company of the Virgin Mary and St. Nicholas, the famous plenary indulgence known as "the pardon of Assisi." The inclusion of St. Nicholas may be accounted for by the fact that the painting had been commissioned by a Nicolò Ventura, who had died in 1574. The presence of the Virgin, shown mediating between Christ and St. Francis, is included because the chapel was contained within the church dedicated to S. Maria degli Angeli.

According to legend, one night in 1216 while at prayer in the little chapel of Portiuncula, St. Francis asked Christ to deliver sinners from their bondage. Hearing his prayer, Christ appeared to St. Francis accompanied by the Virgin Mary and a court of angels. The request was granted on condition that Francis go and present his supplication for the indulgence to Pope Honorius III, who was then in Perugia. Because it had been granted directly to St. Francis in person, the indulgence was of particular importance to the Franciscans who celebrated it at Assisi on the first two days of August. Barocci's painting brought special attention to the indulgence at a time when plans were underway, initiated by Pius V in 1569, to construct the church of S. Maria degli Angeli over the Portiuncula chapel.

That the image in the print is to be identified as pertaining to the indulgence is made clear in the wording of the *privilegio*: "pro fidelibus Ecclesiarum Sanctae Mariae Angelorum Visitantibus ab omnipotenti Deo Indulgentiam obtinuisse." St. Francis is shown on the steps of the Portiuncula chapel. In the lower right of the print Barocci is identified as the inventor and the engraver with the date, 1581, with the notice of the ten-year *privilegio* below: "GREGORII·XIII· PRIVILEGIO / AD·X·" Despite copyright protection, however, the print was copied by Francesco Villamena seven years later.[36]

---

[35] The print is listed in Bartsch, 17: no. 4; Harald Olsen, *Federico Barocci* (Copenhagen, 1962), 107, 160; Andrea Emiliani, *Mostra di Federico Barocci* (Bologna, 1975), no. 76; Simonetta Prosperi Valenti Rodino, "La Diffusione nell'iconografia Francescana attraverso l'incisione," in *L'Immagine di San Francesco nella Controriforma* (Rome, 1982), no. 94; Andrea Emiliani, *Federico Barocci (Urbino 1535–1612)* (Bologna, 1985), 117; Edmund P. Pillsbury and Louise S. Richards, *The Graphic Art of Federico Barocci: Selected Drawings and Prints* (New Haven, 1978), no. 73; and Sue Welsh Reed and Richard Wallace, *Italian Etchers of the Renaissance and Baroque* (Boston, 1989), no. 42. The painting is discussed in Olsen, 159–160; Emiliani, *Mostra di Federico Barocci*, no. 75; Prosperi Valenti Rodinò, 163; and Emiliani, *Federico Barocci*, 105–113.
[36] Villamena's print is inscribed: "FEDIRICVS BAROCIVS VRBINAS / INV.

Matteo Perez d'Alleccio

In August 1581 the painter Matteo Perez d'Alleccio returned to Rome from Malta where he had been busy working on various painting commissions for the Knights of St. John of Jerusalem.[37] In Rome it was apparently Perez's plan to have engravings made of the various paintings he had executed for the Knights. The engraver whom he employed to undertake this task was Pieter Perret.

Born in Antwerp in 1555, Pieter Perret may have worked briefly in France before traveling on to Rome.[38] His earliest dated print, signed and dated "P Perret fe 79," is after an anonymous French painting of the School of Fontainebleau which shows a young woman choosing between youth and old age. In the margin below are verses in French, and the name of a French publisher, Le Blond.[39] From the evidence of other prints, by 1581 Perret was in Rome where he was employed initially by the print publisher Claudio Duchetti. For Duchetti he produced four prints of antique statues, three of which were subsequently included in the *Speculum Romanae Magnificentiae* (for Duchetti, see Chapter 7).[40] Over the next two years he also engraved prints after Hans Speckaert and Bernardino Passari.[41]

EOR. Franciscus Villamena Fecit 1588." An example is in the BN, Paris, Eb 15, fol. 58.

[37] His name, "Mathio da Lecchio," appears for the first time in the records of the Accademia di San Luca on 31 December 1581 (ASASL, vol. 41, fol. 18v.). Baglione, 31–32, refers to him as Matteo da Leccio, but his name also appears written as de Alesio, d'Allecio, de Alecchio, de Alleci, and in Latinized form as Matthaeus Perezius Lecciensis. In 1582, he was one of several artist-members of the Virtuosi al Pantheon who, for the feast day celebration of the company's patron saint, St. Joseph, in the Pantheon, provided paintings for display in the porch outside the church. According to a description of the celebration, which took place on 19 March 1582, recorded in the company's minutes (Archivio della Pontifice Insigne Accademica Artistica dei Virtuosi al Pantheon, Verbali, fol. 53v.–54r., typescript, p. 180), Perez exhibited a newly painted tondo picture of St. Joseph ("essendo di novo fatto un Sancto Joseph per manno di messer Matheo Perez de Alecchio in un tondo di palmi sei").

[38] Perret's first name, depending on the country he is in, is variously given as Pieter, Pierre, Pietro, Pedro, or is Latinized as Petrus. Pieter Perret is believed to be the brother of the calligrapher Clement Perret.

[39] An example of the print is in the Farnesina, Rome, 37 H 11, inv. no. 44428. The painting is today in the Musée des Beaux-Arts, Rennes. Another version is owned by the Earl of Elgin, Broomhall, Fife.

[40] Three of the prints are listed in Huelsen, "Das Speculum Romanae Magnificentiae," nos. 120, 121, and 122. The fourth print, of the *Laocöon*, is probably that listed by Huelsen under no. 59 B.C. but unrecognized as engraved by Perret. An example is in the Casanatense, Rome, vol. 20.B.I.90/27.

[41] The prints after Speckaert are a *Joseph and Potiphar's Wife*, an *Allegory of Painting*,

In 1582 Perret was engaged by Perez to produce a series of prints of Perez's paintings in Malta. Perez's most important undertaking in Malta had been the decoration of the Great Hall in the Palace of the Grand Master of the Knights of Malta with a series of twelve fresco panels depicting the siege of Malta by the Turks in 1565. That Perez considered the printing project an important undertaking is indicated by his desire to obtain copyright protection, which was granted him by Gregory XIII on 30 May 1582.[42] Individual prints of the frescoed scenes, plus an allegorical frontispiece and a sheet inscribed "Al Lettore" (sixteen sheets in all), were issued by Perez in 1582.[43] In the inscription on the frontispiece, Perez explains that he himself "adapted with very diligent accuracy" his designs to the copperplates. Although Perret is not named, it is likely that it was he who undertook the etching of the plates. Another inscription in the lower left of the frontispiece makes it clear that Perez was also responsible for their publication: "IN ROMA APPRESSO MATTEO PEREZ D'ALECCIO." The *privilegio* is indicated below: "Cum Priuilegio/GREG. XIII. PONT. MAX./Ad Decennium MDLXXXII." The series was dedicated to Cardinal Ferdinando de' Medici.[44]

---

and an *Allegory of Sculpture*. All three are dated 1582. Examples of all three prints are in the Farnesina, Rome, 37 H 11, inv. nos. 44422, 44429, and 44430; and the Marucelliana, Florence, vol. LXIV, nos. 120, 121, 122. Examples of *Allegory of Painting* are also in the Casanatense, Rome, vol. 20.B.I.76 bis/155; and BN, Paris, Ed. 10. rés. fol. 114. A print by Perret after Bernardino Passari of a *Holy Family with Saints*, dated 1583, is in the Farnesina, Rome, 37 H 11, inv. no. 44425.

[42] The document is recorded in ASVat, SB, 52, fol. 396r.–v.; *Motu proprio* unnumbered, interleaved between fols. 398 and 399.

[43] The prints are listed in Borroni Salvadori, *Carte, piante e stampe*, 1: 52, no. 150 (frontispiece); 53, nos. 152 (2), 154 (3); 54, no. 156 (4); 55, nos. 158 (5), 160 (6); 56, nos. 162 (7), 164 (8); 57, nos. 166 (9), 168 (10); 58, nos. 170 (11), 172 (12); 59, nos. 174 (13), 176 (14); 60, no. 178 (15). See also Vincenzo Melillo, *Matteo Perez da Lecce, incisore in Roma* (Rome, 1980), 5, c. The series is mentioned by Baglione, 32. The prints were re-engraved (shifting the text to the margin below) in 1631 by Antonio Francesco Lucini and published by Nicolò Allegri who added a seventeenth plate of small portraits of all the Grand Masters from 1099 to 1631 (fol. 2). All the original plates were also renumbered. The 1631 edition has been re-published more recently in Calnan and Testaferrata, *The True Depiction of the Investment and Attack Suffered by the Island of Malta in 1565* (Malta, 1965).

[44] A story, the source for which I have been unable to trace, tells that Perez ran into trouble with the publication of the series. Apparently he had issued the prints without the approval of the recently elected Grand Master of the Knights of Malta, Hugues Loubenx de Verdalle, who may also have taken offense to the fact that the series had been dedicated not to him but to Cardinal Ferdinando de' Medici. Steps were apparently taken by Loubenx de Verdalle to suppress their publication.

Included in the same project is an engraving by Perret of the *Baptism of Christ* after a design that Perez had painted for the main altar in St. John's Cathedral at Valletta.[45] In the dedicatory inscription, addressed by Perez to Cardinal Ferdinando de' Medici, the print is described as after Perez's painting on the main altar in the church and as accurately drawn on copperplate by Perez. The print is signed with Perret's name as engraver.

The *privilegio* also mentions a print of St. Catherine invented by Perez, which may possibly be identified with Perret's print of the *Martyrdom of St. Catherine*, inscribed "Mattheus P. F. Romae" and dated 1583. The print is evidently after a painting by Perez in Malta but which has not been identified.[46] An Adam and Eve mentioned in the *privilegio* has also not been identified.[47]

The notice of *privilegio* also appears on a *Conversion of St. Paul* by Perez, dated 1583. The print was dedicated by Perez to Enrico Guzman, Count Olivares, the Spanish Ambassador who had arrived in Rome on June 6 the previous year. Inscriptions on the print show clearly that it was both designed and published by Perez, and engraved by Perret.[48] Arguably, the print, with its praise-filled dedicatory inscrip-

---

Unable to sell them, Perez may have encountered financial difficulties. The story is found repeated by Calnan in Calnan and Testaferrata, Introduction (unpaginated); Alberto Ganado, "Matteo Perez D'Allecio's Engravings of the Siege of Malta of 1565," in *Proceedings of History Week 1983*, ed. Mario Buhagiar (Malta, 1984), 130, n. 15; Ian C. Lochhead and T. F. R. Barling, *The Siege of Malta 1565* (London, 1970), 59; and in Melillo, 5, c.

[45] An example of the print is in the Farnesina, Rome, 37 H 11, inv. no. 44424. The painting remained on the main altar until around 1700 when it was transferred to the Sacristy where it is now to be seen. Melillo, 4, a, refers to the same print as a "Storia di S. Giovanni Battista," dedicated to Giovanni Giorgio Cesarini, and inscribed "Mattheus Perez de Allecio inventor incidebat Romae cum privilegio Greg. XIII Pont. Max. A.D. X MDLXXXII."

[46] The print is listed by Henri Hymans in Alfred Von Wurzbach, *Niederländisches Künstler-Lexikon* (Vienna and Leipzig, 1910), no. 9, but mistakenly dated 1582. It was dedicated by Perez to Cardinal Guglielmo Sirleto, Prefect of the Vatican Library.

[47] At the conclusion of his *vita* of Perez, Baglione, 31, states that besides having produced the Siege of Malta prints, Perez also produced a Triumph of Christ with many figures. It is unclear whether this print, as yet unidentified, is to be associated with those produced in connection with Perez's work in Malta.

[48] The dedication in the margin below reads: "ILLmo. ET EXCmo. Dno. HENRIQVIO GVZMANO COMITI OLIVARIENSI LEGATO REGIS HISPANIARVM PHILIPPII APVD GREGORIV[M]/PONT. MAX. VIRO RELIGIONE PROBITATE GENERIS SPLENDORE CONSILIO ET PRVDENTIA INCOMPARABILI. MATTHAEVS/PEREZIVS LECCIENSIS AFFECTVS ET OBSERVANTIAE CAVSA DEDICABAT. ROMAE ANNO D[OMI]NI M.D.L.XXXIII."

tion, brought Perez and Perret to the attention of Olivares. It is possible that it was through Olivares that Perret was given the commission to engrave Herrera's prints of the Escorial. Certainly later that same year Perret was in Spain engraving the first of the Escorial prints (see Chapter 11).[49] Perez also traveled to Spain that year. His reasons for doing so are less clear. Perhaps financial problems urged him to abandon Rome, or possibly Olivares had offered to recommend him for a commission in Spain. Whatever the case, by October that same year, Perez had already received an advance payment for an enormous fresco of *St. Christopher* eight metres high for the cathedral in Seville, which he completed in 1584. In Seville, Perez also worked in Santiago el Viejo (1586–87), and S. Miguel (1587). At some point, under the auspices of the Jesuit missionaries, Perez decided to try his luck in the New World. On 6 November 1587 he arranged for a transfer of money and soon thereafter left Spain for Lima, Peru, where he successfully established himself as a painter and where he remained for rest of his life.[50]

Tarquinio Ligustri

On 2 April 1596 the painter Tarquinio Ligustri from Viterbo was granted a ten-year *privilegio* for a print of the "Hortus Balnearius." In his supplication Ligustri explained that he wanted to make prints of his figurative work and other things, and for the present refers to the design of the hunting park ("barco") at Bagnaia.[51] He went on

---

The arms of Olivares appear in the centre. To the right of centre above the margin is written: "Petrus Perret Fe," and to the left: "M. P. de Aleccio Inve. Formis Romae," "1583," and "Cum Privilegio." An example is in the MM, New York, Whittelsey Fund 1962, inv. no. 62.572.11. Another example is in the BM, London, C. 59, inv. no. 1949–10–8–197.

[49] Delen, *Histoire de la gravure dans les anciens Pays-Bas & dans les provinces belges* (Paris, 1924), 105, who mistakenly believes that Perret went to Spain probably in 1585, says that he entered the service of the Spanish king, Phillip III. Besides the Escorial prints, Perret also engraved some frontispieces for Spanish books, and some portraits.

[50] Perez's career in Seville and Lima is discussed in Francisco Stastny, *Perez de Alesio y la Pintura del Siglo XVI* (Buenos Aires, 1970); Josè de Mesa and Teresa Gisbert, *El Pintor Mateo Pérez de Alesio* (La Paz, 1972); Jorge Bernales Ballestreros, *Mateo Perez de Alesio, pintor romano en Sevilla y Lima* (Seville, 1973); and Martin S. Soria, "Pintores italianos en Sudamerica entre 1575 y 1628," *Saggi e memorie di storia dell'arte* 4 (1965): 128.

[51] Ligustri's activities as a painter (with no mention of his prints) are noted in

to ask for a *privilegio* for ten years and "for each of his works to be published, with the usual penalties and restrictions proper in the privileges for prints so that he may enjoy the reward of his labours" and so that his prints would not be counterfeited to his detriment and loss. The print named in the *privilegio* can be readily identified as that showing a plan of all the gardens of the Villa Lante at Bagnaia with each part numbered and the key to the numbering given in the upper right. In the upper left is a dedication by Ligustri to Alessandro Peretti, Cardinal Montalto.[52] In the lower centre is inscribed "Con Priuilegio" with the date "1596" below.

Ligustri's engraving would appear to reproduce in large part a view of the gardens painted in fresco on the end wall in the loggia of the garden casino known as the Palazzina Gambara. The casino had been built, beginning around 1568, and decorated for Cardinal Giovanni Francesco Gambara who had succeeded to the Bishopric of Viterbo in 1566. At Gambara's death in 1587, Sixtus V (Felice Peretti Montalto) gave the Villa Lante "for life" ("donato in vita"), as reported in an *avviso*, to Alessandro Damasceni, his grand-nephew whom he had created cardinal at age fourteen and to whom he had given his name, Peretti di Montalto, and family coat of arms.[53] The decorations, including those on the vault of the loggia, which have been attributed to Raffaellino da Reggio and dated to between 1574 and 1578, show, besides the Villa Lante, views of three other villas, the Palazzo Farnese at Caprarola, the Villa d'Este at Tivoli, and the Villa Medici at Pratolino, as well as a view of the Borgo of Bagnaia.[54]

Baglione, 168. Ligustri's *privilegio* and supplication are recorded in ASVat, SB, 238, fols. 29r.–v., 30r.

[52] The example of the print in the BN, Paris, Topographie d'Italie, Vb 132.s., vol. 13, was trimmed along the right-hand edge clipping off the ends of the four lines of inscription. The print is illustrated and discussed in Claudia Lazzaro-Bruno, "The Villa Lante at Bagnaia: An Allegory of Art and Nature," *Art Bulletin* 59 (1977): 553–560.

[53] The *avviso* is noted in Francesco Negri Arnoldi, *Villa Lante in Bagnaia* (Rome, 1963), 9; and Angelo Cantoni, "Cenno Storico," in *La Villa Lante di Bagnaia* (Milan, 1961), 27 (and Tav. 21).

[54] The attribution and dating of the loggia frescoes are discussed in Maria Vittoria Brugnoli, "Le Pitture della Palazzina Gambara," in *La Villa Lante di Bagnaia* (Milan, 1961), 109–119. The identity of the buildings depicted are given in David R. Coffin, "Some Aspects of the Villa Lante at Bagnaia," in *Arte in Europa: scritti di storia dell'arte in onore di Edoardo Arslan*, vol. 1 (Milan, 1966), 570. The view identified by Coffin as the Villa Medici at Pratolino is identified as the Palazzo Farnese at Capo di Monte by Negri Arnoldi, 38.

As the view of the Villa Lante shows the garden design before it was completed, it is presumed that the fresco was based on the original architect's drawings for the whole project.[55] Neither the fresco, nor Ligustri's print, show the second casino built by Carlo Maderno which was presumably begun soon after 1596 and evidently completed by 1612 when its fresco decorations were underway.[56]

---

[55] The original architect is believed to have been Vignola.

[56] Negri Arnoldi, 9, however, believes that the second casino was completed about 1589. Besides the second casino, Alessandro Peretti also had built the fountain in the parterre, the Fontana dei Mori, which is not shown in Ligustri's print but also does not appear in Giovanni Guerra's drawing, inscribed "FORMA IN RISTRETTO DI TVTTO IL CONTENTO DEL GIARDINO DI BAGNAIA," which Jacob Hess, "Entwürfe von Giovanni Guerra für Villa Lante in Bagnaia (1598)," *Römisches Jahrbuch für Kunstgeschichte* 12 (1969): 196, dates to 1612. In 1612, Ligustri's print was copied in large part by Jacopo Lauro, inscribed "DESCRIPTIO. ACCVRATISS. HORTI. AMAENISS. QVI. VVLGIO. DICITVR. BARCO DI BAGNAIA," and included in his ANTIQVAE VRBIS SPLENDOR. For Jacopo Lauro, see Chapter 8.

CHAPTER TEN

MAPS AND GEOGRAPHICAL PRINTS

Privileges for maps far outnumber those in every other category of prints. It was noticed in Chapter 5 that before 1517 several privileges were granted in Venice for maps and that indeed the first *privilegio* granted for an independent print by the Venetian authorities was for a map. Maps continued to be produced in large numbers after 1517. Some publishers, like the Tramezzino brothers, Giovanni Francesco Camocio, and Donato Bertelli, were more active in publishing maps than others (see Chapter 6). Privileges for maps were also granted to engravers of maps, and to mapmakers, such as Giacomo Gastaldi. In Rome, numerous maps were issued by the print publisher Antonio Lafrery, including some with a *privilegio* (see below). Lafrery's successor, Claudio Duchetti also published maps in Rome (as he had when he worked in Venice), as did Bartolomeo Faletti and Mario Cartari (see Chapters 7 and 8). As we noted in Chapter 4, a measure of the importance of maps is Lafrery's inclusion of over one hundred examples in his inventory of 1573. In an age of navigation and discovery geography was of special interest.

In the following pages, as a means of organization, maps granted a *privilegio* have been grouped as follows: World Maps, Regions and Countries, Cities, Islands, and Maps and Geographical Prints in Books and Atlases. This is followed by two sections devoted to copyright granted for maps by Giacomo Gastaldi, and a *privilegio* for maps engraved by Domenico Zenoi.

World Maps

It was noted in Chapter 5 that on 19 September 1508, Benedetto Bordon had been granted a *privilegio* for a *mappamondo* ("world map"). The next reference to a world map occurs in 1529 when Giovanni Piero de' Marini ("Zuan Piero de Marin"), in his supplication to the Senate, described having made a *mappamondo*, a print he claimed had not been made before by anyone else and had been made by him alone. The Senate granted him a ten-year *privilegio* on 10 May.[1] That same year, Matteo de' Bardolini submitted a request for a *Planispherio*.[2] Copies of neither print have survived, however.

On 18 January 1556 [1555 m.v.], Antonio Floriano was granted a twenty-year *privilegio* by the Senate for a two-sheet copperplate *mappamondo* ("il Mapamondo dal p^{to}. Floriano formato essendo però nova, et non piu da altri posta in luce").[3] In his supplication, Florian states that:

> I, Florian, the very loyal servant of Your Highness and of the Illustrious Republic, with my diligence and knowledge having made a *mappamondo* which has never been made before, with the aid of which one can easily study and learn cosmography and see the entire picture of the world, since it can be reduced to spheric form as Your Highness can ascertain with Your own eyes and have of it whatever information You like.

He adds that the map was made "with so much drudgery and sweat, with more heavy toil [than] Your enlightened judgement can imagine." The map, which is copied from Gerard Mercator's double-cordiform map of 1538, is inscribed "ANTONIVS FLORIANVS UTIN."[4]

On 28 July 1554, Michele Tramezzino published with a Venetian *privilegio* and a papal *privilegio* a two-part, circular *mappamondo* engraved by Giulio de' Musi Veneziano (see Chapter 6).

On 18 August 1561, Mattheo Pagano, who is described as a "libraro et stampator" with a shop, "all'insegna della Fede," in the Frezzaria, was granted a fifteen-year *privilegio* for a *mappamondo* printed on twelve large royal sheets ("Mapamondo in fogli dodeci grandi reali").[5] The map, by Giacomo Gastaldi, was published in conjunction

---

[1] The document is recorded in ASV, ST, reg. 25, fol. 132v.–133r. (150v.–151r. n.n.) and filza.

[2] The document is recorded in ASV, ST, reg. 25, fol. 188v. (207v. n.n.).

[3] The documents are recorded in ASV, ST, reg 40, fol. 83r.–v. (103r.–v. n.n.) and filza.

[4] The map is discussed in Rodolfo Gallo, "Antonio Florian and his Mappemonde," *Imago Mundi* 6 (1949): 35–38. Antonio Floriano, and his older brother Francesco, from Udine, were architects, as is made clear in a document in which both, plus Antonio Canciano da Tolmezzo, apply for a building patent (ASV, ST, reg 40, fol. 113v. [135v. n.n.]). Francesco Floriano is mentioned in Vasari, 1568, 5: 110.

[5] The document is recorded in ASV, ST, reg. 43, fol. 96v. (116v. n.n.). Another document dated 1535 indicates that Mattheo Pagano had earlier worked as an engraver. Incidentally, the Frezzaria is a street in Venice winding from the Piazza

with a booklet written by Gastaldi (for Gastaldi, see below). The booklet is inscribed "La Vniversale Descrittione Del Mondo, Descritta Da Giacomo de' Gastaldi Piamontese. Con Gratia, Et Privilegio. In Venetia, per Matthio Pagano, In Frezzaria, al segno della Fede. M. D. LXII." In the document granting the license to Pagano, the Chiefs of the Council of Ten declare that "nel libretto il quale va insieme col mappamondo di Jac°. piamontese di Gastaldi non vi è cosa alcuna contraria alle leggi." The booklet was printed also in a Latin edition the following year. The woodcut map no longer survives.[6]

A *privilegio* for another *mappamondo* was granted to Marc' Antonio Giustignan on 13 May 1568.[7]

Regions and Countries

Maps of regions and countries form a major category. On 18 August 1554, the Flemish cartographer Gerard Mercator from Rupelmonde near Antwerp (known in Italy as Gerardo Mercadante Rupelimontano) submitted a request for a *privilegio*, granted by the Senate, for his huge fifteen-sheet map of *Europe*, "made with very heavy expenses, toil and diligence," which he dedicated to Antoine Perrenot de Granvelle, Bishop of Arras.[8] On 1 April 1563, Giovanni Piero Contarini, the son of the nobleman Bernardo Contarini, was granted a fifteen-year *privilegio* for a map of Europe and part of Asia which he had engraved himself ("da lui ridutta in intaglio di rame").[9] The

---

San Marco northwest to the Rialto. It, together with the Merzaria, a street running parallel to it, comprised the printmakers' quarter in the city in the sixteenth century.

[6] See Roberto Almagià, "Intorno ad un grande mappamondo perduto di Giacomo Gastaldi (1561)," *La Bibliofilia* 41 (1939): 259–66.

[7] Giustignan's *privilegio* is recorded in ASV, ST, reg. 47, fol. 10v. (31v. n.n.). The document states that Giustignan's *mappamondo* was "in Arabo con le graduationi delle provincie, et città osservate da Sultan Ismael, et raccolte per cagi Acmat, et radotte dal Membre, et Cambi." For Membre (that is, Michel Membre), see n. 49 below.

[8] The document is recorded in ASV, ST, reg. 39, fol. 151r. (172r. n.n.). The map is listed in Karrow, 386, no. 56/13. David Woodward, *Maps as Prints in the Italian Renaissance: Makers, Distributors and Consumers* (London, 1996), 68, comments that the *privilegio* seems to have worked, for no copies were made of Mercator's map until 1571 when it was copied by Paolo Forlani and printed by Claudio Duchetti. The Forlani copy is listed in Karrow, 386, no. 56/13.2.

[9] The document is recorded in ASV, ST, reg. 44, fol. 118v. (138v. n.n.).

map, inscribed "Ioannis Petri Contarini . . . totius Europae, ac partis Asiae nec non littorum Africae descriptio . . . qui . . . eam ab egregiis Geographicis passim colligens, et in aere postmodum incisam praebuit," was printed in Venice in 1564 on sixteen sheets.

On 6 July 1536, the Siennese mapmaker, Girolamo Bell'armato, writing from Rome, submitted a supplication to the Senate for a ten-year *privilegio* for a map of Tuscany, which, he says, will be of use to the military. On 14 July 1536, the Chiefs of the Council of Ten issued Bell'armato a license, and on 26 August 1536, the Senate granted him the *privilegio*.[10] Two days later, on 28 August, Bell'armato was granted a ten-year papal *privilegio* for his "tabula toscana . . . ab eo vocata, in qua provincia Tuscie sive Etrurie depicta ad eo atque designata est."[11] The four-sheet woodcut map, *Chorographia Tusciae*, was printed in Rome the same year with a long dedication by Bell'armato to Valerio Orsini dated 5 August 1536.[12]

On 11 September 1536, Francesco Torresani d'Asola (the son of Andrea Torresani d'Asola) submitted a supplication to the Senate for a twenty-year *privilegio* stating that he had received some bales of books from Paris together with a map of France designed by Oronce Fine. But, he explains, the shipment was ruined, so he made a new map of France, which he now wished to protect with a twenty-year *privilegio*.[13] As Robert Karrow notes, the map of France by Oronce Fine referred to by Torresani must be that published on six sheets by Simon de Colines in Paris in 1525, but for which no single copy survives. This was the first large map of France made and printed in France. The 'copy' for which Torresani is seeking a *privilegio* must be the four-sheet woodcut map dated 1536 by Giovanni Andrea Vavassore. Within a year or so of the expiration of the *privilegio* (i.e. in 1556), the map was copied by Pirro Ligorio, engraved by Sebastiano del Re, and printed with a new Venetian *privilegio* and a papal *privilegio* by Michele Tramezzino in 1558 (see Chapter 6).

---

[10] Bell'armato's Venetian *privilegio* is recorded in ASV, ST, reg. 29, fol. 50r.–v. (71r.–v. n.n.) and filza. His license is recorded in ASV, CCXN, reg. 11, fol. 12r.

[11] The papal *privilegio* (ASVat, Arm. 41, vol. 3, n. 156, fol. 164) is cited by Pierina Fontana, "Inizi della proprietà letteraria nello Stato Pontifico (Saggio di documenti dell'Archivio Vaticano)," *Accademie e biblioteche d'Italia* 3 (1929–1930), 213, who gives the date as 28 August 1538 instead of 28 August 1536.

[12] The map is listed in Roberto Almagià, *Documenti cartografici dello Stato pontificio* (Vatican City, 1960), 10; Woodward, *Maps as Prints*, 10; and Karrow, 78, no. 10/1.

[13] The document is recorded in ASV, ST, reg. 29, fol. 53r.–v. (74r.–v. n.n.).

Three years later, in 1561, Oronce Fine's original map, rather than Vavassore's 1536 copy of it, was copied and printed in Venice by Domenico Zenoi.[14] For Zenoi, see below.

On 9 December 1550, Fra Vincenzo Paletino de Curzola was granted a Venetian *privilegio* for a map of Spain, which was printed on 15 April 1551 with a dedication to Francis of Navarre.[15] In 1558 the book printer Vincenzo Luchini in Rome published a map of Italy, *Italia Nvova*, with a papal *privilegio*.[16] Another map of Italy, with the same title, *ITALIA NVOVA*, had been printed anonymously with a *privilegio* in 1554.[17]

Cities

On 14 April 1547, Eufrosino della Volpaia from Florence submitted a supplication to the Senate for a map of Rome "et contorni." He had already acquired a license from the Chiefs of the Council of Ten, and was subsequently granted a *privilegio* by the Senate.[18] He also received a papal *privilegio* from Paul III, and a ducal *privilegio*

---

[14] Oronce Fine's map of *France* is noted by Konrad Gesner is his *Bibliotheca universalis, sive catalogus omnium scriptorum locupletissimus . . .*, published in Zurich in 1845, fol. 530v.: "Galliæ totius nova descriptio, gallice ædita Parisiis, apud Simonem Colinæum 1525, in tabula circiter sex chartarum magnitudine." There were several later editions, the earliest of which to survive is dated 1538. The map is listed in Lucien Gallois, *De Orontio Finæo gallico geographo* (Paris, 1890), 55–66; and Karrow, 176, no. 27/3. Oronce Fine (1494–1555) was the royal professor of mathematics in France.

[15] The document is recorded in ASV, ST, reg. 37, fol. 81v. (102v. n.n.). The map is listed in Karrow, 444, no. 60/1. In 1558, three years after the *privilegio* had expired, a very close copy of the map, described as *Hispania Brevis descriptio*, was printed by Matteo Pagano.

[16] The map is inscribed "Elegantorioris Italiae Topographiam aeneis nostris formis excursam atq[ue] ita quidem ut nihil amplius desiderari possit Romae con privilegio 1558 Vincentij Luchini aereis formis ad Peregrinum." It is listed in Tooley, 34, no. 327. It may be noted in passing that on 15 December the following year (1559), the Cardinale Camerlengo granted Luchini, and his heirs, *in perpetuo*, the exclusive right to build a paper-mill in Rome and to buy rags "nella spazio di 20 passi intorno della Città." The document is noted in Bertolotti, *Artisti bolognese, ferraresi ed alcuni altri* (Bologna, 1885), 122.

[17] The map is catalogued in Borroni Salvadori, *Carte, piante e stampe*, 15, no. 38; and listed in Tooley, 34, no. 326.

[18] Eufrosino della Volpaia's Venetian *privilegio* is recorded in ASV, ST, reg. 35, fol. 12v. The map is discussed in Thomas Ashby, *La Campagna romana al tempo di Paolo III: mappa della Campagna romana del 1547 di Eufrosino della Volpaia* (Rome, 1914).

from the duke of Florence. On 23 April 1551, Leonardo Bufalini was granted a *privilegio* for a map of ancient Rome.[19] The map, for which Bufalini was also granted a papal, imperial, and a French royal *privilegio*, was printed the following month, on 26 May.

In 1557, two topographical maps of Rome, both engraved by Nicolas Beatrizet, and each one carrying a papal *privilegio*, were printed in Rome in the shop of Antonio Lafrery. One, the so-called "della guerra di Napoli" map, is inscribed in the lower right: "FORMIS ANTON LAFRE/RII. SEQVAN. DILIGENTISS. EXPRESS./AN. M. D. LVII./CON GRA[TIA] ET PRIVILEGIO."[20] The other is Francesco Paciotto's panoramic map of *Modern Rome* inscribed in the upper left: "EX TYPIS ET DILIGENTIA ANT LAFRERII/SEQ-VANI AN[NO] M. D. LVII./CVM GRATIA ET PRIVILEGIO SVMMI PONT[IFICE]."[21] In the latter case, Paciotto, a military architect and engineer, who had dedicated the print to his patron Ottavio Farnese, Duke of Parma, may have contracted with Lafrery to print it.[22] Also published by Lafrery, in 1565, is a map of *Antique Rome* designed by the noted antiquarian and ecclesiastical historian Onofrio Panvinio, which carries not only a papal *privilegio* but also Venetian, imperial, royal, and ducal privileges ("Cum priuilegeis Pontificis, Imperatoris/Regum, Reipublicae Venetae, et Ducum").[23]

---

[19] The *privilegio* is recorded in ASV, ST, reg 40, fol. 117v.–118r. (138v.–139r. n.n.). Bufalini's map is listed in Huelsen, *Piante icnografiche e prospettiche di Roma*, 38, no. 1.

[20] The print is listed in Bartsch, 15: 272, no. 107; Castellani, *Catalogo Ragionato*, 246, no. 85; Huelsen, *Piante icnografiche e prospettiche di Roma*, 15–17, and 49, no. 25; Tooley, 41, no. 472; Destombes, "Les cartes de Lafréri," 250, no. 104; McGinniss, no. 3; Borroni Salvadori, *Carte, Piante e Stampe*, 71, no. 217; and Silvia Bianchi, "Contributi per l'opera incisa di Nicolas Beatrizet," *Rassegna di studi e di notizie* 9 (1981): 120. Another map of Rome, entilted *ROMA CON LI FORTI*, engraved by Sebastiano del Re, derived from the "guerra di Napoli" map, was also issued with a *privilegio* in 1557. The map is listed in Huelsen, 50, no 26; and Tooley, 41, no. 487 (with no reference to the *privilegio*). An example is in the Farnesina, Rome, Sc. 30, FN 36644.

[21] The print is listed in Bartsch, 15: 272, no. 108; Huelsen, *Piante icnografiche e prospettiche di Roma*, 51, no. 29; Destombes, "Les cartes de Lafréri," 250, no. 105; McGinniss, no. 4; and Borroni Salvadori, *Carte, Piante e Stampe*, 71, no. 215.

[22] See Clare Robertson, '*Il Gran Cardinale' Alessandro Farnese, Patron of the Arts* (New Haven and London, 1992), 86; and George Kubler, "Francesco Paciotto, Architect," in *Essays in Memory of Karl Lehmann*, ed. Lucy Freeman Sandler (New York, 1964), 177–178.

[23] The map is listed in Borroni Salvadori, *Carte, Piante e Stampe*, 70, no. 212; and Huelsen, *Piante icnografiche e prospettiche di Roma*, 57, no. 47.

On 13 October 1593, the enormously productive engraver Antonio Tempesta was granted a *privilegio* for his famous map of *Rome*.[24] His supplication begins as follows:

> Antonio Tempesta, Florentine painter in this city [Rome] having published as a print a work of "Roma nuova" of which he was not only the inventor but also drew and engraved with his own hand, at great expense, trouble, and labour over several years, and doubting that someone will not come and usurp this work by copying it, and consequently reap the fruit of his labours . . .[25]

Tempesta then humbly asks for the pope to grant him a *privilegio*, such as is given "to every inventor of new works," so that "no one in the Papal States may for ten years print, or make for printing, or print the said work for others." He also asks that the same *privilegio* also extend to cover, "all the other works" that he might invent or publish with a "licenza de superiori."

The large map (108 × 243 cm) was printed on twelve sheets. Copies of the first edition survive in the Vatican Library and in the Royal Library, Stockholm. It was derived in part from Mario Cartari's large map of *Rome*.[26] In the lower margin can be read: "RECENS PROVT HODIE IACET ALMAE VRBIS ROMAE CVM OMNIBVS VIIS AEDIFICIISQVE PROSPECTVS ACCVRATISSIME DELINEATVS." In a large *cartello* in the lower right (on the twelfth sheet) appears: ANTONIVS TEMPESTA/FLORENTINVS INVENIT/DELINEAVIT ET INCIDIT/ANNO. MDXCIII" with notice of the *privilegio* below: "Romae, cum priuilegijs summorum Principum/per Decem Annos/Superiorum Permissu." The map was dedicated by Tempesta to Jacopo Bosio.

---

[24] The *privilegio* is recorded in ASVat, SB, 208, fol. 74r.–v. The map is listed in Bartsch, 17: no. 1460. It is also mentioned by Baglione, 315.

[25] Tempesta's supplication is recorded in ASVat, SB, 208, fol. 76r.–v. My translation.

[26] The Stockholm edition was believed by Huelsen, *Piante icnografiche e prospettiche di Roma*, 74, no. 84, to be the only surviving example. It had been discovered by Isak Collijn, *Magnus Gabriel de la Gardie's samling af äldre stadsvyer och historiska planscher i Kungl. biblioteket* (Stockholm, 1915), 6, and published by Henrik Schück, *Några Anmärkningar till Antonio Tempesta's Urbis Romae Prospectus 1593* (Uppsala, 1917). Lamberto Donati, "Un secondo esemplare della pianta di Roma di Antonio Tempesta (1593)," *Maso Finiguerra* 1 (1936): 67–68, discovered another example in the Vatican Library. The map is fully discussed by Schück and more recently by Franco Borsi, *Roma di Sisto V: la pianta di Antonio Tempesta, 1593* (Rome, 1986). The 1606 edition is listed in Huelsen, 75, and discussed in Franz Ehrle, *Roma al tempo di Clemente VIII: la pianta di Roma di Antonio Tempesta del 1593: riprodotta da una copia vaticana del 1606* (Vatican City, 1932). Mario Cartari's map is listed in Huelsen, 65, no. 72.

Besides maps of Rome, on 6 May 1564, Giovanni Varisco was issued a license by the Chiefs of the Council of Ten and a fifteen-year *privilegio* for a map of the city of Milan by the painter Alessandro Prola ("Il medesimo concedono per lo dessegno della Citta di Milano fatto per Alessandro Prolla pittor").[27]

Islands

On 6 October 1550, Fra Vincenzo Paletino de Curzola was granted a fifteen-year *privilegio* by the Venetian Senate for a map of the island of Curzola (i.e. Korčula, off the coast of Croatia) by Mattheo Pagano.[28] In 1556, George Lily's *Britanniae Insulae*, first printed in 1546, was re-issued on a smaller scale in an engraving by the Master IHS with a papal *privilegio* ("CVN PRIVILEGIO. SVMI PONTIFICIS. M.D.LVI."). The map is probably a copy of that printed by Thomas Geminus in London in 1555.[29]

A papal *privilegio* also appears on a map of the island of *Malta* engraved by Beatrizet dated 1563 ("Romae 1563. cum gratia et priui-legio").[30] Besides the inscription identifying Beatrizet as the engraver ("Nicolaus Beatricinus Lotharingius incid."), another indicates that he may also have been the map's publisher ("Melita N. Beatricino formis"), and thereby perhaps also the recipient of the *privilegio*. Towards the end of his career, beginning in 1558, Beatrizet was publishing many of his own plates.

In 1565, another map of *Malta*, engraved by Nicolo Nelli, was issued with a Venetian *privilegio*. It is inscribed "Nicolo Nellj Ven. F.

---

[27] The license is recorded in ASV, CCXN, reg. 20, fol. 11; and the *privilegio* in ASV, ST, reg. 45, fol. 27v. (47v. n.n.). The map is catalogued in Ettore Verga, *Catalogo ragionato della Raccolta cartografica e saggio storico sulla cartografia milanese* (Milan, 1911), 23, 90, no. 14. The map appears to have been reprinted in Rome by Antonio Lafrery in 1573.

[28] The map is listed in Marcel Destombes, "La grande carte d'Europe de Zuan Domenico Zorzi (1545) et l'activité cartographique de Matteo Pagano à Venise de 1538 à 1565," in *Studia z Dziejów Geografii i Kartografii*, ed. Jósef Babicz (Warsaw, 1973), 127.

[29] The map by the Master IHS is catalogued in Borroni Salvadori, *Carte, Piante e Stampe*, 9, no. 22; and Tooley, 31, no. 269. It is not in Bartsch, or Karrow. The map printed by Geminus is listed in Karrow, 253, no. 31/2.

[30] The map is listed in Borroni Salvadori, *Carte, Piante e Stampe*, 76, no. 229; and in Tooley, 36, no. 375.

addj Agosto 1565 con Priuilegio."[31] Nelli's was one of a number of maps of Malta issued in 1565 in response to public interest in the siege of the island in that year by the Turks. Nelli's map was one of the first prints to show a graphic view of the siege. The first state is dated July 8, less than a month after the first events of the siege had occurred. In the second state, dated 4 August, the annotated graphic information is brought up-to-date with the news of the siege. A fifth state, with further changes, was issued later in August.[32]

Many prints produced in the sixteenth century were devoted to the subject of the Turks and frequently were issued immediately in the wake of important events, such as battles and sieges, and thereby served as a sort of visual *avviso*, an illustrated news item. Public curiosity about the Turks and the Turkish threat was constant, and printmakers could respond quickly with informative prints about recent events. For example, the configuration of the Christian and Turkish fleets in the Battle of Lepanto in the four-hour period from 5:00 p.m. to 9:00 p.m. on 7 October 1571, was available on the streets of Rome five weeks later in a print by Giovanni Battista de' Cavalieri on 14 November.[33] Particular interest was shown in the places where the Turks were being confronted on land and at sea. Besides Malta and Lepanto, the Turkish siege of Rhodes, for example, was depicted in a print by Giovanni Andrea Vavassore in 1522.[34] Into this same category can also be placed a print by Agostino Veneziano showing *The Positions of the Armies of Charles V and of Suleiman II*.[35] The print is dated 1532 and shows in a panoramic view the sites in Hungary and Austria where, in September of 1532, were to be found the forces of Emperor Charles V and Ferdinand King of the Romans in the war against the Turks. It is singled out here because, below the lengthy explanatory inscription in the lower part of the print appears the words "CON GRATIA ET PRIVILEGYO."

---

[31] The map is listed in Tooley, 36, no. 366.

[32] The same plate was later issued in Rome by Claudio Duchetti. The various states are discussed in Woodward, *Maps as Prints*, 94–99.

[33] An example of the print is in the BM, London, inv. no. 1874–6–13–612. It is inscribed "VERO RETRATO DELARMATA CHRISTIANA et Turchesca . . . la gloriosa Vitoria tra lepanto . . . Posta in luce adi 14 nove[m]b[re] anno sudeto per giovanbaptista de Cavalleri . . . inprocinto de combater come si vede ali 7 de octobre 1571 dalle 17 ore sina alle 21 . . ."

[34] The print is listed in Leo Bagrow, *Giovanni Andreas di Vavassore. A Venetian Cartographer of the 16th Century. A Descriptive List of His Maps* (Jenkintown, 1939), no. 2.

Although the inscription omits the name of the granting authority, it was probably the Venetian Senate.

Maps and Geographical Prints in Books and Atlases

The *privilegio* was also granted to cover maps and prints of a geographical nature included in books. The miniaturist Benedetto Bordon, who had received several privileges in the past (see Chapter 5), on 6 March 1526 was granted a ten-year *privilegio* for a book on all the islands of the world, including Venice. The book, entitled *Isolario*, was published in Venice by Nicolò d'Aristotile (Nicolò Zoppino) in 1528.[36] On 12 October 1568, Bolognino Zaltieri was granted a *privilegio* for several books, including Giulio Ballino's *Disegni delle più illustri città et fortezze del mondo* which contains views and descriptions of fortified sites in various locations and countries.[37] Zaltieri published the book in Venice in 1569 ("Venetiis M.D.L.XIX, Bolgognini [sic] Zaltierii. Typis et Formis, cum privilegio") with a frontispiece engraved by Nicolo Nelli in 1568 (for Nelli, see Chapter 8).[38]

Also popular were books recording travels or voyages to different parts of the world. On 28 August 1546, for example, the engraver Domenico delle Greche submitted a supplication to the Senate for a *privilegio* for a series of woodcuts made after drawings, including

---

[35] The print is listed in Bartsch, 14: 315, no. 419. An example is in the BN, Paris, Eb. 7. fol. 59. A later state carries the address of Antonio Salamanca: "Ant. sal. exc." (an example is in the BN, Paris, Eb. 7. fol. 58).

[36] The *privilegio* is recorded in ASV, ST, reg. 24, fol. 74v.–75r. (92v.–93r. n.n.). The book was reprinted by Zoppino in 1534, and by Federico Torresano in 1547. A facsimile of the 1528 edition was printed in Amsterdam, 1966, and a facsimile of the 1534 edition was printed in Modena, 1983.

[37] Zaltieri's *privilegio* is recorded in ASV, ST, reg. 47, fol. 50v. (71v. n.n.). Among the cities illustrated are *Metz* (Tav. 23), showing the positions occupied by Charles V during the siege of October 1552–January 1553; *Messina* (Tav. 15); *Augusta* [Bavaria] (Tav. 29); *Wittenberg* (Tav. 33); *Eger* [Hungary] (Tav. 35); *Tripoli* (Tav. 47); *Fano* (Tav. 2); *Jerusalem* (Tav. 44); *Frankfort* (Tav. 30); *Geneva* (Tav. 31); *Vienna* (Tav. 39); *Comar* [Hungary] (Tav. 37); *Mirandola* (Tav. 3); *Parma* (Tav. 17); and a panoramic view of a battlefield with the legend "Con questa bellissima et ordinatissima ordinanza suole il Gran Sig^r. Turco presentarsi alla batteria . . . ."

[38] It may be noted that the year before (1567), Nelli had engraved a plan showing the siege of the fortress at Grimesteim: "Alli 25 di Gennaro 1567/fu posto l'assedio sotto la gr/an fortezza di Grimesteim/insieme con la citta di Gotta. . . . Nicolo Nelli Venet F. 1567." An example of the print is in the BN, Paris, Ba 1 (XVI), vol. 5.

maps, that recorded his pilgrimage to the Holy Land earlier that year. The Senate granted the *privilegio* for ten years.[39] In his supplication to the Senate, Domenico explained that he already had in hand a papal *privilegio* granted him by Paul III five months earlier, on 1 April 1546, and included the details of the papal *motu proprio*. In the papal *privilegio* itself it is recorded that Domenico's patron in this endeavour was Pietro de Carate Cantabri, a knight of the Order of St. John of Jerusalem.[40]

On 21 January 1561 [1560 m.v.], Vincenzo Valgrisi requested a *privilegio* for all the engraved plates and the text, translated from the Greek into Italian, of Ptolemy's *Geografia*.[41] The name of the translator is given on the title-page as Girolamo Ruscelli ("Nuovamente tradotta di Greco in Italiano da Girolamo Ruscelli").[42]

On 23 September the same year, Francesco de' Franceschi Senese, "libraro," was granted a fifteen-year *privilegio* for the first part of Strabo's *Geography*, translated into Italian by Alfonso Buonacciuoli.[43] The two-volume work, *La prima [-seconda] parte della Geografia di Strabone, di greco*, was published the following year, 1562, "appresso Francesco Senese."

---

[39] The documents are recorded in ASV, ST, reg. 34, fol. 140r. (163r. n.n.) and filza. The *privilegio* reads in part "... di anni X prossimi dummodo el disegno fatto da lui delli loci della Terra Santa sia cosa nova et da latri non stampata per nianze."

[40] The inscription on the book of prints reads: "Particularis et vera descriptio plateae sancti sepulcri per M. D. Petrum de Carate militem hierosolimitanum ornatu, et diligentia DOMINICI DELLE GRECHE VENET. PICT. descripta MDXLI [sic] cum gratis S. D. N. P. Pau. III et venet. Senatus" (the date is evidently incorrect and should be MDXLVI). The woodcuts in the book are discussed in Erich Bier, "Unbekannte Arbeiten des Domenico dalle Greche," *Maso Finiguerra* 2 (1937): 207–218. It can be noted that three large paintings of maps of Jerusalem, Venice, and Cairo, were painted in the Palazzo Ducale in Venice by Domenico delle Greche between 1546 and 1549. The paintings are discussed in Rodolfo Gallo, "Le mappe geografiche del Palazzo Ducale di Venezia," *Archivio Veneto* 32–33 (1943): 43–113.

[41] The text of the *privilegio* reads in part "... tutte le tavole della geografia di Claudio Tolomeo cosi nelle moderne come nell'antiche, et dappoi intagliate in Rame ... Et medesimamente el testo di essa geografia tradutta dalla lingua greca, nella nostra italiana." The document is recorded in ASV, ST, reg. 43, fol. 39v. (59v. n.n.).

[42] This corrects the claim made in Karrow, 222–223, that the book was published by Girolamo Ruscelli.

[43] The *privilegio* is recorded in ASV, ST, reg. 43, fol. 107v. (127v. n.n.): "la prima parte della Geographia di Strabone tradotte in volgare da D. Alfonso Bonaccioli."

Copyright Granted for Maps by Giacomo Gastaldi

The cosmographer Giacomo Gastaldi from Piedmont was the most prolific among the mapmakers working in Venice in the decades around the middle of the century.[44] A number of his maps were printed either by himself or by others with copyright protection. His earliest recorded *privilegio*, granted in 1545, was for a map of Sicily. It was intended to be used in conjunction with a *libretto* by Francesco Maurolico, entitled *Descrittione dell'isola di Sicilia*, that was published in Venice the following year, 1546, by Nicolò de Bascarini.[45] Two years later, maps by Gastaldi were printed in a new edition of Ptolemy's *La Geografia* published by the "libraro" Giovanni Battista Pedrezano from Brescia. Pedrezano had submitted a request for a *privilegio* on 5 November 1547 to print *La Geografia* in an Italian translation by Pietro Andrea Mattioli. In his request, Pedrezano explains that the book will be printed with "ancient and modern plates" engraved in copperplate with many additions of modern names of cities of the world. The book was printed in Venice with a ten-year Venetian *privilegio* ("In Venetia, per Gio[v]a[nni] Baptista Pedrezano. Co'l Privilegio dell'Illustriss. Senato Veneto per anni. X.").[46] The colophon reads: "In Venetia, ad Instantia di Messer Gio[v]a[nni]battista Pedrezano libraro al segno della Torre a pie del ponte di Rialto. Stampato per Nicolo Bascarini nel Anno del Signore 1547, del mese di Ottobre."[47]

In 1550, Gastaldi and Michel Membre together sought permission to publish a map of Asia with "all the cities and regions" covering an area that they described as "beginning at the Mediterranean Sea and going to the right [i.e. east] where there is all of Anatolia, Syria and Persia, with the country of the Sufi, and then towards the

---

[44] Gastaldi's activities are summarized in Karrow, 216–249.

[45] The print is inscribed in the upper left corner: "Descrittione della sicilia con le sue isole, della qual li nomi Antichi et Moderni et altre cose notabili per un Libretto son breuemente decchiarati, con gratia et priuilegio per Giacomo Gastaldo Piemontese, Cosmographo in Venetia. 1545." It is listed in Tooley, 43, no. 514; Borroni Salvadori, *Carte, Piante e Stampe*, 25, no. 66; and Karrow, 217, no. 30/2.

[46] The *privilegio* is recorded in ASV, ST, reg. 35, fol. 79v.

[47] The book is listed in Karrow, 220; Mortimer, *Italian 16th Century Books*, no. 404. Roberto Almagià, *Documenti Cartografici dello Stato Pontificio Editi dalla Biblioteca Apostolica Vaticana* (Vatican City, 1960), 12, incorrectly states that this edition of Ptolemy's *Geografia* was printed in Venice by Gabriele Giolito.

northeast where there is the country of Cathay, and then towards the south where there is India and the spice islands."[48] They were granted a ten-year *privilegio* on 15 July 1550.[49] Nothing seems to have come of this project, however.

In 1559 Gastaldi was granted further privileges. On 29 April, he obtained a ten-year *privilegio* from the Senate for two works described as "Corograffia della Anatolia," and "Viaggio de Costantinopoli à questa Città."[50] At this time, Gastaldi was also working on two large maps, one a three-part map of Asia, and the other a map of southeastern Europe to be printed on four sheets. It was evidently his plan to publish the three parts of the Asia map separately, and the April 29 *privilegio* was intended to cover only the first part showing Turkey and the Middle East. The map, engraved by Fabio Licinio, was accompanied by a separately printed gazetteer giving ancient and modern place names.[51] Similarly, the map of southeastern Europe was conceived so that the four sheets composing it could be sold separately. The April 29 *privilegio* covers the two northern quadrants. The map, engraved by Fabio Licinio, was printed in Venice by

---

[48] "far uno dissegno particolare di tutte le citta et regni nella parte del'asia incomminciando dal mare mediterarenco [sic] et andante al dritto per levante dove è tutta la Natolia, Soria et persia, cum il paese dil Sophi, et de poi verso griego tramontana, dov' è il paese dil Catagio, verso mezo di dove e lindia et isola delle speciarie." The document is transcribed in Richard J. Agee, The Privilege and Venetian Music Printing in the Sixteenth Century, Ph.D. diss., Princeton University, 1982, 224, no. 29.

[49] The document is recorded in ASV, ST, reg. 37, fol. 35v.–36r. (56v.–57r. n.n.). In another document, Michel Membre identifies himself as the Venetian government's interpreter of the Turkish language (ASV, RSP, Filze 284, no. 22).

[50] The *privilegio* is recorded in ASV, ST, reg. 42, fol. 12r. (31r. n.n.). The approval had been granted by the Riformatori dello Studio di Padova a month earlier on 29 March (ASV, RSP, Filze 284, no. 200).

[51] The map is identified in the upper right as "IL DISEGNO DELLA PRIMA PARTE DELL' ASIA," and carries the inscription "Con gratia & Priuilegio dell'jll^mo senato di venetia p[er] anni XV." The printed sheet of place names is inscribed "I NOMI ANTICHI, ET MODERNI/DELLA PRIMA PARTE DELL' ASIA" and with the words "Con gratia & Priuilegio del Illustriss./Senato di Venetia per anni. 15." In the dedication to the Duke of Savoy, Gastaldi explains: "I nomi antiqui et moderni di questa parte sono separati del disegno in uno foglio di carta. Presto manderò a la stampa le altre due parti del Asia, che seguitano la prima verso oriente e verso Austro, con la Grecia che la sequita verso ponente, le qual parte seranno descritte con i nomi moderni et antiqui come è questa prima parte et similmente farò all'Italia e a molte altre provincie che saria lungo scriverle, ma presto le manderò all'vostra Altezza." The map is discussed in Roberto Almagià, "A proposito di una presunta carta dell'Asia Anteriore di Giacomo Gastaldi," *Rivista Geografica Italiana* 69 (1962): 2–9.

Donato Bertelli. On the right-hand side of the right quadrant a table in a column is headed "Viaggio da Venetia a Constantinopoli per Mare" with below "Viaggio da Ragusi a Constantinopoli per terra" followed by the words "Il dissegno particolare delle Regioni che sono da Constantinopoli, a Venetia, da Venetia, a Viena et da Viena a constantinopoli."

Three months later, on 29 July, Gastaldi was granted a fifteen-year *privilegio* for the second and third parts of the three-part map of Asia, both engraved by Fabio Licinio.[52] They were not published however until 1561. Possibly the delay was caused by Gastaldi waiting for the ten-year papal *privilegio*, eventually granted by Pius IV, which appears on both prints. Like the first part, the second part was also accompanied by a gazetteer giving ancient and modern place names, but for the third part Gastaldi printed the names on the right side of the same sheet as the map.[53] At the same time he also re-published the first part, adding to it the papal *privilegio*.

The *privilegio* granted Gastaldi on 29 July also included maps of Greece, Italy, and Lombardy. The map of *Greece* was engraved by Licinio and published on two sheets in 1560. As in the case with the first two parts of the three-part map of Asia, for the map of Greece Gastaldi provided separately printed indexes of place names, one in the form of a broadside, and another as a booklet. The map of *Italy* was printed in 1561, and also includes a separate gazetteer of place names. The map also carries notice of a ten-year papal *privilegio* granted by Pius IV.[54] The map of *Lombardy* is known only

---

[52] The document is recorded in ASV, ST, reg. 42, fol. 42v. (61v. n.n.). The Riformatori dello Studio di Padova had granted approval the previous month, on 24 June (ASV, RSP, Filze 284, no. 209). The *privilegio* document is noted in Borroni Salvadori, *Carte, Piante e Stampe*, 16, no. 39, but reference is made only to the map of Lombardy.

[53] The map of the second part is inscribed "IL DISEGNO DELLA SECONDA PARTE DELL' ASIA" and dated 1561. The sheet of place names is inscribed "I NOMI ANTICHI E MODERNI DELLA SECONDA PARTE/DELL' ASIA." It is dated 1561 and also inscribed "Con gratia & priuilegio del summo Pontifice Papa Pio/quarto per anni X. Et dal Serenissimo Senato/di Venetia per anni XV." The map of the third part is inscribed "IL DISEGNO DELLA TERZA PARTE/DEL-L'ASIA" engraved by Licinio, and is printed with "I nomi Antichi e moderni della Terza parte dell'Asia per me Giacomo di castaldi piamo[n]tese cosmographo in Venetia 1561" on the right side of the map.

[54] The maps of *Greece* and *Italy* are probably those engraved by Fabio Licinio and printed in 1559 and 1561 respectively. They are listed in Borroni Salvadori, *Carte, Piante e Stampe*, 96, no. 289; and 16, no. 39, respectively. The map of Italy

through copies the earliest of which is that engraved by Giorgio Tilman and published in Rome by Antonio Lafrery in 1570.[55]

Gastaldi's map of *Germany*, engraved by Enea Vico, was printed with a *privilegio* in 1552 by Gabriel Giolito de' Ferrari: "Opera di Iacopo di Gastaldi Cosmografo In Venetia, 1552. Cu' privileg." with, in the upper left, "In Venetia appressso Gabriel Giolito al segno della Fenice" and below "Enea Vico Parm. f[ecit]."[56] Four years later, in 1556, Giolito also published, with both Venetian and papal privileges, Gastaldi's map of *Piedmont*, engraved by Licinio. The map had been granted a license by the Chiefs of the Council of Ten on 24 July 1555. A fifteen-year Venetian *privilegio* was granted to Giolito the following 12 September.[57] The map is inscribed "In vinegia appresso Gabriel giolito de' ferrari Con priuilegio del Sommo pontefice paulo IIII. e della Illustriss. Sig. Di Vinegia." Interestingly, it would appear that the map was actually first published without a *privilegio* in woodcut by Mattheo Pagano in Venice in 1555, and that the version engraved in copperplate by Fabio Licinio for which Giolito was granted a *privilegio* is a version of the original on a reduced scale.[58] For a *mappamondo* by Gastaldi, and an accompanying booklet written by him, published by Mattheo Pagano in 1561, see above.

On 11 September 1564, Gastaldi received another fifteen-year *privilegio* for more maps of modern Africa, Asia Minor ("la Natolia Caramania de Turchi"), and Lombardy.[59] The map of Africa was

---

is also listed in Castellani, *Catalogo Ragionato*, 243, no. 36; Tooley, 32, no. 328; and Almagià, *Documenti Cartografici*, 12.

[55] Giorgio Tilman's copy of the map of *Lombardy* is catalogued in Borroni Salvadori, *Carte, Piante e Stampe*, 17, no. 44.

[56] The print is listed in Karrow, 225, no. 30/70; Borroni Salvadori, *Carte, Piante e Stampe*, 92, no. 276; and Tooley, 30, no. 250.

[57] The license is recorded in ASV, CCXN, reg. 16, fol. 41r. The *privilegio* is recorded in ASV, ST, reg 40, fol. 55r. (75r. n.n.): "il disegno dil piamonte fatto per m°. Giac°. Cosmografo."

[58] The copperplate map is catalogued in Borroni Salvadori, *Carte, Piante e Stampe*, 85, no. 256; Tooley, 40, no. 448; and Karrow, 228, no. 30/76.1. The woodcut map published by Mattheo Pagano, is listed in Bagrow, *Matheo Pagano*, no. 6; and in Karrow, 228, no. 30/76.

[59] The document is recorded in ASV, ST, reg. 45, fol. 58r.–v. The maps are listed in Karrow, 244, no. 30/98.3; and 246, no. 30/103. The map of *Asia Minor* was dedicated to Cosimo Bartoli. A second edition was printed by Giovanni Francesco Camocio in 1566, and a third edition by Bolognini Zaltieri in 1570. The map of *Modern Africa* is discussed in R. Biasutti, "La carta dell'Africa di Gastaldi (1545–1564) e lo sviluppo della cartografia africana nei sec. XVI e XVII," *Bollettino della Reale Società geografica italiana* (1920): 327–346, 387–436.

engraved by Fabio Licinio, and the map of Asia Minor by Paolo Forlani.

A Privilegio *for Maps Engraved by Domenico Zenoi*

Domenico Zenoi, who describes himself as "a Venetian engraver of prints," was active in the 1560s and 1570s. In 1566 he submitted a supplication to the Senate in which he stated his "intention of printing or having printed or selling [prints of] pious figures, portraits and maps of Europe, Asia, Africa and other separate provinces, such as a Europe, an Asia, an Africa and other separate provinces such as Italy, France, Spain and others that from time to time will be made, which have not already been made by others in the form and scope that he will make them." He explains that he has already completed some of the engravings and is now requesting a *privilegio* for fifteen years "so that he will be protected against these malicious people who do nothing else than offend their neighbours by engaging in re-engraving." The license was issued to Zenoi by the Chiefs of the Council of Ten and on the same day, 5 December 1566, the Senate granted him the *privilegio*.[60]

A month later, on 11 January 1566, a second license was issued which included the stipulation that Zenoi "shall be under the obligation of showing each of these [prints] and those which he will have printed from time to time to the Executors so that one should see if there is not any obscenity."[61] Among the prints published by Zenoi with this *privilegio* are two maps, one of *Vienna*, dated 1566, and a *Descrittione dell'Austria, et Ongharia, Transiluania, Bauiera, Stiria, Carintia, Dalmatia, Venetiano*, dated 1567 and inscribed "Dnco. Zenoi cum priuilegio."[62]

---

[60] The license is recorded in ASV, CCXN, reg. 21, fol. 56v, and the *privilegio* in ASV, ST, reg. 46, fol. 100r. (124r. n.n.). The *privilegio* is noted in Woodward, *Maps as Prints*, 68; and Roberto Almagià, *Monumenta cartographica vaticana* (Vatican City, 1944–55), 2: 116.

[61] Zenoi's second license is recorded in ASV, CCXN, reg. 21, fol. 65v. A short while later, however, Zenoi was indeed found guilty of engraving obscene prints (see Chapter 3).

[62] The map of *Vienna* is listed in Tooley, 46, no. 597; and Gallo, "Gioan Francesco Camocio," 99, no. 58. The other map is listed in Tooley, 23, no. 125. For two maps of Europe engraved by Zenoi and published by Giovanni Francesco Camocio, see Chapter 6.

CHAPTER ELEVEN

PRINTS AND BOOKS ON ARCHITECTURE

The sixteenth century saw many books and prints published on the subject of architecture. A number of them were printed with a *privilegio*.

Vitruvius

Mention has already been made of the privileges granted to Francesco Cattaneo for an illustrated edition of Vitruvius in 1495, and to Giovanni Tacuino for Giovanni Giocondo's edition of *De architectura* in 1511 (see Chapter 4). Further editions of Vitruvius (or books based on his ideas and principles) printed with a *privilegio* in Venice include Sebastiano Serlio's book on the five architectural orders published in 1537 (for which, see the section on Serlio below). Twenty years later, on 30 June 1556, the printer Francesco Marcolini was granted a ten-year *privilegio* to publish Daniele Barbaro's translation of and commentary on Vitruvius.[1] Besides the architectural title-page and full-page woodcut at the beginning, Barbaro's book contains one hundred and thirty-one woodcuts, including eight double-page blocks, the designs for which were supplied by Andrea Palladio. Some of the woodcuts have been attributed to Giuseppe Porta Salviati. Ten years later, when that *privilegio* had expired, on 10 May 1567 the "libraro" Francesco de' Franceschi Senese was granted a *privilegio* for a revised and enlarged edition of the book.[2] It was printed the same year by Franceschi with the title *I dieci libri dell' architettvra di M. Vitrvvio, tradotti, & commentati da Monsig. Daniel Barbaro . . . da lui riueduti. & ampliat*. Most of the one hundred and twenty-one woodcuts it contains

---

[1] Marcolini's *privilegio* is recorded in ASV, ST, reg. 40, fol. 120r. (140r. n.n.). The book is catalogued in Scipione Casali, *Annali della tipografia veneziana di Francesco Marcolini da Forlì* (Forlì, 1861), 265–269, no. 109; and Mortimer, *Italian 16th Century Books*, no. 547.

[2] Francesco de' Franceschi's *privilegio* is recorded in ASV, ST, reg. 46, fol. 131r. (155r. n.n.). The book is catalogued in Mortimer, *Italian 16th Century Books*, no. 549.

are reduced copies of those in the earlier Marcolini edition. On the reduced copy of Marcolini's title-page, Giovanni Chrieger is named as Francesco de' Franceschi's associate. In the address to the reader, Franceschi names Chrieger as the cutter of the blocks.

Vitruvius' *I dieci libri dell' architettura* was published again in 1590, with a *privilegio* granted on 16 June 1590, to Giovanni and Giovanni Paolo Gioliti de' Ferrari. The book, *Della architettura di Gio. Antonio Rusconi: con centosessanta figure dissegnate dal medesimo, secondo i precetti di Vitruuio, e con chiarezza, e breuità dichiarate libri dieci*, includes one hundred and sixty illustrations designed earlier by Giovanni Antonio Rusconi. Rusconi had begun designing the woodcuts as early as 1553, but the project may have been delayed by the appearance in 1556 of Daniele Barbaro's translation of Vitruvius noted above. After Rusconi's death in 1587, it was decided to publish the woodblocks with only a summary in Italian of the passages in Vitruvius they were designed to illustrate.[3]

Leon Battista Alberti

The original Latin version of Alberti's treatise, *De re aedificatoria*, edited by Angelo Poliziano, had been first printed in Florence in 1485 by Nicolaus Laurentii. An edition edited by Geoffroy Tory was printed in Paris by Bertholdi Rembolt and Ludovici Hornken in 1512. The first *privilegio* granted for the book was to the "libraro" Vincenzo Valgrisio in Venice on 20 August 1543. Three years later, on 28 August 1546, Valgrisio was granted a second *privilegio* for Pietro Lauro's translation of Alberti's book from Latin into Italian.[4] Lauro's translation, however, was effectively superceded four years later by that of Cosimo Bartoli. Bartoli had been granted a Venetian *privilegio* for the book, which was published by Laurenzo Torrentino in Florence in 1550.[5] It was the first edition to be illustrated. Thirteen years

---

[3] Giolito's *privilegio* is noted in Horatio Brown, "Privilegi veneziani per la stampa (1527–1597)." Manuscript in the Marciana, cod. ital. VII, 2500 (12077), Venice, c. 1890, fol. 857. The book is catalogued in Mortimer, *Italian 16th Century Books*, no. 551.

[4] Valgrisio's *privilegio* of 20 August 1543 is recorded in ASV, ST, reg. 32, fol. 193r. His *privilegio* of 28 August 1546 is in ASV, ST, reg. 34, fol. 139r.–v. (162r.–v. n.n.).

[5] Bartoli's *privilegio* is recorded in ASV, ST, reg. 44, fol. 187r. (207r. n.n.). Bartoli's 1550 translation is catalogued in Mortimer, *Italian 16th Century Books*, no. 12. It may be noted that on 19 July 1568, a *privilegio* was granted to Francesco de' Franceschi

later, on 22 December 1563, Bartoli was granted another Venetian *privilegio* for "il libro di Architettura . . . da lui novamento ritrovato," which would appear to be for the first quarto edition of *L'Architettura di Leonbattista Alberti*, which was printed in Venice two years later, in 1565, by Francesco de' Franceschi.[6]

* * *

Living architects were also publishing their own works with both Venetian and papal copyright.

Sebastiano Serlio

In September 1528, the architect Sebastiano Serlio and the engraver Agostino Veneziano [Agostino de Musi Veneziano] together applied to the Venetian Senate for a *privilegio* to protect prints Serlio had designed and which were being engraved at the time by Agostino illustrating the four architectural orders: Tuscan, Doric, Ionic, Corinthian, and Composite. In addition to these prints, Serlio and Agostino explained in their supplication that they were planning also to produce other prints of various buildings and various other pleasing things of antiquity ("non solo li sopra ditti ordini, ma anchora intendemo stampare varij Edificii in perspicientia et altre varie cose antiche dilettevoli a qualunque"). Serlio, who described himself as a professor of architecture and Agostino Veneziano as an engraver ("Io Sebastian Serli Bolognese professor di architectura et Augustino de musi da Vineggia tagliator di bullino"), asked that for ten years anyone who counterfeited, or printed, or sold the said pieces would be fined one gold ducat per piece and the material confiscated. Unusually, he requested that the fine be divided into only two parts, with one part for the judge and the other for the "accusator." He also requested that the case be brought wherever in Venetian territory the fraud was perpetrated. The *privilegio* was granted by the Senate on 18 September with a vote 118 in favour, 13 against, and 7 abstentions.[7]

---

for Cosimo Bartoli's translation from Latin into Italian of Leon Battista Alberti's *Opuscoli morali* (ASV, ST, reg. 47, fol. 24r. [45r. n.n.]).

[6] Bartoli's 1563 *privilegio* is noted in Horatio Brown, "Privilegi veneziani per la stampa (1527–1597)." Manuscript in the Marciana, cod. ital. VII, 2500 (12077), Venice, c. 1890, fol. 510.

[7] The *privilegio* is recorded in ASV, ST, reg. 25, fol. 70r.–v. (88r.–v. n.n.). Serlio's *privilegio* is discussed in Deborah Howard, "Sebastiano Serlio's Venetian Copyrights," *Burlington Magazine* 115 (1973): 512–16.

At the end of the document, Serlio explained that "our designs [i.e. his and Agostino Veneziano's] will have this sign, that is S.B. and A.V." ("Lì nostri dissegni haveranno questo segno zoe. S.B. et A.V."). Agostino Veneziano had apparently already produced separate prints of the bases, capitals, and entablatures of three of the orders, Doric, Ionic, and Corinthian (nine prints in all), each one, as Serlio pointed out, carrying the initals of Agostino Veneziano ("A.V.") and Serlio ("S.B." i.e. Sebastiano Bolognese). The prints also carry the date "1528," and the name of the order depicted. After it was granted, a notice of the *privilegio* was added to each print: "Cautum sit ne aliquis imprimat, ut in privilegio constat" ("Beware not to copy as it is covered by a privilege") (Fig. 30).[8]

The plan was evidently to produce a book but the project was apparently abandoned. Nine years later, on 5 October 1537, Serlio submitted another supplication to the Senate for a fifteen-year *privilegio* (reduced to ten by the Senate) to publish "some of my books on architecture composed and illustrated by me" ("alcun miei libri de architettura per me composti et figurati . . ."). Serlio asked for penalities that included a fine of ten ducats per book, and one ducat for each design counterfeited ("sotto pena de' ducati X per libro, et di uno ducato per pezo di ogni dissegno"). The book, *Regole generali di architetvra sopra le cinqve maniere de gli edifici, cioe, thoscano, dorico, ionico, corinthio, et composito, con gli essempi dell'antiqvita, che per la magior parte concordano con la dottrina di Vitrvvio*, printed "CVM PRIVILEGII" in Venice by Francesco Marcolini in 1537, contains none of Agostino Veneziano's engravings.[9] Perhaps when it became clear that Serlio was not going to use Agostino's engravings, they were released from

---

[8] The prints are listed in Bartsch, 14: 382–83, nos. 525–533. The translation of the inscription is given in Landau and Parshall, *The Renaissance Print*, 302. The prints are discussed by William B. Dinsmoor, "The Literary Remains of Sebastiano Serlio," *Art Bulletin* 24 (1942): 64–65. Dinsmoor, however, was unaware of the document for the *privilegio* already published by Horatio Brown in 1891 and assumes the copyright was issued only to Agostino Veneziano. It may be noted that Agostino's presence in Venice at this time is also recorded in two documents dated 3 February 1527 [1526 m.v.] and 4 December 1527 concerning payment for engravings he had made (ASV, S. Croce alla Giudecca, Busta 10, fasc. 489).

[9] The *privilegio* document is recorded in ASV, ST, reg. 29, fol. 166r.–v. (187r.–v. n.n.) and filza. The book is catalogued in Mortimer, *Italian 16th Century Books*, no. 471. A copy is in the BA, Vatican, Cicognara VI.662. Passavant's claim (6: 64) that Agostino Veneziano's engravings appear in the 1537 edition of the book is incorrect (although, Veneziano's engravings were in some instances later inserted into published editions of Serlio's fourth book, for example in the 1544 edition).

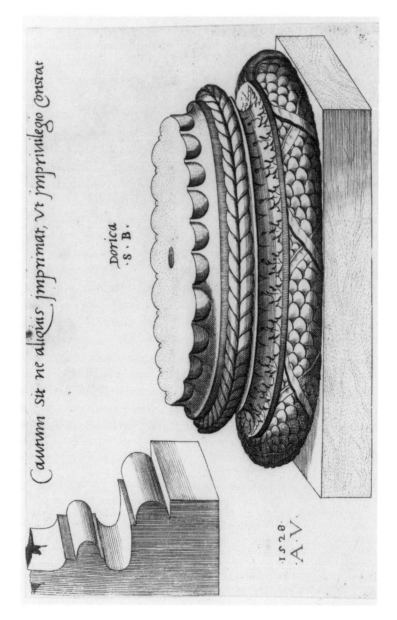

Fig. 30. Agostino Veneziano, *Doric Base* (after Sebastiano Serlio). 1528. Engraving. Photo: Warburg.

copyright restrictions, at which point Agostino made copies (Serlio, no doubt, as the initiator of the project, would have kept the original plates), omitting in each case the *privilegio* and Serlio's initials, but keeping his own "A.V." and adding the new date, 1536. The print publisher Antonio Salamanca in Rome later acquired these plates, to which he added his address, and reprinted them in a second state.

Possibly the delay in Serlio's project had something to do with Baldassare Peruzzi who was at this time accumulating material for his own treatise on the orders of architecture. Serlio's book, which in form and content was transformed from that planned in 1528, was based on material left by Peruzzi who died on 6 January 1536.[10]

On 19 July 1568, the Senate granted a *privilegio* to Francesco de' Franceschi to print Giovanni Carlo Saraceni's translation of Serlio's *De architectvra libri qvinqve*, which was published the following year.[11] The book contains four hundred and fifty-nine woodcuts.

Antonio Labacco

Antonio da Sangallo had been appointed the chief architect of St. Peter's in Rome in 1536.[12] Ten years later, in 1546, his pupil, the architect Antonio Labacco, initiated a project to produce a series of engravings of Antonio da Sangallo's wooden model, which Labacco had constructed of Sangallo's design for the new basilica. A papal *privilegio* was granted for the series by Pope Paul III. The three prints show the façade (Fig. 31), a lateral section, and a lateral elevation.[13] All three prints are inscribed along the top: "FORMA TEMPLI D. PETRI IN VATICANO," with the *stemma* of Paul III below. In the upper right Sangallo is identified as the inventor and Labacco as his pupil and *effector*: "ANTONIVS S. GALLVS INVENTOR./ ANTONIVS LABACCVS EIVS DISCIP./EFFECTOR." Each is also inscribed with the notice of the copyright: "CVM GRATIA ET

---

[10] This explanation was proposed by Rudolf Wittkower, *Architectural Principles in the Age of Humanism* (London, 1962), 18.

[11] The *privilegio* is recorded in ASV, ST, reg. 47, fol. 24r. (45r. n.n.). The book is catalogued in Mortimer, *Italian 16th Century Books*, no. 476.

[12] The record of the confirmation of his appointment, dated 28 May 1536, is in ASVat, Arm. 41, no. 2, fol. 12.

[13] The prints are listed in Huelsen, "Das Speculum Romanae Magnificentiae," 168, nos. 144, 145, and 146.

Fig. 31. Mario Labacco (?). *Façade of Antonio da Sangallo's model for St. Peter's.* 1546. Engraving. Photo: Avery Architectural and Fine Arts Library, Columbia University in the City of New York.

PRIVILEGIO." In the lower right corner of each print is inscribed the publisher's name, Antonio Salamanca, and the date. It may be noted that Labacco and Salamanca knew each other; on 9 May 1546, Labacco, together with the painter Livio Agresti, had proposed Salamanca as a new member of the Virtuosi del Pantheon in Rome.[14]

Due to the script and its small size, the dates on the prints are difficult to decipher and various scholars have put forward readings ranging from 1545 to 1548.[15] After careful scrutiny of all three prints and after taking into consideration the likely reason for their production, it is argued here that the prints had begun to appear in 1546. According to Vasari, it was Labacco who caused the prints to be made after Sangallo's death, which occurred on 26 September 1546.[16] In the months that followed Sangallo's death there ensued a furious struggle between Sangallo's supporters (whom Vasari calls the *setta sangallesca*; the "Sangallo sect") who wished to continue their

---

[14] The record is transcribed in Orbaan, "Virtuosi al Pantheon," 23.

[15] Thomas Ashby, "Il Libro d'Antonio Labacco appartenente all'Architettura," *La Bibliofilia* 16 (1914): 291, n. 1, believes that the Longitudinal Elevation is dated 1546, the Façade 1548, while the Longitudinal Section he says is undated. The same dates are given by Christof Thoenes in *The Renaissance from Brunelleschi to Michelangelo* (Milan, 1994), cat. no. 370. However, Henry A. Millon and Craig Hugh Smyth, "Michelangelo and St. Peter's: Observations on the Interior of the Apses, a Model of the Apse Vault, and Related Drawings," *Römisches Jahrbuch für Kunstgeschichte* (1976), who illustrate the Longitudinal Section in their Fig. 4, are unsure of the date and give it as "1546 (?)," as does Mario Pepe, "I Labacco Architetti e Incisori," *Capitoleum* 38 (1963), 25, n. 11, while James Ackerman, *The Architecture of Michelangelo* (New York, 1961), in his fig. 51c, reads it as 1545. Huelsen, "Das Speculum Romanae Magnificentiae," 168, nos. 144, 145, 146, lists all three prints but refers only to the Façade as dated 1548 (no. 144). Marianne Fischer, "Lafreri's *Speculum Romanae Magnificentiae*: Addenda zu Hülsens Verzeichnis," *Berliner Museen* 21 (1972): 15–17, also reads the date of the Façade as 1548. Lawrence McGinniss, *Catalogue of the Earl of Crawford's "Speculum Romanae Magnificentiae"* (New York, 1976), who catalogues only the Façade and the Longitudinal Section, gives the date 1548 for both (nos. 222, 224). The date 1548 is given to all three prints in Catherine Wilkinson-Zerner, et al., *Philip II and the Escorial* (Providence, Rhode Island, 1990), 122, nos. 50, 51, 52. Similarly, Suzanne Boorsch, "The Building of the Vatican: The Papacy and Architecture," *The Metropolitan Museum of Art Bulletin* 40 (1982–83): 10–11.

[16] Vasari, 1568, 5: 467: "dopo la morte d'Antonio Sangallo, messi in stampa dal detto Antonio d'Abaco." Oskar Pollack, "Ausgewählte Akten zur Geschichte der Römischen Peterskirche (1535–1621)," *Jahrbuch der Preuszischen Kunstsammlungen* 36 (1915), Beiheft, 51, notes an entry in a document in the Archivio della R. Fabbrica di S. Pietro dated 3 October 1546 recording the death of Sangallo that occurred on 26 September. Vasari, 1568, 5: 472, reproduces the inscription on Sangallo's epitaph in St. Peter's that had been placed there on 3 October by Sangallo's widow, Isabella Deta (the epitaph no longer exists).

control of the project, and the supporters of Michelangelo who was the prime candidate for the now-vacant position of architect-in-chief of St. Peter's. Vasari explains that Labacco wanted the prints made in order to show everyone Sangallo's merits as an architect, and also because "new plans had been proposed in opposition by Michelangelo Buonarroti."[17] The prints, therefore, may be seen as part of a campaign to stimulate continued interest, especially Paul III's, in Sangallo's design. Perhaps, with the support of the *setta sangallesca*, Labacco himself may have entertained the possibility of stepping into his master's shoes and being appointed chief architect of St. Peter's. Paul III finally decided to approach Michelangelo, who in fact turned down the position explaining that architecture was not his proper art. However, after seeing Sangallo's model, of which he was very critical, he agreed to make a model of his own design.

A blow to the Sangallo sect was Paul III's appointment, on December 1, of the architect and administrator Jacopo Meleghino as architect for the *fabbrica* of St. Peter's.[18] A fortnight later, two joint deputy architects were appointed: Luca di Benedetto de Bencivenis on December 16, and, two days later, on December 18, the Spaniard Giovanni Battista de Alfonsis.[19] Meanwhile, on December 11, money was made available for the purchase of wood and materials for Michelangelo to make a new model.[20] Payments covering the expense

---

[17] Vasari, 1568, 5: 467: "dopo la morte d'Antonio Sangallo, messi in istampa dal detto Antonio d'Abaco, il quale ha voluto per ciò mostrare quanta fusse la virtù del Sangallo, e che si conosca da ogni uomo il parere di quell'architetto; essendo stati dati nuovi ordini in contrario da Michelangelo Buonarroti."

[18] The reference for Meleghino's appointment is recorded in ASVat, Index 297, fol. 381v.: "Pro Joanne [sic] Meleghino Architecto fabricae S^{ti}. Petri augumentum Salarij ... Die p^{ma}. [1 December 1546]. The reference in the document to Meleghino's salary being increased gives credibility to Vasari's story (5: 471) of a spoken exchange between Paul III and Sangallo in which the pope, in a response to Sangallo's comment that "Meleghino is but an architect in jest," is quoted as saying: "Antonio, it is our wish that Meleghino should be an architect in earnest, as you may see from his salary." Three years earlier, on 26 September 1543, Paul III had placed Meleghino in charge of the fountains in the Piazza of St. Peter's ("Pro Jacobo Meleghino, Officium curandi fontem Plateae S^{ti}. Petri in Urbe"). The reference for the document is in ASVat, Index, 297, fol. 365v. Meleghino, who had served Paul III since 1534 in various capacities, was also the supervisor of the Belvedere and the antiquities in the Vatican.

[19] The reference for documents for the appointments of Bencivenis ("Lucas de Bencivenis deputatur Coadiutor Architectorum Fabricae S S^{ti}. Petri in Urbe") and Alfonsis ("Similis deputatio pro Joanne Bapta. Hispano") are recorded in ASVat, Index 297, fol. 381v.

[20] The payments to Michelangelo for the model are given in Pollack, "Ausgewählte

of making the model are recorded up to 5 August 1547. Around this time Paul III appointed Michelangelo chief architect of St. Peter's. An undated copy of Paul III's brief appointing Michelangelo is generally dated by scholars to the last months of 1546 or early 1547.[21] In a *motu proprio* of 1549, the pope gave his full support to Michelangelo's design and declared that it could henceforth not be altered or changed.

With the death of Paul III later that same year (10 November 1549), Labacco and the *setta sangallesca* may have hoped that their fortunes might change under a new pontiff. Perhaps this was why in 1549, only three years after they were first issued, all three of Labacco's plates were copied in reverse and printed again with several alterations made to the details of Sangallo's design and several changes made to the prints. In the print of the façade, for example, a number of apertures on the upper façade and the campaniles have been eliminated or reduced in size (compare Figs. 31 and 32).[22] Several of these alterations are seen in the model as it survives today. Very possibly, changes in the prints reflect actual changes made to the model itself between 1546 and 1549 by Labacco. Vasari notes that Labacco "finished" the model *after* Sangallo's death.[23] Moreover, on 7 May 1547, nearly a year after Sangallo's death, Labacco is still being described as the "master of the model of St. Peter's" in the records of the Virtuosi al Pantheon.[24] The changes seen between the 1546 prints and the 1549 prints are perhaps the result of Labacco's intervention in the model. These adjustments may have been made either to suit his own ideas about the design, or more possibly in response to the criticisms of Michelangelo and his supporters. Also

---

Akten zur Geschichte der Römischen Peterskirche," 52–53. Another payment for the model, covering the period from 9 July to 5 August 1547, is given in Millon and Smyth, "Michelangelo and St. Peter's," Appendix 1, 200, document no. 2.

[21] The date of "early December, or perhaps November, 1546" is given in Millon and Smyth, "Pirro Ligorio, Michelangelo, and St. Peter's," in *Pirro Ligorio: Artist and Antiquarian*, ed. Robert W. Gaston (Florence, 1988), 216. The substance of the brief was first published by Filippo Bonanni, *Numismata summorum pontificum templi vaticani fabricam indicantia, Chronologica ejusdem Fabricæ narratione, ac multiplici eruditione explicata* (Rome, 1696), 77. Bonanni used an undated copy of the brief written in Italian at that time in the hands of Filippo Buonarroti.

[22] Changes in the architectural details are discussed briefly by Fischer, 16.

[23] Vasari, 1568, 5: 467: "Finito dall'Abaco tutti i detti modelli, poco dopo la morte d'Antonio."

[24] The record is transcribed in Orbaan, "Virtuosi al Pantheon," 23: "Antonio Labaccho, mastro del model di San Pietro."

Fig. 32. Mario Labacco (?). *Façade of Antonio da Sangallo's model for St. Peter's*. 1549. Engraving. Photo: Avery Architectural and Fine Arts Library, Columbia University in the City of New York.

immediately noticeable in the design of the print is the omission of the papal insignia and the arms of Paul III. Salamanca's name as publisher was retained, though inscribed differently, as is the notice of copyright. At the same time a fourth print was added to the original set of three showing the plan for Sangallo's design, with "AEDIS D. PETRI IXNOGRAPHIA EX IPSO ANT SANCTGALLI EXEMPLARI ROMAE M.D.XLVIIII/CON GRATIA ET PRIVILEGIO" inscribed in the lower margin. In the lower right appears Salamanca's address ("Ant Sala. Excudebat").

Whatever hopes Labacco and the *setta sangallesca* had placed in the newly-elected Julius III, however, were dashed when in February 1552 the new pope confirmed in a new *motu proprio* his predecessor's decision to proceed with Michelangelo's plan.

In the meantime, Labacco was evidently writing a book on architecture. On 30 April 1552, he was granted a ten-year Venetian *privilegio* for his *Libro d'Antonio Labacco appartenente a l'architettvra nel qval si figvrano alcvne notabili antiqvita di Roma*, for which he also received a papal *privilegio*.[25] The engravings in the book are the work of Labacco's son, Mario Labacco, as Labacco himself points out in the section "A LI LETTORI" at the beginning of the book: "Mario mio Figliuolo . . . per insin all'intagliare parte di esse stampe."[26] Mario Labacco is also an obvious candidate as the engraver of the Sangallo model prints. His activities as an engraver are recorded in only one other print, a copy, dated 1567, he made of Beatrizet's 1559 print *St. Peter Walking on Water* after Giotto (the so-called Navicella mosaic at St. Peter's), which was printed with a papal *privilegio*.[27]

Pietro Cataneo

Pietro Cataneo was a mathematician who worked both as a military engineer and as an architect in Siena and its vicinity. His sister,

---

[25] The Venetian *privilegio* is recorded in ASV, ST, reg. 38, fol. 92v. (113v. n.n.).

[26] Labacco and his book are discussed in Ashby, "Il Libro d'Antonio Labacco," 289–309. Labacco's "A LI LETTORI" is reproduced by Ashby, 295. The 1559 edition of the book is listed in *Mostra del libro illustrato romano del cinquecento* (Rome, 1950), 28, no. 69.

[27] The print, listed in Zani, 2, 7: 41, Copy B, is inscribed: "Marius Labaccus faciebat Romae cum privile[gio]. MDLXVII." Beatrizet's print is listed in Bartsch, 15: 246, no. 16, but without mention of Labacco's copy. The print was also copied by Giovanni Battista de' Cavalieri in 1564.

Caterina, was married to the Sienese painter Domenico Beccafumi. Cataneo's first book was on mathematics, *I primi due libri delle matematiche*, which was published in Venice in 1546. A second edition, *Le pratiche delle dve prime matematiche, di Pietro Cataneo, con la aggionta, libro d'albaco e geometria con il pratico e uero modo di misurar la terra, non piv mostro da altri*, was printed in Venice in 1569, the year of Cataneo's death.

On 12 May 1554, following the approval of the Riformatori dello Studio di Padova, Cataneo was granted first a license by the Chiefs of the Council of Ten and then, on the 28 July, a fifteen-year *privilegio* by the Senate to publish the first four books of his treatise on architecture: *I quattro primi libri di architettura*.[28] The four books, printed (in a single volume) in Venice by Paolo Manuzio that same year, are devoted respectively to the city and fortifications, building materials, churches, and domestic architecture, and are illustrated with forty-three woodcuts. Thirteen years later, in 1567, Cataneo re-issued the first four books, with additions, and added four more books for which he was granted a twenty-year *privilegio* on 19 February 1567 [1566 m.v.].[29] The four additional books are devoted to the orders, water and baths, geometry, and perspective. The eight books, illustrated with one hundred and fifty-eight woodcuts, were printed in one volume by Paolo Manuzio in 1567 with the title: *L'architettvra. Alla quale oltre all'essere stati dall'istesso autore riuisti, meglio ordinati, e di diuersi disegni, e discorsi arricchiti i primi quattro libri per l'adietro stampati, sono aggiunti di piu il quinto, sesto, settimo, e ottauo libro*.[30]

Andrea Palladio

On 21 April 1570, a twenty-year *privilegio* was granted to Domenico de' Franceschi to publish Andrea Palladio's "il libro di Architettura."[31]

---

[28] Cataneo's license is recorded in ASV, CCXN, reg. 15, fol. 123v., and his *privilegio* in ASV, ST, reg. 39, fol. 146r. (167r. n.n.). Besides the fifteen-year Venetian *privilegio*, Cataneo had also been granted a ten-year papal *privilegio*: "Con priuilegio del sommo pontefice per anni X. & dell'illustrissima signoria di Vinegia per anni XV." The book is catalogued in Mortimer, *Italian 16th Century Books*, no. 113.

[29] Cataneo's second *privilegio* is recorded in ASV, ST, reg. 46, fol. 112v. (136v. n.n.).

[30] The book is catalogued in Mortimer, *Italian 16th Century Books*, no. 114.

[31] Franceschi's *privilegio* is recorded in ASV, ST, reg. 48. The book is catalogued in Mortimer, *Italian 16th Century Books*, no. 352.

The book, published the same year with the title *I qvattro libri del-l'architettvra*, contains two hundred and seventeen woodcuts.[32] Five years later, on 5 March 1575, Palladio himself was granted a fifteen-year *privilegio* for his *proemio* together with prints illustrating the commentaries of Julius Caesar.[33] The book was published in Venice by Pietro de' Franceschi the same year with the title *I Commentarii de C. Givlio Cesare: con le figvre in rame de gli alloggiamenti, de' fatti d'arme, delle circonuallationi delle città, & di molte altre cose notabili, descritte in essi.* In the preface, Palladio explains that the illustrations had originated out of a project he had set for his two sons, Orazio and Leonida. Palladio decided to complete the project and publish the illustrations after the death of both his sons in 1572. Palladio dedicated the book to Giacomo (Jacopo) Buoncompagni, the natural son of Pope Gregory XIII. The Latin text of Julius Caesar's commentaries had been translated into Italian by Francesco Baldelli. Baldelli's translation of Caesar's commentaries had already been published twenty years earlier by Gabriele Giolito de' Ferrari who had been granted a fifteen-year *privilegio* for the book, "con le sue figure, et disegni," by the Senate on 26 February 1553 [1552 m.v.].[34] By the time Palladio published his edition, Giolito's *privilegio* had expired.

Juan de Herrera

To commemorate a Spanish military victory over the French at Saint-Quentin in 1557, Philip II built near Madrid the huge monastery and palace known as San Lorenzo de El Escorial. Begun by the architect Juan Bautista de Toledo in 1563, the building had been completed by his pupil Juan de Herrera in 1584. On 23 June 1584, Herrera applied for and was granted a fifteen-year papal *privilegio* by Gregory XIII for a series of eleven prints of the Escorial together

---

[32] Some of the woodcuts have been attributed to Cristoforo Coriolano and Cristoforo and Giovanni Chrieger.

[33] Palladio's *privilegio* is recorded in ASV, ST, reg. 50, fol. 121r. (143r. n.n.). In its response to the supplication, the Senate explained that Palladio "havendo ... redette in figure tutti gl'ordini militare de Romani, cavati dalli commentarie di Giulio Cesare." The book is discussed in J. R. Hale, "Andrea Palladio, Polybius and Julius Caesar," *Journal of the Warburg and Courtauld Institutes* 40 (1977): 240–255.

[34] Giolito's *privilegio* document is recorded in ASV, ST, reg. 38, fol. 193r. (214r. n.n.). The book was printed "Appresso Gabriel Giolito de Ferrari e fratelli" with the title *I Commentari di C. Givlio Cesare* in 1554.

with a *Sumario*.[35] The project to produce prints of the building had been initiated at least six years earlier. From the beginning Herrera had evidently envisioned it as being a significant commercial venture and in order to protect his investment of time and money had applied to the major granting authorities for copyright protection. The first had been granted on 14 August 1583 by the Cámera de Castilla in Madrid.[36] The following year, on 12 March 1584, the Council of the Indies granted Herrera the right to sell the prints in Spanish territories overseas. Other privileges were awarded by the Emperor, the King of France, and the Senate of Venice.[37]

The list of privileges that appears on plates 9 and 10 must have been added by Herrera after June 1584 (the date of the papal *privilegio*). The inscription reads: "con priuilegio del summo pontifice, y emperador, y rey de España y Francia, y los demas potentados, y principes christianos." The same list also appears on plates 3, 4, 5, and 6, but with the addition of the words: "y de la Señoria de Venecia." Plate 5 is signed and dated 1587, as is plate 7, which appears to be the date by which the majority of the prints had been completed.

The plates were engraved by Pieter Perret (see Chapter 9). Evidently Perret had begun work on the project already in 1583 as plates 9 and 10, and the elevation of the tabernacle in plate 11, are signed by him with the date 1583. However, a contract between Herrera and Perret was not signed until the following year, on 21 October 1584.[38]

---

[35] The document granting Herrera the papal *privilegio* is recorded in ASVat, SB, 59, fol. 409r.–411r. (a copy of the *Motu proprio* is on fol. 410r.). The *Sumario* was published with the title: "SVMARIO/Y/BREVE DECLA-/racio delos diseños y estam-/pas dela Fabrica de san Lo-/rencio el Real del Es-/curial . . . CON PRIVI-LEGIO./EN MADRID/Por la viuda de Alonso Gomez/Impressor del Rey nuestro se-/ñor, ano de 1589." An example is in the BA, Vatican, Barberini N. VI. 190.

[36] The text of the Spanish *privilegio* is given in Luis Cervera Vera, *Las Estampes Y El Sumario de El Escorial por Juan de Herrera*, vol. 1 (Madrid, 1954), 35, and n. 12.

[37] A list of all the privileges granted is given on fol. 32v. of the *Sumario*: "El dicho Iua[n] d[e] Herrera tiene priuilegios del Rey don Philippe nuestro señor, para que en todos sus Rey nos y señorios, ninguna persona pueda estampar, ni hazer estampar, ne ve[n]der los dichos diseños, sino el, o quien su poder tuuiere, Y lo mesmo tiene del summo Pontefice, Y del Emperadori: Y Rey de Francia: y señoria de Venecia."

[38] Noted in Cervera Vera, 39–41; and in John Bury, "Philip II and the Escorial," *Print Quarterly* 8 (1991): 78.

Michelangelo's Architectural Projects

In 1564, an anonymous print of the *Elevation of the South Apse of St. Peter's* after Michelangelo's design was published in Rome with a papal *privilegio* by the book publisher Vincenzo Luchini (Fig. 33).[39] It has been suggested that the print is most likely that referred to by Michelangelo's assistant, Tiberio Calcagni, in a letter dated September 1564.[40] The print most likely reproduces the design of the already completed portions of the south apse and shows in all likelihood Michelangelo's original design for the attic, with arched window openings, as completed in 1558. After Michelangelo's death, on 18 February 1564, his successor, Pirro Ligorio, who served as chief architect of St. Peter's from 1564 to 1566, introduced in the attic of the north apse a different design with rectangular apertures, as is seen today.

A few years later, in 1567, another book publisher, Bartolomeo Faletti, printed with a papal *privilegio* Stefano Dupérac's four engravings of Michelangelo's architecture on the Campidoglio—*Campidoglio*, *Porticus et Palatii Capitolini*, and *Areae Capitolinae*—and at the Vatican— *Areae et Palatii Pontificii Vaticani*.[41] All four were republished in 1568. Other prints published with a *privilegio* by Faletti in 1560 and 1561 are noted in Chapter 7.

---

[39] The print is listed in Huelsen, "Das Speculum Romanae Magnificentiae," 161, no. 96. It is inscribed: "FORMA PARTIS TEMPLI DIVI PETRI IN VATICANO MICHAEL ANGELVS BONAROTVS INVENTOR," with the words: "ROMAE VINCENTIVS LVCHINVS EXCV[debat] in the lower left, and CVM PRIVILEGIO MDLXIIII" in the lower right. Millon and Smyth, "Pirro Ligorio, Michelangelo, and St. Peter's," 232 and notes 13, 110, 112, have noted that Luchini apparently also intended to publish another print showing the interior of the apse. It may be noted that Luchini also published maps, but none with a *privilegio*. In 1558, he published three maps, of *Greece*, *Sicily*, and *Lombardy*, each inscribed: *Romae Vincentij Luchini aereis formis ad Peregrinum 1558*. In 1564, he published a map of the *Marches of Ancona*.

[40] The suggestion was first put forward by John Coolidge, "Vignola and the Little Domes of St. Peter's," *Marsyas* 2 (1942): 98–99, note 54. The letter is reproduced in Frey, *Der Literarische Nachlass Giorgio Vasaris*, 2: 211–214.

[41] The prints are listed Huelsen, "Das Speculum Romanae Magnificentiae," 161, nos. 91 and 92; and 168, nos. 151–152; McGinniss, nos. 200, 202, 203. See also Hermann Egger, "Die Darstellung einer päpstlichen Segensspendung aus dem Verlag Bartolomeo Faleti (1567)," *Maso Finiguerra* 1 (1936): 62. The words *cum privilegio* appear on each. It would appear to have been issued only for these architectural and topographical prints. It does not appear, for example on a portrait, *Pope Pius V Flanked by Saints Peter and Paul*, engraved by Mario Cartari and published by Faletti that same year ("Romae M. D. LXVII. ex Typis Bart. Phaletij") (Bartsch, 15: 293, no. 21).

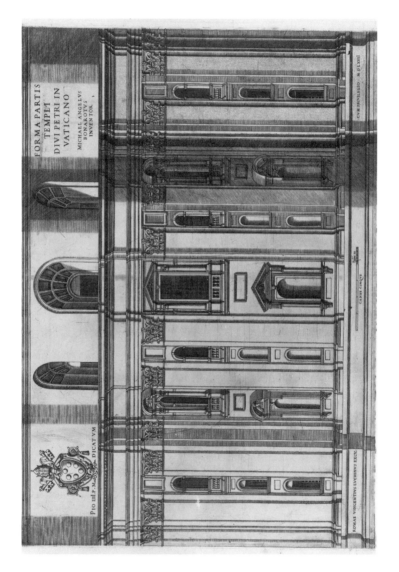

Fig. 33. Anonymous, *Elevation of the South Apse of St. Peter's* (after Michelangelo), 1564. Engraving. Photo: Avery Architectural and Fine Arts Library, Columbia University in the City of New York.

The Santa Casa di Loreto

Beginning in 1567, a series of prints of the Santa Casa di Loreto, engraved by Giovanni Battista de' Cavalieri and printed by Perino Zecchini Guarlotti, were published with a *privilegio*. Although no record of the document granting the *privilegio* has come to light in the archives, a contract drawn up on 13 March 1567 between Cavalieri and Guarlotti describes the terms of the project.[42] In the contract, Guarlotti decribes himself as a printer at S. Maria de Loreto ("stampatore in Beata Maria de Laureto"). The contractual arrangement was for a period of four years during which time Cavalieri was obliged to engrave seven prints, which are described as the four façades, the Madonna inside the chapel, and other "subjects and inventions" that Guarlotti found for Cavalieri. The contract specifies that Cavalieri should consign the completed plates to Guarlotti, who would see to their sale in Loreto and elsewhere, while reserving for Cavalieri the "piazza in Rome" (the phrase would appear to grant Cavalieri the right to sell the prints in Rome). The contract continues by specifying that the prints will be sold for "scudi 3 il centinaio" from which would be deducted the cost of paper and printing at seven *giuli*. Each year, Cavalieri and Guarlotti were obliged to render account of the sale of the prints. After four years, at the conclusion of the partnership, the plates would remain in the hands of Guarlotti, who would continue to give to Cavalieri half of the earnings of subsequent printings while leaving him free to sell or engrave other prints provided that he does not do so in Loreto. The cost of the engraving and printing was to be divided equally between Cavalieri and Guarlotti. The contract makes it clear that Guarlotti initiated and directed the project and retained possession of the 'original plates', and therefore was most likely the holder of the copyright.

The project might possibly have stemmed from a print by Cavalieri, dedicated to Cardinal Giulio Feltre della Rovere of Urbino (and Archbishop of Ravenna), showing a plan of the church at Loreto with the location of the "Sacra domus." According to an inscription in the lower right, the print was protected under a three-year *privilegio*

---

[42] The contract is reproduced in Gian Ludovico Masetti Zannini, *Stampatori e librai a Roma nella seconda metà del Cinquecento: documenti inediti* (Rome, 1980), 208–209, and 231–333, doc. 9.

apparently granted Cavalieri in March 1567, the same month in which the contract was drawn up with Guarlotti: "Joannes Baptista de Cauallerijs industria æneis tijpis representata/Cum Apostolico ad triennium priuilegio Anno .D. 1567. Mense Mart." Guarlotti's name does not appear on the print. It might be suggested, therefore, that it was this print which gave Guarlotti the idea for the project, and he then immediately entered into the contractual arrangement with Cavalieri as described above.

In accordance with the contract, four of the prints show each of the four exterior walls of the Santa Casa.[43] The print of the western end wall ("ad occidentem"), dated 1567, is inscribed in the lower right with the words "Io: Baptistae de Cavallerijs diligentia æneis tabulis excussus ROMÆ/Cum Apostolico priuilegio, Perinus de guarlotis excudebat anno .D. 1567," while the eastern end wall ("ad orientem") is inscribed in the lower left "Opus Johannis Baptistae de Cauallerijs Cum priuilegio/Perinus de guarlotis excudebat Anno .D. 1567." The lateral wall "ad merideum," dated 1567, is inscribed "Opus Johannis Baptistae de Cauallerijs Cum priuilegio/Perinus de guarlotis excudebat Anno .D. 1567." The other lateral wall "ad aquilonem," dated 1568, is inscribed "Ioa baptista de Cavalleris incidebat Cum priuilego/Perinus de guarlotis excudebat Anno .D. 1568" (Fig. 34).

A print of the *Madonna di Loreto*, dated 1569, would appear to be that described in the contract and was part of the same series.[44] The project may have capitalised on the special interest shown by Pope Pius V, who issued the *privilegio*, in the sanctuary of Loreto and to which he contributed bronze doors for each of the four entrances in the marble casing of the Holy House.[45]

---

[43] All four prints are in the BM, London, c. 56, inv. nos. 1872–5–11–791, 792, 793, and 794.

[44] An example of the print in the Uffizi, Florence, is illustrated in Evelina Borea, "Stampa figurativa e pubblico dalle origini all'affermazione nel Cinquecento," in *Storia dell'arte italiana*, part 1, vol. 2 (Turin, 1979), fig. 271.

[45] Pius V's interest in the Santa Casa is noted by Pastor, 17: 124. Evelina Borea, "Stampe da Modelli Fiorentini nel Cinquecento," 245, no. 599, notes however that at the time Cavalieri produced the engravings the bronze reliefs for the doors of the Santa Casa had not yet been executed.

Fig. 34. Giovanni Battista de' Cavalieri, *Lateral Wall ("ad aquilonem")*, *Santa Casa at Loreto*. 1568. Engraving. Photo: © Copyright The British Museum, London.

Nicolaus van Aelst and Sixtus V's Architectural Projects

Nicolaus van Aelst was born in Brussels in 1526. By 1550 he was living in Rome, where he died on 19 July 1613.[46] Van Aelst made his living as a print dealer and publisher. His address appears on numerous prints, most of them issued in a second or later state.[47] A number of the plates Van Aelst printed had previously been owned by Antonio Salamanca (died 1562). It seems likely that he may have acquired these from Salamanca's heir Francesco Salamanca, who died in 1585.[48] Other plates had been previously owned and published by Tommaso Barlacchi, Antonio Lafrery, Claudio Duchetti, and Pietro Facchetti, or Van Aelst had copies made of them. The earliest Van Aelst address appears on a print is 1582. In 1587, Van Aelst published a book of twelve engraved plates entitled *Alfabeti e saggi di scrittura in diverse lingue*.[49]

On 13 December 1588, a fifteen-year papal *privilegio* was granted to Van Aelst for several prints all having to do with the various architectural projects undertaken in Rome during the reign of Sixtus V.[50] The first two items listed in the *privilegio* are the Column of Marcus Aurelius (*Columna Antonina*) and the Column of Trajan (*Columna Traiana*), each shown with the statue placed on its summit by Sixtus V—St. Paul on the column of Marcus Aurelius, and St. Peter on the column of Trajan. Each print shows the column centrally placed with lines of Latin verse in the upper part either side of the statue. The arms

---

[46] The dates of van Aelst's birth and his move to Rome are given in Alfred Von Wurzbach, *Niederländisches Künstler-Lexikon* (Vienna and Leipzig, 1910), 1: 4. The date of his death is derived from an entry in the Liber mortuorum, Parocchiae SS. Mariae et Gregorii in Vallicella, fol. 122: "Die 19 julii 1613. Manifius Nicolaus Vanhelst flander qui primo exercito vacabat mercature venditionis figuram que e suis regionibus tranferri hic Rome curabat ultimo loco habitans in parrocchia S. Blasii de Fossa in aedibus S. Mariae de Anima . . . sepultus in sepulcro comuni." The document is transcribed in Bertolotti, *Artisti belgi ed olandesi a Roma* (Florence, 1880), 227.

[47] Heinecken, *Dictionnaire des artistes*, 1: 46–47, has catalogued several prints as engraved by Van Aelst, but this is a misinterpretation of his name as printer or publisher.

[48] Francesco Salamanca's death, on 18 September 1585, is recorded in AVR, S. Lorenzo in Damaso, Liber Matrim. et Defunt., 43, fol. 139v.: "settembre 1585. 18. Mr. Franco: Salama[n]ca." Other plates acquired by Van Aelst had once been owned by the mysterious Antonio D. Salamanca, who may have been a brother or a nephew of Francesco.

[49] The book is listed in Ascarelli, *Le cinquecentine romane*, 293.

[50] The *privilegio* is recorded in ASVat, SB, 138, fol. 337r.–v.

of Sixtus V are shown below on the left. Among the inscriptions on the lower right can be read the words "Nicolaus van Aelst Bruxellensis/formis aeneis incis dicavit/Anno M. D. LXXXVIIII." Below the base of the column is inscribed "Motu proprio Sixti · V · Pont · Max · per · an · XV· Superioru · permissu." On the base of each can also be seen the monogram of the engraver Ambrogio Brambilla.[51]

The *privilegio* document then lists three obelisks: that by S. Giovanni in Laterano, that by the Basilica of S. Maria Maggiore, and that by S. Maria del Popolo.[52] There then follows the *Acqua Felice* near S. Maria degli Angeli, the *Seven Churches of Rome*, and the *façade of the Gesù*.[53] The print of the *Façade of the Gesù*, titled PARS EXTERIOR TEMPLI SOCIETATIS IESV, carries a dedication by Van Aelst to

---

[51] An example of the *Column of Marcus Aurelius* is in the Farnesina, Rome, 44H30, inv. no. 70350. A later state has the address of Giovanni Giacomo de Rossi, with Brambilla's monogram, the *privilegio*, and Van Aelst's address erased (Farnesina, 44H30, inv. no. 70349). An example of the *Column of Trajan* is also in Farnesina, 44H30, inv. no. 70347. A later state has the address of Giovanni Giacomo de Rossi, with the *privilegio* and Van Aelst's address erased (Farnesina, 44H30, inv. no. 70346)

[52] The obelisk at S. Giovanni in Laterano is inscribed above in the upper frame on the left "SIXTVS.V.PONT.MAX .CRVCI .INVIC ./TISSIMAE .AD BASILIC. S.IO.IN.LATERANO" with, below Sixtus's name, "Nicolaus van Aelst Belga for. aeneis/incis. dicavit. Anno M. D. LXXXVIIII." In the lower left corner, Domenico Fontana is given credit for moving and erecting the obelisk. In the lower right corner is the notice of copyright, and Brambilla's name as engraver: "Ambr.s Bramb. fecit." An example of the print is in the Farnesina, Rome, 34H5, inv. no. 30325. A later state in which the plate has been heavily reworked, with many small additions and erasures, carries the address of Giovanni Giacomo de Rossi, with the *privilegio* and van Aelst's address erased (Farnesina, 34H5, inv. no. 30324). An example of the obelisk at S. Maria Maggiore is in the Farnesina, 44H30, inv. no. 70356. A later state, again with many extensive changes to the plate, including a new façade given to S. Maria Maggiore, has the address of Giovanni Giacomo de Rossi, with the *privilegio* and Van Aelst's address erased (Farnesina, 44H30, inv. no. 70355). An example of the obelisk at S. Maria del Popolo is in the Farnesina, 44H30, inv. no. 70358. A later state has the address of Giovanni Giacomo de Rossi, with the *privilegio* and Van Aelst's address erased (Farnesina, 44H30, inv. no. 70357).

[53] I have been unable to trace the print of the *Acqua Felice* near S. Maria degli Angeli. The *Seven Churches of Rome*, according to Huelsen, *Piante icnografiche e prospettiche di Roma*, 10, n. 1 (b), is a reprint of the 1575 engraving issued by Antonio Lafrery. However, this would not be Van Aelst's plate but the print issued in 1590 by Giacomo Gherardi. Gherardi was the heir of Claudio Duchetti, who was in turn the heir of Antonio Lafrery. The print, which updates Lafrery's 1575 *Le Sette Chiese di Roma* to include most of Sixtus V's recent accomplishments, including obelisks in place at S. Giovanni in Laterano, S. Maria del Popolo, S. Pietro, and S. Maria Maggiore, the completed dome of St. Peter's, the Scala Santa, Lateran Palace, etc., is inscribed: "Iacobi Gherardi heredis Claudij Ducheti Formis/Romæ 1590." The print is discussed by Fischer, 12–15.

Ranucio Farnese dated 1 January 1589 ("Al Ser.mo Sig.re Ranuccio Farneso Principe di Parma et Piacenza... In Roma a di p.o di Gennaro 1589"). The *Motu proprio* appears at the right, with the monogram of Brambilla below (Fig. 35).[54] Although the articulation of both stories of the façade is almost identical to the design ultimately employed by Giacomo della Porta a dozen years earlier in the completed façade, the proportions of the upper storey are not those of the completed structure but of the design seen in Vignola's 1568 medal. There is no obvious explanation for this. The last item on the list is an unidentified print referred to as "Iconas Principium apostolorum de Vrbe."

Five of the prints, and perhaps all of them, were engraved by Ambrogio Brambilla from Milan, whose presence in Rome is first recorded in November 1577.[55] On 12 April 1579, he was proposed for membership in the Virtuosi al Pantheon.[56] It was noted in Chapter 7 that Brambilla had produced several prints for Claudio Duchetti, the earliest of which are dated 1579. He subsequently produced numerous other prints for Duchetti including those of topical subject matter, numerous maps, engravings of antiquities, modern architecture and sculpture, plus a book of portraits of emperors (1582), and a book of portraits of popes (1585). The majority of Brambilla's prints published by Duchetti (many of these prints, it should be noted, were copies of other engravings issued earlier mainly by Antonio Lafrery and Antonio Salamanca) are dated to the years 1581–1582. Although Brambilla returned to Duchetti for the publication of the book of portraits of popes in 1585, after 1582 the address of other printers is found on Brambilla's prints. In 1583, for example, his engraving of the *Baths of Agrippa* was printed by Paolo Graziani and Pietro de Nobili.[57] In 1584 he engraved for Nobili the

---

[54] An example of the print is in the Farnesina, Rome, 34H5, inv. no. 30330. It may be noted that Van Aelst also published a print showing the catafalque for the obsequies of Cardinal Alessandro Farnese in the Gesù on 28 March 1589.

[55] The name "ambroxo milanesi" appears in a document in ASR, Archivio de Tribunale del Governatore di Roma, vol. 255, Costituti dal 26 Ottobre 1577 al 18 Gennaro 1578, D. Ascanius Caracciolus pro Charitale Notus, fol. 28r.

[56] The record is given in Orbaan, "Virtuosi al Pantheon," 28. Brambilla was officially accepted as member the following 14 June.

[57] The *Baths of Agrippa* is listed in Huelsen, "Das Speculum Romanae Magnificentiae," 164, no. 116. It may be noted that the following year, on 6 November 1584, "Ambrogio Brambilla pittore milanese" is named as present in an inventory drawn up on that date for Pietro de Nobili of prints to be sent to Pietro Springher. See Bertolotti, *Giunte agli artisti belgi ed olandesi in Roma* (Rome, 1885), 91.

Fig. 35. Ambrogio Brambilla, *Façade of the Gesù*. 1589. Engraving.
Photo: Avery Architectural and Fine Arts Library, Columbia University in
the City of New York.

frontispiece to the *Vita et miracula santi Francesci de Paula*.[58] After Duchetti's death, on 5 December 1585, Brambilla occasionally worked for his heirs, engraving, for example, a map of *Pozzuoli* in 1586.[59] He also worked for other printers. In 1585 he engraved a map of *Parma* that was printed by Marcello Clodio, and in 1587 he produced a "new" map of Rome, *Nova Urbis Romae Descriptio*, for the publisher Girolamo Francini.[60] Brambilla's first work for Van Aelst would appear to be the prints listed in the 1588 *privilegio*. In 1589, the same year Van Aelst published the prints, Brambilla independently produced a print of Michelangelo's *Last Judgement*.[61]

It may be noted that a ten-year *privilegio* granted by Sixtus V appears on a political print by Philippe Thomassin that also carries a dedicatory inscription by Van Aelst dated 1 January 1588. The print shows Sixtus V before a crucifix with King Henry III of France, the French cardinal François de Joyeuse, and the Duc de Guise.[62]

The Moving of the Vatican Obelisk

Van Aelst's *privilegio* had been secured at a time when the activities of Sixtus V were generating much interest and excitement in Rome. In 1587, Girolamo Francini, who in that same year had published Brambilla's updated map of Rome, noted above, had also been granted a *privilegio* for the extremely popular guidebook to Sistine Rome by Muzio Pansa, *Le cose maravigliose dell'alma città di Roma*, which he published in 1588.[63] On the frontispiece particular reference is

---

[58] A copy of the frontispiece to the *Vita et miracula santi Francesci de Paula* is in the BN, Paris, Rd. 84. 4o.

[59] The map of *Pozzuoli* is listed in Tooley, 40. The print is inscribed "apud haeredes Claudij Ducheti." An example is in the BN, Paris, Ed. 105. fol.

[60] The map of *Parma* is listed in Tooley, 39, no. 444. The "new" map of Rome is listed in Huelsen, *Piante Icnografiche e Prospettiche di Roma*, 71, no. 80. The map is inscribed "NOVA VRBIS ROMAE/descriptio anni 1587 Per Ambrosium Brambillam/pictorem delineatum et incisum." Francini's address is given as at the "sign of the fountain" ("Rome apud Hieronimum Francinum ad signum fontis").

[61] The print of the *Last Judgement* carries the inscription: "Ambrosius Brambilla in aere incid./AN. D. 1589." Examples are in the Casanatense, Rome, 20.B.I.74/28; the Marucelliana, Florence, Vol. XXXI, no. 1; and the MM, New York, inv. no. 17.50.19–150.

[62] The print is listed in Edmond Bruwaert, *Recherches sur la vie et l'oeuvre du graveur troyen Philippe Thomassin* (Troyes, 1876), 83, no. 60.

[63] The *privilegio* is indexed in ASVat, Index 756, fol. 130v. Pansa's book is listed in Ascarelli, *Le Cinquecentine Romane*, 189.

made to the moving of the obelisks and to the building of the aqueducts to convey water to the Acqua Felice. Sixtus's architectural projects are also the focus of Giovanni (Joannes) Pinadello's *Dom Invicti quinarii numeri series quae summatima superioribus pontificibus et maxime a Sixto Quinto res praeclare quadriennio gestas adnumerat ad eundem Sixtum Quintum, Pont. Opt. Max.*, published in Rome by Francesco Zannetti in 1589. The frontispiece, engraved by Giovanni Battista de' Cavalieri, shows, arranged around a portrait of Sixtus V, the pope's various *imprese* together with depictions of his accomplishments, including the obelisks of S. Giovanni in Laterano, S. Maria Maggiore, S. Maria del Popolo, and St. Peter's, the columns of Trajan and Antoninus (i.e. Marcus Aurelius), the Acqua Felice, and the façade of the Gesù.[64] In this same context, but somewhat more specialized, is a study by Giuseppe Castiglione (Iosephi Castalionis) of the inscriptions on the base of the obelisk at S. Maria del Popolo entitled *Iurisconsulti Explicatio ad Inscriptionem Augusti, quae in Basi est Obelisci statuti per S.D.N. Sixtum V Pont. Opt. Max. ante Portam Flaminiam, alias Populi*, printed in Rome by the heirs of Giovanni Gigliotti in 1589. The following year, 1590, Gigliotti's heirs also printed a commentary by Castiglione on the column of Marcus Aurelius: *De Columnia triumphali imp. Antonini Commentarius.*[65]

The event which stimulated the most interest in Rome, however, was the moving of the Vatican obelisk. The task had been given to the architect Domenico Fontana who began work on the project on Wednesday, 25 September 1585.[66] The erection of the framed timber tower and all preparations for the lowering of the obelisk were completed on 28 April 1586. The following day, 29 April, all the workmen involved were given confession and received Holy Communion and on 30 April the operation was begun. On the first day the

---

[64] The book is listed in Ascarelli, *Le Cinquecentine Romane*, 204, and in *Mostra del libro illustrato romano del cinquecento* (Rome, 1950), 33, no. 97. The frontispiece is illustrated in Franco Borsi, *Roma di Sisto V: la pianta di Antonio Tempesta, 1593* (Rome, 1986).

[65] Copies of both books are in the Biblioteca Hertziana, Rome, Raro Dy 180–1863.

[66] Domenico Fontana's first major commissions in Rome had come from Cardinal Felice Peretti (elected Pope Sixtus V in 1585) for the mausoleum of Pope Nicholas IV in 1574, and the Cappella del Presepio in S. Maria Maggiore. Fontana's presence in Rome in 1581 is recorded in a notary document, dated 22 March of that year, which identifies him as "Dominicus Fontanus de mili como dioc. in urbe Murator et Architetor" and as living in Regione Campitelli (ASR, CNC, no. 1770, fol. 547r.).

obelisk was successfully raised up approximately two feet. On 7 May, after eight days of preparation (and following another Mass), the obelisk was lowered onto a long, low wooden carriage. The carriage was then drawn forward on rollers along a specially constructed cause-way to the site where the obelisk was to be re-erected. All prepa-rations for the re-erection were completed by 10 September 1586, when a service was held, and on 11 September the obelisk was suc-cessfully raised on its new base. Another service was held on 17 September, and on 5 October a ceremony was performed to bless the cross that had been placed on top of the obelisk and "to exor-cise and consecrate the Obelisk."

The various stages of the project—the lowering, moving, raising, and blessing of the obelisk—were recorded in a series of at least four prints, all issued with a *privilegio*, made by Natale Bonifacio after designs by Giovanni Guerra. The first of the prints shows the prepa-rations being made for the lowering of the obelisk on the south side of St. Peter's. An inscription in an elaborate frame in the lower left is followed by an explanatory key to lettered portions of the print.[67] In the centre of the frame appears a portrait of Domenico Fontana, at age forty-three, with, in an oval cartouche above, the words: "DOMENICO FO[N]TANA DA MILI/DIOCESI DI COMO ARCHIT./E CONDVTTORE." Also in the frame appears Bonifacio's name and the date, August 1586. In the lower right of the frame are inscribed the words "Cum privilegio." To the right, just above the lower margin of the print, an inscription identifies Guerra not only as the designer but also as responsible for having the plates printed and published: "IO. GVERRA MVT. LINEAVIT/ET IMPRIMI. CVRAVIT." In August 1586, presumably when Bonifacio completed the etching, the obelisk had not yet been re-erected in Piazza di San Pietro.

The second print in the set, which arguably dates to after 11 Sep-tember 1586, shows the entire operation with, from left to right, the obelisk standing in its original location, the lowering and transportation,

---

[67] An example is in the MM, New York, inv. no. 59.508.102. The design was re-engraved by Bonifacio in a different form and without many of the details and inscriptions and printed as illustration no. 22 in Domenico Fontana's *Della Trasportatione dell'obelisco vaticano* in 1590 (see below). Virtually the same scene was also repro-duced in a fresco over the door of a room in the Sistine Library in the Vatican in 1588.

and the obelisk standing in Piazza S. Pietro (Fig. 36).[68] The date, 1586, appears above in a *cartiglio* in the upper right, and Bonifacio's name as engraver ("NATALIS BONIFATIVS SEBENICENSIS IN ÆRE INCIDEBAT") below in the frame of the central *cartiglio*. In the lower left corner appears Guerra's name as designer ("IO. GVERRA M. LIN") and Bonifacio's initials ("N.B. F."). A small *cartiglio* towards the lower right is inscribed "DOMENICO FONTANA DA/MILI DIOCESI DI COMO/INVENTORE ET CONDVT-TORE." To the lower left of centre appears the words "CVM PRI-VILEGIO." The plate was evidently later acquired by the publisher Bartolomeo Grassi who added his address in the lower left.[69]

The third print shows a view of the Piazza di S. Pietro on the day of the erection of the obelisk. To the left appears Guerra's name as the designer, printer, publisher, and Bonifacio's name as the engraver. The print carries the notice of *privilegio* and the address of Bartolomeo Grassi.[70]

The fourth print, dated 1587, depicts the ceremony of the consecration of the cross on the newly-erected obelisk in Piazza di S. Pietro, an event that took place, as noted above, on 5 October. In an oval cartouche at the bottom of the rectangular framed inscription on the left appears Guerra's name as designer, printer, and publisher. Bonifacio's name as engraver appears in the lower centre, plus the date, 1587. Just to the right of centre above the lower margin has been added Bartolomeo Grassi's address with below the words "Cum Privilegio."[71] The print also carries, among the numerous word-filled cartouches, ten lines of verse addressed "AD SIXTVM.V PONT MAX DE OBELISCO VATICANO" composed by Giulio Roscio Ortini.

---

[68] An example is in the MM, New York, inv. no. 41.72 (3.47). A drawing by Guerra for this print in the Bibliothéque de l'École des Beaux Arts in Paris (inv. no. 2556) is discussed by Catherine Monbeig Goguel, "Giovanni Guerra da Modena, disegnatore e illustratore della fine del Rinascimento," *Arte Illustrata* 7 (1974): 166.

[69] Bern Dibner, *Moving the Obelisks* (New York, 1952), Plate 1, shows the state before Grassi's address was added.

[70] See Elena Parma Armani, et al., *Libri di immagini, disegni e incisioni di Giovanni Guerra (Modena 1544–Roma 1618)* (Modena, 1978), 87, no. 79.

[71] Both this print and the first one described were inserted into some copies of a book by Cosimo Gaci in which the author, in the form of a dialogue with Monsignor Giovanangelo Papio, defends and praises Sixtus V's various enterprises, including the moving of the obelisk. The book, entitled *Dialogo di Cosimo Gaci. Nel quale passati in prima [. . .] Si parla poi delle valorose operationi di Sisto V. P.O.M. & in particolare del trasportame[n]to dell'Obelisco del Vaticano* was printed "In Rome. Appresso Francesco Zannetti. 1586."

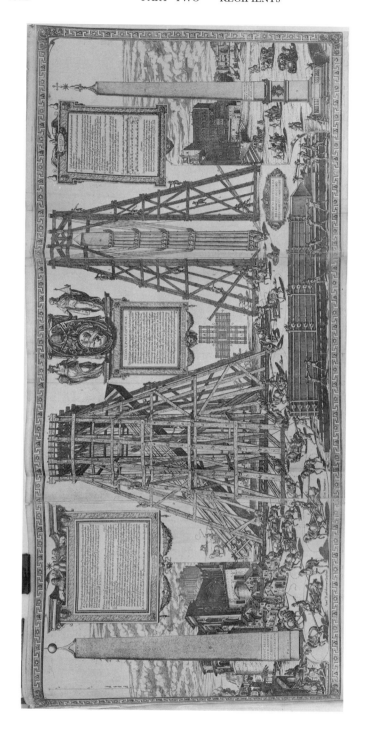

Fig. 36. Natale Bonifacio, *The Moving of the Vatican Obelisk* (after Giovanni Guerra), 1586. Engraving. Photo: The Metropolitan Museum of Art, Harris Brisbane Dick Fund, 1941 ([41.72 (3.47)]).

The moving of the obelisk stimulated numerous other publications, including several more books printed by Bartolomeo Grassi.[72] In 1586, for Giacomo Ruffinelli, Grassi printed a volume of prose and verse, *ORDO/DEDICATIONIS/OBELISCI*, by the Apostolic protonotary Pietro Gallesino. Following a brief history of the project, Gallesino reproduces the text of the rituals of exorcism, dedication, and benediction of the cross undertaken by Sixtus V on 5 October 1586. The book contains a small engraving by Bonifacio of the obelisk standing alone already in its destined location surrounded by a marble balustrade.[73] The same print also appears in Guglielmo Bianchi's *Epigrammata Gulielmi Blanci Albiensis Iurisconsulti in obeliscum* published by Grassi the same year.[74] In 1586 Grassi also published a variant of this same print, with clouds in the sky, human figures, and other details added, in *Commentarius de Obelisco* by Pietro Angelio da Barga.[75] Also at this time, although without any engraved illustrations, Grassi published Filippo Pigafetta's *DISCORSO . . . D'IN-*

---

[72] It may be noted that the idea of moving the obelisk to the front of St. Peter's was by no means new and can be traced back to Nicholas V in the fifteenth century. The idea had been revived by Paul II, Paul III, and Gregory XIII. During the reign of Gregory XIII, Camillo Agrippa had written a treatise on the subject: *Trattato di Camillo Agrippa Milanese di trasportar la guglia in su la piazza di San Pietro*, printed in Rome by Francesco Zanetti in 1583.

[73] Below in the print are six lines of Latin verse. In the bottom left corner is Bonifacio's monogram "N.B." and in the bottom right corner the monogram "S.F." Also inscribed to either side of the lower part of the obelisk is: "Gulielmi Blanci Iun. Albiensis. I. C. ~ Hexastium in Obeliscum." On the title-page is inscribed "ROMÆ, Ex Typographia Bartholomaei Grassij. 1586," while the colophon reads: "ROMAE Apud Iacobum Ruffinelum 1586." It may be noted that the same print also appears added to the second edition, published in 1640 by Giovanni Battista de Rossi with the title *Varie Antichità di Roma Racolte* [sic], of Giovanni Antonio Dosio's album *Urbis Romae aedificiorum illustrium*, containing fifty views of Rome engraved by Giovanni Battista de' Cavalieri, that had first been published in 1569. In the upper part of the print, either side of the summit of the obelisk, is now inscribed "VARIE ANTICHITA ~DI ROMA RACOLTE [sic]/Da Giovanbatista de Rossi ~ in Piazza Navona. 1640."

[74] The full title is *Epigrammata Gulielmi Blanci Albiensis Iurisconsulti in obeliscum mirae magnitudinis ex Aegypto quondam a Caio Caligula Romam advectum et deinde in Circo Vaticano erectum*. The book was printed by Paolo and Tito Diani.

[75] The book was published "CVM PRIVILEGIO ET AVCTORITATE SVPERIORVM" in Rome "Ex Officina Bartholomæi Grassi. 1586" (the colophon reads: "Ex Typographia Bartholomæi Bonfadini. 1587"). In the sky to either side of the cross at the top of the obelisk is written: "SANCTIS ~ SIMÆ CRVCI/SAC ~ RAVIT/XYSTVS. V. ~ PONT. MAX./E' PRIORE SE ~ DE AVVLSVM/ET CÆSARIB ~ AVGVSTO ET TIB/I. L. AB ~ LATVM." The print is signed "NB" in the bottom left and "S.F." in the bottom right.

TORNO ALL'HISTORIA/DELLA AGVGLIA, a two-volume anthology of verse composed on the subject of the obelisk entitled "SEQVVN-TVR CARMINA/A VARIS AVCTORIBVS/IN OBELISCVM CONSCRIPTA/ET IN DVOS LIBROS DISTRIBVTA," and a booklet in which Gonsalvo Ponce de Leon briefly describes each of the four religious services held over the course of moving the obelisk on 29 April, 7 May, 10 September, and 17 September (see above).[76]

In 1589 Bonifacio was also completing the plates for Domenico Basa's edition, printed with a *privilegio*, of Domenico Fontana's *Della trasportatione dell'obelisco Vaticano*, published in 1590.[77] Bonifacio produced the frontispiece and numerous other etching-engravings of which the first twelve illustrate the moving of the obelisk. The book also contains (at "page" 75) in reduced form and less detail Bonifacio's large print produced the previous year, 1589, for Fontana showing each of the four sides of the obelisk at San Giovanni in Laterano.[78]

---

[76] Pigafetta's book, printed "IN ROMA,/Appresso Bartolomeo Grassi," is dedicated by Grassi to Alessandro Peretti, Cardinal Montalto (dated 25 March 1586). In the two-volume anthology, "Sequuntur Carmina," Grassi's name appears on the title-page of the "LIBER PRIMO": "Ex officina Bartholomæi Grassij. 1586." The colophon reads: "ROMAE/Ex Typographia Bartholomæi Bonfadini/M.D. LXXXVII." The "LIBER PRIMO" contains forty-four authors, including Julius Roscius Hortini, Pietro Angelio da Barga, and Castor Durante. It would appear that a second edition was published by Grassi the following year, 1587. The book, titled "Obeliscus Vaticanus Sixti V . . . praeclaris eruditorum virorum litteris laudatus egregie," has on page 5 a list of the contributing authors: "Obelisci Vaticani Scriptores quorum commentarii vel espistolae, vel carmina, de eo impressa ho volumine continentur. Galesini, Ponce de Leon, Angeli P., Aguilar Juan de Leblanc, Pigafetta, Gaci, Guerra, Durante." Ponce de Leon's booklet is titled "FAMILIARIS/QVAEDAM EPIS-TOLA/E ROMA IN HISPANIARVM/MISSA,/In qua quid actum sit die xxix. Aprilis,/vij. Maij, x. & xvij. Septembris in translatione Obelisci brevi-/ter explicatur." The booklet was published in Rome, "Apud Alexandrum Gardanum, & Franciscum/Coattinum Socios. Impressis Bartholomæi Grassi Bibliopolæ Romani. 1586."

[77] Only the first section of Fontana's book is devoted to the moving of the Vatican obelisk (though it also contains most of the text in the book). Other sections deal with other projects undertaken by Fontana for Sixtus V: the Villa Montalto, the Cappella del Presepio in S. Maria Maggiore, the Acqua Felice, the Loggia della Benedittioni at S. Giovanni in Laterano, the Palazzo del Laterano, the Scala Santa, the obelisks at S. Giovanni in Laterano, S. Maria del Popolo, and S. Maria Maggiore, the "Portone della Vigna" (at the Villa Montalto), the Vatican Library, the Cancelleria, and Tabernacle. With the exception of the Scala Santa (in this edition), each project is illustrated (with an accompanying lettered key) with one or more etchings by Bonifacio.

[78] Fontana had undertaken the moving and erection of the Lateran obelisk in 1588. The print, dedicated by Fontana to Sixtus V, is inscribed towards the lower right "Impress./Romae/Anno/MDLXXXIX/Natalis Boni=/fatius Dal=/matinus/incidit." In Fontana's *Della trasportatione dell'obelisco vaticano* the print is inscribed

Tiberio Alfarani and a plan of St. Peter's

In 1590, Natale Bonifacio also engraved a large plan of the basilica of St. Peter's for Tiberio Alfarani's planned book, *De Basilicae Vaticanae Antiquissima et Nova Structura*. Alfarani had been granted a papal *privilegio* for his book on 13 September 1589.[79] The granting document describes the general contents of the book ("antique noveque basilice huiusmodi ac sacellorum Altarium sepulchrorum necnon illi adiacentium ecclesiarum descriptionem in scriptis seu libri aut volumine") and also draws attention to a large plan of the basilica engraved and printed at Alfarani's expense (". . . et etiam ut dici solet in planta magno labore summaque industria composuerit et illam propria impensa tipis excudi et imprimi facere desiderot vereaturque ne si opus ipsum per alios absque eius licentia in lucem edatu[r]. impense et laborum suorum iacturam ineurrat"). The engraving shows a plan of Old St. Peter's faintly overlaid with a plan of New St. Peter's with each part numbered and a key to the numbering shown to the sides and below (Fig. 37).[80] On a banderole at the top is written "ALMAE VRBIS DIVI PETRIS VETERIS NOVIQVE TEMPLI DESCRIPTIO." To the left are the arms of Sixtus V and Cardinal Pallotto. A long dedication to Pallotto is dated 10 December 1589.[81] The book was not published, however, until 1914 (with an introduction and notes by Michele Cerrati).

---

in lower centre: "Natalis Bonifacius Si=/benicensis Incidebat./Romæ. MDL XXXIX." An example of the print is in the Casanatense, Rome, vol. 20.B.I.79 bis/161, and a copy of book is in the Houghton, Harvard, Typ 525.90.402F (A).

[79] The *privilegio* is recorded in ASVat, SB, 149, fol. 178r.–v.

[80] Examples of the print are in the BM, London, C.56, inv. no. 1925-7-28-6; and the BN, Florence, Pal.15,1,11,3.

[81] The dedication reads in part: "Illmo. e Rmo. D.D. Eva[n]gelista Pallotto. S.R.E. Presb. Car. Case[n]tino Tit./S. Matthei in Merulana S.D.N. Sixti. V. Prodatario Sacr. S. Basilice . . . Vale aetatis nostrae Decus KL. Xbris 1589." From left to right across the bottom the inscriptions read: "Cum Privilegio Sum[m]i Po[n]tific[i]ˢ. per An[n]os. X. e Sub Excommunicationis Poena"—"Romae Anno Domini .M.D.L.XXXX"—"TIBERII ALPHARANI/HIERACEN AVTHORIS"— "Natalis Bonifacius Sibenicen. Incidebat"—"Cum Licentia Superiorum."

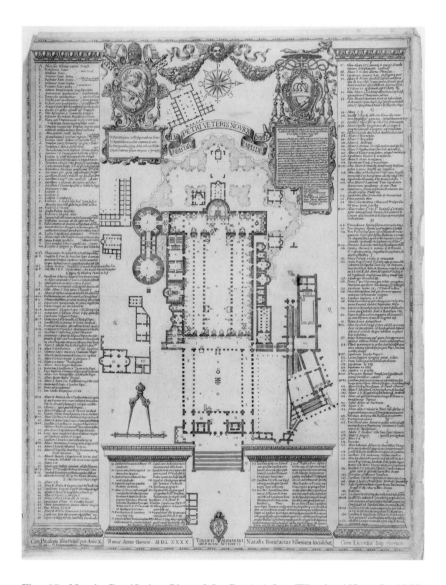

Fig. 37. Natale Bonifacio, *Plan of St. Peter's* (after Tiberio Alfarani), 1590.
Engraving. Photo: © Copyright The British Museum, London.

CHAPTER TWELVE

WRITING MANUALS AND PATTERN BOOKS

Writing Manuals

Writing manuals illustrated with woodcuts and engravings were popular throughout the sixteenth century. A number of them were produced by noted printmakers and published with a *privilegio*.

An early example is a writing manual produced in 1522 by Ludovico
degli Arrighi da Vicenza (known as Vicentino), a sometime bookseller in Rome and later a writer of briefs for the Camera Apostolica.
His book, illustrated with letters cut by Ugo da Carpi and for which
Arrighi was granted a papal *privilegio*, is comprised of two parts:
Operina di Ludovico Vicentino, da imparare di scrivere littera cancellerescha,
and *Il Modo & Regola de scrivere littera corsiva over Cancellerescha novamente
composto per Ludovico Vicentino*.[1] The following year, 1523, Arrighi's *Il
modo de Temperare le Penne* was published in Venice with blocks cut
by Eustachio Celebrino da Udine.[2] Two years later, in 1525, a revised
edition of the *Operina* was printed in Venice but with all new blocks
engraved by Ugo da Carpi in imitation of the first edition.[3] Ugo

---

[1] The book is listed in Emanuele Casamassima, *Trattati di scrittura del Cinquecento
italiano* (Milan, 1966), 40, 85, no. 4; and A. F. Johnson, "A Catalogue of Italian
Writing-Books of the Sixteenth Century," *Signature* 10 (1950): 19. Ugo da Carpi's
contributions are discussed in H. Sotzmann, "Ueber die ältesten meist xylographischen
Schreibbücher der Italiener aus der ersten Hälfte des XVI. Jahrhunderts und Ugo
da Carpi's Antheil daran," *Archiv. für Die Zeichnenden Künste* 2 (1856): 285–286.

[2] The book, with Eustachio Celebrino named as the cutter ("Sta'pata in
Venetia/PER/Ludovico Vicentino Scrittore/&/Eustachio Celebrino Intagliat-/tore"),
is noted in Luigi Servolini, "Eustachio Celebrino da Udine: Intagliatore, calligrafo,
poligrafo ed editore del sec. XVI.," *Gutenberg Jahrbuch* (1944–49): 185, no. 7; and
in Johnson, "A Catalogue of Italian Writing-Books," 19. It may be noted that in
1525 Celebrino also produced his own book on calligraphy, *Il modo di Imparare lettera Merchantescha*.

[3] Philip Hofer, "Variant Issues of the First Edition of Ludovico Arrighi Vicentino's
Operina," in *Calligraphy and Palaeography*, ed. A. S. Osley (London, 1965), 95–106.
Hofer has argued that there was a dispute between Arrighi and Ugo after the publication of the *Operina* the evidence for which is first suggested by the obliteration
of the words "& Ugo da Carpi Intagliatore" beneath the cartouche on D4v. In
retaliation, Ugo recut all the blocks and issued his own edition of the book in

had been granted a *privilegio* for the book by Clement VII on 3 May 1525 the text of which appears on the recto of the second leaf.[4]

In 1523, Ugo da Carpi also produced the engravings for another book on calligraphy, the *Thesauro de' Scrittori*, printed in Rome two years later, in 1525, by Antonio Blado.[5] The little 48-page book is an anthology of foreign alphabets "all extracted from celebrated authors," especially, as is acknowledged on the title-page, from Sigismondo Fanti, who is described as "the first inventor of proportions and rules for making letters." Below on the title-page it is stated that the work was engraved by Ugo da Carpi ("Intagliata per Ugo da Carpi. Cum gratia et Privilegio"). Another edition was printed by Blado in 1535. The particular source acknowledged on the title-page is almost certainly Sigismondo Fanti's *Theorica et Pratica perspicacissimi Sigismundi de Fantis, Ferrariensis in artem mathematice professoris de modo scribendi fabricandique omnes litteram species*, which was printed with a *privilegio* in Venice in 1514 by Giovanni Rosso ("Impressum Venetiis per Ioannem Rubeum Vercelle[n]sem. Anno Domini. M.CCCC.xiiii. Kalen. Decembris.").[6] Rosso had been granted a *privilegio* by the College in Venice on 18 August 1514. Fanti also produced other writing manuals. On 26 November 1526, he was granted a Venetian *privilegio* for "la Theorica e pratica del scrivere."[7]

Venice. The obliterated words can be seen against a strong light in a copy of the first edition at Harvard (Hofer, 99). The colophon, cited in Hofer, 105, and by Luigi Servolini, *Ugo da Carpi: I chiaroscuri e le altre opere* (Florence, 1977), 18, reads: "Finisce la Arte di scriuere littera corsiua ouer cancellerescha stampata in Roma per inventione No, di Ludovico Vicentino. RESURREXIT UGO DA CARPI." The title of the book reads "LA OPERI/NA/di Ludovico Vicentino, da/imparare di/scriue/Re littera Can-/cellares-/cha/Con molte altre noue littere agiunte, et una bellissima/Ragione di Abbacho molto necessario, à chi/impara à scrivere, & fare conto/vgo Scr." [i.e. "Ugo da Carpi scrisse"].

[4] The *privilegio* is transcribed in Luigi Servolini, "Ugo da Carpi," *Rivista d'arte* 11 (1929): 187–188; and in Johnson, "A Catalogue of Italian Writing-Books," 19–20.

[5] The full title is *THESAVRO DE SCRITTORI Opera artificiosa laquale con grandissima arte si per pratica come per geometria insegna a Scrivere diverse sorte littere: cioè Cancellarescha: merchantescha: formata: Cursiva: antiqua: moderna: et bastarda de piu sorte: cum varii, e, bellissimi exempli & altre sorte littere de varie lingue: cioe Grecha: hebraicha: Caldea & arabicha: Tutte extratte da diversi et probatissimi Auttori: & massimamente dalo preclarissimo SIGISMVNDO fanto nobile ferrarese: mathematico: et Architettore eruditissimo: dele mesure, e, ragione de lettere primo inventore: Intagliata per Vgo da Carpi: Cum gratia: et Privilegio ... M.D.XXV.*

[6] The book is listed in Duc de Rivoli, *Bibliographie des livres à figures vénitiens, 1469–1525* (Paris, 1892), 365–366; Casamassima, *Trattati di Scrittura*, 84, no. 2; and Sotzmann, 284, no. 1.

[7] Fanti's 1526 *privilegio* is recorded in ASV, ST, reg. 26, fol. 134v. (152v. n.n.).

In 1540, the Roman calligrapher Giovanni Battista Palatino produced the *Libro nuovo d'imparare a scrivere tutte sorte lettere antiche et moderne di tutte nationi, con nvove regole misure et essempi. Con un breue & utile trattato de le cifere . . .*, printed in Rome by Benedetto Giunta for Baldassare di Francesco Cartolari with two ten-year privileges, one from Paul III, granted on 12 August 1540, and the other from the Venetian Senate ("Stampata appresso Campo di Fiore nelle case di M. Benedetto Gionta per Baldassarre di Francesco Cartolari Perugino, a di 12, d'Agosto. M.D.XL. CON GRATIE, ET PRIVILEGI").[8] In 1545, Blado printed a revised edition with the title *Libro di M. Giouanbattista Palatino, cittadino romano, nelqual s'insegna à scriuere ogni sorte lettera, antica, et moderna, di qualunque natione, con le sue regole, et misure, et essempi: et con un breue, et util discorso de le cifre.* The year before, in May 1544, the book was also published by Madonna Girolama de Cartolari (the colophon reads: "In Roma contrada del Pellegrino per Madonna Girolama de Cartolari Perugina, Il mese di Maggio"). Other editions followed. In 1561 it was printed by Valerio Dorico, "ad instantia of Giovanni della Gatta," with both a ten-year Venetian *privilegio* and a ten-year papal *privilegio*.[9] In 1566, the heirs of the Dorico brothers ("Per li Heredi di Valerio & Luigi Dorici fratelli") printed the *Compendio del gran volume de l'arte del bene et leggiardramente scrivere tutte le sorti di lettere et caratteri,* with a papal *privilegio* granted by Paul III, which is a revised version of the *Libro nuovo.* The *Compendio* was also published in Venice in 1578 by the heirs of Marchio Sessa.[10]

In 1546, Domenico Manzoni from Oderzo, near Venice, published with a *privilegio* his *Libretto molto utile per impara a leggere, scrivere.* The book was printed "In Vinegia per Comin de Trino."[11] Two years later, in 1548, the Franciscan Vespasiano Amphiareo published

---

[8] A copy of the book is in the Farnesina, Rome, vol. 34 I. 8, inv. no. 32840. It is listed in Casamassima, *Trattati di Scrittura*, 88, no. 9; and Sotzmann, 300–303.

[9] The 1561 edition is listed in Adams, 2: 39, no. 75; Johnson, "A Catalogue of Italian Writing-Books," 27; and *Three Classics of Italian Calligraphy: An unabridged re-issue of the writing books of Arrighi, Tagliente and Palatino* (New York, 1953), Introduction [unpaginated].

[10] The *Compendio* is listed in Francesco Barberi, "I Dorici, Tipografi a Roma nel Cinquecento," *La Bibliofilia* 67 (1965): 236; Johnson, "A Catalogue of Italian Writing-Books," 28; and A. S. Osley, *Scribes and Sources: Handbook of the Chancery Hand in the Sixteenth Century* (Boston, 1980), 84.

[11] The book is listed in Johnson, "A Catalogue of Italian Writing-Books," 28. Earlier editions, dating from 1540, did not include examples of letters. Later editions are dated 1565, 1573, and 1574.

Un novo modo d'insegnar a scrivere et formar lettere di piu sorti, che da altri non prima c'hora usate: novamente da frate Vespasiano minoritano trovato, e da lui pur hora dato in luce. The book, issued with a *privilegio*, was printed "In Vinegia, per Curtio Troiano d'i Nauo/MDXLVIII" and dedicated to Doge Francesco Donà.[12]

On 5 July 1560, Giovan Francesco Cresci from Milan, who is identified as a "Scrittore della Libraria Apostolica," was granted a ten-year *privilegio* by Pius IV ("Con privilegio per Anni X") for his *Essemplare di piu sorti lettere di M. Gio. Francesco Cresci Milanese... dove si dimostra la vera et nuova forma dello scrivere cancellaresco corsivo*, which was printed in Rome, at Cresci's expense, by Antonio Blado. Eleven years later, after the first *privilegio* had expired, Cresci was granted another by Pius V on 7 March 1571 for his two-part *Il perfetto scrittore di M. Gio. Francesco Cresci cittadino melanese: doue si veggono i veri caratteri, & le natural forme di tutte quelle sorti di lettere, che à vero scrittor si appartengono: con alcun' altre da lui nuouamente ritrouate: et i modi, che deue tenere il mastro per ben insegnare*, which was also printed in Rome by Cresci himself ("in casa del proprio autore"). The colophon mentions that "it was engraved by the excellent engraver Francesco Aureri da Crema" ("... & intagliato per l'eccellente intagliator M. Francesco Aureri da Crema"). In 1579, Cresci published the third part, *Il perfetto cancellaresco corsivo... liber terzo*, which was printed in Rome "Appresso Pietro Spada," and again at the expense of Cresci and the Roman book publisher Pietro Paolo Palumbo.[13] Simultaneously, it would appear, the fourth part, *Liber Quarto*, of the same book was printed in Venice, "Appresso Pietro Dehuchino," and again at the expense of Cresci and Pietro Paolo Palumbo.[14]

Yet another manual for writing "cancellaresche corsive Romane nuove" is Marcello Scalzini's *Il secretario*, published in 1581. Scalzini,

---

[12] Amphiario's book is catalogued in Casamassima, *Trattati di Scrittura*, 90, no. 12; and Johnson, "A Catalogue of Italian Writing-Books," 29.

[13] Cresci's books are catalogued in Casamassima, *Trattati di Scrittura*, 91, no. 14; 92, no. 15; and 93, no. 16; Johnson, "A Catalogue of Italian Writing-Books," 30, 32. Copies of *Il perfetto scrittore* and *Il perfetto cancellaresco corsivo... liber terzo* are in the Farnesina, Rome, 34.I.8, inv. nos. 33033 and 32926.

[14] A copy of the Venice edition of the *Liber Quarto* is in the Farnesina, Rome, 34.I.8, inv. nos. 33083. Johnson, "A Catalogue of Italian Writing-Books," 33, lists only a 1596 edition, which Osley, *Scribes and Sources*, 113, n. 1, describes as "attributed to Cresco" and as "a collection of models written by [Cresci] in 1579–80" which had been "put together by a Cistercian monk, Silvio Valesi, who states that they had come into his possession after being lost for ten years."

also known as "Il Camerino," after the city of Camerino, describes himself on the title-page as a "Cittadino Romano, Inventore, Scrittore in Roma." In the book, an engraved portrait of Scalzini by Giacomo Franco ("Giacomo franco fec") is followed by fifty other engraved plates. The book was granted a ten-year *privilegio* by Gregory XIII on 5 January 1580, and twenty-year *privilegio* by the Venetian Senate on 28 October 1580. It was printed in Venice at the expense of Scalzini by Domenico Nicolini ("IN VENETIA, Appresso Domenico Nicolini, Ad Instantia del proprio Autore. 1581").[15]

In 1588, Lodovico Curione's *LA NOTOMIA delle Cancelleresche corsive* was printed with a *privilegio* ("Con privilegio di N.S.") indicated on a frontispiece engraved by Martin van Buyten ("Martin' van buyten sculpsit—hoc opus Romae 1588"), who also engraved the book's 48 illustrations. Four years later, on 8 October 1592, an agreement was drawn up between van Buyten "flandrus" and Curione whereby van Buyten was permitted by Curione to 'retouch' ("retoccare") the book ("revidere aut vulgariter dicitur retoccare secundum librum mostrarum seu documentorum scribendi . . . nuncupatum La notomia delle lettere cancelleresche").[16] The following year, 1593, Curione published, again with a *privilegio*, *IL TEATRO delle Cancelleresche corsive*, with the frontispiece engraved by Martin van Buyten ("Martin' van buyten Hollandus/sculpsit anno D[omi]ni 1593"). It will have been noticed that the skills of the Flemish engraver Martin van Buyten were much sought after by calligraphers. In addition to those mentioned above, he also engraved the title-page and thirty-eight plates of Chancery script ("Martin van buyten sculpsit") in Simone Verovio's *Il primo libro delli essempi*, printed in Rome in 1587.[17]

---

[15] The book is catalogued in Pasero, 338, no. III, and Johnson, "A Catalogue of Italian Writing-Books," 36. The contents of the papal *privilegio*, summarized in Italian, and the Venetian *privilegio* are given on the title-page. A copy in the Farnesina, Rome, 34.I.8, inv. no. 33084, has only the Venetian *privilegio*. The dedication, to Cardinal Sirleto, is dated 6 May 1581. Johnson, "A Catalogue of Italian Writing-Books," 37, also catalogues a 1587 edition and a 1589 edition (the latter also catalogued by Casamassima, *Trattati di Scrittura*, 95, no. 19).

[16] The 1592 agreement is reproduced in Bertolotti, *Artisti in Relazione coi Gonzaga Duchi di Mantova* (Modena, 1885), 63.

[17] *Il Primo Libro delli Essempi* is listed in Johnson, "A Catalogue of Italian Writing-Books," 37. A copy is in the Farnesina, Rome, 34.I.8, inv. nos. 33220–33253. The dedication to Cardinal Agostino Valiero of Verona, dated 31 May 1587, is by Nicolaus van Aelst (see Chapter 11 for Van Aelst). Besides writing books, and Marc' Antonio Rossi's "Carta di Gloria" (see Chapter 7), van Buyten also engraved, among

In 1589, Giacomo Romano was granted a papal *privilegio* to publish his own book *Il primo libro di scrivere di Iacomo Romano, dove s'insegna la vera maniera delle cancellaresche corsive, e di tutte quelle sorti di lettere che a un buon scrittore si appartengono di sapere, & che al presente sono in uso . . .*, which was printed in Rome by Pietro Spada.[18] The book has eighty-four engraved plates, each with a woodcut border. In 1598, the same year he was granted a *privilegio* for a print (see Chapter 7), Marc' Antonio Rossi also published with a *privilegio* his own calligraphy book, *Giardino de scrittori*, which was printed in Rome by Rossi himself ("appresso il proprio autore"). Besides the one hundred and twelve engraved examples of calligraphy, the book also has a frontispiece with a portrait of Rossi engraved by Philippe Thomassin after a design by Camillo Spalucci, and a portrait of Cardinal Pietro Aldobrandini also engraved by Thomassin after a design by Antonio Tempesta.[19]

On 27 July 1596, the publisher and sometime engraver, designer, and dealer in prints Giacomo Franco acquired a Venetian *privilegio* that included, besides a book on sewing for women (see below), also his second writing book, *Del Franco modo di scriver cancellaresco moderno. libro secondo. Raccolte da gli essemplari di piu famosi scrittori de nostri tempi*, which he published in Venice the same year.[20] Franco had published the "Libro Primo" the year before, but without a *privilegio*. In the first book, the title-page and all thirty-two plates were engraved by Franco himself. In the second book, he engraved the title, with an

---

other things, the title-page and the ten full-page illustrations in Cataldo Antonio Mannarino's *Glorie di gverrieri e d'amanti*, printed in Naples in 1596 by Giacomo Carlino and Antonio Pace. Mannarino's book is catalogued in Mortimer, *Italian 16th Century Books*, no. 274.

[18] The book is catalogued in Johnson, "A Catalogue of Italian Writing-Books," 38. The papal *privilegio* for Giacomo Romano's book is recorded in ASVat, SB, vol. 139, fol. 29. An example of the frontispiece is in the Farnesina, Rome, 34.I.8 (no inv. no.). The dedication, dated 22 December 1589, is to Giuliano Cesarini, Duke of Civitanova.

[19] The book is listed in Johnson, "A Catalogue of Italian Writing-Books," 39; and in *Mostra del Libro Illustrato Romano del Cinquecento*, 44, no. 154. The full title reads: *Giardino de scrittori di Marc' Antonio Rossi Romano . . . Nel quale si vede il vero modo di scriuer facilissimamente tutte le sorte di lettere, che al presente sono in vso et che sono necessarie ad ogni qualità di persona. Con vn alfabeto di maiuscole antiche rom, fatte per ragion 'di geometria.* A copy is in the BA, Vatican, Rossiana 3458.

[20] The document is recorded in ASV, ST, reg. 66, fol. 77r. (101r. n.n.). The book is catalogued in Johnson, "A Catalogue of Italian Writing-Books," 38–39. Pasero, 346, no. 16, catalogues the first book and notes the granting of the *privilegio* for the second.

emblematic view of Venice, and forty-one plates of examples of script by Scalzini, Cortese, Cresci, Curione, Sopranini, Tosta of Naples, as well as his own.

Pattern and Costume Books

Pattern books provided instructions for sewing, embroidery, and lace-making with examples of patterns. These activities were considered "women's work," and the books were intended for a female audience. Books of costumes were also popular and of interest to both men and women.

Mention can be made first of two embroidery pattern books published in Venice in 1530 by the publisher Giovanni Andrea Vavassore (for whom, see also Chapter 6): *Corona di racammi*, and *Esempalrio [sic] di lavori*.[21] The title-page of the latter book was engraved by Giovanni Andrea's brother Florio. Both their names appear together as publishers also on an edition of Francesco Pelliciolo's book of embroidery patterns, *Fior de gli essempi*, published in Venice around 1545.[22] After 1545 Florio's name ceases to appear. Giovanni Andrea Vavassore, however, continued to publish pattern books. Around 1545 he published alone another book of lace patterns by Francesco Pellicioli, *Essemplario novo di piu di cento variate mostre belissime per cusire intitulato Fontana de gli essempli*. This was probably the book for which Pellicioli had been granted a *privilegio* on 15 April 1542 ("per alcuni desegni di lavoro di donne").[23] Around 1566, Vavassore published two more pattern books: *Corona de le mostre* by Armenio Corte, and a year or so later, *Ornamenti delle belle et virtuose donne*.[24]

On 30 June 1556, a *privilegio* was granted to the German publisher Giovanni Ostaus for Ostaus' own book on embroidery patterns, *La vera perfettione del disegno di varie sorti di recami et di cucire punti à fogliami, punti tagliati, punti a fili et rimessi punti cruciati, punti a sturora,*

---

[21] The books are listed in Arthur Lotz, *Bibliographie der Modelbücher* (Stuttgart and London, 1963), 119, no. 66; and 123, no. 67.

[22] Pelliciolo's book of embroidery patterns is listed in Lotz, 152, no. 84.

[23] The document granting the *privilegio* to Pellicioli is recorded in ASV, ST, reg. 32, fol. 19v. (90v. n.n.). The book is listed in Lotz, 152, no. 83. Another edition was published by Giovanni Andrea Vavassore in 1550.

[24] Both books are listed in Lotz, 182, no. 107; and 183, no. 108.

et ogni altera arte che dia opera a disegni, which was published in Venice the following year.[25] The book was dedicated by Ostaus to Lucretia Contarini, whose name explains the inclusion of a print by Giuseppe Porta Salviati of *Lucretia*, dated 1557, which appears on the verso of page 2 in the same book.[26]

In 1557, following the approval by the Riformatori dello Studio di Padova and the issuance of a license by the Chiefs of the Council of Ten on 15 July of that year, the engraver Enea Vico was granted a *privilegio* on 29 August 1557 for "books on the various costumes of different nations of the world."[27]

Towards the end of the century, Cesare Vecellio, the nephew of Titian, was also producing books on lace patterns, sewing, and costume. In 1590, he was granted a papal *privilegio* and a Venetian *privilegio* for a costume book that was printed with the title *De Gli Habiti Antichi, et Moderni di Diuerse Parti del Mondo Libri Due Fatte da Cesare Vecellio & con Discorsi da Lui dichiarati. Con Privilegio.*[28] The *privilegio* document states that the book contains "four hundred and fifty woodcut illustrations," which were executed by Cristoforo Guerra ("Cristoforo Guerra, tedesco, da Norimberga") based on drawings by Vecellio. The book was published in Venice in 1590 by Damiano Zenaro. A second enlarged edition, with the title *Habiti Antichi, et moderni di tutto il mondo. Di Cesare Vecellio. Di nuouo accresciuti di molte figure . . .*, was printed in Venice by Sessa in 1598 with the number of plates increased to five hundred and three. The text is in Italian and Latin on the recto of each leaf with the woodcut illustration on the verso. By the time the book was printed again in Venice, in

---

[25] The *privilegio* is recorded in ASV, ST, reg. 40, fol. 120v. (140v. n.n.). The book, which is listed in Lotz, 172, no. 96a, went through several editions in the sixteenth century: 1561, 1564, 1567, 1584, and 1591.

[26] Salviati's print is catalogued in Rosand and Muraro, cat. no. 86. For Giuseppe Porta Salviati, see also Chapter 9.

[27] The license is recorded in ASV, CCXN, reg. 16, fol. 226r. (227r. n.n,) and the *privilegio* in ASV, ST, reg. 41, fol. 43v. (58v. n.n.). Twenty-four prints from Vico's book on costumes of different nations are included in *The Illustrated Bartsch*, ed. John Spike (New York, 1985), vol. 30, pages 137–151 (Bartsch, 15: 329–331, nos. 204–232). Another series of prints shows costumes of Spain. For Enea Vico, see also Chapter 8.

[28] The Venetian *privilegio*, granted on 9 January 1590 [1589 m.v.] for twenty years, is recorded in ASV, ST, reg. 59, fol. 165r. (195r. n.n.). The book's illustrations are discussed in C. Lozzi, "Cesare Vecellio e i suoi disegni e intagli per libri di costumi e di merletti," *La Bibliofilia* 1 (1899): 3–11. The *privilegio* also included an engraving, for which see Chapter 9.

1664 by Combi, Cesare Vecellio is referred to as Titian's brother, and Titian himself is credited with helping design the figures! The 1664 title reads: *Habiti antichi, ovvero Raccolta di figure delineate dal gran Tiziano e da Cesare Vecellio suo fratello, conforme alle nazioni del mondo*.

On 6 April 1591, Vecellio received another *privilegio* from the Venetian Senate for "il premio, 2do et 3° libro de dissegni per lavori et ponti diversi per il cucir delle donne, et per li habiti." The sewing book, which contains seventy-six woodcut lace patterns, was published the same year with the title *Corona delle nobili et virtuose donne. Libro primo [-secondo, -terzo]*. A *Libro quarto*, entitled *Gioielli della corona . . .*, was published in 1593, and a *Libro quinto* in 1596. A fourth impression of the *Libro primo* was printed in Venice in 1592.[29]

On 16 November 1591, the engraver Giacomo Franco submitted a supplication for a *privilegio* for a book with engravings he had done of costumes worn by Venetian women ("il libro delli habiti alla venetiana intagliato da lui"). The *privilegio*, however, was not granted at this time, and the book, *Habiti d'huomeni et donne venetiane: con la processione della ser.ma signoria et altri particolari cioè. Trionfi feste et cerimonie publiche della nobilissima città di Venetia*, was apparently not published until 1610.[30] On 27 July 1596, Franco acquired another *privilegio* (mentioned above, which also included his writing book) for a book demonstrating sewing for women ("mostre da cucir") with sixteen woodcut prints and eight copperplates. The book, entitled *Nuova inventione de diverse mostre cosi di punto in aere como di retticelli hoggi di usate per tutte le parte del mondo: con merletti, mostretti da colari, e da manegheti et merli per cantoni di fazoletti*, was printed in Venice the same year. The book is dedicated by Franco to Signora Adriana Palma.[31]

As was noted in Chapter 8, Isabetta Parasole had produced the drawings, which her husband Leonardo Parasole reproduced in woodcuts, that illustrate Castore Durante's *Herbario nuovo*, published in

---

[29] The 1591 *privilegio* document is recorded in ASV, ST, reg. 61, fol. 19v.–20r. (47v.–48r. n.n.). The book and its various editions are listed in Lotz, 199, nos. 116, 117, 118, 119, and 120; and Edward F. Strange, "Early Pattern Books of Lace, Embroidery and Needlework," *Transactions of the Bibliographical Society* 7 (1902–1904): 242, no. 81.

[30] The dedication, to Vincenzo Gonzaga, Duke of Mantua, is dated 1 January 1610. The book is catalogued in Pasero, 350, no. 28.

[31] The document is recorded in ASV, ST, reg. 66, fol. 77r. (101r. n.n.). The book, which carries the inscription "Giacomo Franco Forma," is listed in Lotz, 230, no. 131; and in Strange, 227, no. 24, and catalogued in Pasero, 348, no. 20.

Rome in 1585. Baglione reports that Isabetta also produced a book "con diverse forme di merletti" and other types of work for women, with a frontispiece engraved by Francesco Villamena.[32] She in fact produced several books of embroidery patterns. None, however, was printed with a *privilegio*. They are included here out of interest and to round out the various activities of the Parasole family.

Isabetta's first book, *Specchio Delle Virtuose Donne Dove si vedono bellissimi lauori in ponto in aria, reticella, di maglia, & piombini disegnati da Isabetta Catanea Parasole*, was printed in 1595 "Ad instantia di Rosato Parasole" (Rosato was Leonardo's brother) in Rome, "Con licentia de Superiori," by Antonio Facchetti.[33] The dedication, dated 20 September 1594, is by Isabetta to her patron the Duchess of Sermoneta, Maria Felice Orsini Caetana. In 1597, Isabetta produced another book on the same subject, this time entitled *Studio delle virtuose dame: doue si vedono bellissimi lauori di punto in aria, reticella, di maglia*. It was printed in Rome, "Con Licenza de' Superiori," by Antonio Facchetti.[34] On this occasion, the book carries a dedication (in both Spanish and Italian), dated 13 January 1597, by Isabetta to "Dona Ioanna de Aragon, y Cardona." In 1598 there followed a third book, *Pretiosa gemma delle virtuose donne: doue si vedono bellissimi lauori di punto in aria, reticella, di maglia, e piombini*, printed in Rome "Ad istanza di Lucchino Gargano." The dedication, dated 10 November 1598, to "Donna Gironima Colonna," is signed by Gargano.[35] A revised second edition was printed in Venice by Gargano ("E di nuouo dati in luce da Lucchino Gargano, con alcuni altri bellissimi lauori nuouamente inuentati.") in 1600. A new edition with the title *Secondo libro della pretiosa gemma delle virtuose donne, doue con nuoua inuentione si vedono bellissimi lauori di varie sorti di merli grandi, e piccioli, punti in aria, punti*

---

[32] Baglione, 394–395.

[33] The book is listed in Lotz, 227, no. 129a. Another edition was printed in 1596 in Rome by Pietro Spada (Lotz, 228, no. 129b), and a third in 1598 "IN ROMA, Appresso Antonio Facchetti. Alla Fontana di Treui" (Lotz, 228, no. 129c). Lotz makes no mention of Francesco Villamena having engraved the frontispiece. A document published in Bertolotti, *Artisti bolognese*, 113, identifies Rosato Parasole as Leonardo's brother. Rosato was a wood engraver and a painter. Payments recorded in the Archivio della Reverenda Fabbrica di San Pietro, Armadi, 162, 30, 30, for work executed in 1598 show that Rosato Parasole also worked as an *indoratore* on three niches on the north side of St. Peter's (the document is in Millon and Smyth, "Michelangelo and St. Peter's," Appendix 1, 201, document no. 7).

[34] The book is listed in Lotz, 231, no. 132; and in Strange, 234, no. 57.

[35] The book is listed in Lotz, 233, no. 135a.

tagliati, punti à reticello, e rosetti diuersi, che con l'aco si vsano hoggidì per tutta Europ [sic], was published by Gargano in 1601.[36] Other books by Isabetta Catanea Parasole include *Fiori d'Ogni Virtu*, printed by Facchetti in Rome in 1610, and *Teatro delle nobili et virtvose donne dove si rappresentano varii disegni di lauori nouamente inuentati, et disegnati*, printed by Mauritio Bona in Rome in 1616, with later editions dated 1619, 1620, and 1636.[37]

---

[36] The book is listed in Lotz, 234 no. 136; and in Strange, 235, no. 58. A copy is in the BA Vatican, Ferraiolo.III.634.

[37] These books are listed in Lotz, 243, no. 143a–f.

HANDLIST OF PRINTS GRANTED AND/OR PUBLISHED WITH A *PRIVILEGIO* 1498–c. 1605

Described or mentioned in the text, including some books

• = print(s)

TITLE	ENGRAVER	DATE	PRIV. HOLDER	AUTHORITY
• view of Venice	?	1498	Girolamo Biondo	Venice College
• Triumph of Caesar	Giacomo di Argentina	1504	Benedetto Bordon	Venice College
• map of Italy	?	1508	Benedetto Bordon	Venice College
• mappamondo	?			
• History of Trajan	?	1514	Giovanni da Brescia	Venice College
book: Fanti, *Theorica et Pratica* . . . *de modo scribendi*	?	1514	Giovanni Rosso	Venice College
• Submersion of Pharaoh's Army in the Red Sea	?	1515	Bernardino Benalio	Venice College
• Susanna	Girolamo Pennacchi			
• Sacrifice of Abraham	Ugo da Carpi			
• "altri hystorie noue"	?			

TITLE	ENGRAVER	DATE	PRIV. HOLDER	AUTHORITY
• view of Venice	Giacomo di Argentina	1515	Giacomo di Argentina	Venice College
• Last Judgement • Triumph of the Virgin • Triumph of Christ	? ? ?	1516	Bernardino Benalio	Venice College
• "Triumpho, et la nativita, morte, resurrection et ascension del nostro pientissimo redemptore" • "destructione de la sancta Cita di Hierusalem" • "multe altre varie et belle inventione"	? ? ?	1516	Gregorio de' Gregorii	Venice College
• "la storia dei Sodoma et Gomorra" • "pharaone perseguitante el populo de Israel"	Fra Ippolito Fra Ippolito	1516	Fra Ippolito	Venice College
chiaroscuro patent • Death of Ananias • Aeneas and Anchises	 Ugo da Carpi Ugo da Carpi	1516	Ugo da Carpi	1. Venice Senate 2. Vatican (1518)
book: *Operina . . . da imparare scrivere lettere cancellerescha*	Ugo da Carpi	1523?	Ugo da Carpi?	Vatican
book: *Thesauro de' Scrittori*	Ugo da Carpi	1523?	Ugo da Carpi	Vatican

Item	Engraver/Artist	Date	Publisher	Privilege
book: *Isolario*	?	1526	Benedetto Bordon	Venice Senate
• prints illustrating book on architecture	Agostino Veneziano	1528	Sebastiano Serlio & Agostino Veneziano	Venice Senate
• mappamondo	?	1529	Giovanni Piero de' Marini	Venice Senate
• planisfero	?	1529	Matteo de' Bardolini	Venice Senate
• The Positions of the Armies of Charles V and of Suleiman II	Agostino Veneziano	1532	?	Venice Senate?
• map of France	A. Vavassore (?)	1536	Francesco Torresani	Venice Senate
• map of Tuscany	Girolamo Bell'armato	1536	Girolamo Bell'armato	1. Venice Senate 2. Vatican (1538)
book: *Libro nuovo d'imparare a scrivere*	?	1540	G. B. Palatino (?)	Vatican
• prints illustrating Ariosto and Petrarch	?	1541	Gabriele Giolito	Venice Senate
book: *Essemplario novo di ... per cusire*	?	1542	F. Pelliciolo	Venice Senate
book: Alberti *De re aedificatoria*	?	1543	Vincenzo Valgrisio	Venice Senate
• map of Sicily	?	1545	Giacomo de Gastaldi	Venice Senate
book: illustrated pilgrimage to Jerusalem	Domenico dalle Greche	1546	Domenico delle Greche	1. Vatican 2. Venice Senate

TITLE	ENGRAVER	DATE	PRIV. HOLDER	AUTHORITY
• Last Judgement	Giulio Bonasone	1546	Bonasone (?)	Vatican
various prints • King Henry II of France • Proserpine Changing Aesculapius into an Owl • Giovanni de' Medici	Enea Vico	1546	Enea Vico	Venice Senate
• St. Peter's Façade • St. Peter's Lateral Section • St. Peter's Lateral elevation • St. Peter's Plan (1549)	Mario Labacco ? Mario Labacco ? Mario Labacco ? Mario Labacco ?	1546/ 1549	Antonio Salamanca?	Vatican
book: Italian translation of Alberti's *De Architettura*		1546	Vincenzo Valgrisio	Venice Senate
book: *Libretto molto utile per impara a leggere, scrivere*	?	1546	Domenico Manzoni	Vatican
• map of Rome	?	1547	Eufrosino della Volpaia	1. Venice Senate 2. Vatican 3. Duke of Florence
book: *Antichita della città di Roma* (1553)	?	1548	Michele Tramezzino	Venice Senate

Work	Author	Date	Publisher	Privilege
book: *Le Imagini . . . de gli Imperatori*	Enea Vico	1548	Antonio Zantani	1. Venice Senate 2. Imperial 3. Royal 4. Papal
book: *Uno novo modo d'Insegnar a scrivere et formar lettere*	?	1548	V. Amphiareo?	Vatican
• maps in Ptolemy's *La geografia*	?	1548	G. B. Pedrezano	Venice Senate
• map of Asia	?	1550	Giacomo Gastaldi and Michel Membre	Venice Senate
• map of Korčula • map of Spain	?	1550	Fra Vincenzo Paletino de Curzola	Venice Senate
• map of Rome	Leonardo Bufalini	1551	Leonardo Bufalini	Venice Senate
• "Via, Verità, et Vita" • "Christo resuscitante"	? ?	1551 June	Michele Tramezzino	Venice Senate
book: *Compendio di Roma Antica*	?	1551 Dec.	Michele Tramezzino	1. Venice Senate 2. Vatican
• map of Germany	Enea Vico	1552	Giacomo Gastaldi	Venice Senate

TITLE	ENGRAVER	DATE	PRIV. HOLDER	AUTHORITY
• map of modern Rome (1552) • map of Rome (1553) • Circus Maximus (1553) • Circus Flaminius (1553) • Castro Pretorio (1553) • map of Germany (1553) • map of Hungary (1558) • "dell'Italia"	? Giulio de Musi Beatrizet Beatrizet ? Beatrizet Sebastiano del Re ?	1552 Dec.	Michele Tramezzino	1. Venice Senate 2. Vatican (1550)
book: *Libro dell'Architettua*	Mario Labacco	1552	Antonio Labacco	1. Venice Senate 2. Vatican
book: *Regola di far . . . Ionico*	Giuseppe Salviati	1552	Giuseppe Salviati	Venice Senate
• Sacrifice of Iphigenia (1553)	Beatrizet	1553	Michele Tramezzino	Vatican
• The Lineage of the Twelve Caesars	Enea Vico	1553	Enea Vico	1. Venice Senate 2. Vatican 3. Imperial 4. Duke of Florence
book: *I Commentari di C. Giulio Cesare* (1554), works by L. Dolce, Petrarch, Dante	?	1553	Gabriel Giolito	Venice Senate
• illustrations in Ariosto, Petrarch, Boccaccio	?	1553	G. A. Vavassore	Venice Senate

Item	Artist	Date	Publisher	Privilege
• mappamondo (1554)	Giulio de' Musi	1554 July	Michele Tramezzino	1. Venice Senate 2. Vatican
• Antique Port of Ostia (1554)	Giulio de' Musi	1554 Nov.	Michele Tramezzino	1. Venice Senate 2. Vatican
• map of Europe	?	1554	Gerardus Mercator	Venice Senate
book: *I quattro primi libri*	?	1554	Pietro Cataneo	Venice Senate
• map of Italy	?	1554?	?	Vatican
• Adonis	?	1555?	Antonio Lafrery?	Vatican
book: *Discorsi sopra le Medaglie de gli Antichi*	Enea Vico	1555	Gabriele Giolito	Venice Senate
• map of Piedmont (1556)	Fabio Licinio			1. Venice Senate 2. Vatican
• illustrations in *La vera perfettione . . . di recame* • Crucifixion	Giuseppe Salviati	1556	Giovanni Ostaus	Venice Senate
book: Vitruvius *I dieci libri dell'architettura*	Giuseppe Salviati?	1556	Francesco Marcolini	Venice Senate
• mappamondo	?	1556	Antonio Floriano	Venice Senate

TITLE	ENGRAVER	DATE	PRIV. HOLDER	AUTHORITY
• map of Britain	Master IHS	1556?	?	Vatican
• Theatre of Marcellus (1558)	Jabob Bos	1557	Michele Tramezzino	1. Venice Senate
map of Norway (?), or				2. Vatican
map of N. Europe (1558)	Jacob Bos			
map of Gelders (1558)	Jacob Bos			
map of Flanders (1555)	Jacob Bos			
map of Brabant (1558)	Jacob Bos			
map of Holland (1558)	Jacob Bos			
map of Naples (1558)	Sebastiano del Re			
map of France (1558)	Sebastiano del Re			
map of Belgium (1558)	Sebastiano del Re			
map of Frisia (1558)	Jacob Bos			
• Baths of Diocletian and Maximian (1558)	Jacob Bos			
book: *Historia de la composicion del cuerpo humano*	Beatrizet	1557	Antonio Lafrery	Venice Senate
book: *Le Imagine delle Donne Auguste* "books on various costumes"	Enea Vico	1557	Enea Vico	Venice Senate
• map of Rome	Beatrizet	1557?	Antonio Lafrery (?)	Vatican
• map of Modern Rome	Beatrizet			

• St. Jerome	Sebastiano del Re	1557?	?	Vatican
book: *Augustarum Imagines*	Enea Vico	1558	Vincenzo Valgrisio	1. Venice Senate 2. Vatican 3. others
• map of Italy	?	1558?	Vincenzo Luchini (?)	Vatican
book: *Vetustissimae Tabulae Aeneae Hieroglyphicis*	Enea Vico	1559	Enea Vico	Venice Senate
• Map of Asia (part 1) • Map of S.E. Europe	Fabio Licinio Fabio Licinio	1559 April	Giacomo de Gastaldi	Venice Senate
• 3-part map of Asia Part 1 (1559) Part 2 (1561) Part 3 (1561) • Map of Greece (1560) • Map of Italy (1561) • Map of Lombardy	Fabio Licinio Fabio Licinio Fabio Licinio Fabio Licinio Fabio Licinio Fabio Licinio (?)	1559 July	Giacomo de Gastaldi	1. Venice Senate 2. Vatican
• Portrait of Pius IV	G. B. de' Cavalieri	1560	Bartolomeo Faletti?	Vatican
• Moses Striking Water from Rock	M. Grecchi Lucchese	c. 1560?	M. Grecchi Lucchese?	Vatican
• Massacre of Innocents • Martyrdom of St. Lawrence				

TITLE	ENGRAVER	DATE	PRIV. HOLDER	AUTHORITY
• The Climbers				
• Holy Family with Saints				
• Mystery of Diana of Ephesus				
book: *Essemplare di piu sorti di lettere*	?	1560?	G. F. Cresci	Vatican
book: Ptolomey *Geografia*	?	1561	Vincenzo Valgrisio	Venice Senate
book: Strabo *Geografia* (1562)	?	1561	F. de' Franceschi	Venice Senate
• mappamondo	?	1561	Mattheo Pagano	Venice Senate
• map of Rome (1561)	Jacob Bos	1561	M. & F. Tramezzino	1. Venice Senate 2. Vatican
• map of Greece (1561)	Sebastiano del Re			
• map of Spain (1559)	Sebastiano del Re			
• map of Hungary (?)	?			
• map of Antwerp	?			
• Visitation of Our Lady	?			
• map of Portugal (1561)	Sebastiano del Re			
• map of Friuli (1563)	Sebastiano del Re	?		
book: *Antiquarum Statuarum*	G. B. de' Cavalieri	c. 1561?	G. B. de' Cavalieri?	Vatican
book: Alberti *L'Architettura*		1563	Cosimo Bartoli	Venice Senate

Subject	Engraver	Date	Publisher	Privilege
• map of Europe and part of Asia	G. P. Contarini	1563	G. B. Contarini	Venice Senate
• map of Malta	Beatrizet	1563?	Beatrizet (?)	Vatican
• Man of Sorrows (1563)	?	1563?	P. P. Palumbo?	Vatican
• Adoration of the Shepherds (1564)	?			
• map of Africa / • map of Asia Minor	Fabio Licinio / Paolo Forlani	1564	Giacomo de Gastaldi	Venice Senate
• south Apse of St. Peter's	?	1564?	Vincenzo Luchini?	Vatican
• Madonna del Silenzio	Philippe Soye	1564?	Antonio Lafrery (?)	Vatican
• print illustrating various proverbs (1564)	Nicolo Nelli	1564?	Nicolo Nelli (?) / Ferrando Bertelli (?)	Venice Senate
• map of Malta (1565)	Nicolo Nelli	1565	Nicolo Nelli (?)	Venice Senate
• Martyrdom of St. Catherine	G. B. de' Cavalieri	1565?	G. B. de' Cavalieri?	Vatican
• map of antique Rome	?	1565?	Antonio Laffery (?)	1. Vatican 2. Venice Senate 3. Imperial 4. Royal 5. Ducal

TITLE	ENGRAVER	DATE	PRIV. HOLDER	AUTHORITY
Temple of Antoninus and Faustina	?	1565?	Antonio Laftery (?)	Vatican
map of Vienna (1566)	Domenico Zenoi	1566	Domenico Zenoi	Venice Senate
"Descrittione dell'Austria, et Ongharia, Transiluania, Bauiera, Stiria, Carintia, Dalmatia, Venetiano" (1567)	?			
St Jerome Reading in the Desert (1565)	Cornelis Cort	1566	Titian	Venice Senate
Roger Saving Angelica (1565)	Cornelis Cort			
Holy Trinity (1566)	Cornelis Cort			
Mary Magdalen (1566)	Cornelis Cort			
Diana Discovering Callisto's Pregnancy (1566)	Cornelis Cort			
Prometheus Enchained on Mount Caucasus (1566)	Cornelis Cort			
Rape of Lucretia (1571)	Cornelis Cort			
Martyrdom of St. Lawrence (1571)	Cornelis Cort			
Cyclops Forging the Arms of Brescia (1572)	?			

Description	Engraver	Date	Publisher	Place
book: *Compendion . . . leggiardramente scrivere*	?	1566?	Dorico heirs?	Vatican
book: *L'architettura*	?	1567	Pietro Cataneo	Venice Senate
book: Vitruvius *I dieci libri dell'architettura* woodcuts	Giovanni Chrieger	1567	F. de' Franceschi	Venice Senate
book: "trattato delli edificij fatti da Papa Pio, iiii. composto da Pirro Ligorio"	?	1567	Michele Tramezzino	Venice Senate
• print of family tree of the principal Ottoman Turks	Nicolo Nelli	1567?	Nicolo Nelli (?)	Venice Senate
• Navicella	Mario Labacco	1567?	?	Vatican
• Battle of Hannibal and Scipio	Cornelis Cort	1567?	Antonio Lafrery (?)	Vatican
• Campidoglio	Stefano Dupérac	1567?	Bartolomeo Faletti?	Vatican
• Porticus et Palatii Capitolini	Stefano Dupérac			
• Areae Capitolinae	Stefano Dupérac			
• Areae et Palatii Pontificii Vaticani.	Stefano Dupérac			
• S. Maria di Loreto – plan	G. B. de' Cavalieri	1567	G. B. de' Cavalieri	Vatican

TITLE	ENGRAVER	DATE	PRIV. HOLDER	AUTHORITY
• Santa Casa – west (1567)	G. B. de' Cavalieri	1567?	P. Zecchini Guarlotti?	Vatican
• Santa Casa – east (1567)	G. B. de' Cavalieri			
• Santa Casa – north (1567)	G. B. de' Cavalieri			
• Santa Casa – south (1568)	G. B. de' Cavalieri			
• Madonna di Loreto (1569)	G. B. de' Cavalieri			
• Visitation (1567)	?	1567	G. F. Camocio	Venice Senate
• Resurrection (1569)	Martino Rota	1568		
• Virgin at the Foot of the Cross (?)	Martino Rota			
• map of Europe *brevis* (1568)	Domenico Zenoi			
• map of Europe *piccola* (1568)	Domenico Zenoi			
• map of Morea (1569)	?			
• map of Istria (1570)	?			
• Attilius Regulus in the Barrel (1570)	G. B. Scultori (?)			
• mappamondo	Marco' Antonio Giustignan	1568	Marc' Antonio Giustignan	Venice Senate
book: Serlio *De architectura*	?	1568	F. de' Franceschi	Venice Senate
• "pictoris aulici Austriacæ gentis imaginum pars prima"	Francesco Terzi da Bergamo	1568	Francesco Terzi da Bergamo	Venice Senate

Subject	Engraver	Date	Publisher	Granting authority
book: *Disegni delle più illustri città et fortezze del mondo* frontispiece	?	1569	Giulio Ballino	Venice Senate
"li dissegni suoi novi"	Nicolo Nelli	1569	Nicolo Nelli	Venice Senate
• Allegory of the Battle of Lepanto 1572	?			
• Madonna and Child with Sts. Anne & Catherine 1574	?			
book: antique busts	?	1569	Antonio Lafrery?	Vatican
book: Column of Trajan	Lorenzo de Rozoli Leonardo	1569	Girolamo Muziano	Vatican
• Finding of the True Cross	G. B. de' Cavalieri	1569?	G. B. de' Cavalieri?	Vatican
book: Palladio *I quattro libri dell'architettura*	?	1570	D. de' Franceschi	Venice Senate
• map of Cyprus	?	1570?	G. F. Camocio	Venice Senate
book: *Il Perfetto Scrittore*	?	1570?	G. F. Cresci	Vatican
• Annunciation with Four Prophets	Cornelis Cort	1571	Antonio Lafrery?	Vatican
• Creation of Eve	Cornelis Cort	1572?	G. B. de' Cavalieri?	Vatican

TITLE	ENGRAVER	DATE	PRIV. HOLDER	AUTHORITY
• Penitent St. Jerome (1573)	Cornelis Cort	1573?	Girolamo Muziano?	Vatican
• St. Jerome Translating (1573)	Cornelis Cort			
• Penitent Mary Magdalen (1573)	Cornelis Cort			
• Penitent St. Onuphrius (1574)	Cornelis Cort			
• St. John the Baptist (1574/5)	Cornelis Cort			
• St. Eustace and Stag (1575)	Cornelis Cort			
• Penitent St. Francis (1575)	Cornelis Cort			
• God the Father supporting the Dead Christ (1573)	Cherubino Alberti	1573?	Cherubino Alberti?	Vatican
• Flagellation (1574)	Cherubino Alberti			
• Agony in the Garden (1574)	Cherubino Alberti			
• Adoration of Shepherds (1575)	Cherubino Alberti			
• Conversion of St. Paul (1575)	Cherubino Alberti			
• Penitent St. Jerome (1575)	Cherubino Alberti			
• Tabernacle (1575)	Cherubino Alberti			
book: Palladio *I Commentarii de C. Giulio Cesare*	?	1575	Andrea Palladio	Venice Senate
• Portrait of Giovanni Parisotto	Martino Rota	1575	Antonio Lafrery?	Vatican
• Christ and the Adultress	Diana Mantuana	1575	Diana Mantuana	Vatican
• Preparations for the Wedding of Cupid and Psyche	Diana Mantuana			

Subject	Engraver	Date	Publisher	Location
• Procession of Horsemen in the Triumph of Caesar	Diana Mantuana			
• Nativity	Diana Mantuana			
• St. Jerome	Diana Mantuana			
• Sacrifice of Abraham	Diana Mantuana			
• Madonna and Child with the Young John the Baptist	Diana Mantuana			
• Christ and Mary Magdalene at the Table of Simon the Pharisee (1576)				
• Holy Family in Egypt (1577)	Diana Mantuana			
• Sancta Roma (1575)	Diana Mantuana			
• Piazza di San Pietro (1575)	G. B. de' Cavalieri	1575?	G. B. de' Cavalieri?	Vatican
book: *I Vestigi dell'Antichità di Roma*	Stefano Dupérac	1575	Lorenzo Vaccari?	Vatican
• a. Stoning of St. Stephen "forma prima" (1576)	Cornelis Cort	1576?	P. P. Palumbo?	Vatican
• b. Stoning of St. Stephen "forma secunda" (1577)	Cornelis Cort			
• a. Last Supper "forma prima" (1578)	Cornelis Cort			
• b. Last Supper "forma secunda" (1580)	Cornelis Cort			
• St. George Killing the Dragon (1578)	Cornelis Cort			
• Birth of the Virgin (1578?)	Cornelis Cort			

TITLE	ENGRAVER	DATE	PRIV. HOLDER	AUTHORITY
• map of Modern Rome (1576) • map of Italy (1577) • map of Antique Rome (1579)	Mario Cartari (?) Mario Cartari Mario Cartari	1576?	Mario Cartari (?)	Vatican
• St. Jerome in the Desert with Two Angels (1577) • Coronation of the Virgin with the Martyrdom of St. Lawrence and Other Saints (1577)	Cornelis Cort Cornelis Cort	1577?	Lorenzo Vaccari?	Vatican
• "figuras sanctorumque imagines et similia"	L. Caccianemici	1577	L. Caccianemici	Vatican
book: *Familiae romanae* plates	Mario Cartari	1577?	heirs F. Tramezzino?	Vatican
book: *Il Perfetto Cancellaresco Corsivo . . . Liber Terzo*	?	1579	G. F. Cresci	Vatican
• Holy Family with a Cat	Cornelis Cort	1579	Anthonie van Santfoort	Vatican
• Body of St. Jerome Supported by Angels • Annunciation • St. Lawrence	Cornelis Cort Cornelis Cort Cornelis Cort			

• map of Perugia • Baths of Diocletian	Mario Cartari (?) Mario Cartari (?)	1580	Mario Cartari (?)	1. Vatican 2. Duke Tuscany
• Youth of Christ	Jan Sadeler	1580	Jan Sadeler	Imperial
book: *Il Secretario* (1581)	?	1580	Marcello Scalzini	1. Vatican 2. Venice Senate
book: *Pontificum romanorum effigies*	G. B. de' Cavalieri	1580	Domenico Basa?	Vatican
• Il Perdono d'Assisi	Federico Barrocci	1581	Federico Barrocci	Vatican
• I Veri Ritratti della guerra, & dell'assedio . . . alla Isola di Malta	Pietro Perret (?)	1582	Matteo Perez	Vatican
• Martyrdom of St. Catherine (1583) (?)	Pietro Perret			
• Adam and Eve (?)	?			
• Conversion of St. Paul (1583)	Pietro Perret			
book: *Omnium Imperatorum*	A. Brambilla	1582	Claudio Duchetti	Vatican
book: *Omnium Pontificum*	A. Brambilla			
• Martyrdom of S. Giustina	Paolo Veronese	1582	Luca Bertelli	Venice Senate
• Madonna and Child with Sts Elizabeth and John (1582)	Cherubino Alberti	1582?	Cherubino Alberti?	Vatican

TITLE	ENGRAVER	DATE	PRIV. HOLDER	AUTHORITY
• Pietà (?) • Madonna of the Rosary (?) • Resurrection (?)	Cherubino Alberti Cherubino Alberti Cherubino Alberti	?		
book: *Romanorum Imperatorum Effigies* (?)	G. B. de' Cavalieri	1584	G. B. de' Cavalieri	Vatican
book: *Ecclesiae anglicanae trophea*	G. B. de' Cavalieri			
book: *Ecclesiae militantis triumphi* (1585)	G. B. de' Cavalieri			
book: "monsters" (1585)	G. B. de' Cavalieri			
• San Lorenzo de El Escorial	Pieter Perret	1584	Juan de Herrera	1. Cámera de Castilla Madrid (1583) 2. Council of the Indies (1584) 3. Vatican (1584) 4. Venice Senate 5. Imperial 6. King of France
book: *Antiquitates Puteolorum*	Mario Cartari	1584	Bartolomeo Grassi	Vatican

book: *Icones . . . misericordiae*	Cristofano Cartari and Mario Cartari			
book: *Delle allusioni, imprese, et emblemi . . . * (1588)	Natale Bonifacio	1585	Bartolomeo Grassi	Vatican
• Marriage of Isaac and Rebecca (1585) • St. Paul First Hermit (1585)	Aliprando Capriolo / P. Thomassin	1585?	Bernardino Passari?	Vatican
• Piazza S. Marco, Venice	L. Pozzoserrato	1585	L. Pozzoserrato	Venice Senate
• Cardinal Carlo Borromeo	Agostino Carracci	1585?	?	1. Venice Senate 2. King of Spain
• lowering the Vatican obelisk • moving the Vatican obelisk • erection of the Vatican obelisk • consecration of the Vatican obelisk (1587)	Natale Bonifacio / Natale Bonifacio / Natale Bonifacio / Natale Bonifacio	1586?	Giovanni Guerra? / Bartolomeo Grassi?	Vatican
book: *Regole per imparar a disegnar i corpi humani*	Giacomo Franco?	1586?	Giacomo Franco?	Venice Senate
book: *Le cose maravigliose dell'alma città di Roma*	?	1587	Girolamo Francini	Vatican
book: *Il Primo Libro delli Essempi*	Martin van Buyten	1587	Simone Verovio?	Vatican

TITLE	ENGRAVER	DATE	PRIV. HOLDER	AUTHORITY
book: *Statues of the Order of St. John of Malta*	Philippe Thomassin	1588	Tolomeo Veltronio	Vatican
• Column of Marcus Aurelius	A. Brambilla	1588	Nicolaus van Aelst	Vatican
• Column of Trajan	A. Brambilla			
• Obelisk, S. Gio. Laterano	A. Brambilla			
• Obelisk, S. M. Maggiore	A. Brambilla?			
• Obelisk, S. M. del Popolo	A. Brambilla			
• Acqua Felice	A. Brambilla?			
• Seven Churches of Rome	A. Brambilla?			
• Façade of the Gesù	A. Brambilla?			
• "Iconas Principium Apostolorum de Urbe"	A. Brambilla (A. Brambilla?)			
• Sixtus V before a crucifix with King Henry III of France	Philippe Thomassin	1588?	?	Vatican
• Vision of St. Catherine of Siena (1588)	F. Villamena	1588?	?	Vatican
book: *L'Anatomia delle Cancellaresche corsive* frontispiece	Martin van Buyten	1588	Lodovico Curione?	Vatican
• S. Anthony of Padua (1588)	P. Thomassin	1588?	Thomassin & Turpin	Vatican
• St. Mary of Egypt (1588)	P. Thomassin			
• Holy Family (1589)	P. Thomassin			

• St. Margaret (1589)	P. Thomassin			
• Four Martyrs (1589)	P. Thomassin			
• S. Maria Maggiore (1589)	P. Thomassin			
• Rest of Return from Egypt	P. Thomassin			
• Jesus Christ	P. Thomassin			
• Virgin Mary	P. Thomassin			
• Entombment	P. Thomassin			
book: *Il Primo Libro di Scrivere*	?	1589	Giacomo Romano	Vatican
• King Alfonso Expelling the Moors from Spain (1589)	F. Villamena	1589?	T. Moneta?	Vatican
book: *Della trasportatione dell'obelisco Vaticano* (1590)	Natale Bonifacio	1589?	Domenico Basa?	Vatican
book: *De Basilicae Vaticanae* plan	Natale Bonifacio	1589	Tiberio Alfarani	Vatican
• Annunciation	P. Thomassin	1589	Thomassin & Turpin	Vatican
• Flagellation	P. Thomassin			
• Adoration of the Shepherds	P. Thomassin			
• Virgin of the Rosary	P. Thomassin			
• Assumption	P. Thomassin			
• S. M. del Popolo (1592)	P. Thomassin			
• St. Sebastian	P. Thomassin			
• Wedding Feast at Cana (1592)	P. Thomassin			
• Baptism (1592)	P. Thomassin			

TITLE	ENGRAVER	DATE	PRIV. HOLDER	AUTHORITY
• Christ after the Flagellation (1596)	P. Thomassin			
• Holy Family (1597)	P. Thomassin			
• Madonna and Child (1597)	P. Thomassin			
• Conversion of St. Paul (1597)	P. Thomassin			
• St. Augustine (1597)	P. Thomassin			
• Rosaries (1598)	P. Thomassin			
• Martyrdom of St. Apollonia (1598)	P. Thomassin			
• God supporting the Dead Christ (159?)	P. Thomassin			
• Adoration of the Magi (1599)	P. Thomassin			
book: *Della architettura di Gio. Antonio Rusconi*	?	1590	G. & G. P. Giolito	Venice Senate
book: *Degli Habiti antichi et moderni . . . del mondo*	Cristoforo Guerra	1590	Cesare Vecellio	1. Venice Senate 2. Vatican
• La città di Venetia . . .	Cesare Vecellio?			
book: *Corona delle nobili et virtuosi donne* (1591)	Cesare Vecellio	1591	Cesare Vecellio	Venice Senate
. . . *Libro Quarto* (1593)				
. . . *Libro Quinto* (1596)				
book: *Habiti d'huomeni et donne venetiane*	Giacomo Franco	1591	Giacomo Franco	Venice Senate

• map of Rome	Antonio Tempesta	1593	Antonio Tempesta	Vatican
• Sylva Sacrae • 4 European Countries (undated) • Four Seasons (undated) • "Kitchens of Sadeler" (1598)	J. and R. Sadeler J. and R. Sadeler J. and R. Sadeler J. and R. Sadeler	1593	Jan & Raphael Sadeler	Imperial
book: *Il Teatro delle Cancellaresche corsive* frontispiece	Martin van Buyten	1593	Lodovico Curione?	Vatican
new method for printing plain chant		1593	Leonardo Parasole & Fulgentio Valesino	Vatican
book: *Antiquarum Statuarum*	G. B. de' Cavalieri	1594?	?	Vatican
• Marriage Feast at Cana	Andrea Vicentino	1594	Andrea Vicentino	Venice Senate
book: *Pontificale Romanum* illustrations	Villamena, Grafico, Lauro	1596	Leonardo Parasole	Vatican
• Miraculous Virgin of Treviso book: *Del Franco Modo di Scriver Cancellaresco moderno* book: *Nuova inventione diverse mostre cosi del punto in aere*	Giacomo Franco Giacomo Franco Giacomo Franco	1596	Giacomo Franco	Venice Senate
book: *Centum Armorum Duces*	Aliprando Capriolo	1596	Aliprando Caprioli	Vatican
• Gardens of Villa Lante	Tarquinio Ligustri	1596	Tarquinio Ligustri	Vatican

TITLE	ENGRAVER	DATE	PRIV. HOLDER	AUTHORITY
unnamed prints of religious subjects	1596		Francesco Villamena	Vatican
• Moses and the Brazen Serpent (1597)	F. Villamena			
• St. Francis with a Vision of the Madonna and Child (1597)	F. Villamena			
• Stigmatization of St. Francis (1597)	F. Villamena			
• Rest on the Return from Egypt (1597)	F. Villamena			
• Presentation in the Temple	F. Villamena			
• Annunciation (1598)	F. Villamena			
• Portrait Clement VIII (1599)	F. Villamena			
• "Carta di Gloria"	Martin van Buyten	1598	Marc' Antonio Rossi	Vatican
"diversas hystorias et figuras"	?	1598	J., R., and A. Sadeler	Vatican
• Trophaeum Vitae Solitariae (1598)	J. and R. Sadeler			
• Oraculum Anachoreticum (1600)	J. and R. Sadeler			
• Portrait of Clement VIII	Jan Sadeler			
• Adoration of the Magi (1598)	Raphael Sadeler			1. Vatican
• Adoration of the Shepherds (1599)	Jan Sadeler			2. Imperial
• Virgin and Child with Saint Catherine of Siena (1599)	Raphael Sadeler			

Subject	Engraver	Date	Publisher	Place
• St. Francis (1599)	Raphael Sadeler			
• Holy Family (1601)	Raphael Sadeler			
• St. Agnes (1601)	Raphael Sadeler			
• The Little Milkmaid (1601)	Raphael Sadeler			
• Charles Borromeo (1604)	Raphael Sadeler			
• Emperor Rudolf II	Aegidius Sadeler			
• Three Marys at the Tomb (1600)	Aegidius Sadeler			
• Virgin and Child	Justus Sadeler			
• Holy Family in Egypt	Justus Sadeler			
• "unnamed engravings of religious subjects"	Jacopo Lauro	1598	Jacopo Lauro	Vatican
• Seven Churches of Rome (1599) book: *Giardino dei Scrittori*	P. Thomassin			
"stampe . . . d'ogni sorte"	?	1599	Marc' Antonio Rossi	Vatican
• "Sancta Maria a Sucurso" (1599)	F. Villamena			
book: *Ritratti di Cento Capitani Illustri* (1600)	Aliprando Capriolo	1599	Gio. Antonio di Paolo	Vatican
• *Articoli del Credo* (1599)	Aliprando Capriolo	1599	Philippe Thomassin	Vatican
• Marriage of Isaac and Rebecca	Aliprando Capriolo			
• Alexander the Great (1600)	F. Villamena			
• plan of Valletta (1600)	F. Villamena	1600?	Francesco Villamena?	Vatican
• Penitent St. Jerome (1600)	F. Villamena			
• Crucifixion (1600)	F. Villamena			
• St. Longinus relic (1600)	F. Villamena			
• Seven Churches of Rome (1600)	F. Villamena			
• Barruffa defending himself (1601)	F. Villamena			

TITLE	ENGRAVER	DATE	PRIV. HOLDER	AUTHORITY
• Madonna and Child with Saints (1602)	F. Villamena			
• King David (1603)	F. Villamena			
book: *Caeremoniale episcopum*	?	1600	Leonardo Parasole	Vatican
book: *Directorium chori*	?	1602	Marc' Antonio Rossi	Vatican
book: "Emperors"	?	1603	Domenico Falcini	Vatican
(unnamed prints) • Portrait of Leo XI (1605) • S. Gio. in Laterano (?)	Matteo Greuter Paolo Maupino	1604	Matteo Greuter	Vatican
• "Emperors"	Leonardo Parasole	1605	Leonardo Parasole	Vatican
book: *Sacro Monte della Vernia* (frontispiece)	Domenico Falcini	1612	?	Vatican
book: *Antiquae Urbis Splendoris* (1612)	Jacopo Lauro	1612?	Jacopo Lauro	Vatican
• Emperor Matthias (1612)	?	1612?	Gio. Antonio di Paoli?	Vatican
• Gardens of Ciriaco Mattei on Monte Celio (1614)	Jacopo Lauro	1614?	Jacopo Lauro	Vatican

	Cherubino Alberti	1628	Lattantio Pichi	Vatican
• Flagellation	Cherubino Alberti			
• Tabernacle	Cherubino Alberti			
• Madonna and Child with Sts. Elizabeth and John	Cherubino Alberti			
• Resurrection	Cherubino Alberti			
• Agony in the Garden	Cherubino Alberti			
• The Cumaean Sibyl	Cherubino Alberti			
• Perseus Changing Atlas	Cherubino Alberti			
• Winged Genius	Cherubino Alberti			
• Triumph of Two Emperors	Cherubino Alberti			
• Antique Vases	Cherubino Alberti			
• Renown Sounding Trumpet	Cherubino Alberti			
• Expulsion of Adam and Eve	Cherubino Alberti			
• Adam & Eve after Expulsion	Cherubino Alberti			
• Sacrifice of Isaac	Cherubino Alberti			
• Prometheus	Cherubino Alberti			
• Venus Ascending Olympus and Venus and Jupiter	Cherubino Alberti			
• Three Graces; Venus with Juno and Ceres	Cherubino Alberti			
• Winged Genius on Cloud	Cherubino Alberti			
• Lybian Sibyl & Prophet Daniel	Cherubino Alberti			
• Prophet Isaiah	Cherubino Alberti			
• Prophet Ezekiel	Cherubino Alberti			
• Adoration of the Magi	Cherubino Alberti			
• Angel Supporting Dead Christ	Cherubino Alberti			
• Tobias and Virgin and Child	Cherubino Alberti			

COPYRIGHT ELSEWHERE IN ITALY AND EUROPE

Besides Venice and Rome, copyright in various forms was available in other locations in Italy as well as elsewhere in Europe, where it was granted by a variety of municipal, ducal, regal, imperial, princely, and religious authorities. The following brief survey focuses mostly on instances when the *privilegio* was first granted in each respective location.

Italy

In Italy in the early years of the sixteenth century privileges mostly for the printing of books could be had in various cities. In Naples, a *privilegio* was granted by King Ferdinand on 22 August 1489 to the printer Giovan Marco Cinico from Parma for an edition of Roberto Caracciolo's *Sermones de laudibus sanctorum*. The book, printed in Naples with the title *Celeberrimum opus de laudibus sancto[rum]* by Cinico's associate Mattia Moravo [Mathias Morauum], carries no notice of the *privilegio*. The *privilegio* remained in effect until Cinico had sold all the two thousand copies of the book.[1]

In 1505 a two-year *privilegio* was granted by the officials of the city of Siena to the Compagnia de S. Caterina for the publication of Giovanni Pollio's *Opera della diva, & seraphica Catharina da Siena*. The book was dedicated to Giovanni Piccolomini, archbishop of Siena, and printed in Siena the same year by Antonina (the widow of the German printer Enrico da Colonia) and Andrea Piasentino.[2] Eight years later, in 1513, the "cartaio" printer Simone di Nicolò

---

[1] The *privilegio* is noted in Mariano Fava and Giovanni Bresciano, *La stampa a Napoli nel xv secolo* (Leipzig, 1911), 74, no. 139, and doc. 19.

[2] The book is discussed in Mortimer, *Italian 16th Century Books*, no. 392. In the same year, Antonina and Piasentino also printed *Rime, strambotti, capitoli, sonetti ecc., intorno a Santa Caterina da Siena di Giovanni Scappoli d'Arezzo detto il Pollastrino*, which is inscribed: "Impresso in Siena per donna Antonina di maestro Enrigh da Colonia et Andrea Piasentino."

di Nardo (Symion Nicolai Nardi, also called Il Rosso) petitioned the Sienese Balìa for a ten-year *privilegio* that would grant him not only the exclusive right to print in Siena but would also prohibit the sale in the city of any book not printed by him.[3] The Balìa did not concede his full request, but did license him to print books in Siena for ten years with a *privilegio* that applied to editions of over eight hundred.[4] Notice of that *privilegio* first appears on an edition of Angelo Poliziano's *Stanze*, printed, "Cum Gratia & Privilegio," in Siena "per Symione di Niccolo: et Giovanni di Alexandro Librai," dated 9 February 1513 [o.s. 1512].[5]

In Genoa, the printer Francesco de Silva from Turin was granted a monopolistic *privilegio* in 1506 (renewed in 1512) by the Governor and Commune of the city.[6] A similar *privilegio* was granted by the Municipality of Rimini on 19 January 1511 to the printer Nicolò Brenta to print in that city.[7] The *privilegio*, granted to "Nicolaus q[uondam] Jac[obo] Brenta de Varenna diocesis Mediolani librorum impressor, qui ex Venetiis dicit se recessurum et huc venturum ad imprimendum libros," was for fifteen years. On 26 February, a month after the *privilegio* was granted, the concession of a rent-free house to Brenta was changed to giving him instead ten ducats a year and the freedom to choose his own accomodations.[8]

In Florence, two printers, Giovanbernardo di Salvestro and Giovanbattista di Cristofano Ottonaio, a priest, were granted a six-year *privilegio* to print music books.[9] In 1518, the "Priori di Liberta &

---

[3] Nardo's petition is transcribed in Fabio Jacometti, "Il primo stampatore senese: Simone di Niccolò di Nardo," *La Diana* 1 (1926): 187 and 190, doc. 3.

[4] The document is transcribed in Jacometti, 187 and 190, doc. 4.

[5] In 1517, Nardo also printed Eurialo Morano's *Epigrammatum libri duo* with a *privilegio*. Editions of books printed by Nardo with a *privilegio* in the 1520s and early 1530s are noted in Jacometti, 199–202.

[6] Noted in Norton, *Italian Printers*, xxiv–xxv. Rudolf Hirsch, *Printing, Selling and Reading*, 79, also notes a fifteenth century example of Clemente Donati who attempted to obtain in 1470 the monopolistic *privilegio* to print in Ferrara.

[7] Nicolò Brenta from Varenna had earlier received several Venetian privileges when he worked Venice. On 19 August 1501, for example, he was granted a *privilegio* for two books (ASV, CN, reg. 15, fol. 44r. [46r. n.n.]). The following year, he formed a partnership with the printer Jacopo Pencio da Lecco (Jacobus Pentius de Leuco) and together they were granted a *privilegio* on 22 June 1502 (ASV, CN, reg. 15, fol. 73r. [75r. n.n.]). A month later, on 16 July, Brenta alone was granted another *privilegio* (ASV, CN, reg. 15, fol. 74r. [76r. n.n.]).

[8] The documents are reproduced in Vittorio Adami, "Nicolò Brenta da Varenna, stampatore," *La Bibliofilia* 25 (1923): 195–96.

[9] Noted in Giuseppe Fumagalli, *Lexicon typographicum Italiae: dictionnaire géographique d'Italie* (Florence, 1905), 143.

Gonfaloniere di Iustitia del Popolo Fiorentino" granted a three-year *privilegio* to Dante Popoleschi for a translation of Caesar, printed the same year by Gian Stephano di Carlo da Pavia (Johannes Stephanus Papiensis).[10] Later, beginning with Cosimo I de' Medici, a ducal *privilegio* was available in Florence.[11] Like many other granting authorities, it was reserved almost exclusively for books. In a few instances, however, it was granted for prints, such as Eufrosino della Volpaia's map of *Rome* (1547), Enea Vico's *Lineage of the Twelve Caesars* (1553), and Mario Cartari's map of *Perugia* and *Baths of Diocletian* (both 1580) (see Chapters 8 and 10). Privileges were also granted by the duke of Ferrara and the duchess of Mantua.

In Milan, with the support of the Milanese ambassador to Venice, Gerardo de' Colli, a five-year monopolistic *privilegio* was granted to Antonio Planella in 1470 to encourage printing within the duchy.[12] On 6 June 1481, a six-year *privilegio* was granted by the duke of Milan to the publisher Antonio Zaroto and his associates for Johannes Simonetta's book *Rerum gestarum Francisci Sfortiae*.[13] The *privilegio* imposed a fine of two hundred ducats against all transgressors. Three years later, in 1484, the duke granted a five-year *privilegio* to Petro Justino da Tolentino for Francesco Filelfo's *Convivio* and other works by Filelfo. The book, *Francisci Philelfi ad Thomam Thebaldum Mediolanense conuiuium primum-[secundum]*, was published in Milan the same year by Simon Magniagus. On 10 March 1488, Galeazzo Maria Sforza granted Bettino da Trezzo a *privilegio* to print the *Letilogia*, and on 26 February 1492 Donato Bossi (Donatus Bossius) received a ten-year *privilegio* for his *Chronica mediolanensi*, which was printed for the author by Antonio Zaroto on 1 March the same year.[14]

---

[10] Norton, xxix.

[11] See Berta Biagiarelli, "Il Privilegio di Stampatore Ducale nella Firenze Medicea," *Archivio storico italiano* 122 (1965): 304–70.

[12] Notice of the *privilegio* first appears in the postscript of a diplomatic letter dated 30 April 1470. The following May 10 the matter came before the Consiglio in Milan, and on September 7, a *privilegio* was granted to Planella by Duke Galeazzo Maria Sforza. The documents are included in Emilio Motta, "Pamfilo Castaldi, Antonio Planella, Pietro Ugleimer e il vescovo d'Aleria," *Rivista storica italiana* 9 (1884): 254–257, and 269, docs. 9 and 10. Planella, however, appears to have printed nothing in Milan.

[13] Noted in Arnaldo Ganda, "Antonio Zarotto da Parma tipografo in Milano (1471–1507)," *La Bibliofilia* 77 (1975): 204. The document is transcribed in Emilio Motta, "Di Filippo di Lavagna e di alcuni altri tipografi-editori milanesi," *Archivio storico lombardo* serie 3, vol. 10 (1898): 67–68, doc. 12.

[14] These privileges are noted in Ganda, 1975, 204–205. Bossi's *privilegio* is transcribed in Motta, 68–70, doc. 13.

Following the French invasion of Northern Italy and assumption of the title duke of Milan by Charles VIII in 1494, privileges in Milan and its territories were thereafter granted by the King of France. The humanist editor Aulus Janus Parrhasius, for example, was granted a French *privilegio* for two works edited by him which were printed in Milan by Guillermo Le Signerre and his brother in 1501. Similarly, a *privilegio* granted by Louis XII on 14 May 1511 is noted in Zaccaria Ferreri's edition of the *Acta* of the Council of Constance printed in Milan by Gottardo da Ponte on 21–29 June 1511.[15] In 1520, Andrea Calvo was granted a six-year royal *privilegio* for an edition of Boccaccio's *Ameto*, printed by Alexander Minutianus.[16]

Besides the French royal *privilegio* granted by Francis I as the duke of Milan, Calvo was also granted a five-year papal *privilegio* by Leo X on 1 June 1520.[17] In 1522 the *privilegio* appears in an edition of Hippolytus de Marsiliis's *Brassae* printed in Milan by Giovanni Angelo Scinzenzeler for the De Lignano brothers.[18] The French *privilegio* also extended to nearby Pavia where it appears, for example, on Michele (Giovanni Michele) Savonarola's *De gotta la preseruatione e cura* printed in 1507 [1505?] by Giacomo Pocatela (Jacob de Paucisdrapis de Burgofranco), and on a book by Leonardus Legius printed by Bernardino Garaldi (Bernardinus de Garaldis) in 1522.[19] Later, the French royal *privilegio* is also found on books printed outside the Duchy of Milan.

Besides the King of France, publishers in Italy also acquired priv-

---

[15] The book is listed in Mortimer, *Italian 16th Century Books*, no. 134.

[16] Calvo's *privilegio* is noted in Norton, xxviii–xxix; Giovanni Mercati, "Su Francesco Calvo da Menaggio primo stampatore e Marco Fabio Calvo da Ravenna primo traduttore latino del corpo Ippocratico," *Notizie varie di antica letteratura medica e di bibliografia* (Studi e Testi, 31) (1917): 62, n. 1; *Mostra dei manoscritti, documenti ed edizioni* (VI Centenario della morte di Giovanni Boccaccio). Vol. 2: *Edizioni*, eds Fabia Borroni Salvadori and P. Innocenti (Certaldo, 1975), 63, no. 53; and in Elizabeth Armstrong, *Before Copyright: The French Book-Privilege System 1498–1526* (Cambridge, 1990), 6. Salvatore Bongi, *Annali di Gabriel Giolito de' Ferrari da Trino di Monferrato stampatore in Venezia*, (Rome, 1890), 1: 256, notes another edition published at Andrea Calvo's expense by Zanotto da Castiglione in Milan on 10 February 1521. The 1520 edition, entitled *Ameto di Messere Giovanni Boccaccio: Con le osservationi in uolgare gra[m]matica sopra esso di Hieronimo Claricioi*, is inscribed: "IMPRESSO IN MILANO/nella officina Minutiana/a ispesa di Andrea Calvo/a Di.X.de Giugnio.M.D.XX."

[17] Noted in Armstrong, *Before Copyright*, 12.

[18] Hippolytus de Marsiliis's *Brassae* is catalogued in Mortimer, *Italian 16th Century Books*, no. 288.

[19] The *privilegio* for *De gotta la preseruatione e cura* is noted by Norton, xxix. Legius's book is catalogued in Mortimer, *Italian 16th Century Books*, no. 252.

ileges from other foreign authorities. An imperial *privilegio*, granted by emperor Charles V (usually referred to in inscriptions as "la Cesarea Maesta" and "Caesarae Maiestatis"), and later Maximilian II, appears on books and prints published in Italy. Privileges granted by the King of Spain, beginning with Philip II, also appear on books and some prints published in Italy. Agostino Carracci's engraved portrait of Cardinal Carlo Borromeo (after Francesco Terzi), dated 1585, carries both a Venetian *privilegio* and one granted by the Spanish king.[20]

In various combinations, one or more of these authorities, both Italian and foreign, might appear listed on a title-page. An edition of Gaspare Tagliacozzi's *De curtorum chirurgia per insitionem, libro dvo*, for example, published in Venice by Gaspare Bindoni in 1597 was printed "Cum Priuilegijs Summi Pontificis, Caesarae Maiestatis, Christianissimi Regis Galliae, Regis Hispaniarum, Senatus Veneti, & aliorum Principum."[21] These authorities, of course, also granted privileges in their own countries (and in other countries besides Italy).

Spain

One the earliest privileges granted in Spain would appear to be that issued in 1498 for Juliáno Gutiérrez's *Cura de la piedra y dolor de la yjada y colica rrenal* [sic] printed in Toledo by Pedro Hagenbach at the expense of Melchor Gorricio.[22] The title-page woodcut shows Saints Cosmas and Damian. On 21 May 1499, the bookseller ("librero") Fernando de Jaen published *Leyes hechas por la brevedad y orden de los*

---

[20] The print is listed in Bartsch, 18: 111, no. 138; and in Diane DeGrazia Bohlin, *Prints and Related Drawings by the Carracci Family* (Washington, D.C., 1979), cat. no. 132. The print is inscribed: "CON PRIVILEGIO DI S. S.^{TA} [E]T DEL RE CATH.^{CO} ET DELLA SIG.^{RIA} DI VINETIA CHE PER ANI XII NON SI POSSA/RISTAMPAR IN MODO ALCVNO. MDLXXXV." Borromeo died in 1584. For a *privilegio* granted to Francesco Terzi in 1568, see Chapter 9.

[21] Tagliacozzi's book is catalogued in Mortimer, *Italian 16th Century Books*, no. 488.

[22] Noted in Konrad Haebler, *The Early Printers of Spain and Portugal* (London, 1897), 136; idem, *Spanische und Portugiesische Bücherzeichen des XV. und XVI. Jahrhunderts* (Strassburg, 1898), 9, no. 8; and idem, *Bibliografía ibérica del siglo xv. Enumeración de todos los libros impresos en España y Portugal hasta el año de 1500* (The Hague, 1903), 2: 86, no. 315. The *privilegio* reads: "Este libro fue taxado por los del muy alto consejo de sus altezas: por precio de setenta & cinco maravedis con privilegio que ninguno lo pueda imprimir ni vender so las penas en el contenidas."

pleitos with a *privilegio*. The same book was also issued with a *privilegio*, granted to "maestre Pedro, imprimidor de libros de molde," and printed in Burgos by Fadrique de Basilea. "Maestro Pedro" has been identified as Pierre Brun, a printer who worked in Seville.[23] In 1500, a *privilegio* was granted by Ferdinand V and Isabella of Spain to Garcia de la Torre and Alonso Lorenzo for *Capitulos bechos por el rey y la reyna nuestros señores en los quales se co[n]tienen las casas q[ue] lan de quar dan y co[m]plin los qouernadores*, which was printed in Seville by Juan Pegnitzer (Joannes Pegniczer de Nuremberga) and Magno Herbst. The *privilegio* was granted for three years, and required that the work be sold for sixteen *maravidis*:[24]

> Por quanto maestre Garcia de la torre librero vezino de toledo é Alonso lorenço librero vezino de seuilla se obligaro de dar los dichos capitulos a precio de xvi mrs: manda su alteza: é los del su muy alto consejo q ninguno no sea osado delos emprimer ni vender en todos sus reynos é señorios desde el dia dela fecha destos capitulos fasta tres años primeros siguientes sin licencia d'los dichos maestre garcia de la torre é alonso lorenço libreros: so pena q el que los emprimiere vendiere sin licencia pague diez mill marauedis para la camara de sus altezas.

The *privilegio* also appears on the same work printed at the same time in Salamanca by Juan de Porras.

Portugal

In Portugal, a royal *privilegio* was granted in 1501 to the printer Valentin (or Valentym) Fernandes for a *Glosa sobre las coplas de Jorge Manrique*. A notice of copyright also appears in a translation of Marco Polo, *Marco Paulo. Ho liuro de Nycolao veneto. O trallado da carta de huu[m] genoues das ditas terras*, printed in Lisbon by Fernandes in 1502, and on two more books printed in 1504.[25] The translation of Marco Polo includes the statement: "With the privilege of our lord the king that

---

[23] Haebler, *Early Printers of Spain and Portugal*, 18.

[24] The *privilegio* is noted in Haebler, *Early Printers of Spain and Portugal*, 95; idem, *Bibliografía ibérica del siglo xv*, 1: 52, no. 117; and Hirsch, *Printing, Selling and Reading*, 85.

[25] Noted in Jorge Peizoto, "Os privilégios de impressão dos livros em Portugal no sécolo XVI," *Gutenberg-Jahrbuch* (1966): 265–72. The colophon of the Marco Polo book reads: "Imprimido per Valentym Ferna[n]dez alemaão. Em a muy nobre çidade [de] Lyxboa. Era de Mil [e] quinhentos [e] dous annos. Aos quatro dias do mas de feureyro."

none should print this book nor sell it in all his realms and lord-
ships without leave of Valentim Fernandes on pain of the penalties
contained in the grant of his privilege, the price is 110 *rais*."[26]

Germany

In Germany a monopolistic *privilegio* was granted on 20 September
1479 by the bishop of Würzburg, Rudolph von Scherenberg, to the
printers Stephan Dold, Georg Reyser, and Johann Beckenhub for a
breviary (the *Breviarium herbipolense*). The following year, 1480, the
bishop of Regensburg, Heinrich von Abendsberg, followed suit by
granting exclusive rights for a *Breviarium ratisponense*, and in 1511 the
bishop of Strassburg granted a three-year *privilegio* for a *Breviarium
argentinense*. These episcopal privileges were effective only within the
respective dioceses.

The Empire

In the Empire, one of the earliest recorded privileges was that granted
in 1501 by the imperial Aulic Council to the humanist Konrad Celtes
of Nuremberg for an edition of the dramas of the nun-poet Hroswitha
of Gandersheim.[27] This was an isolated case, however, and the next
imperial *privilegio* was not granted until 1510, to the printer Johann
Schott. In 1512, it was granted by Maximilian I to the historiographer Johann Stab, and also to Eucharius Rösslin for his treatise on
obstetrics, *Der swangern Frauwen und Hebammen Rosegarten*.[28] Rösslin's
privilege was for six years. The first edition, edited by Johannes
Adelphus, was published in Strassburg by Martin Flach. A second
edition was published in Hagenau by Heinrich Gran in 1513.

   The imperial *privilegio* was granted infrequently and was at first
expensive to obtain. Application was made through a *Reichshofrat*. By

---

[26] The translation is in Armstrong, *Before Copyright*, 8.
[27] The same year, 1501, Celtes was granted a similar privilege from the magistracy of Frankfort, then the site of the book-fair.
[28] Noted in Bowker, *Copyright: Its History and Its Law* (Boston and New York,
1912), 11.

the middle of the century the procedure had become fairly standardized. A fee of ten *guilders* was paid and the privileges were recorded in the *Reichregister*. According to the *Reichregister*, between 1522 and 1556, under Emperor Charles V, forty-one privileges were granted. From the evidence of their appearance in books, however, many more than forty-one imperial privileges were granted during this period. They varied in duration from three to thirty years.[29]

Poland

In Poland, the first *privilegio* was granted by King Alexander in 1505 to the printer Johann Haller in the form of a limited monopoly whereby no one else could print, or sell, or import from elsewhere any works he printed. The following year, 1506, Haller printed in Cracow *Co[m]mune incliti Polonie regni priuilegium, co[n]stitutionu[m] [et] indultuu[m] publicitus decretorum, approbatoru[m]q[ue]: cum no[n]nullis iuribus ta[m] diuinis q[uam] humanis.*[30]

Sweden

In Sweden the earliest *privilegio* would appear to be that granted to Paul Grijs in 1510 for a Psalter he printed in Uppsala, the *Psalterium Upsalense.*[31]

---

[29] This information is found in Karl Schottenloher, "Die Drucker privilegien des 16 Jahrhunderts," *Gutenberg-Jahrbuch* (1933), 89–111; and Hirsch, *Printing, Selling and Reading*, 87.

[30] The book is recorded in Joannes Ptasnik, ed., *Monumenta poloniae typographica xv et xvi saeculorum*, vol. 1, *Cracovia impressorum xv et xvi saeculorum* (Leopoli, 1922), nos. 105, 108. The colophon reads: "Explicit dextro sidere: Co[m]mune incliti regni Polonie priuilegium, omni studio ac diligentia Cracouie in edibus Joha[n]nis Haller ad co[m]missione[m] reuerendi pr[incip]is D[omi]ni Johan[n]is de Lasko . . . impressum . . . Anno Domini 1506 xxvij. Januarij."

[31] Isak Collijn, *Sveriges bibliografi intill år 1600*, vol. 1, *1478–1530* (Uppsala, 1934–8), 202–09.

Denmark

In Copenhagen in 1519, Poul Raeff printed with a *privilegio* an edition by Christiern Therkelsen Morsing of Johannes Murmellius' *De latina constructione xxv praecepta*, as well as Johannes Bugenhagen's *Regulae grammaticales*, and Johannes de Spauter's (Johannes Despauterius) grammar book *Rudimenta*.[32] A *privilegio* also appears on an edition of the *Canon Roschildensis* printed by Raeff in Nyborg in 1522.[33]

Scotland

In Scotland a patent was granted by King James IV to Walter Chepman and Andrew Myllar on 15 September 1507 to print in Edinburgh books of "Lawes, actis of parliament, cronicles, mess bukis, and portuus efter the use of our Realme, with addicions and legendis of Scottis sanctis, now gaderit to be ekit tharto, and al utheris bukis that salbe sene necessar." In the patent, King James goes on to state that:

> And becaus we wnderstand that this cannot be perfurnist without rycht greit cost labour and expens, we have grantit and promittit to thame that thai sal nocht be hurt nor prevenit tharon be ony utheris to tak copyis of ony bukis furtht of our Realme, to ger imprent the samyne in utheris cuntreis, to be brocht and sauld agane within our Realme, to cause the said Walter and Androu tyne thair gret labour and expens.[34]

England

In England, the earliest book-privilege, dated 15 May 1518, appears to be that granted by the chancellor of Oxford University, the archbishop of Canterbury, William Warham, for a period of seven years

---

[32] Lauritz Nielson, *Dansk Bibliografi 1482–1550* (Copenhagen, 1919–1935), vol. 3: *Registre* (Copenhagen, 1935), no. 190.

[33] Nielsen, no. 38.

[34] A transcription of the patent is given in Robert Dickson and John Philip Edmond, *Annals of Scottish printing from the introduction of the art in 1507 to the beginning of the seventeenth century* (Cambridge, 1890), 7–8. Among the books printed by Chepman and Myllar at their press situated in the Southgait of Edinburgh, is the two-volume *Aberdeen Breviary* (1509–10), and *The knightly tale of Golagros and Gawane* (1508).

to John Scolar for a commentary, *Questiones moralissime super libros Ethicoru eruditissimi*, by John Dedecus on Aristotle's *Ethics*. The colophon reads "Impressumq[ue] in celeberima vniuersitate Oxoniensi per me Iohannem Scolar . . . Anno dñi. M.CCCCC. decimooctauo." Six months later, on 13 November 1518, Richard Pynson printed an oration by Cuthbert Tunstall on the proposed marriage of Henry VIII's daughter, Princess Mary, and the Dauphin of France with what appears to be the first English royal *privilegio*:[35]

> cum priuilegio a rege indulto, ne quis hanc orationem intra biennium in regno Angliae imprimat, aut alibi impressam et importatam in eodem regno Angliae vendat.

The book, *Cvtheberti Tonstalli, In lavdem matrimonii, oratio, habita in sponsalibvs Mariae potentissimi regis Angliae Henrici Octavi filiae, et Francisci christianissimi Francorvm regis primogeniti*, was also published the following year in Basel by Johann Froben. The colophon reads "Basileae apvd Io. Frobenivm, mense febrvario. Anno M.D.XIX."

The Netherlands

In the Low Countries privileges were granted by the Council of Brabant in Brussels. The earliest example is dated 1512 when Claes de Grave, a printer in Antwerp, sought copyright protection for the 1513 edition of Gaspar [Jasper] Laet de Borschloen's popular *Almanack*.[36] In 1512 Claes also printed with a *privilegio* an edition of Johannes Ketham's *Fasciculus Medicine*.[37] That same year, Thomas van der Noot was granted a three-year *privilegio* by the Council for any books he should be the first to print in Brabant.[38] The following year, 1513, Claes de Grave and Thomas van der Noot together published a Bible with a *privilegio* ("Cum gratia et preuilegio").[39] Six years

---

[35] Noted in Armstrong, *Before Copyright*, 10–11; and Bowker, 19.

[36] Noted in Prosper Verheyden, "Drukkersoctrooien in de 16e eeuw," *Tijdschrift voor Boek- en Bibliotheekswesen* 8 (1910): 208, no. 1. Claes paid a fee of 12s 6d, which he paid again when he was again granted the *privilegio* in 1519 for the 1520 edition. See Wouter Nijhoff and M. E. Kronenberg, *Nederlandsche Bibliographie van 1500 tot 1540* (The Hague, 1940), no. 3332.

[37] Listed in Nijhoff and Kronenberg, 2: no. 1223.

[38] Noted in Verheyden, 209, no. 2; and Armstrong, *Before Copyright*, 17.

[39] The books is listed in Nijhoff and Kronenberg, no. 365.

later, around 1519, after he had moved to Brussels, Van der Noot alone printed *Boecxken van de ordene van S. Birgitten met drie revelacien* with a *privilegio*.[40] Besides the Council of Brabant, the Privy Council also granted copyright. In 1517, for example, a four-year *privilegio* was issued to Jan Seversz., a printer in Leiden, for the *Cronycke van Hollandt, Zeelandt ende Vrieslant*, adapted and translated by the scholar Cornelius Aurelius. The book includes 243 woodcut illustrations printed from 110 woodblocks. Eleven of the woodcuts (plus two repeats) have been attributed to Lucas van Leyden, while others are copies after woocuts by Hans Burgkmair.[41] A supplement to the book, printed by Jan van Doesborsch in Antwerp in 1530 with an imperial *privilegio* granted by Charles V, also contains numerous woodcuts, including a large portrait of Charles V and another of the siege of Vienna.

France

In France privileges were granted through the royal chancery, the Parlement of Paris (and other sovereign courts), and the Prévôt of Paris.[42] The earliest French royal *privilegio*, issued through the royal chancery, would appear to be that granted in 1498 for five years to Johannes Trechsel, a German printer working in Lyons, for an edition of Gerardus Cremonensis's translation of *Primus canonis Auicenne principis: cum explanatione*, edited by Jacques Ponceau.[43] Another was granted by Louis XII nine years later, in 1507, to Antoine Vérard for three years for an annotated edition of St. Paul's *Epistles*.[44] That

---

[40] The book is listed in Nijhoff and Kronenberg, no. 2514; and noted in Collijn, 1: 269–271.

[41] The woodcuts attributed to Lucas van Leyden are discussed in Ellen S. Jacobowitz and Stephanie Loeb Stepanek, *The Prints of Lucas van Leyden and His Contemporaries* (Washington, D.C., 1983), cat. no. 55; Franz Dülberg, "Lucas van Leyden als Illustrator," *Repertorium für Kunstwissenschaft* 21 (1898): 36, 42–44; Campbell Dodgson, "Beschreibendes Verzeichniss der Buchillustrationen Lucas van Leyden's," *Repertorium für Kunstwissenschaft* 23 (1900): 144, no. 6a; Gustav Glück, "Zu den Holzschnitten der Leidener Chronik von 1517," *Repertorium für Kunstwissenschaft* 23 (1900): 455; and Delen, *Histoire de la gravure dans les anciens Pays-Bas & dans les provinces belges*, 67–69.

[42] This and some of the following information comes from David T. Pottinger, *The French Book Trade in the Ancien Régime, 1500–1791* (Cambridge, Mass., 1958), 212.

[43] Noted in Armstrong, *Before Copyright*, 140, 209.

[44] The book, *Les epistres sainct pol. glosées*, was printed in Paris on 17 January 1508

same year, the Parlement of Paris granted a one-year *privilegio* to the Paris bookseller Eustace de Brie for two books, *La louenge des roys de France* by André de La Vigne, and *La chronique de Gennes*. In the colophon of each book is printed a summary of the terms of the *privilegio* that reads in part:[45]

> Et lui a donné la court de parlement et procureur du roy ung an de temps à vendre lesditz livres. Et ont esté faictes deffences et inhibitions à tous librayres et imprimeurs et à tous autres de non imprimer ledit livre jusques à ung an prochain venant . . .

In 1508 a one-year *privilegio* was granted to Martin Alexandre, and on the 12 January 1509 [1508 o.s.] Berthold Rembolt received a three-year *privilegio* for an edition of St. Bruno. A two-year *privilegio* was issued a month later, on 28 February, to Michel La Troyne, followed by three more that same year. At the same time (1509), the royal chancery issued a two-year *privilegio* to the author Nicole Bohier and one for three years to the author Jean Lemaire de Belges. The *privilegio* granted to Lemaire de Belges, on 30 July 1509, was for two of his books: *Les Illustrations de Gaule et singularitez de Troye* and a short tract entitled *La legende des Venitiens* (printed in Paris in 1509). The *privilegio* reads in part:[46]

> De la partie de notre bien aimé maistre Jehan Le Maire de Belges, nous a esté exposé qu'il a intention de brief faire imprimer ung certain livre des Singularitez de Troye et Illustrations de Gaule, contenant trois volumes, par lui faitz et compilez . . . et aussi ung petit traictié par lui faict et compilé, intitulé la Legende des Venitiens. Mais il doubte qu'il ne peust ou osast ce faire sans noz congié et licence. Et à ceste cause nous a icelui exposant fait supplier . . .

Meanwhile, privileges were also being issued by the Prévôt of Paris, the first of which was granted, "par l'ordonnance de justice," to the author Pierre Gringore for one year in 1505. Gringore was granted

---

[1507 o.s.]. Another edition of St. Paul's *Epistles* (*Pauli Epistolae*) was printed in Paris in 1512 by Henri Estienne ("H. Stephanus").

[45] Recorded in Armstrong, *Before Copyright*, 37, 241.

[46] Noted in Armstrong, *Before Copyright*, 210; and Augustin-Charles Renouard, *Traité des droits d'auteur* (Paris, 1838), 1: 108. This edition of *Les Illustrations de Gaule et singularitez de Troye* is discussed in Jacques Abélard, *Les Illustrations de Gaule et singularitez de Troyes de Jean Lemaire de Belges. Etude des éditions. Genèse de l'oeuvre* (Geneva, 1976), 70.

three more in 1509, and another in 1510. In 1508 the translator
Jean d'Ivry was granted a one-year *privilegio*, and another in 1509.[47]

On 23 September 1524, the publisher, printer, author, and engraver
Geoffroy Tory was granted a six-year *privilegio* by Francis I through
the Royal Chancery for an edition of the *Hours of the Virgin* (*Horae
in laudem beatiss. semper Virginis Mariae*) illustrated with metal relief
blocks cut in imitation of Venetian woodcuts. The *privilegio*, the first
of its kind in France, specifically protected Tory's "histoires et vignettes"
(illustrations and borders) against being plagiarized with a background
white, grey, or red, and neither reduced nor enlarged, on pain of a
fine of twenty-five gold *marcs*. The document reads in part as follows:[48]

> Francoys, par la grace de Dieu roy de France, aux bailly et provost
> de Paris, senechal de Lyon, et a tous noz autres iusticiers, officiers, ou
> leurs lieuxtenans, et a chascun deulx endroit soy et si comme a luy
> appartiendra, salut. Nostre cher et bien ame maistre Geufroy Tory,
> libraire, demourant a Paris, nous ha presentement faict dire et remon-
> strer que puis nagueres il ha faict et faict faire certaines histoires et
> vignettes a lantique, et pareillement unes autres a la moderne, pour
> icelles faire imprimer, et servir a plusieurs usages dheures, dont pour
> icelles il ha vacque certain long temps, et faict plusieurs grans fraitz,
> mises et despens. A ceste cause, et pour luy subvenir a recouvrer par-
> tie des despens quil ha faictz et soubstenuz a vacquer a faire faire les
> histoires et vignettes dessusdictes, et a ce quil ait mieulx dequoy soy
> entretenir, nous ha treshumblement faict supplier et requerir que luy
> seul et non autre ait a faire imprimer les vignettes et histoires dessus-
> dictes pour le temps et terme de six ans commenceans au iour de la
> date de limpression desdictes heures, et deffendre a tous libraires den
> faire ou faire faire aucun impression, tant soyent en champ blanc, gris
> ou rouge, ne laissant aucunes desdictes vignettes noires, ne aussi les
> reduyre a petit ou grant pied; nous humblement requerant icelluy . . .
> . . . sur peine de vingt et cinq marcz dargent a nous a appliquer, et
> confiscation des heures, vignettes et histoires . . .
> Donne a Avignon, le xxiii. iour de septembre, lan de grace mil cinq
> cens vingt quatre, et de nostre regne le dixiesme . . .

Two years later, on 5 September 1526, Tory was granted a ten-
year *privilegio* for his "histoires et vignettes a lantique et a la moderne,
pareillement frises, bordeures, coronnemens et entrelas" ("illustrations,

---

[47] Noted in Armstrong, *Before Copyright*, 268–69.
[48] The transcription is given in Auguste Bernard, *De l'origine et des débuts de l'imprimerie en Europe* (Paris, 1853), 148–149. The illustrations and borders are discussed
in Jules Lieure, *La gravure en France au XVIᵉ siècle. La gravure dans le livre et l'ornement*
(Paris and Brussels, 1927), 30–31.

vignettes, friezes, borders, headpieces, and ornaments") in *Champ fleury, auquel est contenu Lart et Science de la deue et vraye proportion des Lettres Attiques* printed in 1529. It is clearly stated that:[49]

> Ce Livre est privilegie pour dix ans par le Roy nostre sire, et est vendre a Paris, sus Petit Pont, a lenseigne du Pot Casse, par maistre Geofroy Tory de Bourges, libraire et autheur dudict livre, et par Giles Gourmont, aussi libraire, demourant en la rue Sainct Iacques, a lenseigne des Trois Coronnes.

Subsequently, the French royal *privilegio* was granted to numerous books illustrated with engravings by Jean Duvet, Pierre Woieriot, and Jacques Honervogt. On 28 June 1545, Francis I granted a three-year *privilegio* to Jacques Androuet du Cerceau for "ouvraiges et figures d'architectes, cornices, moresques et compartiments."[50]

French royal privileges were often indicated on the title-page of a book or on a print (see below) with the words "Cum gratia & privilegio Christianissimi Francorum Regis," or "Cum Priuilegio Christianissimi Regis Galliae," or "Cum privilegio Regis," or "Avec privilege du Roi," or "Cum amplissimo Regis privilegio." It often also appeared simply as "Cum privilegio," or "Avec privilege." Privileges in the first half of the century were usually brief. Later, following legislation passed in 1566, they were longer in form and it was required that they be printed in full in books.

* * *

A major printing project might amass privileges from all over Europe. The 1597 edition of Tagliacozzi published in Venice has already been mentioned. An earlier noteworthy example is Christopher Plantin's enormous eight-volume, five-language Polyglot Bible for which the publisher obtained various privileges from Philip II, the project's chief sponsor, between 1568 and 1573, plus further privileges granted by the Privy Council in Brussels (11 January 1571), the Council of Brabant (12 February 1571), Emperor Maximilian II (26 January 1572), King Charles IX of France (13 April 1572), Pope

---

[49] The *privilegio* is partially transcribed in Bernard, *L'imprimerie en Europe*, 123, and 158.

[50] The *privilegio* is noted by David Thomson in the edition of Jacques Androuet du Cerceau's *Les Plus excellents bastiments de France par Jacques Androuet du Cerceau*. Translated from the English by Catherine Ludet (Paris, 1988), 5. I am grateful to Henri Zerner for bringing this reference to my attention.

Gregory XIII (1 September 1572), and the Senate of Venice
(25 October 1572).[51]

Prints Granted the Privilegio *Outside Italy in the Sixteenth Century*

By the mid-century, several of the granting authorities mentioned
above were issuing privileges for prints. In 1543, Hans Liefrinck, a
printer in Antwerp, was granted a two-year imperial *privilegio* by
Charles V for a print of the *Siege of Heinsberg*.[52] Later, in 1558, the
same Liefrinck evidently received a six-year *privilegio* ("cum gratia et
Privilegio P. AN. 6") for Balthasar Bos's *Rebecca at the Well* after
Lambert Lombard.[53] Bos also published his own engravings, such as
the *Sacrifice of Noah* after Frans Floris ("Balthasar Silvius. Fecit Et
Excudebat") dated 1555.[54] The second state of this print (according
to Zani), is inscribed "Cum Gratia Et Privilegio P. An. 4."[55]

Besides Liefrinck, the printer Hieronymus Cock in Antwerp also
published numerous prints with a *privilegio*. Between 1550 and 1555,
Cock evidently received a number of imperial privileges, granted by
Charles V, and then, from 1556 to 1562 (after Charles V's abdica-
tion as king of Spain in 1556), numerous royal privileges granted by
Philip II. The notice of copyright also appears on several maps and
topographical views published by Cock. A map issued by Cock in
1550 carries an eight-year imperial *privilegio*.[56] The following year, on
4 October 1551, Cock received a *privilegio* for a map of *Piedmont* ("la
vraye description de l'entiere region & pays de piedmont. Imprime
& depaincte en Anvers par Jherome Cock...."), which appeared in
March, 1552, with the following inscription across the bottom: "Niewe
Beschrynvinghe Van Tgheele Landt Van Piemont Met Keyserlycker
Magesteyt Privilegio gheteekent verreycke."[57] In 1553, a six-year

---

[51] Noted in Witcombe, "Christopher Plantin's Papal Privileges: Documents in the
Vatican Archives," *De Gulden Passer* 69 (1991): 142–43.

[52] Noted in Alexandre Joseph Pinchart, *Archives des arts, sciences et lettres: documents
inédits publiés et annotés* (Ghent, 1850–1882), 3: 314–325.

[53] The print is listed in Zani, 2, 3: 28.

[54] The print is listed in Delen, *Histoire de la gravure dans les anciens Pays-Bas*, 70.

[55] Zani, 2, 2: 314.

[56] The print is listed in Riggs, *Hieronymus Cock: Printmaker and Publisher* (New York
and London, 1977), 379, no. 270.

[57] Riggs, 282–283, no. 56, notes that the authorship of the map is not made

imperial *privilegio* appears on a map of *Sicily*, and in 1555 the same appears on a map of *Asia Anteriore* (Turkey and Persia) by Giacomo Gastaldi ("Antverpiae apud Hieronymum Cock cum caesaraee ma[iestatis] privilegio ad sexennium 1555"). Other copyrighted maps followed. After 1555, the royal *privilegio* appears on Cock's prints. A map *Savoy*, for example, dated 1556, was issued with a six-year royal *privilegio* ("Avec privilege du Roy pour six ans)," and another, dated 1557, has a four-year royal *privilegio* ("Avec privilege du Roy pour quatre ans"). A map of the *Netherlands*, also dated 1557, carries a six-year royal *privilegio*.

Besides maps, in 1551 Cock also published with an eight-year imperial *privilegio* a set of twenty-five prints (including the title-page) of his own etchings, *Views of Roman Ruins* (published under the title *Præcipua aliquot Romanæ antiquitatis ruinarum monimenta, vivis prospectibus, ad veri imitationem affabre designata*). The set of twenty-five prints was dedicated by Cock to Antoine Perrenot. Later in the decade, the royal *privilegio* appeared on Cock's set of *Small Landscapes*, dated 1559, and in 1562, on the *Small Book of Roman Ruins* (21 plates) and *Architectural Views* (29 plates), the latter two sets both inscribed "Cum Privilegio Regis." In 1552, a six-year *privilegio* appears on a *Triple View of Antwerp* by Melchisideck van Hooren ("... Melchisideck van Hooren MET GRACIE EN PRIVILEGIE D.K.M. GHEGHEVEN 6 LAREN. 1552").

In the categories of historical and biblical subjects, in 1550 Cock printed Giorgio Ghisi's two-plate engraving of Raphael's *School of Athens* with an eight-year imperial *privilegio*. The print is inscribed: "HIERONYMVS COCK PICTOR EXCVDEBAT. 1550. CVM GRATIA ET PRIVILEGIO P AN. 8." In 1551 appeared Ghisi's print of Lambert Lombard's *Last Supper*, followed in 1552 by his two-plate engraving of Raphael's *Disputà*. In 1554 appeared his *Nativity* after Bronzino, and in 1555 the *Judgement of Paris* after Giovanni Battista Bertani. In these years, Cock also printed with a *privilegio* his own set of ten etchings of the *Liberal Arts, with Pallas, Apollo, and Industry* (1551) after designs by Frans Floris, and a set of four plates

---

clear by the inscription across the bottom. He explains that while "gheteenkent" could mean "drawn," it can also mean "signed." "Verreycke" could be the name of the person who drew the map, or it could be the name of the official granting the *privilegio*. Privileges granted for the printing of maps in Flanders in the sixteenth century are given in Pinchart, 2: 72–73.

engraved by Balthasar Bos of the *Four Evangelists* (1551) the designs of which have been attributed to Floris.[58]

In 1555 Cock also printed with a six-year *privilegio* Hans Collaert's engraving of Lambert Lombard's *Moses Smiting the Rock*, and two prints by Pieter van der Heyden: the *Crucifixion* after Lambert Lombard, and *Moses and the Brazen Serpent* after Frans Floris. The *Crucifixion* is inscribed "Cum/gratia et priui per An. 6./Petrus Mirycinus fecit 1555."[59] In that year he also issued, with a six-year *privilegio*, Cornelis Cort's set of six prints of the *Story of David and Abigail* after Martin van Heemskerck. These were followed the next year by Cort's set of ten prints of Heemskerck's *Story of Tobit*. A royal *privilegio* ("Cum priuileg. Re.") on an undated anonymous engraving printed by Cock of *The Crossing of the Red Sea*, after Bronzino's fresco in the Chapel of Eleanora da Toledo in the Palazzo Vecchio in Florence, would indicate a date after 1556.[60]

Other copyrighted prints followed, including several by Pieter van der Heyden, Frans Huys, and Philippe Galle after Pieter Bruegel the Elder. Mention can be made of Van der Heyden's engraving of Hieronymus Bosch's *Ship of Fools* ("Die Blau Schuyte"), printed by Cock in 1559, and an anonymous two-plate engraving (attributed to Dirck Volkerts Coornhert) of *Calvary* after Martin van Heemskerck, which is inscribed "Imprimé a Anvers avec Grace & Privilege, & approbation du Commissaire de la Ma[iestie] Royale L. Metsuis 1559." That same year, the Antwerp publisher Christopher Plantin printed with a *privilegio* thirty-four plates designed by Cock and engraved by the brothers Jan and Lucas van Duetecum of *The Funeral Procession of Charles V*, an event which had taken place on 29 December 1558.[61] The prints form a frieze more than thirty feet long.

In France, the first *privilegio* for a set of prints was granted by Henry II in 1556, and three years later, in 1559, it began to be

---

[58] Balthasar Bos, whose real name was Balthazar Gheertsen, also latinised his name to Balthasar Sylvius or Silvius.

[59] The latinised form of Pieter van der Heyden's name appears in various spellings: Petrus a Merica, a Meriga, Miricinus, Merecinus, Ameringius, Miriginus, Mirycinus, Myricenis, and Miricinus.

[60] Vasari, 5: 438, describes the print as engraved by Cock.

[61] Noted in Leon Voet, *The Golden Compasses: A History and Evaluation of the Printing and Publishing Activities of the Officina Plantiniana at Antwerp* (Amsterdam, London, and New York, 1972), 2: 194. The full title is *La magnifique et sumptueuse pompe funebre, faite en la ville de Bruxelles, le XXIX. iour du mois de decembre, M.D.LVIII. aux obseques de l'empereur Charles V. de tresdigne memoire.*

granted for single sheets.[62] It appears for example on the second state, dated 1559, of Giorgio Ghisi's engraving of the *Fates* after Giulio Romano, and on Ghisi's *Calumny of Apelles* dated 1560 after Luca Penni.[63] It also appears on prints by Pierre Milan.[64]

---

[62] Landau and Parshall, *The Renaissance Print*, 308.

[63] The print of Ghisi's *Fates*, inscribed "GEOR. MAN./F./MDLVIIII," is after a design by Giulio Romano in the Palazzo del Te in Mantua ("IV. RO. IN./SCVLPTA/IN PALATIO/THE"). An example is in the BN, Paris, Bb. 13, fol. 47. The first state is dated 1558. An example of Ghisi's *Calumny of Apelles* is in the BN, Paris, Eb. 14a. fol. Both prints are catalogued in Boorsch and Lewis, *The Engravings of Giorgio Ghisi* (New York, 1985), cat. nos. 25 and 27, respectively.

[64] Three of Milan's undated copyrighted prints are after Rosso Fiorentino. The prints are catalogued in Eugene A. Carroll, *Rosso Fiorentino: Drawings, Prints, and Decorative Arts* (Washington, D.C., 1987), 212, no. 68; 252, no. 79 (as completed by René Boyvin); and 282, no. 89. The same three are also catalogued in Evelina Borea, "Stampe da Modelli Fiorentini nel Cinquecento," 258, no. 653; 263, no. 684; and 263, no. 686. Two anonymous prints after Rosso also carry a royal *privilegio*. See Carroll, 292, no. 93; and 342, no. 107; and Peter Fuhring, entries in *The French Renaissance in Prints from the Bibliothèque Nationale de France* (Los Angeles, 1994), 315, no. 80; and 317, no. 81, both as "René Boyvin or Pierre Milan."

BIBLIOGRAPHY

Ackerman, James. *The Architecture of Michelangelo.* New York, 1961.

Abélard, Jacques. *Les Illustrations de Gaule et singularitez de Troyes de Jean Lemaire de Belges. Etude des éditions. Genèse de l'oeuvre.* Geneva, 1976.

Adami, Vittorio. "Nicolò Brenta da Varenna, stampatore." *La Bibliofilia* 25 (1923): 193–207, 276.

Adams, H. M. *Catalogue of Books Printed on the Continent of Europe in Cambridge Libraries.* 2 vols. Cambridge, 1967.

Agee, Richard J. The Privilege and Venetian Music Printing in the Sixteenth Century. Ph.D. diss., Princeton University, 1982.

Alberici, Clelia. "Brambilla, Ambrogio." In *Dizionario biografico degli Italiani.* Vol. 13, 729–30. Rome, 1971.

Almagià, Roberto. "La carta d'Italia di G. A. Vavassori." *La Bibliofilia* 15 (1914): 81–88.

———. "Il Mappamondo di G. A. Vavassore." *Rivista Geografica Italiana* 27 (1920): 17–30.

———. "Intorno ad una raccolta di carte cinquecentesche di proprietà del Lloyd Triestino." *L'Universo* 3 (1927): 265–93.

———. *Monumenta Italiae Cartographica. Riproduzioni di carte generali e regionali d'Italia dal secolo XIV al XVII.* Florence, 1929.

———. "Intorno all'opera cartografica di Natale Bonifaco." *Archivio Storico per la Dalmazia* 14 (January, 1933): 480–93.

———. "Intorno alle carte e alle figurazioni annesse all'Isolario di Benedetto Bordone." *Maso Finiguerra* 2 (1937): 176.

———. *La Carta dei Paesi Danubiani e delle regione contermini di Giacomo Gastaldi, 1546.* Vatican City, 1939.

———. "Intorno ad un grande mappamondo perduto di Giacomo Gastaldi (1561)." *La Bibliofilia* 41 (1939): 259–66.

———. "Alcune stampe geografiche italiane dei secoli XVI e XVII oggi perdute." *Maso Finiguerra* 5 (1940): 97–103.

———. *Monumenta cartographica vaticana iussu Pii XII P.M. consilio et opera procuratorum Bibliothecae Apostolicae Vaticanae.* 4 vols. Vatican City, 1944–55.

———. *Monumenta cartografica Vaticana: Carte geografiche a stampa di particolare pregio o rarità dei secoli XVI e XVII esistenti nella Biblioteca Apostolica Vaticana.* Vol. 2, Vatican City, 1948.

———. "A Hitherto Unknown Map of Palestine." *Imago Mundi* 8 (1951): 34.

———. "Pirro Ligorio Cartografo." *Rendiconti della Classe di Scienze morali, storiche e filologiche* serie 3, vol. 11, fasc. 3–4 (1956): 49–61.

———. *Documenti Cartografici dello Stato Pontificio Editi dalla Biblioteca Apostolica Vaticana.* Vatican City, 1960.

———. "A proposito di una presunta carta dell'Asia Anteriore di Giacomo Gastaldi." *Rivista Geografica Italiana* 69 (1962): 2–9.

Amram, David Werner. *The Makers of Hebrew Books in Italy.* London, 1963.

Appuhn, Horst, and Christian von Heusinger. *Riesenholzschnitte und Papiertapeten der Renaissance.* Unterschneidheim, 1976.

Argan, Giulio Carlo. "Il valore critico della 'stampa di traduzione'." In *Essays in the History of Art Presented to Rudolf Wittkower.* London, 1967, vol. 2, 179–81.

Armstrong, Elizabeth. *Before Copyright: The French Book-Privilege System 1498–1526.* Cambridge, 1990.

Armstrong, Lilian. "Benedetto Bordon, *Miniator*, and Cartography in Early Sixteenth-Century Venice." *Imago Mundi* 48 (1996): 65–92.

Ascarelli, Fernanda. *La Tipografia Cinquecentina Italiana.* Florence, 1953.

———. *Annali Tipografici di Giacomo Mazzocchi.* Florence, 1961.

———. *Le Cinquecentine Romane: "Censimento delle edizione romane del XVI secolo posseduto dalle biblioteche di Roma."* Milan, 1972.

Ascarelli, Fernanda, and Marco Menato. *La Tipografia del '500 in Italia.* Florence, 1989.

Ashby, Thomas. *La Campagna Romana al Tempo di Paolo III: Mappa della Campagna Romana del 1547 di Eufrosino della Volpaia.* Rome, 1914.

———. "Il Libro d'Antonio Labacco appartenente all'Architettura." *La Bibliofilia* 16 (1914): 289–309.

———. "Le Diverse Edizioni dei 'Vestigi dell'Antichità di Roma' di Stefano Du Pérac." *La Bibliofilia* 16 (1915): 401–21.

———. "Antiquae Statuae Urbis Romae." *Papers of the British School at Rome* 9 (1920): 107–58.

———. "Impiego degli stessi rami per opere diverse in alcune edizione romane." *La Bibliofilia* 27 (1925–26): 160–62.

Bacotich, Arnolfo. "Giorgio Giulio Clovio, 1498–1578 (Dalmatia?)." *Archivio Storico per la Dalmazia.* 20 (January, 1936): 422–46.

———. "Due stampe assai rare di Natale Bonifacio da Sebenico (1538–1592)." *Archivio Storico per la Dalmazia.* 20 (February, 1936): 478–96.

Baglione, Giovanni. *Le Vite de' Pittori Scultori et Architettori dal Pontificato di Gregorio XIII fino a tutto quello d'Urbano VIII.* Rome, 1649. Reprint, Bologna, 1986.

Bagrow, Leo. *Giovanni Andreas di Vavassore: A Venetian Cartographer of the 16th Century; A Descriptive List of His Maps.* Jenkintown, 1939.

———. *Matheo Pagano: A Venetian Cartographer of the 16th Century; A Descriptive List of His Maps.* Jenkintown, 1940.

Baldinucci, Filippo. *Cominciamento, e Progresso del'Arte dell'Intagliatore in Rame, colle vite di molti de' più eccellenti Maestri della stessa professione.* Florence, 1686.

———. *Notizie dei Professori del Disegno.* Florence, 1846.

Ballestreros, Jorge Bernales. *Mateo Perez de Alesio, pintor romano en Sevilla y Lima.* Seville, 1973.

Barasch, Moshe. *Theories of Art from Plato to Winckelmann.* New York, 1985.

Barberi, Francesco. *Paolo Manuzio e La Stamperia del Popolo Romano (1561–1570).* Rome, 1942.

———. "Le Edizioni Romane di Francesco Minizio Calvo." In *Miscellanea di Scritti di Bibliografia ed Erudizione in Memoria di Luigi Ferrari.* Florence, 1952, 57–97. Republished in abbreviated form in F. Barberi, *Tipografi Romani del Cinquecento. Guillery, Ginnasio mediceo, Calvo, Dorico, Cartolari.* Florence, 1983.

———. "Libri e Stampatori nella Roma dei Papi." *Studi Romani* 13 (1965): 433–56.

———. "I Dorici, Tipografi a Roma nel Cinquecento." *La Bibliofilia* 67 (1965): 221–61.

———. "Stefano Guillery e le sue edizione romane." In *Studi Offerti a Roberto Ridolfi,* ed. Berta Maracchi Biagiarelli and Dennis E. Rhodes. Florence, 1973, 95–145.

Bartsch, Adam von. *Le Peintre Graveur.* 22 vols. in 4. Nieuwkoop, 1982. Reprint of the edition published in Würzburg, 1920–1922, which is a reset copy of the edition published in Leipzig, 1854–1870.

Baschet, Armand. *Aldo Manuzio, Lettres et documents, 1495–1515.* Venice, 1867.

Bean, Jacob. "Two Drawings by Jacopo Ligozzi." In *Festschrift to Erik Fischer: European Drawings from Six Centuries.* Copenhagen, 1990, 211–16.

Beans, George H. *Some Sixteenth Century Watermarks Found in Maps Prevalent in the "IATO" Atlases.* Jenkintown, Penn., 1938.

——. "Some Notes from the Tall Tree Library." *Imago Mundi* 5 (1948): 72–77.

——. "A Note from the Tall Tree Library: A Sixteenth-Century Airway Map." *Imago Mundi* 16 (1962): 160.

Bellini, Paolo. "Printmakers and Dealers in Italy during 16th and 17th centuries." *Print Collector* 13 (1975): 17–45.

——. "Contributi per Diana Scultori." *Rassegna di Studi e di Notizie* 8 (1980): 63–98.

——, ed. *Incisori Italiani del Cinquecento dalla Raccolta di Stampe della Biblioteca Civica di Monza.* Monza, 1981.

——. "Alcuni dati sull'attività romana di Diana Scultori." *Paragone* 38 (1987): 53–60.

——. *L'Opera incisa di Adamo e Diana Scultori.* Vicenza, 1991.

Beretta, Silvia. "Raffaellino da Reggio e i suoi incisori." *Rassegna di Studi e di Notizie* 12 (1984–85): 9–57.

Bernard, Auguste. *De l'origine et des débuts de l'imprimerie en Europe.* 2 vols. Paris, 1853.

——. *Geofroy Tory, peintre et graveur, premier imprimeur royal, réformateur de l'orthographe et de typographie sous François 1ᵉʳ.* 2nd ed. Paris, 1865.

Bernoni, Domenico. *Antonio Blado e la sua stamperia in Roma.* Ascoli, 1883.

——. *Dei Torresani, Blado e Ragazzoni celebri stampatori a Venezia e Roma nel XV e XVI secolo.* Milan, 1890.

Bellocchi, Ugo, and Bruno Fava. *L'Interpretazione Grafica dell'Orlando Furioso.* Reggio Emilia, 1961.

Bertolotti, Antonino. *Artisti Belgi ed Olandesi a Roma nei secoli XVI e XVII.* Florence, 1880.

——. *Artisti Urbinati in Roma prima del secolo XVIII.* Urbino, 1881.

——. *Artisti Lombardi a Roma nei secoli XV, XVI, e XVIII.* Milan, 1881. Reprint, Bologna, 1985.

——. *Artisti Subalpini in Roma nei secoli XV, XVI e XVII.* Mantua, 1884.

——. *Artisti Veneti in Roma nei secoli XV, XVI, e XVII.* Venice, 1884. Reprint, Bologna, 1965.

——. "Lettere inedite di Aliprando Caprioli." *Archivio storico per Trieste, l'Istria e il Trentino* 3 (1884): 117–119.

——. *Giunti agli Artisti Belgi ed Olandesi in Roma nei secoli XVI e XVII.* Rome, 1885.

——. *Artisti Bolognese, Ferrarese ed alcuni altri del già Stato Pontificio in Roma nei secoli XV, XVI, e XVII.* Bologna, 1885. Reprint, Bologna, 1962.

——. *Artisti in Relazione coi Gonzaga Duchi di Mantova nei secoli XVI e XVIII.* Atti e Memorie delle RR. Deputazione di Storia Patria per le Provincie Modenesi e Parmensi, 3. Modena, 1885.

——. *Artisti Francesi a Roma nei secoli XV, XVI e XVII.* Mantua, 1886. Reprint, Bologna, 1975.

Biagiarelli, Berta. "Il Privilegio di Stampatore Ducale nella Firenze Medicea." *Archivio Storico Italiano* 121 (1965): 304–70.

Bianchi, Silvia. "Contributi per l'opera incisa di Nicolas Beatrizet." *Rassegna di Studi e di Notizie* 9 (1981): 47–145.

——. "Apporti per Natale Bonifacio." *Rassegna di Studi e di Notizie* 10 (1982): 189–206.

Biasiotti, Giovanni, and Gustavo Giovannoni. "La Vita a Roma dei Cavalieri di San Giovanni di Gerusalemme." In *Atti del IIᵒ Congresso Nazionale di Studi Romani*, 2, Rome, 1931, 349–66.

Biasutti, Renato. "Il 'Disegno della Geografia moderna dell'Italia' di Giacomo Gastaldi." *Memorie Geografiche* 4 (1908), 29–33.

——. "La carta dell'Africa di Gastaldi (1545–1564) e lo sviluppo della cartografia africana nei sec. XVI e XVII." *Bollettino della Reale Società Geografica Italiana* 9 (1920): 327–46, 387–436.

Bier, Erich. "Unbekannte Arbeiten des Domenico dalle Greche" *Maso Finiguerra* 2(1937): 207–18.

Bierens de Haan, J. C. J. *L'Oeuvre Gravé de Cornelis Cort Graveur Hollandais 1533–1578.* The Hague, 1948.

Bigi, Emilio. "Barbaro, Ermolao (Almorò)." In *Dizionario biografico degli Italiani*. Vol. 6, 96–99. Rome, 1964.

Bilinski, Bronislaw. "*Judicium Ladislai de Cracovia* (Teneczynski) stampato a Roma nel 1494." In *Italia Venezia e Polonia tra Medio Evo e Età Moderna*. Edited by Vittore Branca and Sante Graciotti. Florence, 1980, 201–35.

Billanovich, Myriam. "Benedetto Bordon e Giulio Cesare Scaligero." *Italia Medioevale e Umanisticia* 11 (1968): 187–256.

——. "Bordon (Bordone), Benedetto." In *Dizionario biografico degli Italiani*. Vol. 12, 511–13. Rome, 1970.

Blasio, Maria Grazia. "Privilegi e licenze di stampa a Roma fra Quattro e Cinquecento." *La Bibliofilia* 90 (1988): 147–59.

——. *Cum Gratia et Privilegio: Programmi Editoriale e Politica Pontificia Roma 1487–1527*. Rome, 1988.

Bloch, Joshua. *Venetian Printers of Hebrew Books*. New York, 1932.

Blum, André. "Le *Fasciculus medicinae* de Johannes Kétham." 5 *Byblis* (1926): 95–87.

Boas, T. S. R. *Giorgio Vasari: The Man and the Book*. Princeton, 1979.

Bober, Phyllis, and R. Rubinstein, *Renaissance Artists and Antique Sculpture*. Oxford, 1986.

Bohlin, Diane DeGrazia. *Prints and Related Drawings by the Carracci Family*. Washington, D.C., 1979. [see also De Grazia]

Bonaventura, Maria Antoinetta. "L'Industria e il Commercio delle Incisioni nella Roma del '500." *Studi Romani* 8 (1960): 430–36.

Bongi, Salvatore. *Annali di Gabriel Giolito de' Ferrari da Trino di Monferrato, stampatore in Venezia*. 2 vols. Rome, 1890–1897.

Boorsch, Suzanne. "The Building of the Vatican: The Papacy and Architecture." *The Metropolitan Museum of Art Bulletin* 40 (1982–83).

——. "Mantegna and His Printmakers." In *Andrea Mantegna*. Milan, 1992, 56–66.

Boorsch, Suzanne, Michal and R. E. Lewis. *The Engravings of Giorgio Ghisi*. Metropolitan Museum of Art, New York, 1985.

Borea, Evelina. "Stampa figurativa e pubblico dalle origini all'affermazione nel Cinquecento." In *Storia dell'Arte Italiana*. Part 1, Vol. 2. Turin, 1979, 319–413.

——. "Stampe da Modelli Fiorentini nel Cinquecento." In *Firenze e La Toscana dei Medici nell'Europa del Cinquecento: Il Primato del Disegno*. Florence, 1980, 227–86.

——. "Vasari e le stampe." *Prospettiva* 57–60 (1989–90): 18–38.

——. "Le stampe che imitano i disegni." *Bollettino d'Arte* 7 (1992): 87–122.

Borroni Salvadori, Fabia. "Bonifacio, Natale." In *Dizionario biografico degli Italiani*. Vol. 11, 201–4. Rome, 1970.

——. "Cartaro, Mario." In *Dizionario biografico degli Italiani*. Vol. 20, 796–99. Rome, 1977.

——. "L'incisione al servizio del Boccaccio nei secoli XV e XVI." *Annali della Scuola Normale di Pisa* 7 (1977): 595–734.

——. *Carte, Piante e Stampe Storiche delle Raccolte Lafreriane della Biblioteca Nazionale di Firenze*. Rome, 1980.

Borroni Salvadori, Fabia, and P. Innocenti, eds. *Mostra dei manoscritti, documenti ed edizioni* (VI Centenario della morte di Giovanni Boccaccio). Vol. 2: *Edizioni*. Certaldo, 1975.

Borsi, Franco. *Giovanni Antonio Dosio: Le Antichità di Roma*. Rome, 1970.

——. *Roma di Sisto V: La Pianta di Antonio Tempesta, 1593*. Rome, 1986.

Bottari, Giovanni, and Stefano Ticozzi. *Raccolta di lettere sulla pittura, scultura ed architettura scritte da' più celebri personaggi dei secoli XV, XVI, e XVII*. 8 vols. Milan, 1822–25. Reprint, 2nd. ed., Hildesheim, 1976.

Boucher, Bruce. "Giuseppe Salviati, Pittore e Matematico." *Arte Veneta* 30 (1976): 219–24.

Bowker, Richard Rogers. *Copyright: Its History and Its Law, Being a Summary of the*

Principles and Practice of Copyright with Special Reference to the American Code of 1909 and the British Act of 1911. Boston and New York, 1912.

Brown, Horatio. *The Venetian Printing Press 1469–1800.* London, 1891. Reprint, Amsterdam, 1969.

Brugnoli, Maria Vittoria. "Le Pitture della Palazzina Gambara." In *La Villa Lante di Bagnaia.* Milan, 1961, 109–19.

Brun, C. "Neue Dokumente über Andrea Mantegna." *Zeitschrift für bildenden Kunst* 11 (1976): 23–26.

Brun, Robert. *Le Livre lllustré en France au XVIᵉ Siécle.* Paris, 1930.

Bruwaert, Edmond. *Recherches sur la vie et l'oeuvre du graveur troyen Philippe Thomassin.* Troyes, 1876.

Bulgarelli, Tullio. *Gli Avvisi a Stampa in Roma nel Cinquecento.* Rome, 1967.

Burns, Howard. "Pirro Ligorio's Reconstruction of Ancient Rome: The *Anteiqvae Vrbis Imago* of 1561." In *Pirro Ligorio: Artist and Antiquarian.* Edited by Robert W. Gaston. Milan, 1988, 19–92.

Bury, John. "Philip II and the Escorial." *Print Quarterly* 8 (1991): 77–82.

Bury, Michael. "The Taste for Prints in Italy to c. 1600." *Print Quarterly* 2 (1985): 12–26.

——. "The 'Triumph of Christ', after Titian." *Burlington Magazine* 131 (1989): 188–97.

——. "On Some Engravings by Giorgio Ghisi Commonly Called 'Reproductive'." *Print Quarterly* 10 (1993): 4–19.

Buser, Thomas. "Jerome Nadal and Early Jesuit Art in Rome." *Art Bulletin* 58 (1976): 424–33.

Cadorin, Giuseppe. *Dello Amore ai Veneziani di Tiziano Vecellio delle sue Case in Cadore e in Venezia e delle Vite de' suoi Figli.* Venice, 1833.

Calabi, Augusto. "Marcantonio" *Dedalo* 3 (1922): 24–26.

——. "Note sulla storia economico-sociale degli incisori." *Die Graphischen Künste* 1 (1936) 72–78, 114–18.

Calnan, D. J., and G. E. Testaferrata. *The True Depiction of the Investment and Attack Suffered by the Island of Malta in 1565.* Malta, 1965.

Camerini, Paolo. *Annali dei Giunti.* 2 vols. Florence, 1962–63.

Campana, Augusto. "Intorno all'incisore Gian Battista Palumba ed al pittore Jacopo Rimpacta (Ripanda)." *Maso Finiguerra* 2 (1936): 164–81.

Campbell, Tony. *The Earliest Printed Maps, 1472–1500.* Berkeley and Los Angeles, 1987.

Cantoni, Angelo. "Cenno Storico." In *La Villa Lante di Bagnaia.* Milan, 1961, 9–35.

Cappelletti, Giuseppe. *Storia di Padova.* Padua, Vol. 1, 1874, Vol. 2, 1875.

Cardella, Lorenzo. *Memorie storiche de' Cardinali della Santa Romana Chiesa.* 10 vols. Rome, 1793–97.

Carroll, Eugene A. "Drawings by Rosso Fiorentino in the British Museum," *Burlington Magazine* 108 (1966): 168–75.

——. "Lappoli, Alfani, Vasari, and Rosso." *Art Bulletin* 49 (1967): 297–304.

——. *Rosso Fiorentino: Drawings, Prints, and Decorative Arts.* Washington, D.C., 1987.

Casali, Scipione. *Gli Annali della tipografia veneziana di Francesco Marcolini da Forlì.* Forlì, 1861.

Casamassima, Emanuele. "Ludovico degli Arrighi detto Vicentino copista dell'*Itinerario* del Varthema." *La Bibliofilia* 64 (1962): 117–62.

——. "I disegni di caratteri di Ludovico degli Arrighi Vicentino (notizie 1510–1527)." *Gutenberg Jahrbuch* (1963): 24–36.

——. "Ancora su Ludovico degli Arrighi Vicentino (notizie 1510–1527). Risultati di una 'recognito'." *Gutenberg Jahrbuch* 100 (1965): 35–42.

——. *Trattati di Scrittura del Cinquecento Italiano.* Milan, 1966.

Casciano, P., G. Castoldi, M.P. Critelli, P. Farenga, A. Modigliani, eds. *Scrittura, Biblioteche e Stampa a Roma nel Quattrocento, Aspetti e Problemi (Atti del Seminario 1–2 giugno 1979): Indice delle edizioni romane a stampe (1467–1500).* Vatican City, 1980.

Cassini, Giocondo. *Piante e vedute prospettiche di Venezia (1479–1855)*. Venice, 1971.

Castellani, Carlo. *Catalogo Ragionato delle più rare o più importanti opere geografiche a stampa che si conservano nella biblioteca del Collegio Romano*. Rome, 1876.

———. "I Privilegi di Stampa e la Proprietà Letteraria in Venezia dalla introduzione della stampa nella città." *Archivio Veneto* 36 (1888): 127–39.

———. *La Stampa in Venezia dalla sua origine alla morte di Aldo Manuzio seniore*. Venice, 1889. Reprint, Trieste, 1973.

———. *L'arte della stampa nel rinascimento italiano: Venezia*. Venice, 1894.

Castiglioni, Gino. "'Frixi et figure et miniadure facte de intajo' tra silografia e miniatura in alcuni incunaboli veneziani." *Verona Illustrata* 2 (1989): 19–27.

Catalano, Giuseppe. *De magistro sacri palatii apostolici libri duo*. Rome, 1751.

Cavazzi, Luigi, Anita Margiotta, and Simonetta Tozzi. *L'Incisione a Roma nel Cinquecento nella Raccolta del Gabinetto Comunale delle Stampa*. Rome, 1989.

Cecchetti, Bartolomeo. "La pittura delle stampe di Bernardino Benalio." *Archivio Veneto* 33 (1887): 538–39.

Celio, Gaspare. *Memoria dell'artefici delle pitture che sono in alcune chiese, facciate, e palazzi di Roma*. Naples, 1638. Facsimile edition, edited by Emma Zocca, Milan, 1967.

Charon-Parent, Annie. "Le monde de l'imprimerie humaniste: Paris." In *Histoire de l'Édition Française*. Edited by Henri-Jean Martin and Roger Chartier. Vol. 1: *Le Livre Conquérant*, 237–53. Paris, 1983.

Cicogna, Emmanuele A. *Delle Iscrizioni veneziane*. 6 Vols. Venice, 1824–53.

Cioni, Alfredo. "Benalio, Bernardino." In *Dizionario biografico degli Italiani*. Vol. 8, 165–67. Rome, 1966.

Codazzi, Angela. *Le Edizioni Quattrocentesche e Cinquecentesche della "Geografia" di Tolomeo*. Milan, 1950.

Coffin, David R. *The Villa d'Este at Tivoli*. Princeton, 1960.

———. "Some Aspects of the Villa Lante at Bagnaia." In *Arte in Europa: Scritti di storia dell'arte in onore di Edoardo Arslan*. Milan, 1966. Vol. 1, 569–75.

Collijn, Isak. *Sveriges bibliografi intill år 1600*. 3 vols. Uppsala, 1927–38.

Consagra, Francesca. "The Marketing of Pietro Testa's 'Poetic Inventions'." In Elizabeth Cropper, *Pietro Testa 1612–1650: Prints and Drawings*. Philadelphia, 1988.

———. The De Rossi Family Print Publishing Shop. A Study in the History of the Print Industry in Seventeenth-Century Rome. Ph.D. diss., Johns Hopkins University, 1992.

Consonni, Luisa. "Gerolamo Muziano e i suoi incisori." *Rassegna di Studi e di Notizie* 11 (1983): 169–219.

Conway, William Martin. *Literary Remains of Albrecht Dürer*. Cambridge, 1889.

Coolidge, John. "Vignola and the Little Domes of St. Peter's." *Marsyas* 2 (1942): 63–124.

Cozzi, Gaetano. "Religione, moralità e giustizia a Venezia: vicende della magistratura degli esecutori contro la bestemmia (sec. XVI–XVII)." *Ateneo Veneto*, 177 (n.s. 29) (1991): 7–95.

Creytens, Raymond. "Le 'Studium Romanae Curiae' et le Maître du Sacré Palais." *Archivum Fratrum Praedicatorum* 12 (1942) 5–83.

Cristofori, Francesco. *Cronotasi dei Cardinali di Santa Romana Chiesa nelle loro sedi suburbicarie titoli Presbiterali e Diaconie dal secolo V all'anno del Signore MDCCCLXXXVIII*. Rome, 1878.

Crowe, J. A., and G. B. Cavalcaselle. *Raphael: His Life and Work*. 2 vols. London, 1882–85.

Cumberland, George. *An Essay on the Utility of Collecting the Best Works of the Ancient Engravers of the Italian School . . . from the Earliest Practice of the Art in Italy to the Year 1549*. London, 1827.

Da Como, Ugo. *Girolamo Muziano: 1528–1592; Note e Documenti*. Bergamo, 1938.

Dacos, Nicole. "Tommaso Vincidor. Un élève de Raphael aux Pays-Bas." In *Relations Artistiques entre les Pays-Bas et l'Italie à la Renaissance: Études dédiées à Suzanne Sulzberger*. Brussels and Rome, 1980, 61–99.

D'Amico, John F. *Renaissance Humanism in Papal Rome: Humanists and Churchmen on the Eve of the Reformation.* Baltimore and London, 1983.

D'Arco, Carlo. *Istoria della vita e delle opere di Giulio Pippi detto Romano.* Mantua, 1838.

Davidson, Bernice. Marcantonio Raimondi: the Engravings of his Roman Period. Ph.D. diss., Harvard University, 1954.

——. "Introducing Michaeli Grechi Lucchese." *Art Bulletin* 46 (1964): 550–52.

——. "Drawings by Marcello Venusti." *Master Drawings* 2 (1973): 3–19.

De Bujanda, J. M. *Index de Rome 1557, 1559, 1564. Les premiers index romains et l'index di Concile de Trente.* Index des Livres Interdits, 8. Sherbrooke, Québec, 1990.

De Chapeaurouge, Donat. "Eine Circus-Rekonstruktion des Pirro Ligorio." *Antike und Abenland* 8 (1973): 89–96.

De Grazia, Diane. *Le Stampe dei Carracci.* Bologna, 1984 [see also Bohlin].

De Gregori, Luigi. *La stampa a Roma nel secolo XV.* Rome, 1933.

De Mesa, Josè, and Teresa Gisbert. *El Pintor Mateo Pérez de Alesio.* La Paz, 1972.

Degli Azzi, Giustiniani. "Archivio Alberti." *Gli archivi della storia d'Italia.* Serie 2, Vol. 4. Rocca S. Casciano, 1915, 195–255.

Del Badia, Iodoco. "La bottega di Alessandro di Francesco Rosselli merciaio stampatore (1525)." In *Miscellanea fiorentina di erudizione e di storia.* Florence, 1894, 24–30. Reprint, Rome, 1978.

Del Re, Niccolò. *La Curia Romana.* 3rd ed. Rome, 1970.

Delaborde, Henri. *Marc-Antoine Raimondi.* Paris, 1888.

Delen, Adrien Jean Joseph. *Histoire de la gravure dans les anciens Pays-Bas & dans les provinces belges des origines jusqu' à la fin du XVI* siècle. Pt. 2, Le XVI* siècle.* [a] *Les Graveurs-Illustrateurs,* [b] *Les graveurs d'estampes.* Paris, 1924. Reprint, Paris, 1969.

Derosas, Renzo. "Moralità e giustizia a Venezia nel '500–'600: Gli Esecutori contro la bestemmia." In *Stato, Società e Giustizia nella Repubblica Veneta (secc. XV–XVIII).* Edited by Gaetano Cozzi. Rome, 1980. Vol. 1, 431–528.

Destombes, Marcel. "Les cartes de Lafréri et assimilées (1532–1586) du Départment des Estampes de la Bibliothèque nationale." *Nouvelles de l'Estampe* 5 (1970): 234–274. Addenda et errata, 8 (1970): 353–55.

——. "La grande carte d'Europe de Zuan Domenico Zorzi (1545) et l'activité cartographique de Matteo Pagano à Venise de 1538 à 1565." In *Studia z Dziejów Geografii i Kartografii.* Etudes d'Histoire de la Géographie et de la Cartographie. Edited by Jósef Babicz. Monografie z Dziejow Nauki i Techniki 87. Warsaw, 1973, 115–30.

Deswarte-Rosa, Sylvie. "Domenico Giuntalodi, peintre de D. Martinho de Portugal." *Revue de l'Art* 80 (1980): 52–60.

——. "Les gravures de monuments antiques d'Antonio Salamanca, à l'origine du *Speculum Romanae Magnificentiae.*" *Annali di Architettura: Rivista del Centro Internazionale di Architettura Andrea Palladio* 1 (1989): 47–62.

Dibner, Bern. *Moving the Obelisks: A chapter in engineering history in which the Vatican obelisk in Rome in 1586 was moved by muscle power, and a study of more recent similar moves.* New York, 1952.

Dickson, Robert, and John Philip Edmond. *Annals of Scottish printing from the introduction of the art in 1507 to the beginning of the seventeenth century.* Cambridge, 1890.

Dillon, Gianvittorio. "Sul Libro illustrato del Quattrocento: Venezia e Verona." In *La Stampa degli Incunaboli nel Veneto.* Edited by Neri Pozza. Venice, 1984, 81–96.

Dinsmoor, William B. "The Literary Remains of Sebastiano Serlio." *Art Bulletin* 24 (1942): 55–91, 115–54.

Dionisotti, Carlo. "Notizie su Alessandro Minuziano." In *Miscellania di studi in onore del card. A. Mercati.* Vol. 4. Rome, 1946, 327.

Dodgson, Campbell. "Beschreibendes Verzeichniss der Buchillustrationen Lucas van Leyden's." *Repertorium für Kunstwissenschaft* 23 (1900): 143–53.

Donati, Lamberto. "Martino Rota, Incisore Sebenicense." *Archivio Storico per la Dalmazia* 2 (March, 1927): 29–38.

——. "Natale Bonifacio." *Archivio Storico per la Dalmazia* 3 (April, 1927): 31–42.
——. "Martino Rota: Appunti Iconografici." *Archivio Storico per la Dalmazia* 3 (June, 1927): 123–30.
——. "Un Libro sconosciuto illustrato da Natale Bonifacio Sebenicense." *Archivio Storico per la Dalmazia* 8 (March, 1930): 574–89.
——. "Alcune stampe sconosciute di Martino Rota." *Archivio Storico per la Dalmazia* 13 (April, 1932): 2–11.
——. "Intorno all'opera di Natale Bonifacio. Lettera a Roberto Almagià." *Archivio Storico per la Dalmazia* 15 (August, 1933): 210–38.
——. "Chi fu Leonardo Caccianemici?" *Maso Finiguerra* 1 (1936): 248–49.
——. "Un secondo esemplare della pianta di Roma di Antonio Tempesta (1593)." *Maso Finiguerra* 1 (1936): 67–68.
——. Review of Arnolfo Bacotich, "Due stampe assai rare di Natale Bonifacio da Sebenico (1538–1592)." [published in *Archivio Storico per la Dalmazia* 20 (February, 1936): 478–496]. *Maso Finiguerra* 1 (1936): 75–78.
——. Introduction. *Mostra del Libro Illustrato Romano del Cinquecento*. Rome, 1950.
——. "Di una figura non interpretata di Stefano Pellegrini da Cesena." In *Studi rimanesi e bibliografici in onore di Carlo Lucchese*. Faenza, 1952, 45–51.
——. "Studi sul passaggio dal manoscritti allo stampato: la decorazione degli incunaboli italiani." In *Studi di paleografica, diplomatica, storia e araldica in onore di Cesare Manaresi*. Milan, 1953, 331–43.
——. "Agostino Veneziano." *La Bibliofilia* 57 (1955): 21–22.
——. "Edizioni quattrocentesche non pervenuteci delle Metamorfosi." In *Atti del Convegno Internazionale Ovidiana*. Sulmona, 1958, vol. 1, 111.
——. "Del Mito di Zoan Andrea e di altri miti grandi e piccoli." *Biblioteca degli eruditi e dei bibliofili*. Florence, 1959, vol. 37, 7–50.
——. "I fregi xilografici stampati a mano negl'incunabuli italiani." *La Biblbiografia* 74 (1972): 157–64, 303–27; 75 (1973): 125–74.
Dondi, Giuseppe. "Una famiglia di editori a mezzo il secolo XVI: i Giolito." *Atti dell'Accademia delle Scienze di Torino* 102 (1968): 589–701.
Doni, Anton Francesco. *Il Disegno*. Venice, 1549.
D'Onofrio, Cesare. *Gli Obelischi di Roma*. Rome, 1965.
Dorez, Léon. "Le cardinal Marcello Cervini et l'imprimerie à Rome (1539–1550)." *Mélanges d'Archéologie et d'Histoire* 12 (1892): 289–313.
Dreyer, Peter, *Tizian und sein Kreis, 50 venezianische Holzschnitte aus dem Berliner Kupferstichkabinett Staatliche Museen Preussischer Kulturbesitz*. Berlin, n.d. (1971).
——. "Ugo da Carpi venezianische Zeit im Lichte neuer Zuschreibungen." *Zeitschrift für Kunstgeschichte* 35 (1972): 282–301.
——. "Xilografie di Tiziano a Venezia." *Arte Veneta* 30 (1976): 270–72.
——. "Sulle Silografie di Tiziano." In *Tiziano a Venezia. Convegno Internazionale di Studi, Venezia, 1976*. Vicenza, 1980, 503–11.
Dülberg, Franz. "Lucas van Leyden als Illustrator." *Repertorium für Kunstwissenschaft* 21 (1898): 36–46.
Durling, Richard J. *A Catalogue of Sixteenth Century Printed Books in the National Library of Medicine*. Bethesda, Maryland, 1967.
Edwards, Francis. *Description of a Recently Discovered "Lafreri" Atlas 1553–1580*. Offered by Francis Edwards Ltd. London, 1933.
Egger, Hermann. "Die Darstellung einer päpstlichen Segensspendung aus dem Verlag Bartolomeo Faleti (1567)." *Maso Finiguerra* 1 (1936): 62.
Ehrle, Franz. *Roma Prima di Sisto V: La pianta di Roma Du Pérac-Laféry del 1577 riprodotta dall'esemplare esistente nel Museo Britannico; Contribuito alla storia del commercio delle stampe a Roma nel secolo 16° e 17°*. Rome, 1908.
——. *Roma al Tempo di Giulio III: La pianta di Roma di Leonardo Bufalini del 1551 riprodotta dall'esemplare esistente nella Biblioteca Vaticana*. Rome, 1911.

———. *Roma al Tempo di Clemente VIII: La Pianta di Roma di Antonio Tempesta del 1593*. Vatican City, 1932.

Ehrle, Franz, and Hermann Egger. *Die Conclavepläne: Beiträge zu ihrer Entwicklungsgeschichte*. Vatican City, 1933.

Eisler, Robert. "The Frontispiece to Sigismondo Fanti's *Triompho di Fortuna*." *Journal of the Warburg and Courtauld Institutes* 10 (1947): 155–59.

Elie, H. "Un Lunevillois imprimeur à Rome an début du XVIᵉᵐᵉ siècle: Etienne Guillery." *Gutenberg Jahrbuch* (1939): 186–89 (Part 1); (1944–49): 128–37 (Part II).

Emiliani, Andrea. *Mostra di Federico Barocci*. Bologna, 1975.

———. *Federico Barocci (Urbino 1535–1612)*. Bologna, 1985.

Emison, Patricia. "Marcantonio's *Massacre of the Innocents*." *Print Quarterly* 1 (1984): 257–67.

Essling, Prince d' [Victor Massena]. *Études sur l'art de la gravure sur bois à Venise. Les livres à figure vénitiens de la fin du XVᵉ siècle et du commencement du XVIᵉ*. 3 parts in 4 vols. Florence, 1907–1914.

Faietti, Marzia, and Konrad Oberhuber. *Bologna e l'Umanismo, 1490–1510*. Bologna, 1988.

Faietti, Marzia. "L'incisione di riproduzione in Italia fino alla metà del XVI secolo." *Grafica d'Arte* 8 (1991): 2–8.

Falaschi, Enid T. "Valvassore's 1553 illustrations of *Orlando furioso*: the development of multi-narrative technique in Venice and its links with cartography." *La Bibliofilia* 77 (1975): 227–51.

Fanelli, Vittorio. "Il ginnasio greco di Leone X a Roma." In Vittorio Fanelli, *Ricerche su Angelo Colocci e sulla Roma cinquecentesca*. Studi e Testi, No. 283. Vatican City, 1979, 91–110.

Fava, Mariano, and Giovanni Bresciano. *La stampa a Napoli nel xv secolo*. Leipzig, 1911. Reprint, Wiesbaden, 1969.

Federici, V. "Di Mario Cartaro Incisore Viterbese del secolo XVI." *Archivio della R. Società Romana di Storia Patria* 21 (1898): 535–53.

Fiocco, Giuseppe. "Jacopo Ripanda." *L'Arte* 23 (1920): 27–48.

Fischer, Marianne. "Lafreri's *Speculum Romanae Magnificentiae*: Addenda zu Hülsens Verzeichnis." *Berliner Museen* 22 (1972): 10–17.

Fontana, Pierina. "Inizi della proprietà letteraria nello Stato Pontifico (Saggio di documenti dell'Archivio Vaticano)." *Accademie e Biblioteche d'Italia* 3 (1929–1930): 204–21.

Francia, Ennio. *Storia della costruzione del nuovo San Pietro da Michelangelo a Bernini*. Rome, 1989.

Frey, Karl. *Der Literarische Nachlass Giorgio Vasaris*. 2 vols. Munich, 1930. Reprint, Hildesheim and New York, 1982.

Fulin, Rinaldo. "Gl'Inquisitori dei Dieci." *Archivio Veneto* 1 (1871): 1–64, 298–313; 2 (1871): 357–91.

———. "Primi privilegi di stampa in Venezia." *Archivio Veneto* 1 (1871): 160–4.

———. "Documenti per servire alla Storia della Tipografia Veneziana." *Archivio Veneto* 23 (1882): 84–212.

Fumagalli, Giuseppe, and G. Belli. *Catalogo delle edizioni romane di Antonio Blado asolano ed eredi (1515–1593)*. 2 vols. Rome, 1891.

Fumagalli, Giuseppe. *Antonio Blado, tipografo romano del secolo XVI. Memoria storico-bibliografica*. Milan, 1893.

———. *Lexicon Typographicum Italiae: Dictionnaire Géographique d'Italie*. Florence, 1905.

Fuhring, Peter. Entries in *The French Renaissance in Prints from the Bibliothèque Nationale de France*. Exhibition Catalogue, nos. 80–81. Los Angeles, 1994.

Gallo, Rodolfo. "Gli Incisori Sadeler a Venezia." *Rivista della Città di Venezia* 9 (1930): 35–48.

———. "Le mappe geografiche del Palazzo Ducale di Venezia." *Archivio Veneto* 32–33 (1943): 43–113.

——. "Fra Vincenzo Paletino de Curzola." *Atti dell'Accademia dei Lincei: Rendiconti* 2 (1947): 259–67.

——. "Antonio Florian and his Mappemonde." *Imago Mundi* 6 (1949): 35–38.

——. "Gioan Francesco Camocio and his Large Map of Europe." *Imago Mundi* 7 (1950): 93–102.

Gallois, Lucien Louis Joseph. *De Orontio Finæo Gallico Geographo*. Paris, 1890.

Gamurrini, Eugenio. *Istoria Genealogica delle Famiglie Nobili Toscane et Umbre*. Florence, 1671.

Ganado, Alberto. "Matteo Perez D'Allecio's Engravings of the Siege of Malta of 1565." In *Proceedings of History Week 1983*. Edited by Mario Buhagiar. Published in Malta by the Historical Society of Malta, 1984, 125–61.

Ganda, Arnaldo. "Antonio Zarotto da Parma tipografo in Milano (1471–1507)." *La Bibliofilia* 77 (1975): 165–222.

Garcia, P. J. "Las estampas de la Biblioteca del Escorial." *Religión y Cultura* 27 (1934): 349–60.

Gasparini, Giovan Battista. "La Natura Giuridica dei Privilegi per la Stampa in Venezia." In *La Stampa degli Incunaboli nel Veneto*. Edited by Neri Pozza. Venice, 1984, 103–20.

Gattico, Giovanni Battista. *Acta selecta caeremonialia sanctae romanae ecclesiae ex variis mss. codicibus, et diariis saeculi XV, XVI, XVII*. 2 vols. in 1. Rome, 1753. Photocopy, University of Notre Dame Library, 1983.

Gaye, Giovanni. *Carteggio inedito d'Artisti dei Secoli XIV, XV, XVI*. 3 vols. Florence, 1839–1840.

Geanakoplos, Deno John. *Bisanzio e il Rinascimento: Umanisti greci a Venezia e la diffusione del greco in Occidente (1400–1535)*. Rome, 1967.

Gere, John A. "Two of Taddeo Zuccaro's last commissions, completed by Federico Zuccaro, 2: The High Altarpiece in San Lorenzo in Damaso," *Burlington Magazine* 108 (1966): 341–45.

——. *Taddeo Zuccaro. His development studied in his drawings*. London, 1969.

Gere, John A., and Philip Pouncey. *Italian Drawings in the Department of Prints and Drawings in the British Museum: Artists Working in Rome c. 1550 to c. 1640*. London, 1983.

Gerulaitis, Leonardas Vytautas. *Printing and Publishing in Fifteenth-Century Venice*. Chicago and London, 1976.

Glück, Gustav. "Zu den Holzschnitten der Leidener Chronik von 1517." *Repertorium für Kunstwissenschaft* 23 (1900): 455.

Gnoli, D. "Descriptio urbis o censimento della popolazione di Roma avanti il Sacco borbonico." *Archivio della R. Societa Romana di Storia Patria* 17 (1894): 375–520.

Gnoli, Umberto. "Raffaello e la "Incoronazione" di Monteluce." *Bollettino d'Arte* 11 (1917): 133–54.

Goldschmidt, Ernst Philip. *Catalogue of Illustrated Books 1491–1759*. Catalogue by Robin G. Halwas. E. P. Goldschmidt & Co. Ltd. Catalogue 165. London, n.d.

Goldthwaite, Richard A. *The Building of Renaissance Florence: An Economic and Social History*. Baltimore, 1980.

——. *Wealth and the Demand for Art in Italy, 1300–1600*. Baltimore, 1993.

Golzio, Vincenzo. *Raffaello nei Documenti*. Vatican City, 1936.

Gori Gandellini, Giovanni, and Luigi de Angelis. *Notizie istoriche degli Intagliatori*. 2nd ed., 15 vols. in 5. Siena, 1808–1816. First edition (3 vols.) published in Siena, 1771. On the title-pages of vols. 4–15, the name Luigi de Angelis appears as continuator.

Grande, Stefano. *Notizie sulla vita e sulle opere di Giacomo Gastaldi cosmografo piemontese del secolo XVI*. Turin, 1902.

Grendler, Paul. *The Roman Inquisition and the Venetian Press, 1540–1605*. Princeton, 1977.

Gualandi, Michelangelo. "Memorie intorno la celebre famiglia degli Alberti di S. Sepolcro." In *Memorie Originale Italiane Risguardanti le Belle Arti*. Vol. 2, Serie 6. Bologna, 1845, 50–91.

——. *Di Ugo da Carpi e dei conti di Panico*. Bologna, 1854.

Habicht, Victor Curt. "Miniaturen von Benedetto Bordone in dem Venezianische Bibeldrucke von 1471." *Zeitschrift für Bücherfreunde* 36 (1932): 263–71.

Haebler, Konrad. *The Early Printers of Spain and Portugal*. London, 1897.

——. *Spanische und Portugiesische Bücherzeichen des XV. und XVI. Jahrhunderts*. Strassburg, 1898. Reprint, Naarden, 1969.

——. *Bibliografía ibérica del siglo xv. Enumeración de todos los libros impresos en España y Portugal hasta el año de 1500*. The Hague, 1903.

Hain, Ludwig. *Repertorium Bibliographicum in quo libri omnes ab arte typographica inventa usque ad annum MD typis expressi . . . recensentur*. 4 vols. Stuttgart, 1826–1838. Reprint, Milan, 1948.

Hale, J. R. "Andrea Palladio, Polybius and Julius Caesar." *Journal of the Warburg and Courtauld Institutes* 40 (1977): 240–55.

——. "Venice and Its Empire." In *The Genius of Venice 1500–1600*. Edited by Jane Martineau and Charles Hope. New York, 1984, 11–15.

Hall, Marcia. *Renovation and Counter-Reformation: Vasari and Duke Cosimo in Sta. Maria Novella and Sta. Croce, 1565–1577*. Oxford and New York, 1979.

Haskell, Francis. *Patrons and Painters*. New Haven and London, 1980.

Haskell, Francis, and Nicholas Penny. *Taste and the Antique*. New Haven and London, 1981.

Heawood, Edward. "An Undescribed Lafreri Atlas and Contemporary Venetian Collections." *Geographical Journal* 73 (1929): 359–69.

Heinecken, Karl von. *Dictionnaire des Artistes*. 4 vols. Leipzig, 1778–1790.

——. *Neue Nachrichten von Künstlern und Kunstsachen. 1. Theil*. Dresden, 1786.

Held, Julius. *Dürer through Other Eyes: His Graphic Work Mirrored in Copies and Forgeries of Three Centuries*. Williamstown, Mass., 1975.

Hellwald, Ferdinand Heller von. *Bibliographie méthodique de l'Ordre souv. de St. Jean de Jérusalem*. Rome, 1885.

Hermanin, Federico. "Gabinetto nazionale delle stampe in Roma: Catalogo delle incisioni con vedute romane." In *Le Gallerie Nazionale Italiane* 3 (1897): i–xc.

Herrmann-Fiore, Kristina. *Disegni degli Alberti*. Rome, 1983.

Jacob Hess, "A proposito di un libro di Girolamo Muziano," *Maso Finiguerra*, 2, 1937, 69–75.

——. "Entwürfe von Giovanni Guerra für Villa Lante in Bagnaia (1598)." *Römisches Jahrbuch für Kunstgeschichte* 12 (1969): 195–202.

Hessels, Jan Hendrik. *Abrahami Ortelii (geographi antverpiensis) et virorum eruditorum ad eundem et ad Jacobum Colium Ortelianum (Abrahami Ortelii sororis filium) epistulae. Cum aliquot aliis epistolis et tractatibus quibusdam ab utroque collectis, (1524–1628) Ex autographis mandante Ecclesia Londino-Batava edidit*. Cambridge, 1887. Reprint, Osnabrück, 1969.

Hibbard, Howard. *Carlo Maderno and Roman Architecture, 1580–1630*. University Park, Penn., 1971.

Hilgers, Joseph. *Der Index der verboten Bücher*. Freiberg im Breissgau, 1904.

Hind, Arthur M. *Catalogue of Early Italian Engravings preserved in the Department of Prints and Drawings in the British Museum*. Edited by Sidney Colvin. 2 vols. London, 1910.

——. *A History of Engraving and Etching*. Boston and New York, 1923.

——. *An Introduction to a History of Woodcut*. 2 vols. Boston and New York, 1935.

——. *Early Italian Engravings*. 7 vols. London, 1938–48.

Hinks, Arthur Robert. "The Lettering of the Roman Ptolemy of 1478." *Geographical Journal* 101 (1943): 188–90.

Hirsch, Rudolf. "Pre-Reformation Censorship of Printed Books." *Library Chronicle* 21 (1955): 100–105.

————. *Printing, Selling and Reading 1450–1550*. Wiesbaden, 1967.

————. "Bulla Super Impressione Librorum, 1515." *Gutenberg-Jahrbuch* (1973): 248–51.

Hirth, Herbert. *Marcanton und sein Stil. Eine kunstgeschichtliche Studie*. Ph.D. diss., Leipzig-Münich, 1898.

Hobson, Anthony. "The Printer of the Greek Editions *In Gymnasio Mediceo ad Caballinum Montem*." In *Studi di biblioteconomia e storia del libro in onore di Francesco Barberi*. Rome, 1976, 331–35.

Hofer, Philip. "Early Book Illustration in the Intaglio Medium." *The Print Collector's Quarterly* 21 (1934): 203–27, 295–316.

————. "Illustrated Editions of 'Orlando Furioso'." In *Fragonard Drawings for Ariosto with Essays by Elizabeth Mongan, Philip Hofer, Jean Seznec*. New York, 1945, 27–40.

————. "Variant Issues of the First Edition of Ludovico Arrighi Vicentino's *Operina*." In *Calligraphy and Palaeography: Essays Presented to Alfred Fairbank on His 70th Birthday*. Edited by A. S. Osley. London, 1965, 95–106. The essay first appeared in the *Harvard Library Bulletin* 14 (1960).

Hollstein, F. W. H. *Dutch and Flemish Engravings, Etchings and Woodcuts, ca. 1450–1700*. Vols. 22–23. Compiled by Dieuwke de Hoop Scheffer and edited by Karel G. Boon. Amsterdam, 1980.

Hoogewerff, Godefrid Joannes. *Nederlandsche Schilders in Italië in de XVIᵉ Eeuw (De Geschiedenis van het Romanisme)*. Utrecht, 1912.

————. *Bescheiden in Italië omtrent Nederlandsche Kunstenaars en Geleerden*. The Hague, 1913.

Howard, Deborah. "Sebastiano Serlio's Venetian Copyrights." *Burlington Magazine* 115 (1973): 512–16.

Huelsen, Christian. "Die alte Ansicht von Florenz im Königlichen Kupferstichkabinett und ihr Vorbild." *Jahrbuch der Königlich preussischen Kunstsammlungen* 35 (1914): 90–102.

————. "Das Speculum Romanae Magnificentiae des Antonio Lafreri." In *Collectanea Variae Doctrinae Leoni S. Olschki*. Munich, 1921, 121–70.

————. *Saggio di Bibliografia Ragionata delle Piante Icnografiche e Prospettiche di Roma dal 1551 al 1748* [first published as "Bibliografia delle Piante di Roma," *Archivio della Società Romana di Storia Patria*, 1915]. Revised edition. Florence, 1933. Reprint, Rome, 1969.

Iversen, Erik. *The Myth of Egypt and its Hieroglyphs in European Tradition*. Princeton, 1993.

Jacobowitz, Ellen S., and Stephanie Loeb Stepanek. *The Prints of Lucas van Leyden and His Contemporaries*. Washington, D.C., 1983.

Jacometti, Fabio. "Il primo stampatore senese: Simone di Niccolò di Nardo." *La Diana* 1 (1926): 184–202.

Johnson, A. F. *Periods of Typography: The Italian Sixteenth Century*. London, 1926.

————. "Oronce Fine as an Illustrator of Books." *Gutenberg-Jahrbuch* (1928): 107–109. Reprinted in *A. F. Johnson: Selected Essays on Books and Printing*. Edited by Percy H. Muir. Amsterdam, 1970, 190–195.

————. "A Catalogue of Italian Writing-Books of the Sixteenth Century," *Signature* 10 (1950): 22–48. Reprinted in *A. F. Johnson: Selected Essays on Books and Printing*. Edited by Percy H. Muir. Amsterdam, 1970, 18–40.

Johnson, Jan. "I Chiaroscuri di Ugo da Carpi/Ugo da Carpi's Chiaroscuro Woodcuts." *Il Conoscitore di Stampe/Print Collector* nos. 57–58 (1982): 2–87.

Karpinski, Caroline. *Italian Printmaking: Fifteenth and Sixteenth Centuries; An Annotated Bibliography*. Boston, 1987.

————. "The Print in Thrall to Its Original: A Historiographic Perspective." In *Retaining the Original: Multiple Originals, Copies, and Reproductions*. Center for Advanced Study in the Visual Arts, Symposium Papers 7, Studies in the History of Art, vol. 20. National Gallery of Art, Washington, D.C., 1989, 101–109.

Karrow, Robert W. Jr. *Mapmakers of the Sixteenth Century and Their Maps: Bio-Bibliographies of the Cartographers of Abraham Ortelius, 1570*. Chicago, 1993.

Keith, D. Graeme. Introduction. *The Triumph of Humanism: A Visual Survey of the*

Decorative Arts of the Renaissance. California Palace of the Legion of Honor, San Francisco, 1977.

Kelliher, J. "Privileges (Canon Law)." In *New Catholic Encyclopedia*. Vol. 11, 811–12. New York, 1967–79.

Körte, Werner. "Verlorene Frühwertze des Federico Zuccari in Rom." *Mitteilungen des Kunsthistorischen Institutes in Florenz* 3 (1919–1922): 518–29.

Kristeller, Paul. "Marco Dente und Der Monogrammist SR." *Jahrbuch der Königlichen preussischen Kunstsammlungen* 11 (1890): 242–48.

——. *Die italienischen Buchdrucker- und Verlegerzeichen bis 1525*. Strassburg, 1893.

——. *Il Trionfo della Fede: Holzschnittfolge nach Tizians Zeichnung* (Graphische Gesellschaft 1). Berlin, 1906.

——. "Tizians Beziehungen zum Kupferstich." *Mitteilungen der Gesellschaft für vervielfältigende Kunst* (supplement to *Graphischen Kunste*) 34 (1911): 23–26.

——. *Kupferstich und Holschnitt in Vier Jahrhunderten*. Berlin, 1911.

Kubler, George. "Francesco Paciotto, Architect." In *Essays in Memory of Karl Lehmann*. Edited by Lucy Freeman Sandler. New York, 1964, 176–89.

——. *Building the Escorial*. Princeton, 1982.

Kühn-Hattenhauer, Dorothee. *Das Grafische Oeuvre des Francesco Villamena*. Ph.D. diss., Freien Universität, Berlin, 1979.

Kuhrmann, Dieter. "Frühwerke Agostino Venezianos." In *Munuscula Discipulorum: Kunsthistorische Studien Hans Kauffmann zum 70. Geburtstag 1966*. Edited by Tilmann Buddensieg and Matthias Winner. Berlin, 1968, 173–76.

Kultzen, Rolf. "La Serie dei Dodici Cesari Dipinta da Baldassarre Peruzzi." *Bollettino d'Arte* 58 (1963): 50–53.

Kurz, Otto. "Engravings on Silver by Annibale Carracci." *Burlington Magazine* 97 (1955): 282–87.

Lambert, Susan. *The Image Multiplied: Five Centuries of Printed Reproductions of Paintings and Drawings*. London, 1987.

Landau, David. "Vasari, Prints and Prejudice." *Oxford Art Journal* 6 (1983): 3–10.

——. "Printmaking in Venice and the Veneto." In *The Genius of Venice 1500–1600*. Edited by Jane Martineau and Charles Hope. New York, 1984, 303–54.

——. "Mantegna as Printmaker." In *Andrea Mantegna*. Milan, 1992, 44–54.

Landau, David, and Peter Parshall. *The Renaissance Print: 1450–1550*. New Haven and London, 1994.

Laurent, M. H. "Alde Manuzio l'Ancien, Éditeur de S. Catherine de Sienne (1500)." *Traditio* 6 (1948): 357–63.

Lawner, Lynne. *I Modi nell'opera di Giulio Romano, Marcantonio Raimondi, Pietro Aretino e Jean-Frédéric-Maximilien de Waldeck*. Milan, 1984. Also in English translation: *I Modi: The Sixteen Pleasures. An Erotic Album of the Italian Renaissance. Giulio Romano, Marcantonio Raimondi, Pietro Aretino, and Count Jean-Frédéric-Maximilien de Waldeck*. Evanston, Illinois, 1988.

Layton, Evro. *The Sixteenth Century Greek Book in Italy: Printers and Publishers for the Greek World* (Library of the Hellenic Institute of Byzantine and Post-Byzantine Studies, Nº 16). Venice, 1994.

Lazzaro-Bruno, Claudia. "The Villa Lante at Bagnaia: An Allegory of Art and Nature." *Art Bulletin* 59 (1977): 553–60.

Legrand, Emile. *Bibliographie Hellénique, ou, Description raisonnée des ouvrages publiés en grec par des Grecs aux XVᵉ et XVIᵉ siècles*. 4 vols. Paris, 1885–1906. Reprint, Mansfield Centre, Conn., 1997.

Lehmann-Haupt, Hellmut. *An Introduction to the Woodcut of the Seventeenth Century*. New York, 1977.

Leicht, Pier Silverio. "L'Editore veneziano Michele Tramezino ed i suoi privilegi." In *Miscellanea di Scritti di Bibliografia ed Erudizione in Memoria di Luigi Ferrari*. Florence, 1952, 357–67.

Leospo, Enrica. *La mensa Isiaca di Torino*. Leiden, 1978.

Levenson, Jay A., Konrad Oberhuber, and Jacquelyn L. Sheehan. *Early Italian Engravings from the National Gallery of Art*. Washington, D.C., 1973.

Levenson, Jay A. "Reproductive Engravings, 'Some of the finest Italian prints of the early Renaissance'." *Art News* 73 (1974): 68–70.

Lieure, Jules. *La Gravure en France au XVIe siècle: La Gravure dans Le Livre et L'Ornement*. Paris and Brussels, 1927.

Limouze, Dorothy. "Aegidius Sadeler (1570–1629): Drawings, Prints, and the Development of an Art Theoretical Attitude." In *Prag um 1600: Beiträge zur Kunst und Kultur am Hofe Rudolfs II*. Freren, 1988, 183–92.

———. "Aegidius Sadeler, Imperial Printmaker." *Bulletin of the Philadelphia Museum of Art* 85 (1989): 1–24.

Lincoln, Evelyn. Printing and Visual Culture in Italy, 1470–1575. Ph.D. diss., University of California, Berkeley, 1994.

———. "Making a Good Impression: Diana Mantuana's Printmaking Career." *Renaissance Quarterly* 50 (1997): 1101–1147.

Linzeler, André. *Graveurs du Seizième siècle*. Vol. 1. Paris, 1932.

Lippmann, F. *The Art of Wood-Engraving in Italy in the Fifteenth Century*. London, 1888.

Lochhead, Ian C., and T. F. R. Barling. *The Siege of Malta 1565*. London, 1970.

Lopez, Pasquale. *Sul Libro a Stampa e le Origini della Censura Ecclesiastica*. Naples, 1972.

López Serrano, Matilde. "El grabador Pedro Perret." In *El Escorial 1563–1963. IV° Centenario*. Madrid, 1963, 689–716.

Lotz, Arthur. *Bibliographie der Modelbücher*. Stuttgart and London, 1963.

Lowry, Bates. "Notes on the *Speculum Romanae Magnificentiae* and Related Publications." *Art Bulletin* 34 (1952): 46–50.

Lowry, Martin. *The World of Aldus Manutius, Business and Scholarship in Renaissance Venice*. Oxford, 1979.

Lozzi, C. "Cesare Vecellio e i suoi disegni e intagli per libri di costumi e di merletti." *La Bibliofilia* 1 (1899): 3–11.

Ludwigs, Gustav. "Archivalische Beiträge zur Geschichte der Venezianischen Malerei." *Jahrbuch der Königlich preussischen Kunstsammlungen* 26 (1905): 152–53.

Lugli, Giuseppe. "Una pianta inedita del Porto Ostiense disegnata da Pirro Ligorio e l'iconografia della città di Porto nel Secolo XVI." *Atti della Pontificia Accademia Romana di Archeologia. Rendiconti* 23–29 (1943–1949): 187–207.

Luzio, Alessandro. *La Galleria dei Gonzaga venduta all'Inghilterra nel 1627–28*. Milan, 1913.

Lyell, James P. R. *Early Book Illustration in Spain*. New York, 1976.

Macrea, Mihail. "Un Disegno Inedito del Rinascimento Relativo alla Colonna Traiana." *Ephemeris Dacoromana* (Annuario della Scuola Romena di Roma) 7 (1937): 77–116.

Major, R. H. "On the Map of Africa published in Pigafetta's 'Kingdom of Congo', in 1591." *Acta Cartographica* 1 (1967): 274–79. First printed in *Proceedings of the Royal Geographical Society* 9 (1867): 246–51.

Mâle, Emile. *L'art religieux de la fin du XVIe siècle*. Paris, 1951.

Malvasia, Carlo Cesare. *Felsina Pittrice*. Bologna, 1841. Reprint, Bologna, 1974.

Mancinelli, Fabrizio. "Restauri in Vaticano." *Bollettino dei Monumenti, Musei e Gallerie Pontificie* 4 (1983): 215–19.

Mancini, Giulio. *Considerazioni sulla Pittura*. Vol. 1. Edizione critica e introduzione di Adriana Marucchi. Rome, 1956; Vol. 2. Commento alle Opere del Mancini del Luigi Salerno. Rome, 1957.

Mandowsky, Erna. "Pirro Ligorio's Illustrations to Aesop's *Fables*." *Journal of the Warburg and Courtauld Insititutes* 24 (1961): 327–31.

Manzi, Pietro. "Alcuni documenti di cartografia nolana ovvero: Ambrogio Leone e Gerolamo Mocetto." *L'Universo* 53 (1973): 811–18.

Mariani Canova, G. "Profilo di Benedetto Bordon, Miniatore Padovano." *Atti dell'Istituto Veneto di Scienze, Lettere ed Arti* 127 (1968–69): 99–121.

——. *La Miniatura Veneta del Rinascimento 1450–1500*. Venice, 1969.

Martineau, Jane, and Charles Hope, eds. *The Genius of Venice, 1500–1600*. New York, 1984.

Marinis, Tammaro de. *Appunti e ricerche bibliografiche*. Milan, 1940.

Marzi, Demetrio. "I tipografi tedeschi in Italia durante il secolo XV." In *Festschrift zum fünfhundertjährigen Geburtstage von Johann Gutenberg*. Edited by Otto Hartwig. Leipzig, 1900, 505–578. Reprint, Lichtenstein, 1968.

Masetti Zannini, Gian Ludovico. *Pittori della sconda metà del Cinquecento in Roma*. Rome, 1974.

——. *Stampatori e Librai a Roma nella Seconda Metà del Cinquecento*. Rome, 1980.

——. "Rivalità e Lavoro di Incisori nelle Botteghe Lafréry-Duchet e de la Vacherie." In *Les Fondations Nationales dans La Rome Pontificale*. Rome, 1981, 547–66.

Massar, Phyllis Dearborn. "A Set of Prints and a Drawing for the 1589 Medici Marriage Festival." *Master Drawings* 13 (1975): 12–23.

Massari, Stefania. *Incisori Mantovani del '500: Giovan Battista, Adamo, Diana Scultori e Giorgio Ghisi, dalle Collezioni del Gabinetto Nazionale delle Stampe e della Calcografia Nazionale*. Rome, 1981.

——. *Giulio Bonasone*. 2 vols. Rome, 1983.

——. *Giulio Romano pinxit et delineavit, Opere grafiche autografe di collaborazione e bottega*. Rome, 1993.

Massari, Stefania, Grazia Bernini Pezzini, Simonetta Prosperi Valenti Rodinò. *Raphael Invenit: Stampe da Raffaello nelle Collezioni dell'Istituto Nazionale per la Grafica*. Rome, 1985.

Massari, Stefania, and Simonetta Prosperi Valenti Rodinò. *Tra Mito e Allegoria: Immagini a Stampa nel '500 e '600*. Rome, 1989.

Massing, Jean Michel. "Jacobus Argentoratensis: Étude préliminaire." *Arte Veneta* 31 (1977): 42–52.

——. "*The Triumph of Caesar* by Benedetto Bordon and Jacobus Argentoratensis: Its Iconography and Influence." *Print Quarterly* 7 (1990): 4–21.

McGinniss, Lawrence. *Catalogue of the Earl of Crawford's "Speculum Romanae Magnificentiae" now in the Avery Architectural Library*, Columbia University. New York, 1976.

Matraia, Gioseffo. *Historia della Miracolosa Imagine della B. Vergine detta S. Maria in Portico*. Rome, 1626.

Mauroner, Fabio. *Le incisioni di Tiziano*. 2nd ed. Padua, 1943.

Mayor, A. Hyatt. *Prints and People: A Social History of Printed Pictures*. New York, 1971.

Mazzariol, Giuseppe, and Terisio Pignatti. *La Pianta Prospettica di Venezia del 1500 Disegnata del Jacopo de Barbari*. Venice, 1962.

Mazzariol, Giuseppe. "Urbanistica nella Pianta di De Barbari del 1500." In *La Stampa degli Incunaboli nel Veneto*. Edited by Neri Pozza. Venice, 1984, 97–101.

Melillo, Vincenzo. *Matteo Perez da Lecce, incisore in Roma*. Rome, 1980.

Merlos, Johann Jacob. *Kölnische Künstler in alter und Neuer Zeit*. Dusseldorf, 1895. Reprint, Nieuwkoop, 1966.

Mercati, Giovanni. "Su Francesco Calvo da Menaggio primo stampatore e Marco Fabio Calvo da Ravenna primo traduttore latino del corpo Ippocratico." *Notizie Varie di Antica Letteratura Medica e di Bibliografica*. Studi e Testi, 31 (1917): 47–71.

Meyer, Julius. *Allgemeines Künstler-Lexikon*. 3 vols. Lepizig, 1872–1885.

Millon, Henry A., and Craig Hugh Smyth. "Michelangelo and St. Peter's: Observations on the Interior of the Apses, a Model of the Apse Vault, and Related Drawings." *Römisches Jahrbuch für Kunstgeschichte* (1976): 140–206.

——. "Pirro Ligorio, Michelangelo, and St. Peter's." In *Pirro Ligorio: Artist and Antiquarian*. Edited by Robert W. Gaston. Florence, 1988, 216–86.

Millon, Henry A., and Vittorio Magnago Lampugnani. *The Renaissance from Brunelleschi to Michelangelo: The Representation of Architecture*. Milan, 1994.

Minonzio, Donata. "Novità e apporti per Agostino Veneziano." *Rassegna di Studi e di Notizie* 8 (1980): 273–320.

Monbeig Goguel, Catherine. "Giovanni Guerra da Modena, disegnatore e illustratore della fine del Rinascimento." *Arte Illustrata* 7 (1974): 164–78.

——. "'Filippo Bellini da Urbino della Scuola del Baroccio'." *Master Drawings* 13 (1975): 347–70.

Monssen, Leif Holm. "Rex gloriose martyrum: A Contribution to Jesuit Iconography." *Art Bulletin* 63 (1981): 130–37.

——. "The Martyrdom Cycle in San Stefano Rotondo." *Acta ad archaeologiam et artium historiam pertinentia. Serie altera in 8°* 2 (1982): 175–317 (Part One); 3 (1983): 11–106 (Part Two).

Moro, Giacomo. "Insegni librarie e marche tipografiche in un registro veneziano del '500." *La Bibliofilia* 91 (1989): 51–80.

Moroni, Gaetano. *Dizionario di erudizione storico ecclesiastica.* 103 vols. Venice, 1840–1861.

Mortimer, Ruth. *Harvard College Library Department of Printing and Graphic Arts Catalogue of Books and Manuscripts Part 1: French 16th Century Books.* 2 vols. Cambridge, Mass., 1964.

——. *Harvard College Library Department of Printing and Graphic Arts Catalogue of Books and Manuscripts Part 2: Italian 16th Century Books.* 2 vols. Cambridge, Mass., 1974.

Motta, Emilio. "Pamfilo Castaldi, Antonio Planella, Pietro Ugleimer e il vescovo d'Aleria." *Rivista Storica Italiana* 9 (1884): 252–74.

——. "Di Filippo di Lavagna e di alcuni altri tipografi-editori milanesi." *Archivio Storico Lombardo* Serie 3, Vol. 10 (1898): 28–72.

Mukerji, Chandra. *From Graven Images: Patterns of Modern Materialism.* New York, 1983.

Mundy, E. James. *Renaissance into Baroque: Italian Master Drawings by the Zuccari 1550–1600.* Milwaukee and Cambridge, 1989.

Muñoz, Antonio. *Domenico Fontana, Architetto, 1543–1607.* Rome, 1944.

Negri Arnoldi, Francesco. *Villa Lante in Bagnaia.* Rome, 1963.

Nelson, Mary Jones. An Analysis of Sixteenth Century Venetian Title Pages of Medical Books. 2 vols. Ph.D. diss., University of Kansas, 1976.

Nielson, Lauritz. *Dansk Bibliografi 1482–1550.* 3 vols. Copenhagen, 1919–1935. Vol. 1: *1482–1550*, Copenhagen, 1919; Vol. 2: *1551–1600*, Copenhagen, 1931–1933; Vol. 3: *Registre*, Copenhagen, 1935.

Niero, Antonio. "Decreti pretridentini di due patriarchi di Venezia su stampa di libri." *Rivista di Storia della Chiesa in Italia* 14 (1960): 450–52.

Nijhoff, Wouter, and M. E. Kronenberg. *Nederlandsche Bibliographie van 1500 tot 1540.* 2 vols. The Hague, 1923–1940. Vol. 1, 1923; Vol. 2, 1940. Reprint, 1965.

Nissen, Claus. *Die Botanische Buchillustration. Ihre Geschichte und Bibliographie.* Stuttgart, 1951.

Nolhac, Pierre de. *La Bibliothèque de Fulvio Orsini.* Paris, 1887. Reprint, Paris, 1976.

Nordenskiöld, Nils Adolf Eril. *Facsimile-Atlas to the Early History of Cartography.* Translated from Swedish. Stockholm, 1889. Reprint, Liechtenstein, 1970.

Norton, Frederick J. *Italian Printers 1501–1520.* London, 1958.

Nunn, George E. *Antonio Salamanca's Version of Mercator's World Map of 1538 in the George H. Beans Library.* Philadelphia, 1933.

Oberhuber, Konrad. *Die Kunst der Graphik III: Renaissance in Italien 16. Jahrhundert; Werke aus dem Besitz der Albertina.* Vienna, 1966.

——. ed. *Rome and Venice, Prints of the High Renaissance.* Cambridge, Mass., 1974.

——. "Titian Woodcuts and Drawings: Some Problems." In *Tiziano e Venezia: Convegno Internazionale di Studi Venezia, 1976.* Verona, 1980, 523–28.

——. "Raffaello e l'incisione." In *Raffaello in Vaticano.* Milan, 1984, 333–42.

Oberhummer, Eugen, and Franz von Wieser. *Wolfgang Lazius Karten der österreichischen Lande und des Königreichs Ungarn aus den Jahren 1545–1563.* Innsbruck, 1906.

Ogg, Oscar. Introduction. *Three Classics of Italian Calligraphy: An unabridged reissue of the writing books of Arrighi, Tagliente and Palatino.* New York 1953.

Ohl des Marais, Albert. "Jacquemin Woeiriot, graveurs sur bois du xvi^c siècle." *Byblis* 10 (1931): 13–17.

Olivato, Loredano. "La Submersione di Pharaone." In *Tiziano e Venezia: Convegno Internazionale di Studi Venezia, 1976.* Verona, 1980, 529–37.

Olsen, Harald. *Federico Barocci.* Copenhagen, 1962.

O'Malley, John W. *Praise and Blame in Renaissance Rome: Rhetoric, Doctrine, and Reform in the Sacred Orators of the Papal Court, c. 1450–1521.* Durham, NC, 1979.

Omodeo, Anna. *Mostra di Stampe Popolari Venete del '500.* Florence, 1965.

Orbaan, Johannes A. F. *Sixtine Rome.* London, 1910.

———. "Virtuosi al Pantheon." *Repertorium für Kunstwissenschaft* 36 (1915): 17–52.

———. *Documenti sul Barocco a Roma.* Rome, 1920.

Osley, A. S. *Luminario: An Introduction to the Italian Writing-Books of the Sixteenth and Seventeenth Centuries.* Nieuwkoop, 1972.

———. *Scribes and Sources: Handbook of the Chancery Hand in the Sixteenth Century.* Boston, 1980.

Ozzola, Leandro. "Gli Editori di Stampa a Roma nei Secoli XVI e XVII." *Repertorium für Kunstwissenschaft* 33 (1910): 400–405.

Pagani, Valeria. "Adamo Scultori and Diana Mantovana." Review of Paolo Bellini, *L'Opera incisa di Adamo e Diana Scultori*, Milan, 1991. *Print Quarterly* 9 (1992): 72–87.

Paratore, Ettore. "Beroaldo, Filippo, junior." In *Dizionario biografico degli Italiani.* Vol. 9, 384–88. Rome, 1967.

Paribeni, Roberto. "La Colonna Trajana in un codice del Rinascimento." *Rivista del R. Istituto di Archeologia e Storia dell'Arte* 1 (1929): 9–28.

Parker, Karl T. *Catalogue of the Collection of Drawings in the Ashmolean Museum. 2, Italian Schools.* Oxford, 1972.

Parma Armani, Elena, Enrichetta Cecchi Gattolin, Veronika Birke, and Catherine Monbeig Goguel. *Libri di immagini, disegni e incisioni di Giovanni Guerra (Modena 1544–Roma 1618).* Modena, 1978.

Parsons, William Barclay. *Engineers and Engineering in the Renaissance.* Baltimore, 1939.

Partner, Peter. *The Popes Men: The Papal Civil Service in the Renaissance.* Oxford, 1990.

Paschini, Pio. "Un ellenista romano del Quattrocento e la sua famiglia." *Atti dell'Accademia degli Arcadi* 19–20 (1939–40): 45–56.

———. "Un ellenista veneziano del Quattrocento: Giovanni Lorenzi." *Archivio Veneto* 73 (1943): 114–46.

Pasero, Carlo. "Giacomo Franco, editore, incisore e calcografo dei secoli XVI e XVII." *La Bibliofilia* 37 (1935): 332–56.

Pasquali, P. Luigi. *Memorie Insigni di S. Maria in Portico in Campitelli.* Rome, 1923.

Pasqualitti, Maria Grazia. "La Colonna Trajana e i disegni rinascimentale della Biblioteca dell'Istituto d'Archeologia e Storia dell'Arte." *Accademie e biblioteche d'Italia* 46 (1978): 157–201.

Passamani, Bruno. "Caprioli, Aliprando." In *Dizionario biografico degli Italiani.* Vol. 19, 209–10. Rome, 1976.

———. "Cavalieri, Giovanni Battista." In *Dizionario biografico degli Italiani.* Vol. 22, 673–75. Rome, 1979.

Passavant, J. D. *Le Peintre-Graveur.* 6 vols in 3. Leipzig, 1860–1864.

Pastor, Ludwig von. *The History of the Popes.* 40 vols. St. Louis, 1923–1952.

Pastorello, Ester. *Tipografi, Editori, Librai a Venezia nel secolo XVI.* Florence, 1924.

———. *Bibliografia storico-analitica dell'arte della stampa in Venezia* (Reale Deputazione di Storia Patrie per le Venezie, Miscellanea di studi e memorie, 1). Venice, 1933.

Peckham, John F. *Early Printing in Italy, with special reference to the classics 1469–1517. A guide to the commencement exhibition commemorating the five hundredth anniversary of the invention of printing.* Princeton University Library, 1940.

Peizoto, Jorge. "Os privilégios de impressão dos livros em Portugal no sécolo XVI." *Gutenberg-Jahrbuch* (1966): 265–72.

Pepe, Mario. "I Labacco Architetti e Incisori." *Capitoleum* 38 (1963): 24–27.

Pesenti, Giuliano. "Libri censurati a Venezia nei secoli XVI–XVII." *La Bibliofilia* 58 (1956): 15–30.

Petrioli, Anna Maria. "Stampe Popolari Venete del Cinquecento agli Uffizi." *Antichità Viva* 4 (1965): 62–7.

Petrucci, Alfredo. "Il Trionfo di Cesare." *Il Messaggero di Roma* 83, no. 274 (3 October 1961): 3.

——. *Panorama della Incisione Italiana: Il Cinquecento*. Rome, 1964.

——. "Il Magnifico Matteo: Dall'Appula Alezio al Nuovo Mondo." In *Pernix Apulia: Pagina sparse di Vita, di Storia e di Arte pugliese*. Bari, 1971, 133–48.

Petrucci, Carlo Alberto. *Catalogo Generale delle Stampe tratte dai Rami Incisi posseduti dalla Calcografia Nazionale*. Rome, 1953.

Pettas, William A. *The Giunti of Florence: Merchant Publishers of the Sixteenth Century*. San Francisco, 1980.

Pignatti, Terisio. "La pianta di Venezia di Jacopo de' Barbari." *Bollettino dei Musei Civici Veneziani* 9 (1964): 9–49.

Pinchart, Alexandre Joseph. *Archives des arts, sciences et lettres: documents inédits publiés et annotés*. 3 vols. Ghent, 1850–1882.

Pittaluga, Mary. *L'Incisione Italiana nel Cinquecento*. Milan, 1928.

Pollack, Oskar. "Ausgewählte Akten zur Geschichte der Römischen Peterskirche (1535–1621)." *Jahrbuch der Preuszischen Kunstsammlungen* 36 (1915) Beiheft, 21–117.

Pohlman, Hansjörg. "Neue Materialien zum deutschen Urheberschutz im 16. Jahrhundert. Ein Quellenbeitrag zur neuen Sicht der Urheberrechtsentwicklung." *Archiv für Geschichte des Buchwesens* 4 (1961): cols. 89–172.

Pollard, Alfred William. "The Transference of Woodcuts in the Fifteenth and Sixteenth Centuries." *Bibliografia* 2 (1895): 355.

——. *Early Illustrated Books: A History of the Decoration and Illustration of Books in the 15th and 16th Centuries*. New York, 1927 (first edition 1893).

Popham, A. E., and Johannes Wilde. *The Italian Drawings of the XV and XVI Centuries in the Collection of His Majesty the King at Windsor Castle*. London, 1949.

Pottinger, David T. *The French Book Trade in the Ancien Régime, 1500–1791*. Cambridge, Mass., 1958.

Prijatelj, Kruno. "Clovio, Giorgio Giulio." In *Dizionario biografico degli Italiani*. Vol. 26, 416–20. Rome, 1982.

Procacci, Ugo. "Una 'Vita' Inedita del Muziano." *Arte Veneta* 8 (1954): 242–64.

Proctor, Robert. *The Printing of Greek in the Fifteenth Century*. Oxford, 1900. Reprint, 1966.

Prosperi Valenti Rodino, Simonetta. "La Diffusione nell'iconografia Francescana attraverso l'incisione." In *L'Immagine di San Francesco nella Controriforma*. Rome, 1982, 159–69.

Ptasnik, Joannes, ed. *Monumenta poloniae typographica xv et xvi saeculorum*, vol. I, *Cracovia impressorum xv et xvi saeculorum*. Leopoli, 1922.

Putnam, George Haven. *The Censorship of the Church of Rome and Its Influence upon the Production and Distribution of Literature*. 2 vols. New York and London, 1906.

Puyvelde, Leo van. "Bernardino Passari, Marten de Vos, and Hieronymus Wierix." In *Scritti di Storia dell'Arte in Onore di Lionello Venturi*. Vol. 2. Rome, 1956, 59–64.

Quondam, Amadeo. "'Mercanzia d'Honore, Mercanzia d'Utile,' produzione libraria e lavoro intellettuale a Venezia nel Cinquecento." In *Libri, Editori e Pubblico nell'Europa Moderna, Guida Storica e Critica*. Edited by Armando Petrucci. Bari, 1977, 53–104.

Rave, Paul Ortwin. "Paolo Giovio und die Bildnisvitenbücher des Humanismus." *Jahrbuch der Berliner Museen* 1 (1959): 119–54.

Rearick, W. R. *The Art of Paolo Veronese 1528–1588*. Washington, 1988.

Reed, Sue Welsh, and Richard Wallace. *Italian Etchers of the Renaissance and Baroque*. Boston, 1989.

Renouard, Antoine-Auguste. *Annales de l'Imprimerie des Alde, ou histoire des trois Manuce et de leurs éditions*. 3rd ed. Paris, 1834.

Renouard, Augustin-Charles. *Traité des droits d'auteur*. Vol. 1. Paris, 1838.

Renouard, Ph. *Bibliographie des impressions et des oeuvres de Josse Badius Ascensius, imprimeur et humaniste 1462–1535*. 3 vols. Paris, 1908. Reprint, New York, 1967.

Reusch, Franz Heinrich. *Der Index der verbotenen Bücher: Ein Beitrag zur Kirchen- und literaturgeschichte*. 2 vols. Bonn, 1883–5. Reprint, Darmstadt, 1967.

———. *Die Indices librorum prohibitorum des sechzehnten Jahrhunderts*. Tubinga, 1886.

Rhodes, Dennis E. *Silent Printers: Anonymous Printing in Venice in the Sixteenth Century*. London, 1995.

Richards, Louise S. "The Titian Woodcut by Domenico dalle Greche." *Bulletin of the Cleveland Museum of Art* 43 (1956): 197–203.

Pillsbury, Edmund P., and Louise S. Richards. *The Graphic Art of Federico Barocci: Selected Drawings and Prints*. New Haven, 1978.

Richardson, Brian. *Print Culture in Renaissance Italy: The Editor and the Vernacular Text 1470–1600*. Cambridge, 1994.

Ridolfi, Carlo. *Le meraviglie dell'arte* (Venice, 1648). Edited by Detlev von Hadeln. 2 vols. Berlin, Vol. 1, 1914; Vol. 2, 1924.

Riggs, Timothy A. *Hieronymus Cock: Printmaker and Publisher*. New York and London, 1977.

Rivoli, Duc de, and Charles Ephrussi. "Notes sur les Xylographes Vénetiens du XVᵉ et XVIᵉ siècles." *Gazette des Beaux-Arts* 32 (1891): 494–503.

Rivoli, Duc de. *Bibliographie des livres à figures vénitiens, 1469–1525*. Paris, 1892.

Robert-Dumesnil, A. P. F. *Le Peintre-graveur français*. 11 vols. Paris, 1835–71. Reprint, Paris, 1967.

Robertson, Clare. *'Il Gran Cardinale' Alessandro Farnese, Patron of the Arts*. New Haven and London, 1992.

Röhricht, Reinhold. *Bibliotheca Geographica Palaestina: Chronologisches Verzeichniss der auf die Geographie des Heiligen Landes Bezüglichen Literatur von 333 bis 1878 und versuch einer Cartographie*. Berlin, 1890.

Roland, François. "Un Franc-Comtois Editeur et Marchand d'Estampes a Rome au XVIᵉ Siècle: Antoine Lafrery (1512–1577)." *Memoires de la Société d'Emulation du Doubs* (Besançon) (1911): 320–78.

Romanelli, Giandomenico, and Susanna Biadene. *Venezia Piante e Vedute: Catalogo del fondo cartografico a stampa, Museo Correr*. Venice, 1982.

Ronen, Avraham. "Un Ciclo Inedito di Affreschi di Cristofano Gherardi a San Giustino." *Mitteilungen des Kunsthistorischen Institutes in Florenz* 13 (1968): 367–80.

———. "Il Vasari e gli incisori del suo tempo." *Commentari* 28 (1977): 92–104.

Rosand, David, and Michelangelo Muraro. *Titian and the Venetian Woodcut*. Washington, D.C., 1976.

Rossi, Vittorio. "Un incendio a Venezia e il tipografo Bernardino Benalio." *Libro e la Stampa* 4 (1910): 51–55.

Rotili, Mario, ed. *Fortuna di Michelangelo nell'Incisione*. Benevento and Rome, 1964–1965.

Röttgen, Herwarth. *Il Cavalier d'Arpino*. Rome, 1973.

Rupprich, Hans. *Dürers Schriftlicher Nachlass*. vol. 1. Berlin, 1956.

Russo, Laura. "Per Marcello Venusti, Pittore Lombardo." *Bollettino d'Arte* 64 (1990): 1–26.

Ruysschaert, J. "Albertini, Francesco." In *Dizionario biografico degli Italiani*. Vol. 1, 724–25. Rome, 1960.

Rylands, Philip. "(Giacomo)[Jacopo] Palma (il) Giovane." In *The Dictionary of Art*. Vol. 23, 878–80. New York, 1996.

Saffrey, Henri D. "Les Images Populaires de Saints Dominicains à Venise au XVᵉ siècles et l'Édition par Alde Manuce des 'Epistole' de Sainte Catherine de Sienne." *Italia Medioevale e Umanistica* 25 (1982): 241–312.

———. "'Imago de facili multiplicabilis in cartas.' Un document méconnu daté de l'année 1412 sur l'origine de la gravure sur bois à Venise." *Nouvelles de l'Estampe* 74 (1984): 4–7.

Salmi, Mario. *Italian Miniatures*. New York, 1954.

Saltini, Guglielmo Enrico. "Della Stamperia orientale Medicea e di Giovan Battista Raimondi." *Giornale Storico degli Archivi Toscani* 4 (1860): 257–308.

Sander, Max. *Le livre à figures italiens depuis 1467 jusqu'à 1530*. 6 vols. New York, 1941.

Santoro, Caterina. *Libri Illustrati Milanesi del Rinascimento*. Milan, 1956.

Sanuto, Marino. *I Diarii di Marino Sanuto*. Edited by Rinaldo Fulin, Federico Stefani, Nicolò Barozzi, Guglielmo Berchet, and Marco Allegri. 58 vols. Venice, 1879–1903. Reprint, Bologna, 1969–1970.

Sarton, George. "Agrippa, Fontana, and Pigafetta: The Erection of the Vatican Obelisk in 1586." *Archives Internationales d'Histoire des Sciences* 8 (1949): 827–54.

Sartori, Claudio. *Bibliografia delle opere musicali stampate da Ottaviano Petrucci*. Florence, 1948.

Scamuzzi, Ernesto. *La 'mensa Isiaca' del Regio Museo di Antichità a Torino*. Rome, 1949.

Schmid, Anton. *Ottaviano dei Petrucci da Fossombrone, der erste Erfinder des Musiknotendruckes mit beweglichen Metalltypen und seine Nachfolger im sechzehnten Jahrhundert*. Vienna, 1845. Reprint, Amsterdam, 1968.

Schottenloher, Karl. "Die Drucker privilegien des 16 Jahrhunderts." *Gutenberg-Jahrbuch* (1933): 89–111.

Schück, Henrik. *Några Anmärkningar till Antonio Tempesta's Urbis Romae Prospectus 1593* (Arbeten utgifna med understöd af Wilhelm Eckmans universitetsfond, Uppsala, 20:B). Uppsala, 1917.

Schulz, Juergen. "The Printed Plans and Panoramic Views of Venice (1486–1797)." *Saggi e memorie di storia del'arte* 7 (1970): 1–182.

——. "Jacopo de' Barbari's view of Venice. Map Making, City Views and Moralized Geography before the year 1500." *Art Bulletin* 60 (1978): 425–74.

Scipioni, V. Agostinelli. "Bernardino Passeri e il coro di S. Vittore di Milano," *Arte Cristiana* 63 (1975): 89–102.

Sénéchal, Philippe. Les Graveurs des école du nord à Venise (1585–1620)—Les Sadeler: Entremise et entreprise. 3 vols. Thèse de doctorat de IIIᵉ cycle, University of Paris-Sorbonne/Paris IV, Institut d'Art et d'Archaeologie, 1987.

——. "Justus Sadeler: Print Publisher and Art Dealer in Early Seicento Venice." *Print Quarterly* 7 (1990): 22–35.

Servolini, Luigi. "Ugo da Carpi." *Rivista d'Arte* 11 (1929) 173–94, 297–319.

——. "Ugo da Carpi." *Print Collector's Quarterly* 26 (1939): 31.

——. "Un Incisore del Cinquecento, Cherubino Alberti." *Dedalo* 12 (1932): 753–72. Also published in English translation as "Cherubino Alberti. Italian Engraver of the Sixteenth Century." *The Print Collector's Quarterly* 27 (1940): 216–37.

——. *Jacopo de' Barbari*. Padua, 1944.

——. "Eustachio Celebrino da Udine: Intagliatore, calligrafo, poligrafo ed editore del sec. XVI." *Gutenberg Jahrbuch* (1944–49): 179–89.

——. "Ugo da Carpi Illustratore del Libro." *Gutenberg-Jahrbuch* (1950): 196–202.

——. "Rami Incisi di Cherubino Alberti (37 rami aquistati dalla Calcografia Nazionale)." *Bollettino d'Arte* 36 (1951): 378.

——. "Le xilografie di Ugo da Carpi." *Gutenberg-Jahrbuch* (1953): 105.

——. *Ugo da Carpi: I chiaroscuri e le altre opere*. Florence, 1977.

Shaaber, Matthias Adam. *Sixteenth-century Imprints in the Libraries of the University of Pennsylvania*. Philadelphia, 1976.

Shaw, James Byam. "Titian's Drawings: A Summing-up." *Apollo* 112 (1980): 386–91.

Shiras, Winfield. "The Yale 'Lafréry Atlas'," *Yale University Library Gazette* 9 (1935): 55–60.

Shirley, Rodney. *The Mapping of the World: Early Printed World Maps 1472–1700*. London, 1993.

Shoemaker, Innis. *The Engravings of Marcantonio Raimondi*. Lawrence, Kansas, 1981.

Simar, Théophile. *Le Congo au XVIe siècle d'après la relation Lopez-Pigafetta*. Brussels, 1919.

Sopher, Marcus S. *Sixteenth-Century Italian Prints*. Claremont, Calif., 1978.

Sorbelli, Albano. *Storia della Stampa in Bologna*. Bologna,1929.

Soria, Martin S. "Pintores italianos en Sudamerica entre 1575 y 1628." *Saggi e Memorie di Storia dell'Arte* 4 (1965): 115–30.

Sotzmann, H. "Ueber die ältesten meist xylographischen Schreibbücher der Italiener aus der ersten Hälfte des XVI. Jahrhunderts und Ugo da Carpi's Antheil daran." *Archiv. für Die Zeichnenden Künste* 2 (1856): 275–303.

Spike, John. Marcantonio's Relationship to His School, Qualifying Paper Presented to the Department of Fine Arts, Harvard University, 1974.

Stastny, Francisco. *Perez de Alesio y la Pintura del Siglo XVI*. Buenos Aires, 1970.

Stinger, Charles L. *The Renaissance in Rome*. Bloomington, 1985.

Strange, Edward F. "Early Pattern Books of Lace, Embroidery and Needlework." *Transactions of the Bibliographical Society* 7 (1902–1904): 209–46.

Suida, Wilhelm. "La Giustizia di Traiano." *Rassegna d'Arte* 6 (1906): 135–36.

Suster, Guido. "Dell'incisore trentino Aliprando Caprioli." *Archivio Trentino* 18 (1903): 144–206.

Tacchi Venturi, Pietro. "Il Giubileo del 1575." In *Gli Anni Santi*, 67–84. Rome, 1934.

Tafuri, Manfredo. "Capriani, Francesco detto Francesco da Volterra." In *Dizionario biografico degli Italiani*. Vol. 19, 189–95. Rome, 1976.

Talvacchia, Bette. *Taking Positions: On the Erotic in Renaissance Culture*. Princeton, 1999.

Taurisano, Innocentius, O.P. *Hierarchia Ordinis praedicatorum*. Vol. 1. Rome, 1916.

Tenenti, Alberto. "Luc'Antonio Giunti il Giovane Stampatore e Mercante." In *Studi in Onore di Armando Sapori*. Milan, 1957. Vol. 1, 1023–1060.

Thieme, Ulrich, Felix Becker, and Hans Volmer, eds. *Allgemeines Lexikon der bildenden Künste von der Antike dis zur Gegenwart*. 37 vols. Leipzig, 1907–1950.

Thomas, Henry. "The Romance of Amadis of Gaul." *Transactions of the Bibliographical Society* 11 (1912): 251–97.

——. *Spanish and Portugese Romances of Chivalry*. Cambridge, 1920.

——. *Short-title Catalogue of Books printed in Spain and of Spanish Books printed elsewhere in Europe before 1601 now in the British Museum*. London, 1921.

——. "Antonio [Martínez] de Salamanca, Printer of *La Celestina*, Rome, c. 1525." *The Library* Serie 5, 8 (1953): 45–50.

Thomson, David. *Les Plus Excellents Bastiments de France par Jacques Androuet du Cerceau*. Translated from the English by Catherine Ludet. Paris, 1995.

Ticozzi, Paolo. *Paolo Veronese e i suoi incisori*. Venice, 1977.

Tietze, Hans, and E. Tietze-Conrat. "Titian's Woodcuts." *Print Collector's Quarterly* 25 (1938): 333–60, 465–77.

Tietze-Conrat, E. "La Xilografia di Tiziano 'Il Passaggio del Mar Rosso'." *Arte Veneta* 4 (1950): 110–112.

Tinto, Alberto. "Introduzione agli annali tipografici di Eucario e Marcello Silber (1501–1527)." *La Bibliofilia* 65 (1963): 239–48.

——. *Annali Tipografici dei Tramezzino*. Rome, 1966.

——. "Ludovico degli Arrighi detto Vicentino." In Luigi Balsamo and Alberto Tinto, *Origini del Corsivo nella Tipografia Italiana del Cinquecento*. Milan, 1967, 127–48.

——. *Gli Annali Tipografici di Eucario e Marcello Silber (1501–1527)*. Florence, 1968.

Toda y Güell, Eduardo. *Bibliografia Espanyola d'Italia*. 5 vols. Castell, 1927–31.

Tooley, Ronald V. "Maps in Italian Atlases of the Sixteenth Century, being a comparative list of the Italian maps issued by Lafreri, Forlani, Duchetti, Bertelli and others, found in Atlases." *Imago Mundi* 3 (1939): 12–47.

Troiano, Costantino, and Alfonso Pompei. *The Sanctuaries of Assisi*. Assisi, 1967.

Unterkircher, Franz. "Der erste illustrierte italienische Druck und eine Wiener Handschrift des gleichen Werkes (Hain 15722, Cod. Vindob. 3805)." In *Hellinga:*

Festschrift, Feestbundel, Mélanges: Forty-three Studies in Bibliography Presented to Prof. Dr. Wytze Hellinga. Amsterdam, 1980, 498–516.

Vaccaro Sofia, Emerenziana. *Catalogo delle Edizioni Romane di Antonio Blado Asolano ed Eredi (1515–1593).* Vol. 3. Rome, 1942; Vol. 4. Rome, 1961.

Vaes, Maurice. "Appunti di Karel van Mander su diversi pittori Italiani conosciuti da lui a Roma, dal 1573 al 1577." *Atti del II° Congresso Nazionale di Studi Romani.* Rome, 1931. Vol. 2, 509–19.

Van der Straeten, E. *Notice sur Pierre Perret, graveur Belge du XVI. Siècle.* Antwerp, 1861.

Van Mander, Carel. *Het Leven der doorluchtighe Nederlandtsche en Hoogduytsche schilders.* Haarlem, 1604.

———. *Dutch and Flemish Painters.* Translations from the *Schilderboeck* by Constant van de Wall. New York, 1936.

Van Ortroy, F. "Bibliographie de l'oeuvre de Pierre Apian." *Le Bibliographe moderne* 5 (1901): 89–156, 284–333.

Vasari, Giorgio. *Le vite de' più eccellenti architetti, pittori, et scultori.* Florence, 1550. Facsimile Edition, New York, 1980.

———. *Le vite de' più eccellenti pittori, scultori, e architetti.* Florence, 1568. In *Opere di Giorgo Vasari.* Edited by Gaetano Milanesi. First published, Florence, 1879. Reprint, of 1906 edition, 1981.

Vera, Luis Cervera. *Las Estampes Y El Sumario de El Escorial por Juan de Herrera.* Vol. 1. Madrid, 1954.

Verga, Ettore. *Catalogo ragionato della Raccolta cartografica e saggio storico sulla cartografia milanese.* Milan, 1911.

Verheyden, Prosper. "Drukkersoctrooien in de 16e eeuw." *Tijdschrift voor Boek- en Bibliotheekswesen* 8 (1910): 203–26, 269–78.

Vernarecci, Augusto. *Ottaviano de' Petrucci da Fossombrone inventore dei tipi mobili metallici della musica nel secolo XV.* Fossombrone, 1881.

Voet, Leon. *The Golden Compasses: A History and Evaluation of the Printing and Publishing Activities of the Officina Plantiniana at Antwerp.* 2 vols. Amsterdam, London, and New York, Vol. I, 1969; Vol. 2, 1972.

Volpati, Carlo. "Gli Scotti di Monza tipografi-editori in Venezia." *Archivio storico Lombardo* 59 (1932): 365–82.

Voss, H. *Die Malerei der Spätrenaissance in Rom und Florenz.* 2 vols. Berlin, 1920.

Weiss, Roberto. "Andrea Fulvio antiquario romano (ca. 1470–1527)." *Annali della Scuola Normale Superiore di Pisa* 28 (1959): 1–44.

———. "Traccia per una biografia di Annio da Viterbo." *Italia Medioevale e Umanistica* 5 (1962): 425–41.

Wethey, Harold E. *The Paintings of Titian.* 3 vols. London, 1969–75.

Wilkinson, Catherine, ed. *Drawings and Prints of the First Maniera.* Providence, Rhode Island, 1973.

Wilkinson, Catherine, Christine Patricia Mary Brown, Stephen John Eskilson, et al. *Philip II and the Escorial: Technology and the Representaton of Architecture.* Providence, Rhode Island, 1990.

Wilkinson, Catherine. *Juan de Herrera, Architect to Philip II of Spain.* New Haven, 1993.

Witcombe, Christopher L. C. E. Giovanni and Cherubino Alberti, Ph.D. diss., Bryn Mawr College, 1981.

———. "Giuseppe Porta's Frontispiece for Francesco Marcolini's *Sorti.*" *Arte Veneta* 37 (1983): 170–74.

———. "Cherubino Alberti and the Ownership of Engraved Plates." *Print Quarterly* 6 (1989): 160–69.

———. "Christopher Plantin's Papal Privileges: Documents in the Vatican Archives." *De Gulden Passer* 69 (1991): 133–43.

———. "Privilegio Papale per la pubblicazione degli statuti dell'Ordine di San Giovanni di Malta (Roma, 1588)/The *Privilegio* for the Publication of the Statutes of the

Order of St. John in Malta (Rome, 1588)." *Rivista Internazionale del Sovrano Ordine di Malta* 23 (1991): 28–38 (in Italian and English).

——. "Some Letters and Some Prints Dedicated to the Medici by Cherubino Alberti." *Sixteenth Century Journal* 22 (1991): 641–60.

——. "Herrera's Papal *Privilegio* for the Escorial Prints." *Print Quarterly* 9 (1992): 177–80.

——. "Giovanni Battista Mercati: Notizie sui Dipinti e sulle Incisioni." *Bollettino d'Arte* 76 (1992): 53–70.

Wittkower, Rudolf. *Architectural Principles in the Age of Humanism.* London, 1962.

Woodward, David. *The Maps and Prints of Paolo Forlani: A Descriptive Bibliography.* Chicago, 1990.

——. "Paolo Forlani: Compiler, Engraver, Printer, or Publisher?" *Imago Mundi* 44 (1992): 45–64.

——. *Maps as Prints in the Italian Renaissance: Makers, Distributors and Consumers.* London, 1996.

Würtenberger, Thomas. *Das Kunstlerfälschertum: Entstehung und Bekämpfung eines Verbrechens vom Anfang des 15. bis zum Ende des 18. Jahrhunderts.* Weimar, 1940.

Wurzbach, Alfred Von. *Niederländisches Künstler-Lexikon.* Vienna and Leipzig, 1910.

Zani, Pietro. *Enciclopedia Metodica Critico-Ragionata delle Belle Arti.* Part 2, vols. 2–9. Parma, 1819–22.

Zava Boccazzi, Franca. "Tracce per Gerolamo da Treviso il Giovane in alcune xilografie di Francesco de Nanto." *Arte Veneta* 12 (1958): 70–78.

Zerner, Henry. "L'Estampe Erotique au Temps de Titien." In *Tiziano e Venezia: Convegno Internazionale di Studi, Venezia 1976.* Verona, 1980, 85–90.

——. *L'Art de la Renaissance en France: L'Invention du Classicisme.* Paris, 1996.

Zimmerman, H., and F. Kreyczi. "Urkunden aus d. K. u. K. Reichs-Finanz Archiv." *Jahrbuch der Kunsthistorischen Sammlungen ... in Wien* 3 (1885): 2, nos. 2280, 2550.

INDEX

II. *Places and Locations*